POPULATION AND SOCIETY IN AN EAST DEVON PARISH

The parish of Colyton in Devon has been intensively analysed by historians interested in population trends, analyses which led to similar work on reconstituting the populations of many other towns and villages.

Pamela Sharpe builds on the work of the Cambridge Group to take the demographic history of the parish a stage further. In this book she places the changing demographic patterns of Colyton's population within the context of the economic, social and political life of the parish and region. She makes use of material from a wide range of sources—from court records and poor relief materials to the details of the lives of ordinary families during the early modern period—to stress the diversity of local experience. The parish is set in its global context by considering its contact with the trade across the Atlantic as well as its trading links with Europe.

The book provides valuable new material on religious radicalism, agricultural changes, economic development, local politics, poverty and welfare policies as well as the history of the family and the lifecycle in a small town in the early modern period. It also offers consolidation and critique of demographic research carried out on this area since the early 1960s.

POPULATION AND SOCIETY IN AN EAST DEVON PARISH

REPRODUCING COLYTON 1540–1840

Pamela Sharpe

UNIVERSITY
of
EXETER
PRESS

For Derek, fellow traveller, with love and gratitude over a long haul.

First published in 2002 by
University of Exeter Press
Reed Hall, Streatham Drive
Exeter, Devon EX4 4QR
UK
www.ex.ac.uk/uep/

© Pamela Sharpe 2002

The right of Pamela Sharpe to be identified as the author of this work
has been asserted by her in accordance with the
Copyright, Designs and Patents Act 1988.

British Library Cataloguing in Publication Data
A catalogue record for this book is available from the British Library

ISBN 0 85989 655 2

Typeset in 11½/12½pt Garamond 3 by Kestrel Data, Exeter

Printed in Great Britain by
Antony Rowe Ltd, Chippenham

Contents

List of Illustrations	vii
Abbreviations	x
A Note on Sources and Dates	xi
Publication Permission	xii
Acknowledgements	xiii
Prologue: Investigating Colyton	1

PART ONE: DOCUMENTS AND DISSENT

1.	Interpreting Colyton	5
2.	Dissenting People: The Politics of the Very Godly	29
	Overview of Part One	65

PART TWO: ECONOMY AND LOCALITY

3.	Industrious Dealers: Trade and the Commercial Imperative	67
4.	Resourcefulness: Farming a Wood-Pasture Economy	120
	Overview of Part Two	160

PART THREE: POPULATION AND SOCIETY

5.	Demographic Experiences in a Devon Parish	161
6.	Inside the Parish: Management at the Margins	208
7.	Viable Households: Life-Cycle and Family in Colyton	250
	Overview of Part Three	303

Epilogue: Reinterpreting Colyton: Explaining Population Change in the Parish   305

Appendix: The Methodology of Total Reconstitution	318
Notes	326
Bibliography	
Manuscripts	364
Unpublished Theses and Papers	372
Published Primary and Secondary Sources	373
Glossary	394
Index	397

Illustrations

Tables

1.1	Number and percentage of FRFs with status designation 1538–1837	13
1.2	Distribution of FRFs with status by cohort 1538–1837	13
1.3	Number and percentage of 'marriage only' case FRFs 1538–1799	22
1.4	Status of 'marriage only' FRFs 1538–1799	22
1.5	Percentage of dummy FRFs with status designation compared to FRFs with marriages and status designation 1538–1799	23
1.6	Status designation of dummy FRFs 1538–1799	24
1.7	Number and status of individuals with no FRF linkage 1538–1837	26
3.1	Social status of Colyton households in the 1674 Hearth Tax	69
3.2	Status of Colyton plague victims	85
4.1	Marriage seasonality in Colyton 1538–1837	128
4.2	Wheat prices at Exeter 1730–1819	155
5.1	The sex ratio in Colyton 1550–1837	163
5.2	Number and percentage of Colyton-born children to marry in the parish 1538–1799	166
5.3	Sex ratio at burial in Devon parishes 1650–1699	168
5.4	Age of women at first marriage by status group of FRF 1550–1837	176
5.5	Age of men at first marriage by status group of FRF 1550–1837	177
5.6	Calculated ages at marriage for dummy marryers compared with men marrying at Colyton church 1550–1837	180
5.7	Age of 'all women' at first marriage by status group of FRF 1538–1799	181
5.8	Age of 'all men' at first marriage by status group of FRF 1538–1799	182
5.9	Remarriage chances for men and women in Colyton 1538–1837	187
5.10	Remarriage chances in Colyton for amalgamated cohorts 1538–1837	189
5.11	Birth intervals and marriage age in Colyton 1560–1769	190
5.12	Marital fertility rates in Colyton 1560–1837	190
5.13	Family limitation behaviour by status 1550–1837	191

5.14	Family limitation behaviour in Colyton for amalgamated cohorts 1550–1837	192
5.15	Birth spacing by the Dupaquier-Lachiver method according to status 1538–1837	194
5.16	Birth spacing in Colyton for amalgamated cohorts 1538–1837	195
5.17	Infant and child life-table death rates in Colyton 1538–1774	198
5.18	Infant and child mortality by status of father 1538–1799	199
5.19	Infant and child mortality in Colyton for amalgamated cohorts 1538-1799	200
5.20	'Midpoint' expectation of life at birth in Colyton 1538–1774	203
6.1	Sex and age comparison of those receiving casual poor relief in Colyton in 1682/3, 1742/3 and 1763/4	225
6.2	Poor disbursements in Devon parishes per head of population in the Compton Census 1676	226
6.3	Type of jobs for women recorded in the overseers' account book 1741-1769	245
7.1	Number of pauper apprentices in Colyton 1550–1837	259
7.2	Sex ratio of pauper apprentices in Colyton 1550–1837	260
7.3	Number of cases of pauper apprenticeship by month in Colyton 1598-1830	262
7.4	Mean ages of male and female apprentices in Colyton 1598–1830	263
7.5	Family circumstances of pauper apprentices in Colyton 1598–1830	264
7.6	Family circumstances of pauper apprentices listed in the register and indentures 1598–1740	265
7.7	Status grouping of never-married females 1538–1799	283
7.8	Never-married females of 44+ for amalgamated cohorts 1538–1799	283
7.9	Baptisms of illegitimate children in Colyton 1538–1837	284
7.10	Status of mothers of illegitimate children in Colyton 1538–1837	286
7.11	Number of prenuptial conceptions in Colyton 1538–1799	288
7.12	Status of FRFs with prenuptial conceptions 1738–1799	288
A.1	Status derivation of total reconstitution documents	320
A.2	Status derivations in the listings	322
A.3	Documents giving occupations	323

Figures

1.1	Baptisms, burials and marriages by decade for Colyton 1541–1830	9
5.1	Sex ratio at burial: Colyton 1538–1837	164
5.2	Mean age at first marriage of women and men 1550–1837	175
5.3	Mean age at first marriage of women by status group of FRF 1550–1837	178
5.4	Mean age at first marriage of men by status group of FRF 1550–1837	179
5.5	Mean age at first marriage for 'all women' and 'all men' 1538–1837	180
5.6	Mean age at first marriage of 'all women' by status group of FRF 1538–1799	183

5.7	Mean age at first marriage of 'all men' by status group of FRF 1538–1799	183
5.8	Mean age at first marriage of gentry group of FRFs 1538–1799	184
5.9	Mean age at first marriage of poor group of FRFs 1538–1799	184
5.10	Mean age at first marriage of unknown group of FRFs 1538–1837	186
6.1	Yearly poor law disbursements for Colyton 1740–1769	239
6.2	Percentage of average yearly disbursement for decades by month: Colyton 1740–1769	240
6.3	Percentage of disbursement by month: tithings of Colyton 1763/4	241
6.4	Amounts of Colyton poor relief including and excluding extraneous payments 1763/4	242
6.5	Male and female percentage of annual disbursement by month 1763/4	242
7.1	Parish apprentices in Colyton and Exeter wheat prices 1590–1829	261

Maps

1.	Main features of Colyton parish	xvi
2.	Detail of Colyton town from the Ordnance Survey Map of 1887	6
3.	Detail from Benjamin Donn's map of the County of Devon 1765	7
4.	Detail of the Axe estuary	137
5.	Detail of Seaton Marsh	139
6.	Detail of Tithe Apportionment of Colyford Meadow 1844/5	141

Plates

1.	The tomb of Sir John and Lady Elizabeth Pole (1658) in Colyton church	42
2.	Interior and exterior of Loughwood Meeting House, Kilmington	44
3.	The merchant's mark and tomb of Jane Vye (1655) in Colyton church	109
4.	An apple press, frontispiece to J.W. Gent, *The Second Parts of Systema Agriculturæ* (1689)	133
5.	Contemporary views of the Axe Estuary and area of land reclamation	136
6.	Contemporary view of the town centre of Colyton	156
7.	Shute Barton House	215
8.	The Old Church House (1612)	314

Abbreviations

BM	British Museum
COLYFILE	Compendium of Statistics for Colyton, Cambridge Group
CRO	Cornwall Record Office
DCNQ	*Devon and Cornwall Notes and Queries*
DH	*The Devon Historian*
DRO	Devon Record Office
DSRO	Dorset Record Office
ECL	Exeter Cathedral Library
EHR	*Economic History Review*
FF	Chamber of Feoffees Archives, Colyton Town Hall
FRF	Family Reconstitution Form
LPS	*Local Population Studies*
n.d.	No date
PCC	Prerogative Court of Canterbury
PP	Parliamentary Paper
PRO	Public Record Office
QS	Quarter Sessions
QSBb	Quarter Sessions Bundles
SRO	Somerset Record Office
TDA	*Reports and Transactions of the Devonshire Association*
UBSC	University of Bristol Library Special Collections
V&A	Victoria and Albert Museum
VCH	Victoria County History
WCS	Westcountry Studies Library

A Note on Sources and Dates

Unless otherwise stated, the source of the information contained in the tables and figures is the enhanced reconstitution for Colyton. The Colyton aggregates, the FRFs and machine-entered parts of the reconstitution, and COLYFILE (containing statistical work carried out on the demography of Colyton) are all kept by the Cambridge Group for the History of Population and Social Structure at the University of Cambridge.

The biblical passages are taken from the King James version of the Bible dating from 1611.

With regard to dates, whenever possible, Easter, Midsummer, Michaelmas or Epiphany is identified for Quarter Sessions bundles. For all sources used, the year is taken to begin on 1 January to provide consistency with the previously assembled demographic data. However, specific dates cited follow the Julian 'Old Style' calendar before 1752.

In general, and except in cases where meaning was obscured, quotations from original sources retain their original spelling, capitalisation and punctuation.

Publication Permission

Some sections of this text have been previously published as journal articles. I am very grateful to the publishers and editors of the following journals for permission to reprint the material contained in these articles:

'Literally spinsters: a new interpretation of local economy and demography in Colyton in the seventeenth and eighteenth centuries' *Economic History Review*, 44:1 (1991), 46–55.
'Poor children as apprentices in Colyton 1598–1830' *Continuity and Change*, 6:2 (1991), 253–270.
'The total reconstitution method: a tool for class specific study?' *Local Population Studies*, 44 (1990), 41–51.
'Marital separation in the eighteenth and early nineteenth centuries' *Local Population Studies*, 45 (1990), 66–70.
'Locating the "missing marryers" in Colyton 1660–1750' *Local Population Studies*, 48 (1992), 49–59.
'Further analysis of the victims of plague in Colyton 1645–6' *Local Population Studies*, 54 (1995), 66–68.
'Time and wages of west country workfolks in the seventeenth and eighteenth centuries' *Local Population Studies*, 55 (1995), 66–68.
'Women's names—some problems for reconstitution analysis' *Local Population Studies*, 59 (1997), 60–61.
'Dealing with love: the ambiguous independence of the single woman in early modern England' *Gender and History*, 11:2 (1999), 209–232.

I am most grateful to John Fowles and Jonathan Cape for permission to reprint the extract from *The French Lieutenant's Woman* in Chapter 4.

Acknowledgements

Writing about Colyton invests one with an awesome sense of responsibility to 'those who have gone before'. This research project was conceived by the members of the Cambridge Group for the History of Population and Social Structure and is the direct outcome of forty years of research about the parish of Colyton by members of the Group. Other people's written work, thought and a multiplicity of questions about Colyton have provided the crucial groundwork for my book.

This project started life as a doctoral dissertation and I am especially indebted to my supervisor, Roger Schofield, for his help until his serious illness in the summer of 1988. I am immensely grateful to Tony Wrigley who then stepped in as supervisor at the least enviable point in the creation of a Ph.D. thesis. As Tony was also the instigator of the Colyton reconstitution my debt to him is more than obvious. Peter Laslett, Richard Wall and Jeremy Boulton also gave lots of advice at the right times. David Souden gave access to his file of Exeter court deposition cases and Larry Poos translated and transcribed Colyton court rolls. In the early days of research, Jean Robin shared both her room and her accumulated wisdom about Colyton. I am particularly grateful for her more recent support during the trying days leading up to publication when we both experienced the fallout from the decline of the specialised monograph. At the Group in the late 1980s, Ros Davies and Carol Lee were of invaluable assistance with the computer side of things. These were the halcyon days of early computing and Colyton's data has only ever been partly computerised. Ruth Bridgen helped me to find last-minute references and Oly Skulsky gave me a sense of *bonhomie*, along with the paper clips and envelopes.

The research was made possible by a linked award from the Economic and Social Research Council. I also acknowledge the financial assistance of the Prince Consort and Thirlwall Fund, and the Ellen McArthur Fund held at the History Faculty of the University of Cambridge. I was pleased to be the holder of a Michael Postan Award from London School of Economics for the session 1987/8. I have more recently been given financial support by the Bristol University Faculty of Arts Research Fund; a Scouloudi Foundation Historical Award for further research on Colyton; and the Pasold Research Fund for research on the early modern lace industry. The book really took shape when I was awarded a Nuffield Foundation Social Science Research Fellowship during 1997/8. For one term of the fellowship, I held a visiting scholarship at Wolfson College, Cambridge University, and towards the end of the year was visiting professor in the Department of Economic History in Uppsala, Sweden. Finally, to make publication a possibility I received an Aurelius Foundation Award and a Scouloudi Foundation grant-in-aid of publication provided in association with the Institute of Historical Research.

Turning to the south-west, the investigation would not have been possible without the co-operation of the Colyton Chamber of Feoffees, who gave me access to their archive. I thank the late Mr R.J. Phillips as bailiff, Mr Ted Long as chairman and Mr Colin Pady as archivist in particular, and the feoffees in general, for their permission to microfilm their valued documents. Subsequently, I enjoyed Devonshire farmhouse hospitality and some emergency research assistance from the Pady family. Most recently I am grateful to John Cochrane of Colyton Parish History Society for his efforts on my behalf. I must thank Devon Record Office for various services and carrying out the microfilming operation, especially Mrs Margery Rowe, then archivist in charge. Mrs Audrey Erskine, the keeper of Exeter Cathedral Library until September 1987, assisted in locating Colyton documents. The staff of the Westcountry Studies Library in Exeter were helpful with many aspects of the work. I would like to thank the Carew-Pole family for access to their archive held at Antony House in Torpoint. I acknowledge Prebendary H.H. Rann, the former vicar of Colyton, and Mrs M.J. Forsaith, the church PCC secretary, for their help with finding records. Fellow Devon researchers, the late Dr H.J. Yallop and Mrs Ena Cummings, made constructive and friendly comments on parts of the project. Sandra Cavallo let me house-sit her flat for one long Exeter summer, thus providing an excellent base for research. In Bristol, Nick Lee and Michael Richardson provided much help beyond the call of duty in the Special Collections department of Bristol University Library, and I am most grateful to the trustees for access to the Pinney collection.

I have delivered many academic papers on Colyton and thank everyone who provided feedback. Keith Wrightson and Rab Houston made judicious comments on the original dissertation. Over the years, Jonathan Barry, Harold Fox, Todd Gray, Pat Hudson, Steve Hindle, Anne Laurence, Maryanne Kowaleski, Mark Overton and Mark Stoyle can be singled out for sharing their great expertise and scholarship.

Just before I began work on Colyton, I spent a few months in Western Australia and (strangely enough) the project has also ended in Perth, where the University of Western Australia (UWA) gave me an honorary fellowship for a few months prior to my being awarded a Queen Elizabeth II Research Fellowship by the Australian Research Council. For help with the applications for these awards, for reading sections of the text and for valued friendship and encouragement, I am indebted to Patricia Crawford. For aid with maps of east Devon I am grateful to Viv Forbes, UWA's map librarian. For unqualified assistance with international transit of research materials, I am grateful to Ove Arup and Partners.

Last, but certainly not least, Michael Stanford, formerly of the University of the West of England, and Jonathan Barry of the University of Exeter, both did a brilliant job by reading the text from beginning to end. Dot and Dennis Sharpe have always encouraged my local history pursuits and provided up-to-date information and most of the photographs in the book. And above all, Derek Pennington has lived with this project almost from the outset and has accompanied me on trips to Colyton as well as many more far-flung places. At times I have wondered whether there is a perverse correlation between the smallness of the settlement and the length of time necessary to begin to understand the history of the people who lived and worked there. Without complaining, Derek accompanied me on that long journey, and by way of some small recompense I have dedicated the book to him.

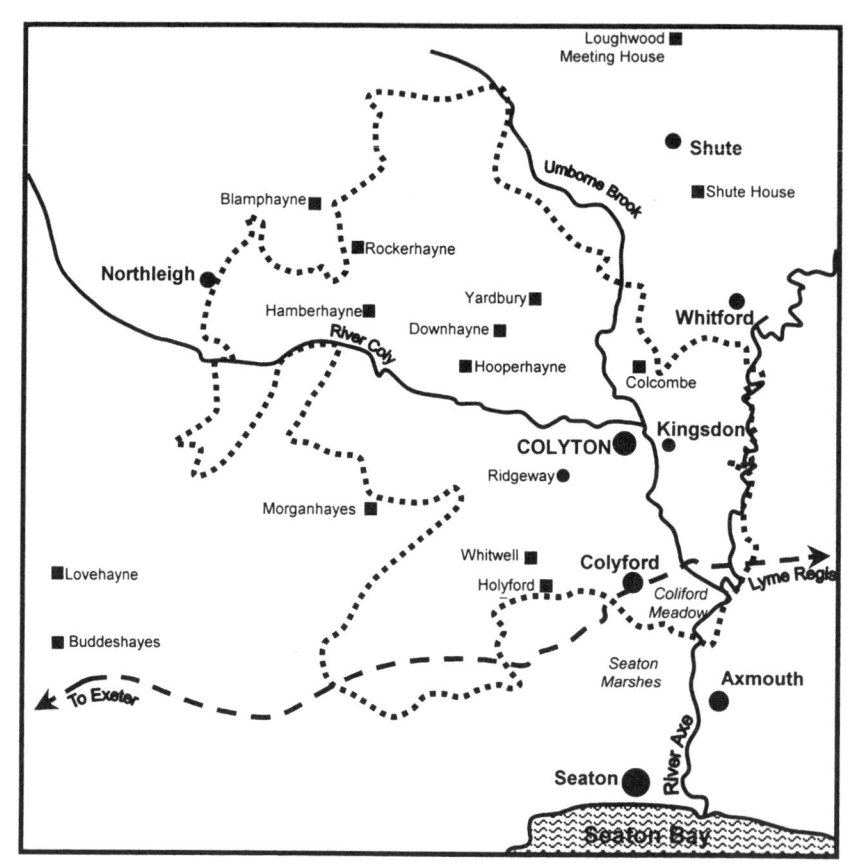

Map 1. Main features of Colyton parish.

Prologue

Investigating Colyton

This book is a study of the local origins of demographic change in a Devon parish in the early modern period. Colyton is well known to economic and social historians as the first English parish to have its population reconstituted (see pp. 11–14). The historical investigation of Colyton was followed by the reconstitution of many other parishes, both in England and elsewhere, such that it is now possible to place the results in a comparative perspective.[1] The details of the demographic history of the parish will be reiterated here, but the book intends to take the study a stage further by suggesting possible explanations for demographic change within the local environment. The time-consuming nature of demographic recovery tends to mean that existing studies stop somewhere short of placing the results in a wider context. Where explanations are offered, they relate population patterns to economic circumstances. I have been more ambitious and attempt not only to offer a detailed description of economic factors but also to place the demographic patterns within the context of social and political life. It became apparent to me that economic, social, political and religious circumstances were inextricably connected in early modern Colyton, and, as a result, this book offers a holistic attempt to reunify areas of academic enquiry which are usually treated separately in the many fields of specialised historical enquiry now pursued. As Richard Vann has recently suggested, with more than a passing reference to Clifford Geertz, a 'thickly textured study' of reconstitution parishes is needed.[2]

The use of 'reproducing' in the title of this book is double-edged. The book encompasses the demographic historian's concern about when, why and how often humans reproduce, but it also aims to reproduce the town and parish of Colyton in as far as it is possible to do so. Yet rather like reproduction furniture, the historian's attempts to recreate a community must always fall short of perfection. Nevertheless, reproduction usefully encompasses the generative and imaginative efforts of the historian. The chapters to follow make a full exploration of the demographic, economic, social, political and religious lives of the 1,500 or so individuals who resided in early modern Colyton. I also consider evidence from other parishes in the same locality in order to cast light beyond the parish of Colyton. The application of social science methods runs alongside the exploration of small stories, culled from local records, about the people of Colyton. Not only does this enliven the statistics, but it emphasises the agency of certain individuals in the history of Colyton. It means that this book is a contribution to the type of history that attempts to analyse a community 'from below'. Yet while recent academic studies of local communities have generally sought to uncover the experience of ordinary people and their livelihoods, it is difficult to leave an immersion in the circumstances of life in this town without an awareness of the importance of local politics and political structures. For convenience I have divided this book into sections considering politics and religion, then the economy and trade, and finally demography and society, but reference to anthropological studies of local communities makes it obvious that these sectors would have been overlaid and interwoven in the early modern parish, perhaps like the complex patterns fashioned in the lace that Colyton people made and traded. The texture will always evade us, however, and therefore the analogy might have been imitation lace, rather than reproduction furniture.

Much is unknowable about ordinary life in a society where many people could not write. To the reader, indeed, in some senses, I may appear to be embarking on 'mission impossible'. As Crafts and Ireland put it, 'It must be stressed that the "true structure" of the demographic system of Colyton or any other pre-industrial village is unknowable'.[3] And how much more unknowable are the motivations behind marriage decisions and timing, the sexual practices of seventeenth-century parishioners, or the true biological reasons for deaths of infants or adults. Even today, in permissive and explicit modern Western society where reproduction, sexuality and death are far more understood and controlled than they were for our forebears, people rarely divulge their motivations or feelings about these natural events. We still have very little understanding of what element of fertility decisions is rational and what is instinctive. As a result, and with no wish to force a pun, we are certain to be groping in the dark when trying to explain the intimate actions of a diverse community of people who lived many generations back in time.

I employ a mixture of tactics to help with this problem and it is as well to be candid about my approach from the outset. First, this study has only become possible by building on a great deal of collaborative research that has resulted from the endeavours of members of the Cambridge Group. I was very fortunate to be able to draw on an already completed reconstititution; but it is also the case that I have benefited from the increasing sophistication of demographic history over the past three decades. Secondly, my approach has been influenced by the work of the great Devon historian W.G. Hoskins and the wider research and writing of the 'Leicester School' of English local history. I try to pay attention to the topography and landscape of the parish as based on personal observation. I have also attempted to consider the local distinctiveness of Colyton alongside its place within a region. Interestingly, employing the full armoury of the local historian has enabled me to see Colyton in a different way from that in which it is treated in some literature. Colyton was not an isolated, rural village. We can set the parish within a global context by considering its contacts not only with London, but also with areas ranged around the Atlantic economy (Ireland, Newfoundland, New England, Virginia, the West Indies, even north and west Africa), as well as its trade links and traffic in ideas with Continental Europe. Colyton parish in fact comprised a small town, a failed borough and several hamlets (Map 1). Here there is a third input, and this is the development of separate disciplines of rural and urban history. The study of a parish like Colyton not only builds on the work of historians who have developed new methodologies but also suggests that these fields can profitably come together when considering a small country town and its hinterland. Fourthly, I have certainly benefited from the work of those historians who constitute what might be termed the 'Wrightson School' of early modern English history. This is not to deny the input of other early modernists, but the study of social history from the sixteenth to the eighteenth centuries has certainly been invigorated by the nuanced and insightful approach of these (originally) Cambridge-based scholars.

Finally, I employ a measure of personal experience that, I believe, has aided my thinking about the relationship between resources and population. I grew up in a mining village where early and general marriage perhaps resulted from relatively high male wages and a defined sexual division of labour plus a large dose of 'ranter' Methodism. Yet even as mines started to close and employment diversified, the universal impetus to youthful marriage remained. It had become an ingrained cultural norm. I later completed my doctoral thesis on Colyton while living in the west of Ireland. This was still a country with bitter memories of demographic nemesis. Before European Community funding had really taken effect, demographic adjustment was ever apparent in and around our village from emigration, bachelor houses, marriages which were managed if not arranged, Catholic piety and a network of rural debt and credit that was as familiar to contemporaries as it will always be impenetrable to the historian. There was a complex mixture of economic and religious factors comparable in some ways with the situation in seventeenth-century Colyton after the area was devastated by Civil War and plague. Later still, in 1997, I found myself assisting with an aid project in a remote part of Tanzania. Despite AIDS, malaria and a very high rate of infant mortality, the region was densely settled and suffering shortages of cultivable land. As a result bridewealth and the age of marriage had risen. Here again, living at a Catholic mission hospital, it was impossible to ignore the religious impetus in the dynamics of the local community that meant that no contraception was available in this region. My interest in Colyton, situated amid England's green and pleasant land (quintessential thatched cottage and cream tea country), may seem incongruous in comparison. But it lies in the process of demographic adjustment and in the interaction between structures that ordinary people live by, particularly economic resources and religious preoccupations, and the way they are able to manipulate these life experiences to their own ends and for the benefit of the community.[4] Such an endeavour has to be alive to politics and it has to delve for the essential haphazard humanness of the actors it seeks to describe. After all, I made my first ever visit to Colyton in 1986, when the town was awash with blue flags. They had just had a visit from Margaret Thatcher.

PART ONE
Documents and Dissent

1

Interpreting Colyton

> ... a great deal of exploration remains to be done by the devoted band of local historians and topographers, whose work, though it may be bounded by their own parishes, is nevertheless of great potential value. The history of each parish, viewed in this way, is a contribution to the history of England: it no longer remains a collection of unassimilated facts but has its own particular theme and continuity. From the histories of such remote and unknown parishes, wherever they may lie, the economic and social history of the county will one day be written with a full mastery of the facts; and from these histories of the counties and provinces we shall be able to write the general history of England that calls to be written.
> (W.G. Hoskins in W.G. Hoskins and H.P.R. Finberg, eds, *Devonshire Studies*, 1952: 228)

Colyton lies at the heart of the home territory of the great English local historian W.G. Hoskins and some of his richest writing concerns this corner of south-east Devon. Colyton is a small market town situated in the Axe Valley some 20 miles from Exeter and 6 miles inland from the sea. Today, the parish looks prosperous, pleasantly situated among green rolling hills with the rivers Axe and Coly flowing through the farmland. In comparison with other Devon parishes, Colyton embraces a fairly large land area. It has been divided into several different parts. First, there is the town itself, arranged around a figure-of-eight road, to a common medieval plan (see Map 2). Secondly, there is the hamlet of Colyford lying to the south of Colyton town astride the main road. Colyford is an incorporated borough and has had a mayor since 1340. It used to be a larger place: Stukeley wrote in 1724 of 'Cullyford where there have been many inns and houses and a considerable town'.[1] Thirdly, there are the

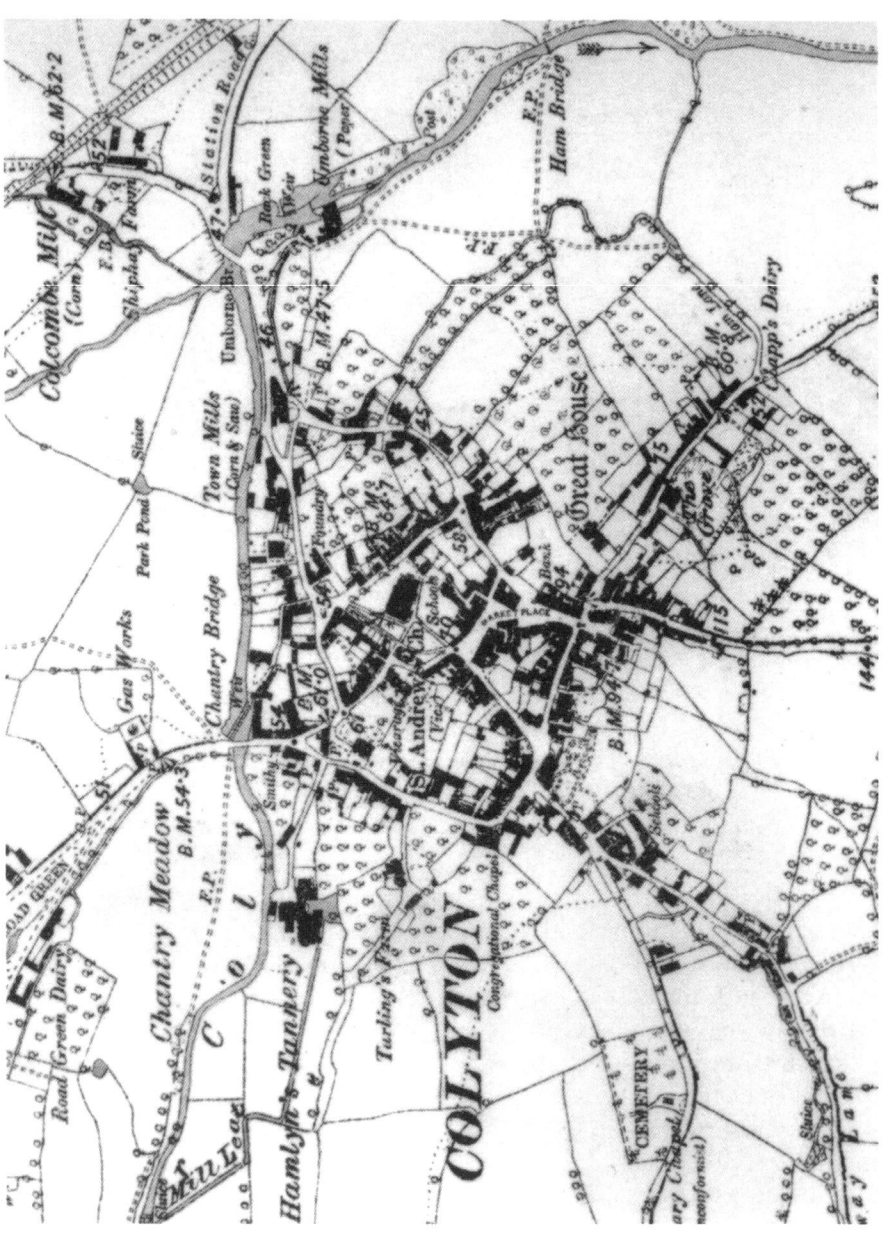

Map 2. Detail of Colyton town from the Ordnance Survey Map of 1887.

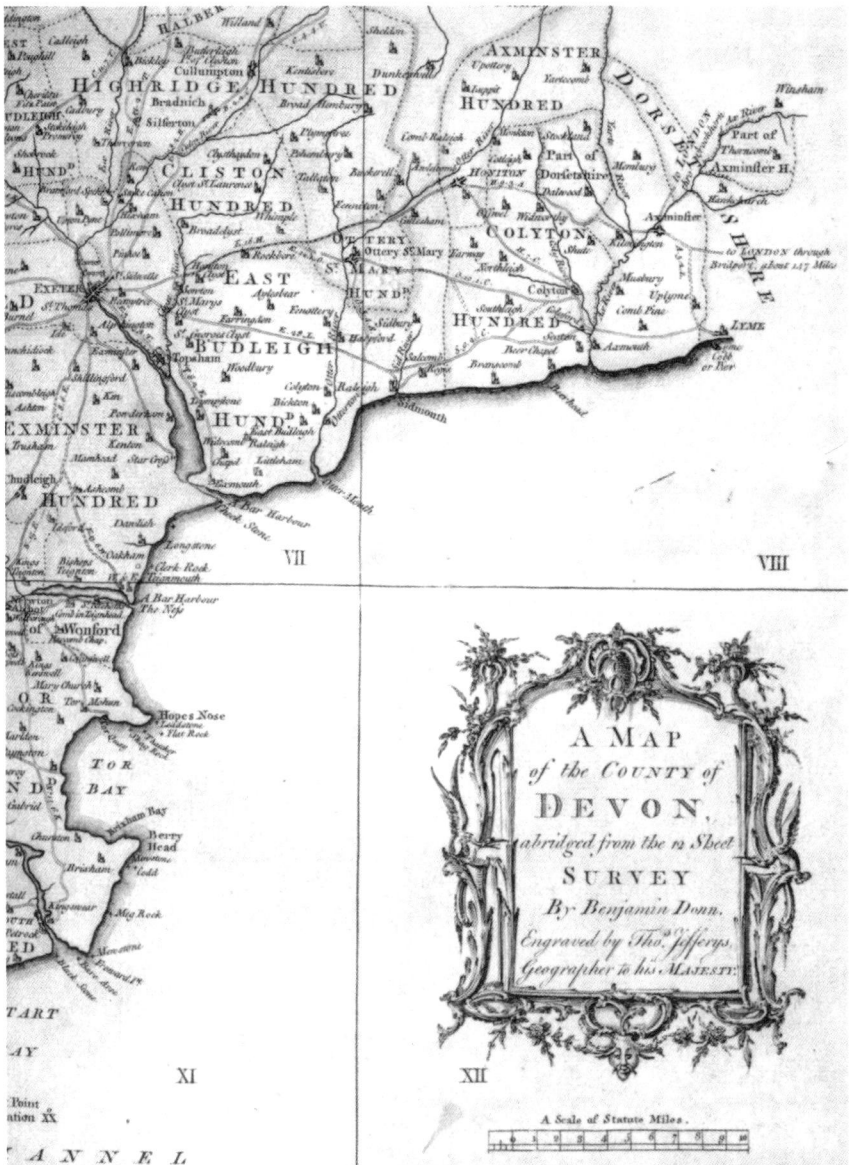

Map 3. Detail from Benjamin Donn's map of the County of Devon 1765, reprinted with permission from the facsimile by Devon and Cornwall Record Society and the University of Exeter (1965).

country 'tithings', or medieval subdivisions, variously known as Farwood, Woodland, Watchcombe and Minchingholme. A good part of the population in the past lived there, in or around the ancient farms that derive from medieval enclosures. The names of the substantial farms consist of a compound of a medieval personal name with 'hayes' or 'hayne' added to it.

Although the present parish covers more than 7,000 acres, the church was once the centre of an ecclesiastical district covering some 22,000 acres. The coastal settlements of the neighbouring villages of Beer, Seaton and Branscombe were derived from lands originally part of Colyton. Shute, Northleigh and Southleigh were chapelries of Colyton and it is probable that Farway, Offwell and Widworthy formed part of the original Colyton estate (see Map 3). Along with other areas of east Devon, Colyton was settled early—the land is fertile and was easily cleared and the parish was populated by customary tenants. While the hillsides remained flinty and formed rough pasture, the sunny bottoms of deep, south-facing coombs were conducive to crop cultivation.[2] When walking today along the medieval tracks that linked the large farms and observing the hedges which enclosed the medieval land parcels, it is not difficult to envisage the early modern rural aspect of the parish. But the town was also significant in the late medieval period for cloth trading. In 1523 Colyton was the fourth wealthiest parish in Devon. The leading parishioners were merchants and the parish held noted markets and fairs.[3] Today, Colyton has 2,400 inhabitants, the same as the parish population in the 1841 census. There are only a few indicators of the seventeenth-century population level. The Compton Census of 1676 seems to be highly suspect since it gives the conformist population as exactly 1,000, and puts nonconformists at a mere 19. Multipliers used on the Protestation Return of 1641 and the Hearth Tax of 1674 produce estimates of 1,610 and 1,712 respectively, which seem to be more accurate.[4] Gregory King made an estimate that the population was 1,554 on the implementation of the 1695 Marriage Duty Act.[5]

Colyton and the Cambridge Group

Colyton is well known to social and economic historians as the parish has been the focus of a long-term project by the Cambridge Group for the History of Population and Social Structure. The project originated in the early 1960s when Tony Wrigley used the complete and unbroken series of parish registers to pioneer the family reconstitution method of nominal record linkage. Colyton's registers date from just after the original injunction of Henry VIII in 1536 and are contained in an enormous book.[6] When Wrigley published the results of the reconstitution study one startling discovery attracted attention to Colyton. Where

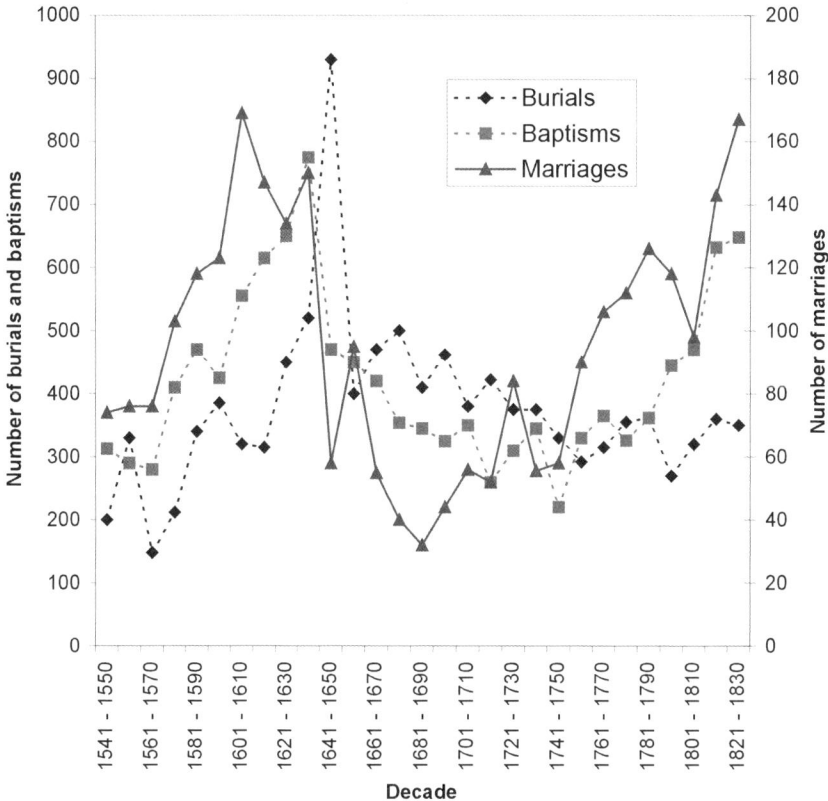

Fig. 1.1 Baptisms, burials and marriages by decade for Colyton 1541–1830.

marriages and baptisms dipped in the late seventeenth century, Wrigley claimed to find evidence of family limitation.[7] Yet the age at marriage results proved to be even more significant. Women in the 1650–99 cohort married over two years later than women who had married in the 1550–99 cohort. After the 1650–99 'high' there was a steady fall in age at marriage such that average age of marriage in the early nineteenth century was a full five years earlier. Later work by Wrigley examined, among other aspects, adult and child mortality and further measurement of registration defects.[8] Subsequently Colyton data have been used in many academic studies. The parish register aggregates provide the broad outline of population change in Colyton and are presented in Figure 1.1. The fall in numbers of marriages and baptisms in the second half of the seventeenth century, and their subsequent recovery by the second half of the eighteenth century, have proved to be one of the most intriguing aspects of Colyton's population history.

The publication of Wrigley and Schofield's *The Population History of England 1541–1871* set the parameters of demographic history for the 1980s.[9] Colyton was included in the sample of 404 parishes. The results provided confirmation that the town could be taken as a 'typical' parish since Colyton's demographic data resembled those of other English parishes. Wrigley and Schofield's central finding was that the age at marriage was the crucial determinant of population trends. Vital changes in female marriage age occurred across the parish sample. Celibacy was also seen as important. Wrigley later summarised this by saying that increases in fertility were 'attributable to changes in age of marriage and in the proportions never marrying, which between them determine what proportion of women of childbearing age is married or was once married'.[10] The Wrigley and Schofield hypothesis postulates that age at marriage and marriage chances are crucially affected by trends in real wage levels. The level of real wages determines when a couple have reached the necessary threshold of income to establish an independent household. Regional specialisation might affect the wage rate. Suggestively for Colyton, this point was taken up by Weir, who argued that 'if the economic opportunities of men and women differed greatly between regions, then migration of the unmarried might have created distorted sex ratios'.[11]

With this in mind, Wrigley and Schofield, and later Weir, argued that the demographic adjustment processes were likely to affect a sector of the population. If real wage factors were entirely responsible, it could be expected that the labouring or impoverished part of the population would either not marry or delay marriage. It is this argument which provides the basis for further investigation into Colyton's past by providing a complementary body of socio-economic information to enhance the demographic details provided by the reconstitution. Enhanced reconstitution methods allow for the full exploitation of parochial records to provide a stratified analysis of one community. Thus, by establishing the social and economic context of life experiences in Colyton and linking the reconstitution results to further details about the individuals and families, it was possible to look at the demographic results by status, and by gender, and to attempt to examine the effect of factors such as income levels. Historical demographic work to date has, generally, been devoid of a status perspective.[12] This omission is most glaring in the analysis of age at marriage trends. Where indicators, such as early marriage age, have been related to certain societal groups, it has not been possible to examine them on a systematic basis over time. The tremendous advantage of an enhanced reconstitution analysis is that it gives a picture of status-specific demographic behaviour. Differences in male and female demographic behaviour in the past have been noticed. For example, whereas female ages at marriage were variable over time in Colyton, male ages did not vary to the same degree. By focusing on these important sex-specific differences it became possible to provide more convincing explanations for demographic patterns.[13]

It has been Cambridge Group practice to provide a full assessment of sources and methods. While this can be tedious, a description of the methodology and documentation follows because it may be useful for other historians carrying out similar investigations. The question of document quality and survival is linked to the political and religious circumstances of the early modern parish and this is explored in Chapter 2. Readers who want to avoid the technical detail may wish to skip straight to Chapter 2. Chapters 3 and 4 provide a thorough examination of the local economy. Chapter 5 gives the results of the analysis of the population by sex and status and considers the connections with the socio-economic conditions in the parish. Chapters 6 and 7 consider the implications of local politics and policy on the family and household in Colyton. Of course, few irrefutable conclusions have been based on a study of one parish and questions of typicality have always arisen over the patterns found to have existed in Colyton. Therefore in the chapters which follow, some attention will be paid to considering whether Colyton was an unusual parish. However, while the Cambridge Group's analysis tends to assume that there was a fundamental homogeneity of demographic behaviour across parishes, as more detailed studies have appeared, it is local diversity which emerges as one of the most interesting facets to be explored.

The Total Reconstitution Method

The technique of family reconstitution was developed by the French demographer Louis Henry in the 1950s as an analytical tool to be used in his search for 'natural fertility'.[14] The method of nominal linkage onto family reconstitution forms (FRFs) was subsequently adopted by Tony Wrigley for the Colyton parish registers. 'Total reconstitution', a phrase coined by Alan Macfarlane in 1977 for his project on Earls Colne in Essex, involves incorporating historical data beyond the parish registers into the nominal linkage process.[15] Macfarlane suggested that all records appertaining to a parish should be linked together rather than just the parish registers of baptism, marriage and burial. Linkage of two or more records is now a common technique in social and economic history studies.[16] Total reconstitution methods facilitate a longitudinal analysis, thus preserving the fluidity and continuity in social change that can be stifled in a more static representation. The result is a useful way to approach the investigation of the family and household using developmental models.[17]

While reconstitution methods in general have received some criticism, it seems likely that linkage quality can only be improved by employing more sources of information.[18] The methodology used here is described in Appendix 1. The main drawback of all reconstitutions is that there is only a minority of people who can 'be reconstituted'. In the entire Colyton reconstitution there are only 206 completed marriages—that is FRFs containing the baptisms, marriage and burials of a particular couple. This forms a mere 6.5 per cent of FRFs with marriages. This is in itself only a part of the total sample, which also includes 'dummy FRFs' where the marriage date has to be 'manufactured' from baptism evidence since the ceremony did not take place at Colyton church. It is on this limited sample of 'completed' FRFs that some of the work on demographic dynamics in Colyton has been based.[19] The linkage technique of incorporating extra records inevitably shows up a core population with a high propensity to appear in the records. The question is then to assess the typicality of the characteristics they show. One obvious problem is that the core population is bound to be the least migratory. As David Levine eloquently put it, 'In most village studies —using the technique of family reconstitution—this problem is simply ignored and the results are thereby quite unrepresentative of the larger population processes. In this sense, most village population studies are rather like the sound of one hand clapping'.[20] There is also evidence that the families for whom a full life history can be produced are larger and more agricultural than others who do not show up.[21] Now that linkage can be carried out by computer it should be possible to produce a total reconstitution covering a group of parishes or a region which would make reconstitution a more useful tool to analyse local migration patterns.

For Colyton, the results of the reconstitution divide the population with a deliberately simplistic partition into four rigid social status groupings which seem to reflect the differentiated social structure which existed in Colyton. This division was inevitably difficult, however, and the number of individuals who cannot be given a status or occupational group of any type is large. Table 1.1 shows the number of FRFs in each category that could be given a status group. As might be anticipated, in general the proportion follows an upward trend over time, but there was a good coverage of records in the first cohort due to documents surviving from the payment of subsidies as well as those made when the Chamber of Feoffees was established.

The population was divided into the following groups: gentry and landed wealth; craftspeople and middling wealth; labourers; poor; status and occupation not known.[22] Table 1.2 shows the distribution of all the FRFs which can be given a status grouping.

While the documentation was reasonably spread across the groups in

Table 1.1 Number and percentage of FRFs with status designation 1538–1837

Cohort	No. of total FRFs	No. with status designation	% with status designation
1538–49	202	86	42.6
1550–99	786	228	29.0
1600–49	1168	473	40.5
1650–99	773	350	45.3
1700–49	669	344	51.4
1750–99	739	425	37.5
1800–37	494	279	56.5

Table 1.2 Distribution of FRFs with status by cohort 1538–1837

Cohort	No.	Gentry		Crafts		Labourer		Poor	
		No.	%	No.	%	No.	%	No.	%
1538–49	86	61	70.9	19	22.0	6	6.9	–	–
1550–99	228	67	29.4	35	15.4	85	37.3	41	17.9
1600–49	473	132	27.9	129	27.2	81	17.1	131	27.7
1650–99	350	113	32.3	49	14.0	37	10.6	151	43.2
1700–49	344	65	18.9	56	16.3	44	12.8	179	52.0
1750–99	425	94	22.1	131	30.8	136	32.0	64	15.0
1800–37	279	78	27.9	79	28.3	107	38.4	15	5.4

some cohorts, a heavy weighting towards the gentry was apparent in the first small cohort. There is a shortage of craft and labourer designations in the period 1650–1749, and a relative lack of recordings of the poor after 1750.

Index cards also contain extra information which, while not concerning the individuals' status grouping directly, was considered to be useful for some part of the study. A typical example of a card is presented here:

> ISAAC DROWER
> 1663 Feoffees Bailiff's Accounts 'pd for mending of ye
> plantchent in Joseph Mayett's own chamber'
> 1674 Hearth Tax 'Pauper'
> 1678 Bailiff's Accounts Apr. 13th 'pd for stocking
> parish musketts 2d'
> Aug. 10th 'pd for making ye schoolhouse court and mending
> others as of his bill 6s 5d'

1681 July 26th 'pd for his work and his boy 3 days to mend parish chamber 6s 6d'
1682/83 Poor Account. Contributed 3s.
Feoffee Document 18/1 (4) 'Isaac Drower's Bill; works at 18d per day together with Zarkey'
1685 (Wigfield) Monmouth Rebel, yeoman. Returned to Colyton after Sedgemoor.

Isaac Drower was a carpenter and he was literate because he wrote and signed his own bill. 'Zarkey', we find from the attached card, is likely to be his son, Zachariah, a joiner, and also a rebel at Sedgemoor in 1685. The Hearth Tax attribution of 'Pauper' probably reflects a temporary stage of life-cycle poverty (as has been found in other cases), and it would seem to be fairly safe to put Isaac Drower into the craftsperson category. Nevertheless, the difficulties are shown by the fact that in the only listing of Monmouth's rebellion giving occupational information, Isaac is described, along with many of his fellow Colyton rebels, as a 'yeoman'. Turning to the FRF number 10683, there is something of a shortage of demographic information about Isaac. No baptism is recorded for him or his wife Mary, and they did not marry in Colyton. But Isaac appears in a marriage bond of September 1663.[23] He was a joiner born in Topsham who married Mary Trawle, a spinster from Colyton. They had three children, baptised from 1664, and Zachariah married in Seaton in 1691 at the age of 26.

Documents

While Colyton has a good overall coverage of documents, this could not be considered in any way superior to other parishes and in some respects the documentation is disappointing. No complete listing or census type of document exists for pre-1837 Colyton, and no record, apart from the parish register, spans the entire 300-year period of this project. Colyton was originally chosen for reconstitution study because of the quality of the parish register rather than any criteria based on the survival of other records. The coverage of the register will be considered in some detail in the next section. Three problems apply to many of the documents. First, they tend to be 'official' in conception and form. They show the authorities acting in their governmental capacities. So, for example, informal charitable relief to the poor is not recorded. There is little evidence of the attitude of Colyton parishioners to those who wrote most of the records. The only exceptions are the few surviving letters to poor relief officers that survive from the late eighteenth and early nineteenth centuries. Secondly, evidence about women is sadly lacking in the document collection. This is a huge problem, common to almost all historical projects but particularly apposite here since it is women's marriage patterns which change over time, yet occupational data refers almost exclusively to men. Thirdly, as will be shown in the chapters to follow, in many cases the reason for the existence and survival of many documents was political. As is common to all community studies, the documents are biased towards recording the lives of the responsible, rich and moral rather than the feckless, poor and immoral.

About eighty documents or sets of documents were used in the total reconstitution process. Appendix 1 provides a complete list of them. More documents than these were involved in the whole project but some of them were not suitable for linking and provided background information. Some records from other Devon parishes were also used to provide supplementary data. To consider tax documents first, several lay subsidies, collected between 1524 and 1624, were linked, as well as the Ship Money collection of 1636. Some local rates were collected such as the 1726 rate to restore Colyton church. The 1780 and 1798 Land Taxes were incorporated and the end point was the 1832 Land Tax. All these lists were used to provide a basic indication of wealth status for the adult male population above the poor.[24] Several lists and subsidies dating from the mid-sixteenth century provided a complementary body of data. The 1546 feoffees' charter, for example, shows women holding property which does not appear on the nearly concurrent 1544/45 lay subsidy roll. It was not possible to use the Poll Tax document of 1660 since Colyton town is missing from it, and the returns for the areas of Stoford, Colyford, Whitwell and Gatcombe are partial. A good-quality Hearth Tax document exists for 1674.[25] This lends itself to comparison with other communities.[26] Pauper householders are named and this provided a useful comparison with the seventeenth-century poor accounts.

Court roll material and manor surveys were used in the project. Family papers were examined from the Sampson, Rolle and Petre collections, but principally from the Carew-Pole estate. The Carew-Pole family are still lords of the manor of Colyton. Several survey books are extant for Colyton but they rarely mention more than the tenant's name. Land disputes, particularly about common land, generated documents. Some court rolls have survived, specifically for the manor of Whitwell, which was in the southern part of the parish. Material has also been included from the Pinney family papers.[27] The Pinneys farmed in Axmouth in the sixteenth century. By the seventeenth century some members of the family lived in Colyton, others in Axminster and in western Dorset. The importance of this very full collection of papers is that they give us an insight into the detail of the lives of a nonconformist 'middling family' involved in the local lace trade and colonial merchandising as well as in farming. Family papers from Colyton also include the diary of Walter Yonge, written at Colyton and Axminster in the first half of the seventeenth century.[28] Yonge was the writer of a famous journal of the Long Parliament.

Probate material and ecclesiastical court records were the weakest area of recording coverage. Wills and probate inventories have been important to much early modern social history but the probate collection for the county of Devon was destroyed in 1942 when Devon Record Office was bombed. The lack of original wills is in part compensated for by those of the Prerogative Court of Canterbury which were transcribed for Colyton and Shute and by a collection of printed probate material. Some of these wills can be matched with a scattering of inventories now kept in the Public Record Office. These were wills of people who held land in other dioceses and were thus the wealthiest individuals in Colyton. Some will abstracts, indexed by name only, were collected by Miss O. Moger and Sir Oswyn Murray between about 1921 and 1941.[29] Wills and inventories provide information on kinship links, religious networks, inheritance practices, consumption of material goods, debt and credit networks, and some idea of the economic activities of local communities. As a result their loss is sorely felt in the case of Colyton. Probate material has added great richness to other 'micro-studies' and can critically enhance a 'total reconstitution'.

As Colyton was a peculiar of the Dean and Chapter of Exeter it was not covered by the ecclesiastical courts and only a few references to Colyton can be located. A survey was made of the records for the Devon ecclesiastical courts for the period 1661 through to 1681, to provide background information and to search for Colyton people who gave evidence in court in other places.[30] While the post-Restoration records are full and well maintained, the early seventeenth-century ones are more patchy and the cases for 1620–1634 are missing altogether. A full search was made for Colyton cases in the quarter session records. The evidence used from court records comprises the immediate local district to provide full details on the social, economic and political context of changes in south-east Devon.

Another archive of records survives for the Colyton Chamber of Feoffees. The feoffees were incorporated in 1546 when the parishioners of Colyton bought part of the manor from the crown for £1,000 after Henry, Marquis of Exeter, was executed for treason. He had owned the whole of the parish and much of the surrounding area. Thenceforth the feoffees were to be nominated by the majority of the parishioners. Their funds derived from selling and letting the estate. Feoffees were essentially public governing bodies. Clause 5 of the charter of the Colyton Chamber of Feoffees stated that letting was to be carried out in a public place where strangers could make offers and parishioners could see what was being done. However, the charter was in Latin and was not translated until 1792. There were twelve elected feoffees and twenty helpers who were called the 'twenty men'. All of them had to hold property in Colyton to qualify for the job. Among other assets, the chamber owned the farms of Buddlehayes and Lovehayne, the church houses, and rights to the market and tolls. The feoffee property was sold in 1918 but the organisation is still in existence today.[31] As the original charter stated, the feoffee funds were to be devoted to 'good, godly and commendable uses and purposes'. These included the repairs of the market house, a salary of £30 a year to the master of the free school and his housekeeping, the payment of a salary to a bailiff and the expenses of the town water. Funds were also used to mend the bridges and roads and to provide for soldiers to serve the King in a time of war. From 1641 the feoffees maintained a fire brigade. All the money was for the 'common utility and profit of the parishioners of Colyton'. The parish church was also maintained by the feoffees but repairs were made from the church's own rate from the early eighteenth century. The remainder of the money was to be distributed among the poor, which, in the seventeenth century, was mainly done by providing doles and paying house rents. As the feoffees' historian, White, put it, 'they became a complete parochial corporation, with whom, and to whom, by common consent, all the social machinery of the town, short of the administration of the law, seemed to devolve'.[32]

An assortment of different poor relief documents has been linked to the reconstitution. Apart from the feoffees' accounts, pauper apprentice indentures and registers, bastardy records establishing paternity and maintenance in the case of poor illegitimate children, workhouse records, settlement and removal documents, as well as the accounts of the overseer of the poor, were used. All these records were patchy in coverage. A particular problem is the absence of any overseers' accounts after 1770 when these are readily available for other Devon parishes. Various miscellaneous work agreements and payments for work completed appeared in the family papers and feoffees' accounts. These ranged from arrangements for Colyton workmen to work on the Poles' large house in Shute, to payments for craftsmen for completing small jobs like plumbing in the church. This type of data embellished the linkage process by providing occupational information. The documents linked to the reconstitution ranged from single sheets such as the Bridge Building Account of 1704, which merely gives a short list of men engaged in building a bridge in Colyton, their precise tasks and the wages paid to them, to much larger documents like the overseers' account book covering the period 1740–70, which details all casual payments made to the poor. Linking this huge volume took three months in itself. In choosing the documents for linkage an attempt was made to include a balanced group in each cohort section. There was a paucity of records relating to the first half of the eighteenth century. On the whole, however, a representative distribution of records was available for use in the total reconstitution.

Keith Wrightson has argued that the choice of a parish for detailed community study should be based on the survival of six key sources: well-kept parish registers, manorial records, tax records, testamentary records, quarter sessions and ecclesiatical court records.[33] Colyton sadly fails on one of these counts—testamentary material—and is not impressive on some of the others. It could be argued that the omission is more serious in the sense that the parish comprised far more than one village. On the other hand, it is important to study the less recorded parishes as well as the better documented places. Some of the best-recorded communities are such because they have not experienced change and conflict; perhaps, for example, they have had a stable leading family in charge over several centuries. As the Colyton story unfolds, it becomes apparent that some of the patchy documentary cover results from a fairly tempestuous and contested history in which record creation was in itself sometimes a political action and where some secrets have been deliberately erased from the record. The task may appear dry, but the local historian is behoven to examine the history of the documents that survive, and why they survive, at the same time as constructing the history of the parish.

The Parish Register

Since the parish register provides the framework on to which the additional Colyton documents have been hung, it follows that some assessment of its accuracy must be made. While Wrigley was fairly certain that the parish register was comprehensive, others (and Devon historians, in particular) have been more circumspect.[34] The feoffee accounts for 1597 contain a payment for the parish registers to be copied on to parchment according to law, and later they were well presented in a book bound by the feoffees in 1792. Some marginal notes were made on the registers at that time. There are three periods of exceptional detail in the registers—1609–21, 1765–79 and 1813–19—for which it has been possible to make an estimate of the occupational structure of Colyton.[35]

Linkage suggests that the earliest registers cover only the wealthy sector of Colyton's population. In the first cohort of 1538–49, 70 per cent of the FRFs which can be given a status grouping are classified as 'gentry'. At the same time 55 per cent of individuals who cannot be linked to an FRF in this cohort fall into the 'labourer' category. It is difficult to provide any certainty on this important point, however, since all the lower social groupings might be found in the 57 per cent of the group who appear on FRFs but cannot be given a status grouping because they do not appear in any of the documentation. The bias has disappeared by the next cohort. There is little reason to doubt that the burial registers are accurate. Poor relief records do indicate that corpses were carried to other parishes if the deceased's settlement had not been in Colyton.[36] More controversy surrounds the accuracy of the baptism register, especially regarding the recording of infants who died at or shortly after birth, as well as the representativeness of the marriage register, which shows a dip in marriages celebrated in Colyton between the mid-seventeenth century and the mid-eighteenth century. These problems will be considered in this section.

On the first issue, the accuracy of a baptismal register is usually measured by its recording of endogenous infant mortality. Endogenous infant mortality, as defined by the Bourgeois-Pichat method, generally refers to mortality taking place in the first month of life. It is mortality associated with the birth process, rather than external influences, which have greatest effect after this first month. The variability in recording endogenous infant mortality has been the subject of several studies.[37] It is clear that a proportion of births will always be excluded from baptisms, and estimates range from a tenth in the seventeenth century, to a third in the late eighteenth century and early nineteenth century.[38] For Colyton, Wrigley and Schofield regard that an endogenous rate of 31 per 1,000 births is low but seems dependable.[39] The parish apprentice register for Colyton also provides a check on the baptism of poor children during the period 1598–1711.[40] Since the parish would have been reluctant to support children who could not be considered as belonging to Colyton, it could be expected that most of them would have been born in the parish. Indeed, for a brief period between 1675 and 1682 the children's baptism dates were stated in the register. Overall, baptism recording was almost complete. The only significant omissions were the under-recording of illegitimate children in the mid-seventeenth century and particularly in the 1660s, and some patchy baptism recording at the end of the apprenticeship register period. A minor amount of mismatching of births and deaths of children occurs in the reconstitution at the end of the seventeenth century and in the early years of the eighteenth century. Some of these cases are where parents have given a child the same name as a deceased sibling, and only one baptism is recorded as having taken place. These omissions seem to coincide with periods that William Salter was vicar of Colyton, from 1684 to 1714. This may explain some of the apparent fall in endogenous infant mortality which occurs in the 1700–49 cohort for Colyton.[41] In general, cases of late baptism were remarkable and worthy of comment, as was the case with Elizabeth Bull. She was born in 1673 and baptised on the 28 September 1676. The parish register records this was 'when she came by herself to the church to see her younger sister baptised'. Linkage of the overseers' account book with the baptism register indicates that poor children in the eighteenth century were generally baptised within two weeks of birth. It seems likely that the Settlement Laws placed a new emphasis on the legality of baptism for defining a settlement, which was of great importance to the poor and potentially poor. Birthplace was always resorted to as a settlement qualification if no other claim, like a yearly hiring, could be made. As an initial insurance for the maintenance of the family it was necessary to register all births in the parish as feoffee and poor relief was normally distributed only to those who had been born in Colyton.[42] The overseers' accounts show that officials would often journey to other parishes to check on people's settlements in their baptism registers.

The story of the hopefully christened Lazarus Colyton, which can be followed in the overseers' account book, shows that once a child had been born in the parish it would be cherished, baptised and entitled to parish funds, however sickly it might be. The overseers' account book records for 1 November 1767: 'pd for bringing a male infant from Borcombe Gate near ye highway it being left there (by person unknown) to Colyton which child was afterwards Baptised Lazarus Colyton and soon after dyed 2s. 6d.' Another expense was incurred before the death and the entry was made: 'pd Joan Edwards for taking care of Lazarus Colyton and for brandy to sprinkle it with as it had lain on ye ground all night and almost dead and other necessaries about it 3s.'. Thereafter expenses were paid for a trip to 'Sidford, Sidbury, Awliscombe, Honiton, Farway, Northleigh, Offwell etc.' in search of the people who had left Lazarus because a description of a strange man and woman travelling around had been given to the poor relief officers. This first trip cost 7s 6d. It was not successful so the next day horse hire was paid for two men to continue the search. Meanwhile Lazarus's body was examined by a coroner, brought from Honiton at a cost of 1s, and a coffin, grave and bell were paid for at the sum of 2s 3d.

Wall showed that about 20 per cent of people who claimed to be Colyton-born in the 1851 census were not actually recorded in the parish registers.[43] The nonconformist registers for the early nineteenth century accounted for 27 per cent of these. If the rest were older people some of the explanation may lie in the note in the flyleaf of the original register that the 1783 Stamp Act carried a tax of 3d and that this led to many omissions in the register until it was repealed in 1794.[44] An alternative possibility is that they had invented their birthplace in order to have a claim to one of the sources of relief in the parish.

With reference to the second issue, there seems to have been no similar incentive to marry in Colyton church. As we have seen, the demographic research that has been carried out for Colyton shows a falling-off in the number of marriages celebrated in Colyton church. This is most apparent

20

after 1660. It is important to establish at this stage whether this was a real fall in marriages or a feature of defective registration. It is apparent, however, that the fall in marriages far exceeds the fall in baptisms, which seems to indicate that it was unlikely to be due to poor recording, but rather that the marriage ceremony was being avoided in Colyton church. This phenomenon, which affects not only the recorded information used for demographic analysis but also our understanding of the social circumstances of the parish, will be examined in detail.

One possibility is that Colyton parishioners married in secret. Historians have shown the importance of clandestine marriage centres in other parts of the country.[45] Prior to the 1753 Hardwicke Act, marriages which happened in any place, and at any time, were valid even if the calling of banns or purchase of a licence was avoided. However, it seems likely that under normal conditions spouses would find it most convenient to marry in one or other of their parishes of residence. They had to make a legal payment to the incumbent if they did not marry there. Admittedly, however, there is little evidence that this was strictly enforced. Wrigley demonstrated that in the 404 parish sample aggregate tabulations compiled at the Cambridge Group the baptism/marriage ratio rose during the seventeenth century to the point where only an estimated 90 per cent of marriages were recorded in the parish registers.[46] Schofield inflated the missing 10 per cent to a possible 14 per cent.[47] Wrigley suggested that couples of low status were most likely to engage in clandestine marriage to avoid the cost of a ceremony, but the evidence from the Fleet prison indicates that, in London at least, a cross-section of the population avoided normal marriage procedures.[48]

In a situation where there appears to be a high proportion of 'missing marryers', Souden noted that Colyton had a drastically reduced proportion of couples who only married in the town in the period 1650–1750.[49] These are the cases where the FRFs feature no baptisms or burials of the marital couple and no baptisms of children. This suggested that there could have been a clandestine marriage centre in or near the parish. But Table 1.3 shows, contrary to Souden's observation, that as a proportion of FRFs with marriages (as opposed to 'dummy' FRFs), 'marriage only' cases increased to form nearly half of all marriages celebrated in Colyton in the 1650–99 period.

Table 1.4 gives the status of people involved in 'marriage only' cases according to the categories set out at the beginning of this chapter. It is clear that most of the 'marriage only' individuals came into the 'unknown' category. That is, they were not people who participated in the economy or social life of Colyton to an appreciable extent. They certainly did not own or occupy any land, and none of the poor law documents indicate that they had a settlement in Colyton. They probably fitted into either the top or bottom rungs of Colyton society. They were likely to be

Table 1.3 Number and percentage of 'marriage only' case FRFs 1538–1799

Cohort	No. of 'marriage only' cases	No. of FRFs with marriages	%
1538–49	22	81	27.2
1550–99	185	501	36.9
1600–49	220	650	33.8
1650–99	121	266	45.5
1700–49	149	353	42.2
1750–99	203	559	36.3

Table 1.4 Status of 'marriage only' FRFs 1538–1799

| Cohort | No. | Gentry | | Crafts | | Labourer | | Poor | | Unknown | |
		No.	%	No.	%	No.	%	No.	%	No.	%
1538–49	22	2	9.0	1	4.5	–	–	–	–	19	86.4
1550–99	185	16	8.6	6	3.2	23	12.4	1	0.5	139	75.1
1600–49	220	18	8.2	6	2.7	6	2.7	10	4.5	180	81.8
1650–99	121	12	9.9	4	3.3	1	0.8	12	9.9	92	76.0
1700–49	149	9	6.0	7	4.7	3	2.0	35	23.5	95	63.7
1750–99	203	30	14.8	28	13.8	20	9.8	9	4.4	116	57.1

either mobile sons or daughters from gentry families or, farm servants who moved around and did not marry in their home parish. The marriage register actually states that these were 'servants' in many cases. These people were not likely to have made a conscious decision against marrying in Colyton church, as they were not deeply embroiled in village disputes or loyalties. Perhaps they were using the church rather like a modern-day registry office, as a setting for a wedding rather than with any particular symbolic significance? This raises the question of whether due to a shortfall of locals marrying in Colyton church, the incumbents encouraged marriages of non-locals. Colyton would have been an ideal location for extraordinary marriages, being an ecclesiastical 'peculiar' and therefore exempt from direct episcopal jurisdiction and regulation.[50] But there is no evidence of an established clandestine marriage centre in Colyton.[51]

At the same time there is evidence of considerable ecclesiastical disruption in mid-seventeenth-century Colyton. The vicar was ejected in 1647 and replaced by a Puritan, John Wilkins. During the period 1653–60 justices of the peace married people. This period of civil registration meant a minor revolution in marriage practices in Devon.[52] An ecclesiastical court matrimonial case of 1672 describes the marriage of Nicholas Dowdling and Prozett Wreford of Dunchideock, who had gone to Exeter fifteen or sixteen years previously to be married by a justice 'according to ye Lawe and Manner at that time'. This was an impersonal wedding that seems to have taken place as quickly and with as little ado as possible. It was a 'group' wedding: 'there was a great company there, there being sev'all others then & there to bee married'.[53] Around the same time the parishes of Colyton and Shute were separated and then rejoined.[54] A clear feature of the 1650–1750 period is that Colyton residents were marrying outside of the church. Children were being baptised in Colyton but their parents were not marrying there. Only 145 marriages were celebrated in Colyton in the period 1650–99 for couples who subsequently baptised their children there: an average of a mere 2.9 marriages a year. In the period 1700–49 only 204 marriages were celebrated by couples who later baptised their children in Colyton, an average of four per year. Close attention has been paid through the 'total reconstitution' to the 'missing marryers' in the cohorts 1650–99 and 1700–49. This is the group that appears on dummy FRFs which have been manufactured from baptism or burial details. Table 1.5 shows in how many cases the status of dummy FRFs can be established in comparison with normal FRFs. In the period 1650–1749 a slightly greater proportion of dummy FRFs have status designations than FRFs with marriages. Table 1.6 shows the distribution of these dummy FRFs according to status.

By comparing Table 1.6 with Table 1.2, in the first cohort the missing marryers showed a similar status distribution to marryers in Colyton. In the 1550–99 and 1600–49 cohorts rather more of the poor and crafts categories showed a tendency not to marry in Colyton. In the 1650–99 cohort, while the poor category seems high, it is lower than in the distribution in the total collection of FRFs; conversely, the craft category is double the proportion in the total collection of FRFs. Some 28 per cent rather than 14 per cent of them appear in the dummy FRFs. This trend is also evident in the 1700–49 cohort with 26 per cent of dummy FRFs

Table 1.5 Percentage of dummy FRFs with status designation compared to FRFs with marriages and status designation 1538–1799

Cohort	Dummy	With marriages	% difference
1538–49	42.2	39.5	+2.7
1550–99	25.0	36.7	–11.0
1600–49	35.5	42.5	–7.0
1650–99	48.3	43.6	+4.7
1700–49	50.4	49.9	+0.5
1750–99	44.5	47.9	–3.4

Table 1.6 Status designation of dummy FRFs 1538–1799

Cohort	No.	Gentry		Crafts		Labourer		Poor	
		No.	%	No.	%	No.	%	No.	%
1538–49	51	42	82.4	3	5.9	6	11.7	–	–
1550–99	71	20	28.2	19	26.8	10	14.1	22	31.0
1600–49	184	43	23.4	71	38.6	24	13.0	46	25.0
1650–99	245	51	20.8	69	28.2	33	13.5	92	37.5
1700–49	159	28	17.6	42	26.4	9	5.7	80	50.3
1750–99	80	9	11.3	30	37.5	26	32.5	15	18.8

being classified as crafts, while there were 16 per cent in the cohort as a whole. Crafts are still 7 percentage points higher for dummy FRFs than for the entire collection of FRFs in the cohort 1750–99.

It is evident from these tabulations that in the period 1650–1749 non-marryers in Colyton church were not disadvantaged in terms of income. In fact, they comprised the central core of the Colyton population. They were craftsmen, small landholders or labourers in regular employment. They were neither the gentry nor the poor but the 'middling orders' of the parish. Where did they marry? The first check was made on parishes surrounding Colyton. It was possible to search the registers of nine nearby parishes for the period 1650–99.[55] Four neighbouring parishes do not have registration covering this period.[56] Of the sample, most marriages of Colyton couples were found in Shute in the 1680s, and Seaton and Beer in the 1690s. Marriages of Colyton couples were found throughout the Farway register. All the registers contained a few cases where one or both partners came from Colyton. In the case of Farway, the Reverend Mallocke seems to have married Colyton people to bring the weddings he performed up to an average of five or six a year, possibly to augment his income by marriage fees, which he could not otherwise collect in such a tiny parish. Marriages may have taken place in other churches because of their geographical proximity to people's homes. Colyton is an extensive parish, and some of the outlying farm hamlets were nearer to other churches than to the parish church. In a few cases it is apparent that children married in the same parish outside Colyton as their parents had done.[57] Interestingly, these couples generally had their children baptised in Colyton. In other cases the marriages may have taken place in other parishes to legitimise a child or take place immediately before one is born. For example, Robert Sweetland, son of Samuel Sweetland, was baptised in Colyton on 18 September 1697. He was not recorded as 'base', but the marriage of Samuel Sweetland and Jane Drower only took place two months later on 22 November in Seaton and Beer. Robert Sandy and Ann Crow were married in Seaton and Beer on 23 September 1699. Two days later their daughter Ann was baptised in Colyton where they lived.[58] In two cases the marriages involved Colyton widows, which is fairly remarkable since only three or possibly four widows can be identified as remarryers in Colyton church in the period 1650–99. A few Colyton marriages could be found in the register of St Sidwells in Exeter where a large increase of 'by licence' marriages of people from all over the county of Devon took place after 1660. William Hake and Ann Mills of Colyford, who married at St Sidwells on 5 May 1670, were presumably new migrants to the city.

But geography was far from the entire explanation of marriage patterns. Some of the marriage places seem to be based on other considerations. Thus on 11 February 1682, Edward Harper and Alice Hawker married in Shute, but they were both born in Colyton and resided in Colyford, thus nearer to Seaton and Beer parish if they had wanted to marry outside of Colyton. There are two possible explanations. One is likely to be short-term, short-distance migration that evades the record. As was the case with the Colyton 'marriage only' cases, many of these weddings are of farm servants who do not seem to have generally gone 'home' to marry in seventeenth-century Devon. A second and strong possibility is that the pattern of weddings reflects the exercise of sophisticated choices based on preference for certain clergy rather than others. It seems likely that some Colyton people gravitated towards clergy who had Puritan inclinations, not all of whom had left the Established Church. This suggests a long history of independent-mindedness among the Colyton parishioners. When the 1851 religious census was taken in Colyton, Arthur Dene, the curate, commented: 'Many parishioners always attend neighbouring parish churches at Southleigh, Seaton and Beer, Widworthy'.[59] Indeed, more suggestive of religious preferences than economic vicissitudes are the Colyton marriages which have been found in the early eighteenth-century registers of Exeter Cathedral.[60] The people who married in the Cathedral can be readily identified as the descendants of the more prominent Colyton nonconformists. The Cathedral had in itself been a symbol of the expression of differing religious interests in Devon—in the 1650s a wall was run up from the choir screen to the roof to divide the congregation in half to accommodate both those with Congregationalist and those with Independent leanings. But the tendency for those associated with nonconformist families to marry there in the early eighteenth century is extraordinary and defies ready explanation because the end of the division and the literal 'restoration' of 1660 was an expression of just the type of worship that Colyton Dissenters of the time would have opposed.[61]

In terms of overall numbers, however, the marriages found in other churches take us only so far towards explaining the bulk of missing marriages in this period. Furthermore, linkage of this particular subset of 'dummy marriages' shows them to be either gentry or the poor, and thus the same sort of people as those who continued to marry in Colyton church. Their age structure was also similar to those caught in the registration process, though the women were slightly older at marriage than those in the overall Colyton sample. A further search for the missing marryers was made in the Devon marriage bonds.[62] All the bonds for the period 1660–99 were scrutinised. In thousands of bonds, only twenty-four cases involving at least one marriage partner who came from Colyton were discovered. Sample years from the eighteenth century did not reveal any Colyton cases at all. In comparison with other dioceses, the Devon documentation is disappointing. Unlike allegations, bonds do not give the spouses' dates of birth or ages, or the occupation of the bridegroom or any details of the couple's parents. Only two Colyton cases were marriages of widows. In eleven cases it was possible to establish the age of the bride from the reconstitution, but this varied, from 16.5 to 41.1 years. Social status was also variable but tended towards the upper end of the social scale. A few cases were marriages of labourers or craftsmen, and these usually involved prenuptial pregnancies. However, the fact that at the end of an extensive search most of the missing marryers are still missing is surely indicative.

Dummy FRFs form 64 per cent of all FRFs in the 1650–99 cohort and this investigation suggests that some individuals were simply not caught in the reconstitution process at all, and although they lived in Colyton they are not recorded in the baptism, marriage or burial registers. Table 1.7 shows individuals who appear on records in Colyton but not in the reconstitution. Those individuals for whom there is evidence that they may have had residency outside of Colyton (for example, in a settlement case) have been excluded from this table. Individuals for whom there was not enough information to make a reasonable identification in the

Table 1.7 Number and status of individuals with no FRF linkage 1538–1837

Cohort	No.	Gentry		Crafts		Labourer		Poor	
		No.	%	No.	%	No.	%	No.	%
1538–49	253	39	15.4	72	28.5	141	55.7	1	0.4
1550–99	50	9	18.0	4	8.0	30	60.0	7	14.0
1600–49	91	12	13.2	22	24.2	18	19.8	39	42.8
1650–99	316	24	7.6	139	44.0	103	32.5	50	15.8
1700–49	121	21	17.4	55	45.5	6	5.0	39	32.2
1750–99	170	28	16.5	22	12.9	41	24.1	79	46.5
1800–37	300	38	12.6	70	23.3	117	39.0	75	25.0

reconstitution have also been excluded. The cohorts have been chosen according to the individual's first year of record appearance. The first cohort, 1538–49, is inflated by the inclusion of individuals who could only have been expected to appear in the burial register. The last cohort, 1800–37, has been checked against the full index.

Table 1.7 indicates that a substantial group of Colyton inhabitants was excluded from church registration. The largest number of individuals with no FRF linkage is in the 1650–99 cohort. Some 44 per cent of these individuals are in the craft category and 32 per cent are in the labourer category. In the subsequent cohort of 1700–49, 45 per cent of missing individuals were in the craft category. Of course, it is accepted that the reconstitution only covers a proportion of the population and this covers only periods of high migration. Some of these people appear to have never married and were born and died outside of Colyton, but they spent a part of their working life in the town. As will be shown in later chapters, the period 1650–1750 saw gender-specific migration patterns which probably affected registration. The high level of trade in the town would also have encouraged these patterns. However, while it is not empirically possible to prove that baptism and burial figures were affected by under-registration, the suggestion can be made that the broad middle of the Colyton population eschewed Anglican registration of marriage. The main reason for this was the strength of nonconformity in the region, as will be explored in the next chapter. It has become apparent in the course of analysing the linked registers that there was a broad spectrum of engagement with the Anglican church. Some people were conformists and all their life 'events' are recorded, others seem never to have crossed the threshold of Colyton church. For the majority, however, a pattern of occasional conformity can be identified, with a far greater tendency for couples to baptise and bury in the church than to marry there.

A Summary so Far

'Total reconstitution' seems to provide the ultimate database for a single community history. Ultimately, however, this process relies on the quality of the local records. Colyton was not particularly well endowed with documentary material; in fact it probably represented an average parish on this score. The parish registers provide the essential backbone to the 'total reconstitution' and, at the last resort, it is their quality that matters most. In the case of Colyton, the registers cannot be viewed with the certainty that their position in so many demographic studies seems to merit. In the years 1650–1750, in particular, many marriages have evaded registration in Colyton. These involved the crafts or 'middling' people in Colyton throughout this period, but also the labouring sector in the second half of the seventeenth century. This seems to have been due to the existence of a nonconformist congregation in Colyton, and gives rise to the possibility that in other communities a similar hidden deficiency might exist. Other Devon historians have found that nonconformism has seriously affected registration to the point of making reconstitution impossible.[63] Putting the spotlight on Isaac and Zachariah Drower exemplifies the problem because while they lived, worked and socialised in Colyton, neither father nor son married in the Anglican church. However, this means that if the 'dummy marryers' were generally resident in Colyton at the time of their marriage, their 'manufactured marriage' date was probably reasonably accurate. These cases can then be included in the age at marriage analysis to substantiate the data for the missing classes. This adds a new dimension to the work already carried out on the Colyton marryers. If, of course, it were proven that the gentry and the poor marryers included in the 1650–99 and 1700–49 cohorts married at different ages from the rest of the population, the exclusion of the broad middle of the population would be very significant.

2

Dissenting People
The Politics of the Very Godly

> ... oh alas! we are too apt to settle our affections on wrong objects & to scatter those great excellencies on earthly things, and for this reason God is often times pleased to cross our greatest desires here, when they are employed on anything else beside himself.
> (Nathaniel Pinney to John Pinney, 1 January 1679/80, in G.F. Nutall, ed., *Letters of John Pinney 1679–1699*, 1939: 6)

Writing to his parents, on the death of his 25-year-old brother who had recently become a Dissenting minister, Nathaniel Pinney's faith was fervent and exuberant but he rejected the world. Nathaniel himself was 20 years old at this time. Five years later, when Nathaniel's brother Azariah also reached the age of 20 his commitment to Protestantism was so strong that he became one of Monmouth's rebels. It is clear that by the year of the rebellion, 1685, Colyton was a Dissenter's stronghold, with viable alternatives to Anglicanism, and quasi-political implications that particularly appealed to the broad 'middle' of Colyton society. The largest proportion of those who followed a different path from the Church of England were Presbyterians, but some of them were Independents, Quakers and Baptists. These groups, which we can collectively term 'Old Dissent', had despised each other since the 1650s and in 1685 they were united only in their rejection of Popery.[1] As young men with a politicised sense of gut faith, Nathaniel and Azariah Pinney were typical of their times in this area.

In the previous chapter, the linkage of the reconstitution 'dummy' FRFs to other records contained in the total reconstitution of Colyton, as well as consideration of people for which there was no FRF linkage, showed that the missing marryers in the 1650–1750 period were drawn from the 'middle' section of Colyton society.[2] Typically the 'missing marryer' was fully integrated into community life in Colyton, had probably been brought up there and was very likely to have lived in the town before marriage. He or she was probably partially literate and had partaken of what educational provision was available in the parish and district. We would expect to find his or her signature on receipts for a variety of small trade deals that would have been commonplace in this busy market town. The evidence suggests that these people belonged to Dissenting congregations. Unfortunately it has been necessary to piece together the history of nonconformity in Colyton from a disparate set of sources. This is a result of the fact that for some of this time period, Dissent was persecuted and constituted an underground movement. In these circumstances it is not surprising that few records have been left to posterity. Dissenters were concerned to cover their tracks so we should not expect them to have left minutes of meetings or a register of marriages if, as seems likely, these were performed by a minister who operated outside of the Established Church. There are some focal points for the history of Dissent in Colyton, such as the decisions on whether to emigrate as a community in the early seventeenth century, the enormous upheaval of the Civil War, and the mass insurrection of Monmouth's rebellion. These events were flashpoints for the forming of Dissenting identity in the parish, but the less spectacular happenings—the smaller contests played out in the arena of Colyton parish—are also important. The aim is not simply to identify the 'missing marryers' but to understand more of their view of the world, because local Dissent must have bred ideas about economic and social relationships.

Sitting for God: Nonconformity in East Devon to 1640

A link between east Devon and nonconformity can be made as early as the Reformation. Two presentments were made in the law day court of the manor of Axminster in 1535. Both cases involved local surgeons. Perhaps influenced by Lollardy, Richard Worth denied the doctrine of transubstantiation. This shows a radical turn of independent thought but was not as heinous as Philip Samon's denial of the Virgin Birth. An influence on Samon's belief was the Swiss Anabaptists and he had perhaps adopted the beliefs of radical Protestantism while studying medicine abroad, indicating that east Devon was not isolated from wider trends in Continental thought.[3] In 1555 a tax was levied on every house towards the repair of the parish church and in disbursing the amounts collected the churchwardens presented their accounts to the Chamber of Feoffees, thus establishing the connection between this body and the Church at this early date.[4]

Having established that one of the manifestations of nonconformity in late seventeenth-century Colyton was the tendency not to marry in the Established Church, it is interesting that one of the signs of independent religious thought in Devon was illegal marriages. On Easter Monday 1603, Bartholomew Stevens from Spreyton, self-styled 'Reader to the Lazar people in St Mary Magdalenes and also in the Wynardes', had conducted a disorderly wedding and the consequent court case affords us some detail.[5] Not only was this not a permitted time but the marriage took place in an apparently unlawful location, there were no banns, Stevens did not wear a surplice and he had refused to use the ceremony of the ring. When pressed with the charges, Stevens stated his objections to the vestments, calling them 'Mass smock' or 'Popish Rags'. Further ecclesiastical crimes were revealed. Stevens did not make the sign of the cross when baptising infants and he administered the sacraments to people whether they were standing, sitting or kneeling. On the reverse side of this presentment is the charge against an ordinary member of a congregation who refused to kneel to receive communion. In interpreting this document, Gowers says it shows how Puritan principles could be publicly demonstrated by a layman even where the administering clergyman was not sympathetic to the cause. The number of disorderly marriages prosecuted in the county as a whole is suggestive for the Colyton case, indicating that avoidance of church marriage was a definitive statement by some Puritans.

In 1632 Henry Parsons and Francis Reede of Colyton were prosecuted in the church courts for seldom or never kneeling at communion in direct rejection of Archbishop Laud's insistence that communicants must kneel. The route from refusal to conform at an Anglican church service to the formation of an alternative venue for religious meetings is apparent in one case prosecuted at Axminster. Roger Slade refused to kneel for the Easter communion in 1630, but his rebellion had started a decade earlier. When a minister had insisted that he must kneel for communion, Slade's noisy answer was along the lines of 'there is no such matter'. He departed the church swiftly and created a commotion. His disturbance of the congregation was an apparent strike against authority. He embarked on a 'do-it-yourself' solution, calling conventicles at his own house, where he 'undertaketh to expound and interpreat the scriptures'. Yet Slade remained what we might call in more modern terms 'an occasional conformist', as is shown by his attendance on Easter Day 1630. This was perhaps because the curate at Axminster also had nonconformist leanings, as the court revealed that he was unlicensed and did not wear the surplice or read the Litany as he was required to do. Moreover, the vicar at Axminster at the time was William Knolls, a close friend of the diarist Walter Yonge, and therefore probably himself a man of Puritan inclinations.

As early as the 1590s there were cases of ministers being evicted in Devon. In 1590 Melanthon Jewell lost his position at Thornbury. He had earlier been prosecuted for failing to keep to the Book of Common Prayer. In the later interrogation before Star Chamber, Jewell was said to have referred to episcopal government as 'That of AntiChrist, bishops polluting themselves even as they sought to purify others'. Fourteen years later he was arrested returning from London. He was carrying legal papers containing questions posed by the new ecclesiastical canons along with answers supplied by Puritan-leaning lawyers. This case also demonstrates the area's receptivity to ideas circulating in the wider world. On his travels, Jewell had illegally preached in several locations. Apart from at four places in Cornwall, these included the house of Mr Edmund Prideaux in Farway and his text there was Revelation 2:2: 'I know thy works, and thy labour, and thy patience, and how thou canst not bear them which are evil: and thou hast tried them which say they are apostles, and are not, and hast found them'. As Gowers suggests, Jewell's demeanour shows 'a fighting and flattering harangue' and an appreciation that now the struggle of Puritans could no longer be legally waged in Parliament or local churches, adherents needed to cultivate lay patrons like Prideaux. The Bishop said that since Jewell had been dismissed from office he had lived as a vagrant minister. He 'was never of anie universitie but a baskettmaker and sent up lately to London by the Puritans of Devon and Cornwall touching theire busines'.[6] To try to infuse him with some sense, he had been committed to common gaol and lodged with a Catholic recusant. Presumably their conversations were fiery!

Prideaux was not the only local that Jewell cultivated in the Colyton area. They also included Richard Harvy, the vicar of Axmouth, who stands at the head of a long line of staunchly Puritan incumbents in that village. His successor's patron was Sir Walter Erle, an influential Parliamentarian during the Civil War and Commonwealth. By the 1620s Colyton's neighbouring village was a hotbed of Puritanism. In 1625 men were prosecuted for absence from the church because they preferred to meet at a demolished chapel to hear a Puritan preacher.[7] In their defence, the Axmouth Puritans called on 'tradition from their forefathers' in their use of the chapel and with regard to the church 'they stubbornly refuse to come unto as if they were a parish by themselves'. Apparently, the men drew on a legitimate claim as Bishop Stafford (1395–1419) had permitted some parishioners 'to find a minister . . . at their owne cost or otherwise come downe to the mother Church'. In the 1620s these were men 'w[hi]ch no way like of the Church government yt now is neither yet our Liturgie but are privy whisperers agt both the Bishops & it'. One man, George Hardy, was described as:

> a p[er]emptory enterer into men's consciences to judge them damned if they conforme not to him and his like: insowmuch that

> he pronownced plainly to Mr Barnard Frye that wth the parish of Kilmington (where the said Fry dwelleth) there were but 4 that could be saved and he named them unto him. This he spake as one displeased because the said Frye would not yeld to remove one yt was their curate upon a sodaine & to accept into that cure of Kilmington another whom the said Hardye proposed. And what was he? Verely that most excellent man of God sent down from heaven (said this Hardy) even Walter Leyman who now preacheth at Newton Poppleford unlicensed as I suppose: than whome there cannot be of his sort a more unlearned one in himselfe (as will in proofe appeare) nor a greater enemy to the prsent government of the Church: a p[er]fect separatist in heart and a most dangerous Anabaptisticall fellowe whispering and inveighling the people secretly from howse to house . . . what he dareth not openly pronounce. Of whom there are many things else to be enfourmed if my Lo. [the Bishop] were at home & it is pitie so factious a fellow were not silenced the while.[8]

The ecclesiastical authorities were rattled by a man like Hardy. An uneducated upstart, but prepared to be strident, he was insistently persuasive with ordinary people and appeared to have a network of contacts around the region. But the depth of the authorities concern suggests there was yet more to the case because Hardy had some sympathy from the local gentry. And his characteristic posturing even seemed to convince those in doubt that he had some sort of divine justification. Walter Leyman, mentioned in the presentment, had been licensed to serve the cure of Axmouth in 1619. As Gowers remarks, some of this Puritan influence came from Dorset and points east.[9] There might also have been the impact of incomers since not a few of the Puritans had Scottish or Dutch connections. The influence from Lyme Regis is clear in the Axmouth situation. As the presentment continued:

> John Alderman & his wife two others of the same sorte late commers into Axmouth who kept their church dulye as long as Leyman . . . was preacher there but as soone as another a more learned and conformed Minister had the place . . . this Alderman hath taken a chamber wth in the towne of Lyme (as who say they are not now of Axmouth) & thither he & his wife repaire every Saturday night & there remaine Sunday and Monday morning they come to Axmouth againe where there dwelling is and there continue all the weeke till Saturday come againe. A fellow more headstrong & furious than any of the rest and herein more madly caried than they yt he will not receave the sacrament but sitting and at his first co[mmun]icating in Axmouth did sit all the rest kneeling and Leyman above

mentioned did minister the bread unto him sitting & when the vicar comiing after wth the cup found him sitting & wth some adoe made him to kneele downe: thensoforth he never comunicated in Axmouth any more but at the next comunion tyme rid into Dors:shire & the next quarterly comunion after that kept himselfe close at home & on the week daies following it is supposd that the said Leyman then curate of Axmouth ministred the communion to him and his wife at home in their own house sitting at wch the said Leyman and his wife dined wth the said Alderman by a solemne invitation. These things are neither tollerable in one nor in the other and we desire it yt this Alderman and his wife may by yor authoritie be strictly enjoyned to be at their owne parish church at Axmouth every Saboth day where [or when] they have tow sermons without misse & the exercise of catechizing betweene wherein the grounde of faith and true religion are explaned and laid open unto the people and that [they be] enjoyned sub pena and let them know they live under lawes & may not do what they list [like or wish?]. The example is evil & wilbe drawne into worse.

What is apparent about the Axmouth situation is that Dissent was extreme to the point that some people could not accept the moderate but Puritan-leaning ministers who were supported by the local Puritan gentry. This brand of nonconformity was extreme, decisive and drew on more than theological disagreement. The politics of the dispossessed became the politics of the very godly. Dispossession was economic, as will be demonstrated in Part 2 of this book, but there was also an intellectual rift. The men of Axmouth were not the educated elite like the clergy and strikingly, they refused to kneel in subservience to the altar. This was the Dissent of the independent practical worker who crafted with his or her hands rather than creating philosophical arguments. Another notable point about the Alderman case is that Mrs Alderman was as involved in the evangelising circuit as her husband. Local churches allotted a separate place for women. For example, in neighbouring Farway church in the seventeenth century there were separate 'rooms' for women.[10] It is impossible to know whether Mrs Alderman sat or knelt in her own area of the church.

As Gowers puts it, 'Soon a Puritan belt of influence was to form which would stretch almost continuously from Exeter to Lyme'.[11] As one of the market towns, Colyton became one of the focal points of this Dissenting area. Honiton, Axminster and Ottery St Mary served similar functions and the patronage of local sympathetic gentry grew in the early seventeenth century. In 1613 John Traske was a preaching curate or lecturer at Axminster and Honiton and was subsequently charged with heresy.[12] Hugh Gundry served a similar role in the 1630s in Ottery, later moving to Seaton.[13] Patronage came from families such as the Yonges, who were prosperous Colyton merchants and interconnected with other leading families such as the Prideaux. The diary of Walter Yonge (b.1581) shows the strength of his Puritan convictions and abhorrence of dancing and plays. The original Calvinist and Zwinglian influences on his thinking in the 1610s and 1620s are evident and the diary is full of international news.[14] As Samuel Hieron described Yonge when looking back in 1678, he was 'a young man of sober conversation and by the other party counted a Fanatick. His family wel order'd, himself praying in it, morning and evening.[15]

Corporate objections to church policy appear to have arisen in counterpoint to Laud's innovations and hardening national attitudes. By the 1630s Puritan resistance was officially sanctioned by the Colyton Chamber of Feoffees.[16] We have already seen that in 1632 two men were prosecuted for sitting for communion—the action we might identify as the most usual sign of refusal to co-operate with higher authority even within moderately Puritan leaning churches. But by the end of the decade the entire local government of Colyton, perhaps influenced by the London Feoffees, had declared themselves to support Puritanism. A letter written in the 1680s recalled the situation fifty years earlier. John Gould was the Dissenting clerk and churchwarden of Colyton in the 1680s:

> In Colyton there are twenty ffeofees who have the management of certain lands given for repair of the church and other pious uses of which number this John Gould is one. And in their Booke of accounts they have entred & agreede to an order, That if any of their Body being elected Churchwarden and prosecuted by the Ecclesiastical Court for refusing to take the Oath of Churchwarden, That the person so prosecuted should have his charges allowed him out of the said publick stock. This order was entered in their said Booke about fifty yeares since and still stands recorded therein. And wee have reason to believe that tis observed by the prsent ffeoffees for that we have not gotten one of that Body to take the oath of Churchwarden (since his Maties restauration, tho[ugh] several of them have been elected into that office) without a great deale of charge and trouble.

Thus by the 1630s Colyton was a Puritan stronghold with established 'insurance' proceedings to back up the convictions of the majority of the parishioners. It was the custom in many parishes in Wiltshire and Dorset to balance the factions within parishes by choosing one Puritan and one non-Puritan churchwarden, but in Colyton the choice of churchwardens was a deeply contentious issue.[17] As Stoyle comments, the refusal to take oaths indicates entrenched attitudes.[18] There had been ongoing agitation over non-payment of tithes in Colyton for years, with the incumbents taking members of the parish to the ecclesiastical court.[19] Refusal to pay tithes was a form of resistance against the ministers. In the case of Colyton, as an ecclesiastical peculiar, the Dean and Chapter of Exeter appropriated the great tithes and were patrons of the vicarage, and it had been common for clergymen to be appointed who were very close to the Bishop.[20] With the existence of the strong corporate body of feoffees, who were charged with maintaining the church fabric and the direct interest of the Bishop in the parish church, it is perhaps not surprising that Colyton proved to be a tinderbox for religious and political feuding. Indeed the background to this was the conjunction of an ecclesiastical peculiar in a parish that had seen resistance to direct governance from the throne, as would have happened had not the feoffees bought the estate in 1546.

Popular Puritanism is also suggested by child-naming practices. The names of Charity, Patience and Grace, all common among non-conformists who tended to name children after Christian virtues, were frequently found in Colyton. There was also the occasional christening of a female child as Pentecost or Worship and a male as Gentle.[21]

Another ecclesiastical court case concerning Axmouth and Shute in the 1630s well describes the deeply radical convictions of the local population and, enigmatically, the way in which these interacted with their demographic experiences.[22] In 1637 John Salway, curate at Shute, was suspended for speaking against the King's Book[23], refusing to wear a surplice and other offences typical of Puritans trying to push a point, such as forbidding revels after evening prayer. The trial record reveals that Salway had been preaching in Axmouth for three years in the absence of the normal vicar. During this time he had been upright and blameless, peaceable and conformist, but recently he had become more outspoken. He pronounced against the King's Book, he forbade feasting on a Sabbath, and he and his mother fasted on a Friday but had a banquet on All Hallows evening. He preached against swearing, providing an example which would have been vivid to the contemporary audience: of a man swearing at his stumbling horse. He did not wear the surplice, did not publish fasts in the church and did not read the Lesson. But his sermons were extraordinarily prolix: 'he goeth upp in the pulpitt and continueth there an hower and a halfe or more wch is contrarie to the kinges order'. Some of Salway's preaching concerned sexual restraint. As Salway was a single man himself, these sections of his sermon seem to have been particularly memorable to the congregation: 'hee did preach that it was a breach of the commandment for a man to lye with his wife after she was delivered; before she was purified, and also tells us of spillinge of seede like that of Aranonon'. In other words, Salway urged self-control especially for men. But historians would argue that preaching against the sin of Onan was a reference to coitus Interruptus rather than masturbation at this time.[24]

Salway told his parishioners that their forefathers were damned because they had not been uged toward sexual restraint. Many clergy of the time directed their sermons at the educated but Salway also addressed the poor, recommending that they become cobblers and tinkers.[25]

Six men of Shute were summoned to appear before the Bishop at the same time as Salway. The Bishop had commanded that churchwardens should take notice of incomers to the church. Gill, the churchwarden, publicly proclaimed before the whole congregation that if any came from other parishes to the church his Lordship had commanded that 'the wardens should plucke them out by the shoulders out of the seates & thrust them headlong out of church so that in my judgement he [Salway] much abused your Lordships authority'. This suggests that Salway attracted a congregation from a wide area. Amy Person and Dorothy Pinney testified against Gill's character. He was characterised as:

> a lewd p[er]son of ill name & fame & of little or no credit or worth, one that hath byn presented for Drunkennes, a comon swearer, full of strife & contention. One who lately attempted women's chastity sollicitying them to uncleaness. Giving threatening speeches that he would hew one of them in pieces because she revealed it & threatened the other to throw her in a pond. This much the women affirme.

By contrast to this monster, Salway had conspicuous support. One certificate was signed by eight parishioners of Axmouth who had found nothing blameworthy in his conduct during three years of his curacy there. The first two signatories were gentlemen, and the influential Puritan vicar William Hooke also signed. A second certificate was signed by all the local Puritan clergy. Salway also commanded adherence from Shute parishioners. The result was that the Bishop ordered Gill to make a public declaration in Shute church both at the beginning of morning prayer and after the second lesson that he had spoken disgraceful words of Mr Salway and 'words tending towards blasphemy against the Prophetts', and the rector of Musbury certificated that he did so. Gill had ruined his case by muddled thinking in the accusations against Salway. Salway had alleged that Gill had called him 'a base snobnose boy' and that when reproved with words from the Book of Zachariah for swearing, Gill 'sayd he did not care a pin for the prophet and demanded what matter it was what the prophet sayd'. Salway was suspended for twenty-four days. His most serious offence seems to have been condemnation of the revels: 'a piece of real anti-Laudian audacity', as Gowers put it. Five neighbouring ministers appealed for his early release from the suspension, including the minister of Seaton, the vicar of Axmouth, the curate of Colyton and the curate of Combpyne.

As this case demonstrates, by 1640 there was huge popular support for Puritanism in east Devon and particularly in the immediate Colyton area. While we might associate this with the middling orders, there is considerable evidence that Puritans were to be found among the gentry and the poor. Spufford noted that Dissent was commonly found in parishes with multiple manors and argues:

> The nonconformist churches which formed under the Commonwealth were very different bodies from the 'natural' parish communities which they replaced . . . These 'gathered' churches cut across the boundaries of parish and village. And enforcedly drew in their members from a wide area . . . The physical problems of getting to meetings and communications were therefore absolutely fundamental to the villages who formed the congregations of the dissenting churches.[26]

Colyton lay in the middle of a swathe of countryside that was broadly Puritan in matters of religion. Yet clearly local people argued amongst themselves about the nature of belief and the form of worship. The gentry were resistant to the Bishop and generally increasingly critical of the Established Church, and there were some signs of separatism. Nevertheless although nonconformity in itself created fissures, the antagonism to the Anglican church meant there was also a sense of local communitarian self-government that encouraged some people to look for a future beyond the English shores.

Colyton and the Dorchester Company

An enigmatic scrap of paper within the Colyton feoffee records is entitled 'Reasons shewing the Benefit of a Planting in New England 1623'.[27] Unfortunately, the content has been obliterated and scrutinising contemporary feoffee records gives no clue as to what had been written within. Did the feoffees debate the idea of emigrating as a corporate body? The evidence suggests more moderate beginnings and the impetus for this comes from John White and the Dorchester Company.[28] The wider context is that special efforts were being made by the King in 1623 to interest the merchants of 'Western Parts' in settling plantations in New England. The King sent out an encouraging letter to the Lords Lieutenant of Somerset, Devon and Cornwall suggesting that the western counties were conveniently located to be both a trade outlet and to receive the products of the plantations. Colonisation would, it was argued, produce employment and reduce the burden of the poor.[29] In fact, as early as 1616, Captain John Smith had tried to persuade West Country adventurers to found another American plantation. He spent the summer of 1617 visiting the towns and most of the gentry in Cornwall and Devon.[30]

John White was a moderate Puritan who devised the scheme of the Dorchester Company to form an agricultural and fishing colony in New England.[31] The primary purpose was to propagate Puritan views and to form a refuge for those of moderate disposition. The colony would initially be peopled by men engaged in the Newfoundland fisheries who were not currently needed to work on board ship, with a ruling order of merchants and gentry drawn from Dorset and east Devon. In February 1623 (new style) the Council for New England authorised the Dorchester Company expedition. It appears to have been Sir Walter Erle of Axmouth who applied and paid for the indenture. From small beginnings, the number of investors in the Company soon rose to 120, of whom about six were Devon gentry, and over £3,000 was collected. The Devon contingent was an interconnected group of pro-active Puritans centred on Colyton and Axmouth. First, Erle was related by marriage to Sir William Pole, as was another investor, Thomas Southcott of Mohuns Ottery. Pole's 35-year-old daughter Elizabeth was another investor and she emigrated to New England with her brother William. His son, John, also invested. Other investors were Walter Yonge, the diarist, and William Fry of Yarty, who had conducted the marriage of John Yonge. John Yonge's daughter Jane had married an Axmouth gentleman, Richard Mallock, another investor who would have been connected with Erle.[32] Presumably the paper sent to the feoffees was an advertisement to find further business sponsors. The mixture of a business undertaking that would exploit the cod and fur industries but was also grounded in piety would have appealed to moderate, wealthy and entrepreneurial Colyton Dissenters. Yonge's diary suggests he would have seen this venture as akin to Dutch explorations in the New World at the same time period.

There is much debate among historians of early emigration to New England as to whether religious or economic motivations lay at the forefront of emigrants' endeavours.[33] Yet the Dorchester Company's history shows that there was no tension surrounding this issue in the minds of contemporaries—Puritanism and the exploitation of business opportunities were inextricably connected. The first boats bought by the Dorchester Company were fishing boats and Erle very soon sent over cattle to be pastured in New England. The Winthrop papers show White's references to cutwork and lace being sent to New England, which perhaps reflects thoughts of developing other sorts of business opportunity based on local industries. Under the influence of the moderate John White, in New England the Dorchester contingent opposed separatism, although there is also some evidence that White founded a church that repudiated the Anglican communion.[34] However, the trading schemes, which were neither practical nor economic, lay at some distance from the down-to-earth materialism and dedication to worldly business of the average Colytonian Dissenter.

Colyton did not produce many migrants before 1650, but those who did leave had clear religious motivations. Thomas Gates, born at Colyford in 1561, left for America in 1603 on a voyage 'to deduce a Colony of people into that part of America called Virginia'.[35] He became Deputy Governor of Virginia in 1609. Hotten's lists show that many did emigrate from the south-east Devon area through the ports of Dartmouth and Weymouth. 'A Booke of Entrie for Passengers' from 1634 shows spinsters emigrating from the towns around Colyton.[36] In a will of 1646, John Newton of Colyton, a surgeon, left money for his son and daughter now in New England.[37] Brother and sister William and Elizabeth Pole, mentioned above, went to America and Elizabeth founded Taunton, Massachussetts, where she died in 1654.[38] William Hooke, vicar of Axmouth, must have left for North America very soon after the Salway affair but returned during the Parliamentary supremacy. He was vicar of Taunton, Massachussetts, from c.1638–44.[39] Colyton was not a major source of migrants to the New World and those that went were mainly from the higher echelons of society. The contest for parish beliefs was fought on home territory and among more lowly inhabitants.

Separatism 1640–1685

According to Pulman, writing in 1875, Dr Manson (who later became one of Cromwell's own chaplains) laid the foundations of nonconformity in Colyton in 1640.[40] As we have seen, however, the background was a long-held strong sense of independent thought and moderate Puritanism in the parish. But either just prior to or during the Civil War, nonconformity became not a matter of degree but an overtly politicised standpoint. The 1630s saw leading parishioners increasingly at odds with national government and the policies of Archbishop Laud, drawing strength from the local alliances centred on Axmouth and Lyme. Notably, in 1630 the parsonage of Beer and Seaton was also bought by the Puritan John White's parish of Dorchester. Walter Yonge was active in galvanising resistance to the Ship Money levies in 1634–40. In fact, Colyton had the largest number of defaulters in the country (69), providing further evidence that the parish was a Puritan stronghold.[41] Coming from a town of merchants, this was a ringing objection to taxes imposed by the King. Stoyle finds that the east Devon parishes varied greatly in their allegiance. Whereas Lyme was a Parliamentarian bastion, Ottery St Mary and Axminster showed strong Royalist leanings during the Civil War. Indeed, maimed soldiers' petitions show a clear split of allegiance, with east Devon containing 32 per cent of Parliamentarian petitioners and 32 per cent of Royalist petitioners.[42]

In 1641 twenty-six of Colyton's townsmen refused to take the Protestation Oath, the national oath of loyalty. One assured the Parliamentary authorities that he was 'not obstinately refusing but scrupulously forbearing'.[43] In the Civil War Colyton was first occupied by the Royalists but in July 1644 they were driven out by the Parliamentarians. The Colyton area was particularly susceptible to the Parliamentary garrisons in Lyme and Axmouth, which sent out demands for men, money and supplies.[44] In 1642 two east Devon husbandmen were overheard 'conferringe together in their worke . . . concerning the raiseing of forces in Cullyford, Beere and Seaton . . . or rifling howses in these tymes of trouble'.[45] Failure to provide what was demanded was punished by 'plundering' or legal confiscation. These demands became particularly acute during the siege of Lyme in 1644. Here we have evidence of direct involvement by some Colyton men. Edward Drake of Colyton, for example, was active in defending the garrison.[46]

In 1647 John Wilkins, an Oxford-educated Puritan, replaced the ejected Thomas Collyns, to become vicar of Colyton at the age of 23. While an uncertain source to use for events that had taken place over two hundred and fifty years earlier, the *Parish Magazine* of September 1907 shows that this went down in posterity as an unwelcome change for at least some of the parishioners.[47] It said that Wilkins was 'forced on to people' and that Collyns, the 'rightful clergyman', was persecuted. His house was plundered, he was forced into hiding and he had to sell his possessions to maintain his ten children. The magazine claims that he was well loved in the town so that a tailor in charity maintained one of his children, two or more were kept by weavers (whose wives nursed them), and the rest were put into service. Reading between the lines then, Collyns did not have the support of any substantial sectors of the population who could have been expected to keep him in a little more dignity. Wilkins was supported under the financial arrangements for adherents to Parliament by Cromwell in 1655.[48]

In the Commonwealth period several separatist congregations developed in Colyton and the surrounding area, as they did in other areas of the country. In Lyme in 1650 the ultra-Royalist mayor, Gregory Alford, constantly reported the Reverend Ames Short to the Privy Council as a man 'who distilled poison into the hearts of the simple and weak' and described his meeting house in George's Court as 'the head conventicle of the country' which had more than once been broken up. Short is recorded as preaching in Colyton in 1669 and was likely to have been there much more often before that.[49] The development of the Exeter Assembly over the period 1655–9 perhaps marks the beginning of

Plate 1. Views of the tomb of Sir John and Lady Elizabeth Pole (1658) in Colyton church. Note detail of local lace. (D. Pennington and D. Sharpe)

official nonconformity. The assembly administered a fund with two objectives. The first was to assist country churches to pay their ministers adequately. The second was to make grants to young men for education.[50] In Colyton itself, in spite of Wilkins's incumbency, a subtle shift was taking place within the Anglican church. The ostentatious tomb built for the Courtenay-Pole family in 1658 is the most visible symbol of the fact that it no longer remained the base of a moderate Puritanism (see Plate 1). The family were large-scale lace customers, buying the best-quality local lace for both consumption and heirloom purposes, and on their tomb, they made full display of the local product. While reflecting local industry, this type of dress was anathema to Puritans. That Sir John had been the reluctant collector of the Ship Money, and that his son was a Royalist in the Civil War, were further markers of allegiance. The erection of Sir John and Lady Elizabeth's tomb, made by Gerard Johnson of Southwark, must have signalled to those of more plain and modest pretensions that the church now represented alien space.[51]

It is clear that some Colyton people sought alternative places to worship. Loughwood Meeting House in Kilmington parish, built by the Baptists in 1653, is an early example of a nonconformist meeting house (see Plate 2). While meeting outside of the parish church was not illegal during the Commonwealth, from soon after the Restoration meeting houses became illegal and remained so until the Toleration Act of 1688. Loughwood was built on land donated by a member in dense woodland, half hidden by the hillside into which the building is dug, and deliberately sited exactly on the county border so that the preacher had a chance of escape from officials by fleeing into either Devon or Dorset. The meeting house was built with stables for travellers' horses and with two retiring rooms with fireplaces and simple cooking facilities so that congregations could spend whole days there. One of the early lists shows a congregation of 219 people, with seventeen travelling from Colyton and sixteen from Shute.[52] Some Colyton Baptists were apprehended in 1661.[53] In the 1680s Quakers are recorded as travelling from Colyton to Membury to attend conventicles in considerable numbers.[54]

Other people turned to more unorthodox solutions and a declaration of their own right to rule. At nearby Sidbury, for example, two brothers reported to the quarter sessions the presence of two men who 'did expressly deny the sacred Scriptures to be the Word of God, of Rule of ffayth, or Lyfe, or to have . . . been the Instrument of any mans Conversion or Conviction', 'And that they . . . and such as they, had the proper Right to the Office and Honour of Magistracy in the Nation, and they had both been together at the house of Mrs Woolacott in Sidbury.' One of the accused brought with him a woman 'whom they say was a Prophetesse'. The other testified that he denied that the Old Testament and New Testament were the word of God 'or a Pale of ffayth and lyffe,

Plate 2. Exterior and interior of Loughwood Meeting House, Kilmington.
(D. Sharpe)

or that they were ever Instruments of Converting or of Convincing any man since the Apostles tymes. But that the Spirit alone worketh.'[55] Others also took religion into their own hands—the innkeeper who boasted of baptising a child himself was not unusual.[56]

The aim of the Act of Uniformity in 1662 was to bring all of those who had departed back to the national church, but it had the opposite effect. John Wilkins was himself ejected from Colyton church for refusing to sign the Act because it required full acceptance of the Book of Common Prayer. Thomas Collyns took the oath under the Act of Uniformity and recovered the living of Colyton in August 1662. Other records suggest there was a gap of three years after Wilkins's removal during which Colyton had no vicar. But even if Collyns was nominally in charge, this indicates some confusion or lack of a clear lead. Wilkins could not be described as radical; in 1666, for example, he took the Oxford oath with the clause 'I will not at any time endeavour any alteration of government, either in Church or State'.[57] Whereas neither Collyns nor his children appear in the parish registers, Wilkins's youngest child was baptised in Colyton church after his ejection, which confirms that nonconformists only partly rejected Anglican registration. It is also the case that two of Wilkins's sons became clergymen. In 1678 Wilkins's son Edward lodged with John Clapp, a merchant and later one of Monmouth's rebels. Edward Wilkins was then a plateworker and part of the very craft and workshop tradition from which the rebels sprang. Perhaps he combined making pewter objects with preaching, as Calamy records him to have taken Anglican orders. This is one indication that it is very easy to be too black and white about Colyton as a self-defined community of Dissenters. Some people were occasional conformists, others spent periods of their lives as Dissenters and other times as conformers. Yet others may have conformed because their employers were churchgoers. Many of those who argued with the Anglican church would not have seen eye to eye with each other. The very many Presbyterians in the parish, for example, had little in common with those who followed radical sects. This begs the difficult question of to what extent there was a community of Dissenters in Colyton. Through the linkage process a network of exchange and marketing between Dissenters can be established and there are indications that they gave each other mutual help, but the fault lines must still have been evident. Perhaps the only unifying political force was the Chamber of Feoffees.

Few first-hand accounts of the ejections of ministers are available, but John Pinney described his ejection in a journal. 'I departed from the ministry at Broadwindsor AD 1662–Augt 24 on wch day my last sermon to the people was preached. Farewell. Farewell.' Observations on this day included 'Much noise of plots & no pr[oo]f of any' and 'Godly people much ofended for my going to ye Bp [Bishop] & ordin[ary]'. On 2

December he went to see the Bishop, 'but did nothing in wch time the psh petitioned for Mr Clarke whose succeeding me was to ye griefe of some & ye joy of others'.[58] John Pinney 'was much a gentleman, a considerable Scholar, an eloquent charming Preacher; very facetious, but always grave and serious'. After his ejection in 1662, 'he had many Troubles by Excommunication and Fines: he was twice imprisond: Once in England, and once in Ireland. He was twice ejected and silenc'd.' Nevertheless, Calamy says 'he was always satisfied in his Nonconformity'. In the difficult days following his ejection, he had various temptations to conform and even went as far as obtaining episcopal orders, but 'No good man pswaded me to conform but all deswaded me'.[59] In the days of persecution his house was watched at night and he dared not pray in it and tried to disguise the fact that he was at home.

The ejections saw the onset of much persecution. For Axminster the 'Book of Remembrance' records a Sabbath in 1663 when several Dissenters met together in a hidden spot in a great wood. In a break between services some soldiers 'observing the motions of the people, Riding furiously by the place, brake in amongst the people & disperst them; some persons were apprehended & taken by them (whereof some of them were members of this Church) & carryed them away'. Those who escaped spent the night in prayer but at the next assizes the ministers were heavily fined.[60] Meetings of more than four persons and preaching in fields were completely outlawed by the Conventicle Act of 1664, which drove them underground. The second Conventicle Act in 1670 was followed by worse persecution. The legislation required attendance on Sundays and holy days at both morning and evening services of 'all and every person and persons inhabiting within this realm not having lawful or reasonable excuse to be absent'. Apart from the penalties, three or four men were to be appointed in parishes to ensure that parishioners went to church. These restrictions, imposed under the Clarendon Code during 1661–5, provided Dissenters with a common focus for protest.

In Axminster, during this period, the Independent congregation remained hidden from the persecutors by 'appointing such seasons and places for their assembling together to worship the Lord . . . sometimes in one obscure place, sometimes in another in woods and solitary corners'.[61] Lyme, the solidly Puritan town of the Civil War, retained its complexion despite many local contests. The Bishop of Exeter described it as being 'overrun with ffanaticks'. Ames Short stayed on in the town after his ejection and established a large Independent congregation, as well as a Dissenting Academy where he taught boys from the local area and Exeter both 'logic and seditious principles'. The Bishop wrote that his house was a 'nursery of sedition' from whence 'young plants' were sent to London.[62] The mayor, Alford, kept a close eye on the other seedbed of sedition in the area, Prideaux's Ford Abbey. The abbey had a non-conformist chapel in it, described by Alford as the 'receptacle of all Fanaticks'.

In Colyton persecution was particularly acute because in 1665 Thomas Tanner had been appointed to replace Collyns. Tanner was an Oxford academic and barrister. According to the *Parish Magazine* of June 1909, he was unpopular, being seen as 'forward' and 'conceited'. But the real problem was political and because national politics impinged on Colyton. Tanner waged war on the Puritans, particularly separatists, and had no time for the practical religion of the artisan. He stayed in Colyton until 1676. Robert Simson was then incumbent for a year. He was succeeded by William Salter, whose ministry contains the only tendencies to occasional registration defects in Colyton's history.

The 1682 evidence of James Harris (whose brother had been in a plot to depose Charles II) gives some detail on radical religion and the impact of national politics in the remoter regions of south-east Devon. Harris reported that William Raddon of Stockland, a Baptist lawyer who was well-connected and spent some of this time in London, said, rehearsing the turbulent history of his lifetime, 'Nothing but a Commonwealth will satisfy us. Between Michaelmas and the time you call Christmas we will fall upon the King and Queen and all his duchesses and whores, and the Duke of York, and his duchess and whores with all the Court Party that were against the Exclusion Bill.' Thomas Parsons of Membury, another 'free-willed Baptist', declared that as they had fought against Charles I and his bishops so they would 'do more cruelly against the present prelates'. John Trowde of Upottery, who had fought with Cromwell, said he hoped again to fight as willingly as he had done for the Old Parliament. Harris said Raddon and Parsons had been employed to send 'scandalous and libellous' news to all of the area, indicating the possible strength of the underground movement.[63]

Of the total 160 licences granted for meeting houses in Devon in 1672, 119 were Presbyterian.[64] In 1670 Robert Collins, Presbyterian minister of Ottery, was fined for keeping conventicles on Sundays in time of divine service in his own house and was frequently fined and once imprisoned. He was fined £60 in 1670, £20 in 1675 and £20 in 1682, and eventually had to flee to the Netherlands and sell his estate 'to maintain his person and family in their distracted, shattered condition'.[65] This case reveals the nature of these conventicles. Collins had an interconnecting door to his neighbour's house so that the seventeen or eighteen people who worshipped with him could hide there if disturbed by the authorities.[66] Collins was still in Ottery in 1675 when he was dismissed as overseer of the poor and a weaver called Robert Hawkings was convicted for being at an unlawful assembly or conventicle in Collins's mansion. A fine of 15s was imposed on him, 5s for himself and 10s for the offences of Richard Baxter and Mary Card who were paupers convicted with him. Hawkings unsuccessfully appealed at the next quarter sessions. He refused to pay his fine and his goods were seized.[67] Perhaps the most interesting piece of evidence of all concerning the Ottery conventicle was the snatched piece of overheard conversation between two men in Ottery, which in the fraught conditions of the time was immediately reported to quarter sessions.[68] One of the men present had uttered 'shall wee continue to overcome the great men of this world'. The other said that he was sorry he had been involved with the conventicle, to which his friend replied: 'as long as he liv'd in this World hee should have trouble'. In the years of prosecution of the early 1680s, an Ottery apprentice reported to the quarter sessions his master's outbursts against justices and authorities and that his master detained him from church. When the apprentice went to church his master became very angry and said he would beat him soundly if he went again.[69] Although it can be argued that towns took the lead in Dissent during these years, conventicles were also found in rural locations and there is evidence of a circulating network of preachers who would have propagated ideas of sedition. For example, Henry Ham of Luppitt was arrested for preaching at an unlawful assembly at the house of Margaret Shepherd within the parish of Membury in 1684.[70] It is, of course, particularly difficult in troubled times to unravel slander and hearsay from reliable evidence of what people did and said. However, in an effort to weave small stories into the larger structures of parish life, such political rumblings merit consideration even if only as the sort of threats that people claimed others were uttering.

In Colyton in 1670, the parish constables—John Holwill, Roger Satchell, Thomas Clapp, Edward Bond and Thomas Parsons—signed a statement that they had received a warrant from the clerk of the peace, and delivered by the head constables, concerning the taking up of the bodies of John Bagwell, Henry Hooper and William Stocker: 'Wee have binn often times to take them up but cannot finde them'.[71] Here men on both sides of the law were extreme Protestants, later involved in Monmouth's rebellion, and this must have influenced their inability to find their friends. Some of the men were in similar trades; both Satchell and Bagwell had cordwaining businesses.[72] The persecution of 1672 was the worst of the Restoration period, with many men employed (now by the King) to track down conventiclers. In Colyton, when the Declaration of Indulgence was passed in 1672 which allowed Protestant nonconformists to worship freely, two licences were granted for Presbyterian meetings at the houses of Widow Drake and Bernard Dwight.[73] It can be demonstrated by comparing the Compton Census results with episcopal and archdeaconal visitations as well as the constable's returns to the quarter sessions that in many cases the presence of nonconformists was ignored.[74] Certainly the figure of thirty-five nonconformists in all of the parishes in the Honiton Deanery seems much too low and the mere nineteen recorded for Colyton is wildly inaccurate. When the members of Colyton conventicle were arrested at the house of Alice Drake, their names included many of the substantial yeomen both of the parish and from further afield, journeying from places like Honiton to worship in Colyton.[75] The 1673 Test Act obliged all officeholders to be Anglicans and this caused immense difficulties in Colyton. The Devon public order of 1682, reinforced in 1683 and 1684, sought to 'deliver up to us those ungrateful monsters (Nonconformist Ministers wee meane) who in the late rebellion preached up sedition and treason'.[76]

Jackson also describes Colyton as a parish rife with religious divisions in 1674, where the strength of Dissent and the responsibility for a large number of paupers meant the office of churchwarden was expected to 'cost more trouble then in former yeares' and 'the imployment was dreaded by many that at other times would have taken it'.[77] It took 'manni perswassions' by justices to get a local attorney, Thomas Sampson, to accept the office, and only a few months later he wrote to the justices asking to be relieved of the office. Yet while assuring the episcopal authorities of Sampson's loyalty to the Anglican church, they requested that he be exempted from strict observance of the oath, writing to the Bishop:

> it will cost much morr troble this year then in fformr yeares; the poor being growin more numerousr and corn so dear, that the imployment was dreaded by man is that [sic: by a man who] at other times would have taken it; [you] well know his abilities to performe this office, and his judrmrkt [judgement] stanright to the Church of Englande . . . [Knowing] . . . as we believe you also doe the general dissent of that part to conformite so that if he shoulde strictly observe the Oath that used to be given to that office [it] will not only be impossible for him to observe it but will render him violently hated by the generality of the p[ari]sh.[78]

It was therefore requested that no oath be imposed on him. Francis Bagwell, a substantial yeoman, was chosen to serve with him but he was also exceedingly reluctant. Bagwell tried to avoid the office by claiming that he had been called to serve in a neighbouring parish so could not carry out the office in Colyton. Investigations soon revealed that he had anyway not taken communion in Colyton church for eight years! The conservative Tanner went on to grumble: 'maybe if he heard me now & then, he would not be so ready to do me ill offices as he is . . . He is a man of £100 a year estate: pray let him know that we may have somewhat to do with such as he is, when they are not contented to have had their owne way; but are pragmaticall in every faction agt ye Church'.[79] Tanner's weakness and insecurity in his role as the vicar of Colyton is made evident by his final request that his letter be kept secret.

As Jackson points out, with such an intimidated incumbent even a conforming churchwarden would have found himself publicly isolated. It appears that the nonconformists indeed gained the political upper hand in the parish during the churchwardenship of Sampson and Bagwell, because at the end of their term Tanner again wrote to the Bishop with a list of complaints. They had failed to provide wine for communion, they did not attend communion to collect the offertory, they had not gathered money for briefs, and perhaps most signficantly of all, they had failed to provide the Book of Common Prayer and of the Homilies, Canon and the Thirty-Nine Articles. As if opening the inside of the ancient church to let everyone in, they made doors to the churchyard where there were none before (creating a door in the huge west window) and left hatches unhinged so that the church was not secure. Tanner's tone was fear; he was particularly worried about the service of communion and did not know how to have a communion at Easter for lack of wine, mentioning that at this time there was none sold in the town, perhaps part of the Puritan clamp-down on drunkenness.[80] Such a dispute might look like a local argument, but could hardly be so in the context of a national political situation where Dissenters may have been insignificant in number, but nevertheless opposed the association between Anglicanism and the Court at a time when the monarch showed evident Catholic leanings.

In the early 1680s the issue of the churchwardens' recalcitrance at Colyton became a national affair as the Bishop of Exeter wrote to the Archbishop of Canterbury asking him to obtain an order from the Lord Chancellor to make Colyton a precedent to keep peace and order within the church. Gould, as clerk and churchwarden, had refused to take 'the oath which is generally given to all Churchwardens in my Diocesse' and ignored all attempts to bring him to law. The Bishop continued: 'this inclosed paper will inform your Grace of a combination agst ye oath, as it concerns *ecclisiasticall* affaires, for yt ys ye word he [Gould] stumbles at'. He went on to disclose that 'If this Gould be absolved without taking ye Oath it will disattisfy all ye loyal Gentry who are very much concerned with persecution of this Person'.[81] Sampson was again churchwarden in 1683/4 when he provided the justices with a list of absentees from church for prosecution at the quarter sessions.[82] Absence lists continued to be kept until mid-1684. One list was headed by Daniel Toupe, mercer, and his wife Mary, plus William Lymbrey, mercer, and his wife Grace. No systematic analysis of the other Dissenters is possible as occupations are not always recorded, but the list includes cordwainers, weavers, taylors, spinsters and a number of those involved in farming. Toupe's business was tobacco cutting.[83] Several widows and single women appear on the list, such as 'Ann Flood (widow) & Ann & Hester her daus and, in another household, 'Jane Cox (widd), Elizabeth her dau and (living separately) Mary Cox (s)' (the (s) probably denotes 'servant'). Humphrey Tilman, a weaver, who had been disciplined by the Bishop in 1671, also appeared on the list.[84] Daniel Toupe was certainly prosecuted and forced to take communion in Colyton church so was probably seen as a leading Dissenter. But he clearly did not change his opinions since in 1685 he was one of Monmouth's rebels.[85]

Colyton's Rebels in 1685

The Gould affair is very significant in Colyton's history for it clearly demonstrates the antipathy of the local gentry to the crown and Anglicanism. It was in many ways a manifestation of a type of conservatism rather than radicalism. If we were able to time travel and press one of Colyton's landholders or merchants on their political and religious stance, we would see them less as rebels and more as upholders of a simple and solid Protestantism that stood in stark opposition to the perceived extravagant Catholic threat from the Continent.

Peter Earle argued that an organised scheme of resistance had been developing in the West Country since 1682.[86] Government informers in 1685 who spied on Dissenters and raided conventicles described 'an enemy in our bosomes that is so secret, so cunning, so industrious, and haveing a cause that steeles them with courage even to desperatenesse'. As a result it was in hidden refuges such as Reverend Stephen Towgood's 'church under the ground' in the 'secret caves of the earth' in the hills above Axminster where Monmouth's rebellion was planned and men prayed for the success of a godly uprising. Towgood had regular members from Taunton, Colyton, Chard and Lyme Regis. Even late in 1684, when repression was intense, he held services at night, one near Axminster on the eve of the Sabbath and the other near Chard towards dawn. According to the Axminster congregation's 'Book of Rememberance', Towgood's sermons spoke to the circumstances of these services of subterfuge with verses from Revelations 12. 'And I heard a loud voice saying in heaven, Now is come salvation, and strength, and the kingdom of our God, and the power of his Christ: for the accuser of our brethren is cast down'.[87]

The Duke of Monmouth was Charles II's illegitimate son and although historians have labelled the rebellion as an anachronism which ended in an abject failure that was apparent from the outset, the very large involvement of men from Colyton and the immediate region begs further investigation. As Little put it, the rebels 'embodied a continuity with the Puritanism and Republicanism of Commonwealth days'.[88] Of any parish, Earle judges that 'The most rebellious place in Devon was the large village or small town of Colyton'. Not only were Colyton's men desperate in their Dissenting beliefs and therefore enthusiastic members of 'the last godly army in English history', but in Earle's argument they were also true democrats who sought to recreate a leveller society. As a result his view is that the Duke of Monmouth emerged as a leader simply because he was available as a leader. Stephen Towgood saw him as 'a deliverer for the nation, and the interest of Christ'. In a snatch of conversation reported to the authorities early in 1685 in Axminster, a group of ordinary men were more equivocal. George Perram, a glazier, and John Perram, who was perhaps his brother and a lockmaker, took sides in the debate about Monmouth. George dismissed Gilbert Copp, who thought Monmouth a coward, with 'goo about thy business & go to work'. Copp replied 'that he was no Kinge'.[89] These debates are about the nature of authority, which was obviously much discussed at the local level at this time. Of the rising level of tension and its effect on local businesses there was little doubt. As John Pinney wrote from Dublin to his daughter about their lace trade and regarding her widowed sister Jane Hoare's business in Colyton in June 1685, 'I see nothing but trouble & misery comming on these kingdoms. wee have Rumrs fro the North evry other day & some from ye West . . . I see it will not be yor Wisdome to keep on yor trade: here is no trade for anything . . . Let yor sistr Hoar be carefull in tyme to limit her trade & trust.'[90]

The mustering which happened in Colyton on a regular basis had prepared the local people for armed rebellion and suggests a different picture from the impression that Monmouth's badly organised army fought with pitchforks and little expertise. The feoffee accounts record an armoury of swords and muskets that were regularly maintained. The feoffees employed a 'Muster Master' and kept barrels of gunpowder with boats next to them for the ready conveyance of the ammunition. One record suggests that they held an additional secret arsenal. There was a complaint to quarter sessions that around September 1667 there was about 150lb of powder with a 'extortionable' [sic: extortionate] quantity of bullets left in custody of the constables of Stoke Gabriel which belonged to the magazine of the parish of Colyton and was left by the order of Captain Bragg on trust to be redelivered when desired.[91]

Monmouth started his campaign in Holland and landed at Lyme, but this was not his first visit to the area. In 1680 he had travelled between Chard and Axminster on the way to Exeter. As he passed through Crewkerne he had cured a 20-year-old local girl, the daughter of a poor widow, of 'king's evil' or scrofula, thus affirming his royal blood to the local populace. His early tours also allowed him to make contact with local Puritan gentry. In 1680 he also visited Edmund Prideaux at Ford Abbey. Prideaux was responsible for outspoken comment on the subject of Protestantism. At a ceremony in connection with the redemption of

English captives enslaved by the Mahometans he once said it was better to live 'in slavery under the Turks than in England under popery', a remark immediately recorded and passed to the authorities in London by the ultra-Royalist mayor of Lyme, Gregory Alford.[92] In 1682 Monmouth returned to east Devon and lodged in Colyton, at the Great House as a guest of Sir Walter Yonge. In spring 1685 an agent called Christopher Battiscombe was sent over from Holland to see Monmouth's confederates in London and then his connections in the West Country such as Walter Yonge, to ask them to meet Monmouth on landing. But the letter giving plans of Monmouth's immediate arrival was intercepted and taken to the Catholic King James II. Yonge never became directly involved and the advance party actually landed near Chideock, ironically a village with a strong Catholic influence. The first meeting of the Duke's party was with some loyalist fishermen who, only after they had partaken of Monmouth's sumptuous landing picnic of canary and neat's (ox) tongues, said they hoped there would be no rebellion. As Monmouth sailed into Lyme, the pro-Stuart mayor, Gregory Alford, who effectively worked as a government agent, rode to Honiton after some prevarication, to send a letter telling the King of his arrival. On the way, he seems to have passed on the news of Monmouth's campaign.

In Lyme, Monmouth was greeted with joyful shouts of 'A Monmouth! A Monmouth! The Protestant Religion!' His standard was set up and recruits started to enlist. Hundreds did so between 11 and 14 June. On 15 June, they made a rapid departure from Lyme following the news that Albermarle and the Duke of Somerset were closing in. Monmouth headed for Axminster where he recruited more local men. The eighty-six Colyton rebels probably assembled in both places, although we are aware that Roger Satchell was amongst the first at Lyme. As persecution had intensified and permeated Colyton society, and because resistance was divided, Monmouth offered the chance to turn small and local battles into a larger, national campaign. Monmouth offered a unifying agenda of annual Parliaments, no standing army without Parliament's consent and equality for all Protestants. It was said of Roger Satchell that 'he always hated the name of a papist' and 'no sooner had the news of the Duke's being landed, but he set himself to work to serve him, desireing all he knew to join with him, and was one of the first that went with him at Lyme and was with him to the end'.[93] Satchell was a merchant cordwainer and a landowner in both Colyton and Honiton. He had recently served as constable, then as overseer of the poor, in Colyton. Proud, haughty, misogynist, and fiercely anti-Catholic, some of his remarks suggest that Satchell also viewed himself as a king—king of the little world of Colyton.[94]

Stephen Towgood's entire congregation fell in behind their pastor but were also among the first to flee when the episode culminated in the execution of Monmouth and bloody defeat on the marshy battlefields of Sedgemoor on 6 July.[95] The first news back to east Devon was full of muddled optimism. Two women from Sidmouth reported to quarter sessions that at Ottery market they had overheard a cheesemonger who had travelled from Aylesbeare say that a post had come into Exeter bearing the news that Monmouth had routed the King's party and had killed 'ten to one & that the posts rid with ropes about their necks and the Bells that before rang for the good news thereupon ceased'.[96] Henry Marker of Ottery reported seeing a great company of mainly women in the town, one of whom told him that Monmouth had come to town, and a man gave his view that Monmouth was alive and well and that he would 'give all he were worth if he was as well as Monmouth'. Another man, however, had been informed that Monmouth was within 8 or 10 miles of Bristol. One woman told another that she believed the Duke of Monmouth to be alive and that 'his head was upon his shoulders as much as this Informants'.[97]

The estimate of the total number of rebels varies from 3,000 to 7,000 at the peak of the army, with 488 from east Devon appearing at the assizes. Rebels hailed from almost all the parishes in the Colyton area, but Clifton is correct to suggest that '1685 was an urban, or more precisely, a small-town rebellion'.[98] Around a quarter of the total adult male population of Colyton fought for the Duke of Monmouth against Catholicism. Considering that they came from different families and that there were also active loyalists in town, the extent of local support for Monmouth is remarkable. We cannot know the full role of the feoffees in raising men, but it is possible to speculate that they interpreted their ancient role of 'raising soldiers for the King', made at the time of the Henrican Reformation, as giving them every justification for providing Monmouth with a good part of his army. Analysis of the background of the rebels shows they could be defined as the 'middle' of Colyton society. They were generally craftsmen, or had trade connections, and they identified with the urban rather than rural parts of the parish or Colyford. Some of the records taken at the trial seem to describe almost all the Colyton men, and particularly the older ones, as 'yeoman'. This was likely to have been a result of the fact that there were so many rebels to deal with that this was shorthand for their real trades. In fact, the total reconstitution reveals a much more convincing mix of town-based occupations. Nicholas Thompson, a doctor, is among them. None of the rebels are recorded as 'paupers', although some had very little material wealth, and this fits with a wider theory that the very poor tended to remain church attenders. William Clegg, a 46-year-old poor weaver, and one of the men executed in Colyton, had land and possessions valued at 15s. Although we cannot be sure how much thought went into the choice of whose hanging was used to make an example, it could be significant that Clegg was one of the poorest Colyton rebels rather than one of the leaders.

Statements taken on the capture of the Colyton rebels reveal that they had deep-seated convictions. These men were religious zealots who believed wholeheartedly in Protestantism as a cause. Joseph Speed, a shoemaker, who was 'somewhat encumbered in the world', was 'A poor man, who could thank God that since the age of sixteen he had had the checks of conscience on me'. Clearly, Speed had been politicised during the Civil War period and this was likely to be the case for most of the rebels since their average age was over 40. His whole design 'in taking up arms under the Duke of Monmouth was to fight for the Protestant religion which my own conscience dictated me to, and which the said Duke declared for'. John Sprague, a mason, who was executed in Colyton along with the weaver Clegg, stated he 'Believed that no Christian ought to resist a lawful power; but the case, being between popery and protestantism, altered the matter, and the latter being in danger, he believed it was lawful for him to do what he did'. These statements reveal the politics of the very godly rather than any articulation of desire for social or economic justice. Indeed, many of the merchants and traders who joined Monmouth would have been in competition with each other in normal Colyton life. Joseph Speed and Roger Satchell were both involved in shoe-making but seem to have been at opposite ends of the economic spectrum. In fact, Satchell may have employed a man like Speed as a worker, for he had accrued substantial cash through trading by the time he wrote his will in 1684. It is therefore difficult to see Monmouth as a straightforward levelling protest because the 'great men' that the rebels variously decried were not the same individuals. At its roots, the rebellion was a show of strength by staunchly independent, Protestant male citizens. Their language was that of the 'Good Old Cause': echoing again the turbulent history of the area since the Civil War.

After Judge Jeffries presided over the 'Bloody Assize', the traitors were executed. Jeffries and his entourage swept through east Devon. The Axminster churchwarden's accounts record a payment to a woman 'for cleaning churchyard after Kings Army' and another 'To ye Ringers when ye Justices sate at ye taking of Monmouth'.[99] Hanging, drawing and quartering was staged in many different towns to illustrate the seriousness of political crime. Apart from the two hangings which took place at Colyton,[100] heads and quarters were tarred and boiled in salt then preserved on poles and sent to towns to create revulsion and act as a warning.[101] Other rebels were publicly flogged in the marketplace in Colyton. In Lyme Mayor Alford tasted his sweet revenge as execution judges were expensively entertained with wine and delicacies such as gammon and sturgeon. The commissioners seized farms or farm produce from captured rebels.[102] Roger Satchell was seized at Chard, perhaps on his way back to Colyton. He was imprisoned at Ilchester, tried at Dorchester and hanged at Weymouth. An application was made to Judge Jeffries to save his life but he was granted only a short dying speech and his estate was sold.[103] His substantial holdings of cash were distributed between family, friends and, by his wish, the purchase of Bibles for the poor of Colyton and Honiton.[104]

Some men were injured. A Colyton husbandman, Robert Sanday, had his skull badly cut by two sabre blows in battle at Norton St Philip and the prison surgeons at Ilchester charged £5 for treating him.[105] The surgeon's report stated that 'with some heavy cuting instrument on his head at two places; on the hinder parte a piece of his skull was cut off and left hanging by the flesh as bigge as a five shilling piece and ye brayne left naked, only a thin skin to keep it in, on ye foreparte was a large wound out of which I took severall pieces of skull'.[106] Surprisingly Sanday or 'Sands' survived, then found himself *en route* to Barbados where he was sold. Many of the rebels were transported as slaves to the West Indian plantations to be used as skilled workers. A few Colyton men went to Jamaica, St Kitts and Nevis, but Barbados was the most common destination. Some did not survive the journey. William Greenaway, a 21-year-old woolcomber, died at sea on Christmas Day. Edward Venn, a cordwainer and an older man (he had married thirty years earlier), also died at sea. Philip Cox was on the same boat and died in transit. His small estate worth £30 was forfeited and his widow and daughter were reduced to beggary.[107] William Marthers, a 28-year-old carpenter, survived the sea journey but died before he was sold as a slave. John Truren, another Colyton man and a woolcomber, had been destined for Barbados after being imprisoned in a workhouse but he and his wife died in Dorchester gaol.

Two other Colyton rebels, John Whicker and Peter Bagwell, made a dramatic escape from the West Indies. They were shipped to Barbados in *The Betty* from Weymouth with fifteen other Colyton men. Whicker and Bagwell formed a crew for Dr Henry Pitman, Monmouth's surgeon, who attempted to sail back to England. As Dr Pitman subsequently published his story we have a full account of the fate of these two men. They chose the evening for their escape when the Governor of Barbados was entertaining the Governor of Nevis and they employed 'two lusty blacks' to carry out a boat. After a week at sea they landed on the Spanish island of Tortuga (Tortola, Virgin Islands), where their boat was burned by pirates. They had sailed some 450 miles. On Tortuga, they bought an Indian slave from some pirates thinking he would help them to fish. They ate turtles and turtle's eggs, fish, young birds and wild vegetables. After three months a man-of-war arrived, an English privateer, but the crew would only agree to pick up Dr Pitman, leaving the Colyton men with a cask of wine, some bread, some cheese, a gammon of bacon, some cloth and needles and thread. Meanwhile, Pitman returned to his home in Lyme where he was greeted as one risen from the dead. Whicker, the older man of the two, then took command of the castaways. Some pirates tried to ambush them but Whicker and his men got the upper hand, tied them up and took possession of their boat. They then set sail towards Puerto Rico but had to land again to dig a well for fresh water. Whicker wrote to Pitman in his description of this 'Lying ashore all night to take up the water as it sprang, we were almost stung to death with a sort of flies called Musquitoes', but they managed to collect some 40 gallons of water. They set sail again and sighted a ship they took to be a Jamaican sloop, 'for she had our King's Jack', but when they anchored alongside her, Spaniards armed as pirates overpowered them. They 'carried us aboard their sloop, stripped us naked, and put us down in their hold'. They were fed on short rations, taken to St Jago, Cuba, and kept as slaves. They fell ill with ague (malaria). However, when the Governor was informed that the Duke of Albermarle had arrived in Jamaica all English prisoners were released. Whicker reported that as free men they were sent from Cuba to Jamaica then England. They probably arrived in the summer of 1688, still 'desiring God Almighty to deliver us, and all our dear countrymen Protestants from the barborous cruelty of the Spaniards and Papists' and obviously having gained a little more experience of their enemies to put behind their convictions than their fellow Colyton rebels. Whicker's wish was also just about to be granted with the arrival of William of Orange at Brixham in November 1688.[108]

For those who escaped from Sedgemoor, the aftermath of the rebellion was many months spent in hiding. In Colyton, one fugitive was with his family when the soldiers arrived. He ran into the garden and threw himself down amid the cabbages, but when the soldiers asked his children where their father was they simply told him and he was arrested. Soldiers were stationed on Chantry Bridge to prevent fugitives entering the town. One man was chased around the streets and hid under straw that was being used for thatching in a narrow court. A dragoon reputedly put his sword right through this man's thigh but he was not discovered.[109] John Clapp, the 51-year-old Colyton mercer who had lodged Wilkins's son, made his way home from Sedgemoor and was in bed when his house was searched. He escaped through a trapdoor on to the roof. The soldiers noticed that his bed was warm and realised that he could not be far away but failed to notice the exit to the roof.[110] Isaac Drower and his son Zachariah, our archetypal Colyton reconstitution subjects, both returned to Colyton after Sedgemoor. When their house was searched, Zachariah hid under the wheel of the family's watermill, presumably used for sawing wood for their carpentry business. Having searched the house the soldiers were leaving when one of them noticed something unusually white hanging from the wheel—it was Zachary's shirt sleeve. He was imprisoned but proposed for pardon at Dorchester. Despite being only 21 years of age, Zachary already owned some land that was forfeited and sold.[111] Other rebels seem to have been successful in lying low throughout the searches. John Marwood is only recorded as being 'at large' in the documents but he died in Colyton in 1710. For others, the rebellion had tragic consequences. Humphrey Mitchell, aged 27, was hanged at Nether Stowey. His wife died in February of the following year, leaving their three children under 6 as orphans. Sir Walter Yonge's servant, known to posterity only as 'Soundy', was last 'seen in Monmouth's Camp'. Others possibly had a lucky escape. Nicholas Warren was to be transported but was inexplicably omitted from the shipping lists. Yet others were recommended for the King's pardon, such as John Woolmington, a 24-year-old Colyton weaver who was wounded at Sedgemoor and imprisoned at Wells.

It is easy to romanticise this period but a general pardon was not issued until March 1686. Before this many fugitives had been camping out in the woods and some were forced in by the winter. The soldiers' searches through the houses of Colyton sound benign or even comical in the accounts of their examinations of the households of the Clapps or the Drowers, but there is every evidence that they shared the brutality of the Judge Jeffries trials, raping and pillaging as they searched. For three-quarters of the old style year of 1685 Colyton was, in effect, under a military occupation. The Calendar of State Papers records that in December 1685 the King requested a full enquiry into the holding force in the West and specifically ordered an enquiry into the looting of lace from the house of an honest citizen in Colyton, 'intending that the offenders should be punished according to the utmost severity of the law and that full reparation should be made'. Thirty-three out of the eight-six Colyton rebels had been captured and their whereabouts and fate would have been largely unknown to their families.[112] There is also evidence that in towns as politicised as those of south-east Devon, rebels had many local enemies only too ready to turn them in. On return to Axminster, eight fugitives were caught and captured by fellow townsmen who were paid at the rate of £1 per rebel and 5d. for the cord to bind them.[113] The Lyme magistrates records show other evidence of 'treachery'. John Bailes of Axminster gave the names of twelve men from his own town and four from Colyton whom he had seen in Monmouth's camp and he provided more evidence to incriminate the minister Towgood, construing him as a political leader 'and saith that one Toogood a minister did often use the house of one Bryan a clothier in Axminster before Monmouth's landing'.[114]

In 1689 a petition was lodged in the State Papers from the mercer John Clapp, Joseph Pitts, and another man now familiar to us, John

Gould, all from Colyton, with Daniel Cleveland and Nathaniel Smith, of Honiton naming forty-one persons described as 'men of sober and industrious lives, [who] were after the defeat of the Duke of Monmouth taken into custody, some having joined in arms with him, some having supplied provisions, but others of them in nowise [no ways] having assisted'. The five men argued their neighbours had been persuaded to plead guilty otherwise Judge Jeffries would have had them immediately executed. They had been terrified into compliance and as a result banished as slaves to the colonies for ten years. Perhaps it was an excuse, or at least the use of a non-political and mercantalist rationale, but the petitioners argued that they should return due to a labour shortage —'That by reason of the great number so banished the country wants inhabitants, artificers and labourers'—so they prayed that these men may return home to their wives and children. This petition was authenticated by Sir Walter Yonge, who, once out of danger, persuaded King William to pardon and recall the Monmouth transportees.[115] Although supposedly free men after ten years, their labour was so valuable to the colonies that they were only slowly released with delays in passing the recall through the various assemblies on the islands. Some men, like Azariah Pinney, who had turned in evidence and left for Nevis as a free man, were able to take provisions, clothing and even a sword. He established a successful plantation but his title to leases back in England was never again secure.[116] The release took much longer to go through the Barbados assembly than elsewhere and some of the Colyton men had set up homes and farms in Barbados by the time they were free to travel back. Others returned as a result of the petition. For example, John Skiffes, a 22-year-old shoemaker who was wounded at Sedgemoor, then transported to Jamaica on the *Port Royal Merchant*, was named on the petition and returned to Colyton and baptised children there in 1694 and 1697.[117] The Monmouth rebellion was no spontaneous reaction on the part of Colyton citizens but an event that embattled parishioners had planned and trained for. Yet it was an external expression for convictions which found no easy outlet within the parish itself because loyalties were divided and personalities intruded. It was also a decisive end to a principled fight that had been in train for half a century.

Nonconformity after Toleration

Following the Toleration Act of 1689 that granted the right of religious worship to Protestant nonconformists, there was a spate of applications to register meeting houses in the Colyton region. The first were for the Presbyterian meeting houses built at Honiton in 1689 and Membury in 1690.[118] In Colyton itself, the original George's Meeting House was a dwelling house converted in 1693 with John Kerridge as first minister.

Kerridge had been ejected as schoolmaster at Lyme Regis in 1662.[119] The house was purchased by the mercer, William Lymbery and the subscribers included Daniel Toupe.[120] Kerridge also seems to have been involved with a school in Colyton and Lyme from as early as 1682, run in conjunction with the son of Ames Short.[121] At some point in the late seventeenth century Matthew Towgood, undoubtedly a relation of the Axminster rebel, was appointed assistant minister at George's Meeting House in Colyton. He also ran a nonconformist academy for young men in the town from 1690 to 1716 and instructed them in classical and theological learning, 'an office for which his solid attainments well fitted him, but his habits of study and absence of thought often led him into many singular and laughable mistakes and blunders'.[122] There had been an academy in Exeter since 1662 and the curriculum comprised not only religion and classics but also mathematics, history and morals.[123] We cannot know who actually attended these schools, and they could have been mainly patronised by the gentry, but the classical curriculum at least hints at an expectation that the sons of merchants and practical men would use this route to learning to rise in the world.

In 1707 a Colyton Baptist church was formed after a rift although in the Presbyterian church, but in 1715 the Presbyterian church alone had a congregation of two hundred people.[124] According to Eyre Evans, the popularity varied with different ministers.[125] It is evident that there were differences between a minister, Mr Rosewell, and some of the hearers in 1711.[126] Rosewell was not prepared to take on an assistant, and from the case heard in the Exeter Assembly we learn that some of the Dissenters returned to the Anglican church. Eventually Rosewell left the chapel and took about twenty-five of his communicants with him, preaching at his own house. As a result, the Assembly minutes record, 'several have left the meeting and are gone to Church: they desire to have a Minister to administer the Lord's Supper to them'. Two years later members from Colyton wrote to the Assembly to ask them to support their meeting, 'some being dead, some remov'd, others unable to pay what they subscrib'd'.[127] Yet the dwindling number of hearers recorded in 1712 soared to 220 during Youatt's ministry from 1714 to 1729. In Colyton as a whole, there were two congregations with a total of 360 hearers in 1715.[128] In July 1717 the will of Benjamin Slade, a merchant, granted money 'towards the maintenance of the meeting now held in my uncle's, Willm Lymbrey's meeting house'. William's widow, Grace, left £29 in 1725 towards the Presbyterian meeting in Ottery St Mary, 20s per annum for the Presbyterian meeting in Beer for twenty years, but a triumphant £200 for supporting the Presbyterian meeting in Colyton.[129] This era was the height of popularity for Devon nonconformity after which numbers started to fall.

By the late seventeenth century Dissent was retreating from rural areas and from the elite in Devon. It was increasingly only common among those of middling status in industrial parishes.[130] Labourers seem to have returned to marrying within the ambit of the Anglican church in the early eighteenth century. In fact, a particularly low number of labourers married outside of the Established Church in Colyton in the 1700–49 cohort. It is also possible that more rigid enforcement of the 1662 Settlement Act underlined the need for the labouring poor to be officially recorded. Certainly, parish registers were often consulted to determine a person's settlement by the mid-eighteenth-century overseers of the poor. In 1761 a new Unitarian chapel was built to replace the old George's Meeting House. The registers of this chapel are still extant but include only 9 per cent of Colyton's population.[131] Some correspondence dating from 1772 regarding the appointment of a new minister mentions that 'the glorious cause of Religious Liberty for which our pious ancestors made such a noble stand in the last century have been on the decline for two or three years last past in the Presbyterian society at Colyton for want of a settled and serious minister'.[132] This was something of an elegy to times past, for Colyton had been without a minister for four years and the next pastor would have difficulty in preventing 'a great diminuition of the flock'.[133] Polwhele's *History* records eighty Dissenters in Colyton in 1793.[134] Clearly, nonconformity was losing popularity amongst all classes in the second half of the eighteenth century and this trend seems to have continued. Indeed in the first half of the nineteenth century one of the ministers of George's Meeting died of starvation.[135]

Religion, Politics and Demography

A particularly detailed case in the ecclesiastical court in 1689 considered the conduct of an errant minister who had upset many of the parishioners in the small east Devon village of Membury.[136] A man from Aylesbeare deposed that a year and a half after Monmouth's rebellion he had visited his father's house in Membury which was full of 'ye Rebels that Skulkt up & downe' and the soldiers who searched for the rebels abused him. He believed the majority of the parish were Dissenters. The vicar had been in the King's service during the rebellion and had been in danger from the rebels. More people had become nonconformists since he had departed, such that something of a religious free-for-all now existed, with Mr Mayowe, a former curate, taking the upper hand. Mayowe may have also been being framed by his neighbours: they said he was a tippler, he had a hot temper and he was accused of sexual harrassment. A farmer's wife deposed that he had talked obscenely to her, touched her bosom and made indecent proposals. She was afraid he would follow her into the fields when she went milking. Perhaps the most damning evidence came from Nicholas Rogers, a worsted drawer and the former parish clerk. He said that although Mayowe had been a curate he had no licence to preach, he had challenged dinner guests to a fight when drunk, had two children with his 'pretended wife', and when it became obvious that she was pregnant Mayowe had started to miss out the Seventh Commandment in Church. As in all of these disputes, there was an element of the personal feud: Mayowe had stopped Rogers performing his office after he turned over two pages together while reading the psalms in church; his replacement was subsequently accused of living in incest by marrying two sisters.

However, this case also reveals several details about local irregularities in recording ceremonies. Abraham Balster of Membury, a yeoman, had been married in Stockland without banns or licence. Mr Harvey, who conducted the service, was believed by the local constable not to have taken the oath of allegiance and not to be a true minister. Shortly after this marriage Mayowe demanded a fee of half a crown from Balster, despite the fact that he had not performed the service, and then confiscated Balster's marriage certificate. Yet Mayowe himself was accused of conducting clandestine marriages elsewhere. Charles Stocker of Dalwood, cordwainer, deposed that Mayowe came into his house with a couple and married them there 'rather than going into an alehouse'. Another man from Broadclyst gave the bride away. He did not know whether they had a licence or banns but Mayowe gave them a certificate of marriage. Jacob Turner of Membury, carpenter, went to Mayowe's house to ask him to baptise a child who was very ill. Mayowe was very unwilling to baptise it, 'saying hee believed some Phanaticall women had putt it into this deponts head to baptise it at home'. Mayowe told Turner of the parishioners' unkindness to him and that they had endeavoured to turn him out. But Turner said 'He Plague ye North end of ye psh as long as I live in ye psh'.

These are depositions of fear and confusion, but coming from the neighbourhood of Colyton they only leave us in greater doubt about trusting church registration. They reflect local power struggles and also the promiscuous local attitude to church attendance and recording. The ecclesiastical authorities doubtless either overlooked or did not know about a mass of idiosyncratic practices which only occasionally surface in the documents. This situation seems quite different from that in Wiltshire during the period 1660–1740 where Spaeth argues Anglican rites of baptism, marriage and burial were thought to be essential and only to be carried out by the Church of England clergy.[137] Mayowe, and men like him, may have been conducting weddings for Colyton's inhabitants. Being an essentially 'anti-establishment' activity it is hardly surprising that there are no records to make this clear. To confirm this, Monmouth's rebels' marriages were analysed. The rebels can be linked to fifty marriages, only fifteen of which took place in Colyton church. The other thirty-five fall into the 'missing marriage' category. The rebels had to be at least in their late forties to have married at Colyton church during Wilkins's ministry, and five of the fifteen cases fall into this category. In fact, only one rebel seems to have married outside of the church in the pre-1662 period. After 1662 and before the Act of Toleration, only six marriages of rebels took place in the church. They were the poorest rebels and it is possible that they were employed by other rebels who persuaded them to fight, or perhaps more likely they fit into the category of occasional conformists. Marriages are similarly under-registered in Lyme and Taunton.[138] In the years immediately preceding Monmouth's rebellion the number of marriages celebrated in Colyton church numbered four in 1681, two in 1682, three in 1683, six in 1684, and five in 1685 itself. Colytonians not only rejected marriage, they also resisted oaths and here an overtly religious stance became political because the Dissenting inhabitants refused to participate in those acts which qualified early modern men for citizenship.

At different dates the population of seventeenth-century Colyton and the region were 'hot Puritans' and 'godly people'. Their membership of different Dissenting congregations meant that they formed networks around the region. Charismatic preachers provided the focal point for these congregations and their popular appeal drew hearers from the surroundings.[139] It was the existence of a corporate body, the Chamber of Feoffees, that transformed an otherwise confusing situation into a coherent protest movement in Colyton. For the period up to the Civil War, David Underdown links ecological types in the West Country with religious allegiance and his thesis has been extended to Devon by Mark Stoyle.[140] Within this scheme, Colyton is a typical Puritan parish, being industrial, open, with a 'wood-pasture' local economy and not dominated by one lord, one of the 'wild and hilly parishes of the Blackdown hills and its outliers'.[141] Yet the above close analysis makes us wary of too close an association between religious behaviour and geographical boundaries. Some local gentry effectively resisted Dissent in their parishes, but in the Colyton area the well-springs of Puritanism seem to have been local gentry networks supported by trade links. They centred on market towns, propagating radical religion and the percolation of ideas among local dealers and craftsmen. As is apparent in Colyton, the role of small-town merchants and shopkeepers was very important in generating faith and levelling political views, yet the involvement of local gentry and some of the poor also suggests that this was not a clear-cut class-based protest movement. The next two chapters will consider this further by exploring the economic world of early modern Colyton, and Part 3 will examine how the religious and political circumstances of the parish impacted on demography, social control and the family. The free thinking apparent in Colyton makes this a fascinating parish to study. But unfortunately the independent-minded make poor reconstitution subjects. This quandary and the political implications of document survival will be analysed as further details emerge. By 1720, non-conformity was evidently a spent political force and another challenge of the sections to follow will be to consider the cultural implications of the transition from passionate, intense religious fervour to a much more moderate urban Dissent accompanied by a large-scale return to conformity. In 1753/4 Hardwicke's Act meant that, in any case, all Dissenters except Quakers had to conform to the rites of the Anglican church.

Overview of Part One

Chapter 1 delineated the aims of this book. We started to place Colyton's demographic history into the broader context of the history of the parish. By piecing together evidence from court cases and poor relief records we can analyse local society from the bottom up rather than gaining a picture only of the life of local elites. We are trying to understand the reasons for the seventeenth-century population doldrums due to the rising age of marriage in the parish and non-marriage. The total reconstitution method allows us to consider demographic patterns by status but it relies on good-quality documentary recording; while analysing the shortfall in marriages, we needed to examine whether this could be a result of recording deficiencies.

Chapter 2 attempted to answer this question. Through the investigation of religion in the parish, Colyton emerges as a Dissenting stronghold in the seventeenth century with a strong tradition of independent thought. The corporate nature of the Chamber of Feoffees provided backing for this, and a counterpoint to the Established Church. The opposition to the Anglican church is shown by the extent of support for Monmouth's Rebellion. Nevertheless, it would be a mistake to assume that all the people involved were united. We can imagine that the solid nonconformity of Isaac Drower, for example, may have jarred with self-opinionated views of Roger Satchell. Overall the degree of nonconformity casts doubt on the reliability of the reconstitution results.

PART TWO
Economy and Locality

3

Industrious Dealers
Trade and the Commercial Imperative

> And yet I knowe that all or the most pte of the other provinces and sheres be rich profitable and stored some wth corne and catle some wth frutes some wth sheepe and wolls and some wth one commoditie or other. But yet generally they cannot compare wth so many as this litel corner yeldeth in sundry respects both for the publyke welth and private proffites and specially for corne and cattell for clothe and woll for tynne and metalls and for fishe and sea commodities all wch out of this have passaged into all naions and be verie beneficiall to the whole common welthe.
> (John Hooker, in W.J. Blake, 'Hooker's Synopsis Chorographical of Devonshire', 1915: 338)

In the early modern period, Devon was the most industrialised area of England. Contemporaries, such as Hooker in 1600, certainly saw the wealth of natural resources in the area and the ways in which they were being turned into wealth. Historians of 'wood-pasture' regions like south-east Devon suggest that the populace engaged in rural industry because agricultural pursuits were insufficient to occupy them fully after the demographic growth of the late sixteenth and early seventeenth centuries.[1]

One attempt has already been made to link Colyton's demographic patterns to the local economy. David Levine argued that economic changes in Colyton were entirely responsible for the fall in population that took place in the second half of the seventeenth century.[2] As the next two chapters demonstrate, close local inspection suggests a more complex picture. Levine thought that Colyton had a thriving woollen industry which collapsed in the late seventeenth century when the new draperies bypassed Colyton. This, he believed, gave rise to a later age at marriage for women. However, he had little documentary evidence for the economic trends and used the population statistics themselves to back up his 'economic stagnation' argument.[3] Levine also argued that lace-making, which employed women and children, became important enough in the second half of the eighteenth century to account for the fall in female age at marriage though providing women with attractive dowries which allowed them to marry earlier.[4] The next sections will examine the documentary basis for industrial trends in Colyton in some detail.

But there are some theoretical problems with Levine's arguments. First, Levine makes the implicit assumption that women wanted to marry early through time and were only constrained by economic circumstances. The alternative argument can be advanced that women would use the access to financial means to preserve their independence. This, in turn, depends on just how remunerative their jobs were. Unfortunately, however, women's wage rates are difficult to establish. Secondly, the assessment of marriage age in Colyton in the second half of the seventeenth century may be flawed by the 'missing marryer' syndrome. Since, as was established in Chapter 1, the marriage data which Levine used refers to the gentry and the poor, he did not, in fact, make an assessment of the marriage age of the wool-working population who fit into the craft and labourer categories, unless it can be proved that economic demise had put all these individuals into the 'poor' category. Nevertheless, the proven influence of Dissent described in Chapter 2 and the combined influence of capitalism and extreme Protestantism must be woven into the picture. Thirdly, subsequent work on other English parishes has shown that there was general population stasis between 1650 and 1750, so that localised, structural shifts in Colyton's economy may prove to be less important than changes in the regional or national economy.[5] The first section of this chapter will analyse the social structure in Colyton and help to inform our analysis of the extent of industry and the distribution of wealth in the parish. The second section will describe Colyton's vigorous trading links and connect these with a buoyant demand from local consumers. The third section will analyse the woollen trade and try to determine whether this can be associated with demographic trends. Finally, I will consider the lace industry in the parish and assess its affect on economic change and local population dynamics, along with the activity of women in this area in the early modern period.

The detailed examination of the culture of Dissent in seventeenth-century Colyton outlined in the last chapter suggests that Puritan projects were a major influence on industrial development in parishes like Colyton where nonconformity helped bring about a renaissance of trade. The detail to follow is drawn from a variety of sources and the evidence should be considered with the caveats on document coverage discussed in the first chapter kept firmly in mind. In terms of 'reproducing Colyton', even in the absence of probate material, there is a breadth of source material that can be applied to the investigation of the economic past.

Social and occupational structure

Only three short periods of detail in the registers give an insight into the occupational structure of the parish. Wrigley found that there was little change between the three periods of 1609–12, 1765–79 and 1813–19. Labourers formed between 30 and 40 per cent of adult males. Owners and occupiers of land comprised between 7 and 13 per cent of this group.[6] As early as 1524, those assessed on wages alone constituted a third of the population of Devon. In the nine parishes of the Colyton hundred the average was already higher than this at 39 per cent.[7] The Hearth Tax return can be used to provide a guideline to the wealth structure in Colyton and this is shown in Table 3.1. This classification scheme follows that adopted by Wrightson and Levine in their detailed study of the parish of Terling.[8]

Table 3.1   Social status of Colyton households in the 1674 Hearth Tax

Number of hearths	Social position	Number of households	%
6–20	Gentry	7	3.7
3–5	Yeoman/wealthy craftsmen	75	40.1
2	Husbandmen/craftsmen	43	22.9
1	Labourer/poor craftsman/poor widow	62	33.1

Source: The Colyton Hearth Tax transcription in Stoate 1982: 6–8.

For those householders who did pay the tax, wealth was more widely distributed than it was in Terling. This is a difficult comparison to make, however, since Terling's capitalist agriculture has been described as a 'precocious variant' of the national pattern.[9] Colyton had a far greater proportion of those who might broadly be termed 'middling'—whether they drew their livelihood from farming, or industry, or a mixture of the two. However, Colyton also had a large proportion of those who were too poor to be assessed at all. Indeed in Colyton less people paid the tax than were classified as paupers: 53 per cent of Colyton's households fell into this category. Terling had rather less at just over 32 per cent of the population omitted in 1671. For England as a whole an average of 35 per cent of households were exempt from the Hearth Tax, constituting an estimated 30 per cent of the population.[10] Hoskins's analysis shows that, by this reckoning, poverty was higher in large rural communities in Devon than in either towns or small villages. For comparison, Exeter had 40 per cent, and the neighbouring parishes of Honiton, Membury and Upottery had 37–40 per cent of households assessed as poor.[11] Colyton was one of the parishes with the largest number of paupers in the county. The figure seems particularly high when placed in the context of an estimate that labourers, cottagers and paupers together comprised some 47 per cent of the national population at the end of the seventeenth century.[12] The Colyton result chimes most readily with other parishes which had a textile-making population and it can be suggested that many of those who could not pay the tax were migrant incomers to the parish. Colyton thus shows one of the characteristics of an 'open' parish with a wood-pasture economy—a large population of immigrants.

Contemporary comment supports the finding that the parish was poverty-stricken in the second half of the seventeenth century, but it is nevertheless possible that the Hearth Tax assessment was affected by the pronounced anti-authoritarian stance of many of the inhabitants. As we have seen, Isaac Drower was a pauper according to the Hearth Tax, yet he had clearly done carpentry work for the feoffees ten years earlier and ten years later he appears to have had a fairly substantial business. Isaac Drower may have been experiencing life-cycle poverty in 1674 but it is equally possible that he had no intention of contributing to national taxation during a period of religious persecution. Even if we were to reclassify Isaac Drower and similar people, however, we are still left with a fairly stark division of the population between a sizeable middling group—who formed perhaps 15 per cent of the population—and a group without much material wealth. There was also a dwindling proportion of cottagers and craftspeople who held some land. This latter category comprised perhaps 25-30 per cent of the population in the second half of the seventeenth century. A sociological picture of Colyton can be drawn from the analysis of who paid the tax and who did not. In the urban area there were merchants and their workers, as well as a large sector of struggling semi-independent craftspeople (who form the subject of this chapter). Their rural counterparts were the yeomen, the dwindling population of smallholders and cottagers, and the agricultural labourers whose livelihood will be discussed in Chapter 4.

Specialist Producers

The father of the diarist Walter Yonge was John Yonge of Colyton, an eminent merchant associated with several others in a royal patent granted in 1588 for 'a trade to the river Senegal and Gambia, in Guinea'. In the Cobb Receivers' accounts for Lyme appears the entry of the sailing of the 'bark Yonge' for the Barbary coast. There is evidence from the 1590s of other voyages from Lyme to West Africa.[13] Lyme was the hub of seafaring adventurers, and when the Axmouth estuary was open in the medieval period, they probably also congregated in Colyton. Some late medieval adventurers bought estates in the Lyme area having made enormous profits on East India voyages. Throughout the early modern period Lyme vessels traded with Newfoundland, Barbados, Virginia, Malaga and Tangier.[14]

While there is evidence of Colyton's wide trading links, this did not automatically translate into economic prosperity. As early as 1540 Leland commented: 'The Toun self of Colington is no very notable Thing'. Colyford, a medieval borough failed to develop into a town despite its main road position. Hoskins suggests that Colyford like other failed boroughs was the optimistic speculation of the lord of a rural manor which did failed to mature owing either to bad siting or lack of productive hinterland.[15] Yet neither of these explanations seems to satisfy fully the Colyford case. Colyford was almost dead around 1724 when Stukeley visited it, but his report suggests that there had been some economic prosperity within living memory. He thought Colyford was probably the site of the last Roman station of Moridunium. 'Here have been many inns and houses and a considerable town. They talk of great stone vaults being found; so that it probably arose from the destruction of Moridunum, as Culliton adjacent, from it. Further, it was a corporation and they now keep up their claim by an annual choice of mayor, who has a mace too, but not I suppose of great elegance.'[16]

We cannot assume that the entire parish had a slow trajectory of decline from the medieval period. Westcote in 1630 described it as 'Colyton a pretty market town, where there is a good resort every Thursday, and in May-day a fair, and the like on St Andrews day'.[17] Perhaps during this period the proximity of several small towns meant there was ample trade between them. Nevertheless the fact that Colyton was not a port town after the silting up of the estuary was of some significance. When Walter Yonge heard from his local head constable that Axminster and Axmouth were to be charged under the Ship Money Act of 1634 he protested that they were decayed towns not port towns and had no man of worth living in them.[18] Of course, this may also reflect political evasion, but there must have been some truth in the statement. Clark and Slack argue that whereas the increase of political stability under the Tudors had encouraged trade in small market towns, improvements in transport benefited larger towns at the expense of the smaller.[19] By the second half of the seventeenth century market towns were no longer one of the most buoyant areas of English urban society. Other research concurs with the idea that transport services determined the success or failure of market centres in the seventeenth and eighteenth centuries.[20] However, Dyer's argument finds that the loss of markets in the south-west in the first half of the seventeenth century was due to economic and social polarisation, but they enjoyed some recovery after 1670. His explanation seems pertinent to Colyton as he suggests that rural industry created local markets for raw materials and food for wage-earners, thus in wood-pasture districts 'we may expect that increasing industry and the spread of production of stock and dairy products for distant consumers together led to the penetration of these previously inward-looking districts'.[21]

There were many marketing opportunities for farm goods and it is clear that by the early seventeenth century local people purchased both corn and meat in the markets. In a 1640 court case John Royers of Shute, husbandman, said that for the last four years he had bought all his corn at the Honiton market.[22] In the late seventeenth century there was a market in Colyton town on three days of the week, every Tuesday, Thursday and Saturday.[23] A court case of 1652 also gives a glimpse of the market. Some butchers, one from Southleigh and one from Farway, described unloading their goods and then going off for a drink. While they were away from the market area a leg of mutton was stolen.[24] In 1797 there were two fairs a year in Colyton and a considerable annual cattle fair in Colyford on 1 March from which the profits went to the portreeve.[25] By the early nineteenth century there were only two markets in Colyton and based on the Lysons' comments we can judge that they were much reduced compared to earlier days. These had now diminished and the Thursday market now sold little except butcher's meat.[26] We can infer from this that markets in the surrounding towns became the focal points and largely took on the functions of the Colyton market. These also provided outlets for the produce of cottagers and small farmers. Celia Fiennes in the 1690s described Exeter market as 'The markets for meate fowle fish garden things and the dairy produce take up 3 whole streetes'.[27] In 1662 a court case involved a butcher from Payhembury whose wife sold sheepskins in Honiton and Ottery markets.[28] The Honiton market was described in the Dean Milles survey, conducted in 1747–57 by the Precentor of Exeter, who was intending to write a book on farming methods in Devon, as selling 'Bullocks, Pigs, fowls of all kinds, Grain of all sorts, Fish, all kinds of shambles, meat, Butter and cheese, all wearing Apparel & in short all the Requisites for the support & convenience of life'.[29] On the road to Honiton in 1788, Reverend Shaw observed. 'We now met numbers of market people with panniers, crooks and gambades'.[30]

Despite the trade between towns and villages, if we were able to visit Colyton in the early modern period we would be struck, as were contemporary observers, by the poor state of the roads. Levine argues that this was one of the factors that made the parish increasingly economically isolated in the seventeenth century. The Dean Milles survey showed that Colyton's rivers were likely to flood and became impassable on spring tides. In the late eighteenth century, Marshall speaks of the roads as 'in the more recluse valleys are nearly in a state of nature: the antient Horse-paths of the Forest state: crooked, narrow, numerous and full of sloughs'.[31] The main method of transportation of goods was packhorse. A court case of 1649 described the loads of agricultural produce carried by Musbury husbandmen on horses: various sorts of corn, pease, wheat, barley and vetches.[32] Outside observers wondered why roads were not repaired considering the availability of flinty stones.[33] This seems even more surprising when we consider the fact that Colyton's feoffees were a centralised authority responsible for road repairs. Yet again, in the seventeenth century the political situation may be relevant. Poor relations with local lords of the manor and a dogged concern to maintain Colyton's cultural isolation from government intervention were perhaps important.

Nevertheless, despite the fact that Colyton was 153 miles from London, evidence suggests close links with the capital and elsewhere. Families like the Pinneys, who traded in lace, spent much time travelling the roads and seas between this area and both Dublin and London in the second half of the seventeenth century. Perhaps it was both the vigour of trade and the exuberance of youth which made Azariah Pinney write to his intended wife, Mary, from Axminster: 'have benn allmost every day on horseback for a month past, an all tho was so full of busynesse the last weeke that did not sleepe 24 hours in 6 days and nights, yet I thinke it doe me good beinge I thank god, as well as ever in my life'.[34] At the same time, his brother, Nathaniel, wrote from London to say that he was heading for Bristol fair. Two cases from the early seventeenth century also show personal and business links between this area and London. In 1619 Nicholas Castle of Axminster, a tucker, commented on the trade of the area with the capital. He described a journey of James Tilman of Aylesbeare, an apprentice tailor, who was going to London but fell sick and had to spend a fortnight in Colyton, then various spells elsewhere and finally Bristol, where he stayed until he died.[35] One Colyton widow, describing the paternity of her illegitimate child, attributed it to a man from Whitechapel in London, a silk weaver who had been in Colyton.[36]

The continuing important involvement of this area in global markets based on seafaring is brought into perspective in a graphic way by an entry in the book of one of the parish officials of Ottery St Mary.[37] In 1699 John Burwell recorded his merchandise on board a ship bound from London for Guinea 'for Old or New Callibar or Bandy Ship'. The shipment included pewter, beads, 36 'Bla[ck?] Casters & Carolinas Laid & Lacd' (Carolinas were a type of late seventeenth century hat), as well as caps and bands, plus 'four and half dozen [y]ells Lace', some coats and 'men's shirts', pieces of cloth, tobacco, and spirits. He went on to mention sundry goods bartered at 'Crue Setera & Coast of Guinea'. Using these goods, Burwell bought slaves. This entry shows that a diversity of fancy consumer goods, some of which were locally made, such as pewter and lace, were used for trade with West Africans. His consignment also shows products such as tobacco that were presumably being exported by Burwell after importation from Virginia and the West Indies. Burwell's consignment of goods travelled a long stretch of the West African coast from current-day Guinea Bissau to Nigeria. Although early modern historians usually characterise the development of rural industry as producing luxury goods for domestic and especially metropolitan markets, this case alone makes it evident that overseas trade should be considered a significant factor within certain local economies. It is also apparent that Burwell traded in some mass-produced items which were probably made locally.[38] The second half of the 1690s saw merchants break the monopoly of the Royal Africa Company in the slave trade along the Guinea coast, and it is apparent that the small ports of this area were not slow in exploiting this victory.[39]

The best documented example of a colonial import that was apparently purchased by even the poorest was tobacco. Celia Fiennes on her journeys in the 1690s found everyone to be smoking in the West Country, commenting on 'the custome of the country, which is universall smoaking both men, women and children have all their pipes of tobacco in their mouths and soe sit round the fire smaoking'.[40] Even a poor woman like Dorothy East, a Luppitt widow in receipt of regular relief who was accused of witchcraft in the 1690s, wandered the countryside with a pipe in her mouth. One of the informants in her case, Jane Ham, said that when passing East's house she had been invited in to smoke a pipe of tobacco but then had been bewitched by East when she refused to linger in her company.[41] Tobacco was sold both in local shops and by pedlars and was readily available in Colyton. For example, a court case of 1647 makes it evident that John Bowen, whose occupation was described as tucker and who hailed from Mywood in Somerset, was travelling the country with a parcel of tobacco to sell.[42] Court cases provide us with evidence of tobacco purchase within the context of other consumer items available at local stores. In 1677 a man entered his local shop in the village of Dalwood to purchase a tobacco pipe. Later several goods were missing and the list provides us with evidence of the variety of haberdashery products sold in the shop including some which might be considered luxury items. The ribbon, serge, stuff, buttons, stockings and cotton tape might be fairly mundane but the several remnants of gold and silver lace that were stolen were not.[43] In towns an even wider range of products, many of them imported, was on sale. When a burglar was at large, Daniel Cleveland, a mercer of Honiton, reported the theft of a new pair of 'greene yarn stockings' which bore his merchant's mark on them. But this case also revealed that the mercer's shop across the road sold imports—nutmeg, sugar of candy, 'raisins of the sun', as well as hops which were probably grown locally. The fact that someone loitering in the shop had put some raisins in their pocket was noticed by 'some women of the country standing by, and taking notyce thereof', suggesting an interesting dichotomy between village and town identity.[44] Tobacco was the most valuable item of plantation trade with Exeter.[45] In 1677 farmers in Lyme started to grow a local tobacco crop but were soon prevented by orders from London which claimed that the venture presented unfair competition with the colonies.[46] Lyme certainly traded in tobacco from the colonies and this would be the product that mercers like Daniel Toupe processed.[47]

For the specialised production of consumer goods, small craft businesses proliferated in the town area of Colyton parish. The linkage process resulting in FRFs shows that these craftsmen would serve one of two distinct markets. There were the plumbers, carpenters, glaziers, blacksmiths and artisans of various luxury goods who traded with the large farmers and local gentry.[48] Their work was of fine quality, they paid attention to detail and were relied upon as a source of local craftsmanship. Secondly, there were the poor shoemakers and poor tailors who had learned their trade as parish apprentices to other paupers. They subcontracted work from proto-manufacturers in the town and they produced the shoes and garments which the poor relief authorities ordered.[49] The larger surrounding towns had an even greater diversity of occupations. Settlement certificates for eighteenth-century Ottery show craftsmen, small tradesmen and families moving in.[50] Boys were apprenticed as taylors, blacksmiths, fishmongers, carpenters, tallow chandlers, sadlers, masons and cordwainers. More mundane items like nails were made by specialists; family accounts from the late 1660s record payments to a 'naileman' in Uplyme.[51]

The wealth of local yeomen expanded with the profits from the wool trade until the early seventeenth century. The way in which these gains translated into spending on material goods is more difficult to determine in the absence of any probate material. From a different area of Devon, however, the consumer spending of local yeomen is shown by the journal of William Honnywell, who farmed in Ashton and Trusham parishes, near Bampton, and made entries in his diary from 1596 until his death in 1614.[52] He frequently journeyed to London where his brother lived. In 1596 he spent three and a half weeks there and bought a watch and a velvet purse in which to keep it, three pairs of shoes (two edged with velvet), a pair of knives, two dozen silk points, and thirty gold buttons for a hat band, which were fashioned for him in Cheapside. In autumn of the following year he spent seven weeks in London and again spent large amounts mainly on fine dress, but also on tobacco. His local purchases were far more prosaic, such as twine, or lime for the farm. Although he had considerable arable land, his prosperity came from sheep farming —he pastured sheep on the commons and sold wool and lambs. He drew wood, also from the local commons, and his workmen made faggots by the dozen.

Honnywell can hardly have worn his London finery for walking in the fields; and his expenditures are indicative of the fact that such yeoman farmers were conspicious consumers who aspired to be gentlemen. Colyton's yeomen demonstrate that there was sometimes a tendency to purchase luxuries rather than more basic items; these men provided the market for some of the specialist items that John Burwell's book demonstrates were being shipped to West Africa to bargain for slaves. As a result the towns of the Colyton area had some specialist craftsmen, including some occupations rarely found in English country towns before the eighteenth century. A court case of 1656, for example, records the theft of a silver spoon from Henry Muston of Honiton, goldsmith.[53] Nevertheless, even in the late seventeenth century, middling and elite households would obtain goods from London, as the Pinney family correspondence makes apparent. Azariah Pinney's letter mentions a present from his sister of a silver tobacco box and a 'bigge golde ringe'.[54] Mary Pinney in 1693 mentioned buying her son a toothpick and a watch in London as a present.[55] Other correspondence in 1696 concerns the purchase of 'Lattaine ware' in London (a sort of milled brass).[56] Pinney accounts from the 1700s and 1710s reveal the purchase of furniture and interior decoration. The Pinneys were fully aware of metropolitan fashions: for example in 1704/5 they paid the bill of 'henri declassr', a japaner, for black lacquer furniture in the Japanese modish style. A bill from 1709 shows the expenses of a very special bedstead. It had carved mouldings, 35 yards of very broad green and gold colour diamond lace, 106 yards of broad lace, 120 yards of cheaper narrow lace and embroidery on the valence laces![57] As the family's wealth grew, based on lace-trading, then money-lending within Presbyterian circles, so did their metropolitan tastes and the gulf from their neighbours became palpable. As the correspondence shows, the neighbours viewed their property improvements and evident commercial success with some suspicion and jealousy. While, as was shown for Honiton, country people were identifiable in the towns, there was a gulf between cosmopolitan tastes and those of locals. Nathaniel Pinney discussed with his sister Hester the delivery of a barrel of sturgeon from London and commented 'ye Country knoes not what it is'.[58]

Even if few people ate caviare in this area, there was a demonstrable demand for more durable luxuries. The inventory of Edward Wilkins, son of the ejected minister, shows he was able to make a business fashioning luxury goods in pewter in Colyton until his death in 1678. As well as 'in the shoppe a presse', there were '1 barbers bason', '1 dozn of tobacco boxes', 'cheesetosters', 'flower boxes', 'pepper boxes' and a 'sugar dish'.[59] Pewter items were made from the melding of tin and lead. In medieval times, when the Axe estuary linked a system of main roads to the sea, many metals would have passed through this area. However, by the second half of the seventeenth century the few extant inventories show far more use of pewter as tableware than had been available earlier. Moreover, as Wilkins's stocks show, the tobacco craze of the 1670s generated its own demand for the 'tobacco box'. This could be a decorated item perhaps ostentatiously placed on show in the house. This certainly seems to have been the case in 1673 when Richard Perry of Farway accused his servant of stealing money from a tobacco box which had been placed on the tableboard.[60] Several other court cases mention pewter in Colyton.[61] In 1638 Robert Lewson of Colyton, brazier, mentioned missing a chamber pot and basin from his house. He believed that they were stolen for the pewter by John Cleeve for his trade of glazing.[62] Skillets are mentioned so often that they were probably manufactured locally. In 1639, Lady Pole's skillet was stolen and it was pawned in Colyton,[63] perhaps to Nathaniel Sweete, Colyton buttonmaker, who acted as pawnbroker for a variety of silver items such as spoons.[64]

There were surgeons and physicians in this area from at least the late sixteenth century. A 1591 deed names Thomas Marwood of Blamphayne as 'phisitian'. He was, in fact, physician to Elizabeth I, and his descendant 'Dr Thomas II' was physician to James I.[65] In 1648 Thomas Blackmoore alias Hill of Widworthy was suspected of eating a stolen sheep sold to him by a poor woman from Ottery who had visited him several times.[66] This 'strange' woman would not reveal her name to the constable but when Thomas arrived he said that she was his wife's kinswoman who was staying at his house in order to consult a local surgeon who was treating one of her legs. This suggests that surgeons would not only aid the wealthy. Diocesan records mention Thomas Blackaller, who was both a 'professr of Physicke and Chysrgene', and his son, who had been trained in both of these areas by his father for twenty years.[67] In 1675 the medical practitioners in the area were not thought sufficient. There was one physician but there was no nearer surgeon to Colyton than Exeter.[68] In 1697 nineteen signatures confirmed that the inhabitants of Colyton and Seaton testified that 'Anthony Overmarss hath dwelt and inhabited in Colyton aforesd severall years past & their practiced as a Churgeon and hath performed in this place and parts adjacent many eminent and notable cures and allways behaved himself civilly'.[69] In a list of freeholders and jurymen for the Colyton hundred made in 1698 there were two 'doctors of physick' mentioned and one 'drugster'.[70] The apparent ease with which Colyton people could consult medical personnel is another suggestion of the relative prosperity of the town and that it was a place which offered 'urban' services in the late seventeenth century.

Despite being a relatively small town, Colyton supported a surprisingly wide range of small businesses. Some used local resources but other manufactures were clearly introduced because they met a need for the local populace. We have already seen that most of the craftspeople in Colyton town formed a large part of the Dissenting community. However, the major production of the parish was textiles. Here again we see a dichotomy between production using local materials, as the wool trade certainly did at the beginning of our period, and the production of a lace—a luxury item that aimed to meet the needs of more conspicuous consumers and both sourced its raw material from distant parts and found markets out of the area.

Making woollens

Local supplies of wool, suitable rivers, perhaps some spare entrepreneurial capital from seafaring merchants and a movement of the focus of trade to Exeter formed the basis of Colyton's woollen industry. According to D. and S. Lysons, the market for wool and cloths was moved from Crediton to Exeter in 1538.[71] The 1524 lay subsidy showed Colyton to be one of the wealthier towns in Devon, with twelve merchants having incomes of more than £40 per annum.[72] The Lysons write that:

> Devonshire kersies had acquired celebrity, and were an important article of commerce to the Levant in the early part of the sixteenth century. Fine kersies, of divers colours, coarse kersies, and white western dozens were sent in English ships . . . from the year 1511 to 1534, by several London merchants . . . Each ship that sailed to these ports took from 6000 to 8000 kersies . . .[73]

A statute of 1593 speaks of the Devonshire kersies as being formerly in great demand and much admired, both at home and abroad, but they had subsequently lost popularity because of the frauds of the manufacturers. There is no detail of the nature of these frauds but it is possible that some were selling cloth that was substandard or short measured.

Touring Devon about 1540 Leland observed some of the river innovations for the woollen industry. He rode past the place where Ottery water was divided into four streams to power grist and tucking mills to grind corn and finish cloth.[74] By the 1540s the feoffees' charter mentions that there were six fulling mills along the small River Coly, most situated in the area of Puddlebridge.[75] There were nine racks for drying wool, several of which were sited on Colyton common. Most of the evidence for Colyton in the sixteenth century suggests that involvement was mainly in the relatively capitalist and specialist finishing occupations of dyeing and fulling after the cloth had been collected and redistributed from Exeter. Fox has shown that it was common to find a fulling mill associated with several cottages in late medieval east Devon.[76] This suggests that much cloth-making was in the hands of the landless and near landless in these parishes. In the case of Colyton it seems likely that some of the cloth was woven elsewhere in Devon. Among the first feoffees were John Byrde, silk and sergemaker, John Buckland, wool merchant, and John Maunder, cloth manufacturer. A feoffment of 1572 also gives us an idea of the type of operations in Colyton. It mentions

> the tucking mill bylded and all the rackes called vii dozen of rackes in the same parcel of land buyelt and also one other fulling mill, and the house to the same mill annexed and all the rackes called three dozen of rackes of late in the tenure of John Tyggen . . . also one house called the dyehouse in the west part of Queens highway.[77]

It seems likely that these local enterprises were a response to the fact that from the mid-sixteenth century wool cloth began to be exported directly to the Continent from Exeter, whereas formerly such processes had been carried out in London prior to export.[78] A court case involving evidence from Sidbury in 1606 gives a further indication of production processes.[79] Robert Westcotte's tucking mill was broken into and 3¼ yards of white raw cloth were removed and presented at a dyehouse elsewhere in the parish for the next stage. It is evident that the stages of the manufacturing operations were subdivided and undertaken by different operators.

John Hooker in c.1600 gives a fairly detailed description of the spinning of wool as an almost universal household employment in this locality:

> The second comoditie of the countrie is clothe and woll of clothe there be foure sortes or kyndes the pyne whites ffryses and newe bayes: but the cheffest is the kersey clothe and this so comon a clothe that there is no market nor village nor scarse any privat

> mannes house where in theise clothes be not made, or that there is not spynninge and cordinge for the same: as the daylye travellers can so witnes it for wheresoever any man doth travell you shall fynde at the hall dore as they do name the foredore of the house he shall I saye fynde the wiffe theire children and theire servantes at the turne spynninge or at theire cardes cardinge and by wch comoditie the comon people do lyve.[80]

On the face of it, the expansion of the industry in the rural districts of south-east Devon in the sixteenth century might seem to be a classic case of proto-industrialisation. Certainly the industry worked to distant markets. However, it is difficult to argue that control lay outside of the community. These were capitalised businesses partly controlled by landowners, using both independent skilled workers for some processes, but also essentially proletarianised workers in the fulling mills and dyeworks. As such the woollen industry largely determined the shape of social relationships in east Devon parishes in the early modern period.

Yet the basis of production remained the small, independent unit. As Westcote described the wool cloth-making process in 1630, the first stage was farmers sending their wool to the market. This was bought by either the comber or the spinner, who produced yarn for the weavers. The weavers then sold the resulting cloth to the clothier who sent it to London (or presumably Exeter), or to the merchant who transported it after it had been processed at the fuller's mill and the dyer's vat. These more capitalised operations provided local investment opportunities. In Uffculme, one Devon parish for which probate material has survived, Marye Leyman died a spinster in 1623. She owned the lease of a mill and lent money. The total value of all her assets was £60.[81] In late seventeenth-century Colyton Alice Weekes had a cottage, an acre and a half of land and one rack.[82] Another important aspect is the interrelationship between the local elite and industry. Not only did manorial customs favour local industry, but it is evident that younger sons of the elite participated in the textile trades. For example, the Marwood family owned much land and several farms in late sixteenth- and early seventeenth-century Colyton. Yet whereas some of the Marwoods were members of the squirearchy, others were tradesmen and craftsmen. Younger sons were apprenticed to trade and some became fullers or feltmakers.[83]

The great increase of the woollen manufacture mentioned by Westcote in the early part of the seventeenth century was due to the revival or extension of the sale of English cloths in Italy, Turkey and the Levant, and diversification into new types of fabric. 'New drapery' production involved the manufacture of serges rather than kersies. At the measurable level of the Exeter market, there was no mention of serge in 1612, but by

1615 it was well established.⁸⁴ The commercial contacts of Exeter merchants with the European ports facilitated this speedy switch. The new serges were of a similar construction to the old kersies, but they had a smooth finish and a twill weave.⁸⁵ They were in fact a modification on, rather than a replacement of, the old draperies. The new draperies used long staples of good-quality combed wool, whereas the old draperies had short, curly, carded wool staples, thus drawing more readily on the local supply. Levine argued that with the new predominance of serge came an extension of capitalist power as wool supply had to be obtained from further afield.⁸⁶ As the mercantile element wrested control over production processes, the corollary was an increasing class of landless proto-industrial workers. Hoskins writes that this reorganisation of production was essentially complete by the beginning of the eighteenth century, by which time merchant manufacturers controlled the whole process.⁸⁷

Levine believed that the differentiation of production led to regional specialisation within Devon but that Colyton was excluded from this process due to the poor condition of the roads and therefore began to deindustrialise. He argued: 'It may be suggested that the critical factor in Colyton's demise as an important woollen town was the shift to Irish wool that led to a radical restructuring of the geographical organization of production. Thereafter, spinning and weaving continued in Colyton, to be sure, but they became vestigal'.⁸⁸ However, this assumes that an integrated system of wool manufactures based on comparative regional advantage emerged, and puts great emphasis on Colyton's inaccessibility. In fact other evidence, such as the commercial links with both London and surrounding towns, suggests that a system of pack horses served the area well enough. Some of the Devon villages which Hoskins shows to have been fully integrated into the woollen industry were certainly more remote than Colyton.⁸⁹

There is enough evidence of cloth-making in the seventeenth and eighteenth centuries to indicate that the trade had not disapppeared. It appears that old and new draperies co-existed in the town for some time. On purely theoretical grounds it would have been unusual if cloth manufacture had disappeared from Colyton at the height of its expansion elsewhere in Devon. In 1640 Dorchester and Lyme, two towns with which Colyton was closely associated, were both listed as among the most important clothing towns in the country.⁹⁰ Westcote described these new draperies in 1630: 'The late made stuff of serge and perpetuanos is now in great use and request with us, wherewith the market at Exeter, is abundantly furnished of all sorts and prices; fine, coarse, broad, narrow, the number will hardly be credited'.⁹¹ Almost every extant inventory for Colyton from the seventeenth century shows evidence of cloth-making or storage. For example, the inventory of William Hill, the vicar who died in 1627, mentions, 'In the little room next to the study about a 100 weight of woolle'. In the hallway was 'Woolle, Yarne, boardes, tressells and some other things of little worth'. In the bakehouse there was 'one paire of woollen loomes with ye furniture with a peece in the same and a brake stocke'. Hill also had a small farm with 'a hive of bees, 25 sheepe, 11 lambes, 1 pigge, a gedling, an acre of wheate in ground'.[92]

Nevertheless, the 1620s were a period of depression for wool-workers all over Devon. William Ham, a merchant of Tiverton, left in his will 'to the parish of Colyton £20 to be lent to two poor clothiers of [the] said parish which shall be skilled in the trade and mysterie of making and weaving of woolcloth'.[93] Yonge's diary recalls that in this year justices called clothiers before them due to the deadness of trade, and that there were 300 poor weavers in Exeter 'which go about the streets to crave relief by begging, because they can get no work'.[94] The Venetian ambassador reported in 1622 that there were risings and other riots in the country for lack of work and money, and at one fair corn was carried away by force.[95] He had earlier written that impoverished cloth-workers in bands of up to 3,000 were stealing food but that they had declared that they were not against the King or the government and that they merely wanted work to feed themselves. But as Todd Gray points out, there is little corroborative evidence that such events actually occurred. The Devon quarter session order books show that in 1621 county justices were concerned about relief for those affected by cloth 'decline', but there was no evidence of disturbances.

The greatest threat to the Colyton wool trade in the seventeenth century was neither temporary slump nor technological change, but the Civil War and then plague. As we have seen, Colyton was the battle-ground between the Royalists stationed at Axminster and the Parliamentary garrison from Lyme. Both sought any opportunity to plunder. The ruination of one Colyton man, John Hewes, is well documented.[96] To offset temporary trade depressions the churchwardens would lend a stock to a wool factor and in 1643 they lent John Hewes, a serge-maker of Colyton, 'The sume of three score pounds of lawful English money, being part of a sum of money rated upon the inhabitants and occupiers of land within the parish of Colyton aforesaid, for a stocke to set the poor people on worke, by the space of the whole year and no other person or persons whatsoever'. Apparently, the parish authorities feared that there might be trouble and decreed that if Hewes's goods were 'plundered, rifled, spoiled or taken by force and violence of means or any rebellious manner' the monies to be repaid were to be reduced accordingly. The account of the losses rendered by John Hewes demonstrates the disruption and uncertainty to production which the wars caused. It also shows the way that manufacture was divided between several small businesses in Colyton. Hewes wrote that on 16 January

1643 'my shoope was broken up and my cloth carried away to the vallew of £20. 0s. 0d.', and at the same time 'carried from mee out of William Stocker's house, the tucker, 25 yards of cloth wor[t]h £6. 0s. 0d.' and 'Moore a piece of 13 yerds which William Stocker putt to drynge for mee, which was plundered, wor[t]h £2. 10s. 0d.'. Two months later he reported further problems. The second time the fleeing army from Lyme had gone through Colyton, the soldiers were searching for men and arms; they found Hewe's cloth hidden in a cock loft and carried away £10 worth. Hewes gave one of the captains a suit cloth to save the rest of his goods. About the same time 'Those that garensed [garrisoned in] Colcomb House in [stole] wostard [worsted] woole and wostard yearn and other yearn from the spinstry, and a peece of sarge [serge] torn out of the Racke work £5. 0s. 0d.'. He suffered two repeated attacks later in the year. On 26 July 1644, 'Perlys men when they came back after they were rowted carried away the worth of £16. 0s. 0d.'. And around 13 October in the same year he reported: 'Caried away from me by those that gariensed Axminster 3 broads which was cost to me £10. 0s. 0d.'. He added: 'Besides the cloth i had lost i hid in such places where it was spoiled by weather, and that i sould in those tymes of trouble to a losinge band, to save it from plundering'.

Judging by the processes he mentions and the materials he employed, Hewes was a new draperies serge-maker but the different types of cloth produced suggest both diversity and adaptability. He was ruined by the wars, his business was abandoned thereafter and the prospect was not good for his ten children. His son, John, was a pauper, given employment as parish clerk because he was able to write. As is evident from these accounts, however, Hewes's business operations do not quite fit the methods of production described by Westcote in 1630. Hewes did not merely see through the finishing operations of a piece of cloth but controlled production through from the yarn to the finishing while putting-out to a series of subcontractors. The other interesting aspect of these accounts is the mention of a spinstry in Colyton. This suggests that Hewes did not collect yarn from different independent spinners but that this was a proletarianised part of the business directly under his control. The fact that worsted yarn is mentioned suggests that the spinners dealt with the higher quality imported wool bought or brought in by Hewes and kept under his control. According to the Lysons, the chain of the serge was made of worsted.[97] Theft cases from the 1650s suggest that a variety of different types of cloth were being made in the locality. In Ottery in 1657 it was 'mixed serge' that was stolen from a rack, in Musbury the following year it was 'two yards and one naile of linzey woollsie' and around the same time Richard Hellier, cloth-worker of Axminster, was charged with stealing a 'Molly Kersey' from a tucking mill when drunk.[98]

Another possibility, given the details of the distribution of the stock, is that the spinstry was a parish-organised project to employ poor women. It seems entirely credible that the two went together: spinners were no longer independent workers spinning the wool of local sheep but proletarianised labourers spinning Irish yarn. A court case from Ottery in 1636 makes it clear that servants who lived in clothiers' houses were employed in the business. A man was accused of cutting off and stealing 2 yards of woollen cloth from his master. He worked in his master's house and slept in the room where the wool was stored.[99] A case from Ottery in the 1650s shows that a married woman, Emlin Minifie, was hired to work as a spinner by a yeoman's wife.[100] Minifie was accused of stealing some yarn '& having a good quantity of wooll intrusted with her. Did much abuse it by holding much of the yarne & then she or some of her family did sell much yarne of the same colour or near the same colour.' While serge-makers like Hewes may have been increasingly exerting control over business, it was still possible for small operators to see a single piece of cloth through the process. In 1639 George Seller, a Sidbury tucker, reported that a year earlier 4 ½ yards of blue cloth had been removed from his horse's panniers at Ottery market and later taken to a tucker of that town to be dressed. Some of the tucker's men knew Seller's mark and sent word to him that they had discovered the stolen cloth. The man he accused claimed to have just found the cloth in the street and said that he put it to dressing by a tucker after keeping it for a while.[101] The final point we can draw from the Hewes case is the unusual extent to which the parish was expected to underwrite his business losses in an effort to employ the poor. In this way, the Hewes case provides a historical spotlight on a typical Puritan project—it aimed to employ the numerous poor in a useful way while creating local wealth. It suggests that the textile industry may have continued in Colyton even if it was not very profitable, because it formed an integral part of the wider social programme that many of the substantial inhabitants supported.

Hard on the heels of the Civil War chaos came plague. Analysis of the Colyton plague victims by linking them to the total reconstitution shows that all the families who were involved with the wool trade were affected by the disease. That cloth-workers were particularly vulnerable to catching plague is also suggested by the study of the disease at Eyam as well as other textile centres.[102] Fleas were the ultimate source of the infection and the disease may have spread with the producing and marketing of woollen cloth simply because this took place in populous centres with much human interaction. In Colyton the linkage produces a clear pattern. The plague started amongst cloth-workers and within the second or third month spread to the wider craft community. Only later did the disease attack all sectors of the population. It is noticeable that the agricultural population was far less affected than the industrial, and consequently, sickness remained fairly confined to the town area of the parish. Plague affected individuals in family groups,[103] and a breakdown of the victims' socio-economic status is made according to families in Table 3.2. In 147 cases the families could be given a status attribution.

Table 3.2 Status of Colyton plague victims

Status	No. of 1600–49 FRFs	Plague families	% affected by plague
Gentry	132	27	20.5
Crafts	129	56	43.4
(not wool)	101	43	42.6
(wool)	28	13	46.4
Labourer	81	26	32.1
Poor	131	38	29.0

The socio-economic standing of plague victims was compared with the status distribution of all FRFs in the 1600–49 cohort. This indicates that relatively few plague victims were from the gentry class, whereas a roughly similar proportion of plague victims were labourers and poor as in the population as a whole. The craft sector was the most seriously affected group as 43 per cent of families had plague victims. Within this group, the wool-making population was worst afflicted, with 46 per cent of families containing plague victims. The dual existence of the old and new draperies can be demonstrated from the occupations given in the parish register. Whereas 'woolcomber' indicates a worker on the new serges, 'fustian weaver' implies a rough, old drapery type of fabric that was probably still made for the local trade. There were thirty woolcombers in the parish register in the period of occupational detail from 1765–79, but there were still eight fustian weavers.[104]

Since Wrigley's analysis showed that the woollen industry accounted for 12 per cent of occupations in the 1609–12 period, and 10 per cent in the 1765–79 period, it is difficult to argue that the woollen industry disappeared from Colyton in the second half of the seventeenth century.[105] Coleman believed that the new draperies were only partly a process of a diffusion of a new technique. They were also the response of a commercialisation of peasant techniques, 'a drawing into the market economy stimulated by market demand'. As such they were an adaption, 'their novelty was built up from many mutations upon traditional techniques'.[106] Had the wool trade disappeared from Colyton in the early seventeenth century, it would have been nonsensical for a man to build a new fulling mill. However, in a late seventeenth-century lease book for the manor of Yardbury, Robert Dyer held a plot of land 'upon which he hath now built a fulling mill in length 32 foot by 20 foot overthwart the river'.[107] In his will of 1670 Thomas Holmes left his nephew, John Holmes, a fulling mill.[108]

The cloth trade seems to have been buoyant enough to survive the devastating effect of the plague on the textile-making community. In 1660 there was enough cloth-making in Colyton for it to create a public nuisance, as the feoffees agreed at a meeting 'that no person or persons whatsoever shall after this present day put, dry or hang any wool on the Lyddes [leads] of the church',[109] although considering the degree of nonconformity by this time some behaviour may have been politically motivated. But the trade was subject to cyclical prosperity and depression. Landless weavers could maintain a good living in prosperous times, but in depression they could sink into poverty in a year or two. Through the record linkage process some spectacular declines in fortune can be charted. Thomas Parsons of Kingsdon, a weaver, was wealthy enough to leave a will in 1651 which divided his property between his eight children.[110] Perhaps this division was the downfall of his family, for by the 1680s his grandchildren were in receipt of materials from the poor relief authorities to enable them to make the cheapest quality of woollen clothes. While involvement in the woollen industry covered the social scale, it would appear from the total reconstitution process that seventeenth-century fullers were middling status and their enterprise was speculative and sometimes short-term. The sixteenth-century fullers were, by contrast, often landed gentry and the mill was just one part of the interests of their estate.

A diversification from wool was paper-making which seems likely to have developed in the last quarter of the seventeenth century in Colyton when there was some geographical expansion in paper mills elsewhere in the country.[111] As paper was made from rags this may have been associated with the cloth trade, perhaps as a by-product of fulling mills which could have been used to pound the rags. As we have seen in the Monmouth rebellion proceedings, Zachary Drower lived in the 'Higher Paper Mill', suggesting that the family had diversified from carpentry and wood and that there was also a 'Lower Paper Mill' at this time.[112] By the time of Dean Milles survey around 1750, there were two paper mills in Colyton,[113] and later in the century there were a reputed seven mills. There was a mill on Umborne Brook which specialised in brown paper. Coarse rags of flax and hemp made brown and common papers whereas spring water with linen rags made white papers. Pigot's *Commercial Directory* of 1830 described paper-making as 'the principle branch of manufacturing in the town, producing blue, brown and common white paper'.[114] English paper was generally poor quality and said to be used by shopkeepers for wrapping thread, gloves and tobacco.[115] Paper-making required a clean, flowing river and therefore cannot have been compatible with the tannery, although it is possible that their operations may have differed by the season. Each mill probably employed between ten and twelve women and children. In 1799 John Morgan was a master paper-maker in Colyton and in 1803 he insured his paper-drying house.[116]

Stephens saw the period 1659–1667 as a depression in the textile trades in Devon, and 1676–1688 as a boom period.[117] These findings are controversial, however. De Lacy Mann, who managed to make some assessment of wages, argued that there was unemployment for weavers, tuckers and spinners from 1666 until an upturn of trade in 1694.[118] She thought that the low level of the weavers' income placed them with the labourer and outservant class rather than among the artisans. It is the case that the period 1688–1714 saw the height of the serge trade with the Dutch as the major buyers.[119] Certainly by the time Celia Fiennes visited Exeter on her travels in 1698, the woollen districts appeared prosperous.[120] Describing Exeter, she said: 'a vast trade is carried on; as Norwich is for coapes callamanco and damaske soe this is for Serges—there is an increadible quantety of them made and sold in the town'. Going into more detail she found:

> besides the large Market house set on stone pillars which runs a great length on which they lay their packs of serges, just by it is another walke within pillars which is for the yarne; the whole town and country is employ'd for at least 20 mile round in spinning, weaving, dressing, and scouring, fulling and drying of the serges, it turnes the most money in a weeke of anything in England, one weeke with another there is 10000 pound paid in ready money sometymes 15000 pound; the weavers brings in their serges and must have their money which they employ to provide them yarne to goe to work againe . . . serge is the chief manufacture; there is a prodigious quantety of their serges they never bring into the market but are in hired roomes which are noted for it, for it would be impossible to have it altogether . . . The carryers I met going with it as thick all entring into town, with their loaded horses, they bring them all just from the loome and soe they are put into the fulling-mills.

Fiennes's personal observation also allowed her to detail processes in fulling mills, and she found the merchant's exchange near the Cathedral in Exeter which met twice a day to be very similar to the one in London.

A survey book of Colyton dating from this successful period shows very many fulling and tucking mills and racks, situated along the River

Coly in the town itself.[121] The prosperity this could bring to a local clothier is demonstrated by the inventory of James Batt from Uffculme.[122] He was fully active as a clothier when he died in 1691. He was owed £541 by London, Bristol and Tiverton merchants for cloth and had five packs of cloth *en route* to Flanders worth £120 and assorted wool (serges, broads, kerseys, druggets, yarn and white and dyed wool) waiting to be spun. He had no cloth-making equipment of his own but put out wool and yarn. Cloth accounted for 90 per cent of his total estate of £1,182 but he also farmed in a small way. Batt's operations are those of the dealer and manager rather than being an active producer himself. Moreover, his goods show that he still had an 'old drapery' element in his business as late as the 1690s.

Settlement certificates from the early eighteenth century suggest that woolcombers and serge-weavers were moving into Colyton.[123] In 1721, for example, Henry Wey, a woolcomber, arrived from Cullompton, and Henry Woodgate, a serge-weaver, came from Exeter with his family. Defoe first mentioned the extent of serge manufacture in Devon and the amount of trade with Holland when he arrived at Honiton:

> Here we see the first of the great serge manufacture of Devonshire —a trade too great to be described in miniature, as it must be if I undertake it here, and which takes up this whole county, which is the largest and most populous in England, Yorkshire excepted . . . But Devonshire, one entire county, is so full of great towns, and those towns so full of people, and those people so universally employed in trade and manufactures, that not only it cannot be equalled in England, but perhaps not in Europe.[124]

He echoed Celia Fiennes in finding that the serge market was well worth seeing and although we cannot place too much value on his exactitude, Defoe remarked that 'The people assured me that at this market is generally sold from sixty to seventy to eighty, and sometimes a hundred, thousand pounds value in serges in a week'.[125]

Spinning was still undertaken in Colyton beyond this date. Two settlement examinations were taken of Ann Snell in 1781, when she was a single woman aged 66. At the age of 18 in 1735 she had lived in Colyton with Sarah Newbury as an 'inmate' and had 'spunned for her living'. Interestingly, linkage shows that Sarah was a compeer. She was two years older than Ann and seems to have maintained her own household at the age of 20.[126] However, by the 1740s a slump in the wool trade resulted from competition with Yorkshire and East Anglia.[127] But the second half of the eighteenth century saw a steady recovery. Chapman has made a study of the extent of the textile industry in eighteenth-century Devon using the details obtained for Sun Life fire insurance policies.[120] Obviously those who held insurance policies were the better-off sergemakers and clothiers, but from this research Chapman demonstrates that Colyton was a minor textile centre. Those involved in the trade generally had a building next to their house in which they carried on the serge-making business. The inventory details show there was still a bias towards the finishing processes. In a rate made in 1726 for the repair of Colyton church, William Berry was assessed for tucking mills.[129] In her inventory, Elizabeth Vicary, a widow, had 'linneys around the Court' but also the machines for finishing 'poundho., poundengine and press and stable all adj[acent].', which were insured for £300 in 1766. In the same year, John Spurway insured 'workshop, warerooms over, dyehos adj[acent]' for £40.[130]

In 1750 when Dean Milles made his enquiry about all the parishes in Devon, he wrote for Colyton: 'clothing and serge the only manufacture. The trade and manufactures in this parish—cloth, serges are disposed of at Exeter and Eastwards' but 'having neither trade nor thoroughfare it is not wea. hy'.[131] The situation was much more buoyant in the larger towns. For Axminster it was reported that the 'chief Trade' was 'narrow Cloth wch is here made very good, and cotton or Manchester Tapes—of late years Broadcloth has been here made, and very good. And very lately a carpet Manufacture has been there set up—wch seems for Strength, Goodness and Beauty to equal any that I have seen.' The Lysons believed that the Axminster carpet factory was established in 1755.[132] The Reverend John Swete was taken on a guided tour of the carpet manufactory in the 1790s.[133] The operation started with worsted-winding carried out by children, and went on to carpet-weaving carried out by women, 'for females were the sole artists', as Swete put it. In Honiton the economic prospects also seemed relatively rosy: 'The woollen goods are partly sold to the Merchants in Exeter & partly sent to diverse parts of the Kingdom'. The *Western Flying Post* contained an account of a fire which destroyed the premises of Mr James Maynard, clothier and serge-maker of Honiton, in 1752. His premises were insured to a value of £1,400 but this was well short of the real value. Maynard kept 'upwards of a thousand persons at work'. This suggests that serge-making was in a flourishing state in this town. Maynard was still in business as a clothier in 1763.[134] By the late 1750s, the *Topographical Dictionary* still found the ordinary weekly sales of the area to be £10,000 and that Exeter was esteemed the greatest wool market in England next to Leeds. Trade suffered in the American Wars but afterwards overseas exportation increased. Nevertheless, there was an almost complete collapse of trade in the French Wars when the revolutionary armies cut off markets. By the time the Lysons were writing there was still some trade with the East India Company and a revival of Spanish and Portugese markets. Ottery still produced a few woven goods and had a large factory for spinning the yarn used in manufacturing serges which were sent to the Exeter market.[135]

Well before this happened, however, we can see an association between the cloth trade and poverty. The overseers' account book for Colyton for the period 1740–70 frequently mentions buying spinning equipment for poor women.[136] For example, from 1743 is the entry 'pd for a spinning Turne for Pol Hawker 1s'. As in the seventeenth century, poor women were expected to work together in a spinstry organised by the poor law authorities. Elizabeth Leighton was bought a spinning turn in 1743 and at the same time the relief officers paid for 'Instructions to bring her to work at several times'. Esther Gill of Chudleigh, who was examined in 1839, told of her work in her childhood in the 1760s when she lived with her aunt in Nether Exe. She 'went to work in the fields for farmers in that parish. She went to Broadclist when about 20 years old and went to work for different people and at home spinning.'[137] An inventory of goods in Colyton workhouse taken in 1779 mentions a workshop with 'Nine spinning turns and one skaining turn'.[138] Men were also set up in the weaving trade by the poor officers when they were in dire economic circumstances. In the overseers' account book in 1768 is the entry 'pd for a pr of weaving looms and carriage for John Ford'. They cost the parish £1. 1s. 6d.[139]

William Marshall describes cloth being manufactured in the home in Devon in the 1790s: 'in private families by men, women and children, who by this employment are kept at their own houses, are enured to habits of industry, are enabled to support themselves at all seasons and are always at hand, to assist in the works of husbandry, whenever the production or the preservation of the necessaries of life requires their assistance'. He said that the manufacture of the lighter kinds of woollen lingered on to the present time: *'women have there, been employed, as weavers*, during a length of years'. But he described the lack of female employment except where they were employed in lace production. 'About fifteen years since, it is notorious that a good spinner would earn 3s 6d per week, her time is now, through the general failure of that employment, too frequently spent in rummaging about for a few loose sticks, in order to procure a scanty supply of fuel.'[140] Although Polwhele still found that in the village of Widworthy 'the women spend the greater part of their time in spinning wool',[141] Hoskins has calculated what a poor living an entire family could expect to gain from the woollen industry at the end of the eighteenth century.[142] Maton comments that Ottery St Mary in 1794–6 was 'a place of some trade, manufactories of flannel, serge, &c having been lately established here'. This seems to have been due to the efforts of the local elite and presumably the encouragement of industry was a form of poor relief.[143]

In 1791, the *Universal British Directory* named fourteen people who were involved in the cloth industry in Colyton. Half of them were concerned with retailing the finished product.[144] In the 1819 poor rate assessment listing there was still a pressing iron and shears at Little Watchcombe in Colyton owned by Richard Kittle. This was a relic of the finishing process which had been carried out in Colyton for hundreds of years.[145] Celia Fiennes had described this dressing process. The fabric was teased to raise a nap on the surface, then closely cropped by a shearman to give a smooth finish. After 'burling' to pick out all the knots, the wool was pressed between plates heated by a furnace.[146] But by the early nineteenth century the wool trade was almost past history in Colyton. In a settlement examination of 1815, John Turner's apprenticeship to Elisha Bennett, a weaver, was terminated, 'trade being very bad'.[147] Colyton was now in a process of deindustrialisation in common with other Devon parishes.

The other textile industry, the production of flax for local linen, seems minor and never a thriving concern. Flax production may have started to produce lace thread in the seventeenth century but was soon superseded by imported thread. The hemp and flax bounty papers for 1786–90 show that flax was grown and manufactured in Colyton by Joseph Restorick.[148] In 1788 Joseph and his wife and nine children had flax bought for them by the feoffees to prevent them from becoming a parish charge. The bounty papers show a limited local linen manufacture in Colyton. In 1781 two brothers who kept a house in the parish for dressing flax were warned that it was a dangerous nuisance and needed to be pulled down.[149] Evidence points to flax being made into rope for both agricultural and seafaring use, rather than into linen.[150]

In summary, in the period 1600–1800 Colyton had a small community of wool-workers. There were a few spinners, a few weavers, some people involved in the finishing sector, and some merchants who traded the finished product. There is certainly more evidence of industry than that suggested by Clapp. He argued that there was 'no evidence for much industrial employment in Colyton at any period during the last four hundred years'.[151] At the same time the cloth trade never involved a large enough proportion of the population to have affected demographic trends in the drastic way that Levine suggested. There is no evidence of industrial demise in the second half of the seventeenth century. In fact, under the influence of a pro-active local government the cloth industry seems to have made a remarkable recovery from the havoc caused by plague and Civil War. Decline is a story that belongs to the second half of the eighteenth century.

Dealing with lace

While Levine portrayed the demise of the woollen industry as having a negative effect on population growth, leading to the late age at marriage of women, he viewed the effects of lace-making much more positively, causing the age at marriage to fall.[152] The evidence for the rise and decline of lace-making, and its effect on women's marriage age in Colyton, will now be examined in some detail. The lace industry merits particular attention, because it was overlooked by many of the earlier economic historians who viewed female manufacturing pursuits as being of less consequence than the West Country trades in which males were largely involved, such as cloth production or tin mining.

A variety of explanations have been advanced for the timing of, and the influences on, the introduction of lace-making to east Devon. Yallop, who has written the most detailed account of the industry, suggests that it may have been introduced from Venice around 1560.[153] Venice was Europe's foremost entrepôt in the sixteenth century and also the most advanced industrial city in Europe. The city was the world leader in technical crafts including textiles and Europe's chief repository of skill.[154] However, a strong tradition associates early lace with refugees from Flanders and France from the 1560s onwards, but particularly following the St Bartholomew's Day Massacre in 1572. An alternative explanation is that English lace may have more indigenous origins, developing out of either the gold and silver thread industry or from linen embroidery, moving out of London to the provinces at the end of the sixteenth century.[155]

In 1600 John Hooker commented on the Devon yeomanry. 'And now of late they have entred into the trade of usurye buyenge of clothes and purchasinge and merchandises clymmynge up daylye to the degrees of a gentleman and do bringe up theire children accordingly'.[156] This comment could be referring to several branches of trade but indicates the willingness of the middling orders in Devon to embrace trade. Point-makers are mentioned in the records at Honiton in 1573 and at Colyton in 1609 and 1612.[157] In 1609, for example, the marriage of William Vale, a point-maker of Colyford, appeared in the Colyton marriage register. The lace industry fits the description of Joan Thirsk, who has shown how new projects and industries were fostered by deliberate government policy in the sixteenth and seventeenth centuries in order to meet domestic demand.[158] As the seventeenth century advanced, colonial markets became more important, and as evidence such as John Burwell's books shows, they even stimulated local trades through small-scale endeavour. While the industrialisation of the seventeenth century meant new opportunities for women, Ann Kussmaul argues that this had most force in an arable area which had just become pastoral because arable practices require more labour per acre and a move to pastoralism thus released labour.[159] As will be shown in the next chapter, such a transition took place in Colyton. Yet economic determinism does not provide the entire explanation.

Spenceley believed that the lace industry thrived in south-east Devon because the local economy of a sheep/corn husbandry area meant poverty and unemployment were endemic.[160] But the dairy industry did supply some all-year-round work and from the second half of the seventeenth century provided employment for women in milking, butter-making and cheese-making on a commercial scale. Westcote also makes it clear that the woollen industry was not seasonal, although as we have seen, this accounted for only a relatively small sector of Colyton's industry. Could it have been the case that we can explain the rise of lace-making by associating it with periods of downswing in the woollen industry, in communities which had some background in textile production, and therefore had established marketing connections outside of the parish? Analysis of this proposition soon shows that it does not provide an explanation. The dealers in the lace industry are different families from those in the woollen industry and the lace trade focused on London and the colonies rather than Exeter. There was little apparent connection between the two trades. Moreover, their periods of prosperity were reasonably similar: the lace trades were also booming at the end of the seventeenth century, at the same time as serge. Lace-making was a skilled operation, learnt in childhood, whereas spinning and other cloth operations in Colyton seem largely proletarianised. Surprisingly, there is possibly a closer connection between fishing and lace-making. The Newfoundland fisheries grew in the late sixteeenth century, and peaked in the early seventeenth century. While fishing perhaps made little direct impact on Colyton, some of the coastal fishing communities also became renowned lace centres. There is a close similarity between weaving fishing nets and making lace and this may be one repository of the skill. Moreover, fishing involved long absences at sea for men and it is possible that their wives met for sociable lace-making gatherings that became the basis of commercial production.

This is a connection, but it does not explain the sustained growth of the trade in inland towns. In Colyton and neighbouring parishes several conditions interacted to produce the conditions for the steady expansion of lace production. The prosperity of yeoman farmers before 1630 was largely due to wool profits. When wool prices fell, many farmers may have sought different areas of investment. Other farmers found themselves at the sharp end of land improvement and consolidation and sought new ways to make money. Moreover, the landholding structure meant that many of the younger sons did not inherit farms and, as in the wool trade, this caused many of them to move into other types of trade.

The lace industry relied on contacts outside of the area, crucially with fashion centres and the metropolis. A few families emerged as dealers with the mobility and willingness to foster these links. Closer to home, the lace industry met local elite demands and would have been in part encouraged by local landowners. Yet another factor was the well-established artisan production of the area which, as we have seen, can be associated with a strong strain of Dissent that gathered ground from the early seventeenth century. Stoyle's analysis of Devon Puritanism finds that it corresponds exactly with the lace-making districts.[161]

Lace manufacture was also particularly well suited to the extreme Protestant mindset. It was seen as employment for the poor in England as early as the end of the sixteenth century.[162] A 1617 memorial in Honiton church commemorates James Rudge, bonelace seller, who gave the parish poor £100 in a charity to last 'for ever'.[163] Rudge's generous benefaction issued with the stern message 'Remember ye poore' is a clear indication of the association between Puritanism and the use of lace-making to employ the poor. Almost all seventeenth-century commentators on the east Devon region mention the association between lace manufacture and the employment of the poor. For example, Chamberlain wrote in 1683 that bonelace was 'the chief of the Ornamentals worn in this Nation' and that 'so general is this Manufacture in many Parts of England that the Poor of Whole Towns are almost totally employed, and in a great measure maintained thereby; Particularly Honiton in Devonshire is a Noted Town for this Sort of Workmanship'.[164] In fact, the seventeenth century saw a transition to the mass production of lace in this area, with many workers no longer artisans but rather outworkers. The growth of these lower branches perhaps dates from the 1620s and 1630s when lace-making became a notable industry. In these turbulent years of harvest failure and overseas war, lace-making became a panacea to poverty in parishes where a strongly Protestant ethic infused local government. Lace-making was the work ethic in action. It provided a discipline for children and a saleable end product. In the other major area of English lace-making, Buckinghamshire and Bedfordshire, persuasion from the local elite meant lace training was obligatory for poor parish children, with payments provided from the parish stock. At Great Marlow, Sir William Borlase founded a workhouse in 1626 in which twenty-four 'women children' were taught 'to make Bonelace, to spin, or knit'.[165] Such worthy pursuits could flounder or flourish. The bonelace trade flourished in both the Midlands and in Devon. By the late 1630s it had apparently absorbed the local poor population and attracted migrants from the surrounding area. By the second half of the seventeenth century, low population growth and stable prices for agricultural products only meant further stimulation to the middling orders to move into manufacturing. By the

1670s, even the poorest inhabitants of Colyton appeared to want to purchase goods like tobacco and probably worked in the market to do so. Such was the onset of what Jan de Vries has described as the 'industrious revolution' in seventeenth-century Colyton.[166] It expanded the potential for household production well beyond the increasingly intensified and specialised economy of the cottager.

Is it possible to flesh out these general outlines with some evidence? First, it is necessary to correct the erroneous impression of historians that the lace industry was only being established on a commercial basis in south-east Devon in the 1630s.[167] Westcote, writing in 1630, says that Honiton lace (in fact the name given to lace produced all over this region) was sent to London by the week, and he commented on 'the abundance of bone lace, a pretty toy, now greatly in request, being made at Honiton and Bradridge'.[168] Westcote was describing a rapidly developing industry rather than its inception. He also mentioned the fine spinning of flax thread to be used in the lace trade and placed the trade within the context of the other textile manufacturing industries:

> Ottery St Mary, with divers other places, hath mixed coloured kersies. Cullimton [sic], kersey stockings; and Comb Martin serves the whole county, and other places with shoemakers thread. This might be enlarged with other petty commodities belonging to other towns, besides the generalitye of knitting worsted and yarning stockings, spinning of worsted thread for women's working in every town.

Three court cases give us an indication of the existence of the trade in the early years of the seventeenth century. In 1611 Elizabeth Packett, a Honiton spinster, admitted that she had found bonelace on a pillow at the house of Robert Searell of Honiton on Easter Tuesday, which she took and subsequently sold for 6d. She was also found to be carrying georgett, thin silk dress material, taken from Searell's court and she was accused of stealing money from the box of Robert and Hugh Searell.[169] The Searell brothers were perhaps traders in fine fabrics. Notably, the piece of lace was not of high value. There is also a court case from the fishing village of Sidmouth in 1621.[170] Here a girl or woman was sent to Honiton market by her mother to sell four pieces of lace, worth 5s 6d, 1s 2d, 1s 5d and 2s 8d. The different values presumably reflect different sizes of piece or quality of work. The girl seems to have sold these from her basket which she set down on a bench in someone's house. This suggests that at this stage this was a small-scale craft industry which did not generate major profits. An interesting third case, significantly also from Honiton, involved John Satchell of the town, a bonelace-maker.[171] Satchell said that lace was not the trade he had been apprenticed in, so we can assume that he changed tack and learned the skill because it was increasingly in demand. However, Satchell visited a fortune-teller who told him that he was born to ill-fortune. The fortune-teller told him that he should not have altered his trade: 'She told him that if he had keep his trade he was first bound in he would have done very well'.

The clearest detail of the influx of poor migrants is provided by the petition to the assizes at Exeter Castle in 1638:

> Whereas this Court is enformed by the humble peticion of the Churchwardens and overseeres of the poore of Honyton that there be a greate many strangers come into the towne of Honyton than have ben placed on other parishes as pore and are from them placed into the towne aforesaid, besides other poore out of diver places that are brought into the trade of bone lace makinge, whereby the towne is like to come into greate poverty, For prevencion whereof this court dothe thinke fitt and order that yf any master in any other parish, havinge takne a poore child an apprentice by the appoyntment of the justices of peace, shall afterwards for his owne ease place away the same apprentice in Honyton aforesaid without the consent the justices of the peace att the sessions then the churchwardens and overseeres of the poore of Honyton for the time beinge are to to acquaint the said next justice of the peace therewith, and the said justice of the peace is hereby designed to send for the master of such apprentice againe and keepe him accordinge to his indentures of apprenticeshipp which yf he shall refuse to doe, then the said justice is hereby desired to bynde the master refusinge to doe the same to the next assizes that such order may be taken therein as shalbe fitt.[172]

The gender of lace-makers is not apparent from this petition but the association of lace-making with child labour is clear. As the above examples show, however, it is evident that there were many male lace-makers in the 1630s. Samuel Goyings of Lympstone is mentioned in the quarter sessions of midsummer 1638.[173] Colyton tithe disputes mention the deposition of Thomas Pinckley, husbandman, who was born and had always lived in the town. About 1638 he was 'being then a young man and getting his living by lace making within the parish of Colyton'. This shows that he was a bachelor lace-maker at the age of 27 and there were others in the parish in the 1630s as the same case mentions several other similar single men, earning their living not as covenant servants but by their own hands.[174]

The lace historian Santina Levey sees the period 1620–75 as the 'triumph of bobbin lace'.[175] The technique of lacemaking on a pillow lent itself to large-scale production in comparison with the other type of

English lace, the more intricate and intensive needlepoint which was produced in the Midlands. This expansion in production, which absorbed increasing amounts of labour in the lace towns and villages of east Devon, was fashion-led. Copious amounts of lace were needed for trimmings: for example, 25 yards were needed to edge a standard ruff. The diary of Samuel Pepys from the 1660s shows that it was common to overhaul garments with trimmings and even shoes were decorated with lace. London was always the major market for Honiton lace, but it was also exported to the colonies and lines such as 'Bath Brussels lace' were developed for early modern tourists to the leisure towns.[176] As fashions rapidly changed and because the markets were distant from the area of production, the role of the dealer was vital to the success of a lace business. The lace patterns used in the seventeenth century were also rarely original but copied from the Continent. As a result, as Campbell much later put it bluntly in his 1747 career manual *The London Tradesman*, in bone lace making 'we are bunglers in this work compared to France'.[177] Precisely because both France and Flanders made higher-quality lace, government protection was introduced in 1662 and stimulated the trade in the second half of the seventeenth century.

As we have seen, however, the local population were also consumers and there is plenty of evidence of local demand for high-quality lace from the elite. The Courtenay-Pole family bought lace for presents, internal decoration and also as a store of value for the future.[178] The Easter Account for 1669 records 'pd for 13 dozn of lace for Liberii [children] at 3s per dozen £1-19-0'. 'Jane's Accompte' for one of the children in 1668 records the purchase of 13 yards of pillow lace and gold and silver lace for Shute. In January 1668/9 the family purchased 'Erloom' [heirloom] Laces & Silk'. As we have seen in Chapter 2, the elaborate tomb in Colyton church (see Plate 1), constructed in 1658 for Courtenay-Pole with figures of himself and his wife adorned in local lace, became a symbol for Puritan alienation and confirms that members of the family were major local customers for the high-class branches of the local lace industry.[179] There is an ambiguous relationship between religious and political allegiance and the market for lace. The nineteenth-century lace historian Mrs Bury Palliser saw the 'Puritan' period of c.1630–60 as holding back English lace development as nonconformists condemned lace as a frippery and tainted with royalism.[180] But as we have seen, local evidence does not really support Palliser's case, for this was a period of unprecedented expansion in the lace trade. The Winthrop papers contain writings probably by the moderate Puritan and Dorchester Company initiator John White from c.1630, where he says orders for cutwork, lace, etc. were being sent over to New England, indicating a love of luxuries and pride among the newly settled and supposedly devout populace.[181] Local middling-status people also bought lace. In 1639 the wife of a Musbury yeoman reported the theft of 'small clothes' including a 'quoyfe [coif], two faire handkerchiefs, one ruffe band, and a table napkin'. She suspected that these lace items had been stolen by her servant who was the wife of a Musbury husbandman. The servant's story was muddled. On the one hand she said she found the coif in the hedge and that the lace was being aired. But she also claimed that her mistress had asked her to keep some of these clothes as she had separated, 'to lay it upp for her she then liveing from her husband'.[182] This case is a clear indication, as reflected in many other similar court cases, that textiles were a female store of value under English property laws which subsumed a wife's legal standing into that of her husband. For wealthy women, lace could be worn, or it could be stored to gain value. The papers of the Gay family of Bristol show that in the 1670s portions (or dowries) were given to female members in the form of fine fabrics or garments.[183] A letter from Naomi Gay in 1690 reports her distress in losing her suit of bonelace on a journey with the Exeter carrier. The loss meant she no longer looked fashionable but suggests that the suit was Naomi's savings. The contents of her portmanteau were:

> all out besides the lace which makes me fear tis lost that way and the more because here is the peice for the caule [a net worn on the head] behind with it. And methinks they should not have sent that from the sute. If tis lost I shall be quite broke . . . I want that and the rest of my things so mightily and had rather have paid carriage for the box than not to have had it send attall. I am ashamed of the trim I have gon in ever since I came to be seen by all sorts as I have been.[184]

The extensive archive of the Presbyterian Pinney family gives us a fascinating insight into the operations of dealers in Honiton lace. Like some other ejected ministers in the area, John Pinney and his wife Jane established a lace-dealing business after he was ejected from the living of Broadwindsor in Dorset in 1662.[185] Thereafter he set himself up as a gentleman farmer in Bettiscombe, a few miles nearer to the Devon lace-making area, and gradually passed the lace-trading business over to his daughters. Pinney's daughters were middlewomen—apparently both organising workers in the east Devon region, and marketing lace and buying imported thread in London or exchanging it for lace. The 1662 Act prohibiting importation of bonelace makes clear that most lace-making thread was imported[186] and in 1679 John Pinney wrote: 'We have sent a pcell of 4 peices of lace to Mr Hill to Exchange for thred, wch if he refuse to doe, Its ordered hm to delivr it to you what of it he liketh not'.[187] In 1679 when extensive correspondence starts, two of the Pinney sisters, Sarah and Rachel, aged 29 and 27 respectively, were running the lace business in the recently rebuilt Royal Exchange. Hester Pinney, the youngest daughter, who was to take forward the business, left home in the summer of 1682 just before her father moved to Dublin to take on a new congregation.[188] Some flavour of the business can be gleaned from early correspondence as John wrote to Hester apparently suggesting that she organised specialist work in Devon and 'There was sent to you a parcel of lace by Morris as I understand last week. The remnant you sent downe shall speadily be cut & sent & a ruffel lace of 2 nailes broad.'[189] Hester and Rachel lived in a tavern, next to the shop, in the 'Seaven Stars' below stairs in the Inner Walke of the Exchange. Hester never married nor did she ever establish a permanent residence in London. Over the coming years her father was greatly concerned about her living in taverns. Such places were multi-functional in this era and Hester would not only have been on the spot for customers but also able to store bundles of lace. Hester must have had a professional relationship with people whom she later lodged with, such as attorneys and apothecaries. She based much of her trade on personal contacts. A Chancery case in 1693 regarding the debts of an MP, the late Henry Wallop, shows Hester's retailing operations in action. They had dealings for ten years 'in Linnen po[ints], bow laces etc.' which she bought by order. She washed and starched lace for him. Over several years he had sent his servants to the Pinneys' lodgings to fetch handkerchiefs or ruffles which he failed to pay for. When in town he had sometimes visited a barber in Covent Garden and had asked the barber's wife to fetch haberdashery items from the Pinneys such as 'some Linnen . . . box of Cravats & Ruffles' which he had on credit.

The Pinney business ran into difficulties in 1685, largely as a result of the prevailing political and religious conditions. At this point, Sarah Pinney seemed to be nominally in charge of lace-trading. John, writing to Hester in 1686, said their sister had made an inopportune marriage and had 'yt lost 600l & upwards in money & goods when she came hither in her trust & now not yet not know what is become of a penny of it'.[190] It was largely John Pinney's wife, Jane, who had to deal with the fallout from this bankrupcy and her industry is always recognised in discussions about the trade. Jane Pinney made a revealing comment about their Devon lace-workers in a letter to Sarah: 'I am trobelled gretly, what you can doe with the workkers thes times, for heare is no trade, and I greatly fare that it is as bad theare . . . I should advise you to be red of sum of the workkers, not to trune them of, but to bat thim away'.[191] Evidently then, the Pinneys employed regular lace-makers. Historians believe that lace-makers worked on a self-employed basis, though often exclusively for one manufacturer with the manufacturers supplying designs and thread.[192]

In the same summer of 1685 the youngest of the two surviving Pinney sons, Azariah, rallied to the support of Monmouth as he sailed into Lyme Regis. He was captured and sentenced to hang and it is at this point that Hester's trading acumen becomes evident, for she very quickly produced £65 as a bribe for one of the chief agents arranging to transport the rebels and he convinced the Lord Chief Justice to commute Azariah's sentence to transportation. Azariah also traded some evidence to be shipped as a free man. Nevis was selected as his destination. Azariah left with a fever and was shipwrecked along the way. His name had been confused with another Pinney who was executed and for a few weeks his father had given him up for dead. Nevertheless, John Pinney felt the transportation was a missed opportunity and that he should have gone to the colonies furnished as a factor. From the Pinney accounts it appears that Azariah took with him a parcel of lace sent by his sister worth £5 2s and another sent by his mother worth £1 13s.[193] He had no sooner arrived than the family started to ship bonelace to him. They sent over £150 worth and Azariah quickly established a market across the West Indies, returning cargoes of sugar from his plantation. The family shipped over £263 worth of lace to Jamaica alone in 1688, representing a large proportion of the lace transported from England to the West Indies at this point.[194] The colonial lace business was risky but it could make large profits very quickly.

It was also not the family's first experience of overseas trade. The Pinneys sold both narrow and broad lace and many variant lengths and qualities.[195] A 1686 account also records the valuation of 'old fashion Lace', suggesting second-hand lace or discounted lace which was no longer fashionable in London but might be passed off at a profit in the colonies.[196] A box shipped in 1686 contained 144 yards of bonelace showing the extent of production in east Devon.[197] High-value lace was sent to Jamaica on a sale or return basis. The value of high-quality separate pieces is evident here. A parcel containing twenty-nine separate pieces of bonelace was packed into one box with the very high value of £263 7s 5¼d. But one return shipment of sugar and indigo in 1691 was captured by the French and the Pinneys lost every penny. Profits of over 100 per cent were possible if a cargo had a safe passage and found its market, but the losses could be severe. Nevertheless, a comparison between the amounts laid out to the workers and the profits accrued suggests that the manufacturing costs were very slight indeed. While some production was highest quality, much of the bonelace was produced by children or workers whose conditions we might describe as 'sweated'.[198] Nevertheless, whether or not to engage in the lace trade remained a speculation. In 1685 John Pinney wrote to Sarah that his son Nathaniel 'wrote to me of 50£ which he had to spare, but to buy it out in lace is dangrous at this tyme'.[199] Later in this difficult year John wrote that over half of their stocks of lace were not sold.[200] The family also sold lace to haberdashers in Bristol and Bath who bought parcels of lace worth from £4 to £17.[201]

During the 1690s the profitable lace sales in both the domestic and overseas markets moved both Hester and her brother Nathaniel away from commodity trading towards money-lending. Hester Pinney's subsequent success as a businesswoman is evident from her bank books and financial accounts. She bought bonds in merchant trading companies, she tenaciously chased up debts and mortgages, she had success in the South Sea Bubble and she made a personal alliance which resulted in a fortuitous inheritance. By the 1730s she had amassed fortunes but sought to invest them in a traditional way, by purchasing a farm in her native area. She died a wealthy woman. All the Pinney women were actively involved in the trade regardless of their marital status and relative lack of education. The Pinneys were traders to the marrow and energetically exploited all the opportunities which came their way. John Pinney was a well-known preacher and the family's commercial imperative was inextricably connected to their Presbyterian ethos. Indeed, their trade links and especially money-lending networks involved fellow Presbyterians. Religion formed not only lateral but also vertical societal links. The Pinneys exploited the patronage of elite Presbyterians to gain influence in debt repayments but also to sell lace to aristocrats. As we have seen, the family travelled extensively. This case example alone belies a picture of deindustrialisation due to poor roads in east Devon. The dogged, calculative and ruthless attitude to business of this family, and their sheer capacity for hard work, contradicts the notion that the lace districts suffered from their geographical isolation.

Exactly how the Pinneys managed their business at the local level is not clear from the records. They did a good deal of trade with Mr Bird, the major Colyton lace dealer, and we gain glimpses which suggest that subcontracting was common. (William Bird of Colyton appears in state papers as a prime mover in the anti-lace-smuggling faction after an act was passed against lace smuggling in 1662).[202] After Monmouth's rebellion, troops plundered Colyton and stole £325 17s 6d worth of lace from Bird.[203] The value of his losses is another suggestion that this was a fairly important industry. It was possibly his father who struck the trade tokens dated 1657 and bearing a feathered tribe as a pun on 'Bird'.[204] Most of these tokens were issued by large employers of manual labour and they are common in the textile trades. This suggests that men like Bird were employers of many workers and operated some sort of a truck system. In many senses, such tokens were the coinage of the poor and in some places local officials manufactured them for this purpose.

A complex system of subcontracting and local barter and exchange is revealed in a court case from Ottery St Mary in 1686.[205] Dorothy Baron ran her father's mercers shop and had lost several parcels of lace-making thread of number 12 and 13. She suspected the wife of a cordwainer who was supposed to have sold the same sort of thread to several persons of the town. As the case subsequently unravelled, it became evident how many shops in the town were involved in lace-making and supported a system of subcontracting. The suspect, Elizabeth Martin, had taken twenty skeins of lace-making thread number 12 to another shop to exchange them, telling her servant that she had bought them from a mercer's wife. Evidently some women were involved in the thread business separately from their husbands. For example, Johan, the wife of John Ashford, a cooper, testified that she had not sold any lace-making thread or employed Martin to sell any during the last month although she normally did so. Mary Sanders, a lace-maker, said she had bought five skeins of thread from Martin for 5d. which Martin said she had bought at the shop of a widow called Mrs Mary Hare. This case also reveals local networks of credit and barter. In one supposed transaction, thread was exchanged for goods. Martin's own defence was that the thread was given to her in exchange for running errands for the Barons and all the other shopkeepers. It seems likely that merchants and local shopkeepers advanced small loans to lace manufacturers, perhaps as a means of keeping their loyalty.[206]

A result of the demand generated for lace was the proliferation of mercers and tailors in east Devon.[207] Even small parishes sustained haberdashery businesses. For example, the Uffculme probate material includes an inventory for Samuel James who died in 1682. He was a prosperous haberdasher with an estate worth over £80. His stocks included silks, buttons and assorted finery.[208] Mrs Deborah Tucker, an Exeter widow who died in 1694, stocked an enormous range of textiles, lace and haberdashery in her shop, along with various weights and colours of thread for lace-making. She also sold ready-made laces.[209] In the country districts, lace was also on sale from chapwomen and the consumption of fine fabrics permeated the outer extremeties of the Devon economy.[210] For example, in 1662 Joan Taylor, a married woman from the fairly remote parish of Rackenford, went to Tiverton market, leaving in her chamber 'red, blue and green silke, galume [galloon] lace and women's dressings'. When she returned later in the day it had gone. The people who had been to the house 'professed to sell som bone lace to the people of Sandford towne as they came homewards'. This case is a little mystifying for we cannot be sure whether Taylor was herself a trader in lace and fine fabrics and lost her merchandise, or whether she lost her personal possessions. Recent research, showing the extent of the second-hand clothing trade, suggests that this may have been an arbitrary distinction: clothing was both a personal possession and an item to be sold.[211] A huge volume of local court business concerned clothing theft and reveals the confusion of disputed ownership. In 1681 Elizabeth

Carter of Sidmouth reported having three laces made for her of one sort for 'three severall dressings'. Two of the laces were taken from her house at different times. Agnes Potbury of Sidmouth said that she had sold the lace now supposedly owned by Carter to one Agnes Serle a year and a quarter ago, and that around the preceding Easter she had bought two pieces of this same lace from a Scotchman who was at her house and her sister had taken one piece.[212]

As we have seen, there were some men who made lace, particularly in the early seventeenth century. Later lace employed far more female workers and many children, but lace still provided an occupation for displaced, disabled or elderly men. From the mid-1660s there was a huge number of both maimed soldiers and prisoners of war reported to quarter sessions. The Frenchmen found wandering in Honiton in 1666,[213] and the five Dutch prisoners of war clapped into Honiton workhouse and paid 2d a day each were possibly set to make lace of the lowest and simplest quality.[214] Many of the ministers ejected in 1662 turned to lace-making. Yet lace-making was a skill for which a training was required. It is rare to find evidence of formal apprenticeship of children to lace-makers, especially for the lower branches of the trade. However, four indentures survive for Honiton at the height of the trade in the 1690s. Martha Richards was apprentice to a tailor, William Chard, in 1689 with £5 premium for her to be taught bonelace-making and housewifery until the age of 21.[215] Only Martha's mother is mentioned on the indenture so she was evidently the daughter of either a widow or a single woman, and her apprenticeship was likely to be partly a fostering relationship. In 1690 Ruth Hollet was apprenticed to Robert Darke. No occupation is mentioned but the obligation was for 'Darke or his wife to instruct'.[216] Martha Forde was 'bound to John Forde & after him to his daughter Christian Forde' in 1691. Christian Forde was a spinster and she had a merchant's mark of 'c'. It seems likely that Martha, who was described as the daughter of Walter Fforde, mason, was a relation and it is notable that she bound herself apprentice.[217] In 1697 Hannah Bishop was apprenticed to Mary and Elizabeth Abbott, lace-makers.[218] Hannah appeared to be an orphan: 'M & E Abbott doth covenant & promise to bring up, or cause their sayd Apprentice to be brought up in the arte & Science of a Lacemaker'. There is a danger of reading too much into the terse wording of a legal document but the latter case appears very little different from the training of girls in urban needlework trades in the nineteenth century. Some of these cases make it clear that lace skills were taught by women, and often by the wife of the person to whom the child was apprenticed. For example, quarter sessions heard in 1676 that Mary Rolls had recently been bound apprentice in lace-making to Jeffrey Wollacott of St Thomas Apostle in Exeter, a weaver, and his wife, but his wife had just died and since 'noe position made nor course taken to instruct her in the said Art or trade' she was discharged. Another case which suggests that marriages of lace-makers to those in other textile trades may have been common is the 1701 Ottery settlement certificate of Deborah Freeman, a poor child of the parish of Bickton who was bound apprentice to John Carpenter of Ottery St Mary, a serge-weaver until the age of 21 'to be instructed in Housewifery, Lace Making and Reading'.[219] The inclusion of reading here is interesting and may again suggest the Puritan influence on apprenticeships. Bicton was a 'closed' village dominated by the Rolle family and this may have been a route for a bright girl to move into an urban trade. A later indenture from 1756, between Anna Bartlett, daughter of John Bartlett, husbandman, and Samuel Bartlett of 'Whemple', cordwainer and likely a relation, records that Bartlett would instruct Anna in lace-making or spinning. Whimple was an agricultural parish with many orchards but notably located not far from the main Exeter–Honiton road along which passed most of the traffic of lace.[220]

By the time of the French Wars there are references to girls being trained in lace schools. In Sidbury in 1800, a poor girl referred to as 'French's Daughter' (probably indicating her surname not her nationality) was put to a lace school as an apprentice. Three months later it was decided that she should be paid 2s a week for a half year for instruction in lace-making.[221] In the settlement examination in 1829 of Susan Willman at Colyton, she mentioned that in 1824, at the age of 16, she 'went to Chard and there remained about seven weeks learning lace'.[222] The fact that lace-making could be a skill which was transportable is shown by a settlement case from Ottery St Mary in 1815.[223] Mary Salter, who now received poor relief, was born in Honiton and continued to live with her parents until she was about 16 'when she went to London and lived with her cousins & got her living by mending & joining of Lace & after living in London about four years she returned to her parents at Ottery St Mary', with whom she lived until she married George Salter. Ten years before and after fourteen years of marriage, Salter 'left her with one child which she brought up & bound out an Apprentice by her own Industry'. She now pointed out that since she was married her husband had sold his right and interest in some land in Ottery and received some £120 for it. This, perhaps not an entirely unusual case of a skilled woman's parlous livelihood, also shows the value that Mary Salter placed on her own training. She must have been aware that it was a tenuous route to financial independence.

Mary Salter was in late middle age when she appealed for financial help. Her case also reflects that women could have a short livelihood as a lace-maker and that the prime age for the work was when women were in their twenties. They suffered from failing eyesight because exposure to light spoiled the lace and so they often worked in fireless, damp conditions for fear of making the lace dirty and unsaleable. The awkward posture led to dyspepsia and back and neck pain. Nineteenth-century parliamentary reports associated lace-making with the increased incidence of diseases such as consumption. Perhaps as a result, there is evidence that by the late eighteenth century women saw lace-making as a resource for now and then rather than as a job for life. The agricultural writer Vancouver commented, 'The making of bone lace occupies a large part of the time the females in the lower class of life (whether in town or in the country), can conveniently spare from their other concerns'.[224] When describing pillow lace in the Honiton area to parliamentary commissioners in 1843, Sarah Hart, a native of Otterton and mother of a child in a lace school, thought lace-making 'a great advantage to a girl' as when 'out of work they have always an advantage in lace-making'.[225]

A lace-maker's remuneration depended on her level of skill, her commitment of time to lace-making, and perhaps the extent to which she was able to exert control over some section of the business. Many workers in the ordinary branches would have described this in the same terms as a 23-year-old single woman from Honiton in 1663, Agnes Winston: 'That she lives by her p[ro]fession in makeing of lace. And that she is worth but little.'[226] However, there is evidence that lace-making could be a very remunerative trade. Spenceley thought that lace-workers could earn 7s a week.[227] This is a lot more than the wages fixed by Devonshire quarter sessions in 1679 for wool-spinners—'all spinsteres shall take by the week in private houses not above 12 pence with meate and drinke and not above 2s 6d. without meate and drinke'—and even this was double the rates fixed by the justices in 1684 of 6d with meat and drink, or 16d without.[228] Horn has shown that women and children's employment in pillow lace-making and straw-plaiting could be very remunerative in the nineteenth century in comparison with other areas of female employment.[229] However, the lack of evidence has led to a possible over-reliance on the 1699 House of Commons Journal which reported on the lace-makers' petition to Parliament of 1698. Here it was stated that a 'good lace-maker' could earn up to 7s a week and a child of 6 making 'two penny lace' for sale in London could earn 20d a week. This was a prosperous time for the trade and may therefore exaggerate the normal remuneration. The estimate is derived from the report of a Buckinghamshire lace-buyer and it is not clear whether he had included the payments lace-makers had to make to purchase thread. Moreover, lace was evidently most profitable during the London 'season' and lace-workers would have experienced lulls in trade in between. The Pinneys closed their lace shop in the Exchange at times of year when trade was not brisk. In ecclesiastical court records for late seventeenth-century London Earle found 5s a week to be the average.[230] By comparison 3s a week was the average for a week's work by a woman in agriculture in Devon.[231] Yallop in his book on Honiton lace thought high earnings were general in lace-making and argues that 8s a week, commensurate with a skilled craftsman, was common, but an average might have been 5s.[232] Payment to skilled lace women at the same level as those paid to men were reported in the Flanders lace districts.[233] But we can be sure that high-class work was vastly exceeded by work in the poorer branches which gave employment to innumerable children.

By the 1690s the lace trade was extremely profitable indeed. In 1698, when the Devon lace-dealers joined those from the Midlands in petitioning Parliament against competition from foreign lace, there were four thousand lace-workers in the Colyton district. In Colyton there were 353 lace-makers. So, an estimated 21 per cent of the population were directly involved in the trade.[234] If the Parliamentary petition figure is correct, and there is no way of verifying it, lace-making was a large industry in seventeenth-century Colyton. By comparison, there were only 185 lace-workers recorded in the 1851 census after lace had enjoyed a fashion revival in the 1840s.[235] Further analysis of these figures by Yallop reveals the extent to which lace-making was an urban occupation, as 63 per cent of lace-makers in 1698 lived in towns.[236] He also finds that lace manufacture was an occupation of the valleys rather than upland settlements. When considered using the Compton Census, the Otter valley has the highest proportion of lace-makers at 31 per cent of the population involved in the trade.[237]

At the turn of the seventeenth century Celia Fiennes commented on the skill of the work in the Honiton area: 'They make the fine Bonelace in imitation of the Antwerp and Flanders lace and indeed I think its as fine, it only will not wash so fine which must be the fault in the thread'.[238] But from the early eighteenth century, the tide started to turn away from Devon lace. The Pinneys seemed to be all but out of the trade by the 1700s as the fashion turned away from Honiton lace to Bedfordshire and Buckinghamshire light laces.[239] An Act of Parliament in 1707 also removed protection. Yallop's analysis of the importation of sister's thread—the main type of thread used in lace-making—shows it fell off after 1730.[240] The history of eighteenth-century and nineteenth-century lace was then one of steady decline with localised episodes of good trade. The Dean Milles survey still observed that for Honiton 'The lace is chiefly disposed of in London, Bath and other noted places', that Sidbury had a trade of cordwainers and bonelace in which 'The Lace-makers are employed by persons of Honiton who sell their Laces at London & Bath chiefly', and that in Sidmouth 'The women are mostly employed in making Lace'. A great fire in Honiton in 1756 caused great distress among lace-workers.[241] While Levey finds that the third quarter of the eighteenth century saw English lace at its most prosperous, it seems likely that a decreasing share came from Devon. In 1769 Mary Williams, aged 26, was apprehended for 'wandering up and down and laying in the open air' at points between Ottery and Shoreditch along a route through Southampton, Winterslow and Shaftesbury. Seventeen years previously, at the age of eight or nine, she had been bound apprentice to Mary Maynard, widow of Ottery, 'to learn housewifery and to make Lace and Spin'. She probably served out her time for she was with her mistress for twelve years. But there seemed to be nothing to do at the end of this time and she appeared to have no parents to resort to as she was now travelling with her younger sister, aged 18, who had been previously bound apprentice in Ottery.[242]

When visiting Honiton in 1760, Mrs Lybbe Powys went to see lace being made and asserted with some stridency that this 'gave us great pleasure, and much more to see it was our own country women that could arrive at such perfection in this work, as I hope will prevent our ladies from forming the least wish to have the right Flanders: for really, on comparing the two pieces ours had the first preference; and if so how very cruel not to encourage the industrious poor of our own land'.[243] This passage suggests some of the conditions now long-standing in the trade—the competition from the Continent and the fact that lace-making was now seen as job creation. An Exeter newspaper announced in 1766 the opening of 'A new manufactory for lace, in the fashion of Flanders'.[244] Serious decline set in during the American War of Independence (1775–83), which destroyed the colonial markets just at the same time as European fashions were adopting muslin and gauze in place of lace. This was offset locally only by the way in which some of the coastal Devon towns were beginning to fashion themselves as resorts with outlets for selling lace to tourists.[245] The Reverend Swete in the 1790s passed particular comment on Sidmouth as 'the gayest place of resort on the Devon coast and every elegancy, every luxury, every amusement is here to be met with—iced creams, milliners shops, cards, billiards, plays, circulation libraries, attract notice in every part, and as I saw a smart gentleman take a novel from his pocket in the public shed, I presume such to be the fashion of the place'.[246]

The potentially fatal blow to the trade was Heathcoat's invention which mechanised the lace-making technique, especially when his factory in Tiverton was established in 1811. A relief plan was launched in 1816 and the Exeter newspaper announced that 'Honiton, in this county, has long been celebrated for its Manufacture of a particular description of Brussells Thread Lace, which has given employ to a great number of females, who are now in consequence of the decreased demand for that article, out of employ'.[247] A hundred lace-makers were thought to be unemployed and the plan was to produce the lace at wholesale prices for subscribers. In 1817 a list of subscribers was published and it was announced that the scheme was extended to other parishes around

Honiton.[248] It is clear that lace-making was generally in decline in the south-east Devon area in the early nineteenth century. The Lysons commented in 1822, 'about 40 or 50 years since the number of females employed in Honiton and in the neighbouring villages was 2,400, but it had gradually gone into decay . . . and the number at present employed does not exceed 300'.[249] There were many settlement examinations in the 1820s in Colyton of young single women who had been domestic workers and were now unemployed. By the late 1820s lace was factory-made in Chard with manufacturers moving in from Nottingham.[250] Nevertheless a rather idiosyncratic census for Sidbury taken in 1829 still found 129 lace-makers and suggests they were mainly spinsters and widows but there were also eighteen 'man batchelors'.[251]

The history of lace-making in Colyton does not fit the interpretation postulated by Levine. Lace-making seems to have started in Colyton at the very beginning of the seventeenth century, but had expanded into a viable domestic industry, employing a sizeable proportion of Colyton's population under the impetus of Puritan projects in the 1630s and then again in the 1660s. This was the time when women's marriage ages were rising in Colyton. Lace-making seems to have diminished in Colyton during the period 1740–1840, which was a period of falling marriage ages for women in the parish. This chronology suggests precisely the opposite of Levine's theory then, as lace-making is associated with late marriage for women.

It seems inappropriate to close the discussion of the Honiton lace trade without a passing mention of its branch in India. In the nineteenth century, Honiton lace became the focus of another evangelising project with missionary zeal. In 1837 George Beer, a shoemaker, and William Bowder, an indentured labourer, both from Devon and attached to the Strict Baptist Congregation, went to Narsapur as missionaries. Lace-making was the means by which the missionaries tried to help the poor to earn their livelihood. In the first few years they distributed thread and patterns and then dispatched the finished goods to contacts in England and, as the trade developed, to the global market.[252] Here again we see lace becoming the economic currency of disadvantaged women, a religious expression of the work ethic, and a viable project of an insistent consumer-led capitalism.

Women as Parish Traders

The merchant's mark of Jane Vye, dated 1655, can still be seen in Colyton church (see Plate 3). Both male and female traders, even if illiterate, tended to have a merchant's mark, often based on their initial, which they used to sign bills and papers. We also know that at least six female businesswomen, based in Exeter during the seventeenth century,

Plate 3. The merchant's mark and tomb of Jane Vye (1655) in Colyton church.
(D. Sharpe)

had coins struck bearing their names and to be used as trade tokens which were paid to workers.[253] The historian of these tokens further notes that in the case of male issuers, the coins often bear three initials and the second letter is that of the issuer's wife, suggesting her essential role in the business. Such tokens seem to have been in common use until 1672 when Charles II coined a large quantity of copper halfpences and farthings and the existence of small change took away the need for tokens. Unlike many larger towns such as Oxford, the east Devon towns seem to have passed no regulations against women's trade.[254] Indeed, such restrictions would have paralysed the entire economic dynamism of the region.

In 1689 Mary Seaward of Axminster, a single woman, was riding from Lyme Regis on market day, when on the road near Uplyme two men took her horse by the head, forced her down and pushed her into Cornelius Dobson's drinking establishment, the Sign of the Black Dogg, and detained her there for the afternoon and half of the evening, threatening her in an attempt to extort money.[255] While at first sight this looks like a case of aggravated robbery, the proceedings suggest it was a good deal more complicated and involved perhaps blackmail or money-lending. One of the men, Thomas Pole of Axminster, said he had been to Lyme to get an attorney's writ against Seaward for slander. The other man said he was acting 'as a Baylife imploy'd in . . . ye affaire . . . on account of Thos Pole'. We know nothing more about this case but along with many similar incidents it suggests that women were deeply involved in trade in this area, held some economic power, travelled alone on business, and perhaps were not unusual figures in local drinking houses, even if Mary entered under coercion. Did women have an unusual degree of self-confidence in this area in the early modern period? E.P. Thompson suggests that this may have been the case from a glimpse at events such as the Coronation Day celebrations for Queen Anne in Honiton on 23 April 1702. Perhaps because her regal wedding attire stimulated the lace trade, three hundred women and girls marched two by two with three women drummers and a guard of twenty-five young men on horseback up and down the town from 10 a.m. to 8 p.m., hurrahing and weaving long white rods with tassels of white and blue ribbon (the Queen's colours with the addition of bonelace).[256] This procession took place when the local lace trade was still flourishing, but was the source of women's self-confidence entirely economic?

Women were actively engaged in business in the Colyton area, and may have moved into the area because of the work opportunities it presented. This is not to ignore the fact that the extent of pauperism in the parish and the degree of house-sharing suggests that many of the women who moved into lace-making parishes were poor and remained poor. It is to argue that accelerated industrialisation in the second half of the seventeenth century not only exploited some women but expanded the wealth opportunities for others. As the local records make clear, were we able to ride the roads of seventeenth-century east Devon we would have met many women going about their business as fellow travellers. Had we imbibed in the roadside drinking houses, we would not have found them to be the sole preserve of men. Local records show that Colyton women drank and smoked in public. If we happened on one of the towns on a market day, we could not have escaped the stir of female commerce. If we put up at an inn, we would not have been surprised to find lone females staying there. Hoskins writes of the number of wives and daughters who acted as commercial travellers in the heyday of the Devon serge industry at end of the seventeenth century.[257] Perhaps this assertiveness can be linked to the fact that women may have formed a majority in the nonconformist congregations of the area and thus forged independence by taking a stand against authority, and became used to travel for reasons of worship?

A 1646 quarter sessions examination concerned Anne Adams, servant of Kathryn Gould of Great Torrington, 'pettie chapman'.[258] Gould accused Adams of stealing 40s from a bag which she had to carry. This pair went about the countryside selling small goods. While Gould went into a widow's house she left Adams with the money bag. Adams, suffering from the cold, went into the house of Christopher Slowman in Zeale to warm herself by the fire, and then to lodge there for the night. Slowman and his wife, knowing she had money in her bag, plied her with drink for a good part of the night until she began to feel sick. Then Slowman asked her for some money and she lent him 36s. She then went to bed with the money and small wares 'fast knit' but in the morning her money and goods had gone. Slowman said she had given him the money to keep until she got home to Torrington and she had given him 4s to secure this safekeeping. He asked for 6s more for commodities which she bought from him. His wife said Adams had come 'in the nature and habite of a pedler woman'. In 1647 John Lowe of Axminster, an innkeeper, described the wife of a tailor of Exeter wishing to sell him wares and then later desiring lodgings in his inn.[259] In 1641 Elizabeth West, wife of Robert West of Shute, said she was given a peck of meale, another of malte, a bagge and a cheese, by Thomas Mitchell of Rockesbeare, to take to his wife who lived at Seaton. She said that she 'laid in the towne of Otterie the last night but at which house she knoweth not'.[260] In 1669 in Exeter, 'Angell Sparke of the parish of Trinity, woolcomber, and one of the constables of the city of Exeter, informeth on Friday last, a woman of the country had some wool of him for to spin, which wool she put upon her horse in a bag, and having other business in the city, she tied her horse in the street, with the wool upon him, but she coming afterwards to her horse she found the wool wanting'.[261] Lone women's travel for business is far more unusual today than it was in seventeenth-century east Devon. On trips from London, Hester Pinney travelled the distance by side-saddle like Celia Fiennes. As John Pinney wrote to Hester in 1691 regarding a trip from London: 'But if you please to come down this Season in the Coach or have an horse and side sadle of Will Clarke, give us notice of it and an horse shall be ordered for you'.[262]

In a detailed case in 1679 several strident Colyton women came into conflict with the authorities over illegal textile imports.[263] John Carter of Beer, landwatch at the 'Golden Lyon' in Colyton with several other customs officers, secured six baskets of canvas or French linen and loaded them onto horseback to take to the customs warehouse in Lyme. The operation did not run smoothly for they were caught by flooding near the bridge over the Axe. They were advised not to pass this point and so were forced to take the cloth they were carrying back to 'The Swan' in Colyford. While attempting to do this they met with a 'tumultous rout' of people. They waited there for one and a half to two hours hoping the water would abate, but when defeated a second time by the height of the waters they were forced to carry the cloth back to 'The Swan' and lock it in a room. Then the rioters invaded the drinking establishment. Amongst them were Ann Blackaller and Ann Wallersee, who said they were also there to drink a flagon of beer. Charles Sydenham of Lyme deposed that the 'tumult encompassed the house threatening to beat down the house about their ears'. The customs officers stayed at the inn for another two days, then again loaded the packets of cloth for another attempt to reach the warehouse. But as soon as they turned into the street they again found a 'great tumult' of people including men, women and children who attempted to seize the goods. Sydenham was struck by a stone and the people continued to follow them and throw stones as far as Colyford Meadow. The portreeve of Colyford was called to assist the officials. In the same case John Sweetland of Lyme, who had received a severe blow to the leg, deposed that the crowd was about four hundred strong. The officials only lost the crowd when they finally managed to cross the river. Even then a woman in the crowd claimed they had sent forty men ahead, presumably to ambush the officials. Ann Blackaller's husband, William, had refused to co-operate with the officials. He entered the public house to ask who was abusing his wife. When they showed him the King's writ, 'he said he did not care a turd for them nor the kings writ neither'. Sydenham added the names of two other women as ringleaders and the entire account suggests that women seemed to be the prominent actors in the dispute. The wider context of this incident is apparently the religious and political repression in the parish at this time. Anti-royalist sentiments took precedence over the legislation designed to protect industries such as the English lace trade. The overwhelming motivation of the rioters was perhaps for autonomy and non-interference: another instance of the perception of Colyton as a little kingdom. Whatever the motivation, the upheaval brought out a large proportion of Colyton's population, and men like Blackaller, who was a close associate of the rebel leader Roger Satchell, saw themselves as outside of the law. Gregory Alford, the conservative mayor of Lyme, then held the patronage of that town's customs.[264] His actions were empowered by the Commission of Enquiry of 1678 into customs frauds at a time when an interest in smuggling was seen as analogous to adherence to conventicles by those who sought to enforce authority and root out Dissent in the mercantile community.[265] French linen was the main textile seized in these raids and the connection with ultra-Protestant lace-making towns may be essential to understanding this case. The significance of the French linen is unclear, but it may have been used as a backing cloth to mount lace sprigs. Apparently, soon after the riot and after her husband died, Ann Blackaller moved away from Colyton. A scrap of paper, apparently a bond written in 1683 and contained within the feoffee records, records a wager: 'Wm Wolsman 20s if his sister the Wido. Blackaller returns home from London in 3 yeers'.[266] Wolsman was probably the Monmouth rebel 'Willsman'. The scrap suggests that the outspoken, independent Ann Blackaller left for London soon after this incident either on business or perhaps due to her religious leanings.

Inns and drinking houses seem to have been an integral part of the business activities of many local women. Not only did many women buy and sell in drinking houses, they served liquor and they drank in them for pleasure. Such women seem to have not been touched by the Reformation of Manners regulation of drinking. In' the ecclesiastical court that investigated Mr Mayowe, the disgraced, false preacher in Membury in 1687 we are given an insight into both sides of this.[267] Rachel Drewe, a single woman aged 29, was presumably ready to sell cider when Mayowe entered her grandfather's roadside house, where she also lived, and asked for a glass of cider. Shortly afterwards Joane Daniel, a young woman of Axminster, entered the cider house and Mayowe asked her why she looked so unwell and whether she had lost her sweetheart. She replied that she had no sweetheart. Mr Mayowe said he could tell her other things like where she was on Michaelmas Night. She said that she did not mind that she was away from home. Mayowe went on to ask her 'if she knew that place of Scripture where Christ came to ye woman of Samaria that was drawing of water'. Mayowe referred to St John's Gospel 4 where 'Jesus saith unto her, Go, call thy husband, and come hither. The woman answered and said I have no husband. Jesus said unto her, Thou hast well said, I have no husband; for thou hast had five husbands; and he whom thou now hast is not they husband: in that saidst thou truly.' Water and thirst made strong imagery in this cider house, and Mayowe presumably implied that Daniel was an outsider, a woman shunned by other women. He certainly upset her, for Joane Daniel turned tail and left.

Two cases from Widworthy in 1648 concern husbandmen whose wives made and sold drink. Henry Bord the younger recalled that four men came to his house, apparently a common alehouse, who spoke to him and said they desired him to help reap. 'And they having dranke a pipe of Tobacco and a cupp of small Beere' departed from his house without paying for it. Bord then fell under suspicion for having stolen wheat.[268] In the same year, Elizabeth Lovett called the constable to a rabble in her house; when the crowd was told to be quiet, they replied 'they would have Beere for their was Beere to sell'.[269] The constable told them not to 'abuse poore folkes in this kinde'. Jennings said that the Lovetts must have beer to sell as Elizabeth 'kept a Comon Alehouse'. One of the soldiers went up to the chamber and drew some beer. He also drew beer out of a barrel in a lower room and was charged with stealing two cups and a bucket as well as the beer. William Lovett said that his wife was about to bake but they threw the beer among the dough and spoiled it. She had not intended to sell the beer, which she said her husband 'intended to keepe for his refreshment when he goeth to worke taske worke'. The women involved in these drinking house disputes hardly fit the reserved image we might have expected women to present in a area infused by Puritan values.

As well as this symbolic assertiveness of women and their apparent role in local religious communities, there is the evidence of women's pro-activity during the Civil War. In the six-week siege of Lyme, women were busy in building trenches with spades, manning them, and loading and firing muskets. These women wore men's hats with red cloaks which caused the Royalists to think the town had very strong defences armed with ample manpower.[270] One woman, a weaver or thread-spinner, had one of her hands shot off during the siege. According to the vicar's account, being asked what course she would take now she had lost one of her hands, she said: 'I had a hand to loose for Jesus Christ, for whose cause I am as willing and ready to loose not merely my other hand but my life also. A sweet and most saint-like speech indeed.' He also mentioned one woman firing off sixteen muskets. The Reverend James Strong composed a poem in 1645 called 'Joaneridos', which refers to the Joan of Arc epic. The subtitle is 'Feminine Valour eminently discovered in the Western Women at the Siege of Lyme'. The verses are poor quality but contain remarkable passages such as 'To most 'tis known / The weaker vessels are the stronger grown / The vine which on the pole still leans his arms / Must now heave up and save the pole from harms'. The title of the poem also includes references to women fighting, carrying stones, carrying powder and 'overcharging of Peeces [guns] to ease the soldiers'.[271]

Historians have recently been busy demolishing the idea that women ever had a 'golden age' wherein their status and experience of work resembled that of men. Many of these studies take their starting point from the researches of Alice Clark.[272] The widest evidence is for the independence of widows. The number of widows was swelled in east Devon by the death of soldiers in the Civil Wars and other warfare of the mid-century. The evidence from quarter sessions attests to the fact that many widows were forced onto poor relief or to take any work available after these mortalities. A 1666 petition from the inhabitants of Beer concerns William Croker, who had been impressed into the King's service. He had served in a ship ironically named the *Happy Returne*, until he was killed in a fight by the Dutch. His wife was left very poor with four small children and now sought to reclaim the 30s her husband's clothes were sold for.[273] Not only were many men killed but many were maimed and disabled such that they may have been subsequently unable to work. So many men fell into this category that in 1666 a surgeon was employed by quarter sessions to search the maimed soldiers of Colyton and Axminster to inspect their injuries and there was a series of collections of money for their support.[274]

For single women, independence is perhaps a more puzzling issue than for either wives or widows, for they remained under the authority of their father or brother. We can make an immediate connection with work opportunities as women's late marriage ages coincide with the peak period of both lace and wool prosperity in the 1690s and 1700s.[275] In 1689 Nathaniel Pinney advised his ageing parents to leave off the lace trade: 'Not to trouble yourselves at this age to receive in Lace againe, and when I have soe often advisd against the medleing with it, to Improve, and save that is got already . . . here's my Sister Hester workes dayly hard Early and late at her needle for her liveing wch she gets by that, and puting out lynn and laces to wash, and to see other folks in the intrime maintaind in Idlenese wth that shee by birth can chaullendge agreater propriety in'.[276] This reference suggests that apart from the accomplished businesswoman Hester had become, she combined lace-selling with hands-on repair and laundering. Hester Pinney transacted business in taverns in London, much as women were doing in Devon at the same time. For example, in 1691 she met Dorothy Rose in a drinking establishment on the Strand to discuss making table cloths, napkins, caps, shirts, types of callico and embroidery decorations.

Wood-pasture economies have been seen to provide some routes to independence and we can see that there are grounds for this from the evidence on Colyton's economy. David Underdown has suggested that pastoral economies in the south-west provided the basis for a measure of women's independence, arguing that 'it may be that for some women in some places there had been a slight enlargement of their roles in the household economy, leading to a greater sense of independence which men found threatening'.[277] It has been shown that where an arable to pastoral switch had taken place opportunities for marketing dairy products were increasing. Women were also more likely to be involved in cloth-making in wood-pasture areas than in arable areas. Underdown goes on to argue that mainstream values of Puritanism strengthened rather than weakened patriarchial authority but placed a stress on the partnership role in marriage. Relationships were being renegotiated in the first half of the seventeenth century and Underdown suggests that such strained gender relations in early modern England lie at the heart of 'the crisis of order'. The Colyton region does offer evidence of women's role in marketing but no assurance that this applied only to the pastoral sector.

There does appear to be an association between women's apparent independence and the type of parish within which they lived. While parishes are often characterised as 'open' or 'closed' for the eighteenth and nineteenth centuries, such a typology can also be drawn for the seventeenth century in Devon.[278] This distinction is usually used to describe the extent to which a parish was 'open' to in-migration and settlement. 'Open' parishes like Colyton were more populous and had higher poor rates and frequently a labour surplus. They were characteristically controlled by a group of landowners, By contrast, 'closed' parishes, often under the control of a single landowner, had lower poor rates and sometimes a shortage of labour. 'Closed' parishes were those which often excluded industry and this might be seen as an elaboration on the points made by Underdown, whose argument mainly centres on the period before the Civil War.[279] One example of a closed parish is Chudleigh, where in 1675 the yeomen presented a list to quarter sessions of people between the ages of 12 and 40 who are 'duely required to be retained in service . . . and yet doe utterly refuse soe to doe contrary to ye . . . Statute in such case made'.[280] Most of the list were single women. Hoskins describes Chudleigh as a market town but it was also a purely agricultural parish containing the mansion of Ugbrooke with a fine deer park of 600 acres built by Lord Treasurer Clifford of the Cabal in the mid-seventeenth century. This parish was also a Royalist stronghold.[281] By contrast, there seems to have been an association between the extreme Protestantism of parishes like Colyton and women's self-reliance, perhaps reflecting the central emphasis on religious individualism. Protestant religious commitment seems to have complemented the scope and independence that the women's lives already had. In the context of France, Natalie Zemon Davis finds 'Women already independent in the street and market now ventured into the male preserve of theology'.[282]

The contrast between types of work and relative mobility in 'open' and 'closed' type parishes in the eighteenth century can be illustrated by two settlement examinations taken in 1763. Mary Soper was a single woman residing in Ottery St Mary. She said that she had been born in the City of Exeter. When she was about six weeks old her mother took her to Chard in Somerset to her grandmother, with whom she lived until bound pauper apprentice by the officers of the parish to a serge-weaver who did not have a settlement there. She resided with her master for a year and a half before moving with him to the parish of St Thomas the Apostle, Exeter. After five or six months she ran away from him 'and went into the parish of Colyton . . . and lived there about three years under no agreement with any one but weaved by the peice for her living, and from thence she went into the parish of Ottery St Mary . . . and lived there between two and three yeares in the same manner of weaving under no Agreement'.[283] In the same year Joan Jones, a single woman aged about 27, was living in the parish of Talaton. She had lived with her parents; then moved to another parish and hired herself by the week to William Drake for about half a year; the returned to Tallaton and hired herself to one Richard Gater for a year at the wages of 30s; then returned to her father for two months, after which she went to daily labour in Talaton. She then had a yearly hiring, then weekly, with several jobs for varying lengths of time. 'Then her Master went into Ottery St Mary to live and she . . . went with him & his Family as a servant & lived ther with him for half a year, after which she being with child by her master left his service . . . and returned to her father.'[284] Talaton was also in the east Devon area but was a closed 'estate' type village. This proletarianised and servile pattern of female employment reflects this and provides some contrast with Colyton.

Generally, in analysing this type of evidence we are forced to assess women's actions by what they did rather than what they said, and reported actions may be a poor reflection of whether or not women were independent. If women were unusually independent in this region the evidence collected in this section suggests that this might be due to the particular type of economy and the influence of religious factors. Demographic patterns (to be further explored in Chapter 5) are also pertinent. The emphasis on open and closed parishes suggests the importance of local structures of authority but, for Colyton at least, the evidence from the riot in 1679 suggests that women were not reluctant to involve themselves in protests against central government and the crown.

The Industrious Parish

The only analysis which has been carried out to examine Colyton's economy suggests that it was undergoing deindustrialisation in the seventeenth and eighteenth centuries. Levine portrayed Colyton as a backwater, bypassed by industrial change and deindustrialising in the seventeenth century. While the woollen industry was probably never very important in terms of employing a large number of people, there is no evidence of technological change leading to its economic decline. Finishing was the most important branch of manufacture. This was a highly capitalised business, and perhaps employed more waged labourers than self-employed workers. Lace-making seems to have been a far larger industry in Colyton, but being an employer of females and home-based, it has been largely ignored in the historical record. Lace-making probably employed the majority of women in Colyton from the 1630s to the early eighteenth century, when it was replaced by the small wool-spinning sector as the main domestic industry. However, this does not fit into Levine's chronology, which suggested that lace-making led to a fall in the age of marriage of women. In fact, lace-making seems to have promoted women's independence in that they married later. In comparison with other towns, over time Colyton's economic position was waning. The parish's prosperity was at a height in the late medieval period. This was due in part to the openness of the manors to industrial pursuits and economic diversity, but in part also to overseas adventuring. Leading families such as the Yonges achieved their position in the sixteenth century by merchant trading on the seas. By the end of the seventeenth century both the serge and lace trades were at a peak, probably because most of the workers were women, and only a few were paid adequate remuneration for skilled work. Colyton's local markets were not prospering in comparison with larger local towns. Dealers such as the Pinneys made immense gains from the local trade but possibly put little back into the economies of places like Colyton. Their luxury expenditures were made in London (even glass for their farm came from the capital) and other good quality materials were obtained from larger centres. Nevertheless the sheer number of bills extant in the feoffees' archive reveals a busy, working town in the late seventeenth century. Ultimately, however, business people attempted to invest their profits in land and this will be explored in the next chapter.

In Colyton, de Vries's 'industrious revolution' and staunch Protestantism go together. This connection has been the subject of numerous writings and, in its most cogent form, underpins Tawney's *Religion and the Rise of Capitalism* (1922). The 'culture of discipline' in fact brought about a new economic language. The covenant theology of the predominant Presbyterianism enshrined an ethic of time-consciousness and enterprising zeal which was codified in local statutes.[285] Christopher Hill wrote that Protestantism facilitated the triumph of new values in the sense that 'there was no inherent theological reason for the protestant emphasis on frugality, hard work, accumulation; but that emphasis was a natural consequence of the religion of the heart in a society where capitalist production was developing'.[286] Colyton's middling orders were infused with a commercial imperative. They bought lace, pewter and dairy products. Poor cottagers and immigrant workers drank in wayside cider houses and smoked imported tobacco.

By making a slightly unfair comparison it is even possible to detect a different sense of purpose and urgency about people's movements by the end of the seventeenth century which provides a supplementary demonstration that the parish experienced the 'industrious revolution'. Under surveillance in a court case in 1614, William Burd, an ancestor of the lace-dealers who subsequently appear in the records, was asked to account for the whole of one Tuesday in early January.[287] After Burd rose he went to the clerk's house and remained there for three-quarters of an hour. About ten o'clock Burd moved on to Gregory Sampson's house. While there a relation of his called him to dinner. He then went 'upp to Colyton towne' and met his mother who directed him to 'goe to Gill his house who kept an inn to see whether Searle of Musbury, butcher was there'. He drank with Richard Gill, then returned to his mother. It was now three o'clock. He then went to John Sampson's and bought tobacco, then to Murron's house where he and Richard Gill drank a 'quart of burnt ale' until four o'clock or thereabouts, and then returned to his own house about 'candlelighting'. After supper he went to the house of Richard Cox, met another male friend, and about 8 o'clock he went to another man's house, 'Whitemoor', to borrow a horse. He stayed there an hour and spent 2d on cider and apples and 1d on bread. This was a slow day, and possibly the weather was atrocious, but Burd spent the time on sociable, slow contact with a very large number of men. He may have been striking deals along the road but there is no real indication of this. Yet Burd is a consumer, purchasing tobacco even at this early date. We can contrast this with Nathaniel Pinney's life in the country as described in a letter to his sister in 1696.[288] He berated Hester for writing letters which are full of 'many little Nasty Snevelling Sordid pickthank matters'. He has 'soe much businesse on my hands . . . Rideing, leting, siting, buying, placeing, writing with along etCetera for the whole family' yet he complained of being 'soe little in health for performance'. Nathaniel Pinney was busy, and indeed, at the end of the seventeenth century, the countryside was vibrant with trade. Yet during the eighteenth century, with the failure of industry to expand, an economic malaise seems to have eclipsed this sort of bustle as the emphasis moved to the rural sector.

4

Resourcefulness
Farming a Wood-Pasture Economy

[Colyton stands] at the mouth of a beautiful combe which runs back into the greensand outliers of the Blackdown Hills. The whole parish is singularly beautiful, with rolling green hills and deep combes dotted with ancient farmsteads.

(W.G. Hoskins, *Devon*, 1954: 373)

The sweetest scene of cultivation I ever beheld. This may be called the garden of Devonshire, not only from its own intrinsic superiority, but the beauteous order in which it is disposed—a fine amphitheatre of meadow and arable enclosure gradually ascending towards the south, in the highest cultivation, up to its natural boundary of open hills ranged in all the uniformity of a perfect wall.

(Dr Stukeley, in R. Polwhele, *The History of Devonshire*, Vol. III, 1797: 278)

Colyton parish is situated in hill and vale country. Rich pastures with alluvial soil near rivers make this a natural dairying region, but historically the parish has seen mixed farming. The evidence of inventories, leases and deeds suggests that Colyton's diverse but integrated farms proved adaptable to changing economic conditions. In particular, the balance between pastoral and arable production could be altered according to relative price changes. The greensand uplands had heavy loam soils. These lands were too heavy to be used except for turbary, sheep and intermittent cultivation.[1] But when sheep were at a premium this land was extremely valuable. This chapter will examine the elements of the farm system in early modern Colyton, along with the exploitation of other local resources by parishioners. If the exploitation of natural resources within the parish formed the basis of the livelihood of a large proportion of the inhabitants, how can we link this to the demographic changes that have been identified? Land was the basis of the social and economic status of Colyton parishioners throughout our period. Although this was an industrial parish, the goal of those who made money in business was to invest in land and as a result the relationship between the rural and urban areas of the parish requires investigation. We also need to consider whether inequitable land distribution underlies some of the Dissenting protest of the second half of the seventeenth century. Since demographic explanations link population with resources, it is necessary to examine fully the local economy.

Agrarian historians have identified a great diversity of farming types and regions within England.[2] Colyton's geography means that it can easily be characterised within one of these regional types: the parish has a wood-pasture economy. Yet a close analysis of the early modern parish suggests that it does not readily fit all the stereotypes. We have seen that Colyton's parishioners engaged in rural industry and crafts and that they demonstrated an independent spirit in matters of religious non-conformity. But it would be inaccurate to place too much stress on their economic independence. Colyton's early modern farmers were not peasants but commercial operators on a greater or lesser scale. Only a cursory glance at the extant records for the parish reveals a hierarchy of farms and a broad band of capitalist yeoman farmers who employed servants in husbandry, apprentices and day workers. Further investigation also reveals the commercial importance of the manorial structure of the parish. Only detailed local history can reveal the nuances of economic difference between parishes. Harold Fox's detailed studies of medieval manors within the east Devon area, on which I draw in this chapter, reveal subtle distinctions between different parishes which could all be described under the broad title as possessing 'wood-pasture' economies.

Landholding Structures

Underlying the agrarian structure of Colyton were manors. Colyton parish contained four separate manors at the end of the medieval period. These small manors, usually with absentee lords who owned land in several parishes, have often been ignored in parish studies. But manorial influence held some sway throughout this period and needs to be considered in the context of both land improvement and encouragement to local industry. The evidence that can be collected about the individual manors suggests that they helped rather than hindered agricultural improvement and also encouraged industrial development. For example, the eighteenth-century tenants of the tithing of Colyton and their heirs had common of pasture for all cattle, the right to estovers and turbary in the waste and common soils of the manor, the freedom to dig in wasteland for earth and sand to build and repair properties or mills and to use the common 'to make as many new Racks for their Mills as shall be sufficient for their use or trade' but crucially these uses were 'each according to the rate and quantity of their severall Lands and Tenemts (Mills excepted)'. All tenants had the right to fowl and fish in waters running through their own lands, to enlarge their houses and buildings by 12 or 13 feet or less on any side upon any waste and had 'the Antient allowance for Collection of the Lords Rents as hath been accustomed to repair all bridges and chimneys'.[3]

This structure had been influenced by the execution in 1538 of Henry Courtenay, the most important landowner in the parish. As we have seen, the parishioners bought the manor for the sum of a £1,000 and the Chamber of Feoffees was established in 1546 to administer the land. Courtenay's properties were leased to the parishioners by a series of eighty-eight grants including forestry rights.[4] These were recorded on the feoffees' charter.[5] The average size of grant was only 25 acres but there was a great deal of difference in the parcels of land leased. They varied from a rood and a cottage, to that leased by the Strowbridge family. 'John Strobrigge of Howberhayne' received 227 acres whereas 'John Strobrigge of Streathayne' received 132 acres. The feoffees' charter delineated the social and economic structure of Colyton for the few hundred years to come. At the highest social level were a small group of families who had access to most land. The families of Pole, Sampson, Yonge, Drake and Strowbridge predominated in the sixteenth and early seventeenth centuries. It is possible that, given the strength of nonconformity in the parish in the seventeenth century and despite the measures designed to prevent this, the Feoffees may have engaged in leasing land in a partisan way which led to a further perception of land shortage.

These leases combined with a much longer standing freehold element within the parish, termed the 'backwoods gentry' by W.G. Hoskins. Their lands were 'rooted in some ancient free tenement for centuries —many so old that they took names from dwelling places but were not Lords of any manor'.[6] The backwoods gentry not only maintained their ancient home farms but they also possessed farms in other parishes which they had leased or acquired through family marriages. The domain of these 'backwoods gentry' remains fairly clear on the first edition of the Ordnance Survey map published in 1887. In the sixteenth century large farmhouses were built on the former medieval enclosures in Colyton creating farms such as Hooperhayne and Blamphayne. As Hoskins puts it: 'These and others were the homes of small squires and are very characteristic of their period and status'.[7] The basis of the wealth of these farmers was sheep farming and many yeomen rose to affluence in the second half of the sixteenth century with the rapid inflation of wool prices. One of these, the historian W.G. Hoskins's ancestor, George Hoskyns, was a sheep farmer on a large scale on the chalk downland behind Axmouth and Musbury, in an area just to the east of Colyton. By the time of his death in 1625, Hoskyns held land in three or four parishes and owned five hundred sheep, forty-eight cattle and twelve horses. His inventory records little expenditure on interior decoration or fine furniture but men like Hoskyns did spend money on improving their dwellings as a result of their profits from sheep. The sizeable, substantial farmhouses still to be seen in the parish today are the result of this era of wool-based prosperity.[8] The final stage of the development of these new farms was hedging. Like other forms of land improvement, some hedging was done by the manorial lords and some by tenants. At one date in medieval Colyton 77s was spent by the manor on 'marling and hedging'.[9] As Hooker points out, writing about 1600, newly planted hedges yielded a good store of fuel.[10] And hedges, like farmhouses, were made to be both large and substantial in south-east Devon.

The landholding families sought to extend their lands throughout the period of high wool prices from the last quarter of the sixteenth century through to the early years of the seventeenth. The Yonges, for example, greatly increased their possessions in Colyton by purchase in the years between 1622 and 1650, buying both houses in the town and farms.[11] The 'waste' on which ordinary people kept their animals was gradually eroded. Between 1579 and 1599 a dispute raged over Lovehayne Common which was originally 200 acres of common land on which beasts could be raised.[12] Incursions onto the common by landowners seeking to increase their grazing for sheep were happening all over the region at this time. In 1607 there was almost a riot at Kilmington about the use of the common.[13] The evidence of William Smyth was that the tenants of Whitford (part of Shute parish) had of right by usage 'not only common or pasture for their sheep or cattle' but also 'several tenements to cutt and take furzes for fuel'. Several attempts were made to reassess the size of the common in Colyton in the 1620s. The Estreat Rolls of 1625–35 make mention of the conflict between sheep graziers and poor people who cut turves upon the 'Downe' or common.[14] Late medieval and sixteenth-century enclosure from the waste mainly involved the addition of small acreages to existing holdings rather than creating entirely new farms. However, at Axminster in the 1500s new farms were still being created out of waste, and at Southleigh manorial tenants 'by common consent among themselves divided and enclosed' the waste. In Colyton some name evidence perhaps indicates that new farms were being created during the first half of the seventeenth century. Property names from this time carry a welter of meanings. Some (Summerleaze, Cownhayne, Waterleaze) suggest the type of land or the nature of an improved pasture, others suggest the land use (Boatfield, Fishing Meade, Twich marsh, Pressing Iron and Shears) and some clearly indicate family names prominent in the early seventeenth century (Birds, Waldrons, Veryards, Tilmans).[15]

Colyton then fits perfectly into the overview provided by Hoskins and is almost a textbook example of the 'rise of the gentry'. During the period of rising population from 1560 to 1640, the increasing wealth of farmers is evident in the rebuilding of farmhouses, many of which still stand today. The squires and gentry were able to extend the farm lands in their possession. One consequence was the shrinkage of land available to the poor.[16] In this way, we might read the Hearth Tax analysis in Chapter 3 as demonstrating a division into the landed, with three to five hearths in their houses, and the landless. Even for those who did hold land, there are indications that the manorial system imposed an archaic structure on landholding. Men in trade sought to purchase land to secure their investments, but land was either not for purchase or only available in scattered plots situated all around the parish. In some cases, this sort of pattern may suggest piecemeal purchases of land at different times using trade profits. A man like Peter Bagwell (the Monmouth rebel who made the dramatic escape from the West Indies) held 71 acres of manorial land but it was scattered all around the parish. Roger Satchell, the leader of the rebels, was wealthy in cash terms but only owned an estate worth £20, suggesting that he may have had difficulties in purchasing property with his trade profits. As a result, the revolt against the great and the good which was such a prominent theme in the language of political and religious dissent in the seventeenth century, had a proven basis in land shortage. The result was likely to have been an obvious division between town-based merchants and rural yeomen.

Capitalist farming by yeoman was enhanced by developments in the leasehold system. The 1570s also saw the emergence of the three-life lease as the main means of holding land.[17] Such leases were held for three lives or ninety-nine years, whichever was the shorter. New lives could be inserted on the payment of a fine. As one student has described it, 'the system provided a means whereby the countryman could buy a lifetime's security for himself and his immediate dependants'.[18] The drawback was that all the lessee's capital could be absorbed by the initial expenditure. Although by the second half of the seventeenth century the evidence which can be collected for rents in Colyton manors does not suggest they were rising, there was a steep rise in entry fines in the period 1570–1670.[19]

As Bettey points out, such tenures varied widely depending on the customary law of individual manors and could vary between neighbouring manors. For example in Ottery St Mary in the 'Old Barton lands', 'this Lande the Wife of the Tennant Dying leased hath her Life By the Custome paying nothing for her Incombe But so much for an Honorable

Yearly Rent and the Eldest Son or Daughter where no son Inherits'. Elsewhere 'The Wife Hath Widowes Estate by Customs'.[20] In Sidbury where the manor was under the auspices of the Dean and Chapter and still held courts through to the late nineteenth century, widows held two-life leases jointly with their sons.[21] Local custom had a crucial effect on copyholders' lives and especially on the ability to improve farms. In a situation where copyholders had beneficial rights of transfer and inheritance and low rents plus fixed entry fines and heriots, they had the security and wealth to put up substantial buildings and to experiment with agricultural methods. In other cases, entry fines were arbitrary at the will of the lord, rents were subject to rise, heriots posed a heavy burden and tenants were not eligible to nominate their successors.[22]

The second half of the seventeenth century in this area saw a transition from copyhold at three lives to leases for a term of years with a rent that reflected the annual value of the holding.[23] The late eighteenth-century agricultural writer Marshall saw lifeleasehold as a game of chance where possession depended on the leaseholder's own life and this could result in destitution for his wife and children, but also this type of lease tended to 'excite a spirit of speculation and gambling'.[24] As Mary Bouquet points out, the same unsophisticated farm tools recorded by Risdon in 1630 were still in use in nineteenth-century Devon because farmers struggled with the level of capital formation necessary to pay an entry fine.[25] Thus whereas in the sixteenth century the three-life lease may have stimulated improvement, by the nineteenth century, where the system survived, it may have acted as a brake. The use of primitive farm tools may have meant more women and children were involved in farm production than was the case elsewhere in the country. Above all, however, the lifeleasehold system meant that older, male offspring were favoured in the inheritance of land and farms. In other areas of the country, such as the Midlands and east, propertied parents shared the inheritance among their children. By contrast, in this area, parents showed a marked reluctance to divide the patrimony. The Pinney letters make it fairly clear that this was a major reason why women worked. It did mean that, in some cases, daughters were entered on the lease as 'lives', giving them a vested interest in the farm business. As a result the number of female tenant farmers was probably higher than in other areas of the country.[26]

How did lifeleasehold affect individual families? The records of the Pinney family suggest that inheritance systems were not only extremely complex but played a crucially important role in family fortunes. Although a system of lives was in operation, effective management of farms was passed between generations at points other than death. Sons effectively took over farms from their fathers when they married, rather than on their father's death.[27] The correspondence of brothers Azariah and Nathaniel Pinney to their father, John, reflects their anxiety over their lives being added to the lease of the family farm.[28] In the 1690s a family catastrophe concerning relations where the father had died without adding new lives to the lease was discussed in morbid detail. The nonconformist Gundrys through marriage possessed an estate worth about £80 per annum. On the death of the eldest Gundry, 'they are all undon and turned out of doores this Gundry being the only and last life they had on their whole estate'.[29] 'Old Gundry' had never made a will, 'being Exceeding fearefull of Death and said but an hourer or two before he dyed he should be well and Rise againe in a day's time'. As Widow Gundry had confessed to the Reverend John Pinney when he conducted old Gundry's funeral, 'she was undon and knew not which way to turne her selfe nor provide for her Numerouse family'. As Nathaniel Pinney commented, 'And the truth on't is that the whole Country say that its not only Gundry's owne family who are undon by his Death But al the whole Rowe of that fmily of the Gundrys are by his Death quite undon They holding their whole estates by his life only'.

In rural England, and especially fertile parishes like Colyton, land was the valuable commodity underpinning the workings of society. As we proceed to examine actual changes in farming in Colyton, three points need to be borne in mind. The first is the polarisation between the landed and the landless in the parish which, while not new, became more apparent in the early seventeenth century. The second, which we will return to in the next chapter, is that the system of lifeleasehold by tenants may have restricted land availability and affected the likelihood and timing of marriage. The third, which will be considered in more depth in Chapter 6, is that the substantial freeholders cast an important political influence in Colyton in the early modern period. Hoskins's 'backwoods gentry', along with urban merchants and manufacturers, were, until the second half of the eighteenth century, a key presence in Colyton.

Wood-pasture Farming

A substantial acreage of the land within Colyton parish was enclosed in the medieval period, from 1250 onwards, and this process was largely completed by 1500. Farms in the valleys were developed by clearing forests piecemeal for each farm.[30] These old enclosures, many of them linked by a network of medieval lanes, are recognisable from the farm names containing a personal name and the suffix 'hayne'.[31] As Hoskins describes the area around the neighbouring parish of Luppitt as 'a country of deep, winding lanes running from one ancient farmstead to another, haunted by buzzards on the valley, and by curlews on the heaths above, and full of flowers'.[32] The land and climate in the valley bottoms produced a lush, fertile growing environment.

Harold Fox finds that small closes characterised the medieval field pattern of east Devon with a mean size of only 2.9 acres. The closes remained fragmented and intermixed, although inter-tenant exchanges led to some consolidation of strips.[33] These farms produced a prodigious arable crop.[34] An analysis of land use on thirty-seven east Devon manors for the period 1244–1377 shows 68.6 per cent of the total acreage to be arable.[35] The Lysons said that in Henry VIII's time Colyton had a great pitched market for corn with grain markets taking place three times a week.[36] At this time Exeter's hinterland was most significant to the east, and fairs of eight or nine days duration were held in towns such as Colyton.[37] Kowaleski notes that Colyton fair was one of the best known in Devon and that it was usually called the St Calixtus fair, because it ended on that feast day. By 1281 the fair reputedly ran for fifteen days, which indicates its reputation.[38]

The later medieval period saw the beginnings of a transition to a pastoral economy. As Fox argues for the mid-fourteenth century to 1500, 'During this period there developed in East Devon the most well-rounded pastoral system in all of south-western England'.[39] A detailed study of Axminster shows that by 1574 it was dominated by 1–3 acre closes. By the seventeenth century the predominant land type for much of east Devon was permanent pasture with much woodland remaining.[40] John Leland, the antiquary, in 1534–43 described a mixed economy in Colyton with 'good Corne, Pasture and sum Wood'.[41] Norden, probably writing in the 1590s, had described the arable techniques of the West Country as if unremarkable.[42] The transition back to a mainly pastoral economy largely took place within the space of thirty years at the beginning of the seventeenth century at the same time as the population was rising and along with the consolidation of a good deal of land, much of it former common. Whereas about 1600 Hooker boasted of his native county as a great producer of sheep, cattle and corn, Westcote, a generation later, found Devon was barely able to feed itself with grain.[43] Both Chartres and Everitt have described declining exports of grain from the county as the seventeenth century progressed. Through disparate sources we can track these changes in Colyton. Walter Yonge's diary written between 1604 and 1628 makes only a few comments on the weather and its effect upon the crops.[44] The harvests of barley and wheat were his main concern; hay-making seemed to be of lesser importance. A Willoughby family lease of 1591 mentions cattle and pasture, but most of the records indicate that this was a subsidiary to arable farming.[45] When the feoffees leased the two major farms which they maintained, Lovehayne and Buddlehayes, in 1600, they arranged to take a proportion of tillage of 'corne or graine'.[46] The Colyton tithe disputes of the 1610s mention hay from meadows, as well as a tenth of the wheat, oats and pease crop.[47] An inventory of the possessions of John Strowbridge of

Hooperhayne was made by a special commission in 1576.[48] This shows that he did a minor amount of cheese-making, probably just for home consumption. No cloth-making equipment is recorded on his farm. Corn-growing and malt-making were his most important activities. He had a men's chamber with beds to accommodate his farm servants. His household contents are plentiful but not particularly fine, although we cannot know the meaning of the 'out Chamber' containing 'a great deale of other trompery and trashe'.

Following Kussmaul, one way of assessing the relative importance of types of agriculture in Colyton is by looking at marriage seasonality.[49] Table 4.1 shows the percentage of marriages in the cohort which could be described as 'pastoral' affected as they took place in April, May or June, after the busy spring period of calving or lambing. This is compared with the marriages that could be described as 'arable' affected because they took place in September, October or November following the harvest. Since pastoral agriculture had fewer tendencies to seasonality, an all-year-round pattern of marriages also suggests emphasis on dairying or sheep grazing.

As Colyton had an industrial sector the patterns of seasonality could not be expected to be as defined as in a purely agricultural parish, although, as was shown in Chapter 1, many of the crafts marriages are missing in the 1650–1750 period. However, the influence of arable agriculture was strong before 1650 and fell over time, while the pastoral pattern dominated in the 1650–1749 period. Seasonality seems to have had little influence in the 1750–99 cohort and indeed the agricultural trends are most confusing in that time period. The documentary evidence which survives for Colyton lends credence to these general outlines. Kussmaul finds that the West of England was a nearly homogeneous autumn-marrying region in the sixteenth and early seventeenth centuries. But by 1661–1740 there was a wholesale shift from arable

Table 4.1 Marriage seasonality in Colyton 1538–1837

	% of spring marriages	% of autumn marriages
1538–49	20.1	42.6
1550–99	24.8	37.2
1600–49	29.6	34.9
1650–99	35.0	30.5
1700–49	37.5	25.5
1750–99	20.3	23.4
1800–37	31.3	20.0

Source: Parish registers.

employment to rearing as the main agricultural determinant of marriage seasonality.

William Marshall was wrong in thinking that east Devon had been from 'time immemorial' a dairy district.[50] Fox suggests that it began to supply London with dairy from the sixteenth century.[51] This would account for the consolidation and extension of lands in the valleys as well as on the uplands. On the other hand, it is also feasible to argue that the real expansion of the dairying industry was a development mainly of the second half of the seventeenth century as a response both to declining wool prices by yeoman farmers and to shrinking land availability by the poorer sort. The accounts of one of the Colyton manorial lords, the Willoughby family, who had their residence at Leyhill near Honiton, show that in August 1644 they sold 87lb of butter. Over seven months in 1644 their farm retailed 800lb of cheese.[52] Cheese-making was commonly the most important economic activity mentioned in the few extant seventeenth-century inventories for Colyton.[53] The extent of the trade is probably underestimated in inventories taken in winter as dairying was seasonal. Butter and cheese were made from April to November with many cows going dry in winter.[54] In 1797 Polwhele noted that 'Colyton is a good dairy parish; remarkable for its rich butter and its skim-milk cheeses'.[55]

Efforts were made toward land improvement as elsewhere in Devon. Professor Finberg has shown that Tavistock Abbey was using calcareous sea sand extensively in the fourteenth century.[56] We would expect that land in parishes such as Colyton which were within easy range of the sea, and also had accessible patches of chalk, were likely to be improved in this way. The Widworthy manorial court rolls record a 1446 account for the building of three lime kilns by the lord.[57] Hooker went into a great deal of detail on the techniques of liming in this area of Devon. Samuel Colepresse, in his geological survey of the area for the Royal Society in the 1660s mentions both marling and liming along with the use of sea sand and seaweed as a top dressing.[58] In Branscombe, donkeys with panniers were used to collect seaweed to dig into soil and to take away the crops.[59] The valleys of the Colyton area were overlain with a layer of red marl, a fine grained clay which could be used either to improve upland greensand or in brick-making. The value of this material is evident from the number of records of those prosecuted for making illegal marl pits in the area.[60]

The large seventeenth-century farmhouse in Colyton had a buttery, dairy, brewhouse, cheese room and cider cellar. Specialisations in the farm economy arose according to the part of the parish in which the farm lay. A 1684 inventory mentions that John Darby ran a commercial cheese venture in one of the valleys. He had only eight cows and heiffers but a buttery, milkhouse and wringhouse for cheese, and in the cheese chamber there were 'twenty three cheeses, one hundred and half six cheese vats'.[61] On the high ground, in the same period, John Burnard ran a sheep farm. His inventory consisted of 'one hundred twenty two ewes and hogg sheepe, in sheepe's wool £20'.[62] Some farms covered all types of land because, as we have seen, land might be leased all over the parish, and the inventories reflect this. One yeoman's integrated, market-orientated farm is shown by an inventory dating from 1671. John Marwood had three hogsheads of cider in the cider house, thirty empty hogsheads, and three beer barrels. He had a butter chamber and a malt chamber. In the barn he had £5 worth of linen, £40 of hay and £90 worth of wheat, barley and oats, as well as pease to the value of £90. He had a hundred and seventy ewes and wethers, and sixty-three lambs. He had oxen worth £24, twenty-one cows and one bull valued at £66. Furthermore he had forty-five barren beasts and young cattle worth almost £100 and thirteen calves worth £8. He also had 'ii mares, i nag, ii hogg colts, xiii hoggs and poultry'. He had at least ten labourers to work on the farm since he had ten beds: 'i in the milkhouse chamber, iv in the kitchen chamber, iii in the entry chamber, ii in the men's chamber'.[63] Some textile manufacture was incorporated into the farm economy. Raffe Teape's farm in Whitwell in 1647 had not only a bakehouse, a buttery and dairy, along with a lodging and cider house, but there was also plenty of evidence of wool manufacture with 'ii rooms containing v spools' and over the lodging room 'a linney with v spools', as well as a hayloft.[64]

Yeoman farmers consolidated and extended their lands, and also took measures to improve their quality. Small closes in the the river valleys were used for stock rearing and moors were used for summer grazing as well as to provide furze for animal bedding. Land use was much enhanced by the development of water meadows, which put a thin film of water over a meadow in winter to keep it frost free. By this means, early spring fodder was produced and a greater crop of hay in summer than could have otherwise been expected. Water meadows were perhaps the most significant agricultural improvement of the seventeenth century and their development required both a good deal of work and a significant capital outlay to construct the channels and drains. As a result water meadows were constructed by wealthy yeoman farmers who had already made money, perhaps in sheep farming and the wool trade.[65]

Colyton's pastures were used not only by farmers for their own animals but also as commercial grazing for drovers who passed through the parish. Fox has shown that even in large villages there were meat markets and leather trades in the later medieval period.[66] As early as 1207 the men of Axmouth paid 20s to site rural tanneries in that town.[67] Kowaleski writes that tanning much expanded in rural areas with suitable rivers in the later medieval period. This was partly associated with the growth of pastoral farming which gave tanners a regular supply of hides outside of the larger urban centres, thus keeping them immune from the polluting, foul effluence. Fox finds that by the sixteenth century Colyton's rich pasture was let at high rents to carriers accustomed to 'eate the grasse of the same with their travailling horses'.[68] The mid-eighteenth-century Dean Milles survey shows a cattle trade of droving towards east Devon, Dorset and London.[69] Uplyme, for example, had 'a large quantity of Horn Cattle—cows & heifers of a small sort & some sheep—Dorset sheep'. At Seaton 'There were very good sheep, and fine pasture at Beer, bought by graziers and sold at Weyhill Fair' (near Andover, Hampshire). For Colyton, the survey records very high land values. The parish had the most expensive rough pasture in the survey and meadow reached the high level of £3 per acre, reflecting the value of the pasture on the reclaimed salt-meadows near the Axe.

Wrigley finds leather to be the second most important industry in Colyton in the first two periods for which it is possible to analyse male occupations from the parish register, 1609–12 and 1765–79 and latterly the largest employer.[70] Thus, if anything the trade increased in relative importance over time. In 1673 Edward Cawley of Colyton, a husbandman, was accused of stealing cattle having sold some heifers to a tanner in Kilmington. The will of Aaron Reed of Colyton, made in 1691, mentions a tan works at Puddlebridge on the River Coly.[71] He left the tan house to his son, John Reed, and to his daughter, Rebekah, 'all the leather, bark, millstone and furnaces and all the implements as belong to the trade of tanning'. Cattle and leather were bought and sold by Colyton dealers as far away as Saint White Down fair in Somerset in the mid-seventeenth century.[72] As late as the 1780s there are still both ale tasters and searchers and sealers of green leather as officers of the manor of Colyton, and elsewhere in the district these offices continued.[73] A tannery still exists in Colyton specialising in high quality oak bark tanning. Twenty-four tanners were employed there in the 1851 census.[74] The existence of the tannery seems to have encouraged the development of associated small leather craft businesses such as boot and shoe manufacture and harness-making. For example, it is apparent that shoemakers in the area made ready-made shoes as early as 1627 when Charity Tucker was accused of stealing shoes at Honiton Market and a pair were identified as 'size 12s'.[75] Leather gloves were another local manufacture. In 1634 John Boden, Colyton glover, was charged with taking away eighty-five 'thonges' from Colyton market from Nicholas Dunscombe, Membury tanner.[76] There were also animal-byproduct industries such as soapboiling from tallow.[77] As we saw during the discussion about Roger Satchell, this is the type of production that proliferated with heightened consumer demand during the course of the seventeenth century.

Another feature of the Colyton farm economy was apple orchards and cider production. A 1619 ecclesiastical court case regarding tithes suggests that cider apples had been part of the tithe since about 1580 (see Plate 4).[78] This perhaps suggests that more intensive cultivation of the valleys was the corollary of more extensive running of sheep on the uplands. Historians believe that apple orchards were becoming more important in the second half of the seventeenth century in this part of Devon and the amount of production in the Colyton region and the existence of cider houses suggests that this was a commercial venture not just a supply of cider for farmworkers.[79] An average yeoman farm such as the Pinney farm in Bettiscombe perhaps made twenty hogsheads a season.[80] In the 1642 will of Gideon Hall, a husbandman of Colyton, an apple mill was left for his wife.[81] Ordinary people opened cider houses, perhaps putting out a flag as is done in chicha houses in present-day rural Peru. For example, in a 1687 court case, Rachel Drewe said that her grandfather sold cider: 'he living in ye rodeway and selling cyder'.[82] By the mid-eighteenth century, Colyton was one of the parishes producing the largest amount of cider at 1,500 hogsheads of the total 170,000 hogsheads (10 million gallons) made in Devon as a whole.[83] The cider varied in type and quality. Whereas at Gittisham, where 250–300 hogsheads of cider were made annually, it was a 'Good masculine cider rather of ye rough sort', Ottery St Mary produced 'a mild racy Cyder annually improving'. Apples grew well here and were being propagated. The Sampson account book refers to a cider engine being constructed at Smitten's pit in 1778.[84] The feoffees' minute book mentions apple trees being planted at Lovehayne, and an orchard being developed at Colyford in 1785.[85] As Fraser said of Devon in 1794, 'Throughout a great part of this county, particularly the southern districts, cider constitutes a very material article of rural oeconomy'.[86] Most farms, large or small, had possessed a cider still since the early seventeenth century.

There is little doubt that yeoman farmers were experimenters and improvers. A fascinating early eighteenth-century letter from William Phelps to Azariah Pinney II makes this clear.[87] Phelps had become a servant to an Irish landowner and found himself removed from west Dorset to the townland of Clanfart in County Clare: 'I am in acuntry amongst a strang sort of people nastly ignorant and stubarn thinking thare one ways to be the best and indeed they no nothin att tall of country Bisness'. His strongly Protestant opinions were apparent. The Roman Catholics had too many holidays and did not work hard enough to find their way out of poverty. The hay-making was a prolonged business carried out in the same way as in Devon but only half as well. The Irish let it 'lye a month in stalk, then do nothing to it for a month more then shack it abroad with their hands, then do nothing for a month more'. Phelps had made 100 acres of hay for his lord in the English way but locals felt it would create a fire because he dried it for only four days.

Plate 4. An apple press, frontispiece to J.W. Gent, *The Second Part of Systema Agriculturæ* (1689), reproduced by permission of the Director of Information Services and University Librarian of the University of Bristol.

He went on to harvest wheat as in England. He ploughed above an acre a day but was forced to travel 50 miles to find one of his countrymen who knew how to make ploughs in the English way. Phelps compared local productivity with that of his native area in hay-making, harvest, ploughing and sowing. In ploughing he claimed to have raised their productivity four times over. He could now manage an acre of ploughing a day with his own ingenious invention and the help of two men who understood English agricultural methods. Phelps had a capitalist attitude to farming. He was concerned about the distracting influence of the lord's drunken sister and he felt the farm was overladen with workers.

By the late seventeenth century, Colyton's wood-pasture economy supported a number of substantial and progressive yeoman farms. Encroachment on to wastes, enclosure, water meadows and the presence of fine rich pasture on the saltings, enhanced by the inflation of wool prices and the system of relatively secure leases which did not insulate farmers entirely from market forces, had supported a predominantly grazing, fruit-growing and dairying economy from the early seventeenth century. The small farmer who specialised and was able to adapt prospered, but in these conditions some small producers were eliminated.

Fishing and Commons

The most significant land improvement within the Colyton parish and area resulted from the attempts to re-open the Axe haven. The history of these attempts will be examined in some detail because they have a bearing on the economic development of the parish in general. In the medieval period, there was a wide and sheltered estuary stretching inland from the mouth of the Axe for some four miles. It appears that ships were able to sail as far as Colyton, and Axmouth was probably a considerable Roman port. The estuary connected to the Fosse Way and linked the estuary to a convergence of trade routes from Somerset, Exmoor and Dartmoor, facilitating a trade in furs, hides, wool, lead and silver from Exmoor, tin from the Chagford district of east Dartmoor, and copper from Okehampton.[88] It was possibly as a result of a cliff being destroyed by a great storm in 1377 that a massive shingle bar grew from west to east, diverting the estuary flow. This led to rapid silting and entry to the estuary became barred to all but the smallest boats. Nevertheless in 1513 when ships from the West Country were pressed into the King's service against France, Colyton was still one of ports mentioned in State Papers. The importance of this waterway is shown by the numerous attempts to re-open the haven. Leland described early efforts in some detail in 1534–43:

> Ther hath beene a very notable Haven at Seton, but now ther lyith betwen the 2 Pointes of the old Haven a mighty Rigge and Barre of pible Stones in the very Mouth of it, and the Ryver of Ax is dryven to the very Est Point of the Haven, caullid Whit Clif, and ther at a very smaul Gut goith into the Se; and her cum in small fisher Boates for sucour. The Men of Seton began of late Dayes to stake and to make a mayne Waulle withyn the Haven, to have divertid the Course of Ax Ryver, and ther almost in the Midle of the old Haven, and ther to have trenchid thorough the Chisille, and to have let out Ax and receyvid iin the mayn Se, but this Purpose cam not to effect; me thought that Nature most wrought to trench the Chisil, and ther to let in the Se.[89]

Here Leland is describing a dangerous and failed attempt by the Seaton inhabitants to breach the pebble ridge and by the men of Beer to build a quay. This attempt was supported by letters patent under the Great Seal whereby money was collected throughout the kingdom.[90] The silting up not only affected the trade with other areas of Devon but destroyed Seaton and Axmouth as significant fishing communities. Leland said that 'The Town of Seton is now but a meane Thing, inhabited with Fischar Men, [but] it hath bene far larger when the Haven was good' and that he had 'passid from Seton at Ebbe over the Salt Marshes and the Ryver of Ax to Axmouth, an old and bigge Fischar Toune on the Est side of the Haven'.

As early as 1450 Bishop Lacy of Exeter had offered an indulgence of forty days to all persons who would contribute towards the cost of repair of the haven. A further attempt was made in 1575 on the initiative of the inhabitants of Colyton. With the backing of some leading Devon gentlement including Sir Humphrey Gilbert, letters patent were obtained and a royal proclamation enabled them to solicit contributions from beyond county boundaries. They were authorised to impress both materials (stone, timber, etc.) and labour.[91] Four separate nationwide collections were made in the 1570s and 1580s. In Eltham, Kent, there is record of '1575 paid for makinge the bookes of the collections toward the makinge of Colliton haven, and for carrying the said bokes two severall days to London iis'. Three separate collections, in 1576, 1580 and 1583, were made in Culworth, Northamptonshire.[92] In his will of 1580, Thomas Veale, a yeoman, of Knighton in the parish of Beerhacket in Dorset, gave the princely sum of 12d 'towards [the] making of Culliton Haven'.[93] The urgency of these requests suggests that the opening of the haven would have led to greater prosperity for the wool trade if kersies had been carried out by sea, then possibly exported from Lyme Regis. In the 1590s the Axmouth Erle family made great efforts to open up the haven; as Sir William Pole recorded in his early seventeenth-century

ECONOMY AND LOCALITY

Plate 5. Contemporary views of the Axe Estuary and area of land reclamation.
(D. Pennington and D. Sharpe)

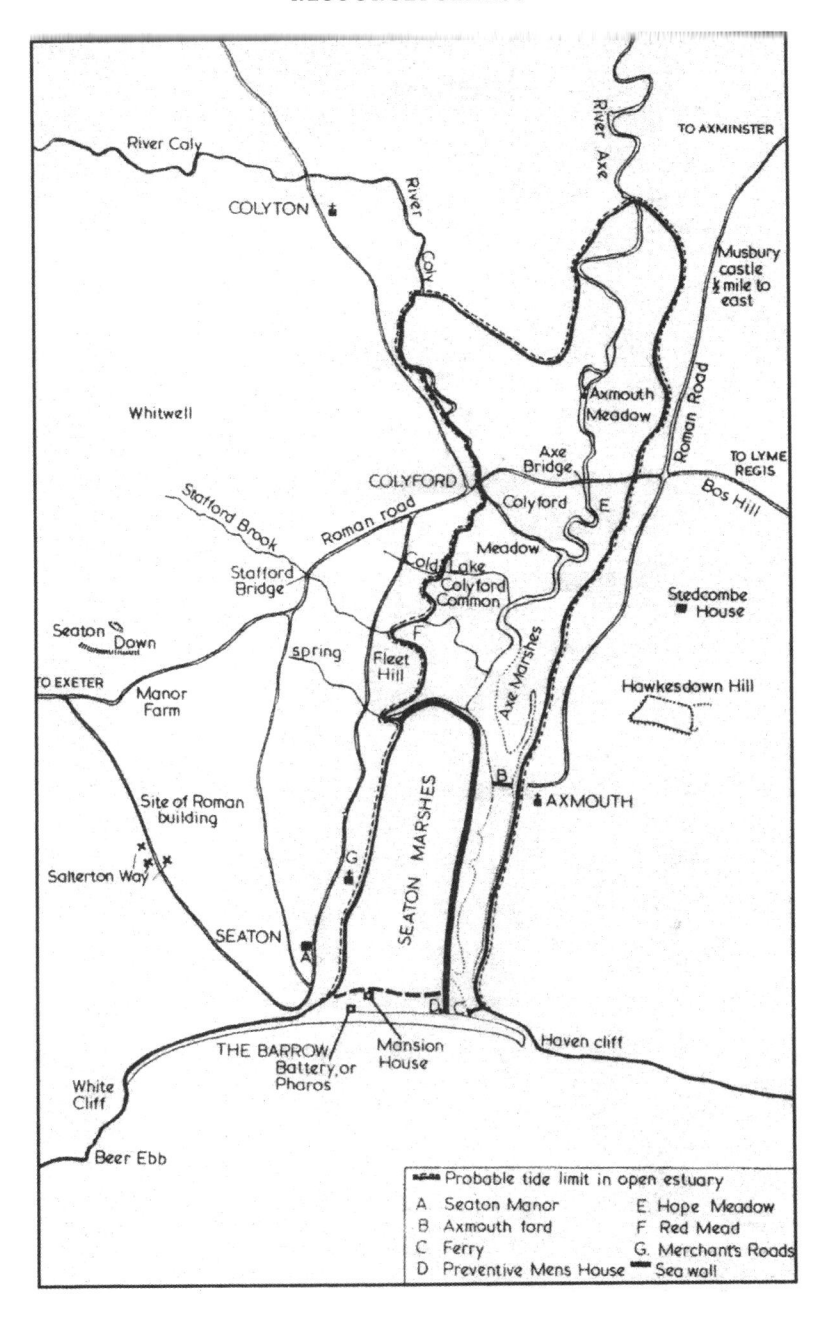

Map 4. Composite map combining features of the Axe Estuary from Roman times, through the medieval period, to the late seventeenth-century, from Margaret Parkinson, 'The Axe Estuary and its Marshes' *Reports and Transactions of the Devonshire Association for the Advancement of Science*, 117 (1985), figs 1 & 2, pp. 21–7, reproduced by permission of the Devonshire Association.

history of Devon, their endeavours involved 'old woorks and piles' and that 'About LV yeeres past theire was a collecion over England, by authority, to collect moneys for the makinge of an haven in this place, but the money was converted to worse use'.[94] But Camden (1623) and Risdon (1630) attribute the failure not to financial factors but to the weather and the inexorable west–east drift of shingle.[95] In fact, no real success came until the early nineteenth century when the efforts of J.H. Hallett at Axmouth were recorded by the Lysons in 1822: 'Piers have been constructed at the mouth of the Axe under the shelter of which vessels of 100 tons discharge their cargoes in safety'. In 1830 Hallet obtained an Act of Parliament to collect quay dues and use the proceeds for harbour upkeep (see Plate 5).[96]

While a disaster for shipping, the importance of the silted-up haven for the local agricultural economy was immense.[97] The saltmarsh produced a rich source of grazing for manorial tenants on Colyford meadow (see Maps 4–6). The mudflats also extended the inland fishing possibilities of the parish beyond the trout, minnows and eels which could be netted in the rivers. Within Colyton, grazing was possible on Colyton Common, Axe Marsh, Hope Meadow and Colyford Meadow. In surrounding manors, such as Seaton, the common was referred to as the 'waste' of the manor, indicating that it was regarded as rough grazing. The quality of the pasture in the saltings was so high that it was worth maintaining a small strip for the hay it would produce. A survey of Whitwell manor shows that Colyford Meadow was so highly esteemed that each tenement in both this and the other three manors within Colyton parish had one or more 'parcells' within it, in addition to the tenants of Seaton manor who still held their rights dating from Saxon times. For example, Elizabeth Pike held 'one acre of meadow in Culliforde Meadow' and John French held 'one acre of meadow lying in Colyford Mead'. While the land was in named parcels, many of these saltings were called 'common meads' because after the occupier of each strip had removed the hay crop, they were thrown open as common pastures for the stock of all occupiers. The 'foreshare' or 'first cut' was property of the occupiers of individual strips but the 'aftershare' was communally managed. By the sixteenth century some aspects of management had been introduced with regulation of the number of animals and commons being fenced off to prevent the stock from one manor straying to another.[98] A 1636 dispute over the cultivation of hay on Colyford Meadow suggested that some of the meadow was common and some was enclosed. It also indicated that the larger tenants had employees making hay on the land.[99]

As a result of the value of this land, in the late seventeenth century the Willoughby family, lords of the manor of Whitwell, decided to reclaim Seaton Marsh and entered into agreements with their tenants to suspend

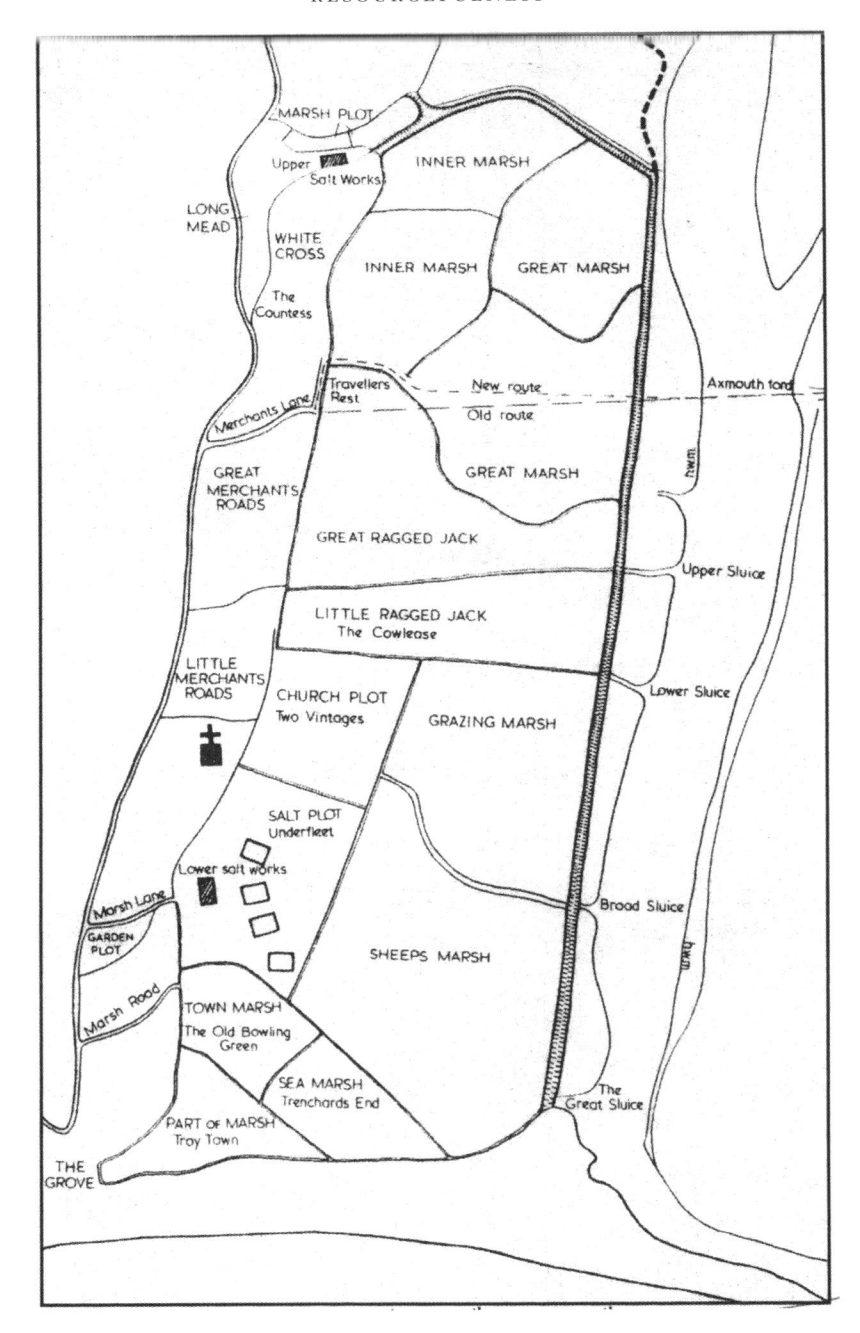

Map 5. Detail of Seaton Marsh from the mid-seventeenth to the mid-nineteenth century, from Margaret Parkinson, 'The Axe Estuary and its Marshes' *Reports and Transactions of the Devonshire Association for the Advancement of Science*, 117 (1985), figs 1 & 2, pp. 21–7, reproduced by permission of the Devonshire Association.

their rights to common pasture there. A reflection of the high value of this land is the agreement with one particular widow for a bond of £100 for agreeing no longer to pasture her sheep or cattle on the common marsh. John Willoughby promised to pay the widow, Mary Coombs of Colyton, £4 a year in lieu of her rights on Seaton Marsh. In another case, one Richard Clarke was allowed to 'have 30 sheep on the lower marsh during my pleasure and no longer'. The diversity of similar agreements indicate that varying amounts of land were held by different individuals and manorial surveys suggest that access to common was allocated according to the value and quantity of land held.[100] After reclamation Seaton Marsh was divided into parcels which could be let separately. Crossing places over ditches were constructed with access gates that confined the livestock within paddocks. One of the phases of work in 1669–72 involved raising the bank and construction of 'the Great Slushe' (sluice). The outbanks of the marsh also needed constant upkeep to avoid flooding. The Willoughbys adopted sophisticated Dutch methods of land reclamation and the works generated considerable local employment and use of resources. Their accounts mention payments to Colyford men for repairing breaches in embankments. Timber was brought from Farway to construct a line of vertical piles 4–6 feet long on the outer seaward edge of the clay core of the bank, along with two hundred piles of alder sourced from a coppice at Branscombe. There are references in the accounts to Colyford and Seaton 'bankers' who worked in teams to pile up stones. New drains were cut and culverts and sluices constructed. This required local ironwork and the Colyton blacksmith was paid a handsome £253 13s 7d. Parkinson shows that the many references to boundary stones in the Willoughby papers indicate resentment at the continued use of unreclaimed grazing for saltmarsh. Something of this surfaces in a dispute between two lords of the manor over Whitwell Common in about 1678. Courtenay-Pole's servant had put his cattle on the land and the tenants of Whitwell had driven them out. The tenants of Whitwell made a distinction between different commons and argued that 'they Enjoyed Whitewell Comon alone & that none else has any right of comon there'.[101]

A hundred years later, in another boundary dispute in 1780, Henry Clarke, who described himself as a labourer, particularised the miniature but diverse plot of land he had held in Colyford Meadow since about 1740. He had a house, orchards and several closes of arable, meadow and pasture ground, all called Square Acre and lying within a close where land was held by fifty people in total. He said that the land was mowed every year and the hay was carried off by landowners or tenants. Each plot was bounded with stones or stakes.[102] Perhaps as a result of these intensively farmed, fruitful little plots, by the late nineteenth century in Colyton, Seaton and Axmouth the allotments were colloquially termed

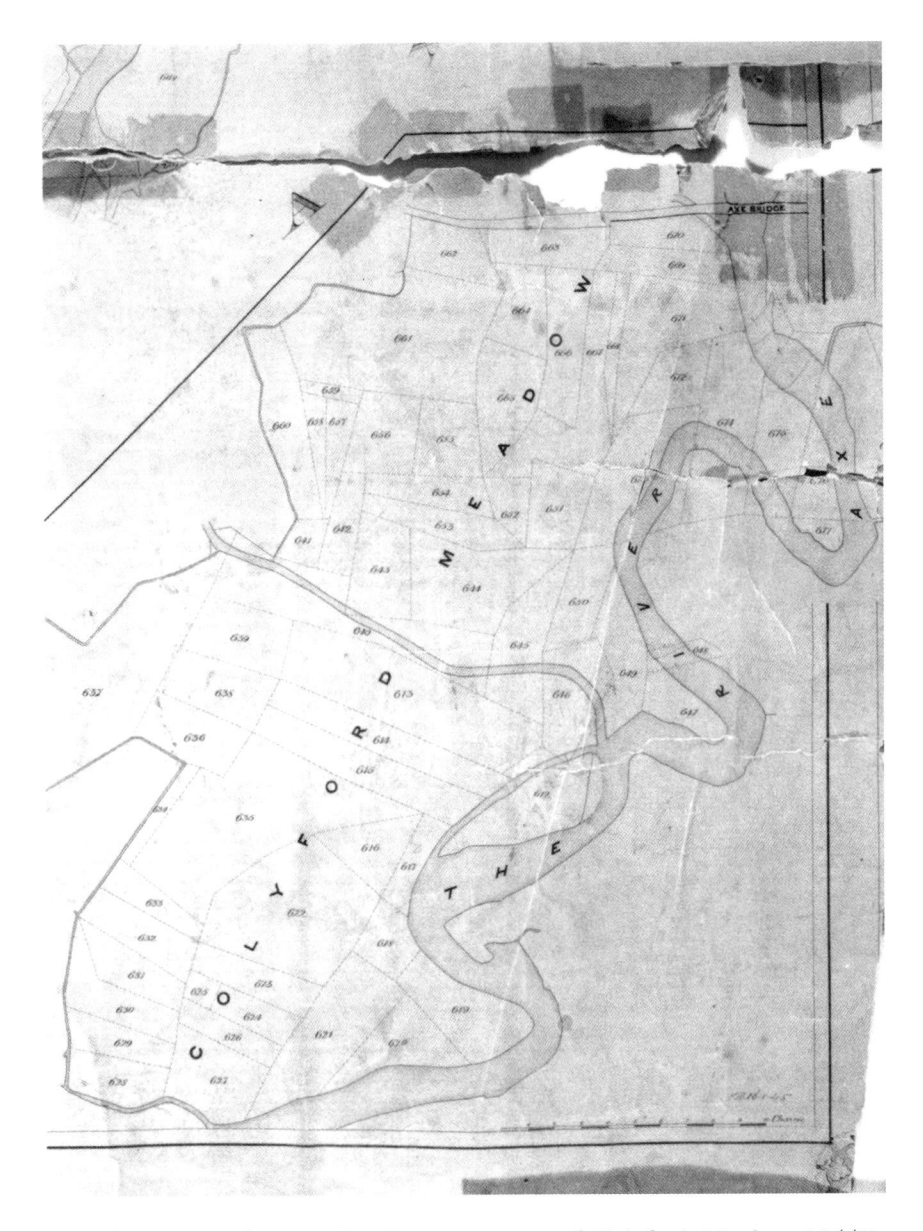

Map 6. Detail of the Tithe Apportionment of Colyford Meadow 1844/5, courtesy of Devon Records Office.

'the vineyard'.[103] The Colyton tithe map shows a complicated picture of land holding reflecting ongoing subdivision over two centuries (see Map 6). The detailed inset shows that the size of parcels varied from just over an acre to a tenth of an acre with over eighty associated individual landholders. The complex pastiche of landholding is apparent when in about 1680 Edward Drake held 'one parcell of meadow about 3 quarters of an acre, lying undivided with Elizabeth Starrs . . . att Comon land, one other parcell of meadow about half an acre bounded out from other of the grounds of the said Eliz Starr near Comon land aforesayd and one other parcell of meadow . . . about 3 quarters of an acre lying in comon with the meadow grounds . . . belonging to the Tenement sometymes in the possession of one Wm Newton'. By the end of the nineteenth century further subdivision meant some of these parcels were too small to be viable. Only 7 acres of Colyford Common was true common with free access and no titles attached to it. This area was known as 'Saltgrass' and named parcels were divided by saltmarsh creeks. A section of the saltmarsh (later known as the 'old bowling green') survived the reclamation as the pitch for an ancient game similar to French boules.

As this chapter progresses, I will explore in some detail the economy of cottagers like Henry Clarke. But the detail on the saltings area of the south of Colyton parish makes apparent that commonable pasture was not open to everyone who lived in the area. The Starrs, for example, were some of the largest and most long-standing tenant farmers of the manor. Except for very small patches, and perhaps then only at certain times of the year, this was land intensively farmed by manorial tenants, some of whom were large proprietors, and in some cases the lord of the manor's own family. As Fox has shown, however, east Devon parishes also had extensive wastes in the late medieval period, forming some 17.4 per cent of the total land area in his manorial survey.[104] These areas were essential to a grazing economy. The wastes at Uplyme were said in 1266 to be able to support fifty ewes and six hundred wethers. Wastes might also provide fuel, gravel and stones and less perceptible benefits like rabbit catching and berry and herb collecting.[105] According to the manorial surveys, the commons did provide access to all for fishing, fowling and hunting.

The documents afford only glimpses into the use of this area of land. They suggest that while access to the small closes and the best pasture may have caused disputes in the seventeenth-century parish, the improvement of this area provided a rich enhancement to farming possibilities within Colyton. But what was the impact of the silted-up estuary on other areas of the maritime economy?

In 1538 Leland described Lyme as 'having good ships and using fishing'.[106] Here the sea and fishing trades linked the town with London. Goods were carried in baskets, known as dorsers, on the backs of pack horses. Inns like 'The George' in Lyme always kept a quantity of pack horses for hire.[107] Fuller, the vicar of Broadwindsor from 1634, said 'dorsers are carried on the backs of horses . . . Fish-jobbers bring up their fish in such contrivances above an hundred miles from Lyme to London.'[108] As both Maryanne Kowaleski and Todd Gray's research on Devon fisheries has shown, the sea trades and the Atlantic system were important before the time when the colonial trades became central to the English mercantile system.[109] Kowaleski argues that from the late fourteenth century through to the early sixteenth century the expansion of marine fishing was of the greatest importance in the rising prosperity of the region. It was a critical supplement to the many small farmers. It employed many people in ancilliary industries such as fish curing. There was an upturn in capital investment in ships and equipment and the expanding trade gave navigational training and experience to the seamen who formed the Tudor navy. Gray describes the expansion of fishing from Devon to Ireland in the medieval period, the rise of the Newfoundland fisheries in the sixteenth century and the extension to New England in the reign of Elizabeth I.

The trade employed an estimated 15,000 men along the Devon and Cornwall coast in the early modern period and an unknown number of women who unloaded, washed and packed fish and hawked it between parishes.[110] A fisherman could be in Newfoundland for summer, north New England for spring and autumn, and Ireland from March to December. Many men were certainly away for six to nine months of the year battling with the elements and the dangers of piracy and shipwreck. The Newfoundland trade saw its greatest expansion during the period 1570–1600 when the French, Portugese and Spanish withdrew from the fisheries, and the peak was 1610–30 when Devon had some 10,000 men at sea.[111] The harvest of the great Newfoundland fisheries was available well inland. In July 1602 yeoman farmer William Honnywell recorded in his diary that he travelled to Chudleigh and purchased 9d worth of Newfoundland fish.[112] There is much evidence of the extent to which fish were carried inland and formed an important source of food for the poor.[113] The Newfoundland trade also impinged on the local economy in other ways than the fish trade. For example, in 1699 William Pomeroy, a Sidmouth cordwainer, when proving in a court case that a jar of oil was his own said it was bought in Newfoundland.[114]

More locally, just off the south coast, pilchards and herring were caught by boats small enough to navigate amid the sand- and shingle-choked waters. A 1632 court case involved two husbandmen, Edward Mason and John Teape, both of Farway, who travelled to the seaside at Seaton where people were catching pilchards. Although their two stories do not quite tally, they planned to buy fish.[115] By the early seventeenth century the mariner population was spreading inland albeit in a patchy way. The Duke of Buckingham's survey of south Devon in 1619 showed nine sailors in Colyton and also nine in Axmouth.[116] Risdon described Sidmouth in the early seventeenth century as 'one of the especialist fisher towns of this shire, and serveth much provision into the east parts, whereupon her principal maintenance consisteth; but in times past, a port of some account, now choked with chisel and sands by the vicissitude of the tides'.[117] Seaton was 'at this day a poor fishing village'.[118] In 1750 Dean Milles described the inhabitants of Beer as 'mostly fishermen, remarkably strong . . . live to a great age', and said that fish such as grey mullet, bass, salmon, trout and flounder were netted in these coastal villages in the months from May to October. In the 1790s, Reverend John Swete described stakes and poles at Beer for fixing nets to take fish at high water, and at the ebb of the tide.[119] At Budleigh Salterton, he wrote, 'The men are farmers and fishermen, and the women lacemakers, and the natural production which for some years past have rendered the place well known, are its fine lobsters and laver. This last under the class of mosses, is a vegetable growing on the rocks, and for its flavour is in high request at the tables of many.'[120]

Despite Colyton's proximity to the sea, fishing does not seem to have been an important industry, although the availability of fish must have given parishioners a varied diet. Not only are few mariners recorded in the 1610s but Colyton's settlement examinations do not reflect the seasonal nature of reliance on fishing, in the same way that those for Coffinswell do, for example, even though that parish was also without a seashore.[121] Perhaps there was sufficient diversity in Colyton's economy without recourse to the unpredictable and seasonal fisheries. Nevertheless, some local industry was related to the fishing trades. In the 1700s Sir John Trevelyan started salt manufacture with salthouses and saltpans on the reclaimed area of the former haven. This was a summer activity mainly done from May to August. The salt-makers were generally also graziers and at Seaton the lease of marshes for grazing ran alongside the lease of saltworks. The initiative received encouragement from the Newfoundland cod fishery. By the 1730s two salthouses and four saltpans were still there but the business was not a long-term success as it proved to be unable to compete with the French in peacetime.[122]

Court cases also reveal a marginal engagement with the sea trades. We can see that while not many mariners lived and worked in the area, 'going away to sea' would have been a reality for some of the dispossessed and poor of the parish. Likewise some strangers arrived in the parish through commercial connections forged on the waves. In 1631 Thomas Smythe of Lynn in Norfolk (presumably King's Lynn) was examined at Colyton.[123] He had come into St Ives having been bound on a ship at Hull. He was taken by the Turks but relieved by a 'Stateman of War'. His wife joined him in Cornwall when he sent for her, but he then said his pass to travel around the country was burned by the lighting of tobacco! The Smythes were apprehended travelling along the road. Smythe was said by his wife to be unable either to read or to write. Nevertheless they were travelling towards a business associate of Smythe's, as he said he was 'allyed to one Mr Harvey Customer of Lyme' who had visited him in Lynn two years previously. Several men had been pressed into service at sea. In midsummer 1656 Elenor Fursey, the wife of Rafe Fursey of Farway, testified that she was pregnant by the son of a gentleman. He had got her pregnant in an orchard and had often made sexual advances since and offered her £10 to name another father. She said that she presumed her husband had been drowned on his passage to Ireland about five years earlier when he was pressed as a soldier. She had not heard from him since his departure (at which time she had a letter from him).[124] A Colyton man, John Rulty, testified that he had been pressed to serve at sea in 1658. He had sustained a wound and in an apposite description of the value of day labour (or perhaps sexual capacity) had 'lost all he was worth'.[125] In 1679 Christopher Mathew from Ottery St Mary sailed out of Topsham bound for Newfoundland and then Bilbao. On the voyage he was taken and seized by a 'Turkesman of War' and carried captive to Algiers where he was in 1683 still detained in 'most insuferable & wretched Slavery' with a ransom of over £80. He was a poor man with a considerable family and his father petitioned quarter sessions. They agreed to pay the miserable contribution of 50s towards his redemption.[126]

While investment in shipping was an option for the wealthier sections of Colyton's population and probably contributed to some of the land and property investment in the parish, the proximity of the sea seems to have provided no more than limited opportunities for the ordinary dweller in Colyton. The effects described by Kowaleski had only limited impact on the parish, raising interesting questions about the local distinctiveness of the economic structure of parishes. The next section will explore the economic situation of the cottager and the landless labourer.

The Livelihood of the Cottager and Farm Worker

> The Undercliff—for this land is really the mile-long slope caused by the erosion of the ancient vertical cliff face—is very steep. Flat places are as rare as visitors in it. But this steepness in effect tilts it, and its vegetation, towards the sun; and it is this fact, together with the water from the countless springs that have caused the erosion, that lends the area its botanical strangeness—its wild arbutus and ilex and other trees rarely seen growing in England; its enormous ashes and beeches; its green Brazilian chasms choked with ivy and the liana of wild clematis; its bracken that grows seven, eight feet tall; its flowers that bloom a month earlier than anywhere else in the

district. In summer it is the nearest this country can offer to a tropical jungle. It has also, like all land that has never been worked or lived on by man, its mysteries, its shadows, its dangers—only too literal ones geologically, since there are crevices and sudden falls that can bring disaster, and in places where a man with a broken leg could shout all week and not be heard. Strange as it may seem, it was slightly less solitary a hundred years ago than it is today. There is not a single cottage in the Undercliff now; in 1867 there were several, lived in by gamekeepers, woodmen, a pigherd or two. The roe deer, sure proof of abundant solitude, then must have passed less peaceful days. Now the Undercliff has reverted to a state of total wildness. The cottage walls have crumbled into ivied stumps, the old branch paths have gone; no car goes near it, the one remaining track that traverses it is often impassable. And it is so by Act of Parliament: a national nature reserve. Not all is lost to expedience.[127]

When John Fowles describes the coastal track from Seaton to Lyme Regis in *The French Lieutenant's Woman*, the mysterious passageway also captured by Jane Austen in *Persuasion*, he evokes the lost world of the forester, fowler and cottager who dwelt among the farms of the yeomen in this part of Devon. These people form the group who possessed one hearth in the Hearth Tax assessment. Harold Fox's study of villages in this area shows the extent to which they had populations of independent cottagers. In 1394 in Sidbury the mean size of farm holdings was 24 acres but a proportion of the population held only 5 acre smallholdings. Some of the hill and vale country already specialised in dairy in the late medieval period with a combination of livestock management which was intensive in the valleys and areas like the saltings but extensive where sheep ranged on the hills. There were expanding markets for their produce in Exeter and the small towns of the east Devon region.

Woodland or common pasture allowed Sidbury cottagers the ability to pasture animals by right or custom. At nearby Northleigh a lease of a single acre in the fourteenth century gave the right to pasture an unlimited number of animals 'on the hills'. The common wastes also provided ferns and turf on the 'great heath or waste' lying between Sidbury and Ottery. As Fox puts it, 'Sidbury's cottagers in the Later Middle Ages were still people of the verges, people of the ragged "plebian underwood", of the hilltops bright with gorse in spring and sombre, peat black in winter'.[128] Cottagers could also earn income from cloth-working. Sidbury had an official market and fair from 1291, possibly for cheese and cattle. Manors like Sidbury were similar to Colyton with diversified craft-workers who had occupations as smiths, as well as in the wood-related and leather trades. Fox finds butchers, spinsters, glovers, fishermen and prostitutes in fifteenth-century Sidbury, and possible surname evidence reveals a hatmaker, tavernkeeper, baker, smith, carpenter and even a juggler. The parish would have had a population of immigrants, particularly moving from manors with less diverse economies. To what extent did a similar independence in the wood-pasture economy still appertain by the time period covered in this book? The court rolls of neighbouring Farway for 1618–21 also show the cultivation of common land by tenants from time to time. Robert Mason, aged 76, and John Clapp, aged 70, who were manorial tenants, reported that they had long used parcels of common and had topped trees and felled underwoods for their own use. They said that in the 1570s tenants had 'plowed & put in Tillage and grew Corn. And enjoyed herbage and pasture, and taken Furze there.'[129] Clearly, however, access to the commons varied from parish to parish and within Colyton the evidence suggests that free access to commonage was a contested issue and a battle which the cottagers had largely lost by the mid-seventeenth century.

Economic upheavals dislocated the cottager as the seventeenth century progressed. The year 1631 saw severe harvest failure and subsequent textile depression. The Civil War caused some disruption to agriculture in Colyton. Judging by the number of soldiers who appear in the burial register in 1643, fighting seems to have taken place in the parish. A lease map of the late seventeenth century shows where three cottages were burnt down in the wars.[130] Chapple, in his edition of Risdon's *Survey of Devon* published in 1785, wrote of the great check to agriculture of the Civil Wars. Labourers were in the armies, the countryside was overrun by fighting, and fear of crops being destroyed was general.[131] This disruption was reinforced by the outbreak of plague in 1645 in which a fifth of Colyton's population died.[132] Isolated court cases from Colyton and surrounding parishes allow us to glimpse some of the tensions surrounding the shrinking access to the commons. According to Hooker, around 1600, 'ffor the husbond mann be he poore or riche be his bargayn greate or small, he hathe all wayes some sheepe be they more or lesse'.[133] But as the seventeenth century progressed, more court cases suggesting poverty, such as the theft of sheep, became common for Colyton. In 1658 Ralph Teape was arrested by his brother, who happened to be the constable, for stealing sheep on Colyton common.[134] In the 1660s there was a particularly large number of cases in the Devon quarter sessions concerning sheep-stealing and the sale of sheepskins. In 1669 Thomas Seaward, a Colyford carpenter, was asked about the liquor or broth found boiling when his house was investigated. Seaward claimed it was water in which a shirt had been boiled or milk scalded but that it was not broth or potage made of stolen lamb. Evidently not satisfied, the portreeve searched the houses of Seaward's drinking companions at 'The Bear' in the hope of finding the missing lamb.

Several court cases document the theft of firewood and it appears that by the 1630s fuel was bought rather than collected in Colyton, as the woodlands became a commercial resource. Like the saltings, access to the common woodland was confined to manorial tenants and tended to exclude poorer people or recent immigrants. In 1684 William Hooke, a tenant of the manor of Ottery St Mary, climbed a hill and saw two men cutting turves, spinny, furze and heath on the common, with another helping them to load their cart and carry this away. When he asked them to unload he was assaulted as the turf-cutters threatened to kill him or his horses.[135] More extensive commons existed in the parishes originally carved out of woodland such as Stockland and Kilmington, and this was where prolonged and bitter battles took place in the eighteenth century. In 1698 Richard Warren, following his mother's bidding, scaled Stockland Hill to collect a bundle of wood with a companion. They were accused of stealing a flock of sheep by driving it away from Stockland.[136] In 1755 the overseers' account book for Stockland records payment in defence of the custom for poor people to cut furze, turf and heath upon hills and waste places for their winter fuel. The lord of the manor had commenced actions against several of the poor, who by reason of their poverty were not able to defend themselves. In retaliation the main tenants retorted: 'We therefore whose hands are here unto sett at a Parish meeting this Day held being the principall Inhabitants and Payers of the said parish in Order to support the undoubted Rights of the said Poor People do order & Agree that Mr Amos Callard of Axminster, Attorney att Law shall appear for . . . [names of the poor] & defend the said actions'. The costs and charges were to be collected by the overseer of the poor and every inhabitant was ordered to pay as they were rated for the poor.[137] In Kilmington the lords of the manor were in a more dominating position and in alliance with the freeholders destroyed enclosures and housing on the common in 1765.[138] In 1796 vestry orders were passed for protecting the common by preventing the cutting of furze, turf or fuel and digging of stones, sand and gravel. All stock on the common were to be marked and their owners were to pay a fine if their animals were found straying or were not authorised to graze there. People were not allowed to turn their stock onto the common if they were not rated. The use of commons was increasingly regulated, with the parish drawing up 'A list of those that have asked Liberty to cutt Turves in the Marshey Places in Kilmington Common for the year 1790'.[139] Yet this well precedes parliamentary enclosure in Kilmington and as late as 1830 illegal cottagers were still being removed from the common. At the end of the eighteenth century commentators still remarked on the extent of commons still visible in Devon.[140] Polwhele in 1793 observed large tracts of unenclosed ground in the north and south parts of the parish of Colyton but the remaining common was enclosed in 1796.[141] Meetings were held at large farms to divide small commons and define boundaries. In 1806 the commons at Lovehayne and Buddlehayes, the farms leased out by the feoffees, were enclosed. However, as has been made evident, such common land was for the use of manorial tenants rather than for the landless and poor. Moreover in the seventeenth century it is evident that the purchase of a cow plus the cost of the highly valued pasture in the parish would amount to an outlay of more than £5 which was a level well beyond the means of the poorest and certainly not an economical prospect when measured against the earnings of an ordinary lace-making woman.

Mary Bradforde was one manorial tenant whose rare surviving inventory, dating from 1674, allows us a glimpse at the family economy of one of those who had common rights on the saltings to the south of Colyton.[142] Bradforde lived in Colyton but was a tenant of the Erle family of Axmouth for two lives and her land was situated in that parish. Her land had a yearly rental value of £15 per annum and she also had pasturings for sixty-five sheep. Bradforde or someone in her family seems to have had an interest in pewter manufacture. Perhaps as a result, her inventory is much richer in household goods than that of John Strowbridge made a hundred years earlier, even though Strowbridge farmed on a much more extensive scale. Bradforde had far more kitchen ware: brass pots, a kettle, skillets, pots, ladles and candlesticks which would have been made and supplied locally. This is one indication that the lower ranks of Colyton's population survived the increased population pressure, combined with the predatory advances of the larger farmers, by intensifying the dairy/weaving small farm economy. An inventory of widow Alys Markhill's possessions in 1620 shows she had only 8 acres but also '1 mylkehouse with chamber', '1 house called the Bakehouse' and '1 house called the weaving house'.[143] This response was similar to the intensive production which has been described for the Forest of Arden parishes in the early seventeenth century.[144] Westcote described the situation in 1630: 'The meanest sort of people will now rather place their children to some of the mechanical trades than to husbandry (esteemed more painful) whereby husbandry—labourers are more scarce and hirelings more dear than in former times'.[145] Intense production needed a local consumer market and inventories such as Mary Bradforde's suggest that this may have developed among not only the yeomen farmers but also the better-off cottagers. Thus does Colyton appear to distill the essence of de Vries's formulation of the 'industrious revolution'.

From a scattered array of evidence we can gain some insight into the diverse economies of the small-scale producers. The survey of the manor of Colyton carried out in 1696 shows many orchards scattered around the town.[146] Some of the soil is marked as 'good pasturage', elsewhere as 'thin, hungry clay', and in other parts as 'full of flinty down stones now turned for barley'. Small cottages are dotted around the town in closes encircled by hedges. These were the houses of labourers and craftsmen. Nearby were small areas of woodland marked 'cops for kitchen fuel'. Honey was another small industry. Edward Pratt kept bees at Whitwell in the 1650s.[147] This whole area had excellent potential for vegetable production. Dean Milles recorded that in Ottery St Mary a great many families found a living by propagating vegetables fit for the table such as cabbage, carrots, turnips and potatoes to supply the neighbouring markets and countryside. Branscombe had ledges formed from cliff slips, used as frost-free vegetable plots, particularly for potatoes.[148] A 1629 quarter sessions case involved a Northleigh man who was so very hungry that he entered a garden in Offwell because the cabbages there were very good. He not only stole cabbages but also took hens, a furze faggot and leeks which he later claimed he bought in Honiton market.[149] Some idea of the diversity of the local economy can be obtained from the material on tithe collection in Ottery.[150] In 1672 they were collected in hops, hemp, flax, grass, milk, heifers, cider, cows, honey, wax, roots, cabbages and wool. Further tithe details given for 1691 mention 'Carrotts, Cabbage, Parsnips and Plants each pr Acre', and 'Turnips pr Acre paid at Easter'. Added to this were payments for 'calves, [dove] cotts, lambs, broad geese, furrowing sowes, fleeces of wool etc'. In Colyton in 1676 there were different customs in distinct tithings but tithes were made up of wool, lamb, calves, milk, eggs, geese, hen's eggs, hops, honey, wax, coppice woods, apples, pears, herbage, butter and cheese.[151] The accounts of the upper gentry Willoughby family of Leyhill for the mid-1640s show that they purchased many provisions in local markets. For example, they made a payment 'unto John Clarke for a salmon and bringing it from Seaton' and purchased garden seeds including cucumber, carrot, mustard, and turnips, as well as cabbage plants.[152]

Even if commons were not always available, people might lease the produce of land from farmers. Richard Weekes, an Axmouth husbandman, said in 1624 that two of his children had leased certain barley in the ground of one Thomas Seaward of Axmouth, with whom Weekes was working at the time.[153] Leasing a crop, but not the land, was still common in the early nineteenth century. The settlement examination of John Spurway of Shute in 1827 showed that he rented a cottage 'and has also rented about a quarter and a half of quarter of an acre of potatoes at 3 pounds together and no more'.[154] A Dunsford settlement examination of 1838 explained that Martha Hill was dismissed from her apprenticeship in 1828, and then returned home, 'Sometimes assisting her father about cattle and other work . . . at other times helping her mother in the household department and digging her Father's (and her Master's) Potatoes'.[155] Even more common than leasing was the system of dairy letting which Bettey shows evolved in the seventeenth century.[156] The farmer provided the cows, pasture, winter fodder, house and dairy, and the dairyman made his profit from the sale of milk, butter and cheese. Marshall mentioned that the farmer would also allow the dairyman to keep as many pigs and poultry as he wished, and a mare to carry out the butter etc.; the mare, by producing a foal yearly, was considered a further material advantage to the dairyman, who might sell the foal once weaned, for £8–10.[157] The arrangement was for a year only and the dairyman could then be given notice. Marshall commented: 'The dairies in general are managed by making all the cream into butter, and from the skimmed milk, an inferior sort of cheese'.[158] Average annual payments for cows in the late seventeenth century were £2 14s a year; in the early eighteenth century they were £3 per cow, rising sharply in the course of the eighteenth century to £6 per cow in 1793 and up to £8 in very fertile parishes like Broadwindsor where the Pinneys farmed. The fixed price for each cow reflected the quality of the land and the anticipated produce of the beast.[159] Bettey suggests it is possible that the system of dairy letting evolved when rising wealth meant farmers' wives withdrew from this intensive labour.[160] Larger farmers perhaps concentrated on corn and sheep and were reluctant to be involved in day-to-day dairy management. The problems of dairy storage and marketing may have also resulted in farmers renting out dairies. But the practice of dairy letting was not confined to large farmers; the evidence from quarter sessions shows small farmers also letting out dairies in the last quarter of the seventeenth century, perhaps to overcome life-cycle problems of supplying the labour to manage such an enterprise.

Most evidence of individuals who rented dairies comes from poor law settlement papers since a question mark usually hung over the issue of whether renting a dairy qualified a person for a parish settlement. In a case of 1793, for example, Joel Bagwill, an Offwell labourer, had both rented a house and dairy of three cows and moved to another house in Widworthy 'which he had with the cows as a tenant to Mrs Marwood'. Thus as well as renting three cows he had 'a Cow of his own which he pd six pence a week to Mrs Marwood for keeping during the time he had the dairy & one shilling a week since he left the Dairy'.[161] William Baker of Widworthy gave the testimony that he had married in 1807, having been a parish apprentice and a yearly servant. Two years later he rented a dwelling house, land and a dairy of six cows at a yearly rent of £60, which he occupied for twelve years.[162] The most common system was for labourers to rent a dairy directly after marriage. James and Hannah Tucker said in a settlement examination that from 1813 through to 1822 they leased a tenement situated in Colyton which consisted of eight pasture-fed milking cows.[163] The 1822 case of labourer Richard Harries also shows that dairies could be rented over a wide area within this region. His first rental was for two years in Combe Raleigh with six cows at £10 each, the second was for two years in Membury with twelve cows at £10 10s each, and the third for a year in Chardstock with ten cows at £10 10s each.[164] Polwhele stated in 1797 that 'Colyton is a good dairy parish; remarkable for its rich butter and its skim-milk cheeses' and these must have to a large extent been the produce of these let dairies, very often run by the wives of labourers who worked on the larger farms.[165] Vancouver in 1813 thought that in the south-west a cow would produce 140lb of cheese and 20lb of butter a year. One person could make approximately one cheese a day.[166]

The wood-pasture economy presented a diverse set of possibilities for the cottager but access to commons was constrained from the early seventeenth century. Smallholders became specialists, especially in dairying. But increasingly they had not only to sell their produce but also their labour. Yeoman farmers employed labour of three types: servants, apprentices and day workers. Servants and apprentices are considered in the final chapter of this book. Demographic conditions would lead us to expect that day workers might be a more important group before 1650 and after 1750. The only evidence has to be pieced together from assorted court cases which cannot be expected to provide a reliable assessment of numbers of certain types of worker, but it is the case that there are fewer cases describing waged labour in the 1650–1750 period. It is evident that in the 1630s both women and men were involved in hay-making in Colyton.[167] Colepresse in 1677 said that for harrowing 'the labour as proportionate to women as men in our country' and for reaping 'Four men or women may reape an acre per diem and one more will binde, and shocke after them'.[168] A 1684 ecclesiastical court case makes evident the work of Elizabeth Mitchell, who had been taken on as a farm apprentice when she was about 10.[169] She was then 'able to Milck the Cows, make beds, attend ye Children, or any other ordinary worke about the house' all along employed 'in some service [or] other such as her Age and strength was capable to performe . . . as shee increased in Age so likewise incrased in capassity of doeing more and more service'; 'when shee first came there and was then able to doe but little service but as she grew older shee was capable of doeing more, as Milking, or any ordinary indoore worke'.

A case from 1640 involving stolen corn makes evident the nature of day labour. William Roost, a Shute husbandman, left his house on a Saturday morning 'about a quarter of an hour before sunrising and went immediately to the worke of one William Wyett, with whom this examinent then wrought'.[170] When his wife Thomasine was questioned she made it clear that he did not have a regular employer. She said her husband 'rose a little after day light and went to worke, but where she remembereth not'. Evidently, day labourers sometimes had to go further afield than local farms. In 1645 John Courtier of Bere Ferris, husbandman, 'had bin all the weeke abroade at work'.[171] But the more usual experience was likely to be typified by the case of Thomas Blackmoore alias Hill, a Widworthy husbandman suspected of consuming a stolen sheep. His day work was 2 miles away in the parish of Offwell. Another husbandman went to his house 'to call hym to come to worke haveing formerly promised hym for that daye'.[172]

Men's labour was perhaps less used in the summer months because they were employed on their own holdings.[173] Alun Howkins's analysis of the nineteenth-century records of Whitwell Farm shows that this small farm borrowed workers from larger farms at threshing and harvest. Smaller farmers worked for larger farmers at busy times of year and incurred debts were repaid in seed, cheese and cider.[174] By the second half of the eighteenth century there is still much evidence of women's work on farms. The farm account of George Harris of Colyton in 1782 showed that his farmhouse had a 'maiden's chamber' with two beds in it.[175] Girls taken on for the year were described as 'covenant servants' in this area. The settlement case of Elizabeth Froom reveals biographical details which showed that her work had changed little from when Colepresse was writing, bearing out the points made by the anthropologist Mary Bouquet that lifeleasehold stultified technological advance in the long run. Froom was bound apprentice when she was 7 years old in 1786 and she went to live in Taddickshayes in Southleigh.[176] She lived there until she was 12 years of age, then lived with Mr White at Balshayne in Colyton for a year, and then moved with Mr White to Northleigh for three years. She left when she had a child with William Clark who worked on farms and as a carpenter in Northleigh, Southleigh and Colyton parishes. She recalled that agreements over work were made with her employer in the kitchen. She suffered cruel treatment on the farms she worked on. The farmer quarrelled with her over 'not dragging the ground properly and he had me in and said he would teach me the art of memory and gave me a good flogging'. This suggests she had to drag a heavy harrow whose iron teeth would have been pulled over ploughed land to break up clods, pulverise and stir soil, root up weeds or cover in seeds. Yet even using a wide sample of settlement examinations for the region, it is rare to find other references to female agricultural work.[177] There are some women who we might expect to take farm labouring work if it were available but perhaps did not have the skills necessary for the dairy. Anne Gold, a spinster, who is mentioned in a Membury settlement examination of 1750, said 'she hathe been out of service about a year and a half and sometimes goes to washing and other Household work for her support and of late she has been in no employment and is now reduced to want'.[178] By the 1831 census there were 130 labourers employed in agriculture in Colyton. Fifty occupiers employed labourers, twenty-seven did not. There were twenty-three yearly male servants and eighty-eight female servants.[179] Analysis of the length of farm jobs from the settlement certificate sample shows that this shortened over time. Many agricultural labourers had a peripatetic existence. Reuben Radford of Colyton is a typical example. He was apprenticed at Tiverton 'until he was 22 or 23 years of age, then he left Tiverton and went about the country, sometimes working as a flaxdresser, and at other times as a common labourer for four or five years'.[180]

Some analysis can be made of labour on farms in this area from the day labourers book for Shute Barton in 1791–4.[181] Shute was the neighbouring parish to Colyton and this estate, which was owned by the Pole family, employed workers from Colyton (see Plate 7 p. 215). Oats and wheat were the main crops, but timber management, fishing and attending the hounds also feature as significant jobs. Women earned 6d per day for field work and men generally received 7s a week. Women were employed mainly in hay-making, weeding, harvesting in the fields and gathering fruit. One woman ran the dairy, which was probably just for household consumption. This was all-year-round work. The season within which women worked now lasted most of the year: weeding started in March, cultivation of the potatoes and plantations took the work into November, turnips were singled in mid-winter. For example, in January 1794 Martha Strowbridge was '6 days cleaning the Brickyard, putting, washing and cutting of Turnips 3s.'. The labour force was very stable and the same men were employed all year round. As would be expected of an arable farm, the number of women who were employed was much reduced. At hay-making time eleven women and twenty-nine men were employed. The few women who did work on the Shute Barton estate could be linked to the reconstitution of Shute.[182] The women were all single and mainly aged in their early twenties. They were daughters or siblings of the male workers on the estate. Interestingly, there is no record of any of them ever marrying and most of them had had illegitimate children, or went on to have them in the future.[183] By the time of the 1843 Parliamentary Report on Women in Agriculture in Devon, women only seem to have worked all year round in dairying when they were single and lived as yearly servants. Field workers were normally married. They were involved in hay-making, hoeing, and turnip and potato cultivation. They were apparently still paid half the wages of men.[184]

Keith Snell's research into wage levels in Dorset and Devon indicated that female wages rose over time, reaching almost three times their 1730 level in the 1830s. Male wages also rose slightly over time but not by nearly the magnitude of female wages. The result was that male and female wages stood at similar levels by the 1800s.[185] Contrary to this pattern, men's and women's wages were at very different levels in Colyton after 1750. The mean average of all male wages after 1800 stands at £215 7s 0d, which is double that of females which stands at

£109 7s 0d. It is, of course, extremely difficult to compare day and weekly wages, which show a high degree of variability, with those of farm servants which generally contained a large element of 'in kind' payment and included the servants' board and lodging and sometimes the provision of clothes as well. Vancouver's *Devonshire* describes the packages given to labourers in the early 1800s.[186] Wages were 7s per week in winter and summer, 'and from a quart to three pints of drink daily; even in hay-time and harvest, these wages are not increased, although the additional exertions at those seasons are not amply compensated by board, and very extraordinary drinks and sittings over ale and cider. To these wages must be added the standing supply of bread-corn; of wheat at 6s and barley at 3s per bushel.'

It is extremely difficult to compare either wages or conditions of farm work across wide areas of the countryside with those on specific farms and in particular localities. The larger point to emerge from a study of wages and of farm labour is that the labour market within the Colyton area was largely controlled by yeoman farmers in the eighteenth century, and to an extent a similar situation applied before that in a countryside dominated by small squires. The fact that there was a large class of day labourers from the earliest records also mitigates against placing too much emphasis on the universal independence of the livelihood in this wood-pasture locality.

Farming in the Late Eighteenth Century

The capitalist farms of the Colyton district proved adaptable to changing economic circumstances. When grain prices began to rise in Exeter in the late 1780s, as shown in Table 4.2, more men were required on farms for the harvests.

Table 4.2 Wheat prices at Exeter 1730–1819

Cohort	Decennial averages of shillings per quarter
1730–9	30.0
1740–9	33.2
1750–9	39.0
1760–9	42.5
1770–9	49.5
1780–9	53.3
1790–9	70.5
1800–9	90.2
1810–9	110.8

Source: Adapted from Mitchell and Deane 1962: 484–487.

Plate 6. Contemporary view of the town centre of Colyton.
(D. Sharpe)

The number of labourers mentioned in settlement examinations reflect the new male-orientation in agricultural work. At the same time farm sizes were increasing and lands consolidated. More land was owned by outsiders to the town. During the French Wars many of the larger farmers took over leases of smaller properties in the Colyton area.[187] By the mid-1800s tithes were paid in oats, wheat and pease instead of the former apples and hay.[188]

From the 1780s, settlement examinations mention that men returned to Colyton at reaping time. Vancouver, in 1808, described the agriculture in Colyton as mixed, with wheat, barley and turnips being grown. He commented, 'The dry stratum is always prefered . . . whether for winter and spring corn, and the grass grounds, which are generally very good, are employed for the purpose of feeding dairy cows'.[189] Fairly large quantities of hops were also grown on some farms in the Colyton area in the late eighteenth century.[190] Polwhele commented on the 'corn and pasture beautifully interwoven' and that 'The farms are small. The cultivation of them might admit of improvement. Very little of the land is kept in hand except small portions in the neighbourhood of the town: it is chiefly occupied by rack renters.'[191] Rackrents (equivalent to the annual market value of the land) indicate the influence of the landowners in Colyton since Arthur Young had commented on the low rents elsewhere in this area.[192] By the early nineteenth century landlords were introducing fourteen or twenty-one year leases at a rackrent equivalent to the full value of the land.

On his travels in the 1790s, the Reverend Swete remarked that the landscape of this area was a mixture of corn and pasture. The purpose of his tour was to search for the fashionable resort, and he noted the great contrasts between prosperous and poor villages. Dunkeswell's inhabitants, for example, betrayed a 'variety of wretchedness'. Colyford also seemed to him to be 'mean'.[193] Hoare's analysis of the 1797 Land Tax showed that 69.3 per cent of those taxed held between 1 and 9 acres.[194] The largest proportion of land was held by a few individuals, however. In the 1832 Land Tax, for example, £513 4s 7d was collected just from Sir W.J. Pole Bart. By the end of the eighteenth century the gap between wealthy and poor evident in the 1674 Hearth Tax had probably widened.

Soon after the Napoleonic Wars Colyton's farmers reverted to exploiting the region's natural advantage in pastoral production, but in 1822 the Lysons reported that Colyton's economy seemed to be depressed.[195] In 1826 the report of the commissioner concerning charities confirmed that the town's market had 'fallen off considerably . . . corn which used to be brought and pitched for sale has now entirely disappeared'.[196] The growth of smallholdings is evident when Colyton was losing prosperity and in economic terms could only reflect on its buoyant past.

By the late eighteenth century, Colyton was almost wholly reliant on the farming sector in economic terms because, as we have seen in Chapter 3, all industry was by this time in the doldrums. The change to a mainly grain-growing landscape, with fewer of the diversified farming pursuits of the late seventeenth century, also indicates a marked change. What was the connection with social relationships in the parish?

Agriculture and Social Polarisation

Historians have sought the characteristics of wood-pasture regions but Colyton is probably not atypical in containing a diversity of people, providing a complex situation where sometimes we hope for simplicity. Colyton had a diversity of inhabitants: traditional backwoods gentry, aggressive yeoman farmers, successful merchants eager to invest capital, determined small producers, struggling foragers who sought a livelihood amid precarious industrial production and along the by-lanes and forests of the parish, loyal task workers who were mainly employed by one of the farmers, and a few men who 'went to sea'. And there were various large landowners who placed their own stamp on the economy of the parish.

The seventeenth century might be seen as the height of improved farming in this part of Devon. This was the 'agricultural revolution' for yeomen in Colyton. Its counterpart was an intensive sort of production on the small farms of cottagers. In this era the three-life lease seems to have served as a sort of protection and imparted a particular kind of dynamism. But this was not sustained. At the end of the eighteenth century agricultural commentators Fraser, Marshall and Vancouver all noted that although potatoes and turnips had been introduced they were not properly part of rotations, ploughs and other implements were still primitive, and draining was little known. In the mid-nineteenth century, James Caird commented on the 'many cumbersome and unskillful practices' still employed in Devon.[197]

The existing picture of economic conditions in Colyton, which was put forward by David Levine, does not fit the facts. In terms of social structure, there is little evidence of a 'peasant' population in Colyton. Most of the land belonged to large farmers who farmed for the market and formed a yeoman elite in the parish throughout the 300-year period of this study. Cottagers were also commercially orientated and they evolved intensive farming methods to cope with the shrinking land availability. There was always a large group of labourers, craftsmen and domestic workers. Some of these were landless but others farmed small plots and let dairies as well as labouring for others, and it was on these groups that manorial and yeoman land improvement and consolidation had the most concerted impact. It can be established with some certainty that arable cultivation was important in Colyton before 1650 and in some decades after 1750. In the late seventeenth century cattle raising and dairying, especially cheese-making, as well as fruit-growing for cider production, were the pre-eminent types of agriculture. In the period of demographic stasis, from around 1630 to 1730 therefore, the types of agriculture which used a higher proportion of female labour were most common. There is no evidence of a simple Malthusian check to population growth in these years for there was no absolute land shortage in Colyton and no deficit of possibilities for exploiting the resources which did exist. But land was being distributed away from the poorer groups. Those who were industrial workers or craftsmen still aspired to landholding status and it seems reasonable to venture that there was a perception of land scarcity in the late seventeenth-century parish because archaic manorial structures meant that 'new wealth' bought land only on a piecemeal basis and could not establish consolidated farms as was the case on the rich saltings of Colyford Meadow. The eighteenth century saw the parish deindustrialising and the emphasis moved to a farming structure with sharp divisions between the landed and the landless. In both agricultural and industrial sectors, the parish seemed to have lost the dynamism that had been apparent in the late seventeenth century. The 'ruralisation' of the parish came about at the same time as the growing power and influence of Sir John William de la Pole and might be in part attributed to a growing aesthetic element within landownership. As has been found with other large landowners elsewhere in the country, as he purchased much new land and when he built the commanding new Shute House, de la Pole probably sought a view of rolling golden acres of wheat, not shambolic reminders of small-scale industrial production and impoverished shacks of small-scale producers.

Here I will briefly summarise the results of the economic survey of Colyton before we move to looking at the interrelationships between population change and local society in Colyton. A social division into property holders and the poor is evident in Colyton throughout the period in review but it increased with the rise in wool prices and the population increase of the latter part of the sixteenth century and beginning of the seventeenth century. Under the impetus of an anti-authoritarian attitude to politics and religion, this led to a buoyant economic situation in the late seventeenth century when, if ever, Colyton experienced agricultural and industrial revolution but growing poverty. However, there was a sharp change of character in the early eighteenth century. In the eighteenth century industry seemed to dwindle at around the same time as Dissent. There were few merchants in eighteenth-century Colyton and whereas other communities might have seen a transition to greater production in the course of the eighteenth century, the beautiful valleys of the Colyton area lost rather than gained industry. The result was an even starker division into rich and poor in the area. The connection with the balance of power in the parish can be further examined in Chapter 6, but first we must return to Colyton's demography.

Overview of Part Two

Part 2 has analysed the local economy of Colyton and the surrounding area. We have noted a small but thriving cloth industry, an important lace-making sector and many other areas of production such as leather. Even beyond the time period considered here, the 1887 Ordnance Survey map (Map 2, p. 6) conveys an impression of an industrious parish. There is both a tannery that is in use and a disused building, corn mills and saw mills and a foundry. There is a smithy at either end of town. Umborne Brook has paper mills and Rack Green indicates the previous position of cloth racks, while weirs and sluices show how the waterways have been put to economic use. Natural advantage meant that Colyton's land supported a diverse dairy industry that is now in itself only part of history as the last dairy farm ceased production during 2000. Proximity to the sea had given rise to merchant endeavours that underpinned the development of some of the larger farms. In the seventeenth century, with the expansion of the handicraft sector, partly as a Puritan project emanating from the religious intensity described in Chapter 2, Colyton was a far more commercialised parish than at the end of the nineteenth century. In both rural and urban parts of the parish there was an evident division of the population into two distinct 'classes'. The gentry farmers and the urban merchant-manufacturers were an important group in the early modern parish but there was also a significant underclass of landless workers, many of whom were migrants. Linking this picture to the demographic structure we may indeed postulate that access to economic opportunity would produce very different results for these groups. Social stratification became more intense during the relative deindustrialisation of the parish. While the reliability of the total reconstitution is questionable, therefore, it is still worth examining how demographic trends and family formation change with economic vicissitudes.

PART THREE
Population and Society

5

Demographic Experiences in a Devon parish

> Local populations are not miniatures of national populations, like them in everything but size, but fragments of a gigantic mosaic, in which each additional piece, at an early stage of research, may put the whole in new perspective.
>
> (T.C. Smith, *Nakahara*, 1977: 13)

The wheel is rapidly coming full circle in historical demography. While Colyton was the first English parish to be reconstituted, indicating several characteristics of English population change through time, the completion of a number of further reconstitutions means that the Colyton patterns can now be placed within the context of different economic and regional types of parish.[1] The analysis to follow also uses the total reconstitution to 'inject' class and gender analysis into the demographic results for Colyton with the aim of providing more nuanced results. This chapter will first examine migration into Colyton and its distinctive effect on the parish. I will then consider the evidence for marriage patterns in Colyton. The most outstanding feature of the original reconstitution of Colyton was the possible discovery of family limitation in the parish and this will be examined in detail. Finally, both infant, child and adult mortality will be analysed. This chapter will conclude with a speculative explanation for the patterns of demographic restraint that can be identified for the period from around 1630 to 1720. Further elements of reproductive behaviour in Colyton —prenuptial pregnancy, illegitimacy and marital separation—are examined in Chapter 7.

The Structure of the Population

In Colyton, as we have already seen, women were involved not only in dairying and the manufacture of butter and cheese, but also in lace-making, wool-spinning, fruit-gathering from the orchards, pulling flax, and a number of care and nursing jobs. The employment structure of Colyton, especially as the seventeenth century progressed, consisted of many 'female' jobs. However, instead of producing (as theorists of the family economy have believed) households that were enterprises worked jointly and complementarily by husband and wife,[2] the result was spatial and seasonal differentiation between men's and women's work, which complicated the process of family formation. The effect of the gender-specific nature of work on the structure of the population will be considered.

Skewed sex ratios or 'unbalanced populations' are a common feature of the demographic structure of developing societies.[3] While they have been studied in contemporary situations, they have been little explored in historical demography.[4] This is hardly surprising since it is impossible to measure sex ratios in the past with any degree of accuracy. Furthermore, it is important to establish that sex ratios at birth were reasonably normal and mortality chances of both sexes similar, before the sex ratio can be given much meaning as an indicator of migration trends. Since there is little reason to doubt the accuracy of the Colyton burial register it is possible to analyse the sex ratio at burial in the parish and the results are presented in Table 5.1. From the 1620s the sex ratio became distinctly skewed in Colyton. Whereas in the 1550s there were four men to every three women in the parish, by the 1650s there was a reversal of the situation with four women to every three men. Not until the late eighteenth century did the ratio near parity again. This trend is demonstrated in Figure 5.1. It is immediately obvious that the sex ratio transition occured at the same time that more social and economic differentiation became apparent in Colyton. The 1620s and 1630s saw a shift towards pastoral farming and the proletarianisation of cottagers. These decades also saw depression in the wool trade and the beginnings of mass-produced lace. We should also note the concurrence between the sex ratio patterns and the timing of the greater intensity of non-conformist belief in the parish.

How accurate a measure is the sex ratio of the actual circumstances pertaining in the parish? Infant mortality may distort the sex ratio at burial. However, in the case of Colyton, in the cohort 1650–99, male infant mortality rose to a peak of 135 per thousand live births, then fell again, whereas female infant mortality remained steadily around the 90 per thousand mark. So male deaths are, if anything, overstated in the sex ratio at burial over the critical period, while female deaths are not

Table 5.1 The sex ratio in Colyton 1550–1837 (men to women)

	Sex ratio at burial	Ratio excluding deaths under five years
1550–59	133.3	134.8
1560–69	115.9	106.1
1570–79	117.7	100.0
1580–89	113.6	105.6
1590–99	109.2	104.8
Cohort 1550–99	117.5	111.5
1600–09	98.7	87.7
1610–19	96.9	94.0
1620–29	78.4	77.5
1630–39	78.3	68.2
1640–49	86.7	85.7
Cohort 1600–49	86.1	81.3
1650–59	69.8	59.5
1660–69	87.4	87.0
1670–79	84.0	81.1
1680–89	98.6	91.3
1690–99	71.2	60.6
Cohort 1650–99	81.8	75.5
1700–09	71.4	69.4
1710–19	63.6	58.7
1720–29	81.6	77.6
1730–39	77.0	75.7
1740–49	94.1	101.5
Cohort 1700–49	76.3	74.5
1750–59	66.7	60.7
1760–69	78.2	76.4
1770–79	70.4	60.2
1780–89	101.7	95.5
1790–99	81.5	80.4
Cohort 1750–99	79.5	74.0
1800–09	97.4	93.9
1810–19	90.2	87.3
1820–29	97.0	81.1
1830–37	75.4	78.6
Cohort 1800–37	89.5	85.1

artificially inflated. In the 1700–49 cohort, male infant mortality fell so that both male and female infant mortality were in the range of 85 to 100 deaths per thousand live births. In the second column of Table 5.1 the deaths of children under five years were excluded from the sex ratio at burial. The result shows an even more unbalanced population from the

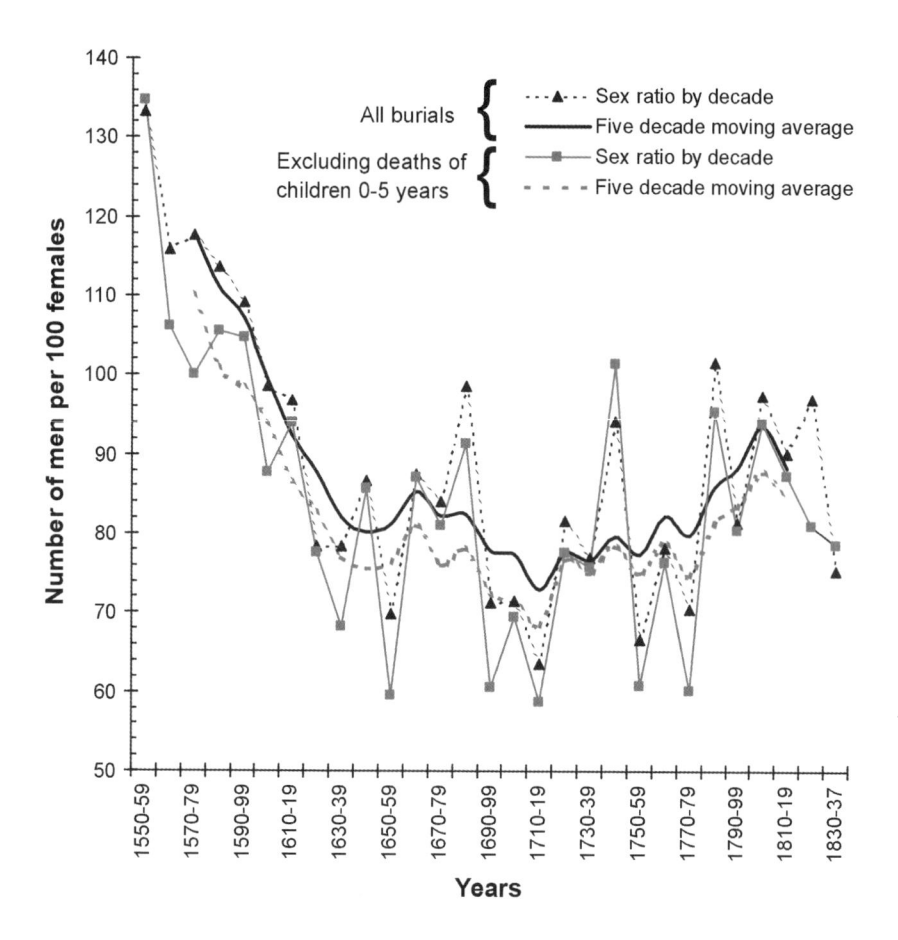

Fig. 5.1 Sex ratio at burial: Colyton 1538–1837.

early seventeenth century. Since corpses were often moved from place of residence to place of settlement, the sex ratio at burial figures may still understate the magnitude of outmigration. Furthermore, they disguise the typical 'servant in husbandry' type of local migration which was a life-cycle stage for many before marriage. Since the sex ratio is thought to reflect economic opportunity in a particular area, it is likely that the sex balance would be even more skewed for those in the marriageable age groups. As Weir remarked, 'if economic opportunities of men and women differed greatly between regions, then migration of the unmarried might have created distorted sex ratios'.[5]

These patterns suggest that while there were economic opportunities and perhaps also poor relief support for females in Colyton, from the 1620s conditions prompted outmigration of men.[6] Souden, in his analysis of migration trends in England based on ecclesiastical court records, found this pattern of migration to be a typical 'urban' one. He makes a distinction between cities and the more important towns 'which tended to have female dominated populations, and smaller, rural settlements which tended to be balanced or male-dominated'.[7] Colyton does not seem to fit well into the 'larger town' category and certainly the parish had an agricultural element. Souden found that women tended to move between towns from one domestic service opportunity to another, whereas men stayed in the countryside, particularly working on 'improved' farms, or moved longer distances to large cities, particularly London. In the case of Devon, movement to Exeter was especially common. Souden's research showed that in the 1660s Exeter proceeded against many 'strangers' who were living in the city and had taken up residence in the poorest parishes.[8]

During the same period in Colyton only women were proceeded against for being 'inmates'.[9] From the 1660s under the ambit of the new settlement law their certificates stipulated that they must return to their own parishes 'a single woman and unmarried'. Clearly the parish officials were concerned about the possibility of migrants marrying and thereby gaining a legal settlement in the parish. The prevention of marriages of the poor has been found in many other English parishes.[10] In 1673 the vicar, churchwarden and two overseers from Seaton certified that 'Jane Beavis of our parish . . . is now resident in Colyton. We shall receive her at any time in the space of a year into our parish provideth that she keepeth herselfe single.'[11] Likewise, in 1682 Susannah Ford of Axmouth was bound an apprentice in Colyton but her native parish expected to take her back at the end of her apprenticeship or 'Whenever she shall become chargeable unto any of you pvided that she Returne Single & Unmarried in Testemony'. Other settlement certificates leave us in no doubt that work migration was the reason for most of these moves. In 1673 Mary Hore of Axmouth was 'willing for her better livelihood' to travel and live in Colyton. Two years later the sisters, Margaret and Joane Smith of Widworthy were 'willing for their better Imployment to Dwell and remaine' in Colyton. After 1700, and perhaps around the same time as the lace trade started to fall off, the same documents start to show the reverse trend, with more settlement certificates being issued by the parish to women moving out than moving in.

Souden describes the ratios in some local populations as 'extremely skewed' and argues that segregation of the young population could have diminished local marriage opportunities. The effect of the sex ratio on marriage chances can be examined with the aid of the Colyton reconstitution. The number of sons and daughters who survived to the age of 16 and then married in Colyton is shown in Table 5.2.

Table 5.2 Number and percentage of Colyton-born children to marry in the parish 1538–1799

Cohort	Male			Female		
	No. 16+	No. marry	%	No. 16+	No. marry	%
1538–49	102	30	29.4	79	54	68.4
1550–99	755	212	28.1	720	202	28.1
1600–49	1181	222	18.8	1275	155	12.2
1650–99	740	166	22.4	713	70	9.8
1700–49	562	140	24.9	572	97	17.0
1750–99	706	158	22.4	726	151	20.8

This table suggests that the possible relationship between the sex ratio and the opportunity of marrying in Colyton was strongest before 1700. In the cohort 1650–99, for example, only 10 per cent of females born in Colyton who survived to the age of 16, subsequently married there. They had less than half of the chance of a Colyton male of marrying in the parish. This can be directly related to the fact that the sex ratio at burial indicates that there were frequently in excess of four women to every three men in Colyton. The sex ratio in fact became more adverse in the next cohort, but women's marriage chances seem to have improved as 17 per cent of them married in the parish. The relationship can only be tentatively established, therefore, and marriage chances were obviously affected by a variety of factors that could mitigate the effects of the sex ratio.

In Colyton the ratio became relatively more balanced between 1750 and 1799, probably due to more emphasis being placed on arable agriculture, which created male work opportunities. By the end of the eighteenth century women's local marriage chances seem to have equalled men's, but the sex ratio was still skewed in the early census. In the 1801 census, females outnumbered males by 119 in Colyton. Recruitment into the militia in the Napoleonic Wars could have contributed to this. Towards the mid-nineteenth century the sex balance disparity became smaller. Of course, the chances of a Colyton-born child marrying in the parish are affected by a number of factors and Table 5.2 is designed only to give a rough indication of the circumstances which were produced by the migration patterns underlying the sex ratio. The table includes sons and daughters who can be linked from dummy FRFs. While this overcomes some of the shortfall in marriages that took place in Colyton church in the 1650–99 and 1700–49 cohorts by adding the marryers who probably married in a nonconformist setting in Colyton, it tends to emphasise male marriages since it is possible to link more dummy male marryers to baptisms than female marryers because children's baptisms always give the father's name but not necessarily the mother's name. The good chances of a son marrying in Colyton would then be 'artificially' exaggerated. If the numbers of males are 'inflated' in this table compared to women who may have married in Colyton but cannot be linked, this may offset the effect of brides marrying in their home parish who then went to live elsewhere. It has been assumed that it was traditional for couples from different parishes to marry in the bride's parish. If this were the case, all things being equal, more females who were born in Colyton could be expected to marry there than males born in Colyton. But aside from this table, when the original 'core' reconstitution alone is considered without the extra 'dummy' men, this effect is only noticeable in the cohorts of 1550–99 and 1600–49 when fifty-three and forty-nine more females than males married in Colyton. In the 1650–99 cohort seven more males than females married in Colyton and in 1700–49 sixteen more did so. In general, marriage place seems to have preceded residence in Colyton and reflects practicality rather than the tradition of marrying in the bride's parish. If a Colyton daughter married a person in the church of another parish she was likely to move to live in that parish.

Of course, the low sex ratio in Colyton cannot be considered in isolation as it is possible that the shortage of men in the parish was offset by the burial of more men in neighbouring parishes. The sex ratio at burial of ten neighbouring parishes with reasonably reliable burial registers is shown for the later seventeenth century in Table 5.3. These are all rural or seaside parishes with the exception of Ottery St Mary, which was a medium-sized town. The results are arranged according to proximity to Colyton and confirm that the whole district had a low sex ratio, with the regional ratio being 90.7, or 86.6 if Ottery is excluded.

Coupled with the lack of marriage partners in the Colyton area for women, the sex ratio affected their marriage ages. It seems likely that women would marry later or not marry at all if there were an excess of women of marriageable ages in the community. The opposite situation applied to men, who were presented with a wide choice of marriage partners. The higher marriage age for women than men in the second half of the seventeenth century appears to be, at least in part, a function of the availability of women in the marriage market rather than a conscious attempt at family limitation.[12] A distinctive marriage pattern of younger men and older women is evident in the post-1630 period.[13] John Scarr married Johane Seward in 1663. He was 27 and she was 39. They had no children. In these cases one child was fairly typical as the women neared menopause when they married. The availability of wives along with the earlier age of first marriage for males made remarriage a possibility for widowers. Many men entered their second or third marriage with a

Table 5.3 Sex ratio at burial in Devon parishes 1650–1699

	1650–9	1660–9	1670–9	1680–9	1690–9	1650–99	No.
Colyton	69.8	87.4	84.0	98.6	71.2	81.8	2,222
Axmouth	117.1	78.0	78.4	132.3	53.6	86.6	405
Farway	82.5	87.5	94.4	160.8*	89.3*	98.2	331
Musbury	118.2	65.6	88.5	86.4	79.3	85.3	402
Seaton and Beer	–	97.1*	85.7	75.0	75.7	80.8	537
Shute	75.7	84.4*	62.2	88.7	144.2	85.6	529
Branscombe	100.0	60.4	66.7	114.3	82.0	82.4	445
Offwell	122.2	82.9	72.5	125.8	109.8	100.6	349
Stockland	82.4	82.4	103.0	144.0	–	94.3	583
Membury	82.0	77.5	89.5	78.2	111.8	87.7	610
Ottery St Mary	100.8	101.7*	93.7	96.1	89.5	96.4	4,088
Total						90.7	10,501

Note: * denotes incomplete recording
Sources: DRO burial registers: Axmouth MF1–2; Farway MF2–4; Membury MF1–3; Musbury MF1–4; Offwell MF1–3; Seaton and Beer MF3–5; Shute MF1–5; Stockland MF1–2. Devon and Cornwall Record Society, *The register of Branscombe, 1539–1837* (1913); Devon and Cornwall Record Society, *The register of Ottery St Mary, 1601–1837* (1908–29).

young wife when they themselves were in their fifties and sixties. The result was that even poor men found themselves raising families when their labour input was diminishing. By contrast, only three widows are known to have ever married in Colyton in the 1650–99 cohort. The important conclusion here is that the sex ratio provides a partial explanation of the limitation of marriage in early modern Colyton.

So far I have emphasised work-related migration as underlying the sex ratio patterns and the wider context of local migration will be explored in more detail in the next section. However, some other factors have a bearing on the patterns that have emerged. The first point, evident from Part 1, is that nonconformism renders all registration dubious during the most interesting period. This also points us in another direction, away from stressing purely economic factors, because the networks of nonconformity described in Chapter 2 clearly have a bearing on the patterns that have emerged. Secondly, for some of the population who were born and died in Colyton and lived in the rural areas of the parish, the patterns could be more connected to land shortage than to the local lace industry and this would seem to be indicated by the number of Colyton women born in the parish who did not marry there. Finally, the history of Colyton in the seventeenth century is also a history of strife. As the petitions of maimed soldiers and the testimonies of 1685 illustrate, the absence of men from Colyton also reflects the Civil War, other military movements, and Monmouth's rebellion.

Migration 1620–1750

What migration patterns lay behind these sex ratio patterns, beyond the extra-local moves of the women who carried settlement certificates? Some characteristics of the parish of Colyton suggest that it may have been well integrated into migratory trends in the country as a whole. Colyton was an 'open' and diverse parish comprising several manors, which offered employment to incomers.[14] Although the settlement laws proscribed the long-term residence of the poor, Colyton offered a fluid society with people moving in and out of the parish. Leases indicate that the common land, moorland and forest areas of the parish became more densely settled as the population expanded before 1650. The land market meant that internal boundaries in the parish were not fixed and land was available for those who had the means to purchase it. The wool and lace trades were volatile, but in periods of expansion created opportunities for 'strangers' and may have relied on their presence to increase production.[15]

An undated (c.1590s) transcript of a petition from 'poor fishermen and other inhabitants' of Colyton, Colyford, Seaton, Axmouth, Beer, Branscombe, Salcombe [Regis] and Sidmouth to Lord Francis, Earl of Bedford (presumably as lord of the manor), complained that they only lived 'very poorly' and that 'there be two tenantes in moste pte of theire howses because the people do encrease verye mytche in all the countrye there', also suggesting the latitude of manorial control as regards migrants.[16] An entry from 1631 in the Farway Churchwarden's Memorandum Book considers who in the parish was to be the next churchwarden and notes those who have 'of late yeares come in dyvers dwellers wch have groundes to their tenements', which perhaps suggests land was being bought up by immigrants in small lots.[17] At the end of the century a similar situation prevailed. Gregory King in 1695 found that there were only 237 inhabited houses in Colyton, suggesting an average of 6.5 persons per house. It seems correct to assume that these houses were full of lodgers who were emigrating to Colyton at a rapid rate, while members of the native population were having relatively few children.[18]

Outbreaks of plague often precipitated emigration in England.[19] Warring armies, moves to impress men into the armies and the severe plague epidemic in 1647 hardly made Colyton a settled place in the mid-seventeenth century. The 1650s were the peak decade of the seventeenth century for emigration to the colonies from England as a whole, and the period through from 1630 to 1660 saw a large volume of movement to America.[20] Surprisingly then, Souden found a 'peak' of immobility in Colyton in the period 1630–60, while reporting the paradoxical result that a large number of women appear in the reconstitution who married and raised children in the parish but do not seem to have been baptised or buried there.[21] His finding of increasing 'closure' is based on male baptism/burial links in the reconstitution. Contrary to his conclusion, this shows mobility of the working age population and suggests that men who had been born there were being buried in Colyton, even though they had not raised a family there, and women who had lived in the parish were not buried there. This suggests that the actual sex ratio of the living population was even more drastically unbalanced than the ratio at burial results indicate.[22]

Many of the women who married and baptised children in Colyton must have been migrants to the parish. The overwhelming reason for these women moving to Colyton, often in their teens and early twenties, was to work in lace manufacture. In the later period of 1765–77, when it was normal for the wife's parish of origin to be given in the marriage register, more of them were born outside of Colyton than in it, even though by then domestic trades were in decline.[23] The earliest settlement certificates for Colyton confirm that while the economic position for men was not always secure in the seventeenth century, there were work incentives for women to move into the parish.[24] Out of a total of 123 cases, thirty-three were single adult women who moved to Colyton on their own, whereas only seventeen cases were single adult males. Twenty cases were male children and thirteen cases were female children who were to be apprenticed in Colyton. Forty cases consisted of groups of people. These were families, many of which were headed by a woman and sometimes seem to have had other, apparently unrelated women with them. An example is the certificate granted to the following group in 1667: 'Floorans Flood of the psh of Offwell in ye Countey of Devon, wid., and Dorothy Flood and Ann Flood her too childrn. And Darkis Fildey of the same psh and countey aforesd are gon to Inhabit in to the towne of Colliton since the acte'. One certificate issued by Colyton clearly indicates that in some cases female earnings were necessary to support a family in Colyton. John Barrett, a taylor, was leaving in 1675 due to 'his being a widd. and therefore not possibley to provide & attend his two naturall children viz. Elizabeth Barrett, Mary Barrett in such manner as they ought to be Provided for in their minority'.[25]

Direct references to people leaving Colyton are difficult to find. The concern of the feoffees and the parochial officials was with the people who remained in Colyton, who paid the poor rate, rented property, or had to be supported by the parish. The bailiff's accounts note that the feoffees gave Philip Wearington a contribution to help his passage to Ireland in 1670.[26] Migration to early America has traditionally been associated with the middling orders.[27] Galenson challenged this by arguing that the emigrants came from a broad cross-section of society. They were mostly male indentured servants who were aged between 15 and 25.[28] This fits the picture which can be inferred for Colyton, where, as we have seen in Chapter 2, migration was limited before the middle of the seventeenth century. Thereafter males who were not able to find jobs as yearly servants or day labourers on the large farms in the parish probably joined streams of migrants to the larger towns and cities and then went overseas. One example is William French from Colyford, who was bound apprentice on a vessel destined for America at Lyme Regis in 1683. He was 21 and came from a labouring family who had suffered life-cycle poverty.[29] The influence of apprenticeship to sea trades and recruitment into the army or navy must also be considered as factors in the migration of males, as many settlement certificates show that many men went overseas or to another part of the country and never came back. Throughout the eighteenth and nineteenth centuries settlement certificates refer to men spending a year or more working in Newfoundland.[30]

In the early 1660s the documentation suggests an upturn in concern about migration into east Devon parishes. Some of this was official, a result of the Settlement Act which coincided with a second wave of the expansion of lace due to protective legislation. The sheer extent of settlement documentation is indicative and suggests the heavy policing of migrancy by Colyton's feoffees. We have already seen that many women traded in this area and must have been drawn to towns like Colyton and Honiton by the business opportunities they presented. Gossip often centred on strangers and migrants and, under conditions where nonconformists were pursued, people's suspicions were further aroused. In 1663 Richard Cornish, an Ottery clothier riding from Exeter back to Ottery, was overtaken by two women on horseback, Frances Browne and Elizabeth Ffloyde.[31] As they came near to him they fell into a quarrel which went on from Heavitree gallows to Rockbeare. Ffloyde (Lloyd) hailed from Wales, and Browne said that when Ffloyde 'first came to Ottery she had not a bed to lie on'. In a reposte now familiar to us from other studies of ecclesiastical court records, Ffloyde asked Browne who told her so and accused her of being a whore. Ffloyde spoke in a 'very angry, . . . rayling, and raging manner, out of envy and passion'. Cornish stated that he was worth £100 and that Browne was giving him 5s to defray his charges. John Manly was another witness and recalled that the quarrel took place at Whitsuntide Fair. The argument had started with 'why Goody ffloyde you need not be so high for I remember when you came first into Ottery you had hardly a bed to ly on'. These opprobrious words were 'tending to the dimunition of the Credit and reputation' of this woman. Apparently, such defamation meant her business reputation was at stake. Interestingly, Ffloyde had been in the area for over ten years yet was still considered an incomer.

Migration patterns differed according to sex in this area of Devon. Some women like Elizabeth Ffloyde had moved fair distances but many women's movements, as reflected by settlement examinations, were extra-local. They moved from one village or small town in the Colyton area to another. The pattern was from smaller settlements and hamlets to the towns of Colyton, Honiton or Ottery St Mary. Within the parish of Colyton, if they were born in country tithings, they were likely to move into the town. Men seem to have moved longer distances. Before they married they could sometimes find hirings as yearly servants near to home or within a small radius of their native places. Some had to stray further afield. Marriage did not bring stability for agricultural workers. When work by the day or week followed marriage, employment was not necessarily steady, and there is evidence of men labouring in other parts of the country. The very skewed sex ratio in Colyton from the first decades of the seventeenth century reflects a labour force which was highly differentiated along the lines of gender. These patterns must also have applied to other parishes in the south-east Devon area, if not in an even larger region. A parish with a highly unbalanced population structure could not be an isolated case as a certain amount of local migration is always marriage-related and would cancel out sex ratio differences between neighbouring parishes. Nonconformity also brought forth its own particular patterns of local migration. Amid the factional differences in seventeenth-century Colyton people gravitated to certain preachers and particular congregations, which would have caused some movement between parishes and restricted the pool of choice and age of marital partners. As nonconformity attracted many women it seems highly probably that the sewing circles of lace-makers may have fostered the anti-authoritarian attitudes shared by their menfolk. Overall, it is no exaggeration to suggest that the experience of migration is one of the defining features of the demographic regime in Colyton.

Marriage and Status Differentiation

Since the Colyton population was widely differentiated on a status basis, the linkage data derived from the total reconstitution provides an ideal testing ground to assess how demographic factors varied with economic circumstances. The demographic variables of age at first marriage, propensity to remarriage, marital fertility, and infant and child mortality can be related to the socio-economic grouping of the population. This type of 'class' differentiation has rarely been carried out for historical populations. It is difficult to achieve without a series of censuses giving occupations.[32] Yet it is of essential value to most of the interpretations of historical population change which have so far been propounded. The central theory that marriage age and the real wage level vary in tandem, for example, suggests that the group in the population who relied directly on wages, the labourers, might be most affected by changing economic opportunities and have significantly varying ages at marriage through time. Taking into account factors such as the unbalanced sex ratio in Colyton means that celibacy should be incorporated with age at marriage patterns in explaining how population growth was held back before 1750. A possible 15 per cent of the English population never married in the seventeenth century.[33] Unfortunately reconstitutions do not lend themselves to systematic analysis of non-marryers and the status-specific analysis must be of those who did marry.

Goldstone argued that after 1750 fertility rose due to the emergence of a group of 'young marryers' who comprised roughly 20 per cent of the population. He thought this was due to the availability of steady employment for proletarianised workers which was provided by the Industrial Revolution.[34] But as we have seen, this chronological outline does not apply to Colyton marryers. Colyton industrialised in the seventeenth century, was bypassed by the classic Industrial Revolution, and was in fact deindustrialising in the late eighteenth century. Analysis of settlement examinations reveals that work was getting less steady and day work was increasingly normal for young men of marrying age. More applicable to the situation in Colyton is the argument that changes in the poor law made it more difficult for young single women to obtain relief at the turn of the nineteenth century, which could have forced them into early marriages.[35] However, as can be shown in the analysis which will be presented in later chapters, at least until 1770 the parish provided work for these unemployed women, and there may have been an expansion in opportunities for domestic servants. The status-specific analysis presented here allows a closer look at the marital behaviour of poor women separately from their employed counterparts.

Sex differences in marriage age in Colyton have already been researched. Whereas male marriage ages were relatively stable, women's were subject to change over time. In particular, women's marriage age was on average two years later in the second half of the seventeenth century than in the first half. By the early nineteenth century, the magnitude of fall of women's marriage ages was far greater than men's. Gender and status differences will be additionally considered with respect to remarriage in Colyton in this analysis. Status-specific changes in two other demographic aspects are also relevant because they are affected by the amount of gender-specific work in Colyton. The extent of women's work in Colyton might be thought to affect marital fertility and so birth spacing behaviour is analysed by status. Infant and child mortality may also be connected with women's work. Women are biologically responsible for reproduction by bearing children, but also historically responsible for social reproduction, which includes the caring and tending of infants. How far did the extent of women's work in Colyton affect patterns of child nurture and child raising? Marriage ages, remarriage opportunities and marital fertility patterns as well as infant and child survival are all considered by demographers to be partially controllable aspects of personal demography and important aspects of what Tony Wrigley has described as a 'fertility strategy'. The total reconstitution database provides an insight into the collective responses of several groups of individuals to prevailing circumstances brought about by gender and status. Other factors, such as large-scale mortality changes, require a societal response which is more readily examined by conventional historical methods of research.

This section aims to take the age at marriage analysis for Colyton a stage further, by dividing the population for whom age at marriage is known into socio-economic groups. The total reconstitution database provides the means to divide about half of the population into four categories according to wealth or occupation. The documentary basis for these groups and the method by which they were determined is given in the Appendix. There are a number of shortcomings to this method; in particular, it is impossible to quantify changes in the social structure over time, which means that the results are, at best, indicative estimates of what was happening in Colyton to certain groups at certain times. In the first place, there are the people for whom demographic information exists but no evidence with which to assign them to a status group. These 'unknowns', as was shown in Chapter 1, formed between 71 and 44 per cent of FRFs in the various cohorts. Due to the balance of documents available, the gentry, followed by the poor, and then craftspeople were the easiest groups to classify by status. Consequently, the results for 'unknowns' are presented in the following tables since they probably represent the demographic behaviour of the labourers and some craftspeople.

Secondly, there is the opposite problem of people for whom there is status information but no full recording of their demographic behaviour. This is a particular difficulty with the 'missing marryers' of the cohorts 1650–99 and 1700–49. As we have seen, most of these were members of a nonconformist sect who baptised but did not marry in the Anglican church. These marryers are recorded on 'dummy FRFs' with 'manufactured' marriage dates derived from their first child's baptism. An attempt has been made to use this additional data to extend the sample size and this will be considered after the original sample has been analysed. The results of the analysis of age of marriage by status are given in Tables 5.4 and 5.5. The most significant results are presented in Figure 5.2.[36]

Figure 5.2 shows the mean age at first marriage of men and women. These results accord with Wrigley and Schofield's results. They show

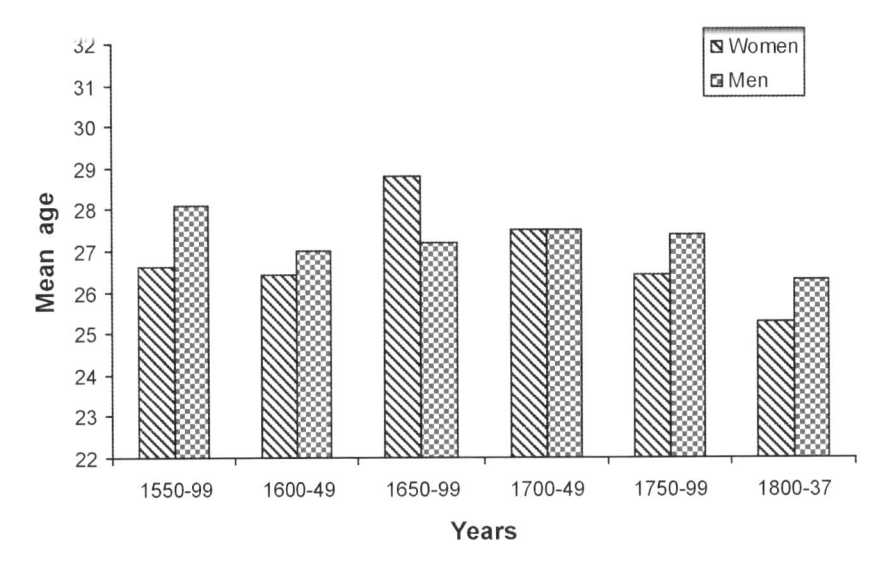

Fig. 5.2 Mean age of first marriage of women and men 1550–1837.

that mean age at marriage for women peaks at a far higher level than average age for men, affirming the result (which some scholars have found surprising) that a significant proportion of women must have married younger men.[37] Wrigley found that over the whole period 1647–1719 55 per cent of brides were older than their grooms whereas in 1800–37 only 29 per cent were. The extremes of average marriage age for women in Colyton stand at 30.7 in 1700–10 and 23.3 in 1825–37.[38] One explanation for the pattern lies with the sex ratio, since there was a shortage of men who were available to be marriage partners. Additionally, I have suggested that this may be a feature of marriage within small religious circles. The 'hump' in marriage ages certainly fits the sex ratio pattern until 1700. Thereafter, while the sex ratio remained 'feminine', female marriage ages were dropping and this trend continued into the nineteenth century. The association between age at marriage and the sex ratio, particularly before the eighteenth century, is the most significant result of this analysis. The trends for the 'whole group' are superimposed onto the Figures 5.3 and 5.4 to show the division into socio-economic or 'status' groups.

In Figure 5.3, which shows age at first marriage for women according to status group of FRF, the problem of a lack of cases for craftspeople and labourers is most evident. The results for the more complete gentry and poor group show that in every cohort poor women married on average a year or more later than their wealthier counterparts.[39] Nevertheless, the gentry group also show a 'hump' pattern in the 1650–1749

Table 5.4 Age of women at first marriage by status group of FRF 1550–1837

Cohort/group	No.	Mean	Standard deviation	Lower quartile	Median	Upper quartile	Trimean
1550–99							
Gentry	15	24.6	5.2	21.0	23.0	27.0	23.5
Crafts	11	25.4	5.0	22.0	23.0	29.0	24.3
Labourer	14	25.6	4.4	21.8	25.5	28.3	25.3
Poor	13	25.2	4.6	21.5	24.0	29.0	24.6
Unknown	68	27.7	6.3	23.0	27.0	30.5	26.9
Total	121	26.6	5.8	23.0	25.0	29.0	25.5
1600–49							
Gentry	32	24.1	3.6	22.0	24.0	27.0	24.3
Crafts	31	25.7	5.6	22.0	24.0	30.0	25.0
Labourer	18	24.2	4.4	21.0	24.0	26.3	23.8
Poor	47	26.5	5.0	23.0	26.0	29.0	26.0
Unknown	118	27.5	6.5	23.0	26.0	31.0	26.5
Total	246	26.4	5.8	22.0	25.0	30.0	25.5
1650–99							
Gentry	13	27.8	5.9	24.5	26.0	33.5	27.5
Crafts	5	–	–	–	–	–	–
Labourer	4	–	–	–	–	–	–
Poor	35	29.5	6.9	24.0	28.0	35.0	28.8
Unknown	45	28.6	6.8	24.0	28.0	34.0	28.4
Total	102	28.8	6.7	24.0	27.0	34.0	28.0
1700–49							
Gentry	12	28.4	8.2	23.0	26.5	34.3	27.6
Crafts	11	22.6	4.4	20.0	22.0	27.0	22.8
Labourer	3	–	–	–	–	–	–
Poor	28	28.6	6.3	23.5	28.5	33.8	28.6
Unknown	27	28.4	6.2	24.0	28.0	31.0	27.8
Total	81	27.5	6.7	23.0	26.0	31.5	26.6
1750–99							
Gentry	24	26.2	5.2	22.0	24.5	30.0	25.3
Crafts	40	26.8	7.5	21.3	25.0	29.8	25.3
Labourer	27	26.8	4.1	24.0	26.0	30.0	26.5
Poor	23	28.0	7.8	23.0	28.0	31.8	27.7
Unknown	50	25.2	5.7	20.0	24.5	29.0	24.5
Total	164	26.4	6.3	22.0	25.0	30.0	25.5
1800–37							
Gentry	14	26.4	5.2	21.8	25.5	29.5	25.6
Crafts	22	24.8	5.4	20.8	23.0	26.5	23.3
Labourer	11	24.4	5.0	19.0	23.0	27.0	23.0
Poor	4	–	–	–	–	–	–
Unknown	47	25.1	6.6	21.0	23.0	28.0	23.8
Total	98	25.3	6.1	21.0	23.0	28.0	23.8

Table 5.5 Age of men at first marriage by status group of FRF 1550–1837

Cohort/group	No.	Mean	Standard deviation	Lower quartile	Median	Upper quartile	Trimean
1550–99							
Gentry	16	29.6	6.6	25.3	28.5	32.0	28.6
Crafts	8	26.5	3.6	23.0	26.5	28.8	26.2
Labourer	13	28.5	5.5	25.0	28.0	30.0	27.8
Poor	5	–	–	–	–	–	–
Unknown	28	27.5	5.0	23.0	28.0	30.8	27.4
Total	70	28.1	5.5	24.0	28.0	31.0	27.8
1600–49							
Gentry	18	26.1	5.8	21.8	23.5	31.5	25.1
Crafts	31	26.6	5.6	23.0	25.0	30.0	25.8
Labourer	21	24.1	2.9	22.0	24.0	25.5	23.9
Poor	28	25.6	5.3	22.0	24.0	28.5	24.6
Unknown	82	28.2	7.1	27.0	23.0	30.5	26.9
Total	181	27.0	6.6	23.0	25.0	29.0	25.5
1650–99							
Gentry	10	28.0	6.4	22.8	27.0	33.8	27.6
Crafts	7	27.3	6.9	23.0	25.0	29.0	25.5
Labourer	5	–	–	–	–	–	–
Poor	20	26.4	4.9	22.3	25.0	30.3	25.6
Unknown	30	27.1	5.1	23.0	26.5	30.3	26.6
Total	72	27.2	5.7	23.0	25.5	30.8	26.2
1700–49							
Gentry	8	28.8	8.0	21.5	25.0	38.8	27.6
Crafts	9	27.3	5.9	23.5	25.0	31.0	26.1
Labourer	7	25.1	5.6	20.0	24.0	31.0	24.8
Poor	42	26.5	6.9	22.0	25.0	28.0	25.0
Unknown	25	30.6	8.3	25.5	30.0	33.0	29.6
Total	92	27.5	8.0	23.0	26.0	31.0	26.5
1750–99							
Gentry	21	27.1	5.2	22.0	27.0	31.0	26.8
Crafts	42	26.1	3.9	23.8	26.0	29.3	26.3
Labourer	27	27.3	6.3	22.0	25.0	32.0	26.0
Poor	19	27.1	5.6	22.0	27.0	30.0	26.8
Unknown	26	29.8	8.3	23.8	26.5	35.3	28.0
Total	135	27.4	6.0	23.0	27.0	32.0	27.3
1800–37							
Gentry	7	26.3	5.6	21.0	26.0	31.0	26.0
Crafts	18	25.2	6.3	20.8	23.0	29.0	23.9
Labourer	11	24.8	5.1	21.0	24.0	28.0	24.3
Poor	2	–	–	–	–	–	–
Unknown	16	28.0	6.5	23.5	27.0	29.8	26.8
Total	54	26.3	6.2	21.0	26.0	29.8	25.7

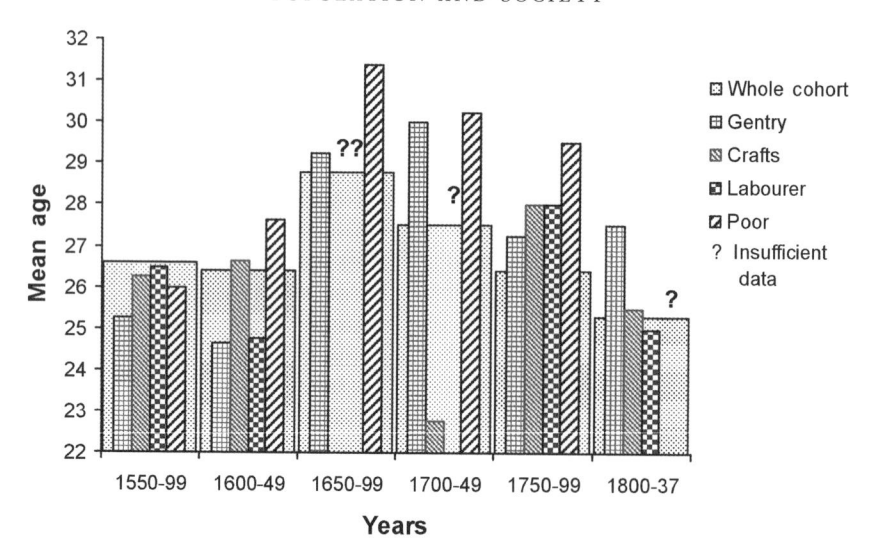

Fig. 5.3. Mean age at first marriage of women by status group of FRF 1550–1837.

period and the implication of this finding is that outmigration of men involved all social levels. Male marriage patterns as shown in Figure 5.4 indicate that, as might be expected for a group where inheritance of land was important (or accumulating the means to buy a farm), gentry marriage age was late.[40] This is a reverse of the pattern for gentry women. Poor men generally married much earlier than gentry men. Labourers may have married even earlier than them, but again the problem is obscured by lack of data. In Figures 5.3 and 5.4, the inclusion of the unknown status category also adds a number of people with older marriage ages. Some attempt to circumvent this of lack of information about the broad middle of the community can be made by adding the data derived from the dummy FRFs. As these mainly represent non-conformist marriages, an assumed marriage date calculated by subtracting nine months from the baptism of the first child on the dummy FRFs would be fairly accurate in a large proportion of instances. So it is possible to incorporate these new cases into age at marriage data, where the baptism date of the spouses can also be established. Since dummy FRFs constituted between a quarter and a third of all FRFs in the 1650–1749 period, this addition is potentially very significant. Without these cases, which were generally craftspeople or labourers, the demographic analysis by status reflects only the top and bottom of Colyton society.

Since the marriage date which has been pencilled in to the dummy FRFs is assumed to be reasonably accurate, the data for 'all men' and 'all

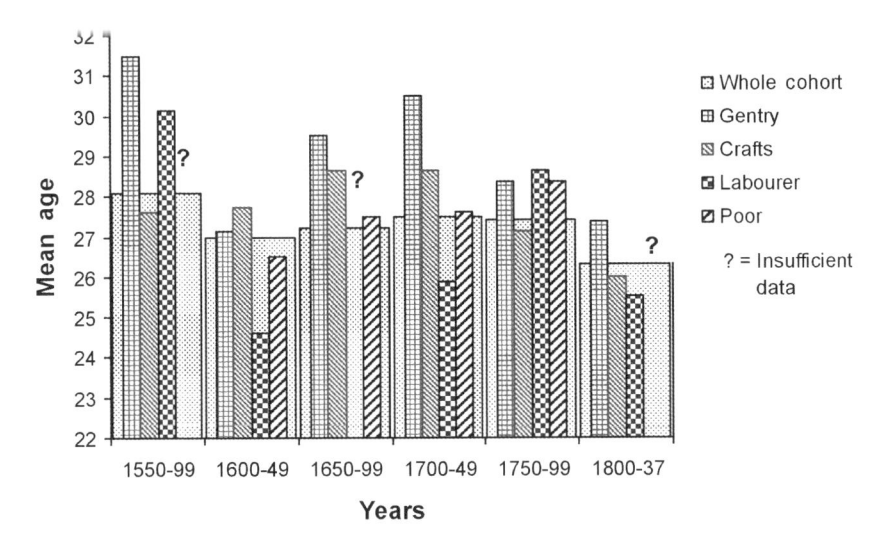

Fig. 5.4 Mean age at first marriage of men by status group of FRF 1550–1837.

women' has been incorporated into the analysis. It is important to note that 'all men' and 'all women' have been cohorted by baptism date, rather than marriage date, in the tables which follow. One advantage of the incorporation of this data is that they add an extra early cohort as the marriages of sons and daughters who were baptised in the first years covered by the reconstitution are included. It is not possible to make an assessment of the marriage age of those cohorted on marriage date in this cohort because the result would represent a truncated sample biased by early marryers. The inclusion of these 'dummy marryers' contibutes most to the male marriage figures, however, since it is much easier to link males to their own baptism than females, because their names were always given when their children were baptised. How does the age at marriage calculated for these extra 'dummy marryers' compare with the ages analysed for men? This is considered in Table 5.6.

The ages of the dummy marrying men are so near to the ages for the men who married in church that they can be used with confidence to extend the sample size by looking at 'all men'. Unfortunately, while the results for women have been included for the sake of balance, they add few cases to the analysis.

Only in 34 per cent of dummy marriages in the period 1630–1700 was any indication given of wife's name at all. In this minority sample, the woman's first name could be established from either a child's baptism or from another document which was used in the total reconstitution. If the dummy marriages took place in Colyton, but are not recorded there, there is reason to believe that a number of the women would be

Table 5.6 Calculated ages at marriage for dummy marryers compared with men marrying at Colyton church 1550–1837

Cohort	Dummy marryers			Church marryers		
	No.	Mean	Std Dev.	No.	Mean	Std Dev.
1550–99	30	29.0	6.2	70	28.1	5.5
1600–49	132	26.9	5.8	181	27.0	6.6
1650–99	134	27.5	5.8	72	27.2	5.7
1700–49	76	27.5	6.1	92	27.5	8.0
1750–99	44	27.4	5.3	135	27.4	6.0
1800–37	29	25.8	4.6	54	26.3	6.2

Colyton-born. Since these cases could not be incorporated into the full analysis of marriage age, a separate attempt was made to discover their age at marriage. Of these named female missing marryers, a sample of seventeen with unusual first names was chosen. Examples of these names are Dorcas, Bashaba, Urith and Tephany. Eleven of the seventeen cases could be linked back to a baptism in Colyton. This produced a range of marriage ages from 21.9 years to 38.2 years. The mean age was 28.7 years, however, which is similar to the mean of 28.8 for women marrying in Colyton church in this cohort. This test indicates that as far as can be proven, the excluded women's marital behaviour did not differ

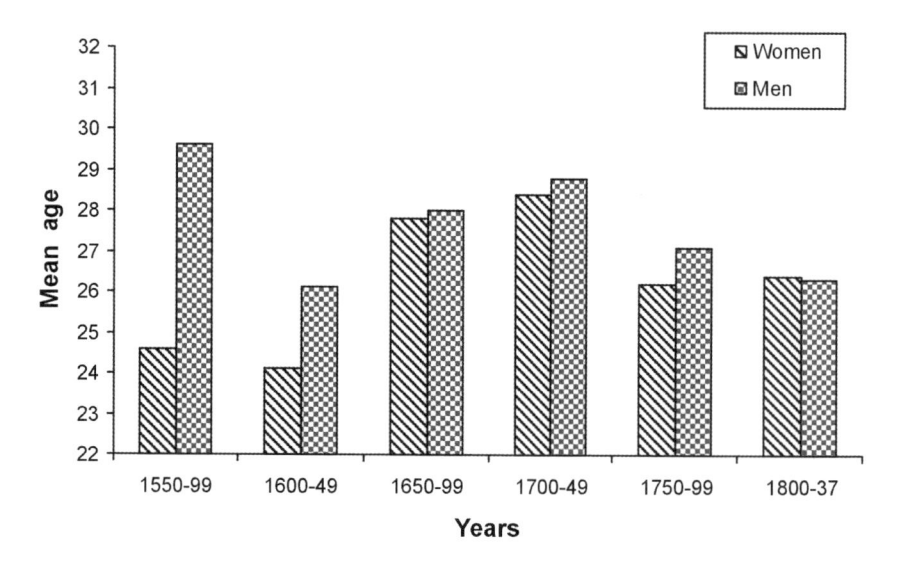

Fig. 5.5 Mean age at first marriage of 'all women' and 'all men' 1550–1837.

Table 5.7 Age of 'all women' at first marriage by status group of FRF 1538–1799

Cohort/group	No.	Mean	Standard deviation	Lower quartile	Median	Upper quartile	Trimean
1538–49							
Gentry	26	27.6	6.2	23.0	25.5	29.3	25.8
Crafts	10	28.2	8.4	22.8	23.0	32.8	25.4
Labourer	7	28.7	4.5	27.0	29.0	31.0	27.0
Poor	0	–	–	–	–	–	–
Unknown	11	30.3	5.6	25.0	29.0	35.0	29.5
Total	54	28.2	6.4	23.0	27.5	31.0	27.3
1550–99							
Gentry	27	25.1	4.4	23.0	24.0	28.0	24.8
Crafts	36	24.6	4.1	22.0	23.5	27.0	24.0
Labourer	29	28.4	6.2	23.0	27.0	31.0	27.0
Poor	25	29.5	6.2	25.0	29.0	33.0	29.0
Unknown	86	28.0	6.5	23.0	27.0	31.3	27.1
Total	203	27.3	6.0	23.0	26.0	31.0	26.5
1600–49							
Gentry	32	26.4	6.4	23.0	26.5	28.8	26.2
Crafts	25	27.1	6.8	21.5	25.0	30.5	25.5
Labourer	17	27.8	7.5	21.5	26.0	36.0	27.4
Poor	27	27.9	6.1	23.0	27.0	30.0	26.8
Unknown	57	29.2	6.9	23.0	27.0	34.3	27.8
Total	158	27.9	6.8	23.0	26.0	33.3	27.1
1650–99							
Gentry	10	26.5	6.9	21.3	25.5	28.3	25.3
Crafts	2	–	–	–	–	–	–
Labourer	4	–	–	–	–	–	–
Poor	22	28.4	4.9	24.0	27.0	30.5	27.1
Unknown	57	29.2	6.9	24.5	27.0	35.0	28.4
Total	95	28.7	6.5	24.0	27.0	34.0	28.0
1700–49							
Gentry	13	24.8	4.8	20.0	26.0	29.5	25.4
Crafts	22	24.0	4.7	22.0	23.0	25.3	23.3
Labourer	7	27.4	7.3	23.0	24.0	31.0	25.5
Poor	26	29.7	5.4	26.0	29.0	32.0	29.0
Unknown	31	28.3	5.8	25.0	25.0	31.0	26.5
Total	99	27.2	5.9	23.0	26.0	31.0	26.5
1750–99							
Gentry	28	24.4	3.9	21.3	23.0	27.8	23.8
Crafts	33	26.0	4.8	22.5	26.0	29.0	25.9
Labourer	24	26.3	4.9	23.0	25.0	28.8	25.4
Poor	26	25.8	6.0	21.8	25.0	29.0	25.2
Unknown	29	24.7	6.2	19.5	24.0	28.0	23.9
Total	140	25.4	5.3	22.0	25.0	28.3	25.1

Table 5.8 Age of 'all men at first marriage by status group of FRF 1538–1799

Cohort/group	No.	Mean	Standard deviation	Lower quartile	Median	Upper quartile	Trimean
1538–49							
Gentry	16	29.1	5.7	25.0	26.5	33.5	27.9
Crafts	2	–	–	–	–	–	–
Labourer	3	–	–	–	–	–	–
Poor	0	–	–	–	–	–	–
Unknown	10	32.2	5.0	28.5	33.5	36.3	32.9
Total	31	30.0	5.5	26.0	29.0	35.0	29.8
1550–99							
Gentry	30	28.1	5.6	23.8	27.5	32.3	27.8
Crafts	32	27.7	4.8	24.0	27.0	31.0	27.3
Labourer	27	27.6	6.3	23.0	25.0	29.0	25.5
Poor	37	26.0	4.9	22.0	25.0	28.0	25.0
Unknown	81	29.4	6.3	25.0	29.0	33.0	29.0
Total	207	28.1	5.9	24.0	27.0	31.0	27.3
1600–49							
Gentry	45	27.6	5.5	24.0	26.0	32.0	27.0
Crafts	39	25.7	5.0	23.0	25.0	28.0	25.3
Labourer	17	25.6	2.5	24.0	25.0	28.5	25.6
Poor	42	25.5	3.7	23.0	24.0	28.0	24.8
Unknown	82	27.1	6.4	22.8	26.0	30.3	26.3
Total	225	26.5	5.4	23.0	25.0	29.0	25.5
1650–99							
Gentry	30	28.5	6.2	24.0	28.0	31.0	27.8
Crafts	10	27.7	6.1	22.0	26.0	34.5	27.1
Labourer	5	–	–	–	–	–	–
Poor	50	27.8	6.0	23.0	27.0	31.0	27.0
Unknown	75	27.6	7.2	22.0	26.0	30.0	26.0
Total	171	27.6	6.9	23.0	26.0	31.0	26.5
1700–49							
Gentry	11	29.6	4.2	27.0	28.0	34.0	29.3
Crafts	24	27.3	5.2	25.0	28.0	30.0	27.8
Labourer	4	–	–	–	–	–	–
Poor	43	25.7	5.6	22.0	24.0	28.0	24.5
Unknown	49	28.7	6.3	25.0	27.0	31.5	27.6
Total	131	27.4	5.9	23.0	26.0	30.8	26.4
1750–99							
Gentry	24	26.8	5.1	22.3	26.5	31.0	26.6
Crafts	40	26.7	5.5	22.3	26.0	30.0	26.1
Labourer	37	27.3	5.8	23.0	26.0	30.0	26.3
Poor	17	25.8	4.6	22.5	24.0	29.5	25.0
Unknown	39	27.9	6.2	22.0	27.0	32.0	27.0
Total	157	27.1	5.6	23.0	26.0	30.0	26.3

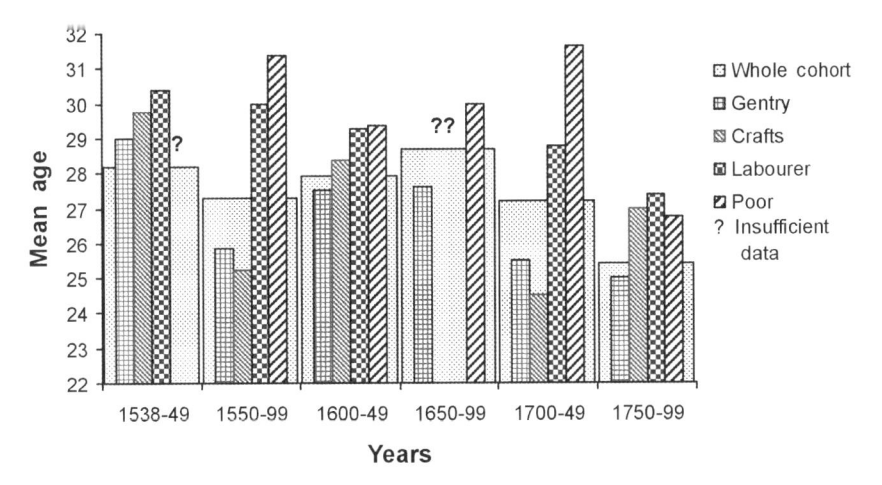

Fig. 5.6 Mean age at first marriage of 'all women' by status group of FRF 1538–1799.

significantly from the women in observation. It would appear that the age at marriage of the Colyton nonconformists was not markedly different from their Anglican counterparts. However, the incorporation of the marriage data for dummy marryers only goes some way towards exploiting the full information contained in the reconstitution. Evidently, there is still a shortage of positively identifiable 'labourer' cases even when the dummy marriages are considered. The socio-economic breakdown of the extended sample is shown in Tables 5.7 and 5.8 and in Figures 5.6 to 5.7.

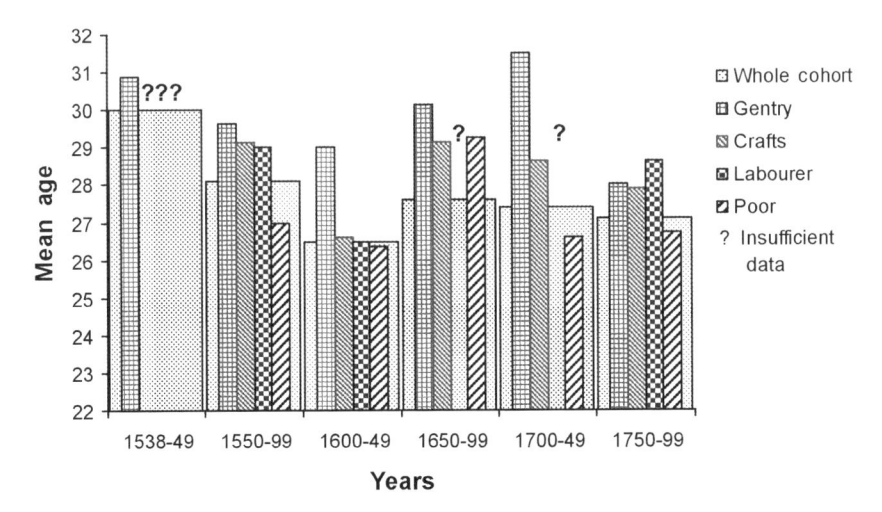

Fig. 5.7 Mean age at first marriage of 'all men' by status group of FRF 1538–1799.

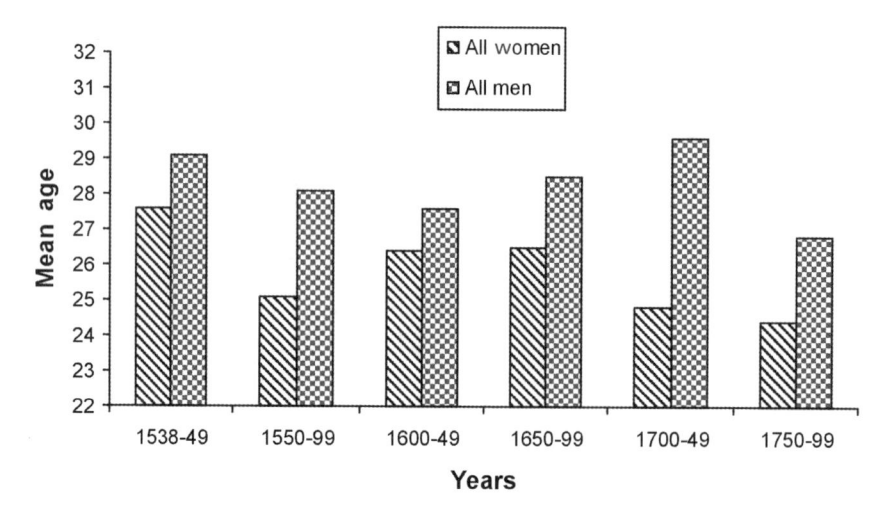

Fig. 5.8 Mean age at first marriage of gentry group of FRFs 1538–1799.

As shown in Figure 5.5, the most interesting new aspect of the extension of the sample to include 'all men' and 'all women', which is brought about by cohorting on baptism, is the high age at marriage for all men and relatively low age for all women in the new first cohort which covers a period where the sex ratio was well over a hundred in the wheat and wool economy of the first half of the sixteenth century. This is a reversal of the situation in the seventeenth century when females

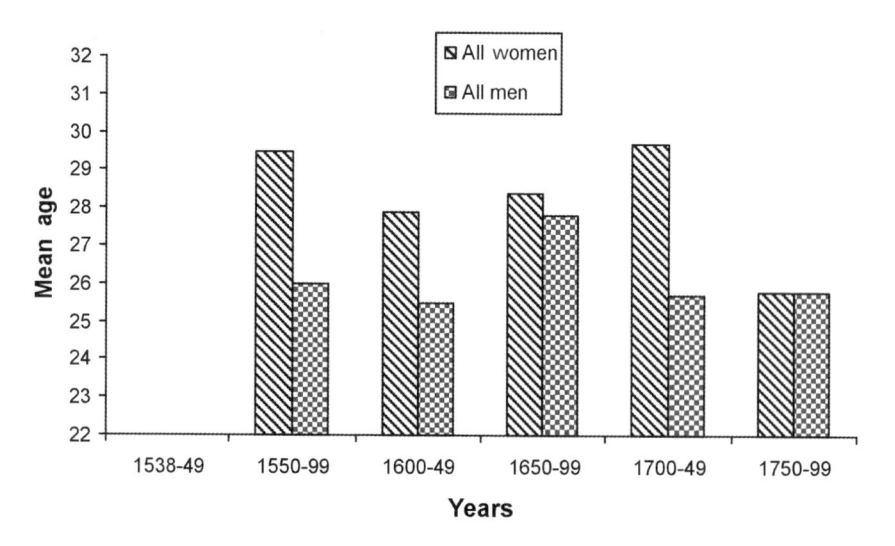

Fig. 5.9 Mean age at first marriage of poor group of FRFs 1538–1799.

exceeded males in the population and marriage age for women was higher. The results for 'all women', shown in Figure 5.6, are more divergent than the earlier results for women. There is still a lack of data for 1650–99. The picture of the poor marrying significantly later than the wealthy is confirmed, however. An association between labourer and poor patterns and gentry and craftspeople patterns is suggested by this figure. The gentry and crafts show an early 'low' in the 1550–99 cohort when the sex ratio was reasonably even. This has only a minor effect on the overall mean due to the divergence of the poor group. The poor cases married at a very late age in this cohort.[41]

An interesting result is produced by the comparison of Figure 5.6 with Figure 5.7, as the pattern for 'all men' is a reversal of the 'all women' pattern. Since this figure incorporates the fullest information because 'dummy' men are added, the outcome is very important. The picture that emerges is a hierarchy of marriage age for sons with the poor marrying earliest, then labourers, then craftspeople, with gentry sons marrying at the older ages of all. Since the most reliable data are available for the gentry and the poor, Figure 5.8 and Figure 5.9 compare the age at marriage behaviour of the sexes within these two groups. Figure 5.8 shows that the gentry women's marriage ages stayed below the men's ages. The rise in male marriage ages within this group in the period of a particularly skewed sex ratio probably reflects social norms which indicated that wealthy men should marry women who were a respectable amount younger than they themselves were. The shortage of marriage partners for women seems to have meant that they married at later ages and sought out even older partners.

A completely contrasting picture is produced of the poor group in Figure 5.9, with female ages being well above male ages throughout. These marriage patterns reflect that inheritance considerations were of less import to this group but they closely mirror the shortage of men and surplus of women.

Figure 5.10 shows the age at marriage of a totally different group of marryers from those presented in the figures so far. These are those for whom no status grouping can be given as they do not appear in any documents. Due to the balance of documentary material, which gives plenty of information about the poor and the gentry, the 'unknowns' are likely to be labourers or former servants in Colyton (this was suggested by the 'marriage only' cases discussed in Chapter 1). The marriage patterns are less sex-specific for this group. The marriage ages were also less variable until 1700 when men and women's ages diverged, with women's ages dropping far lower than men's ages.[42]

In all of the representations of age at first marriage in Colyton, a convergence of the age trends for all of the status groups is evident in the 1600–49 cohort, and then in the 1750–99 cohort. These cohorts

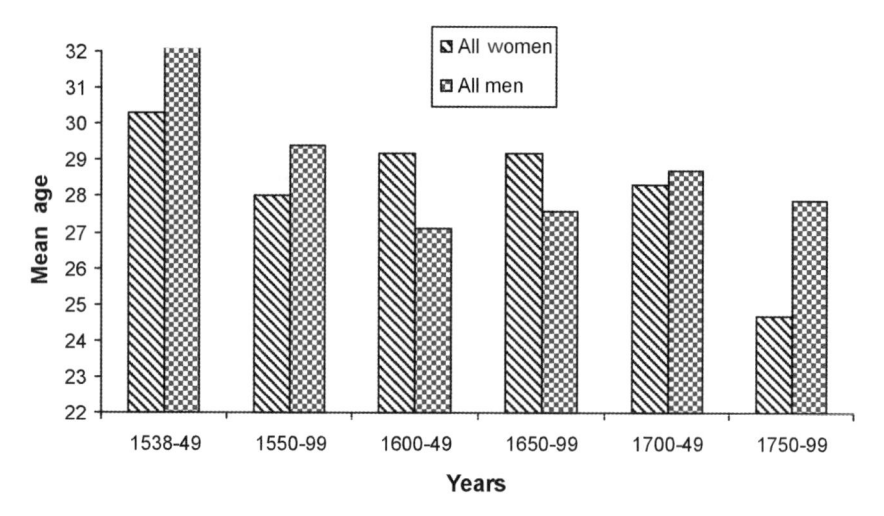

Fig. 5.10 Mean age at first marriage of unknown group of FRFs 1538–1799.

reflected the periods of greatest economic change in Colyton, and it is possible that different parts of the cohort cancel each other out as marriage trends embarked on a new path which reflected adjustment to new economic circumstances. The reconstitution does not provide a method of quantifying numbers of people who never married in the community, but it seems certain that males must have had a far higher chance of marrying than females in most of the period covered here, and that poor females were in the worst position of all. The most significant result of this section is the finding that male and female marriage ages did not move in tandem and that patterns of age at marriage for women from differing status groups showed significant variance, especially before 1750.

Remarriage

Turning to trends in second or later marriages, if the sex ratio seems to have had a significant influence on the chance of first marrying, it must have had even more effect on chances of remarriage. Considering the wider demographic context of the parish, the restriction on remarriage for women who were widowed when they were in their twenties and thirties must have undermined the community's reproductive potential. There are some problems with specifying remarryers in the reconstitution, and therefore the number of those who have been positively identified as remarrying widows or widowers is likely to be a conservative estimate.[43] Not only do the Colyton patterns show sex ratio effects, they

Table 5.9 Remarriage chances for men and women in Colyton 1538–1837

Cohort	Group	Total marriages	Remarriages Men No.	%	Women No.	%
1538–49	Gentry	20	5	25.0	1	5.0
	Crafts	9	2	22.2	1	11.1
	Labourer	3	–	–	–	–
	Poor	–	–	–	–	–
	Unknown	49	4	8.2	2	4.1
	Total	81	11	13.6	4	4.9
1550–99	Gentry	50	13	26.0	6	12.0
	Crafts	30	3	10.0	3	10.0
	Labourer	75	6	8.0	11	14.7
	Poor	29	–	–	3	10.3
	Unknown	317	34	10.7	47	14.8
	Total	501	56	11.2	70	14.0
1600–49	Gentry	56	10	17.9	7	12.5
	Crafts	70	15	21.4	9	12.9
	Labourer	57	5	8.8	4	7.0
	Poor	93	23	24.7	10	10.8
	Unknown	374	81	21.7	40	10.7
	Total	650	134	20.6	70	10.8
1650–99	Gentry	33	23	69.7	–	–
	Crafts	14	4	28.6	–	–
	Labourer	8	5	62.5	–	–
	Poor	61	31	50.8	1	1.6
	Unknown	150	35	23.3	2	1.3
	Total	266	98	36.8	3	1.1
1700–49	Gentry	28	12	42.9	1	3.6
	Crafts	25	5	20.0	3	12.0
	Labourer	25	2	8.0	–	–
	Poor	98	33	33.7	9	9.2
	Unknown	177	16	9.0	3	1.7
	Total	353	68	19.3	16	4.5
1750–99	Gentry	62	5	8.1	3	4.8
	Crafts	101	13	12.9	2	2.0
	Labourer	96	14	14.6	8	8.3
	Poor	55	11	20.0	2	3.6
	Unknown	245	24	9.8	11	4.5
	Total	559	67	12.0	26	4.7
1800–37	Gentry	45	4	8.9	4	8.9
	Crafts	47	6	12.8	9	19.1
	Labourer	42	6	14.3	5	11.9
	Poor	10	2	20.0	1	10.0
	Unknown	141	16	11.3	5	3.5
	Total	285	34	11.9	24	8.4

also indicate national patterns of the likelihood of remarriage of widows and widowers. Wrigley and Schofield found that in fourteen parish reconstitutions for the period 1600–1799, there was a higher incidence of male remarriage than female remarriage, and that there were shorter intervals before the remarriage of widowers compared with widows.[44] The median interval to male remarriage was 12.9 months while to female remarriage it was 19.4 months. The more agricultural the parish the longer the interval to remarriage for women. In the full sample of reconstitutions the mean interval to remarriage lengthened between the early seventeenth century and the early nineteenth century, almost doubling over this time period.[45]

Table 5.9 shows chances of remarrying in Colyton by gender and status grouping. Total marriages by status are compared with the percentage of remarriages by status. The effect of remarriage on reproductive potential obviously depends on the number of females who are able to marry while they are still in their childbearing years. Remarriage chances also depend on the prevailing level of mortality. Unfortunately, however, if only remarryers for whom ages are known were included in this analysis, the numbers would be prohibitively small. Only four of the females in this table are known to have remarried when they were under 40. The effects of the sex ratio are obvious since it was far more common for men to remarry than women in the 1650–1749 period. When the sex ratio stood at 111.5 in 1550–99, women's remarriage chances were better than men's. They were diminishing from the 1600–49 cohort onwards. Only nineteen women can be identified to have married a second time in the entire period 1650–1749. Not until the nineteenth century were remarriage chances of women roughly equivalent to those of men. Furthermore, chances of remarriage seem to have been status-specific, with poor women having less chance of marrying again than their wealthier counterparts.

As the numbers are very small, and there are difficulties in making adjustments for age and adult mortality, the amalgamation of the trends shown in Table 5.9 into an analysis for the whole reconstitution period of 1538–1837 is shown in Table 5.10.

The economic disadvantages of widowhood, for poor women in particular, have been thought to increase widows' desire to remarry.[46] In Colyton the poor relief system was certainly orientated towards women's support in the seventeenth and most of the eighteenth centuries. While this may have reduced the pressure for them to remarry, it seems far more likely that this aspect of poor relief developed as a response to the remarriage chances of poor women being virtually non-existent.[47] The high proportion of marriages that were remarriages of men in the second half of the seventeenth century is fairly striking, although the overall low level of recorded marriages must be considered. To an extent this pattern

Table 5.10 Remarriage chances in Colyton for amalgamated cohorts 1538–1837

Status	Total marriages	Remarriages			
		Male	%	Female	%
Gentry	294	72	24.5	22	7.5
Crafts	296	48	16.2	27	9.1
Labourer	306	38	12.4	28	9.2
Poor	346	100	28.9	26	7.5
Unknown	1453	210	14.5	110	7.6

reflects not just the economic situation but also the outfall from disasters in the parish such as the aftermath of plague.

Family Limitation

Attention was first drawn to Colyton by the discovery of family limitation behaviour in the parish in the second half of the seventeenth century.[48] The possibility that 'stopping' methods of family limitation were used in Colyton will be reviewed first, and then the evidence for 'spacing' methods. Family limitation behaviour in Colyton was indicated by a last birth interval of more than forty-eight months being found for some of the women who had married before the age of 30, and had previously had stable birth intervals. It seemed possible that this might have been caused by a recording aberration, and as we have seen there is reason to suspect that baptismal recording may have suffered a shortfall, especially before 1684 when the church incumbent was deeply unpopular.[49] Alternatively, Wrigley thought that coitus interruptus was being used as a contraceptive method in Colyton, and that a conscious attempt was made to stop reproduction when a certain family size had been reached. Wrigley's case was strengthened by the observation that the fall in marital fertility was age-specific. As Wrigley showed, couples who started their reproductive careers earlier also stopped them before couples who married later. Tables 5.11 and 5.12 summarise the case for fertility restraint in late seventeenth-century Colyton.

As Table 5.11 shows, it is apparent that at the same time as age at marriage rose for women, so did birth intervals (and particularly, the indicative interval to last birth). Wrigley identified a marked decline of fertility in the fifteen years before the plague, and this became more significant thereafter. There was an abrupt change for some of the families who spanned the plague, to the point that it might be suggested that some women became barren as a result of either the prevalence of disease or psychological shock. The patterns which emerged for Colyton

Table 5.11 Birth intervals and marriage age in Colyton 1560–1769

	Mean birth interval (months)	Mean last birth interval (months)	Mean age at first marriage of women
1560–1646	27.5	37.5	27.0
1647–1719	31.4	50.7	29.6
1720–1769	29.1	40.6	26.8

Source: Crafts and Ireland 1976: 605.

were very similar to those earlier identified by Henry for the Genevan bourgeoisie but there they continued into the eighteenth century, whereas there was a reversal in Colyton.[50] In Geneva the background to family limitation was that high-status positions were limited such that adult sons had to emigrate. The adoption of family limitation meant that late seventeenth-century couples stopped childbearing four years earlier than pre-1650 cohorts.

Although Wrigley's findings led to some criticism,[51] the most recent demographic work places greater stress on the role of marital fertility in national population change and affirms the findings for Colyton for at least a section of the population.[52] Other work on local communities, both within and outside of England, has also found patterns which suggest the local population limited their families.[53] This section will attempt to forward the discussion of family limitation in Colyton on two fronts. First, was the use of birth control specific to certain groups within the population? Secondly, in an era well before the use of contraception, how did people limit their families in early modern Colyton?

Stopping behaviour was shown in a sample of 215 FRFs which had completed marriages, and was demonstrated to have become more

Table 5.12 Marital fertility rates in Colyton 1560–1837 (Age-Specific Marital Fertility)

| | Children born per 1000 woman years lived |||||
	20–24	25–29	30–34	35–39	40–44
1560–1629	467	403	369	302	174
1630–1646	378	382	298	234	128
1647–1719	346	395	272	182	104
1720–1769	362	342	392	227	160
1770–1837	441	361	347	270	152

Source: Adapted from Wrigley 1966a: Table 10.4.

Table 5.13 Family limitation behaviour by status 1550–1837

Cohort	Group	Limitation cases No.	Limitation cases %	Normal FRFs No.	Normal FRFs %
1550–99	Gentry	3	6.0	47	94.0
	Crafts	5	16.7	25	83.3
	Labourer	3	4.0	72	96.0
	Poor	7	24.1	22	75.9
	Unknown	12	30.8	305	96.2
	Total	30	6.0	472	94.0
1600–49	Gentry	3	5.4	53	94.6
	Crafts	15	21.4	55	78.6
	Labourer	13	22.8	44	77.2
	Poor	15	16.1	78	83.9
	Unknown	23	6.1	351	93.9
	Total	69	10.6	581	89.4
1650–99	Gentry	2	6.1	31	93.9
	Crafts	2	14.3	12	85.7
	Labourer	–	–	8	100.0
	Poor	10	16.4	51	83.6
	Unknown	10	6.7	140	93.3
	Total	24	9.0	242	91.0
1700–49	Gentry	1	3.6	27	96.4
	Crafts	3	12.0	22	88.0
	Labourer	–	–	25	100.0
	Poor	8	8.2	90	91.8
	Unknown	10	5.6	167	94.4
	Total	22	6.2	331	93.8
1750–99	Gentry	7	11.3	55	88.7
	Crafts	13	12.9	88	87.1
	Labourer	15	15.6	81	84.4
	Poor	15	27.3	40	72.7
	Unknown	15	6.1	230	93.9
	Total	65	11.6	494	88.4
1800–37	Gentry	–	–	45	100.0
	Crafts	1	2.1	46	97.9
	Labourer	3	7.1	39	92.9
	Poor	1	10.0	9	90.0
	Unknown	–	–	141	100.0
	Total	5	1.8	280	98.2

common in the 1600–49 cohort. Table 5.13 shows these FRFs arranged by status group compared with the status distribution of FRFs that do not show this type of behaviour. Not surprisingly, considering the small sample, the results seem highly variable, but it is evident that 'stopping'

Table 5.14 Family limitation behaviour in Colyton for amalgamated cohorts 1550–1837

Status	Normal FRFs	Limitation cases N.	%
Gentry	274	16	5.8
Crafts	287	39	13.6
Labourer	333	34	10.2
Poor	346	56	16.2
Unknown	1404	70	5.0

behaviour was not common among the gentry but was a feature of families further down the social scale. This is particularly important because, as has already been demonstrated, gentry women tended to marry earlier than poor women, and so are more frequently found in the category of 'under 30 marryers'. The 1750–99 cohort provides the clearest indication of a hierarchy in this type of behaviour, with the gentry being least likely to limit their families and the other social groups showing increasing tendencies to birth control. The lack of 'unknown' cases in all cohorts apart from 1550–99 could indicate an association between family limitation and long-term residency in Colyton. Table 5.14 provides the figures for the entire time period.

If marital fertility is assumed to be a variable component, it is helpful to investigate whether birth spacing shows status-specific patterns. Wilson found that Colyton conformed to the typical pattern for the west of England and that was associated with a diverse economic structure. The long birth intervals in Colyton were attributed to breast-feeding, which probably lasted for eleven to twelve months.[54] The effect of this would have been to lengthen the period of post-partum amenorrhoea.[55] The existence of wet nursing in Colyton is also partially confirmed by the findings in Table 5.14, as labourer's and craftsmen's wives (where they are caught in the recording process) show high tendencies to 'stopping' which may have been due to breast-feeding rather than coitus interruptus.

In Table 5.15 birth intervals have been categorised by social status to find out whether different classes showed distinct patterns in the micro-study of Colyton's population. The Dupaquier-Lachiver technique, developed for studying French birth intervals, was used to divide birth intervals into four groups:[56]

1. Short intervals <19 months.
2. Medium intervals 19–30 months.

3. Long intervals 31–48 months.
4. Sterile or 'contraceptive' families >48 months.

The number of cases used in Table 5.15 is larger than those used in the COLYFILE sample as FRFs with more than two baptisms have been used instead of concentrating on completed families with a large number of children. While raising the possibility of including families who baptised outside of the parish as well as in it, this eliminates any bias towards stable families who might not have had typical birth interval patterns. There is also reason to believe that FRFs with large numbers of baptisms are biased towards higher status since wealthier women married earlier and had a longer childbearing period. First and last intervals have been excluded and the cases are those where date at marriage is known. Table 5.16 shows the amalgamated pattern for all cohorts.

Tables 5.15 and 5.16 show a tentative pattern of birth spacing according to status. Through all the cohorts, the higher the social status of the family, the more likely it is to appear in the 19–30 month category with 'medium' birth intervals; the lower the status, the more probable it is to appear in the 31–48 month category of 'long' intervals. One explanation for this may be that gentry families were employing wet nurses, and families lower down the social scale were acting as wet nurses. However, apart from the number of alternative employment opportunities that were available for women in Colyton, there is no evidence for England to suggest that wet nursing was ever a social institution on the same scale that it was in France and what evidence there is points to most wet nursing taking place on the periphery of metropolitan areas.[57] The patterns shown here are more likely to reflect community-based wet nursing among poor and labouring women, while indicating that gentry women breast-fed for a relatively short time. Even if this is not the explanation, the tendency for craft, labourer or poor group women to space their births when compared to gentry women is striking.[58]

How was marital fertility limited in Colyton? Breast-feeding provides one explanation but Wrigley suggested that Colyton couples practised coitus interruptus. Although the evidence is lacking, the possibility that rural prostitution functioned as a form of birth control is presented in Chapter 7. Another probability is that abortion and infanticide were more common than historians have assumed.[59] There is little doubt that these were used in illicit relationships. In a Devon quarter sessions case in 1651, Deborah Brackley, a servant from Lamerton who was able to sign her deposition with a fine hand, said that she had been got with child by a fellow servant, George Jewell. As well as pressing her to name another father 'hee told her she could not be with Chile & though the doctors tould her soe yet they were fooles. And if shee were with Child shee knew what things to take to bring it goinge & advised her to take Phisicke.'[60]

Table 5.15 Birth spacing by the Dupaquier-Lachiver method according to status 1538–1837

Cohort	Status	<19 months No.	%	19–30 months No.	%	31–48 months No.	%	>48 months No.	%
1538–49	Gentry	3	10.7	19	67.9	6	21.4	–	–
	Crafts	1	7.1	5	35.7	8	57.2	–	–
	Labourer	–	–	1	–	–	–	–	–
	Poor	–	–	–	–	–	–	–	–
	Unknown	5	18.5	7	25.9	11	40.7	4	14.8
	Total	9	12.8	32	45.7	25	35.7	4	5.7
1550–99	Gentry	3	7.0	26	60.4	14	32.6	–	–
	Crafts	–	–	17	58.6	10	34.5	2	6.9
	Labourer	4	12.5	16	50.0	12	37.5	–	–
	Poor	1	2.6	14	35.9	21	53.8	3	7.7
	Unknown	7	5.1	61	44.5	59	43.1	10	7.3
	Total	15	5.3	134	47.8	116	41.4	15	5.3
1600–49	Gentry	2	9.1	13	59.1	7	31.8	–	–
	Crafts	4	9.1	19	43.2	19	43.2	2	4.5
	Labourer	–	–	17	50.0	16	47.1	1	2.9
	Poor	4	6.8	25	42.4	28	47.5	2	3.4
	Unknown	8	10.3	36	46.2	32	41.0	2	2.5
	Total	18	7.6	110	46.4	102	43.0	7	2.9
1650–99	Gentry	5	10.2	26	53.1	15	30.6	3	6.1
	Crafts	1	5.2	9	47.4	9	47.4	–	–
	Labourer	2	13.3	6	40.0	6	40.0	1	6.7
	Poor	3	3.7	34	42.0	39	48.1	5	6.2
	Unknown	4	4.7	40	46.5	35	40.7	7	8.1
	Total	15	6.0	115	46.0	104	41.6	16	6.4
1700–49	Gentry	–	–	17	63.0	9	33.3	1	3.7
	Crafts	–	–	9	56.3	5	31.3	2	12.5
	Labourer	–	–	2	33.3	4	66.7	–	–
	Poor	5	5.5	43	47.2	40	44.0	3	3.3
	Unknown	3	5.0	24	40.0	26	43.3	7	11.7
	Total	8	4.0	95	47.5	84	42.0	13	6.5
1750–99	Gentry	2	7.7	17	65.4	5	19.2	2	7.7
	Crafts	2	3.8	23	43.4	27	50.9	1	1.9
	Labourer	4	11.8	12	35.3	15	44.1	3	8.8
	Poor	3	8.3	17	47.2	15	41.7	1	2.8
	Unknown	14	22.6	17	27.4	28	45.2	3	4.8
	Total	25	11.8	86	40.8	90	42.6	10	4.7
1800–37	Gentry	6	42.9	6	42.9	2	14.2	–	–
	Crafts	2	11.1	9	50.0	6	33.3	1	5.6
	Labourer	5	17.2	13	44.8	10	34.5	1	3.5
	Poor	1	33.3	2	66.6	–	–	–	–
	Unknown	2	10.5	11	57.9	6	31.6	–	–
	Total	16	19.3	41	49.4	24	28.9	2	2.4

Table 5.16 Birth spacing in Colyton for amalgamated cohorts 1538–1837

Status	<19 months No.	%	19–30 months No.	%	31–48 months No.	%	>48 months No.	%
Gentry	21	10.0	124	59.3	58	27.8	6	2.9
Crafts	10	5.2	91	47.2	84	43.5	8	4.1
Labourer	15	9.9	67	44.4	63	41.7	6	4.0
Poor	17	5.5	135	43.7	143	46.3	14	4.5
Unknown	43	9.2	196	41.8	197	42.0	33	7.0

The clearest evidence of the use of abortion in Colyton dates from 1682 and is worth examining in some detail.[61] This was a case reported with more witnesses and evidence than the run of quarter session cases. This is not because the facts of the case were unusual, indeed we might surmise that it suggests that abortion was a fairly routine occurrence. In fact, the attention given to this case is because it involved the extremist Protestant hothead Roger Satchell and should be read as an attempt by the authorities to frame him by casting his reputation in sexual scandal.

Patience Morley deposed that Satchell's servant Mary Pease complained of not being well on 17 May 1682. The next evening she came out of Satchell's house carrying a cup which she warmed by the fire then drank. She said it was some stilled waters and some syrup and that she had been taken very ill in Satchell's house and nearly fainted. When she took off her shift, it was evident from it and from the bed clothes that 'it was not wth her as wth a virgin'. Seeing this, Patience Morley sent for Mary Burrough, the Colyton midwife, who viewing the linen agreed with her and desired a further search at the house of Joseph Bird. But by this point Mary Pease had escaped back to Satchell's house. When she returned and saw a gathering of women she went to a neighbour's house. It took some hours before they could 'capture' her, then as was usual at the time 'the women had the view of her & tryed her'. The midwife, Mary Burrough, stated that she 'hath seen linnen so from a woman that hath miscarried & to her judgmt could be no otherwise'. The other seven women present signed a statement using their distinctive trader's marks, 'all of them having the sight of the linnen & all of them being the mothers of Children never did see any such linnen come from a virgin and cannot judge it to be otherwise than what Mary Burrough the midwife hath given in her informacion'. James Batten, apparently a male servant of Satchell's, deposed that he had seen Mary Pease collapse after taking a drink and then 'ly as dead in the window'. When Batten asked Satchell what was the matter, Satchell answered he did not know 'what ailed the cramp ass jade' and told Batten to look after her as he believed she was dead! Mary Pease's stepmother deposed that Mary often frequented the house of Roger Satchell and sometimes stayed there all night, 'he having no wife nor other in his family but himself'. Her father often reproached her for this and found a place for her three miles away, but she came back again, left her father's house and spent most of her time with Satchell, saying that he was 'her Master & that she was in Covenant with him'. Mary Pease herself claimed 'that shee never was with child & shee knows no cause why it should be so with her linnen unless it be for want of the benefitt of nature which she wanted nine or tenne weeks'.

Mary Burrough then deposed again with details of a second trial by the women (or provided further description which may be fabrication). The women had sent for Pease and searched her breasts 'and found in them such milk as women wth child usually have' so they asked her to declare who got her with child. Pease was silent for a long time, she then replied 'that it was no married man's'. The other women when asked about this examination said they found in her breasts 'some waterish matter'. Pease restated 'that shee would free her Master for it was no married man's'.

Satchell was at this point a former constable, and current overseer of the poor, who refused to cooperate with county justices and was politically allied with the recalcitrant churchwardens as well. This court case was an attempt to check his progress which ultimately failed because Satchell became an ardent follower of Monmouth. Even if the real point of this case was to mire Satchell in sleaze to diminish his local reputation, his opponents doubtless mounted a credible case: in other words, foetuses were terminated in this way. It is also necessary to consider this case in the light of the fact that there is no evidence of real prosecution of illegitimacy cases as was pursued in other early modern parishes like Keevil and Terling, and this may be another indication of the fractured nature of authority in early modern Colyton.

Mary Pease was an incomer to the parish and none of her vital events are recorded. Much fuller information is available for the group of women who tried Pease. They were the wives of village craftsmen and small-scale retailers and resolutely local. While Pease implied that she was Satchell's covenant servant she also suggested her willingness to submit to him. But an important emphasis of the case was that Satchell was an unmarried householder. Pease's defence implied that this made her crime far less serious than adultery and she perhaps had in mind Hebrews 13:4: 'whoremongers and adulterers God will judge'. The syrups and herbs used here were not known as abortifacients, although Pease may have lied about the content of the drink. Riddle argues that the means to abortion and contraception using a variety of readily available herbs such as pennyroyal, a mint toxic taken as tea, was widely known.[62] For example, pennyroyal was mentioned in Culpeper's directory of 1651 as a remedy for midwives to stimulate menstrual flow.⁶³ One of the most interesting aspects of this case is the fact that Satchell was a lone householder yet we know from his will that at his death he left a wife, two children and some grandchildren.⁶⁴ He also owned land in Honiton and the most likely explanation is that his family lived there. Satchell himself would have needed a residence in Colyton to further his political ambitions there.

Wrigley believed that coitus interruptus was the technique of birth control probably used by married couples. Nevertheless, onanism was roundly condemned by the Bible. As we have seen, John Salway in Shute in 1637 preached against the practice and the intellectual forefathers of the Protestant impetus in seventeenth-century Colyton outlawed withdrawal. Luther called coitus interruptus 'a most disgraceful crime'; Calvin went further to damn the practice as an 'act of monstrosity'. We might argue that the thoughts of these theologians were a world away from the everyday practices of ordinary people in Colyton, but the diary of Walter Yonge in the 1600s shows a clear concern with Calvinism. For example, he makes a point of recording the death of Mr Beza, head of the Genevese church after Calvin.⁶⁵ Nevertheless, this was a sin difficult to detect in the homes of private families. Santow argues that withdrawal is more efficient than generally believed and more common.⁶⁶ For the seventeenth-century West Country, in the court cases collected by Quaife, one wife complained not only that her husband's attentions were infrequent but 'what seed should be sowen in the right ground he spent about the outward part of her body'. Another woman 'took it out when it was half in', while a third claimed that her lover 'had fouled her clothes'.⁶⁷

Coitus interruptus may be relevant but the use of herbs and potions to bring about abortion were also known. However, the coincidence between the onset of family limitation and the rise of religious Dissent in Colyton is also apparent. The natural decline of fertility with age, combined with baptismal recording aberrations, is probably sufficient to provide an alternative explanation to deliberate birth control, especially when the coincidence of the long birth intervals with the very social groups who were active Dissenters is noted. Yet there is perhaps more to say than this. Family limitation was a feature of the same time period as saw high celibacy, late age at marriage and low prenuptial conceptions. The apparent onset of family limitation coincides not only with plague but also Puritanism, and it is necessary to probe some way beyond the recording deficiencies to speculate about the effects of extreme Protestantism on restraint.

Infant and Child Mortality

Infant and child mortality patterns in Colyton are summarised in Table 5.17. The west of England pattern described by Wilson was typified by low infant mortality which is associated with breast-feeding.[68] Infant mortality levels were low in England as a whole in comparison with other pre-industrial communities in nineteenth-century Europe, but the patterns for the period 1675–1749 in all the reconstitution parishes suggest that market towns were far more unhealthy than agricultural parishes.[69] Commerce, exchange and the general mobility of people spread diseases to a far greater extent than they had previously. Such effects were certainly felt in the industrious parish of Colyton where the period 1625–99 saw substantially higher mortality than earlier or later periods, with a rising death rate among young children, particularly boys in the second half of the seventeenth century.[70] Mortality was never as high as in parishes elsewhere in the country which were more poorly endowed with land or suffered from endemic disease regimes, but nevertheless there is a noticeable change from Tudor Colyton. Such a picture holds even when account has been taken of a fall in recorded baptisms around the time of the plague and this may be suggestive for the analysis of familial fertility strategies.[71]

This section will look more closely at the status-specificity of infant and child mortality and will then go on to consider whether the raised level of mortality in industrialising Colyton was a result of the disease environment, which may have affected all groups in society, or whether it was affected by social and economic conditions which mainly impacted on the poor.[72] Table 5.18 examines the mortality of infants and children up to the age of 5 years and groups them according to status. All children who appear in the reconstitution, including those on dummy FRFs have been incorporated. Three baptisms were excluded because the sex of the

Table 5.17 Infant and child life-table death rates (1,000 qx) in Colyton (sexes combined) 1538–1837

Age	1538–99	1600–49	1650–99	1700–49	1750–1837
0–1	108	81(77)*	79	98	72
1–4	80	93(85)	113	82	75
5–9	27	50(32)	65	23	28
10–14	21	44(24)	35	23	20

Note: * Figures in parentheses for 1600–49 show the death rates which result after deducting all deaths which occurred during the plague period 1645–6.
Source: Wrigley 1968: Table 7.

Table 5.18 Infant and child mortality (0–5 years) by status of father 1538–1799

Cohort	Group	Live births	Mortality No.	%	Male No.	%	Female No.	%
1538–49	Gentry	114	25	21.9	13	11.4	12	10.5
	Crafts	104	17	16.3	10	9.6	7	6.7
	Labourer	20	4	20.0	2	10.0	2	10.0
	Poor	–	–	–	–	–	–	–
	Unknown	43	17	39.5	11	25.6	6	13.9
1550–99	Gentry	300	70	23.3	41	13.6	29	9.6
	Crafts	113	19	16.8	13	11.5	6	5.3
	Labourer	212	29	13.7	13	6.1	16	7.5
	Poor	177	28	15.8	16	9.0	12	6.7
	Unknown	1099	229	20.8	141	12.8	88	8.0
1600–49	Gentry	473	72	15.2	33	7.0	39	8.2
	Crafts	461	81	17.6	46	10.0	35	7.6
	Labourer	264	49	18.6	29	11.0	20	7.6
	Poor	489	90	18.4	46	9.4	44	8.9
	Unknown	1372	251	18.3	151	11.0	100	7.3
1650–99	Gentry	338	77	22.8	41	12.1	36	10.7
	Crafts	138	33	23.9	21	15.2	12	8.7
	Lab	111	28	25.2	15	13.5	13	11.7
	Poor	326	118	36.2	61	18.7	57	17.9
	Unknown	1012	156	15.4	79	7.8	77	7.6
1700–49	Gentry	197	41	20.8	23	11.7	18	9.1
	Crafts	139	19	13.7	12	8.7	7	5.0
	Lab	86	17	19.8	5	5.8	12	13.9
	Poor	527	124	23.5	61	11.6	63	12.0
	Unknown	574	128	22.3	70	12.2	58	10.1
1750–99	Gentry	196	15	7.6	6	3.0	9	5.0
	Crafts	313	70	22.4	32	10.2	38	12.1
	Labourer	192	50	26.0	31	16.1	19	9.9
	Poor	149	48	32.2	20	13.4	28	18.8
	Unknown	920	63	6.8	30	3.3	33	3.6

child was not known. Table 5.19 shows all the cohorts combined. Table 5.18 suggests that until the mid-seventeenth century child mortality was not status-specific but after 1650 infant and child mortality were more common in the lower social groups. In the cohort 1700–49 there is no large disparity between the figure for the gentry and the labourers/poor. But in the 1750–99 cohort there is a very striking fall for the gentry and a rise for the poor and labourers.

By comparison, for Germany Knodel found few socio-economic

Table 5.19 Infant and child mortality in Colyton for amalgamated cohorts 1538–1799

Status	Live births	Mortality	
		No.	%
Gentry	1618	300	18.5
Crafts	1268	239	18.8
Labourer	885	177	20.0
Poor	1668	408	24.5
Unknown	5020	844	16.8

differences in the deaths of children aged under five.[73] The most important reason for this was local customs regarding infant feeding practices, which, he believed, affected the whole community. Early childhood mortality improved over time but infant mortality grew worse. It is possible that a similar result would be found for Colyton if the children's ages were taken into account. There were gender differences in infant and child mortality in Colyton. In every cohort, apart from 1750–99, the figures for mortality of girls were lower than those for boys.[74] The smaller birth intervals identified for gentry children suggest that they were either wet-nursed or breast-fed for only a short period, which might be expected to make them more prone to illness and death. For the lower classes women's work is only one factor contributing to a child's well-being, whereas poverty and disease are certain to have affected a child's life chances. Ideally, it would have been beneficial also to divide the data into rural and urban areas of the parish but the evidence does not exist for such comparison.

The evidence suggests the combined effects of socio-economic reasons for infant and child mortality, but also the existence of independent diseases, particularly prior to 1750.[75] What is known of health conditions in the parish? Contemporary writers saw Colyton as healthy, but Colyford as 'agueish'.[76] Not only was Colyford described as poverty-stricken in the seventeenth century but it was positioned on the main road and thus subject to disease from passing traffic. Perhaps even more significantly, Colyford was not far from the large area of reclaimed marsh on which so many manorial tenants held grazing. In the mid-eighteenth-century Dean Milles survey, Reverend Francis Drake, the vicar of Seaton, commented on the climate as mild but subject to agues 'which was called the Seaton sick but since the recovery of the marsh that complaint ceases'.[77] As the reclamation was an ongoing process we cannot tell exactly what time period Drake is describing, but this suggests that the southern area of Colyton parish was marshy and possibly malarial, as described by Mary Dobson for south-east England. Dobson shows that parishes with natural water had the lowest death rates in early modern England. Death rates also tended to be low in parishes with wells, little surface run-off on chalky soils, or situated on the upper reaches of rivers. Settlements on major rivers and in saline estuaries or marshland were the least healthy. Colyton's mixed topography suggests a variety of countervailing influences. Thus the unhealthy marsh may have been offset in the aggregated figures by the access to fresh water from streams in other parts of the parish. The overall conclusion from Dobson's research is that communities separated by a few miles were, demographically, worlds apart.[78]

In Colyton a water supply for the town was constructed by the feoffees in 1641. Its course can still be traced, for a stone leat conveyed the water from springs at Ridgeway to a large underground tank situated at one end of the town. From there a network of conduits fed most of streets. Broadly similar water systems were in place in surrounding towns. In Honiton water channels ran along streets and a little square dipping place was provided at every door so that, as Defoe put it, 'every family in the town has a clear, clean running river . . . just at their own door'.[79] Similarly, 'At the head of Beer a pure spring rises out of the flint rock, and runs in a clear current through the town', and Ottery St Mary had a sparkling spring in the middle of the town which was even supposed to possess mineral qualities.[80] The Colyton water system was maintained from feoffee income and in the late seventeenth century this was actively pursued. There are many entries such as the bailliff's accounts for 1676 recording a payment to two men 'for mending of the water course in Peter Westcots court', but it is difficult to say whether it was adequately managed during the period of feoffee decline in the early eighteenth century.[81] After all, the feoffees were also supposed to upkeep the roads but no contemporary comment suggests that this was adequately executed. Under circumstances of neglect in the early eighteenth century, the open water channels may have become more of a health hazard than a local benefit. There is little doubt that the rivers would have been polluted with textile dyeing, the tannery and the paper-making operations. The high number of persons per house and the influx of migrants at the end of seventeenth century must have put further pressure on local services. In 1775 the conditions in one of the overcrowded streets near the centre of Axminster probably reflect the poor living conditions in the poorer parts of all of these local towns. It was reported that cottages in the Back Lane 'have noo necessary houses . . . whereby a great nuisance arises . . . by Reason that the occupiers do their occasions in the Town Lake'.[82] The owners of the houses were ordered to improve their facilities.

Infant mortality is an acute barometer of social and economic conditions and infant deaths are unlikely to have been affected by recording difficulties. The Colyton picture then emphasises an 'industrial revolution' in the parish in the seventeenth century after 1625. The rising levels in the late eighteenth century also suggest socio-economic inequalities.

Adult Mortality

Recent research on mortality finds the trends to be 'complex' but at the same time 'strongly patterned'. Wrigley, Davies, Oeppen and Schofield argue that 'They are a salutary reminder that biological, epidemiological, and social history will probably prove at least as important as economic history in enabling better sense to be made of the history of mortality in England'.[83] The analysis of expectation of life in Colyton presented in Table 5.20 bears out the findings for infant and child mortality showing relatively higher mortality levels in the second half of the seventeenth century.

Furthermore, a gender-specific analysis of mortality shows female death rates were higher than those for males in sixteenth- and seventeenth-century Colyton.[84] Clearly a major reason for high death rates in seventeenth-century Colyton was plague. Southern Devon was always susceptible to recurring plague outbreaks which crippled parishes one at a time. Slack argues that infection was probably imported by sea to Colyton in the sixteenth century, then moved along the rivers.[85] There was a rise in burials in Colyton in 1557–9, particularly in August and February, which may indicate the presence of more than one disease. Total burials in the parish in these years amounted to 177, whereas the annual average was only 13.7. Slack disputes Shrewsbury's suggestion that there was bubonic plague in Colyton in 1558 because there is no evidence in other parishes and no evidence of a gradual rise of burials to a summer peak.[86] Strype thought the fevers and 'strange diseases' of 1558 to be especially severe in August and this may suggest insect-borne fevers which emanated from the silted Axe estuary.

Plague was again found in east Devon in 1591, and there were epidemics in 1592 and 1593 in Sidmouth and Colyton, when the disease was possibly reintroduced from London.[87] Plague was in Ottery St Mary in 1604,[88] Otterton and Axminster in 1611–12, and found throughout Devon in 1625–8 and again in 1636–7.[89] In the epidemics in Honiton and Ottery St Mary in 1625 it is suggested that plague entered from the main London road as well as by sea and was affected by the movement of traffic. Several diseases afflicted parishes at the same time in the Civil Wars but typhus, the classic disease of armies, and plague were particularly prevalent. The parish saw high mortality throughout 1643–6 but plague was only marked in the parish register in 1645–6.[90] Of course, a

Table 5.20 'Midpoint' expectation of life at birth in Colyton 1530–1774

Dates	Expectation of life (years)
1538–1624	43.2
1625–99	36.9
1700–74	41.8

Source: Adapted from Wrigley 1968: Table 17.

list of the outbreaks of plague does little to convey its devastating impact on the local community. A mere recording of the number of burials does not provide any picture of the number of people severely debilitated by illness or psychologically wounded by a local disaster. There can be little doubt that plagues would have been considered in biblical terms by the Colyton parishioners. Even after the great and last plague of 1645–6, disease remained at a high level.

Chambers believed that the late seventeenth-century rise in death rate may have been due to an independent disease regime. He thought Colyton was affected by all the diseases which emanated from London after the plague—smallpox, typhus, flu, diptheria, malarial ague, spotted fever, relapsing fevers, or dysentery. When we review the evidence for Colyton's trade links, this explanation becomes all the more likely. The parish had close links not only with London through the lace trade but also Exeter, Lyme and the colonies. Chambers also argued that this amount of disease might have made people sterile if fertility is also affected by psychological insecurity, and he suggested that there was lower coital frequency due to poor health or attitudinal changes. He suspected lower fecundability and more annovulatory cycles.[91] These propositions were tested by Crafts and Ireland, who also suggested that an epidemic of venereal disease could produce such changes in monthly chances of conception.[92] The latter is impossible to prove but might be linked with the military movements in the area (which were not confined to the Civil Wars but in fact continued at times throughout the seventeenth and eighteenth centuries) and the scanty evidence for local prostitution.

The exchange of infectious diseases, exacerbated by the number of incomers and the new levels of trade, is a more realistic explanation than linking raised mortality to a lower standard of living in Colyton. There is no evidence for lower prosperity overall, even if the local industrial revolution worsened conditions for some groups of workers and created an underclass in the parish. Colyton shared in the high mortality rate of market towns all over England after 1650, and they appear in the same category as marshland and city parishes in suffering a relatively high mortality rate.[93] The incidence of epidemic and incoming disease in Colyton makes it impossible to provide an analysis of mortality by linkage to FRFs, especially as it is difficult to disaggregate the rural and urban sections of the population after 1700 and before that we only have the data for males on marriage and not on death. Even this would only provide us with information on stable males not immigrant females.

For adult mortality the results show mixed and not entirely conclusive effects, with the key finding being that adult mortality was higher during the period 1625–99 than in earlier or later times, especially for females. It is possible to speculate that a wealthy yeoman farmer who lived in the hills and drank water from his own spring might enjoy relative longevity, but he could also catch a disease while tending a grazing animal on the Axe marsh or while going about his business in the town. Perhaps because women were such active traders, and the lace trade in particular thrived in congregations of workers, they were even more likely to be contaminated by others in the course of commerce.

Reproduction and Restraint: a Culture of Discipline?

Colyton has been seen as an excellent example of the ability of English local populations to respond sensitively to local conditions. The period from c.1630 to 1720 saw demographic restraint in comparison with the time periods before or after. This period correlates very well with that of the era of nonconformist activity. We have also seen in this chapter that the combined evidence suggests that lower-status families were smaller in this period. Compared to her wealthier counterpart, if a poor woman succeeded in finding a partner not only was she unlikely to conceive prenuptially, she married later, had longer birth intervals, and had a greater tendency towards terminating childbearing a few years before menopause. Her children were more likely to die, and if her husband also died she had little chance of marrying again. It is not new to discover that pre-industrial England was socially and sexually unequal, but the demographic implications of this have not been adequately assessed.

The explanation for demographic change put forward so far equates changes in population with economic conditions. In his early work Wrigley did not commit himself to an explanation of why family limitation was found in Colyton, preferring to argue that 'people respond sensitively to social pressures' and that the new demographic 'regime allows holding of gains in real income'.[94] He believed that Colyton people showed a sort of instinctive prudence after the plague. This is a neo-Malthusian explanation which foregrounds the self-regulating impulse within demographic behaviour: a system described by Wrigley and Schofield as demographic homeostasis. Wrigley argues that 'homeostatic adjustment brought about a favourable balance of population and resources. Explanations for demographic decline in late medieval England are founded on the possibility that the psychological shock of the Black Death meant survivors protected their new-found affluence.[95] However, in the case of Colyton the era of demographic restraint starts to appear some fifteen years before the plague and the industrialisation of the parish in the second half of the seventeenth century should have created prosperity, and stimulated marriage and fertility, rather than inhibiting it. The higher death rate should also have produced a greater access to land through inheritance. The criticism of Wrigley's explanation by Lestaeghe is pertinent here. He suggested that demographic homeostasis and preventative checks are not entirely adequate for they fail to account for aspects of the social system and the immediate interests of the population.[96] In the most recent manifesto from the Cambridge Group it is acknowledged that 'Wider issues linking demographic with economic and social change have been almost entirely neglected, though they are ultimately of greater significance than the attempt to establish the facts of population history'.[97]

Colyton people perhaps did respond to adverse trade conditions for wool in the 1630s and then the periodic disruptions to follow through the century. There can be little doubt of the psychological force of portents to early modern people. Walter Yonge recorded in his diary on 11 June 1607:

> This day fell in Colyton, not far from the town, rain, being as it seemed a thunder shower, and some thunder heard with all, among which were certain drops fell like blood, which stained those things it fell on. I saw a partlet [a woman's neck garment, collar or ruff] slain therewith, and it seemed, as it had been blood; my mother's maid, viz Scar's wife, and one Joan Milles, showed the same coming home from milking.

On 'The 13th of February 1616–17, there was seen in the air like the appearance of a firebrand wrapped in a red cloak and shining at both ends'. Weather often seemed to reflect the winds of change against Puritans and in events in the wider world, such as wars with Moors and Jews. Direct retribution struck those who disobeyed God.

> The 19th of August, 1622, being Monday about one of the clock in the morning, the wind arose and blew so vehemently for six hours, that it brake down divers strong trees. It quealed [curled up] all hedges towards the south that they clavered [withered] as if they had been scorched with lightning. It spoiled standing corn so, as in many places it seemed that all the corn (especially barley and oats)

had been threshed or beaten out of the husks. By report there is 200L. loss and hurt done to corn in Axmouth only by the said wind.

As for the fate of those who went reaping on a general fast day, Yonge declared 'See here God's hand upon the contemners of his ordinances!'.[98]

Colyton saw a powerful impulse to religion at the same time as the expansion of capitalism in the 1620s and 1630s. This Weberian concoction, so amply demonstrated in the abstract, brought both poverty and prosperity to this parish. Committed families, the same people who went on to become Monmouth's rebels, negotiated their place in the industrialising parish with prudence and self-restraint. As William Hunt describes it in the context of seventeenth-century Essex: 'The sermon was the principal means by which new standards of self-restraint could be infused into the populace' and 'Many of the most vigorous advocates of this new culture of discipline, both clerical and lay, believed that a model of an ideally governed community already existed, a community that claimed moreover to have virtually eliminated the problem of poverty. This was Calvin's Geneva.'[99] In their study of Quaker demography, Vann and Eversley suggest a Weberian link between pious and prudent behaviour, arguing that English and Irish Quakers had a 'rational' demographic response including family limitation and conscious control of fertility from the outset.[100]

In some senses the extreme religious impulse—the culture of discipline—was a way of imposing order in an increasingly chaotic local world where disasters assumed biblical proportions and incomers were plenty. Despite the upturn of local trade, many people lived in a state of perpetual anxiety about their wealth. To take one example, Deuteronomy was a powerful Old Testament reminder not to take prosperity for granted. Holy words on marriage were to be taken seriously; according to the Book of Common Prayer, matrimony 'is not to be enterprised, not taken in hand unadvisedly, lightly or wantonly, to satisfy man's carnal lusts and appetites, like brute beasts that have no understanding; but reverently, discreetly, advisedly, soberly, and in the fear of God'. As we will see in the Chapter 7, the period of youth in Colyton was prolonged further, emphasising the stress on restraint and probity. A woman like Hester Pinney came under serious family pressure not to marry.[101] The next chapter will consider the way in which the parish gave boundaries to family life.

Population in the Parish

This chapter has demonstrated the use of a 'total reconstitution' to provide a socio-economic analysis of the demographic patterns in Colyton. The emphasis has been on fertility rather than mortality and the independent features of the disease regime have been stressed. The historiography of English demographic change to date has given fertility rather than mortality a primary explanatory role.

Several salient features of Colyton's early modern demography have become apparent. First, there was the migration of women into the parish in the seventeenth century and the resulting skewed sex ratio elevated marriage age and meant some women never married. This is reflected in the late ages for poorer groups shown in the cohort analysis and the low rates of remarriage. The restraining effect of an unbalanced sex ratio must be seen as of great importance in Colyton's demographic history. In any population with a radically unbalanced sex ratio, fertility must be affected. A comparison with the sex ratio results in Figure 5.1 suggests that a ratio of less than 80 may have had that effect, whereas a minor sex ratio imbalance may be a population stimulus. Secondly, family limitation presents a close 'fit' with nonconformism. It is perhaps the clearest indication of a prevailing culture of restraint in reproductive activities and this chapter has made tentative links to a culture of discipline which was a result of the interactive power of religion and capitalism. Thirdly, mortality, of both adults and children, is more likely to be accurately documented than fertility, leading to confidence in the fact that mortality rates were high in the seventeenth-century parish and suggesting the effect of both disease and a lowered standard of living for some of those involved in industrial pursuits. All told, these factors suggest that early modern industrialisation could exert a powerful restraint on local population growth. The results suggest that while economic factors had an important influence on demographic behaviour, we should also consider the cultural context of population change. The parameters of the culture of discipline in the parish as a whole and in the household will be considered in the two chapters to follow.

6

Inside the Parish
Management at the Margins

> yor brothr Hoar, a dutifull child, a tender fathr, And a most loving husband dyed at Coliton being killed at Muster by a fellowe musket yt stood neer him & broke in shuting that splinters pierced into his Braines about 4 a clock after noon & lived till 4 a clock at morning but never spake one word after he was hurt . . . And just come to be mastr of his trade & had he lived, would have greatly flourished . . . there be very many yt put in to take off his shop, goods & trade to which ye old Hoare is very willing: But yor sister would keep it on herselfe not by my Advise, for I know she will not be able. It would be well if she could, till her boys be grown up. But I se no possibility of it.
> (John Pinney to Rachel Pinney, 28 March 1679, in G.F. Nuttall, ed., *Letters of John Pinney 1679–1699*, 1939: 4)

This letter from John Pinney to his daughter Rachel is the first surviving piece of correspondence from the rich collection of the Pinney family. The incident it describes took place on Lady Day (25 March) 1679 and it encapsulates several elements of social relations in early modern Colyton. Lady Day was the formal start of the year. It was a holiday and the time when many Colytonians would have paid their annual rents. First, although William Hoare had been a husband since his marriage to John Pinney's daughter in 1674 and was a father of several children, he is also referred to as a child and the fate of his business is partly to be determined by his father. The centrality of the family in this world-view is evident. Secondly, we are aware of the hierarchy and gradation of skill, for Hoare had just become a master. The fact that others are keen to take on the business suggests some of the vitality of trade in Colyton, as has been indicated in earlier chapters. Thirdly, there is a question over whether his widow can run the trade, and while there is doubt about this, prevailing attitudes give rise to the expectation that women will work. Within the nonconformist Pinney family, women worked whether single, married or widowed. Finally, the wider context of this case reminds us of the militarism of these local Protestants a few years before they were to rally to Monmouth using the guns stored in the parish armoury,[1] and also the fact that not only illnesses, but also accidents, were quite likely to cut down people in their prime. William Hoare's tragic death by a loaded weapon makes it evident that Colytonians were deadly serious in their belligerence even when only providing a show of strength. It is the argument of this chapter that it was partly in reaction to the inherent instability of life in seventeenth-century Colyton that a Puritan-inspired project sought to impose the skeins of control on the parish. As the balance of power was largely held by the middling orders, this project was shaped by manipulation of the margins—by controlling the young, women and the poor, particularly migrants. The middling orders imposed their own sense of independence and insularity on the parish to try to create a local Jerusalem. The route to moral reformation was to impose an ethos of ordered urban living on the parishioners. This was a partial success in the seventeenth century but in the eighteenth century nonconformity waned, as did the industrial sector of the parish. By the end of the eighteenth century, social relations in Colyton resembled many other parishes that drew their livelihood from agriculture—a deferential and distant relationship between the lord of the manor, wealthy farmers and landless labourers.

Social Relations in Action

The structure of government in Colyton, as in all English parishes, was shaped by Henrican and Elizabethan reforms, yet much older manorial structures continued to exert major local influence. The institution of the feoffees and twentymen in Colyton introduced a counterweight to manorial powers. The prosperity of sheep farming, which exalted some of the local yeomanry, and new trading innovations in the seventeenth century such as the lace industry and the colonial markets, gave rise to some spectacular social mobility and adjustments to the perception of local social 'worth'. In the first half of the century the effects of this became more keen, with the usual uncertainties of high mortality being exacerbated by harvest failure in the 1620s and 1630s. Colyton was in the front line during the Civil War. Royalists had a garrison at Colcombe which was then destroyed by the Parliamentarian influence bearing in from Lyme. Much property was destroyed and few people in the parish can have been unaffected. Civil War was followed by the devastating plague. The second half of the seventeenth century saw the persecution of nonconformists and, finally, the Monmouth fiasco. The effect was both collective and personal insecurity resulting from external factors but manifesting itself in a desire to control other people. This found a language in the 'culture of discipline' of the Puritans and gained reinforcement from some national acts, such as the Settlement Act of 1662 that sought to alienate 'strangers' who might fall on local poor rates. As I have shown, Puritanism in Colyton, while perhaps a stronger force for much longer than in most other parts of the country, infused the middling orders but never formed the basis of a totally coherent group of believers. One reason for this must have been that many of the Dissenters ran rival businesses within the town. We have also seen that while a wood-pasture economy might have been thought to create an independent cottager class, in fact even common land was largely controlled by the squirearchy and small farmers had little choice but to sell their labour for part of the year. Finally, both the wool trade and the lace industry employed workers and drew immigrants to the parish. Parishes not dominated by one lord might appear to have a relatively egalitarian structure, but beneath the surface the parish teemed with potentially conflictual relationships of dominance and deference based on status, gender and whether people were considered to be strangers or natives. The instability of war increased the number of wandering strangers. In 1634, for example, a number of Irish war wounded and their vagrant wives were examined in Colyton.[2]

Studies of other English parishes have also identified a growing sense of social differentiation in the 1620s and 1630s.[3] The basic social division in seventeenth-century Colyton was between the groups described as 'husbandman' and 'yeoman'. Both terms were used very loosely and, as shown in the description of the Monmouth rebels, a yeoman could be a craftsman. A husbandman might be a day labourer but he could have some land as well. Essentially, however, the dynamic between these two groups, and their relationship with gentlemen and poor labourers, formed the major element of social relationships in the parish. This economic polarisation certainly bolstered the confidence and authority of those who became the town-based elite. Yet in Colyton status was manifestly not the only dynamic. Religion was crucial and some of the patterns of local migration resulted from people following certain preachers and congregations. The evidence for piety at the labourer level is limited and this might persuade us towards seeing Colyton as another parish like Terling in Essex, where a godly elite pressed its ideals of order, morals and reform onto an unruly set of parishioners in a way which paralleled the growing gulf between rich and poor.[4] Many other historians have identified the broad outlines of this 'ideology of discipline'.[5] Martin Ingram has contrasted the village of Keevil in Wiltshire with Terling. He also found hardening attitudes to moral failings but could not identify a godly group or a clear drive to reform personal discipline except in sexual matters. Keevil rather saw 'an unexciting process of adaption to economic conditions and to modifications in social structure'.[6] In Keevil feuds between influential families had more effect on local life 'in so far as religious and moral issues in Keevil were socially divisive the splits were as much vertical as horizontal'.[7] Margaret Spufford has also found no support for 'the Terling thesis'.[8] She argues that Dissent was not the prerogative of village elites but that nonconformity is to be found across the whole taxable population. She is not persuaded by the economic determinism of an argument which links religion with industrial communities and gives less import to the influence of a new religious movement.[9] As we have seen, in Colyton there was not one 'godly people' with an identifiable programme but several factions. Some individuals saw themselves as citizens of a corporate body, others were perhaps more self-interested and concerned with personal and material goals. Above all, as Wrightson stresses, Puritanism stood for a pro-active view of religion. Arguably, nonconformism was too strong and widespread in this area to be unified. Given this situation, the clearest manifestation of control came with relief of the poor and this will provide the central concern of this chapter.

Controlling the Parish: The Structure of Local Governance

Colyton parishioners were subject to several interlocking forms of governance in the early modern period. Firstly, the lord of the manor throughout the period covered by this book was variously named members of the Pole family who owned approximately 60 per cent of the acreage of the parish. The fortunes of the family plummeted in the Civil War. Nevertheless, manorial courts existed throughout this period in this area and were still active in the nineteenth century.[10] Very little has been written on the operation of manorial courts in small towns after the medieval period and their influence is underestimated.[11] The evidence which can be assimilated for Colyton and neighbouring parishes suggests that manors played a large part in regulating the economic and social life of the parish. In Ottery St Mary in 1612 manorial documents mention the regulation of the 'great wastes'.[12] By 1812 the manor still appointed water bailiffs, and even pig and duck drivers.[13] The manor court book for late eighteenth-century Colyton announced deaths of copyholders and the transmission of land, the repair of the stocks and houses in the parish, as well as regulating encroachment on the wastes.[14] The manor also exerted some influence over Colyton market. In October 1763, for example, and at the end of the dairy season, 'We present Jane Marchant, Mary [Hookings] and Ann Hookings for forestalling in buying of Butter, bring into this manor for the use of the Inhabitants thereof and selling the same again to the sd Inhabitants for an unreasonable Profit'. By this time, the manor seems to have taken on the function of galvanising the feoffees into action as the court ordered an inspection of the pitching in the market place and keeping water courses flowing there. The feoffees were ordered to do this within a month or face a fine of 40s. Evidence from the Pinney papers also suggests that their lord of the manor took an active rather than a detached interest in the running of farms. They quarrelled with the Worshipfull Robert Browne over the management of woods and in 1701 Nathaniel complained that 'Browne . . . abuses us thus continually for our Extraordinary good husbandry beyond other which thing hath made our Neighbors envy us alsoe'.[15]

Secondly, in general in the seventeenth century, Devon was strongly governed by the justices and the county administration and in the late 1620s and early 1630s weekly meetings of justices of the peace were held in Colyton.[16] The regularity with which cases were filed from Colyton suggests that the appearance of local criminals was a way of ensuring social control. The justices oversaw the structure of local government, appointing constables to the hundreds. In the seventeenth century, Colyton still had tithingmen who were particularly concerned with preventing disorderly conduct and, in effect, were petty constables. In 1670 there were five petty constables who reported to both the head constables and to the quarter sessions. In a 1631 quarter sessions case the head constable is described as a husbandman.[17] The constables took their cases to the hundred's court, which was effectively a form of petty session.[18] At a lower and voluntary level in the hierarchy of law and order were the land and sea watches in operation in the sixteenth and seventeenth centuries, which were particularly activated in times of danger. In 1588, the year of Armada, the watch and beacons were activated in Colyton with 'six discreet and sufficient persons to report to tythingman'.[19] A 1627 order to the constables of Colyton hundred sought to find men to watch the beacons at Seaton every night. They were to be 'five Noble and sufficient men' who were able to use a musket or forfeit 6d for every night.[20]

In the fraught conditions of the late 1670s, when mustering was common in Colyton, a land watch was also reported at Beer. Colyford, as a borough, had its own administrative structure with a portreeve who was the mayor or his bailiff, and some under-bailliffs. The portreeve carried out his duties using the rents and profits of a close of land called Portreeve's plot. The fact that this area was strongly governed underlies the power of resistance apparent in the seventeenth-century parish when we consider the bold statements made in two court cases already mentioned as showing the enterprise of two poor women in 1648 in Widworthy. A house in Widworthy, kept by Elizabeth Lovett, was invaded by troopers who helped themselves to drink, stole goods and vandalised the house. When the local constable arrived, Thomas Rex of

Colyton announced that they lived under noe Justices of the Peaces lawes'. In another case Henry Bord the younger, a husbandman, and his alehouse keeper wife refused to attend church. When investigated by the constable and tithingman they treated the officials with contempt. When asked why he had not attended church Bord said the last time he went there was no minister there 'and for ought he knew he would goe to church noe more,' although when brought before the justices he changed his story and claimed his wife had been ill.[21]

Thirdly, the dispensing of charity and some economic functions were controlled by the twelve feoffees and the twentymen who had to own property in Colyton and were not allowed to benefit personally from the trust dispensing funds for 'good, godly and commendable uses for the benefit of the people of the parish'. As Hunt suggests, in the years before the Civil War a concern with poverty was regarded in itself as a token of Protestantism.[22] After the expenses of town water, the repair of the market house and the costs of the school, the deducted remainder was distributed amongst the poor who were not in the constant receipt of parochial relief. As already indicated, in the seventeenth century the feoffees were the central repository of Dissent and opposition to the Anglican church and the driving force behind the militaristic backing for Monmouth. While very active in the seventeenth century, the feoffees went into decline from the early eighteenth century, perhaps along with the falling popularity of nonconformity and less emphasis on an ethos of incorporation in the parish. In complete contrast to their seventeenth-century vigour, by 1740 the number of feoffees had been reduced to two: 'Thos Marwood & Phil Mitchell each above 80 years of age, the latter often receiving assistance from the parish as a Pauper & it is thought at that time there was not one twentyman surviving, nor had been for many years'.[23] About Whitsuntide 1742 there were several meetings of the parishioners, apparently to revitalise the body and it was reported that twelve persons were nominated as feoffees. A contemporary reported that some of these new feoffees were also in very mean circumstances, such as the miller, John Good, 'who was not worth above 20 pounds a year and several people had been omitted who had greater worth'. In 1742 the vicar announced that tithes would be taken in kind. In a meeting of the new feoffees some of them did not consent to these 'unreasonable pretended customs'. This dispute, which generated a parish-wide quarrel, explains the revival of detailed poor relief records from this point and seems to be an attempt to wrest the entire control of local government, including social welfare, away from the influence of the feoffees. In turn it was argued: 'These trustees of this charity have assumed to themselves power to take into their custody all the publick rates of the said parish, the overseers of the poor instead collect the rates but are compelled to give their accounts to New Trustees, in their Chamber, as it is called and they deny the inspection of any of their papers'. By the early nineteenth century any resurgence of the power of the feoffees was again vestigal as the Lysons reported that there were four feoffees and that only six of the last twentymen to be elected were still living.[24]

In early modern Colyton, as in most other English parishes, local governance rested on a delicate balance between four sources of power: the manor, justices and county administration, a local incorporated body and the church. At times, these could overlap in terms of personnel or they could become confrontational. The periods of consensus or conflict are of crucial importance in the shaping of early modern parishes, but in very many cases conflicts are almost impossible to reconstruct. While they may generate documents, as did the tithe dispute of 1742 in Colyton, the evidence is fragmentary and fractured because so much of the process is subterfuge and secrecy. The possession or destruction of local documents is part of this process. Document creation is also a result of political and religious circumstances. This is most easily seen in the case of Colyton parish register, but it also becomes apparent that the survival of poor relief records for only the years 1682/3, 1698/99 and 1740–70 is the product of particular circumstances. Local historians have perhaps been too ready to attribute the destruction of records to chance happenings such as fire and mice, rather than to the process of legitimating political struggles. This was particularly likely to be the case in a parish such as Colyton where power resided in several different bodies.

In Colyton the loss of political control by the feoffees in the eighteenth century can be related to social division, impoverishment and industrial decline, and the wider diminishing influence of Dissent. It also coincides with the rising importance of the lord of the manor.[25] Sir William Pole (1678–1758), who was Master of the Household to Queen Anne, revived the family's flagging fortunes. But it was his son, Sir John William, who refashioned the family name to 'de la Pole' and placed an enduring stamp on the community. Sir John William bought the Shute lands from the crown (they had formerly been held on lease). By his death he had increased the family estates in the area to over 10,000 acres, adding lands in Colyton, Colyford, the manor of Whitford, and Seaton. In 1787 he built a commanding new Regency dwelling, Shute House and renamed the former residence 'Shute Barton' (Plate 7). Sir John William was no absentee, and the influence of himself and his wife is found in local politics. 'Sir John' is hovering in the background of many poor law and select vestry decisions of the late eighteenth century. Perhaps this tilt in the balance of power could have been offset if Colyton had obtained borough status or obtained a charter of incorporation during the Tudor and Stuart era. Arguably, this would have given wider, less introverted recognition to the town of Colyton than was provided by the feoffees.

It was possible in these east Devon parishes for groups of yeoman

Plate 7. Shute Barton House.
(D. Sharpe)

farmers to override manorial lords and landowners, giving rise to a struggle for power. One instance is the 1755 case of the defence of commoners' rights in Stockland, as discussed in Chapter 4. Another interesting expression of local democracy concerns smallpox inoculation in Shute. In 1789 Sir John William de la Pole wrote to the Shute vestry with a plan for general inoculation of the poor of the parish at his own expense.[26] To his surprise, the offer was rejected but inoculation went ahead at parish expense. Subsequently, in 1803, perhaps to affirm a position in local administration, Lady de la Pole was nominated as overseer of the poor for the parish.

Provision for the poor has been viewed in a rather unproblematic light by historians. As the provision of relief was statutory from the sixteenth century, it is often assumed that there were uniform ways of dealing with it across parishes. Recent research has uncovered differences between the north and south of England.[27] In investigating the management of the margins of a parish like Colyton within the context of other local history studies, it is possible to go further than this—to argue that social welfare provision varied between contingent parishes and also to suggest that it changed over time to reflect political and religious preoccupations. The next section will examine the provision of relief in some detail and later sections will concentrate on the particular marginal groups who were relieved.

The Politics of Poverty in the Local Context

In 1661 Francis Fry, a Honiton shoe-maker, was asked by Mr Richard Levermore, who was the holder of the lease of Honiton market weighbeam, whom he was going to vote for as burgess (Member of Parliament).[28] Levermore was the electoral agent for two of the candidates. Fry said there were few supporters for the Royalist candidates, Sir Peter Prideaux and Sir Courtenay-Pole, except for 'alehouse haunters and poor beggarly rogues and if they should come to the parish to be relieved by it they should have noe more but to keepe them alive, but would not starve them'. Fry had a poor opinion of these candidates: 'if they should carry it they would not sitt in the parliament house long'. Roger Rode, a cordwainer, came into Robert Lee's house and found Levermore and Fry in discussion about the poor of Honiton. Levermore said he wondered 'why soe many poor people should be against the Burrow [Borough]' for 'if they should come to want they must be relieved by the Burrow and he would think upon them that they should have noe more but only to keep them alive', 'then francis fry asked him whether he would starve them and he replied noe, but they should have what needs they must'. The conclusion, spelled out by the clerk, was that those for Prideaux and Courtenay-Pole were 'a company of loose fellowes and pott companions'. Julian Rode, otherwise Bonefield, wife of Roger, also said the poor of Honiton were against the borough. Richard Trood, tailor, who had called for a cup of beer at Levermore's house, said he would vote for Prideaux and Courtenay-Pole. Levermore replied that if he would vote for Sir William Waller and Mr Yonge and persuade others to do the same, he would give him 'ten shillings and halfe ten for Mr Yonge and Waller are very honest men and may do good to the town'. Then Levermore gave him five or six jugs of beer over the next few days, and refused money for it. John Abbot, butcher, was asked by John Bussell, glover, to whom he gave his support and he said Prideaux and Courtenay-Pole. Bussell said 'he had given it to the devills' and Abbott replied that 'they were mortal men and that Sir Peter Prideaux deserved it as he lost two sons in the late King's Service'. John Pulman, tailor, asked Paull Beer, mason, to whom he would give his support when he was working in his court. He said 'Peter Prideaux but that he did not live in the borough'. Pulman retorted that he would give it for popery.

Prideaux and Sir Courtenay-Pole triumphed in this election.[29] Interestingly, most of the candidates had a close association with Colyton. Courtenay-Pole was an old Cavalier who had moved from Colcombe Castle to Shute when the Castle was burned in the Civil Wars. Yonge was a leading property owner in the area and a prominent Presbyterian. Levermore was subsequently investigated for bribery. The voices we hear of in the proceedings are those of the 'potwallers': Honiton was a very democratic parish with an electorate of 300–500 because every inhabitant in the borough who had a family and who boiled a pot had a vote. Indeed Pole had restored this franchise.[30] The detail provided on this case, with depositions taken from a large number of Honiton dwellers, shows the enmeshed nature of questions surrounding the relief of local poverty, with the schisms founded on politics and religion. As a training ground for lace-making, Honiton felt the full force of incomers to a greater extent than Colyton and the discussions here reflect concern over questions of the extent to which the poor should be maintained. The poor are characterised as 'alehouse haunters', which seems ironic in a case which turns on an innkeeper dispensing jugs of beer as political bribes. A concern with social welfare was associated with Puritans, and as we have seen this cannot be entirely separated from their employment of the poor in various works projects. Yet by the 1660s there were many attacks on public provision from their detractors.[31] Interestingly, the poor themselves seem to have retained a deferential loyalty to aristocrats. Their voting allegiances for Prideaux and Courtney-Pole parallel the way in which the poorest still attended Colyton church when it stood in a sea of nonconformity.

One major issue with which local communities grappled in the second half of the seventeenth century was the question of who had the authority and held the purse strings to relieve the poor. In some senses the older belief in casual almsgiving still persisted. Brushfield has documented the many ways in which the elite might dispense alms through church alms boxes, 'bid-ales' or the 'charity bags' carried by the wealthy.[32] In some parishes, such as Colyton, relief had been dispensed by an incorporated body for over fifty years before the national parish poor relief system was defined by the Acts of 1598 and 1601. Surrounding parishes also had poor relief systems that predated the statutes, such as the Elizabethan 'Wardens of the Poore' in Farway. The Colyton feoffees were not an unusual organisation for the county of Devon. Ottery St Mary, for example, incorporated feoffees in 1440 when John Lawrence gave four houses and certain lands to be held by twelve trustees.[33] As in the case of Colyton, the purpose was to distribute the income arising from these properties among the deserving poor. In the course of time, further leases were entrusted to the feoffees, who were not themselves allowed to hold the common property. For most English parishes early records of either the operation of the statutory system or the more informal and discretionary means of relief are difficult to find. One case from quarter sessions which documents a female 'Robin Hood' in Colyton may suggest that in its earliest years there were either serious failings in the relief system or it operated in a partisan way. Elizabeth Kemer was a servant to a mercer in Colyton when in 1607 she was accused of stealing goods which she gave away to others.[34] She gave her father 12d in money and two types of cloth from the shop. She also delivered various small quantities of wheat and other provisions to the elderly wives of townspeople. Several deliveries of money, barley meal, faggots of wood, and cloth were made to William Abbott's daughter. Abbot's wife told her 'that she dydde serve god to steale from her maister and . . . for that they are so misarable'. Kemer also took money from her master's hose in his chamber to give to the poor, perhaps suggesting that he failed to give personal gifts to the needy.

A double structure of relief defined by both the poor law and the corporate system administered by the charitable body of the Chamber of Feoffees seems to have become operative from the 1620s, in response to growing poverty from harvest failure, land consolidation by the yeomen and the vicissitudes of the textile trades. Wales has found evidence that the poor law was becoming more organised in the 1620s, and an inquisition into the charitable works of the feoffees took place in 1623.[35] While it is possible that the totally destitute were relieved, it is likely that a good deal of assessment of character and reputation determined whether the more marginally poor were relieved. An ecclesiastical court case from Seaton in 1619 gives some flavour of the assessments which were made of the parish poor.[36] William Charter was 'a poore man relieved by the Almes of the parrish and allowed 8d a week by the parish of Seaton . . . and hath gonne about begginge'. By contrast, Roger Whicker was 'an honest, sufficient householder and a harmless man'. Elizabeth Crabbe was a 'poore woman & one that doth worke and goeth errands for divers peopole . . . & hath sometymes meate and sometymes money for her paynes'. Meanwhile, Helen Bubb, notably a migrant, 'Is a woman of small creditt and reputation & very much given to drunkeness'. Since she came to live at Seaton she had been 'divers tymes overtaken wth drinke'.

In the early 1630s, as poverty increased, there were several cases of corn theft and cows being milked by unknown persons in the Colyton area. In 1631 Thomas Culme of Colyton was suspected of stealing corn from a farmer, John Cox.[37] John Kerbie, husbandman and head constable, searched Culme's house and found a peck of corn in a bag hidden under the bolster of Culme's bed. Culme's wife implied that Cox had given the corn to her husband after Culme had spent the week threshing in Cox's barn and Mrs Culme had winnowed wheat for Cox. Mrs Culme later admitted that she had taken the corn herself and Culme argued that she had done so without his knowledge as he was out of the barn 'to water a billow sheafe to bind up his billows'. This case is plainly stated but raises questions. Mrs Culme had anticipated, in a time of relative corn shortage, that she and her husband would be given a small share of the crop they worked on. Around the same time Robert Knight of Uffculme, husbandman, threshed in his master's barn. After he had finished work in the evening, he locked the barn doors and went into his master's kitchen, looked for a bag, then took a threshed peck of wheat. He then hid it in a bundle of oaten straw in a pig stall. In court, he claimed that this plan was at the instigation of Bartholomew Woods who came to the farmhouse to ask for wheat every night. His master was [not?] in the habit of 'giving of him Bread sufficient'. Both Knight and Woods appear to have been propertyless.[38]

Individual failures of generosity to neighbours or employees evident in the lean times of the 1630s became more significant with social polarisation, but were dwarfed by much more general destitution in the 1640s. During the Civil War, soldiers made further demands on overstretched reserves of relief. In 1640 four soldiers of the King appeared in a widow's back yard in Seaton.[39] One of them demanded relief. When the widow's daughter refused, he began to rail at her saying he must be relieved because he was a soldier. She called to the widow of a neighbour, Richard French, to help her, crying aloud 'God for French' at which the soldier cried (louder) 'God for duty'! Neighbours gathered, and soon this incident had developed into a fracas with the soldiers threatening the Seaton tithingman with a drawn sword. As we have seen, and as was the case in many other communities, Colyton established parish provision for a stock of £20 in 1641, which was to be 'imployed for the setting on worke of such poore people . . . as shall not be able to procure themselves worke from tyme to tyme' and administered by the feoffees.[40] In January 1646 the presentment of the constable of Axminster said that many strangers had lately take up arms in the King's party and were now resident in the town and living without a calling.[41] By the end of this decade, Devon was described as an 'Exhausted Countie' in quarter sessions, and trade dislocation and plague deepened the crisis. With 473 plague fatalities in Colyton, the parish suffered enormously. Very soon maimed soldiers, many unable to work, presented another problem. John Ffitz had been in Royalist service in the wars; 'he remained Loyal and Constant and never deserted the Service in the worste of times and for his Loyattie was ruined by the Enemie his hows & goods burnd & destroyed'.[42] He described himself as being utterly ruined by 1666.

The mid-century crisis must have affected the tendency for many parishes in this area to attempt a latter day 'Reformation of Manners'. As Clark and Slack put it, 'Towns . . . took the lead in enforcing the Puritan ethic, the suppression of gaming, vice and drunkeness, and the preservation of the sanctity of the English Sunday'.[43] One of the clearest statements of this cultural shift comes from the east Devon parish of Awliscombe. In 1662 Peter Barton, an incoming overseer of the poor who took over the job with reforming zeal, wrote: 'What emulation and contention there is in this parish against order and good government . . . many shameful offences have been committed in this p[ari]she which have made it become odious & contemptible by Remyse Officers, Examples of the same who care not that disorder ther is therein for drunkenesse, fornication, unlicenced alehouses, masterlesse persons, monsters of schysme, decievers of the Relief at own cost'.[44] He had not seen an account from the last overseer of his parish, 'gross faction styll remayning'. Very similar statements and actions followed from other parishes, often amid an undertow of anarchy. In 1671 George Welland of Thorverton, a man accused of beating and wounding his wife, said on arrest that 'he did not care a Turd for any Justice of the peace in England'.[45] In the Ottery hundred, the 'multiplicitie of Alehouses' was presented to quarter sessions several times along with a number of people as masterless persons in the 1660s.[46] In 1663, amid settlement disputes about migrancy and illegal alehouse keeping, the overseer of Ottery was complaining of the abuses of former officers in the previous years.[47] By midsummer 1668 there was a complaint from the inhabitants that the overseers were not carrying out justices' orders and were irregularly keeping accounts.[48] There were many recognisances for alehouses in Colyton, especially over the period 1657–73.[49] The depth of the problems in east Devon parishes largely dependent on trade, and the sheer volume of work necessary to administer the relief of the poor, were made obvious when quarter sessions wrote to the King and Secretary of State about the danger of disease, particularly amongst poor people who were already subject to disorder because of the decay of trade 'upon wch their subsistence too much depends'.[50] This was soon followed by a petition from Sidmouth in 1666 that there were many parishioners in the King's service and a great deal of women and children not able to relieve or subsist of themselves. The parish was too poor to bear the burden.

With this economic and political climate in other parishes, and the atmosphere of factional infighting within Colyton, it comes as little surprise to find that the parish officers were similarly being replaced. In 1665 Stephen Bird was committed to gaol by quarter sessions for cheating the parish in his overseer's account.[51] In 1671 a warrant was issued for John Burnard for contempt of previous justices' warrants and for reproachful language.[52] In 1673 and 1674, under the impetus of the 1673 Test Act that obliged all officeholders to be Anglicans, a succession of constables were replaced in Colyton, with Mr John Collings being discharged in 1674.[53] In 1675 Robert Collings, the conventicler and one of the Ottery St Mary overseers of the poor for the ensuing year, was dismissed from office for 'that Mr Colins is Master of Arts and for other reasons showne unto this Courte'.[54] A petition was presented to quarter sessions in 1684 from Jone Ffarant of Payhembury. Her husband, a nonconformist, had left her six months earlier, leaving a family of five children to be maintained out of her labour. But the justices and parish officers refused to relieve them because of a recent order of the quarter sessions directing overseers to deny relief to absentees from church. The family had now rejoined the parish church. This case is a clear indication of the conditional nature of parish relief. In Colyton when the extreme dissenter Roger Satchell was forced to render his accounts of relief in 1682, there were clearly questions over his partiality. This may have resulted from the case of Joane Ball, a Colyton widow, in 1681. Joane Ball had an order from three justices for relief from the parish of Colyton, but when she showed the order to Roger Satchell, overseer, and John Gould, churchwarden, they contemptuously refused to obey it and said 'that if the Justices had any more paper & Inke to spare they should send it to them, and if they would have the poore p[ai]d they should come & doe it themselves for they (meaning the s[ai]d Satchell and Gould) were Justices themselves in their places and speaking severall other contemptuous words agt the sd Justices'.[55] Both Satchell and Gould showed personal generosity in other instances (for example, Satchell donated money and clasped Bibles to poor children in his will dated 1684 and similarly John Gould left 40s to the poor of Colyton in 1723), so this action was likely to be a political statement.

As we have seen in the analysis of the Hearth Tax, Colyton had one of the highest proportions of paupers in the 1670s in Devon. The control of social responsibility for the poor had both religious and economic underpinnings. First, there is no doubt that the welfare of the poor— especially of their own congregations—was seen as a particular role of Puritans and, later, nonconformists. As John Pinney wrote in his sermon in 1666, 'Twenty Lessons to be Learned from London's Late Burning Written by Me JP': 'charity according to the ability yt God hath given us and others we should largely and cheerfully contribute to their necessety as theres no duty more largely commanded in the word of God than to relieve the poor especially Godly poor'.[56] Secondly, control of the purse strings was an obvious way to draw in new believers. In Colyton the poor had divided loyalties. The analysis of marriage in Colyton shows that some of the poor remained with the Anglican church but that some of the poor were Monmouth rebels. In a wider sense, the control of poor relief also gave some control over cheap sources of labour. The craftsmen, traders, lace dealers and wool merchants who were active Dissenters also employed labourers. There is evidence of overseers perhaps copying from the token system in use for paying lace-makers to operate a type of truck system for parish relief. In 1684 a widow with two small children to maintain said that in 1681 one of the Ottery St Mary overseers had been ordered to relieve her at a rate of 6s monthly. Yet when she went to his house she was unable to obtain money but was forced to take wares from his shop such as wheat, bacon or other small commodities.[57] Thirdly, and perhaps most crucially, in Colyton, which was not a borough and did not have a mayor, the overseer was the most important lay position, followed by the constable, from which it was possible for an ordinary parishioner to exert a particular influence and to effect a moral reformation of the parish. We have already seen the reluctance of the churchwardens to take office in the 1670s. We have also seen that Roger Satchell as overseer refused to pay certain people relief and proclaimed himself to be under no authority but his own. The fact that he presided over an annual budget of over £235 in a parish with a population of an estimated 1,700 people was a source of considerable local power. The overseers of this period stood at the head of an apparatus for poor relief that well surpassed that of the eighteenth century. Only fragmentary poor relief records survive from seventeenth-century Colyton and it seems likely that Satchell was forced to render accounts in the early 1680s (the account for 1682/3 is one of only two years available for the seventeenth century) but otherwise dispensed relief according to his religious and political leanings.

The politics of relief in particular parishes need to be considered by all historians when they approach this subject.[58] In so far as records of seventeenth-century relief survive then, they may not be actual reflections of poverty but political documents. This suggests that poor lists provide an indication of who should be relieved that was more complicated than the division into deserving and undeserving poor identified by historians. It may also have literally been the case that much poverty was ignored during the chaos of changing officeholders. In 1689 quarter sessions reported the appointment of a marshal for apprehending rogues, vagabonds and beggars because of the 'great multitudes of idle and disorderly psons within this county lying aside their lawfull trades & imployments through an idle disposition to wander up and downe the Country begging' due to the fact that their numbers had much increased recently because of the neglect of constables and other officers.[59] Even in 1690 when nonconformists had gained legitimacy, a Sidbury shoemaker said that factions influenced his trade due to 'threates and other irregular and illegal practices by the officers and other parishioners of Sidbury'. He was unable to obtain a convenient habitation to manage and carry on his trade of shoe-making and complained of oppressive and illegal practices.[60] Such complaints are still found today in towns that have become dominated by religious cults. In Colyton, the degree of control was intensified because the feoffees controlled many of the land leases. The next section will consider patterns of the receipt of relief. Some demographic historians have stressed that the inclusive welfare system of English parishes had an important influence on family structure, in particular, facilitating the independence of the parental generation and the separate housing of young couples.

Receiving Relief in the Seventeenth Century

A very late case of witchcraft comes from the rural area near to Colyton.[61] In 1693 Dorothy East, a Luppitt widow, bewitched Joseph Thomas when he would not give her cider. She then begged beer from Bridgett Toods who was saving it for her sick child. When offered water instead, East refused to take it from a dish but asked for the child's cup. The child died three weeks later. Jane Ham smoked tobacco with East but later when East begged tobacco from Ham she refused to give her any. As a result East bewitched her child, who subsequently died. Christopher Rodgers denied her milk, and she bewitched his cows. Finally, Sarah (the only deponent except the physician able to sign), the wife of farmer John Byrd, deposed that East came to them a little before Christmas and begged alms from her for Christmas but Sarah told her that 'she designed not to give anything to such poore people as had monthly Reliefe of the psh, neither should she have anything'. The retribution was that Byrd had very ill fortune with his cattle. Finally, East went to John Worthell and said she wanted to live with him in his house. When he rejected the idea he was subsequently stricken and 'fell into a discontented Condition, running up and down as a mad man, and soe continued for the space of one day and halfe'. Even when his senses returned he reported spending a week in bed with great pains and prickings in his body and limbs.

As in all witchcraft cases, there is a danger of over-interpretation. On the face of it, the East case is very similar to those analysed by Macfarlane for Essex.[62] East appears to be a marginalised character who is being denied neighbourly reciprocity. East seems to assume that she can take pickings from all the households around her and perhaps the traditional type of pre-Reformation alms-giving in the area involved this sort of gratuity to the evidently poor. Two aspects of this case are particularly suggestive. First, when East tried to claim traditional Christmas alms from a farmer's wife, she was denied because she was assumed to be in receipt of regular parish relief. Secondly, East seems to have assumed that her neediness entitled her to move in with one John Worthell, suggesting as appears in other documents that lodging and boarding were common. Whatever, doors closed in East's face and she was at the mercy of local poor relief, which, as we will see, gave a generous living only to those inside the community who seemed to qualify for it. East maintained a traditional view of what she could expect from neighbourly relief, but her ideas clashed with a different conception of relief that was now held by her wealthier, property-holding acquaintances.

The feoffees' operation of poor relief meant they relieved people by two means in the seventeenth century. First, they paid poor people's rents on a regular basis. Secondly, they provided quarterly doles.[63] The rental system was a particularly generous gesture, giving people up to 50 per cent more than their actual rental value in some cases. It seems likely that rents were falling in the seventeenth century as population pressure and demand for housing eased off, but the feoffee payments remained at a fixed level and must have provided a high level of welfare for receipients. For both types of relief the recipients were a selective group who were either single or widowed and generally elderly; sometimes the rent list was even titled 'Widdows Rents'. There were around forty people on the list and the quarterly dole consisted of disbursements of 6s 8d to the same forty people. The relief seems to have been administered rather inflexibly. Once a person was admitted to the feoffees' list, they were given a pension until their death regardless of whether there was any change in their circumstances. Falling prices meant that the feoffees created a 'welfare state' situation in late seventeenth-century Colyton for those able to qualify for this relief.

The total reconstitution method which exploits the information on Colyton inhabitants' life-cycles provides a very effective technique for looking at the poor. Payments were granted to people on an individual basis; payments to families occur in the accounts, but are not normal until the nineteenth century. It was certainly not the case that payment would automatically be given to the male head of a family as was usual over a century later.[64] Married women, children and young adults were often recorded as being given payments in the overseers' account book without reference to the male head of household. This highlights the fact that each member of the family was expected to achieve his or her own maintenance, perhaps reflecting a Puritan-inspired sense of self-reliance. The assumption can also be made that long-term family poverty was a limited phenomenon until after the mid-eighteenth century.

Nevertheless, the presence of local industry led to instability. The situation in late seventeenth-century Colyton had some parallels in Whickham, County Durham, where in the period from the late 1670s to the early 1740s the number of poor in receipt of regular allowances almost trebled because the development of coal mining and an increase in the wage-dependent sector brought about an increase in life-cyle poverty.[65] Poverty affected families with a burden of children who were not yet old enough to contribute to the family budget. An example is George Bird, who appeared in the Hearth Tax as a pauper in 1674. He had four children aged between 5 and 12. By the 1682/83 poor rate collection he was contributing to the rate, being assessed on several sections of property in Colyton.[66] By then he had come through a temporary phase of poverty. But here, however, it is necessary to note a problem of interpretation. Without full records of the meetings, and even sometimes when we have them for later cases, it is impossible to judge why Bird was actually relieved. His family were of long standing in the parish and would have had a legal settlement there. He was

Table 6.1 Sex and age comparison of those receiving casual poor relief in Colyton in 1682/3, 1742/3 and 1763/4

		Child <17	Male 17-50	Female 17-50	Male >50	Female >50
1682/3	Single	5	3	9	2	11
98 cases	%	16.7	10.0	30.0	6.7	36.7
	Married	–	12	–	5	–
	%	–	70.6	–	29.4	–
	Widowed	–	1	3	9	27
	%	–	2.5	7.5	22.5	67.5
1742/3	Single	32	1	19	2	1
102 cases	%	58.2	1.8	34.5	3.6	1.8
	Married	–	7	21	7	–
	%	–	20.0	60.0	20.0	–
	Widowed	–	–	–	4	3
	%	–	–	–	57.1	42.9
1763/4	Single	26	8	24	3	11
163 cases	%	36.1	11.1	33.3	4.2	15.3
	Married	–	21	10	22	5
	%	–	36.2	17.2	37.9	8.6
	Widowed	–	–	1	5	15
	%	–	–	4.8	23.8	71.4

probably related to the lace-making or the farming family of Birds; perhaps he was also a Dissenter and therefore one of the favoured group granted relief. Yet he was not a Monmouth rebel. The increasing wage dependency in Colyton also meant people slipped below the poverty line in old age.

As soon as measures are applied to the poor relief records stark facts emerge. Over half of the population were classified as paupers in the Hearth Tax, but the feoffees who were operating the poor law system appeared to be relieving less than a fifth of them. A breakdown can be produced showing payments made by the overseers of the poor for the three years for which full information is extant. Payments were made from Easter to Easter, and the years covered in Table 6.1 are 1682/3, 1742/3 and 1763/4. The breakdown has been made according to age and marital status where this can be established from the reconstitution. In the 1682/3 listing eleven individuals could not be linked to FRFs, nine of whom were women. In the 1742/3 list five people could not be linked. In the last list twelve people could not be traced, nine of whom were female. These figures in themselves suggest that it was mainly natives of Colyton who were relieved. There were some problems in classifying men

Table 6.2 Poor disbursements in Devon parishes per head of population in the Compton Census 1676

Parish	Population	Amount per Head
Halberton (1685)	1045	6s.1d.
Clayhidon (1687)	341	5s 6d
Zeal Monachorum (1676)	205	5s.5d
Hennock (1676)	220	4s.11d
Nymet Rowland (1675)	40	4s.9d.
Colyton (1682)	1019	4s.7d
Farringdon (1685)	231	4s.6d.
Chudleigh (1676)	646	3s.6d.
Drewsteignton (1676)	550	3s.3d.
Marldon (1676)	206	2s.5d.
Spreyton (1676)	193	2s.5d.
Dunchideock (1680)	114	2s.1d.
Cheriton Fitzpaine (1676)	401	2s.1d.
Upton Hellions (1676)	75	2s.0d
Cullompton (1677)	3061	1s.11d.
Stoke Gabriel (1671)	387	1s.10d.
Ashburton (1678)	2003	1s.9d.
Warkleigh (1676)	139	1s.7d.
Abbotskerswell (1676)	198	1s.5d.
Churston Ferrers (1671)	316	1s.5d.
Newton Ferrers (1667)	324	1s.5d.
Instow (1676)	183	1s.5d.
Tawstock (1676)	960	1s.2d.
Bere Ferrers (1666)	552	1s 0d.
Bovey Tracey (1667)	1623	0s 9d
Kingswear (1677)	334	0s.5d.
Stoke in Teignhead (1668)	400	0s.4d.

as 'single' since they could have married and raised a family in another parish and then returned to Colyton in old age, as their place of settlement, specifically to claim poor relief. It has been assumed in this table that they were single if no family was mentioned in any document linked to them in the total reconstitution. 'Married' was the legal rather than actual status of ten females aged 17–50 in 1763/4 because only in four of these cases did husband and wife actually live together.

The overseers of the poor paid out a similar amount of relief per head of poor in 1682/3 as in 1742/3. In 1682/3 an average of £2 6s 0d was paid for each person. In 1742/3 an average of £2 5s 0d was paid, although the cost of pursuing settlement cases had increased. However, it is evident that the orientation of these payments changed entirely. Whereas payments were directed to the elderly in the seventeenth century, younger sectors of the population were paid in the eighteenth century. Whereas the elderly accounted for 55 per cent of payments in the seventeenth century, in the eighteenth century only 16 per cent of those receiving payments were elderly. While it is not possible to make an accurate assessment of the age structure of the population of Colyton, the tendency to late marriage and smaller families suggests that it contained a large number of the elderly in the seventeenth century. Apparently poor relief supported single or widowed people in the seventeenth century but over the next forty years there was a change to support for a wider section of the population, which took in more married people, and women in particular. Single women in the 17–50 age group were also increasingly supported in the eighteenth century. Overall the poor relief officers supported a greater number of women than men. By the 1763/4 listing the most striking result is the large increase in adult males who claimed relief. These were particularly in the over 50 age group.

The evidence from the feoffees' bailiff's accounts confirms this picture. The ratio of women to men who were in receipt of rent relief was three to one. By linkage to the reconstitution it is apparent that the men who received rent relief were usually between ten and twenty years older than the women. Turning to the amounts paid out for poor relief, in comparison with other Devon parishes for which the data exists, Colyton seems to have been generous in the amount of relief which was distributed. In Table 6.2 the amount of relief which was distributed was compared with the population who were aged 16 or older, as given in the Compton Census of 1676.[67] Twenty-seven Devon parishes which have extant seventeenth-century overseer of the poor accounts were analysed. The relief distributed in the nearest possible year to 1676 was considered. The year which was used is given in brackets. The payments varied widely, but Colyton was near the top of the scale in terms of money distributed.

All the Devon parish accounts show a bias towards more women than men receiving relief.[68] In the parish lists at least two women appeared to every man. In Colyton considering the 'casual' budget alone, women accounted for 51 per cent of the payments given to adults in 1682/3, 65 per cent in 1742/3 and 60 per cent in 1763/4. The female bias has been noted in studies of early poor relief payments carried out for other parts of the country.[69] The reason why women, and widows in particular, were given a disproportionate amount of poor relief have usually been attributed to their lack of access to the labour market and associated societal disadvantages which went with their gender and single status. In the case of Colyton a living was available from the lace trade for single and married women alike but as we have seen the strain on their eyesight may have meant that few of them were able to pursue this in later life. The fact that there were more women in the parish than men, particularly in the town area, goes a further way towards explaining the bias.

Where any hints of residency are given in the feoffees' accounts, most of the poor women seem to have lived within Colyton town rather than in the rural areas. This suggests an unsurprising correlation between poverty and the more industrial area of the parish. Institutional bodies like the feoffees may have maintained a tradition of town relief which was modelled on earlier guild structures whereas paternalistic gestures on the part of farmers were thought to suffice in country districts, as is suggested in the Dorothy East case. Yet yeomen farmers contributed to the poor rate. It may simply be that housing suitable for the poor was more readily available in the town.

The Colyton evidence clearly shows that when some parish women were too old to work for their maintenance they would be fully supported by the parish. A systematic revision of the question about the amount of poor relief that women were given was made by Wales, who argued that it was likely that an individual living alone in the second half of the seventeenth century could survive on 1s a week.[70] This was roughly the average amount of support given in Colyton where it averaged out at 46s a year. The amount of relief given to women roughly correlated with their age if they were not marked down as sick. Whereas some women were only given partial support, others were being fully maintained by the poor relief authorities. Widows living alone in Colyton were given up to 8s a month. Comparison with payments to widows in Axminster, where payments varied between 3s and 6s but averaged 4s, suggests that this was generous.[71]

Taylor estimates that half of the total poor relief in Devon in the period 1780–1840 came from sources which were outside the poor law jurisdiction.[72] Hoskins found 380 parishes with charities in Devon. Only fifty parishes had none and they were generally minute in size.[73] Notably, the Chamber of Feoffees was appointed to administer these private charities.[74] William Poole (Pole) of Shute left 12d to every poor householder in Colyton, Colyford and surrounding parishes in 1587. In 1614 Francis Seller of Kilmington left 20s to the poor of Colyton along with other parishes. An important charity was established by Thomas Holmes in his will of 1670. Twelve sixpenny loaves were to be distributed every six weeks to twelve poor people of the parish to be selected regardless of whether they received poor relief or not, and once chosen they were to enjoy the charity for life. Thomas Tomkins of Axminster left 40s to Colyton and to several surrounding parishes in 1688. In 1812 Isaac Grigg's charity mirrored feoffee relief, as he left £100, the interest from which was to be distributed to the poor of the parish who did not receive parochial relief, in proportion to the size of their families.

In the seventeenth century, Colyton offered generous relief to those who qualified for it and constituted a particular group that we might describe as the honorary poor. But there is little evidence for relief for the shifting migrant group who formed the major part of the workforce for the parish.

Housing the Poor

In Colyton the structure of charity and poor relief supported certain single people and facilitated their separate residency. The nature of the housing market in the second half of the seventeenth century and the early eighteenth century also made it possible for them to establish and maintain households without being married. The evidence from Colyton furnishes several examples of single people living alone. There are more examples of single women than men. In the 1674 Hearth Tax, Anne Grange the elder, a widow, and her single daughter, Anne Grange the younger, appear as separate householders on the list of paupers. In the 1682/3 poor law disbursement the younger Anne was paid her house rent and her mother was given a separate allowance. The parish chamber formed a collection of small dwellings with gardens which were rented at nominal rents of 4s or less per year.[75] This could be easily covered by a single woman who worked as a lace-maker, or even from the allowance of an elderly person who was past work. Maintenance of the property that the poor occupied was carried out by the feoffees. The poor relief authorities in Colyton and surrounding parishes also rented properties for the use of the poor. In 1683 Joane Batt, a widow of Ottery St Mary, complained that for many years the overseers of the poor had placed poor people in three houses of hers and had paid her 16s per annum for each of the houses but now the overseers had stopped paying poor people's rent in this way. It seems that a 'tenant's market' for all rented property existed in late seventeenth-century Colyton. Rents started to rise in the first half of the eighteenth century. By linking properties in lease books it is possible to see that the average rent of a poor person's cottage rose from around 8s a year in the 1660–90 period to £1 a year by 1750.[76] Linkage to the reconstitution shows that households were not only set up on marriage but sometimes before that in the early modern period. In the 1636 Ship Tax return some young men had their own house or land before they married. Edward Wilkins, son of the ejected Puritan minister of Colyton, was living apart from his widowed mother in 1678 when he died at the age of 21. Joseph Tucker alias Baker, a poor man, contributed towards the 1726 Church Rate on a house he rented in Colyton four years prior to his marriage.[77]

Occasionally, family papers referred to cottage leases on the 'waste' or common. In 1690 John Lewes, a shoemaker, rented a cottage and ground on the common.[78] The cottage was a mere 14 feet in length! Court rolls show that these houses had outside ovens which were likely to have been shared.[79] The houses on the common were probably little more than huts which were of a short-term and moveable nature.[80] John Knowles, a Colyton weaver, left his cottage in Colyton to his son. This was subdivided into higher and lower parts. One dwelling consisted of one entry, a cellar, a ground chamber, one other chamber, and 19 feet of ground. The rental payment to the lord of the manor was 8d per year and his son sublet it.[81] Richard Dunning of Exeter commented on the separate housing of the poor in 1698, that 'Several of them have ordinarily one house apiece entirely to themselves, which would conveniently serve three or four of them'.[82] It could be accumulations of independent dwellings under one roof that led to the extreme estimate of Gregory King that there were 6.6 persons per house in Colyton.[83] This was not a representation of the actual situation in rural areas of the parish since a list of Pole family leases for the manor of Yardbury shows that two or three children were the norm to be living in each house with their parents in the period from the 1650s to the late 1670s, but King's estimate probably accurately reflects migrant lodging in houses in the town.[84] A case from Colyton in 1607 shows that lodging and taking inmates was not unknown. Roger Shakell of Colyton was accused of stealing a coffer containing money from Widow Teape. The living circumstances described Shakell's own house, 'where Widd Teape hath a roome to lye in'. He claimed to be retrieving money which Widow Teape owed to the hundred's court, so she had perhaps surrendered her own house on falling into debt.[85] In 1641 Henry Best described the type of houses which were divided in two to produce separate dwellings in Yorkshire: 'Mary Goodare and Richard Miller have a cottage betwixt them. Mary Goodare hath two rooms and the orchard and payeth 6s. per annum and Richard Miller hayth one roomstead and payeth 4s. per annum'.[86] The pattern of subdivision of houses for single women, widows and estranged wives is evident in the overseers' account book for Colyton in the eighteenth century and has been found elsewhere where evidence exists for the residential arrangements of the poor.[87]

Some poor women certainly lived with their peers in eighteenth-century Colyton.[88] In November 1752 the overseer 'Pd Old Widow Venn, Widow Denning and Susannah Auton more than their usual pay when Mr Prince turned them out of his house in the open street'. All these women were certainly over 50 and were frequently sick. All of them had close relatives in the town and while it seems cruel that homeless, ill, old people should not be cared for by their kin, clearly the expectation was held that the parish would provide for them. Susannah Auton (whose husband's death was not recorded but neither was he in evidence) moved in with another two women of similar age. The parish decided to patch up the house so they 'pd John Sweetland for reed and thatching Agnes

Wishlade's house where Grace Long and Susannah Auton now lives'
Widow Denning's house rent was shared with different 'single' women for each year after the eviction. 'Single' here covers a variety of differing marital states. The women may never have married, they could be recently or long widowed or they could be separated from their husbands. In 1753, for example, Widow Denning resided with 'Snell's wife' and 'White's wife'. Her daughter, Thomazine, lived with her on a temporary basis after attempts to make her a parish apprentice met with resistance. Thomazine was 30 and single and living with her mother when Widow Denning died in 1766. After her mother's death she seems to have taken over the rental of her house and taken in Rebecca Hallett, who was a peer and had a series of illegitimate children. She was also paid for keeping Jane Ford's 4-year-old child. Jane Ford was another contemporary. She was also single and had left domestic service when she became pregnant. Although single women appear to have been solitary, it was common for them to take in children or other misplaced people on a temporary basis. They were in fact placed in the centre of a web of relationships of dependency.

It seems likely that these female residential arrangements formed work units for domestic industry. The rationale behind the association of certain women certainly rested upon practicality or friendship rather than kinship. So, Ann Rick, a single woman who was probably a spinner, in a Chudleigh settlement examination of February 1774, went to Chudleigh after her apprenticeship expired 'and there lived with a poor woman and worked for herself ever since'.[89] It is noticeable in the testimony given by Ann Snell, who mentions spinning in Colyton, that when she became sick while in service in Plymouth around 1734, she went back to Colyton and lived with Alice Long.[90] Although her father was alive and living in the town, she did not return to the parental home, but to a poor woman who nursed her. When she recovered she went to live and work at spinning with Sarah Newbury. Sarah was two years older than Ann and seems to have maintained her own household in Colyton town from the age of 20. In the second half of the eighteenth century the renting of houses to the poor seems to have operated on a system of short-term leases which reflected the transience of employment and rapidly rising rent values. The Sampson family account books show how changeable were the occupants of the cottages they rented out in Colyton. On 24 June 1785, for example, 'Let Hooper's house to John Roost for two pounds and twelve shillings a year', then on 26 April 1788 'James Smith came to Hooper's house at 1s. per week'.[91] Most of their houses seem to have changed occupancy three times every ten years.

Denial of housing or land to the poor was one of the characteristics of the 'close' parish in the seventeenth and eighteenth centuries. Colyton, as we have seen, was not dominated by one lord and remained 'open' to incomers. Nevertheless, the picture emerges of two tiers of poor. The honourable poor, supported by the feoffees in the seventeenth century, were given cheap housing for life. The outsiders faced a more precarious future in the parish.

Schooling the People

The establishment of the feoffees in 1546 contained the provision for a parish school. Following an indenture of feoffment in 1599, the feoffees paid the costs of keeping a school from 1600 when the sum of £5 was charged on all the estates in Colyton.[92] A house for the master was built in 1612 and in the mid-nineteenth century the feoffees still paid a salary of £30 a year to the master of the free school for the instruction of twenty boys in reading, writing and arithmetic.[93] This school was designed for the education of poor boys. Reading was essential to Protestant endeavours and the small towns of this area took the lead in educating youth. Some boys from the countryside moved into the towns for schooling. A case from 1629 shows scholars living in a room of a house in Ottery St Mary as boarders while they attended school there.[94] In the 1630s there was a Puritan schoolmaster who was also an assistant preacher at Beer. Two other Puritans were licensed to teach grammar at Ottery in 1629 and at Rockbeare in 1632.[95]

The few surviving inventories for seventeenth-century Colyton show general ownership of Bibles. In 1629 Anne Lowde, wife of a Colyton yeoman, missed her Bible and found a similar one for sale by William Lee of Seaton, and so suspected a theft.[96] Mary Bradforde, in her 1674 inventory, had 'A Grett Bibell and seven other bookes worth £1 10s'.[97] Most people in east Devon could probably read, even if writing was less common. In 1687 in Membury, Nicholas Rogers was a worsted drawer who had been parish clerk. Although he signed with a cross, he had formerly read the psalms in church and was able to recognise others' handwriting.[98]

In the seventeenth century the £30 allocated by the feoffees to pay a schoolmaster seems to have been divided between a Latin master and an English master. The latter does not seem to have been inundated by pupils. He held the school in the porch room of the church until this was forbidden in 1660.[99] The bailiff's accounts for 1663 suggest that his main role may have been in teaching the fatherless poor: 'Payd Edward Clarke for teachinge of thre [3] of Jo Burds children, to. [2] of Jo Goodmans, on [1] of patients Nags 14s'. In 1662 a schoolmaster's licence was issued to Mr James Butter to teach 'Latine school and writing'.[100] In 1676 the feoffees paid him a fee of £15. Ten years later, the rector sent a letter to the higher ecclesiastical authorities about Butter:

'he has divers years before I come officiated as Mr [Master] of the free-schoole here, and hath ledd a sober & inoffensive life . . . He entred into orders upon this account & put himself off from other employments upon this account & was licensed by Bp Garden & encouraged with a double augmentation . . . One from ye towne itselfe & another from ye family of Sr Walter Yonge, whose children he hath taught. But he is now in some doubt of new designes (wch they call great thoughts of heart) to be as much discouraged. Therefore he desireth (& I with him) that he may have a new & a larger licence, then he had before to confirm him, that he may find no objection.[101]

We can see this as embedded in the factional disputes which were then so rife in Colyton, for in the following year Tanner wrote to the Bishop regarding the excommunication of a teacher called Newton, 'a petty teacher of writing & ciphring telleth me & not of reading in ye beggarly borough of Colyford' . . . 'ye fellow was too simp[le], too pore to give them the fee in hand to do it . . . if he persist, he can doe no hurt. I find it a prejudice to the church to publish Excom [except] two sorts viz. ye Quakers & ye Poore.' This decrepit document not only shows that the borough of Colyford was a particularly destitute part of the parish but confirms Tanner's antipathy to the poor.[102]

For older male children, as we have seen, nonconformist academies, offering a broadly based curriculum, opened in this area in the second half of the seventeenth century and in Colyton from about 1690. The academies at Taunton and Exeter taught theology, classics, Hebrew and a practical course in pastoral duties, suggesting that they aimed to educate aspiring ministers.[103] There is evidence of two schools run by the Dissenters in the eighteenth century.[104] Matthew Towgood kept an academy at Colyton in the 1710s and instructed young men in classical and theological learning. Joseph Cornish opened a classical school in 1782 and he taught in the gallery of the Dissenters' Meeting House. In 1796 he bought a house and began to take in boarders. The school closed in 1811. A Sunday school was instituted in Colyton in 1814 with 124 pupils, 'for the special purpose of imparting moral and religious instruction to the poorer class of children and for the enforcing of a more strict observance of the Sabbath'.[105] The pupils were given elementary steps to reading and writing on sand with a skewer. They were also given a uniform, 'six dozen of Drab coloured Hats to be trimmed . . . not to exceed in price three shillings' along with cloaks.

To an extent the partial moral reformation of Colyton must have been founded on this limited access to rudimentary education that the school provided. The late seventeenth-century academy represents a more sophisticated and selective means to infuse the middling population of the parish with Dissenting values.

Providing Parish Relief in the Eighteenth Century

For the eighteenth century, records are not only more readily available, but it is clear that, rather than the feoffees, the parish was the main resort of the destitute. The poor law overseers' account book is an immaculately kept book which details all 'casual' expenditures made by the poor law officers, but not the month-by-month disbursements.[106] In every case the recipient is listed and the reason for the payment is given. The beginning of this book marks the transfer of responsibility for the parish poor passing from the feoffees to the vestry at the beginning of the 1740s, at the same time as the influence of nonconformity was in serious decline.

Under the parish poor law the main method of obtaining relief was by direct application to the overseers, who would then put the matter to a vestry meeting. In some cases people needed immediate relief. This could be granted by overseers or someone in the town who had the means to hand and would later apply to the vestry to be reimbursed. Thus, in a settlement examination of 1742 a woman 'never apply'd for relief but on[e] day this week[s] was complayning to one of the overseer[s] of Colyton that it was hard time with her upon which he gave her one shilling'.[107] The overseers also actually sought out people to help (presumably after they had heard that it might be appreciated) so there are payments such as the one recorded for 1748 in the overseers' account book 'For a journey to old Bakers to see what was wanting'. Regular relief was paid at church and on certain special occasions the bell was tolled at the church when alms were about to be distributed.

In 1776 seventy-five people were on regular relief.[108] In common with other communities this number rose many times over the last quarter of the eighteenth century; in 1803 339 people, forming 22.2 per cent of the population, were relieved permanently.[109] Whereas in 1682/3 the total year's pay and distributions were £235 4s 9d, in 1742/3 they had risen only slightly to £267 0s 7d, but by 1769 the amount stood at £452 16s 8d. When the rise in price of consumables is taken into account, this still represented a rise of around 75 per cent.[110] By 1830, the total amount had reached £576 3s 6d.[111] In comparison with real prices, however, this represented a fall of approximately 50 per cent since 1769. Unfortunately, books recording distributions to the poor have not survived for this period.[112] It is almost certain that most of the extra expenditure met the costs of providing family allowances.[113] By the end of the eighteenth century there was a class of regular poor relief recipients who relied on the poor law payments and family allowances were the normal system of poor relief in Devon parishes.

Furthermore, poor law support was not just financial. Some of the relief was distributed in kind. For example, Mary Parsons was paid for 'providing wood, milk and cabbage for Street family'.[114] Wood for fuel is frequently noted and must have been fairly readily available in a partly forested parish. The officers kept a stock of old furniture, which was usually bought when poor people died. This was redistributed around Colyton as required, bedsteads and cooking pots being the most sought after items. This system was not unique to Colyton; in nearby Sidbury the collection of useful items on which the poor could draw functioned as an alternative to poor relief, including clothing and shoes (especially gowns and shifts), bed linen and also scythes and shovels.[115] Clothing was also shared in Colyton. In March 1766 the entry appears in the overseers' account book: 'Pd for a coat for use of poor and cleaning 6s.'. The coat was made by a poor tailor using local flax. Poor women made underwear. A typical entry is 'pd Mary Torson and Grigg's wife for making Boles Linnen and Old Goodman's shirt and old Buckland's bedlye 4s'. The poor officers paid a few people's house rents, but this was a minor part of the budget by the eighteenth century, although the parish chamber provided some subsidised lodgings. More significantly, the poor law officers were also involved in job creation with typical local industries. John Green, a man with a young family was found 'Papper Stuff' and tilts to make paper in 1752. Four years later, however, John Green seems to have established his own business making cider. In a clash with the law, the poor officers and lord of the manor bailed him out: 'pd John Green when his goods was seized by the excisemen 5s.' and 'pd for relieving John Greens goods, by the order of Sir John Pole, paid the fine levied on them for selling sider £1. 5s. 7½d.'. Obviously fearing what might happen next, the parish bought him a pick axe, shovel and hook to provide him with another form of work. They spent £6 9s 4d on another unemployed Colyton man, Barnard Welsh, to buy him iron, steel and bellows in 1754. They were secondhand and the parish had them mended for him. Additionally he was given a grinding stone, coals, and a sledge. The situation was different in the nineteenth century as the poor law authorities would not allow relieving officers to establish any applicant for relief in trade or business. At this time the feoffees stepped in to provide financial assistance in setting up small trades.[116]

Poor law officers also took it upon themselves to effect small improvements in public health at the local level. During the period covered by the overseers' account book, sums expended on medical exigencies grew. In particular, more had to be spent to meet doctors' bills as attempts were made to reduce susceptibility to smallpox. In an epidemic in 1755 Dr Baron's bill was 'for the poor in the smallpox 12s. 11d.'. Full-scale inoculation took place in 1791: 'Pd Mr Symes and Mr Hathaway their bills for innoculating the Poor £28. 0s. 0d.'.[117]

Furthermore, the amount of neighbourhood nursing increased over time. It was supported and organised by the poor law authorities. There were also specifically appointed, 'semi-professional' nurses. It is noticeable that references to washing became more common in eighteenth-century Colyton. Particularly from 1757, it was noted that underwear, clothes, old people and dead bodies were being washed. From the 1760s soap was given out by the authorities. As we have seen soap-boiling was another local industry and it was sold in Colyton by the hogshead.[118]

The biggest project of the Colyton poor relief officers in the eighteenth century was the establishment of Colyton workhouse in 1767. Previously, a few paupers had been sent to Sidbury workhouse. Now an existing building was converted and the most apparent and immediate benefit of the workhouse was not for potential inmates but the amount of local employment it provided. First, there was structural work on the building; for example, the overseers' account book records 'pd John Pigeon for woodware for the workhouse by receipt £1. 0s. 9d.'. Then there was furniture for the workhouse, such as beds: 'Mr Crago's bill for bedsteads, to filling 3 beds and 3 bolsters for ye workhouse'. Clothes had to be made for the occupants, for example: 'pd Susannah Turl making 5 shirts carried to the workhouse'.

This was a late date for a workhouse to be built under the Old Poor Law. Exeter had a 'Hospital of the Poor's Portion' established under the influence of Puritans in the early seventeenth century. In the 1670s Thomas Firmin was influential in advocating workhouses for the poor. In 1678 he published a pamphlet on his schemes for the poor, *Some proposals for the imployment of the poor* which advocated that every parish with many poor should set up a workhouse for children where they would knit stockings, wind silk, make lace and generally be kept from idleness while being taught to read. For controlling criminals, a house of correction opened in Honiton in the early seventeenth century, and early in the Interregnum a new bridewell was constructed at Ottery St Mary with a stock and implements for the 'keeping, correcting and setting on work of such rogues, vagabonds, sturdy beggars and such other idle and disorderly persons as shalbe from tyme to tyme there committed'.[119] By comparison in seventeenth-century Colyton the feoffees seem to have preferred the relatively expensive solution of out-relief along with some measures which may have been private initiatives such as the spinstry.

Once the workhouse was opened, food was bought from local suppliers by the month. Provisioning was a major expense. For example, there is the entry, 'pd for 50lb of beef to William Beed at 3d. [per] ¾lb for ye workhouse 14s. 7d'. Mutton, veal, 'pig', hops, malt, wheat and treacle were also bought. Cheese was purchased from a neighbouring village, presumably to obtain a poorer quality than that which was produced in Colyton. An oven was constructed in a separate structure next to the workhouse. Kitchen utensils had to be bought and a water pump 'borrowed'. The building could accommodate sixty-six people. It had a men's room and a women's room and a governor's chamber. In 1775 it also contained 'A Washing Kettle, one Jibb, a Pick Axe, one Watering Pott, one Baskett and a Flask'.[120] The workhouse was supervised by a committee of twelve who were chosen from 'gentlemen, farmers and tradesmen'. Two of the committee were to meet at the workhouse every Thursday morning to conduct an inspection.[121] The workhouse became a focus for private (and often 'off the cuff') charity, and provided a more direct means of giving than leaving money in wills. The Sampson family account books, for example, mention 'The sum of £2. 8s. 2d. allowed . . . for a piece of canvas and Oat Meal (which paid for the people in the workhouse)'.[122] As such the workhouse moved the focus of relief away from the church.

It is not quite clear what function the workhouse served. The original reason for building it was to centralise the setting to work of paupers as well as providing some accommodation for the homeless, but the indications are that it was used as a place for outpaupers to go to work rather than having a large number of inmates. An inventory taken in 1779 shows that there were nineteen beds but only one resident.[123] In a breakdown of adult paupers in 1803, 144 were on outrelief and twenty-six lived in the workhouse.[124] But not much work was being carried out there either. No money was spent on purchasing materials for the poor to work with and in the year only £3 17s 0d was earned by the labour of the poor inmates towards their own maintenance, and a mere £2 6s 10d was earned by outpaupers. New rules of the workhouse were drawn up in 1790.[125] Part of the workhouse was to be set aside to be a small penitentiary consisting of two apartments. Offenders were to wear a certain uniform. Children had to be instructed in spelling and reading and in the principles of Christian religion. A doctor was appointed to take care of sick inmates. Within thirteen years of being built, the workhouse had changed from being a house of industry to a prison and orphanage. Unemployed labourers were now being relieved with cash handouts rather than by the provision of parish work in an institutionalised setting.

In the course of the eighteenth century, despite attempts at revival, feoffees' meetings lapsed. There is no evidence that they offered any relief, but this may be because the record has been lost. In 1791 there were only three feoffees left. Suddenly, new feoffees were appointed and business was stepped up.[126] To reinforce the revival, a copy and translation of the charter deed was made. It seems likely that a developing 'poor crisis' prompted the feoffees into action. In 1795 they purchased £50 worth of wheat to be made into bread and their distribution of this reveals the sort of social control which preoccupied the propertied classes, with the spectre of the French Revolution fresh in their minds: 'whoever may be found or known to engage in a riotous manner is not to partake of this charity'. In 1800 an order was passed at a feoffees' meeting that the bailiff should purchase '300 bushells of barley, 100 bushells of pease and 100 bags of potatoes' which were to be deposited in the feoffees' chamber and sold to such persons as should apply, not exceeding 'half a peck of barley, a quarter of a peck of pease, 6lb. of potatoes for each person at any one time'.

Robin has outlined the feoffees' system of payments in the nineteenth century in such detail that it requires little more elaboration.[127] Briefly, they operated a family allowance system, with people applying for payments. Payments were allocated upon marriage and then proportionally according to the number of children a couple had. Those aged 70 and above did not get paid as they were eligible for a pension from the parish relieving officers and those in receipt of parish relief were not eligible for feoffee payments. Proprietors of land were also not given relief. Even a widow who had been left a small amount of property would not be paid. At the same time, the payments helped the propertyless tradesman class who faced fluctuating fortunes in the early nineteenth century. Recipients did not have to be poverty-stricken when they applied. In fact, a measure of respectability helped. Applicants had to have a legal settlement for feoffee relief and linkage to the census proves that few immigrants were paid. By the mid-nineteenth century direct payments to the poor accounted for less than a third of the feoffees' expenditure.[128] In sum, the feoffees again operated in much the same way that they had in the seventeenth century.

Since the line of eligibility was a fine one, some people tried their luck each year. Widow Denman received a one-off payment in 1830, for example, but next to her name was written 'shall not come again'. For William Edwards, a large family was not sufficient to convince the feoffees to pay him, for in the 1832 Land Tax assessment he was holding lands and was an innkeeper and maltster. His application for relief was refused three years in succession. Disability assisted in a claim for feoffee help. James Farmer, a carpenter with a crippled child, was paid year after year. Single women who had had illegitimate children were borderline cases. Mary Davis had an illegitimate child in 1824, and another in 1829. She seems likely to have been in a common-law relationship. Despite this 'moral failing' the feoffees paid her a shilling in 1829 and a shilling in 1830. Others were not so lucky.

Into the New Poor Law period, feoffee relief continued the generous aspects of relief distribution which had become associated with the Old Poor Law before the mass poverty schemes of the late eighteenth century. The allowance system, which seems to have been adopted by the feoffees around 1820, continued into the mid-nineteenth century. In fact, the

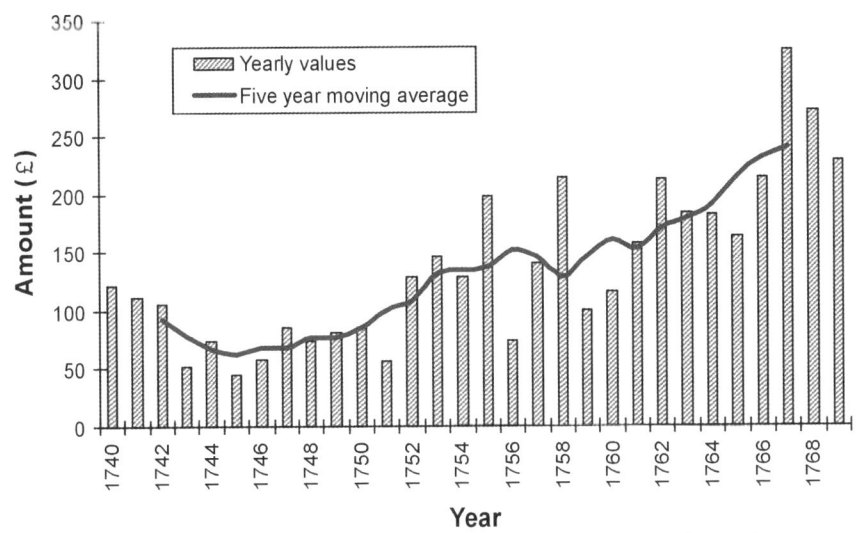

Fig. 6.1 Yearly poor law disbursements for Colyton 1740–1769.

feoffees' policy of giving financial support for employment maintained the 'independence' of the labourer or craftsman in a way which was denied by the 1834 legislation.

Doing and Being in Eighteenth-Century Colyton

Following the settlement statutes of 1662 the records indicate that over time more attention was paid to defining who had and who did not have a settlement in Colyton. The strict enforcement of the eligibility laws was characteristic of parishes in the area, and perhaps generally for England. For example, in Ottery St Mary, Martha Roe, the wife of William Roe, reported in a settlement inquisition that he came from Bodmin in Cornwall but had married locally. After living in Ottery St Mary for four or five years 'about that time there was a meeting in Ottery of some Justices for sending home all strangers or People that were not legally settled there'. He did not want to be removed by an order so voluntarily returned to Bodmin.[129] Other eighteenth-century parishes show every concern to avoid making people parishioners. Elizabeth Pinn, whose case was considered in 1767, was born in Colyton but went to Ottery for her first job, presumably as a domestic servant. She then went to Salcombe. After a three-month trial period she wanted to stay longer but her mistress said she was unwilling to take a maid by the year because it would make her a parishioner and proposed taking her by the week, offering her 14d a week.[130]

By the eighteenth century the overseers' account book reflects that

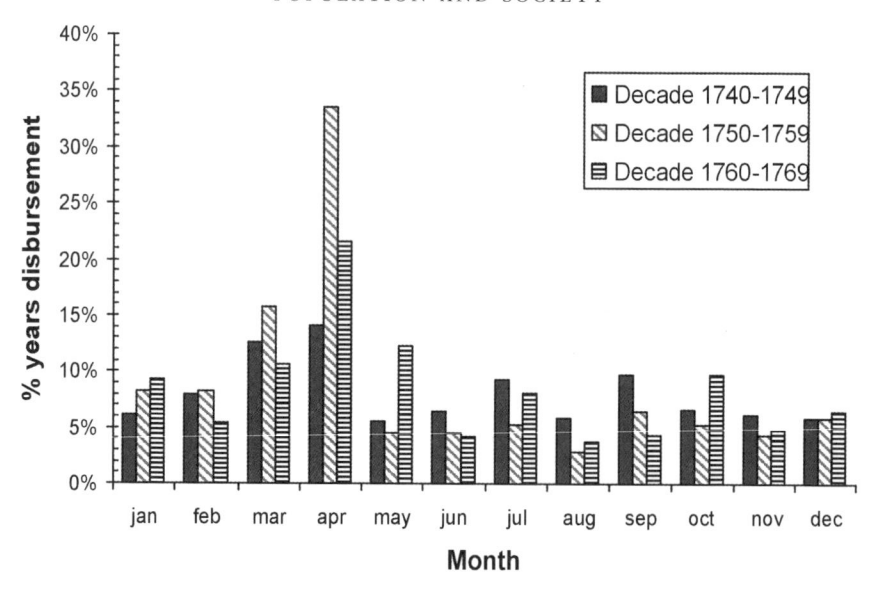

Fig. 6.2 Percentage of average yearly disbursement for decades by month: Colyton 1740–1769.

Colyton had a multifaceted social system within which relief was generously distributed to those who were eligible for it. A settlement was vital to secure relief in Colyton. Now and again the settlement laws were applied rigorously to the point of being rigged against those who must have seen Colyton as their home. Joan Salter had been in Colyton for almost a lifetime when in April 1743 the overseers apparently bribed another parishioner to provide information against her: 'pd Thomas Tilman to give evidence against Joan Salter touching her settlement several times 5s.'.[131] In 1761, in the tithings of Farwood and Watchcombe which comprised the outlying part of the parish of Colyton, there was a summons to warn lodgers and boarders that their legal settlements were to be checked and eighteen examinations were taken.

As has been discovered for other parishes, whereas in the seventeenth century the poor relief system tended to make up a full wage for those disadvantaged by age or disability, in the late eighteenth century able-bodied men increasingly relied on the relief system. Over the period of the overseers' account book, which covered 1741 to 1769, there was a slight increase in adult males who claimed relief, particularly extremity payments over the winter. Where their occupations are given, they appear to have been husbandmen or poor craftsmen. Inflation apart, since there was little rise in population, it is payments to males of working age which account for most of the rise in relief expenditure in Colyton over the thirty-year period, as shown in Figure 6.1. Figure 6.2 shows poor

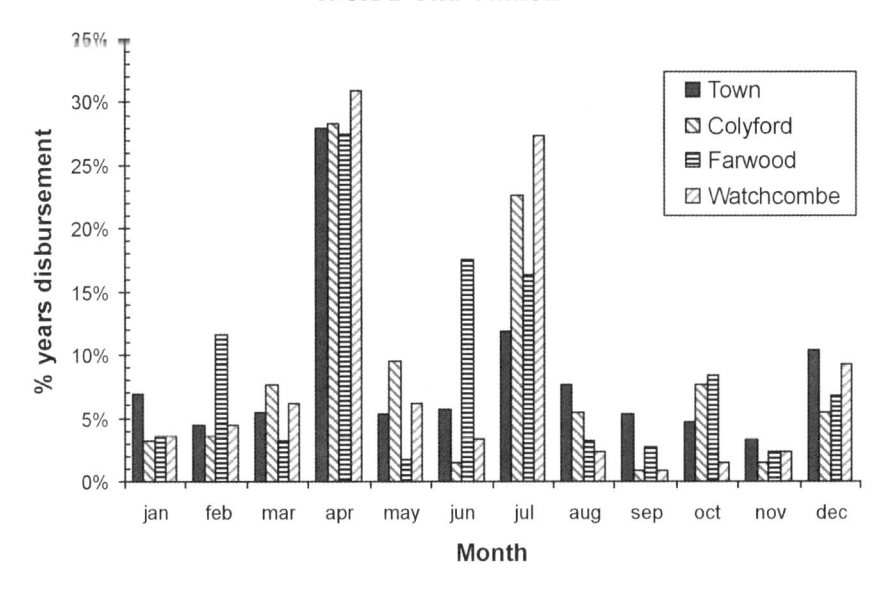

Fig. 6.3 Percentage of disbursement by month: tithings of Colyton 1763/4.

relief disbursements by month in ten-year cohorts. The increasing seasonality of relief payments, which would be expected if a large proportion of the money distributed went to men working in arable farming, was not yet apparent. Colyton's poor relief was still more likely to reflect a pastoral pattern. The peak of payments in April is in fact artificial, as funds which had not been spent during the previous year were then spent on extraneous things like extra sets of clothing for the poor and the payment of annual bills. At the same time, March and May show high rates of relief being paid.

From 1756 poor relief distribution was organised into four sections, each of which had an overseer who rendered an account. The division was made into Colyton town, Colyford, Watchcombe and Farwood. For a few of the years, some of the expenditure details for the country tithings are missing. Full details exist for 1763/4, however, and Figure 6.3 shows that when poor relief disbursements are divided by tithing, a similar seasonal pattern is evident for all of them. The year 1763/4 seemed to be representative as there was no extraordinary expenditure of the type which was incurred when epidemics struck Colyton.

The payments can be dissected into those which were for immediate need and those which solved more general problems. In Figure 6.4 payments which were not directly for relief or could be classed as 'extraneous' are indicated. These include apprenticing and settlement case expenditures, house rent payments, annual bills, tax payments and payments to travellers.

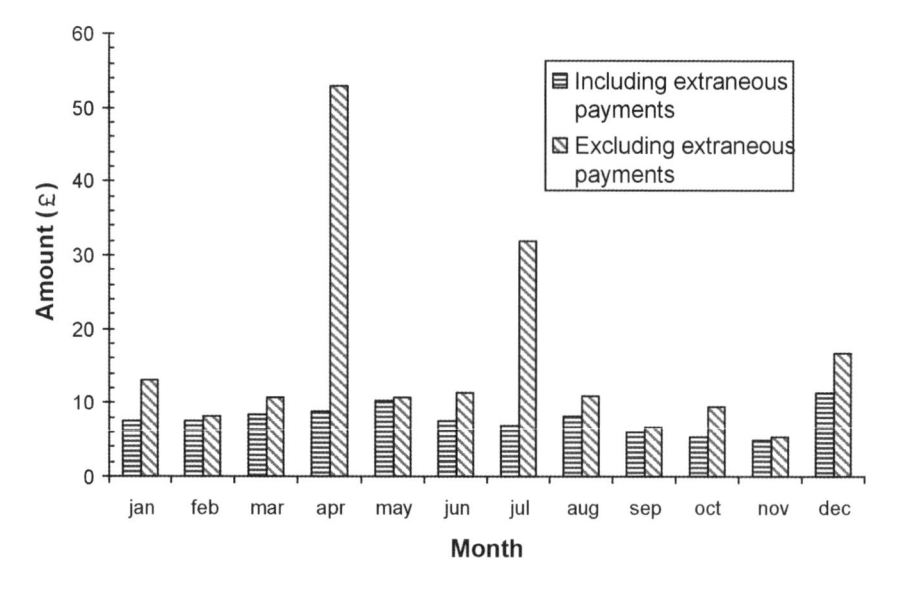

Fig. 6.4 Amounts of Colyton poor relief including and excluding extraneous payments 1763/4.

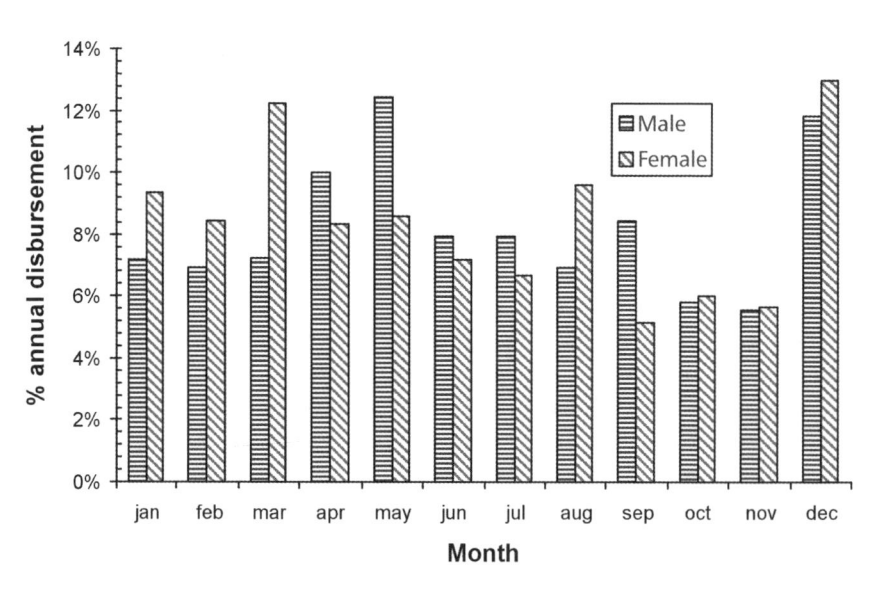

Fig. 6.5 Male and female percentage of annual disbursement by month 1763/4.

Throughout the period when the account book is divided into tithings, payments in Watchcombe show a bias to supporting men, whereas payments to women are more common than payments to men in the town tithing. Figure 6.5 shows the distribution of poor law disbursements in 1763/4 by season according to gender. Payments were missed out in the few cases where the name of the recipient is not given and their sex cannot be determined. Payments for sickness obviously follow different patterns from those determined by work seasonality, but some of the sickness probably disguised unemployment and the compilation of 'casual' payments is thought to provide an indication of the times of year when need was felt in the community. The female pattern shows that women's involvement was still likely to be in dairy farming with year-round employment but had a tendency to precariousness in May.[132] The male pattern shows the tendencies to higher winter unemployment, reflecting some arable influence. The relative 'low' in January was probably due to the Christmas dole given out by the feoffees.[133] Although those in receipt of parish poor relief were not eligible for feoffee charity, it is possible that more people would have applied to the parish had they not had the expectation of Christmas alms. The April peak was much reduced by the removal of extraneous expenditure. The July peak evident in Figure 6.3 also disappears since the expenditure resulted from setting up and paying the premiums for a group of apprentices. As yet, Colyton could not be described as showing a developed 'arable' pattern, but the marriage seasonality results presented in Chapter 2 showed that the 'pastoral' pattern was not strongly evident in the 1750–99 cohort either. The 'arable' influence probably came in the 1780s when there were more men in Colyton. Unfortunately there are no overseers' accounts in existence for the period after 1770.

Winter unemployment was compounded by the expenses of maintaining a household in terms of extra clothing and fuel. Apart from direct references to able-bodied men needing to claim poor relief, such as the one for Joseph Swayne ('In extremity before he could get work 6s.') in February 1753, there were other, less direct indications of necessity.[134] Isaac Bole, a notable resident pauper, was brought home having been found almost dead in a field in March 1767 after a particularly difficult winter. He seems likely to have been starving. In the same month and year, William Bishop, a father of four children, attempted to hang himself. After that he was relieved through the summer with 'garden stuff' in kind. Payments of food and fuel were more often being made directly in this period than in earlier times. Another indication of the amount of want in eighteenth-century Colyton is provided by assessing vermin collection.[135] Payments to parishioners for collecting mice, polecats, foxes and various predatory birds exist among the Colyton accounts from the early seventeenth century. While the payments were nominal amounts, normally 1d or 2d for each creature caught and produced for the overseers' inspection, it is significant who had the time to trap them and valued the small income this provided. Whereas early in the eighteenth century the vermin were collected by young boys, later in the century this was carried out by adult men.

The five or six exceptional cases in the overseers' account book, where men are paid for taking care of other poor people, all took place in the months of March or April in the 1760s and in the 'male-predominant' tithing of Watchcombe. The men concerned were all over fifty: Perhaps strength mattered more than experience in some of the agricultural tasks. Samuel Goff, a husbandman, married for the second time in 1794 and had five children. In 1805 he was granted £6 6s 0d by the feoffees 'in consideration of his age and inability to support his family'.[136] No baptism is recorded for Goff, but his first marriage had taken place in 1779. He is a typical example of a victim of the poverty that commonly overtook widowers who remarried in Colyton.

The regular relief payments for eighteenth-century Colyton do not survive, but the 'casual' payments give a detailed impression of the amount of relief which was paid out to offset temporary and seasonal work shortages. The amounts paid to people which are recorded in the overseers' account book indicate that the payments were often a full maintenance. The estimates of yearly wages made by Snell for Devon and Dorset for the cohort of 1741–5, of £4 18s 0d for men and £2 5s 0d for women, were similar to the amounts of poor relief which, if calculated on a yearly basis, would be £5 4s 0d for men and £2 12s 0d for women.[137] In general, men were given poor relief at exactly double the levels given to women. Whereas men tended to be paid for time which could have been spent in work, women were given specific caring and nursing jobs by the parish. Where their husbands were unemployed they were paid for household duties. In March 1768 Robert Gray, who had been paid 12s a month during a period of unemployment in the winter, was given 'for his wife for boarding and cleaning of house before his wages begun 10s 6d.'.[138] The reasons for which payments were made to women can be divided into 'doing' and 'being' activities. 'Doing' included nursing the sick, being on hand in childbirth deliveries, wet nursing other people's children, laundering, providing lodgings, and organising wakes for the dying. In 'being' activities women were paid in childbed and childbirth and for nursing their own children. The 'doing' jobs are analysed by type and year in Table 6.3. The occupations have been divided into five categories: helping with childbirth, laundering, caring for the sick, taking lodgers, and laying out and preparing corpses for burial. These categories are not always distinct since some of the sick women who were being nursed may have been in childbirth and some of the lodgers may

Table 6.5 Type of jobs for women recorded in the overseers' account book 1741–1769

	1741–9		1750–9		1760–9	
	N.	%	N.	%	N.	%
Childbirth assistance	2	7.7	3	4.7	35	13.8
Laundering	1	3.9	7	10.9	3	1.2
Nursing	12	46.1	17	26.5	108	42.7
Taking lodgers	11	42.3	32	50.0	34	13.4
Laying out the dead	–	–	5	7.8	73	28.8
N = 343	26		64		253	

have been taken in because they were sick and needed looking after. The category has been chosen because it seemed most appropriate from the limited detail given in the overseers' account book.

The provision of a welfare system through the employment of women in parish jobs became significantly more important in the 1760s. This seems likely to be associated with falling employment in the lace and woollen industries.

As 'jobs' all these activities reinforced the gender-specific nature of work. They all took place in the domestic and 'indoor' domain. The women involved might have been either single or married. A breakdown of the women doing these jobs who could be linked to the reconstitution shows that 45 per cent were single, 41 per cent were married and 13 per cent were widows. Most were not permanently associated with a man, since the linkage shows that 80 per cent of these women who were legally married were separated from their husbands. These women were all of typical working age—between their early twenties and late fifties. The widows who are recorded were generally young, but because remarriage was still far commoner for males than females in the 1750–99 cohort due to the skewed sex ratio, they stood little chance of marrying again. A small proportion of women could not be linked to the reconstitution. Since the women who were regularly helped had to have a settlement in Colyton, it seems likely that these were women who married outside of Colyton church before 1753 and are not named on dummy FRFs.

Tending or nursing sick people was sometimes more remunerative than working as a live-in servant. Elizabeth Long was taking care of Joan Edwards in 1763 and was paid 3s per week for her trouble. Sometimes women were paid for tending their relatives. For example, Sarah Goodman, a married woman of 34, was paid 3s in 1754 for tending her mother and sister, and Mary Collier was paid in the same year 'for tending her mother who hath on the book 6s. per month'. Cleaning, whether of people, clothes or houses, was a semi-commercialised activity. When Sarah Hussey died at the age of 19 in 1749, it was not her mother or sister who did her washing, but a non-relative. The overseer records: 'pd Rachel Sargent for watching her cloaths 1s'. Presumably they were to become parish property. Alternatively, this shows a willingness to place an economic value on household tasks which was to disappear subsequently. Whereas other studies of this network of parish care and support systems have described them as 'neighbourly', it is not apparent from the Colyton record that this was exactly the case.[139] Hannah Collins was paid for 'lying forth Turner's wife and waking one night', but whereas the Collins lived in Colyford, the Turners lived almost 5 miles away in the Watchcombe tithing. They were not related and it seems likely that the overseers had an organised welfare care system and appointed poor people to specific short 'jobs'.

The payments for these 'jobs' varied from being a supplement to a full maintenance. How much the woman was paid presumably depended on how much income she could get from other sources. In the minority of cases where married women were with their husbands, the male income did not necessarily disqualify the wife from being given poor relief employment. Mary Restorick was paid independently for giving lodgings to a number of people while her husband was employed as a coffin-maker in the 1760s. However, the largest payments were for 'being' activities and were made to women who were incapacitated and totally unable to work. Joan Bole was paid for every one of her eight pregnancies and the sickness she suffered after each one. She would be paid 'in childbed' in June for a child born at the end of August and payments could go on for several months after a child's birth.

Elsewhere in the country, in arable areas at least, single women were thrown on to poor relief in the late eighteenth century.[140] As their work in agriculture diminished, they might be expected to marry earlier to secure a livelihood. This could only be verified if diminishing opportunities for domestic servants can be assumed to have existed. It seems clear that domestic work in textile-making had fallen off in late eighteenth-century Colyton, and agricultural work was becoming more male-orientated, but many single women must have worked as indoor servants. Certainly, however, the parish provided its own 'job' opportunities for single and married women, and marriage would not necessarily take women off poor lists because, in the period to 1770, they were expected to earn their own income. It is evident that towards the end of the eighteenth century, the poor relief system became more male-orientated as the policy of giving family allowances was increasingly implemented. This occurred after the end of the overseers' account book for Colyton, and most evidence of the policy in operation can be drawn from settlement records and letters to the overseers. During the period of 1762–1853, which is covered by removal orders, 66 per cent of cases of removal back to Colyton were family groups.[141] Some of them were headed by a widow, some by a deserted wife; but increasingly over time the groups who were sent to Colyton consisted of a young labourer, his wife and children. A settlement examination of November 1845 drew evidence from the previous sixty years and demonstrates the way in which the relief system of the early nineteenth century encouraged early marriage and maintained whole families.[142]

Robert Loveridge was born in 1785 in Colyton. He lived with his parents until he was 10 or 11 years old when his mother deposited him at the house of a large Colyton farmer, James Pady at Cadhayne, saying that he was bound apprentice. He worked there for about five years and then hired himself as a servant in husbandry to another large farmer, Mr Samuel White of Hooperhayne, for whom he was to drive horses. He left Mr White at the end of the harvest after he had been there for two years. He then returned to live with his parents and took up day labour. After two years he married. His wife was seven months pregnant at the time of the marriage and Robert was not quite 19. After their marriage Robert and his wife lived initially with his parents until they were able to rent a cottage for £3 a year. After three years residence in Colyton, Robert moved to Southleigh. By this time he had three children and four more were to follow. The Loveridge family were in regular relief according to the allowance system which operated in all the parishes in the Colyton area. Immediately on reaching Southleigh, Robert applied to the Colyton parish officers for relief and he was given 1s a week. When his fourth child was born he applied to Colyton parish for more relief and it was then increased to either 1s 6d or 2s per week (he could not recall which amount). He went on to say: 'as my family increased I applied to the parish officers of Colyton for further relief and they increased my relief to 2s 6d per week which was continued for several years and as my children grew up my relief was decreased'. He received relief on the allowance system for eighteen years overall, spanning 1808 through to 1826. The amount of relief seems to have increased over time. By 1823, 2s 6d was the standard payment for a baby and 2s for a growing child. Additional relief could be claimed in clothes. Mary Loveridge, Robert's wife, explained the process by which these were obtained around 1825: 'The last relief I received was some clothes for my son the said John Loveridge, the pauper and my youngest son, Thomas, this was about 20 yrs ago. I went to Colyton and applied to the Select Vestry of that parish then sitting in the vestry room there for clothes for my said two sons, they granted me the clothes and the week following I went to the then acting overseer who accompanied me to a shop in Colyton and I received the clothes'. There is no mention of Mary doing any sort of work aside from the care of the large family and Robert clearly saw the relief as a supplement to his income, for he said 'I have myself frequently received the relief from the parish officers of Colyton but my wife on most occasions fetched it'.

As well as this settlement document, other sources show that Colyton was fairly generous in supplying allowances to men working in other parishes. The best examples are a series of letters written by Thomas Kingsbury who followed canal building to Bath with part of his family in 1799 and 1800, and appealed to the Colyton overseers every few months.[143] The first letter was dated 21 July 1799 and addressed to the overseer:[144]

> I should bee very much oblige to you if you will send me that money that you Promised me as I Dow wantet verey bad for things is verey Deer heir but I hope it will not be long first Sir you most think that six pipell can not bee maintaind for asmool mater for Breed is averey Der artickell and Every thing Else in per poshen Sir I wish I cold Dow with thoute yet But I cannot . . . Sir ples to give ouer Dutey to mother and Love to mu Dauter and Love to all the famiIey and I hope this will find them well my wife going with mee.

The overseers agreed to pay Thomas £1 12s 0d as a back payment of 2s per week from the previous April. By 3 November, Thomas wrote again and several quotes sum up the contents: 'I hope you will send mee sum money as soon as you can as my family is Inn agoodill of drestness', 'William Bud can tell you how hard I work for a little money', 'I Can not geet onn no Beter at present as Tims is soo very hard at pressent', 'I most Have sum De Rectly or Elis I most send my famiIey home but I hope you will stope that', but despite all this 'I Can Do Beeter with my famiIey her Beter than I can Down in Devonsher'. The overseers immediately sent a £5 Bank of England to Thomas. On 3 February 1800 they received another letter from him: 'Sir I am very sorey to trobell you soo often but I most have sum money to pay my hous Rent as I can not Dow moor for my famley then what I Dow and I hope you will bee so good as tosend mee what was agreed for mee I wish it was in my power to Dow without it but I can not and I hope you will be afrend to my family . . . Ples to give ouer Duty to mother and I hope this will find all well and Love to my Litell Ann'. It was agreed to send him, as he himself suggested, '1 pound not for youse of my famiIey' as he said he 'have not had any for along while'.

Parish Poor Relief

Throughout the period in consideration here, on a superficial level Colyton was a generous distributor of poor relief through a double system of feoffee and poor law payments. Distribution to the parish poor passed through three different phases. In the seventeenth and early eighteenth centuries most relief was directed towards elderly women. In the eighteenth century, with the decline of the lace trade, younger adult women became the main recipients. Towards the nineteenth century married men claimed an increasing proportion of the budget by way of seasonal relief which gradually became an all-year-round supplement. The change from female to male directed poor relief coincided with the re-alignment of the sex ratio to a more even proportion of males and females in the community. Yet poor relief was never all-embracing and indeed the proportion of poor relieved in the seventeenth century was extremely low. The allocation of relief in the seventeenth century served political and moral purposes and the provision of charity housing and schooling were probably to similar ends. The system in operation was exclusive not inclusive. As we have seen, the parish was 'open' yet tightly governed and saw friction in the late seventeenth century to control the purse strings. Even in the era when the feoffees no longer administered the system, it was possible for people to be excluded and they would certainly not be paid if they belonged to another parish. This is not to imply that there was one authoritarian structure that determined life in Colyton. Indeed, it may be argued that local government was more fractured than in many communities.

We have now reviewed the evidence for the religious background of the parish, taken a detailed look at the economy and taken further what is known about the demographic history of the parish. This chapter has tried to place these areas in the context of the governing structure of the parish through an analysis of poor relief. The final chapter will consider the point where all these come together: the history of the family.

7

Viable Households
Life-Cycle and Family in Colyton

> God knos: what will become of our whole family there beeing no Union nor Affection left amongst any, two or three of ym No nor se[c]ondly a sence of any Duty Naturall but they're become all Like Brute Beasts pushing one against another And governed and carryed away According to their divers Lusts by the Wheedles of Every Jilt and JacaNapes to the Division and almost utter ruine of us all I meane Comparatively to what wee might bee Heres Grandfar govrnd wholey by Hester Paul Jane Hore by her son and my Man, her son by Mathew Raw sister Scrimsh by W.C. and my Bror wholey by his wife and young Wm Clarke by his Fathers Boy And this is carried on to that Degree That we are as t'were Aliens one to another not to say worse yt we are become enemyes And our Neighbours at the same instant Envying us all which I looke on as A just Judgmt of God for the punishmt this untoward wicked Defection amongst us of which my Father hath all along shewed himselfe to much Guilty, pray God remove this Descention Dissimulation and haterd amongst us And in his Due time better Unite us in true affection One towards another'.
>
> (Nathaniel Pinney to Hester Pinney, 29 December 1701, in G.F. Nuttall, ed., *Letters of John Pinney 1679–1699*, 1939: 110)

So moaned Nathaniel Pinney in 1701, bewailing household disharmony and neighbourhood jealousy after the family had risen in prosperity. As Margaret Hunt has shown, similar conflicts and anxieties divided many early modern middling families.[1] The Pinneys are an example of spectacular financial success. In the early 1680s Nathaniel's brother Azariah married a servant whose mother (probably a widow) received poor relief. Yet thirty years later Azariah's son John married an heiress to a West Indian fortune with a portion of £10,000.[2] Such transpositions were the currency of local gossip, and even more so when they had a political edge. In his study of the parish of Keevil in Wiltshire, Martin Ingram argues that divisions within the parish fall not only along lines of class and status but are also based on family feuds and rivalries and that fissures might therefore be as much vertical as horizontal.[3] Clearly, however, family loyalties did not necessarily all flow in the same direction.

This chapter considers life-cycle stages and family formation in Colyton in the seventeenth and eighteenth centuries. In Chapter 5 we saw the demographic parameters of family life in Colyton. Chapter 6 considered the management of poverty and the boundaries of social order in the parish. This chapter puts together both of these approaches. Social historians have found that household order was the foundation of social order in early modern England. A particular focus will fall on youth and marital decisions. Not only are there detailed records relating to young people in Colyton, but as much of the emphasis of explanation for demographic trends lies in the importance of the age of marriage it seems necessary to examine the lives of unmarried adults, especially women, in some detail. The structure adopted will be to examine the lives of Colyton inhabitants from birth through to death. A review of this material contains an implicit critique of some of the work on the history of the family to date. Colyton's history shows us that when death rates were high and marriage ages late, many men and women in fact lived outside of traditional families. This was an anomaly apparent to contemporaries: whereas Puritan moralists stressed patriarchy and the importance of the good order of the family, in fact the reality of living arrangements was often at variance with this. Investigation of a parish at a detailed level does much to unsettle a picture of normative experience.

This chapter investigates the areas of responsibility which are shared between families and welfare agencies today and the change from the collective to family concern for welfare. The first area is antenatal and natal care. The circumstances of marriage will then be examined, and finally old age and death in the parish will be considered. While progressing through the life-cycle, it is necessary to consider the factors that lie behind record survival, as the very reason for the sometimes minute detailing of family life in seventeenth- and eighteenth-century records is the attempt by officialdom to impose order on the unruly poor. To counterbalance the material on the poor I also look at the rich detail available in the Pinney records. Indeed, what much of this enquiry exposes is a class divide in early modern Colyton. The detailed record survival for apprenticeship—a major concern of the feoffees—can be contrasted with the lack of recording of illegitimacy in the second half of the seventeenth century, suggesting that this was an area that local officials in this anti-authoritarian parish did not want to expose to the county officials. Yet again, the extant documents are hardly a mirror of the history of the parish and we must interpret the clues provided by record survival in considering how early modern Colyton should be reproduced.

Bearing Children

Childbirth is commonly regarded as having moved from the private to the public sphere since these days it generally takes place in an institutional setting. In the past it is thought to have been a family event which took place in the home. In fact, in Colyton the home in question was often not that of the parents, and childbirth frequently took place with a number of helpers and onlookers which gave the event a particular social and public significance.[4] The prevalence of wet nursing also indicates that child-raising was not considered to be the exclusive duty of the mother.[5]

Wrigley stressed that the national fall in mortality of newly born infants between 1700 and 1850 must have fuelled population growth.[6] He attributed this to changes in maternal nutrition, in parental attitude to newborn children and in childbed practice. As we have seen, in Colyton mortality of all children under 5 fell significantly during the eighteenth century. Payments to women in childbed are frequently mentioned in the overseers' account book, and this form of assistance seems to have permeated a broad section of the labouring poor. From the eighteenth-century record childbirth was a large expense that the parish seemed always to be prepared to meet. The minimum cost of lying-in with a doctor delivering the child, a midwife in attendance and other women helping out was £1 16s 6d. Illegitimate births were given the same treatment as legitimate ones, and overseers paid out the same costs for them. In April 1764 Mary Martin a woman with no legal settlement in Colyton, gave birth to an illegitimate child.[7] It was a difficult birth. The doctor was called, a special midwife was summoned from Kilmington and Mary was given her own nurse. Nevertheless she died and the parish was left to bury her body and maintain the child. The cost to the parish was £2 7s 0d, almost as much as a female domestic servant's annual wages at the time.

The length of childbirth payments can be documented for Colyton in the period of the baptism register where both birth and baptism dates are recorded. For example, Joseph and Benedicta Restorick's first child was born on 11 June 1769. Joseph was a miller and flax grower and was frequently poverty-stricken. In the following November, Benedicta was still receiving payments for the birth. Whereas the normal rate of poor relief for a woman would be between 1s and 1s 6d per month, on the birth of a child this would often go up to 9s. Two sets of bastardy bonds which detail maintenance costs allow some analysis of the rising costs of childbearing.[8] The first set consists of ten bonds covering the period from 1683 to 1744; the second set consists of twelve cases from the years between 1762 and 1810. In these cases, the man named as responsible was expected to meet the costs allotted to him and was generally not poor. Lying-in expenses were to be met by the child's father. In the first period these varied between 1s and 10s, the average being 4s 7d. By the second period, there had been a huge increase in these costs and they now stood at between 7s and £2 3s 0d, the average being £1 0s 6d. This represented a quadrupling of the amount spent on this aspect of childbirth.

The part of the maintenance costs to be met by the father also rose over time. Between 1683 and 1744 this varied from 6d to 1s 2d, the mean amount being 7d a week for as long as the child remained chargeable to the parish, which was normally until the age of 8 when he or she would be apprenticed. Between 1762 and 1810 these costs were between 9d and 2s 6d, with a mean of 1s 2d Thus, the cost to be met by the father each week had doubled over a century and particularly in the period covered by the overseers' account book. However, when inflation of prices is taken into account there seems to have been little 'real' increase. Meanwhile the maintenance costs expected to be met by the mother rose very little. In the first period she was to pay between 6d and 9d, but most women paid 6d which was the mean amount. At the end of the eighteenth century she could be expected to pay between 6d and 1s with the mean amount being 7d. Therefore the single woman's contribution was exactly half that of the male, whereas earlier in the century it had been almost equivalent. This may reflect the relative difference in wage levels, as well as declining employment prospects for women. The total weekly maintenance of a baby had jumped from 1s 1d to 1s 9d. This was a fairly substantial share of the average weekly wage of an agricultural labourer, and highlights why men with several children began to rely more and more on poor relief supplements. The total cost of child maintenance thus almost doubled, reaching £4 11s 0d, with no gender difference, at the end of the eighteenth century. This is similar to the median averages of £5 5s 0d for girls and £5 0s 0d for boys found in early modern probate accounts by Amy Erickson.[9] Some of the increasing cost of childbirth can be accounted for by a rise in the number of women who were in attendance at the birth. Due to unemployment in other 'female' jobs, assistance in childbirth was more frequently given as a form of parish employment.[10] From the 1760s specialised midwives were appointed to all births and two or three other women were to be on hand to look after the mother and child. Certain women, like Rebecca Barjew and Mary Newbury, specialised in deliveries and babies would be born in their houses rather than at the home of the mother. Women in labour were carried to the houses where they would give birth. The increased amounts spent on care in childbirth must have contributed to the number of surviving births. Added to the factors underlined by Wrigley, this suggests a community willingness to pay for nurturance, perhaps indicating an increased emphasis on maternity in the late eighteenth century.

Child-raising was a shared activity for the poor. Wet nursing was a normal practice. Breast-feeding of other people's children provided both an income and a contraceptive for lower-class women, as Maclaren argued. Maclaren examined nurse children in the burial register of Chesham in Buckinghamshire and linked them to a reconstitution of the families who took them in. She argued that it was common to find 'long, regular spacing of births for the poorer sort of teeming women'.[11] By contrast, Fildes argues that seventeenth-century wet nurses tended to be artisan or middling order wives, rather than the very poor.[12] They were normally married women not single women who had borne illegitimate children. They often lived in the hinterland of a city, in a town or village that had trade links with the city through a river or road link. While there are too few documents to indicate just how common commercial wet nursing might have been in England, there are enough to dispel any impression that this was an activity confined to London.

The results of the analysis of marital fertility in Colyton shown in Chapter 5 may indicate that wet nursing took place within the community, since in some cohorts the wealthy classes had shorter birth intervals than those lower down the social scale. The evidence which can be found for wet nursing on a commercial basis in Devon suggests that most of the custom would come from Exeter. Two ecclesiastical court depositions from the second half of the seventeenth century provide examples. In a matrimonial case of 1668, Maria Burd said of Peter Carew, the putative father, 'That he had prvided a place with her, Joan Alford, in ye country to be delive[re]d of child & that it should be well enough & that he had p[ro]vided a Nurse for her & when shee did come againe from ye country hee would marry with her'.[13] In a case of 1679, Jane and Nathaniel Southcombe of Faringdon parish near Exeter were deponents and described the arrangements being made for a baby: 'One Gendells came into Ffaringdon and enquired for a Nurse to Nurse a young child whereupon this deponent (being then a Nurse) was mentioned and recommended to him and sent to come to him at Allesbeare'.[14] The arrangement was made that 'one Roger Channon, a strong waterman of Exeter was to pay her'. She was to receive 12s for each month's nursing. After three weeks the baby died, however, and was buried by the nurse and her husband. Gendells was a hellier (a tiler or slater), perhaps someone who moved around in the course of his work, and passed on information along the way.

In the Colyton burial register for 1641, the burial of Marie, a 'nurse child' of William Michell of Rockerhaine in Colyton, is mentioned. She appears to have been 3 years and 4 months old at her death so there is either some inaccuracy in the record or she was breast-fed for an extraordinarily long time. When the Reverend Collyns was ejected from the incumbency of Colyton in 1647, two of his ten children were reputedly put out to weavers whose wives nursed them.[15] In general, however, there is far more evidence of wet nursing in Colyton from the second half of the eighteenth century when female employment prospects were looking bleak. Judging by the frequency with which references are made to the nursing of children by women who were not their mothers in the overseers' account book, breast-feeding of children was not considered to be the prerogative of the mother by the poor. The reasons why this should be the case are more difficult to discover, but it seems likely to have developed when women's work was plentiful in Colyton. During the first year of their infant's life, women frequently took in other people's children. After an illegitimate birth, single women could make some money by taking in other children. A married woman would take in children after her third or fourth child was born. It is probably indicative of a conscious attempt to space births. Joan Edwards had her second illegitimate child in March 1767.[16] In November she was looking after the foundling Lazarus Colyton, and in December she was nursing Elizabeth Abrahams's child. Elizabeth Abrahams was a soldier's wife who left the parish abandoning her baby. Mary Knight's bastard son Robert was born in February 1757. He was put into the immediate care of a married woman, Margaret Gosling. She was paid 14s 8d from February to April, presumably for wet nursing. Since the Goslings' last child had been born in 1755 and was 21 months old when Margaret took over Robert's nurture, it seems likely that wet nursing extended the 'contraceptive' birth interval as the Goslings' next child was not born until 1760 after a 66-month interval.

Poor children do not seem to have been weaned until they were in their second year. In a case of 1788, Elizabeth Bustel was removed back to Colyton with an illegitimate child called Joseph Corbett who was earmarked 'for Nurture'. His age was given as 'about two years'.[17] Removal proceedings began on John and Sarah Deane just before the birth of their last child, Mariah, who was baptised on 28 January 1752. There was a delay due to wrangling over which parish the Deanes should be sent to. While the family were given constant parish relief, the two children, a boy of 2 and Mariah aged 1 month, were boarded with Elizabeth Legg. 'Old Elizabeth Legg' was probably a widow. For keeping the Deane children, she was paid 12s a month instead of her usual 2s. Her daughter, Martha, who was single and had just had an illegitimate child, probably breast-fed the child. In January 1753, when the family were finally removed to Stockland, the parish supplied '3 Horses, a man and the Nurse with the suckling child'.

By this period wet nursing was far more remunerative, in terms of income, than domestic service or any type of textile manufacture. In a settlement examination of Eleanor Johns taken at Chudleigh in 1820, it is recorded that she left her service position when she was found to be with child, and went to live with her mother.[18] After the child was born she went to live with Mrs Barnes, the wife of an attorney-at-law in Exeter, as a wet nurse. She was paid the extremely high sum of £1 5s 0d per month and stayed there for seven months. She then went into a brief period of hiring, before going back to join her mother, and then replacing her sister in a hiring where she was paid 1s a week. Clearly this was a huge drop in earnings from the financial rewards of wet nursing.

Other women preferred to carry on working while giving their child to another woman for wet nursing. In a Tiverton St Peter examination of 1813, Mary Routley described how she was brought to bed with an illegitimate child in Silverton.[19] Soon after the birth she went into weekly service for six months. After that she went to Tiverton and hired herself to Mr Joseph Grant of Great Bradley House as a yearly servant. She said: 'When she left Silverton she put her child out to Nurse and all the time she lived in Tiverton has paid ninepence per week towards the maintanence of her child to a person at Silverton'. Giving children to strangers to care for seems to have become increasingly rare in nineteenth-century records. Misplaced infants were more often taken in by their kin. In an examination, made in 1847, of Eliza Hoare, who was an indoor pauper in the Axminster Union workhouse and chargeable to the parish of Coombpyne, she explained that after her birth in 1823: 'When I first recollect I was living at Combpyne with my Uncle and Aunt Edward and Amy Maticks. I have been told I was taken to Combpyne from Colyton (where my parents resided) when I was only Ten Days old, as my mother was unable to nurse me by reason of her being subject to fits.'[20]

Childbirth and wet nursing were both activities which fell into the public realm for poor women until the nineteenth century. Procreation may have had some financial benefits since wet nursing of poor children was a lucrative source of local employment. The role of welfare provision for childbirth and child-raising was very important, and probably mirrored community-based provision for childcare, which had evolved as a response to women's work in Colyton.

Boarding Children

Some ten years after the dreadful incident recorded in the last chapter where the Hoare children's father died in a muster parade, the boarding of one of Widow Hoare's children, John, with a Mr Tucker of Colyton is recorded in Nathaniel Pinney's accounts for his father.[21] The residence of children with local people who were not their parents was the usual experience in Colyton and locality. As a busy industrial town, late seventeenth-century Colyton attracted some youth for training. In 1675, for example, Abraham Edwards of Axminster was living with Jonathan Seaward of Colyton who ran a carpentry workshop.[22] Some children were boarded as orphans, others to be scholars. There was a traditional West Country assumption that child training was best done by people other than parents. In 1704 Azariah Pinney wrote to his sister from Nevis asking for one of his nephews to join him: 'But why is none yet sent, or will any be sent on this letter, if there will I can provide for him still: but ye westerne people of England thinke their children out of gods providence when they are gone from theirs, & thus they distrust god at ye same time they pretend to have a lively faith in him'. By this time John Hoare, now in his late twenties and a potential helper for Azariah, was still considered a 'child'— perhaps because he was not in a position to inherit which might have inspired a desire to initiate him into trade.[23] For Dissenters like the Pinneys, the choice of occupation for sons was a serious religious duty and one of the most important parental responsibilities was choice of a trade or profession for the boy—a practical outworking of the Puritan conception of the calling. Of course, a long period of training for youth was inspired by the culture of discipline and was a way of securing orderly workers.

Probably as a result of this, if there is one area in which Colyton could claim to have comprehensive documentation it is in child apprenticeship. The 1562 Statute of Artificers gave justices of the peace and officers of towns the power to bind as an apprentice any unemployed person who was under the age of 21. An Act of 1577 defined the binding out of 'beggar's children' until the age of 24 for boys and 18 for girls. By the 1597/8 Poor Law Act, the age for girls was raised to 21. This was reinforced by the 1601 Act. Justices were now empowered not only to apprentice children of paupers and vagrants, but also those of parents who were overburdened with children.[24] Consequently, the community aspect of caring for poor children was enshrined in legislation. Apprenticing was not only a statutory function of the poor relief officers, but was reinforced by the feoffees, and the influence of this corporate body explains why apprenticeship was even more widespread than in other English small towns.[25] However, Colyton was not unusual. In Ottery in the late sixteenth century bequests for the relief of the poor of the parish were administered by the feoffees and used to give loans to 'young artificers and handicraft men . . . not being any ale-house haunters' to start them in life. For poor children, the governors of the corporation acted in conjunction with the justices and overseers of the parish in administering poor relief and particularly in the binding of apprentices.[26] In Colyton, the feoffees provided much more extensively for poor children than in similar parishes. About 1690, for example, when the Widow Paule's daughter took up her indentures she was given linen smocks, aprons, a coife, underclothes, a pair of bodices and stockings and a pair of shoes, with the small linen made up for her.[27]

Colyton started to record the apprenticing of children after the passage of the 1598 Act in an Apprenticeship Register that extends to 1711. Apprenticeship indentures cover the period from 1647 through to 1741. There is an Apprenticeship Clothing Account for 1647 and also a list of 'paupers bound forth apprentice' in 1710/11. From 1741 to 1769 the premium paid for apprenticing was always recorded in the overseers' account book, but no records exist for the last thirty years of the eighteenth century. Following an Act of 1802, which ordered the keeping of registers of apprentices, a parish apprentice list was kept until 1830. As we have seen throughout this study, the recording of various aspects of parochial life is selective and therefore the very existence of such a rich archive tells us that apprenticeship was an activity endorsed by those who held power in the parish.

It is within the three documentary periods of 1598–1740, 1741–69 and 1802–30 that apprenticing in Colyton will be analysed. These records all relate to poor apprentices. The indications of private apprenticeship are confined to a few bonds, the mention of bequests to apprentice children in Prerogative Court of Canterbury wills and references in family papers. Nevertheless, the children of the middling sort were apprenticed after schooling. The Pinney family experience was probably fairly typical for a family with wide connections. Nathaniel Pinney was apprenticed to a London merchant, who seems to have been either a relative or a man with local links in east Devon or west Dorset. Nathaniel's master taught him accountancy skills that built on the practical education he had gained at one of the local Dissenting academies. Other boys were apprenticed locally to craftspeople and progressed through the stages of apprentice, journeyman and with the eventual hope of becoming master of the trade.

The background to a child being made a pauper apprentice can be closely examined in the overseers' account book. Normally the child had been maintained by the parish for several years and was in temporary 'keeping' arrangements before he or she was apprenticed. A typical case is Samuel Abrahams, who was apprenticed in 1752. His father went off with a 'wench' and left him as a baby with his estranged mother. The parish paid for his shoes, clothes and maintenance from infancy until he reached his eighth birthday, which, although several years younger than the usual age of indenturing, was a very common time for pauper apprenticing in Colyton.

Table 7.1 shows the number of apprentices recorded in Colyton in the various documents, and compares them with baptisms by cohort. There is a large shortfall in the penultimate cohort because of missing figures for 1770–99. Without that, the number could be expected to be similar to the 1700–49 and 1800–37 figures. There are records of a total of 815 pauper apprentices in Colyton, who comprised nearly 12 per cent of baptisms in one cohort. The large number of pauper apprentices in early seventeenth-century Colyton can be related not just to feoffee practice but also to the upheavals of the period and orders from the authorities at county level to apprentice children. In April 1631 a certificant covered several hundreds of Devon including Colyton, Axminster and Ottery and ordered: 'In same parishes we have taken views of particular poor families and hath given order for the billeting of divers poor children of such as by their labour are not able to support their charge, others we have placed abroad as apprentices, so that we know not what may remaineth for us to do more, considering the great burthens of the persons of every quality and deadness of the time'.[28]

Table 7.2 shows the sex ratio of pauper apprentices. The sex ratio of pauper apprentices reflects the economic position of the sexes. In the first cohort roughly equal numbers of girls and boys were apprenticed. Into the seventeenth century there was more employment for girls at home in lace-making, so that by the second half of the century half as many girls as boys were apprentices. The ratio equalised in the second half of the eighteenth century as female employment opportunities diminished but male opportunities grew. Since the lace trade did not revive until after 1840, the explanation for the excess of boy apprentices in the last cohort is more difficult but may indicate an increasingly male-orientated labour market or the fact that some girls may have found work in factories in nearby towns.[29]

Large rises in children being apprenticed concur with specific distress conditions. For example, twenty-two children were apprenticed in 1651 on the eve of the Dutch war, and a serious trade depression. Since children were apprenticed when their families were poverty-stricken,

Table 7.1 Number of pauper apprentices in Colyton 1550–1837

	No.	% of baptisms
1550-99	55	2.9
1600-49	208	6.8
1650-99	98	5.1
1700-49	178	11.7
1750-99	84	4.7
1800-37	192	9.1

Table 7.2 Sex ratio of pauper apprentices in Colyton 1550–1837

	Boy	Girl	Ratio
1550-99	28	27	103.7
1600-49	127	81	156.8
1650-99	65	33	197.0
1700-49	102	76	134.2
1750-99	41	43	95.3
1800-37	124	68	182.3

peaks of apprenticing could be expected to follow high wheat prices and periods of high mortality. Figure 7.1 shows that there was some relationship between the number of apprentices and wheat prices. Thus, at Exeter in 1630 when wheat was 54.7s per Winchester quarter, nineteen children were apprenticed in Colyton in the following year. In 1647, wheat stood at 62.7s and there were forty-two apprentices. This relationship did not always hold, however, since 1708 and 1709 saw very high wheat prices but no sharp rise in apprenticing. By contrast 1810 and 1811 had particularly high wheat prices and twenty-eight children were apprenticed.

The great number of apprentices in 1647 necessitated a special account to be taken of clothing which was made for the children before they were bound out.[30] Not only were food prices high, but Colyton experienced a mortality crisis due to the plague outbreak which took hold from November 1645 to December 1646. The beginning and end of the epidemic are marked in the burial register by 'Here ye sickness began' and 'Here ye sickness ended'. On 24 May 1646 the House of Commons ordered a collection for Colyton and Tiverton which were both severely afflicted by the plague. In all, a fifth of Colyton's population died and many children were orphaned, although only 6 per cent of families lost both husband and wife. Before the plague started, Colyton was experiencing high mortality and a lowered birth rate. This must have been due, in part, to heavy fighting in the town, and general disruption caused by the Civil Wars in 1643 and 1644.[31] This probably led to a typhus epidemic that preceded the plague outbreak. Schofield's study of the Colyton plague showed that it was concentrated in certain families.[32] In 73 per cent of cases, the family as a social and economic unit remained intact, and 62 per cent of families escaped death entirely. As shown in Chapter 3, the total reconstitution indicates that the families worst affected were based in the town and had connections with the woollen industry.

Even if the plague was confined to certain groups, the fact that 1647 saw the largest number of children ever apprenticed in the parish

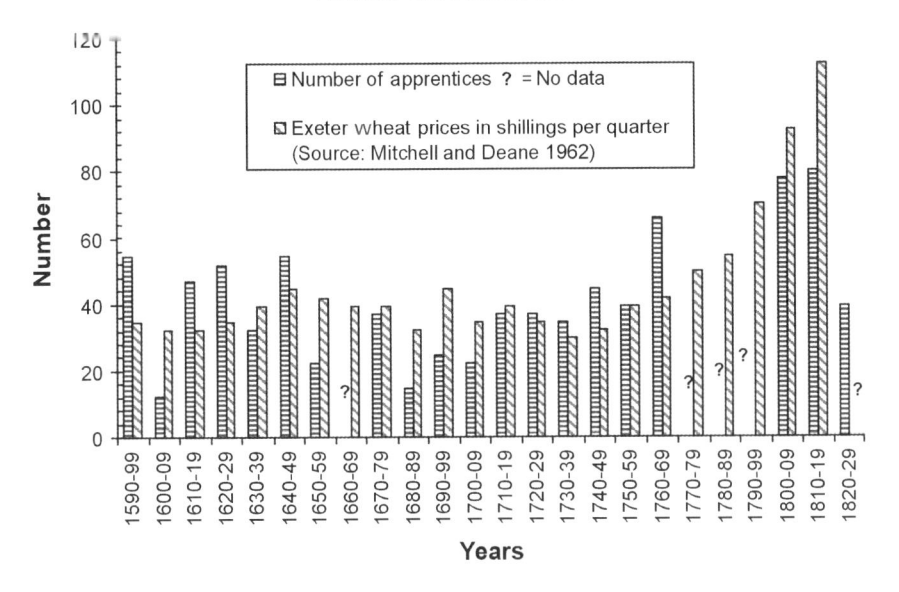

Fig. 7.1 Parish apprentices in Colyton and Exeter wheat prices 1590–1829.

suggests that there was a considerable number of homeless orphans. Children were generally allocated to someone (usually a man) who had lost a marital partner in the plague. Walter Vye, a widower who lost his wife in the plague, was given an apprentice in 'housewiferie' in 1651. While apprentices have been generally thought to come from over-large families in the earlier periods, this was not necessarily the case. The overriding factor that determined the apprenticeship of some poor children was that their labour could be used by another family.[33] Given the Puritan backdrop to this period, we should also see apprenticeship as part of an impulse to place children under household authority and in a position to contribute to the work effort of an industrious parish: the religious basis for apprenticeship was never far from the material.

The association between apprenticing and employment in Colyton can be further examined by considering seasonal variations, although to some extent the patterns of seasonality are distorted by apprenticing children in batches, which was a feature of the eighteenth century. For example, all the children who were apprenticed in the year 1711 were bound on 6 July. This was most evident in the indentures of the early eighteenth century which have not been included in this analysis. There was also some tendency for the register entry to lag behind the indenture date. Worse still, there are long gaps in recording months in the registers, and a few apprentices were just contained in the annual account in the overseers' account book without the month being specified. Despite these pitfalls an attempt has been made in Table 7.3 to find a seasonal pattern for those cases for which there is information in three of the records for the different periods.

Contrary to the expectation that most children would be apprenticed in winter when poverty was hardest felt, it was most common to apprentice children in the summer, with July through to September being the most common months. This could have been to meet farmers' hay-making and harvesting needs, as the children apprenticed in summer normally went to one of the wealthy large farmers in the district. The analysis of poor law disbursements in Colyton suggested that unemployment was low in late summer.[34] A seasonal distribution of Colyton settlement certificates shows that while unemployment was all year around, there was something of a peak in winter which became more defined in the late eighteenth-century period of concentration on arable farming. Apprentices were taken by the farmers who could be expected to be most responsive to price changes that favoured wheat production.

Apprentices as a form of farm labour were particularly common in Devon. As Marshall said in 1796, 'The practice of putting out the children of paupers to farmers, as apprentices in husbandry, is, as an established custom likewise peculiar to this part of the island'.[35] The job designations of apprentices were usually gender-specific, being 'servant in husbandry' if they were boys and 'housewifery' if they were girls. It has

Table 7.3 Number of cases of pauper apprenticeship by month in Colyton 1598–1830

Month	Apprentice Register 1598–1711		Overseers' Account Book 1741–1769		Apprentice Register 1802–1830	
	No.	%	No.	%	No.	%.
January	39	11.1	3	3.6	8	4.2
February	19	5.4	13	15.7	30	15.6
March	16	4.6	10	12.0	3	1.6
April	24	6.8	9	10.8	13	6.8
May	23	6.6	3	3.6	11	5.7
June	30	8.5	4	4.8	10	5.2
July	44	12.5	15	18.0	18	9.4
August	82	23.4	9	10.8	40	20.8
September	26	7.4	4	4.8	40	20.8
October	26	7.4	4	4.8	8	4.2
November	20	5.7	8	9.6	8	4.2
December	2	0.5	1	1.2	3	1.6
Total	351		83		192	

Table 7.4 Mean ages of male and female apprentices in Colyton 1598–1830

	Male	Female	Both sexes
Apprentice Register/Indentures 1598–1740	11.7	12.0	11.9
Overseers' Account Book 1741–1769	11.0	9.9	10.4
Apprentice Register 1802–1830	9.6	10.5	10.3

been thought that this label, for girls at least, covered some sort of training in crafts.[36] Considering the farm economy in Colyton it seems likely that apprenticeship for girls would include some training in spinning and lace-making. Little evidence is available in the records of the economic contribution of children either in their parents' home or in that of their master or mistress. It could be expected that this would depend on age. Premiums for the apprenticeship, which were generally paid by the parish, varied with the age of the child and did not differ according to the gender. Whereas 6s 8d was paid for a 15-year-old boy in 1609, £9 0s 0d was paid in 1621 for a 5-year-old girl. Premiums fell over time. Most of the extant bastardy bonds for Colyton, which cover the periods 1683–1744 and 1762–1810, contain the provision that the putative father should put forward 40s for the child to be apprenticed at the age of 8 years.[37] In the overseers' account book, the parish generally put forward £1 for each child apprenticed.[38] In the nineteenth century higher payments were made for boys to be apprenticed into specific trades, thus £5 5s 0d was paid to a stonemason, £11 0s 0d to a cordwainer and £6 0s 0d to a ropemaker.

Paupers could be apprenticed as early as the age of 4 or as late as 20 in Colyton. The earliest apprentice register gives either supposed age, date at baptism or parents' name. The supposed ages could be wrong in an upwards or downwards direction by a few years, but nevertheless these details made linkage to the reconstitution easy. Table 7.4 presents the ages according to gender from the different records.

The mean age of apprentices up to 1629 was only 8.7. Around that time there was a jump in age, and in the 1630–89 period the average was 11.6, and from 1690 to 1740 the average was 10.0.[39] Colyton apprentices were generally younger than those mentioned in comparative studies.[40] Snell found that the average age for male apprentices in Devon in the period 1700–1860 was 13.4.[41] Devon was one of the counties which showed the earliest ages of children leaving home; elsewhere boys were generally at least 14 when they were apprenticed. Wall compared the

Table 7.5 Family circumstances of pauper apprentices in Colyton 1598–1830

	Both parents alive		Father dead		Mother dead		Both dead	
	No.	%	No.	%	No.	%	No.	%
Register/Indentures 1598–1740	63	20.9	103	34.1	106	35.0	30	9.9
Overseers' Account Book 1741–1769	125	88.6	7	5.0	5	3.5	4	2.8
Register 1802–30	181	94.3	3	1.6	4	2.0	4	2.0

1841 census for Colyton with listings for Swindon in 1697, Cardington in 1782 and Binfield in 1801, and also found that only in the case of Colyton did children as young as 10 live away from home.[42] Some of the Colyton pauper apprentices were older than those entering ordinary indentures. It is not clear how to interpret this—was it an extended period of servility for a poor young adult or a late chance to make a start in training for a trade or craft using public and charitable funds?

It seems possible that limited employment prospects or no access to land for parents might make it more usual for children to leave home early. Table 7.5 shows what is known of the family circumstances of children in Colyton at the time when they were apprenticed.

The striking result of linking apprentices to the reconstitution in Table 7.5 is the apparent change in the mortality of parents.[43] By the second half of the eighteenth century, very few of the apprentices' parents appear to be dead. This probably indicates a change in attitude by the overseers towards the function of apprenticeship. It is possible that orphaned children were kept by another method and may have been domiciled in the workhouse. Alternatively, the settlement examinations suggest that in the nineteenth century they were more likely to be boarded out with relatives who were expected to bring them up as part of their own families.

Ideally, the parental circumstances of apprentices would be compared with the number of children 'at risk', but the reconstitution is not an adequate tool for making such an estimate. In the period up to 1740, while there were no significant differences in sex-specific parental mortality, did the death of a mother or a father make any difference to the chances of a child being apprenticed? The overseers seem to have been assiduous in placing children aged over 8 within a few days of the parental death. Table 7.6 gives a breakdown of parental circumstances by date to the mid-eighteenth century.

This period spans the change from a predominantly arable to a predominantly pastoral agricultural system in Colyton and the patterns

Table 7.6 Family circumstances of pauper apprentices listed in the register and indentures 1598–1740

Years	Both parents alive		Father dead		Mother dead		Both alive	
	No.	%	No.	%	No.	%	No.	%
1598–1649	42	25.4	60	36.4	47	28.5	16	9.7
1650–1699	12	19.4	20	32.3	23	37.1	7	11.3
1700–1740	9	12.0	23	30.7	36	48.0	4	9.4

reflect this. A father's death was more likely to lead to a child being apprenticed before 1650. Thereafter, more children were apprenticed on the death of a mother. Since a mother's chances of remarriage were virtually nil in this period, it is clear that women had some economic standing or more children would have been apprenticed on their father's death.

The apprentices of the second half of the eighteenth century were different. Usually their parents were alive, but could not support them because they had large families and the children were close in age. The overseers used apprenticeship as a means of family support, which predated, and later supplemented, the policy of giving allowances. In some of the cases, the parents were separated, and the child was being maintained by a single parent. Some of the children's fathers were 'decayed tradesmen' supported by the feoffees. Others, in the 1810s, were away in the militia or were war invalids. In some cases the problem must have been a sheer lack of housing space.[44] Henry Milden, whose settlement was examined in December 1817 at Tiverton, said he was born in Tiverton and brought up by his parents until he was 14 when his uncle from Cullompton took him away from his parents 'in consequence of their having a long family'.[45] There must have been some house sharing in Colyton. In the 1801 census there were 257 inhabited houses and 334 families occupying them. The situation eased as houses were built over the next few years, as in 1811 there were 343 houses and 400 families occupying them. By 1821 there were 399 houses and the same number of families occupying them.[46]

The relationship between parental mortality and apprenticeship in the period up to 1741 can be considered in more detail. Linkage to establish social status shows that in some of the cases where a parent was dead, the apprentice came from a 'middling' status family. The families least likely to remain intact on the death of the father were the smaller yeomanry, as farmer's wives do not seem to have resorted to domestic industry. If their husband died there were no marriage partners available for them. Deborah Cross was apprenticed as a pauper in 1677, despite the fact that on his death in 1671, her father had been described as a 'gent' of Downhayne farm. As we have seen in the discussion about the three-life lease, a rapid slide into poverty could also result from a failure of inheritance strategy. In the cases where the mother died, the child being apprenticed was on average five months older than when the father died. The gender differences of apprentices in the cases of parental death are significant. In 103 cases where the father died, sixty sons were apprenticed and forty-three daughters. In the 106 cases where the mother died, sixty-nine sons and thirty-seven daughters were apprenticed. If either parent died, sons were more likely to be apprenticed. This probably indicates that girls could be more of a positive asset to the domestic economy than boys.

The apprentice indenture legally defined the obligations of both parties to the apprenticeship, and resembled a modern adoption document. In Colyton the child was kept for around sixteen years by a 'surrogate parent' who promised to supply sustenance, lodging and washing. In the seventeenth century in the case of craft families where the mother had died, apprenticeship was sometimes of son to father. This might span a father's remarriage. Other children were apprenticed to an uncle or an older brother. This reinforced links between relatives and step-relatives at a time when many men were leaving Colyton.[47] The system seems to have broken down in the 1690s when apprenticeship became defined as 'a head of settlement', in other words, a legal basis for a person having a settlement in a particular parish. Children were increasingly apprenticed out of the parish. Alternatively they were apprenticed not to one person but to several 'contributors' who shared the child in an attempt to circumvent the law and prevent the child gaining a settlement in one particular parish.

In the case of illegitimate children, apprenticing formed 'fostering' relationships. Although bastardy bonds made provision for children to be apprenticed at the age of 8, in the earliest apprentice register only three children can be definitely identified who were born illegitimate. In the register, which covers the period 1802–30, twenty-three apprentices had been baptised as 'base', forming almost 12 per cent of apprentices in this period. It seems likely that their mothers were less able to maintain them after the collapse of domestic industry. Apart from the apprentices who came from a single parent situation, there were some apprentices who had both parents alive. There was always an element of apprenticeship as a life-cycle stage. So, in some families several children would be bound out when they attained their eighth, ninth or tenth birthday. This was a much more common pattern in the nineteenth century when a line of brothers or sisters would be apprenticed on reaching their eighth birthday. In the period of the first apprentice register and group of indentures from 1598 to 1741, 34 per cent of apprentices had siblings who were also apprenticed. By contrast in the apprentice register of 1802 to 1830 75 per cent of apprentices had siblings who were also apprenticed. In a few unusual cases, such as the Roust family where six out of nine children were apprenticed, both parents were dead. Generally, however, parental mortality was unusual in these cases and apprenticeship supplemented the poor law authorities' policy of providing child allowances.

Parental attitudes to the apprenticing of their children were ambivalent. In December 1747 a widow, Hannah Pitfield, had her poor relief cut to a third of its original level when she refused to have her children bound out, despite being destitute.[48] Her deceased husband had been a farmer of some standing in the parish and it seems likely that she found apprenticeship a disgrace. By contrast, other mothers were more than eager to apprentice their children. Mary Ward, a widow who had at least two children after her husband died, was determined to place her daughter. An entry in the overseers' account book for December 1746 states: 'Pd for an indenture for Wid. Ward's daughter but the master (Cap'n Sampson) as Mrs Anning reports, refused to sign the indenture—the child's mother took her daughter and placed her in another parish'.

What effect did apprenticing have on achieving independence? In the early modern period males were apprenticed until they were 24 years old, and females until they were 21. Following an Act of 1778 no apprentice was to be held bound after the age of 21, and nineteenth-century indentures of females normally contain the provision 'until 21 or day of marriage'. The societal constraint on the achievement of independence has been thought to raise the age at marriage.[49] In fact, the indentures do not always seem to have been adhered to as a binding contract. Linkage shows that some apprentices married before they were 24 even though this was prohibited by the indenture stipulations. This leads to suspicion that the pro-forma indentures were not taken literally. There is also no evidence from Colyton that it was common to marry immediately after coming out of indentures; apprentices generally married when they were older. In the 1598–1741 period eighteen apprentices never married, twenty-one died single before they were 30, and for the rest the average age at marriage for males was 30.9 and for females 28.6. Men's ages at marriage were generally more variable than females. In the 1802–30 period the averages differed little from those for Colyton in general, standing at 26.8 for males and 24.6 for females.

Various pieces of evidence can be accumulated from the Colyton information to provide context for the question of when children left home and when their parents rescinded authority over them. The local economy seems to be all-important in determining at what age children were likely to leave the parental home.[50] Children left home earlier in rural than urban areas, and children from the lower strata left their families earlier than those from farmer or merchant households.[51] It seems to have been rare for sons to remain in the parental home in preference to daughters in the country as a whole, although in the late eighteenth and early nineteenth centuries more sons would stay in the parental home than they had earlier.[52]

The evidence for pauper apprentices can be related to the question of when children left home. Even before the removal of legal protection for apprentices in 1814, the institution became much more flexible and began to resemble an inferior type of yearly hiring, as William Marshall described it in 1796 for Devon:

> Instead of treating them as their adopted children or as relations or as a superior order of servants whose love and esteem they are desirous of gaining, for their mutual happiness, during the long term of their intimate connexion, as well as to secure their services at a time they become most valuable, they are treated, at least in the early stage of servitude, as the inferiors of yearly or weekly servants, are frequently subjected, I fear, to a state of the most abject drudgery: a severity which they do not forget, even should it be relaxed as they grow up.[53]

From the late eighteenth century there was a decline in apprentices 'living in'. 'Outdoor apprenticeship' became normal, with apprentices living at home and going out to work for their master each day. Consequently they would be paid a nominal wage. Snell has argued that while children had earlier been passive in the apprenticing process, they increasingly began to organise their own indentures.[54] In the case of Colyton and some other Devon parishes for which settlement examinations survive, it was in fact more common for parents, rather than the parish or feoffees, to set up their children in apprenticeships from the late eighteenth century.

In the settlement case of John and Charlotte Loveridge who were examined in Colyton in 1845, John's mother referred back to her son's childhood: 'When my son was about 8 years of age I agreed with Mr Samuel Newbury (of Southleigh) that he should serve him to drive his plough at the wages of 6d. by the week and the sd Mr Newbury finding him meat and drink and he lodging at home and my husband finding him clothes'.[55] His wages went directly to his mother, who 'received his wages as I required and made up the account with Mr Newbury when we found it convenient'. Fifteen-year-old William Bole was apprenticed to Collan Warmington, a cordwainer, in October 1764. The apprenticeship was for three years with the consent of his father. Warmington agreed to pay 6d in wages weekly to his father.[56]

The 1843 Parliamentary Report into the Employment of Children indicated that apprenticeship, as organised by the parish, was outside of the predominant family system and was effectively an evasion of family responsibilities: 'The parents are not only relieved from the expense of maintaining their children but they are also released from all parental obligations towards them. They cease to consider their children when once apprenticed, as part of their family, and the relief afforded to the parents in the removal of the children is regarded by them as an advantage'.[57] Certainly between periods of service even adult children would return to their parental home, and at what point they made a clear break can be difficult to define. In Sherford, in a settlement examination of 1831 after her master moved, Mary Ann Gillard 'asked him what she was to do, [her master] . . . told her to go home to her mother and tell her to get her a place'.[58] William Weston, examined in Colyton in 1838, said that after working for local farmers as a labourer and living at home, 'his mother placed him apprentice to a stonemason. He resided with his mother who received the said wages and provided for him.'[59]

Paid apprentices were highly vulnerable to trade conditions, and were frequently laid off in trade decline in spite of their indentures. More often, apprenticeships were based on fictitious or verbal agreements 'with no paper signed', which offered no recourse in the case of any breach of agreement. At the same time agreements which included no payment were increasingly being shrugged off in favour of more lucrative arrangements. Seventeen-year-old Mary Anstis in a Colyton settlement examination of 1788 explained that she had been apprenticed to William White until she was 15 years old when the indentures were terminated, 'at which time her master agreed she should go and get her bread which she accordingly did' and hired herself at 40s a year. Mary Ware said in a settlement examination of 1795 that at 16 she was bound out apprentice by the overseer of the poor of Seaton to a farmer, George Harper. Three years later, her father obtained her master's consent to give up her apprenticeship and she went into service for wages of a shilling a week.

By the early nineteenth century the boundaries between apprenticeship and service were certainly not distinct. This is clearly shown by an examination of Thomas Batstone at Seaton and Beer prior to his removal to Colyton in 1835.[60] He was born at Southleigh and lived there with his parents until he was 12. He then lived with Nathaniel Power of Colyton for two years in return for food and lodging. This was an apprentice-type arrangement and 'nothing was said about time or wages'. When he was 14 his father went to see Power to negotiate some wages for Thomas and also obtained a potato patch for him. This was a way of paying his father, however, since 'when potatoe sowing came my Master planted the potatoes for me and afterwards took them up and sent them home [the crop] to my Fathers'. We have seen that leasing crops from farmers was fairly common and may suggest that payment by this method was not unusual. When Thomas parted company with Power he moved back to live with his parents. He then went to learn the trade of shoemaker with William Scriven, 'with whom I was to serve five years' but there were no indentures and Thomas only stayed two years. After living for three months in Southleigh he moved to Colyton with his master, then worked in North Petherton for four or five months, and then at Wellington in Somerset for two years. He was then bound apprentice to a Captain Farrant for four years and lived on board the schooner *Antelope* for about nine months. After being at sea for six months he married.

Defined life-cycle stages fell out of their previous order in the early nineteenth century. Some married men even became apprentices. Thomas Bright was not an isolated case. He explained in a settlement examination of July 1841 that he was born in 1792 and married in 1815 at the age of 23, his wife having borne his child a year beforehand and he had been paying maintenance for it.[61] Three years after his marriage he was apprenticed by his father to William Mayne of Colyton, a tallow chandler, for three years and he lived in his house for three years. Despite this, he and his wife had four children and when he was out of indentures they were able to rent a farm in Colyton.

Many poor children lived outside of a family composed of relatives. Until the second half of the eighteenth century apprenticeship represented a community method of looking after displaced children and young adults. Evidently this later became a family responsibility. Nevertheless, we are only skimming the surface of this practice by looking at official records. Many Colyton children would have been in informal training relationships that never found public expression in indentures. The paucity of surviving evidence for lace-making apprentices perhaps suggests that this was particularly the case for girls. While apprenticeship officially ended in 1814, parish apprenticeship was still evident in other Devon parishes in 1834: in Awliscombe the children of paupers were bound to landholders by rotation from the age of nine and Woodborough also had parish apprenticeship from the age of nine.[62]

Apprenticeship was particularly important in Colyton because the sex ratio and economic structure impaired the formation of strong family ties among the poor. In the seventeenth and early eighteenth centuries a family-based workshop form of production for crafts and textile production ran alongside a pool of workers who sold their labour. By the second half of the eighteenth century this largely proletarian workforce had become the norm. Their household income was partly dependent on welfare and charity, and within a situation where there was a large 'underclass' pauper apprenticeship should be seen as a local 'institution' which was perhaps particularly extensive because of early industrialisation.

Service

We have seen that pauper apprenticeship shaded into service. It is important to recognise that service was not just a labour relationship but should also be seen as a central Christian duty, as an act of kindness which, at least traditionally, held obligations on both sides. In 1600 Johan Whitelocke, a servant in Plymouth, reported a conversation with her next-door neighbour. On telling her that she served the sadler next door, William Dulking's wife said 'Whate doest thou meanne to serve suche a cruell fellowe for his servants doe alwaies come awaie from him'. She advised Johan to 'shift for thie selfe, and take such things as you maie, and so gett from him, and then thou shalte be fitt to serve another; for that the sd sadler will no make after thee, to take thee againe'. Reflecting the typical experience of the mobile servant, Alice Dulking claimed she only said Johan 'wolde staie in town but a likell tyme'.[63] Demographic patterns of late marriage and high celibacy in the 1650–1750 period suggest that life-cycle service would have been a very common experience. The evidence for servants in Colyton and district suggest that life as a servant could have very many permutations. Not all servants lived with their master. In 1599 Edward Rutley was accused of stealing money while he was a servant for William Hore of Colyton, a shoemaker, but he 'did lodge in the house of one Saunders wief in Colyton'. This, and later evidence, reveals the extent of lodging arrangements in Colyton.[64]

In the early seventeenth century there was sometimes little status difference between masters and servants, the crucial distinction being that the master had inherited and now ran his own household whereas his servant could be a younger son or someone spending time outside of the parental household in a period of training. This is evident in a court case that reveals several aspects of life in early seventeenth-century Colyton. In 1624, 19-year-old Phillip Seaward of Colyton, a groom, deposed that a little before Christmas, John Clarke, a 22-year-old servant, stole 6d from Morgan Hayne, his then master.[65] Seaward said to Clarke, 'art thou not a shamed to doe such a thinge seeing they master doth trust thee as he doth'. Clarke entreated Seaward not to reveal it, 'for said he thou knowest I doe it for neede'. It then transpired that three months prior to this, Seaward, Clarke and Hayne had all worked at the house of one Mr Longe in Colyton. One one occasion when Clarke was dressing, Seaward saw a silver spoon fall out of his hose. When Seaward demanded to know where it came from, Clarke said that it belonged to his needy father who had asked Clarke to pawn it for him, but he later confessed that it was Longe's spoon. There was an apparent divergence of fortune here between the young men: while Clarke appears to be attempting to alleviate his family's poverty, Hayne appears to have moved from the position of servant to the status of householder with his own servants over a few short months when he inherited his father's farm. Morgan Hayne's own future was not necessarily economically secure, however, for six years later he was back in court.[66] He claimed to have found in the stable of his mother-in-law, Syth Hayman, a pair of sheets and a pillow tye covered up under the manger. He pawned them for 9s to Nathaniel Sweete, proposing to be able to redeem them again and return them to the Widow Hayman. Sweete, a buttonmaker of Colyton and the local pawnbroker, confirmed that he had the goods in his custody until they were taken away by Syth Hayman.

A case in which a female servant and her female mistress also seemed to be of similar status comes from Chudleigh.[67] Christian Curteise, spinster and servant to a widow, Elizabeth Sexton, had had £5 10 0d in her chest. While scouring the cooking pots in the court, she took a break for a cup of beer and found her mistress to have opened and seized her servant's box, although she had the key in her girdle. The servant called her mother. She had received 20s from her grandmother when she died, as well as other money from her mother. Her mother had given her custody of 12s formerly lent to another woman. Her mistress claimed to be searching for some of her children's things and said that in the box she had found a piece of silk tiffany which was her own. Another woman said she had been in company with Christian on Sunday 'at a gossipinge', presumably a meeting of women which may have been associated with a christening. The woman asked Christian for a loan of £5. Christian denied she had so much credit, saying 'it was a base lye whoever said it for shee never had but ten shillings in all'. Here servant and mistress seem little different in status and the small store of money that it was possible for a servant to collect and lend out are apparent.

There is evidence of Colyton women travelling to other parishes to be servants. Anne Weekes, a single woman, had a chequered career. She deposed that she left Colyton where she was born, about Michaelmas in 1628 'and came into Tyverton , where she was intertayned as a servant by one John Diamond'. She was put into the House of Correction on suspicion of sleeping with Moses Pugsley, a shoemaker, and accused of stealing borrowed clothes to go to see him. She had also travelled to Cullompton and Kentisbeare. In a subsequent case on a fair day 'at about Matthew's Day last she came into Joane White's house at Plymptree . . . with an intent to serve her'. After being left with a blind old man to mind on the first night she ran away to Uffculme.

Yearly service was known as 'covenant service' in this area. A few other cases will furnish a picture of the experience of some young women. Anne Gold, a single woman, had her settlement examined in 1750 when she was aged about 22. When about 15 she had bargained to be a covenant servant with her uncle, a farmer, in Membury for 30s a year. Since then 'she hath been out of service about a year and a half and sometimes goes to washing and other Household work for her support, and of late she has been in No Employment and is now reduced to want'. She was apprehended in Cranbourne as a vagabond.[68] Grace Carmel deposed in 1731 (or soon after) that she had returned to Colyton and lived there with Daniel Skinner as his housekeeper, managing his dairy and 'doing the Business of his whole house to the time of his death' in 1743.[69] Her duties were not specified, but 'only as the said Grace Carmel was able to Shave, the said Daniel Skinner'. He agreed to pay her 4s per year for shaving him, 'which was accordingly paid her every Quarter for above 10 years together'. In his will he gave her liberty to live in his house without paying any rent for as long as she wanted, leaving her a legacy of £7 if she were living with him at the time of his death. The settlement case of Susan Harris provides a picture of someone who began as an apprentice in agriculture, went through various types of proletarianised service, and finally gravitated towards urban employment.[70] She was 18 years old when her settlement examination was taken in 1822. At the age of 9 she had been apprenticed to a Stockland yeoman until the age of 21. But after four years of apprenticeship her master died and she returned home and remained there for about six months. She then she went to Farmer Gill at Axminster and hired herself at 9d a week plus board and lodging and stayed there for a year, then moved to Honiton and hired herself to Mr Berry of the Turks Head Inn for a year at £3 wages plus board and lodging but continued there only six months, and then went to Heavitree and hired herself for a year at £5 wages plus board and lodging. This case history shows gradually rising wages as she grew older and moved nearer to Exeter and mobility.

Jean Robin's research shows that farm service remained part of the life-course of young adults in late nineteenth-century Colyton.[71] She cites a local case reported in the newspapers for 1866 of a 13-year-old farm servant who had been put to drive a cart drawn by two horses but lost control and upset the cart. His master called him a 'mump-headed toad and a brute' and beat him so severely that the matter was brought to petty sessions, where the magistrate said it was the master who was the brute and imposed a fine on him.

This evidence, from case histories, cannot enlighten us as to rising or falling numbers of servants in Colyton. Clearly, stray references in the evidence show that many servants were married women who acted as household helpers. While service endured through our time period, there was an obvious change in the service relationship. Whereas in the early seventeenth century, service to peers was reasonably common, by the early nineteenth century there was a yawning social gulf between masters and their servants and service was less a formalised period of training than a proletarianised form of labour.

Marriage Restrictions

It is evident that almost every child and young adult in early modern Colyton would have been brought up outside of the parental household and lived as an apprentice, boarding scholar or servant. Nevertheless, in the period from 1620 to 1720 some time elapsed from the end of apprenticeship until the average age of marriage. People of both sexes who were in their twenties were servants, many women worked as lace-makers and some young men left the parish. This section will examine the circumstances of marriage. As we have seen, the age of marriage is a crucial demographic indicator and when a large number of people do not marry, there is a demographic brake. Understanding the circumstances surrounding marriage decisions in early modern Colyton is a crucial step towards explaining demographic change.

Most demographic history to date assumes that marriage decisions have been closely associated with economic conditions. It was apparent in Chapter 5 that economic factors certainly influenced the timing and possibility of marriage in Colyton. The lace industry produced a distorted sex ratio, and while providing profits for some, impoverished others, at a time when welfare was conditional and subject to political considerations. The documents which can give us an insight into marriage decisions in Colyton have to take us beyond the statistics into the realm of personal and family strategies, emotions and perceptions. As other commentators such as Wrightson have noted, love, affection and personal choice were only a few of the considerations underlying a marital union.[72] Investigation of the papers of the Pinney family, and various court cases involving local people, demonstrate that marriage was viewed with a great deal of anxiety and trepidation in early modern south-east Devon. The main considerations that affected both the couple and their parents centred on financial matters and religious affiliation. Many years before Jane Austen's writings, and at much lower levels in the social hierarchy than she describes, middling Colyton people worried over 'worth', status and reputation. These criteria were of such great importance that some people were unable ever to find a satisfactory match and never married as a result.

For men in seventeenth- and eighteenth-century Colyton it appears that it was not the status of husband or father that was the essential attribute of manhood, although these would doubtless enhance a man's reputation.[73] Being a householder and leasing land or accruing 'worth' gained through trade or crafts were critical. As such the consolidation of yeoman farms, the validity of the three-life lease and the manorial conditions attached to it, along with changing conditions of paternal mortality in the seventeenth century, could have a determining effect on a man's status and make his life fraught with anxiety into middle age.

His choice of marriage partner could offset some of these difficulties because her marriage 'portion' might add to his worth. However, as we have seen, the seventeenth-century parish was riven by a religious Dissent that was unified only in its rejection of the Anglican church. As is indicated by the fact that most of the middle orders married elsewhere, the choice of a marital partner was also crucially affected by their need to find someone with an identical religious standpoint. Most Colyton people sought partners from the same congregation and thus their choice of husband or wife was quite limited.

The documents of the Pinney family attest to a good deal of kin influence on marriage decisions. Most marriages were viewed as potentially threatening the family patrimony and therefore discouraged by siblings as well as parents. Weddings for this family were rarely public affairs but secret unions, often enveloped in rumour and distrust. The marriages of most of the children of John and Jane Pinney occurred within the period for which letters survive. At the age of 30 Rachel Pinney married a vintner in 1682 to the great disapproval of her father. As he wrote to her: 'Daughter are you at this age & understanding, under such obligations to your father & will you ad such an Affliction to me to favour a person so vile & irreligious, to reproach your family, to undoe yourselfe body & soule?'.[74] As we have seen, two years later Azariah Pinney married a woman not thought to be of his equivalent social standing because she was daughter of a widow who had been in receipt of parish relief, although apparently with the same religious views. His sister wrote that she was sorry for his marriage although Azariah's own comment on this implies that it was a secretive union: 'I thinke but am not certaine shee doo not yet know of it pretending shee did not understand what the meaninge of it was'.[75] Hester Pinney also disapproved of the marriage of her sister, 35-year-old Sarah, in 1685 on the grounds that she should not marry during conditions of trade disruption and the marriage might affect their lace business.[76] Hester's own love matches in the 1690s, notably only when she had amassed a considerable fortune in the lace business and in lending money, were subject to heavy disapproval by her father and brother on the grounds of religion or lack of financial probity, and in the long term she did not marry. She had been subject to heavy censure from her brother Nathaniel regarding her conduct and reputation as a single woman, doubtless because she had a long-term affair with an aristocrat. As the eldest surviving son, Nathaniel's own late marriage was the subject of much discussion and rumour. In 1689 his father, John, received false reports that Nathaniel had married.[77] Nathaniel's reply is a tribute to the degree of family control over marriage:

> I can't but Extreamly wonder att what you reporte, And did not you think soe I can scarcely perswade my Selfe to beleeve, you would say That I am married And that you was told soe in Bristol, I pray then why in Bristol, had you not Sattisfied yourselfe to the Contrary, rather than prsently to Conclude on an error, and att distance in the Country resolve, most wronfully that yor childerene haveing disposed of themselves without yor knowledge or consent, were like to live without yor supporte or assistance, These are things that I must tell you. doeth even at once Crush the very Sperrits of them, and more Espeically Such of them, who have not only borne a great share in the trouble of geting yor family out of the confusion it was in, But have still a reale sence of the wrong it hath received by such confusion, and of the want there may bee of what Substance was then lost, To Sattisfie you now, And pray let this Sattisfie you, That I speake it in the presence of that God, before whome I expect to bee one day accountable, That I am not married to aney person in the world, nor never was, nor never thought of any Such thing, nor never will, as I have often told you, unlesse it bee verry much to my advantadge, And if you can now recomend mee to aney Such person I am ready to Imbrace the same, Therefore I pray doe not on false grounds and erroniouse suppositions Throw away that which should quallifie mee for such promotion. I have bin carefull industriouse and Saveing my Selfe, and question not but by Gods blesseing, and those meanes, I have already, and shall doe in litle tyme put my Selfe in agood way of liveing, and then I can the better recomend my Selfe for the maintainance of others, when its seen I can wel maintaine my Selfe, But if this while wee loose the maine substance at home, Too what purpose all this care and industry.

Nathaniel was 30 and, as he suggests here, had already achieved a measure of business success because he and Hester turned around the lace business in the second half of the 1680s. Nevertheless, like his sisters Nathaniel still relied on his father's support and approval. We should also note his personal providential attitude to marriage. Nathaniel had a cautious and conservative nature but his approach was characteristic of many of his contemporaries. Nevertheless, a year and a half later, Nathaniel's further business success made him much more confident, almost bullish. He wrote to his father from London explaining that he had no wish to become a country squire after sixteen years where his main business had been in trade in the city:

> I hope you are not conserned that I should neglect a women [sic] of Countrey breeding with 800l thinking I should overstand my Market, Indeed, I would not have you concerned att it for a 1000l

fortune I can have dayley when I please, and If ever I take up with such a fortune It shall bee when I am a little older, or with one I can love much better then I could doe that gentlewoman. I thank God I still enjoy my health here, and am not verry Expensive neither, neither doe I waite for places or perfermt altho: both I think are sooner to be got here then in the Country, Bee pleased to asure yor selfe I am very well sattisfied with my condicon and circumstances . . .[78]

Nevertheless, shortly after this Nathaniel was to make a very suitable marriage to Naomi Gay, an heiress from a trade background in the West Country, with the appropriate nonconformist credentials, and soon had 'Gentleman' appended to his name.

Despite (or perhaps because of) the fact that the family never stopped slandering Azariah Pinney for his young and thoughtless marriage, when his own son went on to marry at the age of 20 Azariah was almost inconsolable in his distress. His anger, perhaps fuelled by the heat and brutal conditions in Nevis, spills over from the poor paper and faded ink that reflect the scant West Indian supplies.[79] He wanted to be proved wrong that he had given a liberal education 'to a monster in human form nor to a Child of hell'. He had been in 'many years exile living in a scorching country & sweating my very blood & Trouble for th good of one' he thought would be a comfort. John, the errant son, was expecting to enter the legal profession in London and had entered Oxford (which the Pinneys associated with hedonism) as a gentleman commoner. After the marriage Azariah wrote:

> you'l find a Numerous family will be diversion enough (without your) jolly companions wine & musick . . . you will soon find that when the wyre edge of your rapid inclination is taken off by enyoyment, your head & heart will be cooler & your understanding cleerer, which will cause you to repent when too late & to crie out, a Fortune with lesse beauty had been better, & slavery bro't on my selfe by humor & fancy is insupportible'.

As soon as John married, he and his wife unwillingly took in their spinster aunt Hester as lodger and presumably some sort of guardian, although his young wife particularly objected to her. Four years later, following reports from Hester, Azariah accused his son of being a 'degenerate Wretch' and 'That you mind not Studdy Except to please your wife, but dine & Entertaine Torys Papists and Atheists in it, That you wholly Neglect the Publick [and that you] are a Practicall Atheist your Selfe'.[80] John was accused of lying in bed late, being so 'effeminate as to rise from your wife to make Chocoletta and when you have both drank your fill, goe to bed to her again, cum multis aliis!' He spent too much on wine, and lived extravagantly, 'giving out £1,000 fortune with your wife, who wil not goe to Markett herselfe but Trusts all to servants to buy abroad & manage household affaires at home, where as much againe, by such unhousewifely practices and Negligent Ins[pection] is Expended as is Necessary'. Azariah resented his son's further education and extolled the virtues of a traditional pattern for young adulthood when he canted: 'I repent I ever gave you more than Scoole Learning, I repent I had not bound you an apprentice to have gott your own living long ere this time'.

In 1713, nine years after first asking for a young family member to lodge with him, Azariah's nephew by marriage, William Gundry, was removed from his apprenticeship and sent to join Azariah in Nevis after a secret marriage. Interestingly this marriage was discovered when Gundry's father intercepted a letter to his barber 'interwritten in the style of a Husband'. Hester had all the particulars of the marriage but was accused of being compliant in the subterfuge. Azariah promised to make William fit for business and prevent his wife from following him to Nevis, but in the event Gundry died in the West Indies soon afterwards, 'being given to drink'.[81]

The evidence suggests that women's portions were crucial to the legitimation of a marriage.[82] In some senses the function of portions was more symbolic than material. Hester Pinney was an established businesswoman at the time she thought of marriage. A reckoning of her assets reveals that she easily had the required worth to produce her own substantial dowry but in the event it was the lack of family consent and refusal to produce a portion by her father which meant the assignation was called off. The portion was a sign of female status and reputation in rural society. In a case of suspected adultery of John Restorick with Jane Hooper when they were both hay-making in Colyton in the 1630s, she declared, apparently in an effort to clear her reputation, 'that she is a mayde and knoweth that her mother will bestowe a portion upon her' (her mother was a widow).[83] In a broken engagement in Shute in 1675, John Cox had promised to marry Mary Farrant but he failed to honour it. The reasons cited were that he was much older than her (she was 29) but she also had no portion.[84] More telling is the case of Edward and Ellen Searle of Northleigh, who complained that they were seen as man and wife by the parish but gentlemen jeered at Edward as he had married a wife without a portion and was seen as a cuckold. Robert Moore went on to depose that 'common acceptation of ye word Cuckold in ye pshes of ffarway and Southleigh is that the wife of him is a whore', yet Ellen was described as 'a Modest, Civill woman'.[85] In Ottery St Mary, Axe's charity established in 1691 ordered the governors to pay out of the profits of the Axe estate 'marriage portions' to such young men and women who had served the same master or mistress for seven years without receiving public relief. The marriage portion was £3 but if in five years the couple had increased their stock they could apply for an additional grant.[86]

Finally for the very poor, there is some evidence of parishioners and particularly poor law authorities trying to prevent their marriages or at least dissuade them from becoming a charge on the parish. As we have seen, Steve Hindle has documented a number of these cases.[87] In the quarter sessions of 1678, the parishioners of Colyton petitioned regarding the case of Primus Carpenter, who was described as a masterless person now committed to Bridewell. Since he had been there, the parish of Musbury had tried to marry him to a pregnant woman, Alice Bithy of Musbury, by offering her clothes and money towards the marriage so that they did not have to maintain her after the birth. They were already paying her 2s 6d a week and had now sent Alice to join Primus in prison. As stipulated under the Settlement Acts, she would then become the responsibility of Colyton. The Colyton petitioners were demanding action to prevent the charge should the two people marry.

There is little to suggest that concerns about reputation and material worth were in any way new in the seventeenth century, but several factors made marriage a more hedged and heedful affair. Dissent narrowed the choice of partner. Social differentiation due to the economic changes of the seventeenth century made mismatches of partners with variant prospects all too likely. The culture of discipline, with its Puritan-induced austerity, made for circumspection in marital matters for the aspirant middling sort. They also sought to impose a sense of probity on to the poor whose marriage chances were already limited. Even when a match took place, weddings had few of the modern-day public aspects. The secretive nature of many of these matches added to the rumour and secrecy surrounding marriage. At six o'clock on Sunday morning, 6th July 1707, Moll Hoare, 28 years old and a servant at her aunt and uncle's farm, born the year her father was tragically killed in Colyton, married her cousin, Hugh Gundry, brother of the supposed alcoholic, William.[88] Although both were Presbyterians, they married in the parish church, but in the utmost privacy. Nathaniel Pinney recorded in his account book that 'there being none Else present but my Selfe who gave her in Marriage being cald up about 5 o'Clock by Mr Gundry who came from Broadwindsor that Morning for that purpose pray God make them Happy in Each other'. Four days later Nathaniel paid Mr Gundry her portion of about £500, partly in bonds.

Singlehood and Secret Relationships

Although Hester Pinney never married, she had a long-term relationship with a married aristocrat, the Honorable George Booth, and in his last years, she cohabited with him in his London house. Hester's background was in trade; Booth was from one of the most prominent landed Presbyterian families in the country. Such liaisons, perhaps never openly acknowledged by their families at the time, may have been common but are one of the hidden aspects of the historical picture that we can never completely unveil.

In a situation where many men married into their thirties, and were constrained by wealth disparities between partners, it is hardly surprising that we should find a market for sexual services in the Colyton area. Indeed this was the flip side of the culture of discipline and restraint. With many soldiers stationed in the area in the Civil Wars, rural prostitution was likely to have increased. In 1655 a next-door neighbour deposed that Emlin Minifie of Ottery St Mary had had a bastard when 'in the time of the troubles there was very base order, a notorious whore then living there, and one who is now rotting with the pox and the sd Emlin very loose'.[89] A game of tit for tat is apparent here, for Emlin herself reported that she had seen Anstis Gander and Matthew Chubb together through a hole in the planchet from her house and saw Anstis's naked thigh. Naturally, the evidence is not easily uncovered in such instances, although there are anecdotal accounts in contemporary Colyton of certain courts being the haunt of prostitutes. At least two quarter sessions cases mention the possibility of payments for sex. In 1651 Elinor Landley of Tavistock, widow, said that she was with child by Thomas Pennington the elder and for the first encounter he had given her 2s.[90] In 1653 Jane Barnard, wife of John Barnard of Shute, miller, reported that Robert Newbery, then also of Shute, came to her in the millhouse and propositioned her.[91] She put him off but on his fourth attempt he offered her 40s 'to have to doe with her'. He then approached her in a drunken state when she went to milk her cow. His wife came to know of this and said she was afraid of her life of him. It was possibly a case of prostitution in Membury when two men reported to quarter sessions that on a Wednesday night in May at 10 p.m., Edward Pring and Joane Smith were tumbling together on the ground 'in a very uncivill manner'. An hour later Smith was on the ground in a different garden with the lower part of her body exposed and James Clode lying upon her. When the informant, Gosling, asked him why he was so uncivil, being a married man and having a wife of his own, Clode replied that his wife was not there. Pring confessed that he had subsequently spent the night with Smith.[92]

Some of the cases of illegitimacy and extra-marital sex from the Colyton area have a surprisingly modern ring to them. In 1666 Mary Diamont, a single woman, reported to quarter sessions that she had been made pregnant by one Zachariah Thrale of Colyton with whom she had had sex three times. In every case this had taken place 'at her owne house' and in the afternoon.[93] In a similar case, Elenor Gammage, a widow of Uplyme, said in 1678 that David Wyatt of Axminster sometimes had sex with her at her house. Wyatt sometimes lived with her and had first come into her bed the previous Allhallowtide. Wyatt admitted that he was the father of her illegitimate child. He had promised to marry her but was persuaded to the contrary by his relations because, as may have been the case in innumerable love matches, there was a wealth disparity between them.[94] The consequences of bearing illegitimate children for widows could be even more serious than punishment by the quarter sessions. As Bettey has shown, on some manors widows who had illegitimate children had to forfeit their estates.[95]

As we have seen, due to the skewed sex ratio in Colyton from the second half of the seventeenth century more women than men were, in the last resort, simply left out of the account as far as marriage was concerned. Furthermore, when age at marriage is analysed according to class, it seems that poor women stayed single for longer than their wealthier counterparts. Depending on the predilection of the writer there have been differing portrayals of the lives of single women. Laslett has commented on the traditional role of the spinster that 'for the great majority of them it meant to act as an entirely inferior collaborator in the household where they had been brought up or in which they had been taken as servants'. He underlines 'the failure of those who never got married because they never joined in a familial project . . . they were simply left out of account for many social purposes'.[96] Miriam Slater, in her detailed study of the seventeenth-century Verney family saw marriage as 'a crucial attainment in women's lives'.[97] She argued that:

> If marriage was considered to be a woman's preferment, continued spinsterhood was viewed as a form of social derogation. Spinsterhood condemned one to a lifetime of peripheral existence; it was a functionless role played out at the margins of other people's lives without even that minimal raison d'etre—the possibility of bearing children—which was supposed to comfort and sustain the married woman. For a woman, the single life was hardly an alternative lifestyle to marriage but rather a despised condition which both the woman and her family sought to avoid.

For the eighteenth century Olwen Hufton reminds us that 'Any eighteenth century scholar must be aware that the period sees the emergence in the literature of the spinster as a stereotype—one to be despised, pitied and avoided as a sempiternal spoilsport in the orgy of life'.[98] A more positive view was taken by Amussen, who portrayed women who bore illegitimate children as presenting 'an implicit challenge to the social and familial order by creating a "family" without a head'.[99]

Reconstitutions are not well suited to specifying the proportion of a population who do not marry. The burial of a woman with her maiden name may indicate singlehood, but this was not necessarily the case. In the seventeenth century when marriage age was late, death rates high and remarriage chances for women extremely low, marriage was sometimes a very short-lived episode in a woman's life and her 'town' identity appears to have remained with her maiden name. Several instances of widows who had once been married being referred to by their maiden name can be found in the Colyton record. This has meant that a few linkages have been missed in the reconstitution.[100] For example, Alice Paul was born in 1632 and came from a family which was often in receipt of poor relief. When she was 32 she had an illegitimate son. She married in 1670, at the age of 38, to William Zalway, and bore him one son in 1673. Her husband died in 1679. In the 1682/83 list of those in receipt of poor relief she appeared as Alice Paul. There is no evidence that women who were not widows were buried with their maiden names. In the same way that separated women would often revert to using their maiden names, women in common law relationships would generally adopt their partner's surname. An overseer's letter of 1801 concerned the common law marriage of Hannah and William Harvey who had two daughters.[101] Hannah called herself 'Harvey' even though she was married to John Lugg in 1787 and had had four children with him. Mary Anning called herself 'Mary Facey' in the 1820s when she had two children with John Facey. In the cases which involved single women having illegitimate children in the second half of the eighteenth century, it became fairly common for the children to be baptised with the father's surname. John Hitchcock, a married man who was separated, was the father of Elizabeth Driver's illegitimate daughter who was born in 1763. Elizabeth died in childbirth and her daughter was baptised Majdalene, the unusual name of Hitchcock's mother and sister.

Despite these problems, an attempt has been made to classify by status a sample group of 206 never-married females from the Colyton reconstitution. These were women for whom there were no indications in any of the linked records that they ever married and who also died in Colyton. The results are presented in Table 7.7. The women included lived to be at least 26 years of age, and are cohorted on baptism.

Considering the small number of labourer and craftsperson cases in observation in the 1650–1750 period, it is significant that some spinsters do fall into this category. Particularly from the early eighteenth century there was a tendency for spinsters to predominate among the poor. This supports the idea that poverty made a woman's marriage chances lower than ever and compounded the effects of the sex ratio.[102] It probably explains why spinsterhood seems to have occurred in certain families. The birth rank in the family of these spinsters was variable and being

Table 7.7 Status grouping of never-married females 1538–1799

Cohort	Total	Gentry No.	%	Crafts No.	%	Labourer No.	%	Poor No.	%	Unknown No.	%
1538–49	13	1	7.7	8	61.5	–	–	–	–	4	30.7
1550–99	31	2	6.5	1	3.2	5	16.1	6	19.3	17	54.8
1600–49	66	11	16.6	14	21.2	5	7.6	24	36.4	12	18.2
1650–99	47	12	25.5	7	14.9	5	10.6	13	27.6	10	21.3
1700–49	35	4	11.4	3	8.6	2	5.7	23	65.7	3	8.6
1750–99	14	2	14.3	2	14.4	3	21.4	5	35.7	2	14.4

either an elder or younger sibling does not seem to have affected their chances of marriage. Total reconstitution of an earlier period confirms that many illegitimate mothers were related to each other and lived in the town rather than country.[103]

The more conventional presentation of non-marryers reduces the mortality effects by only considering those who were aged 44 or older. This leaves a small sample of a hundred unmarried women in Colyton over the entire reconstitution period. These results are too limited to divide by status in cohorts but in Table 7.8 the cohorts have been amalgamated to show the status grouping over the whole period in comparison with all marriages.

Table 7.8 confirms that females who never married were most likely to be poor. The low proportion of 'unknown' cases also suggests that never-marrying females were likely to have spent most of their lives living in the town.[104] The 1851 census provides a method of quantifying numbers of celibate men and women. The number who were born in or before 1811 and recorded as 'unmarried' were analysed. Of a total of forty-seven people, thirty-four were female and thirteen were male. Twenty-two of them were born in Colyton. The connection between spinsterhood and poverty can be taken further by looking at illegitimacy. The numbers of illegitimate births in Colyton have been considered by

Table 7.8 Never-married females of 44+ for amalgamated cohorts 1538–1799

Status	All marriages No.	Never-married females No.	%
Gentry	249	13	5.2
Crafts	249	13	5.2
Labourer	199	11	5.5
Poor	331	43	12.9
Unknown	1312	20	1.5

Table 7.9 Baptisms of illegitimate children in Colyton 1538–1837

Cohort	Total First baptisms	Illegitimate baptisms	% Illegitimate
1538–49	180	2	1.1
1550–90	601	59	9.8
1600–49	948	96	10.1
1650–99	652	37	5.7
1700–49	520	98	18.8
1750–99	536	151	28.2
1800–37	342	90	26.3

Laslett and Oosterveen.[105] The data on numbers of illegitimate births is restated in Table 7.9 using different cohorts.

Illegitimacy is considered to be high in Colyton in the seventeenth century compared to national averages, which stood at only 1.5 per cent of all births prior to 1725, rising to 6 per cent after 1775,[106] but there is a change in pattern between the seventeenth and eighteenth centuries.[107] The number of illegitimate births was very high in the eighteenth century, then fell slightly in the early nineteenth century.

In Devon as a whole the 1650 Act suppressing adultery and fornication was rigorously applied and there was a great rise in cases appearing in quarter sessions in the 1650s.[108] Implementation of the central tenets of the 'Reformation of Manners' meant that female offenders would typically be immediately punished by a moderate whipping then sent away to the House of Correction in Exeter for a year's hard labour. Cases of illicit sex were commonly reported by prying, and perhaps jealous, neighbours. In 1656, for example, three single women of Ottery St Mary spied through a hole in the wall at 4.00 a.m. and saw Mary Taylor and John Turner having sex. One of the women taxed Taylor directly with 'her incivilitie', saying that she had played the whore. Taylor replied, 'what is that to thee, there is silver broken between us, in token of marriage'. Moreover she was forced to strenuous denials that sex had actually taken place. She did 'confesse that he was uncivill and more foolishe with her than was fitting for him. But did not any Acte of uncleanes with her.' Turner denied the sex but admitted fondling her bosom. However, the reporting of such cases in Colyton is rare despite the relatively high levels of prenuptial pregnancy and illegitimacy found in the parish. Although the local administration was based on piety in the seventeenth century perhaps a moral clean sweep was impossible because local authority was so fractured. As we have seen stated several times, prominent local people believed they were justices themselves and strongly maintained parish insularity.

Some association can be made between illegitimacy, general dislocation and movement of troops in the Colyton area. Notwithstanding the Civil War, one of the highest decades of illegitimacy of all was 1741–50 when Colyton was often used as a billeting station. In the overseers' account book for 1751 is the entry 'Pd Mr Crowe for a Guarde House and Bagage House for the soldiers on the March'. Seven years previously had been the entry 'Pd for a warrant to summon the officers of Sandford to appear to Colyton at the Removing of Eliz. Dowdel who was left by the soldiers great with child etc.'

An attempt is made to analyse the status of mothers of illegitimate children in Table 7.10. This table bears little resemblance to the numbers in Table 7.9 as the number of women rather than the number of illegitimate children are under consideration. Illegitimacy is, by definition, outside of the reconstitution process that operates by linking legitimate children. A second generation mother of an illegitimate child is automatically excluded from the method. The cases considered here appear as daughters on the FRFs and are related to their father's status, unless they themselves were in receipt of poor relief before they had the illegitimate child. Since the largest status grouping for illegitimate mothers was 'poor', the table has been simplified to show merely 'poor status', 'any other status' and 'status unknown'.[109]

Since mothers of illegitimate children were disproportionately likely to be born in Colyton, with 56 per cent of illegitimate childbearing mothers being born in the parish over the entire period, their status was easy to define in the total reconstitution.[110] The 'repeater phenomenon', of women giving birth to more than one illegitimate child, is far more obvious in the period after 1750. Laslett and Oosterveen showed three phases of repeaters.[111] In the period 1540–1639 a relative 'high' of 11.4 per cent of illegitimate mothers were repeaters. In the period 1640–1739 there was a 'low' with 2.1 per cent of repeaters, and in the last period of 1740–1839 there was another 'high' of 24.7 per cent. In the occasional case this was likely to be the result of prostitution. Honor Stedham, in the mid-eighteenth century for example, had at least six (and possibly eight) illegitimate children and six different fathers were identified.

Where bearers of illegitimate children can be linked to families who had some means, the total reconstitution sometimes shows some tendencies towards wayward behaviour and involvement in activities which were outside of the law. Jayes Bawden, for example, had an illegitimate daughter in Colyton in 1569. Her father was a small landowner and was reasonably well off in terms of paying subsidies and premiums on apprentices, but the court roll also notes that he was frequently involved in disputes over land.[112]

Considering the low economic status of many bastard bearers and the fact that age at marriage and age at bearing illegitimate children were

Table 7.10 Status of mothers of illegitimate children in Colyton 1538–1837

Cohort	Total No.	Poor No.	%	Not Poor No.	%	Status Unknown No.	%
1538–49	4	2	50.0	–	–	2	50.0
1550–99	24	8	33.3	6	25.0	10	41.6
1600–49	33	12	36.4	11	33.3	10	30.3
1650–99	29	14	48.3	3	10.4	12	41.4
1700–49	51	36	70.6	7	13.7	8	15.6
1750–99	44	38	86.4	5	11.4	1	2.2
1800–37	68	58	85.3	6	8.8	4	5.8

similar, illegitimacy has come to be seen as a consequence of 'frustrated marriage' attempts, as in the case of Taylor and Turner who were betrothed.[113] Since prenuptial pregnancy patterns follow the same trend as illegitimacy patterns, some illegitimacy can be seen as prenuptial pregnancies which were never legitimated. Joane Morgaine of Bradninch said in 1649 that Nathaniell Ascott had betrothed himself to her 'and by his flattering and decepfull tongue had the use of her bodye shee being his wife before God: promising her great prefermt but never performed nothing herein, but always tooke his Worde yet . . . he proved false in his promises towards her'.[114] The ecclesiastical court depositions for Devon show that sex normally followed spousals.[115] Pregnancy was not unexpected but was expected to be honoured, so almost all of the couples whose promise was not legitimated had made some arrangements for their marriage and future residency, even if the marriage was to take place after the child's birth. In a Linkinhorne case of 1666, Walter Bale said to Wilmot Laundrie, who was six months pregnant, 'if you intend to Mary this John Staning i wonder you doe not hasten to doe it, for i preine that your Belly is Bigg'. Elinora Bale corroborated this and said 'after They were married ye sd Staning & she would live together in a chamber of one William Bridge'.[116] Analysis of the sample of Devon matrimonial cases in the ecclesiastical court indicates that whereas spousals were an open affair with several symbolic actions like the public promise, the wedding itself was an altogether less formal matter conducted where and when convenient, like that of Moll Hoare and Hugh Gundry. The couples actually saw themselves as man and wife as the promise was a formally witnessed contract. This took place in a public setting, either a public house or a house of mutual friends, and followed private planning. The promise involved a standard wording, not unlike marriage vows, and exchange of gifts, normally rings. For example, in a Manaton case of 1662, John Hart and Mary Bully went into a forechamber and agreed to marry with 'set' words. Mary 'tooke him the said John againe by the hand and said John Hart thou art my husband before God and we are man and wife before God and these people here present. And i doe pmise that I will never marry any other as long as then shall live', after which they 'kissed & imbrased each other'.[117] The sticking point hereafter must have often been an inability or unwillingness by parents to financially underwrite the union.

However, in other cases there was no thought of marriage and these suggest that historians may have been too hasty to attribute most illegitimacy to the unfortunate outcome of economic circumstances. Many of these instances must have resulted from the exploitation of female servants; masters and their sons bore none of the punishment and little of the responsibility for the upbringing of the child. In 1675 Dorothy Purchase, a single woman and a servant in Upottery, said the grandson of her master had 'usually' come to bed with her for two years.[118] A year previously she had borne an illegitimate child and when the father found out he made off and left the country. She told his grandfather and 'hath since had sometimes some small relief' but around the same time the father of her child, who now lived in Axmouth and was described as a husbandman, had conceived an illegitimate child with another woman. Some more unusual cases do describe men taking responsibility for offspring. There are shades of Silas Marner in the case of Charles Markes, a woolcomber from Ottery St Mary, concerning a child called Dorothy in 1752. A letter came to him from Grace Porter, a widow who lived in Sidbury, desiring him to fetch a midwife to a woman who lodged at Grace's house and was in labour. He accordingly carried over Hannah Mitchell, a widow of Ottery, who delivered the woman of a female child. Two hours after the birth, the child was taken back to Markes's house to be looked after by him.[119]

The percentage of marriages for which a child was born less than nine months after the marriage in Colyton is given in Table 7.11. The figures are based on a COLYFILE print-out of the details of FRFs where the date of the first baptism indicates a prenuptial conception. The number of prenuptial conceptions are probably underestimated in the 1650–1750 period since few labourer and craft FRFs are in observation. The cases of prenuptial conception have been divided into two groups. In the first 'early marriage' group the child was born between 2.0 and 9.0 months after marriage, and the parents had married at a relatively 'early' stage in the pregnancy. In the 'late marriage' group the child was born within the first 1.9 months after marriage.

The marriages are given an attribution according to status in Table 7.12.

The pattern for most of the period was for conception to occur just prior to marriage, so the cases fell into the 'early marriage' category. After 1750, however, women increasingly married late in their pregnancy. This

Table 7.11 Number of prenuptial conceptions in Colyton 1538–1799

Cohort	No. first births	No. prenuptial conceptions	%	No. 'early'	%	No. 'late'	%
1538–49	59	6	10.2	6	100.0	–	–
1550–99	316	114	36.0	104	91.2	10	8.8
1600–49	430	87	20.3	80	91.9	7	8.0
1650–99	145	32	22.0	32	100.0	–	–
1700–49	204	55	26.9	46	83.6	9	16.4
1750–99	356	73	20.5	54	74.0	19	26.0

Notes: 'Early' marriage = baptised two or more months after marriage.
'Late' marriage = baptised less than two months after marriage.

is the same pattern that has been found for other parishes in the country.[120] Apart from the fact that prenuptial pregnancy fell to be the lot of women in the higher status families less than half as frequently as for poor women, class differences are difficult to detect. In the 1750–99 cohort when more women probably married and marriage ages fell, prenuptial pregnancy seems to have been the experience of craft, labourer and poor families. Alternatively, the lack of craft and labourer marriages in Colyton in the pre-1749 period may have distorted the results, so that in fact prenuptial pregnancy may have affected all the three lower social groups to a similar extent.

The association between illegitimacy, and women who came from poor families and later went on to claim poor relief themselves, is apparent. Illegitimacy rates rose in Colyton as domestic industry collapsed, and as sex ratios continued to be skewed towards women in the eighteenth century. Under an adverse sex ratio, the chances of a prenuptial con-

Table 7.12 Status of FRFs with prenuptial conceptions 1538–1799

Cohort	Gentry No.	%	Crafts No.	%	Labourer No.	%	Poor No.	%	Unknown No.	%
1538–49	1	5.6	–	–	1	33.3	–	–	4	13.3
1550–99	8	23.5	10	41.7	14	26.9	13	46.4	69	38.8
1600–49	4	10.5	15	23.4	16	31.4	25	30.1	27	13.9
1650–99	1	4.8	4	40.0	–	–	16	32.7	11	19.0
1700–49	4	21.1	2	11.1	2	9.1	26	41.3	21	25.3
1750–99	5	15.6	18	24.7	15	19.7	13	28.3	22	17.1

Notes: No. = Number of FRFs with prenuptial conceptions.
% = Prenuptial conceptions as a percentage of first births.

ception being legitimated by a marriage were far slimmer than when there were roughly equal numbers of men and women.[121] Having been delivered of a child, if a woman could not marry, she would probably try to be hired as a domestic servant, and if this failed she turned to poor relief. If she worked she would board out her children to married women in the village in the early eighteenth century and normally to kin in the nineteenth century. According to a Hartland settlement examination of February 1803, Catherine Coull was born in Hartland and lived with her grandmother until she was 15 when she hired herself as a yearly servant for several years. She became pregnant and after delivery of the child returned to Hartland and hired herself again for two years or more. At this time Catherine's mother received parish pay for the maintenance of the child and Catherine also contributed from her wages.[122] After the revival of lace-making in the nineteenth century, Jean Robin argues for Colyton: 'The measure of economic independence which lacemaking brought to Colyton girls may have caused them to worry less about conceiving a child as a consequence of intercourse before marriage, so contributing to the high level of sexual nonconformism evidenced by illegitimacy and prenuptial pregancy'.[123]

The change in sex ratios affected the chances of mothers of illegitimate children ever marrying. In all cohorts up to 1750, very few bastard-bearers ever married.[124] Those who did normally married in their late thirties. From the second half of the eighteenth century bastard-bearers were more likely to marry eventually. By the mid-nineteenth century, only twenty per cent of bastard-bearers stayed in Colyton and did not marry.[125] Studies based on listings from the second half of the eighteenth century or census returns from the nineteenth century rarely show single households or clusters of 'independent' women.[126] In the nineteenth century illegitimate mothers lived with their parents whenever they were alive, whereas in the overseers' account book they were paid their own house rent or a payment for houseroom.[127] William Berry, who gave a testimony for a settlement examination in November 1853, said he was the illegitimate son of Jane Berry and was born in 1810 in a house occupied by his grandmother which was situated near to Colyton church. Linkage to the reconstitution provides additional information about the family. Jane Berry was one of seven children of William Berry, a cordwainer. He died when she was 10. Her mother was paid 8s of weekly militia men's relief from 1800 as William had been a volunteer doing permanent duty at Honiton. Jane had three illegitimate children born in 1810, 1814 and 1821. She never married and in the 1851 census is recorded as living alone.

Mothers of illegitimate children who did not work in their home parish often returned home for the birth, or directly after it in the nineteenth century. In a Chudleigh settlement examination of 1851,

John Evans described his sister having an illegitimate child thirty-five years previously; after 'she had the Base child she returned to Ideford and lived there some time in my father's house'.[128] By contrast, in the eighteenth century the overseers' account book gives the impression that it was considered strange for adult females to live with their parents. Bartholomew Pound, often referred to as 'Labourer Pound' by the overseers, was 79 in 1754. He had married several times and his three youngest daughters were aged 17, 21 and 24. In March of that year payment was grudgingly made to 'Bartholomew Pound who keeps three Idle ladees at home'; a month later two of them must have found employment, for the entry read: 'Pd Bartholomew Pound who retains an Idle, Disorderly Daughter in his house'.[129]

To a large extent, and perhaps increasingly over time, we can see an association between domestic industry, poverty, singlehood and the probability of bearing illegitimate children for women in Colyton. There is some evidence of rural prostitution. Above all, despite the fact that seventeenth-century Colyton was a godly parish, there is little evidence of sexual continence. In fact, illegitimacy would seem to have precipitated marriage for many Colyton couples. The road from courtship to marriage was a protracted path, often prolonged by the dependence on parental financial decisions. Given these circumstances, it is surprising that there were not more illegitimate births and the reason for this could be the extent of use of herbal abortifacients as described in Chapter 5. To Levine, the illegitimacy patterns in Colyton were difficult to explain on economic grounds. As he perceptively commented, 'It is curious and somewhat fortuitous that the first English village chosen for intensive study by historical demographers proved to be so surprising, interesting, and in many ways unique in its demographic behaviour'.[130]

Marital Separation

Where women lived alone in the second half of the eighteenth century, their residency patterns have to be seen in a context of unstable employment. As the balance of mixed farming turned to arable cultivation, male employment became more plentiful but more seasonal, whereas the two main female sources of employment, dairying and textiles, were eroded. Short-term male migration was common before the system of the poor relief authorities paying family allowances was fully implemented. As with illegitimacy, however, the patterns we can identify from the records may be as much a result of local political conditions and control of parish governance as they are connected with economic conditions.

One result of the lack of year-round male employment was short-term work separations of man and wife. Temporary and long-term migration for work reasons was hardly new, but historians have identified an upturn in movement in the second half of the seventeenth century.[131] A case involving meat stolen from Honiton market in 1675 contains the evidence of a man who was working away from the area in winter at 'dikeing work' and sending for salted butchered meat.[132] The sample of settlement examinations for Devon shows that the length of stay in farm jobs was getting shorter over time in the eighteenth century and that day work often involved tramping around neighbouring towns and villages. Sometimes married men went further afield for a spell of work. A letter from James Machin, a canal digger resident in Burlescombe in Devon, to the overseers of Tiverton St Peter, when his wife's settlement was being examined in October 1810, explained that he had been a shepherd and a servant before going to work on the canal.[133] A letter to his wife (which she presumably never received) was contained within the one to the overseers, and showed that high wages were the major reason why he was working away from her. He sent her his affection and explained how she could visit him, and then he added that 'them that tel you it is a Bad Country or Bad Work are Liers for the Men get 5 shillings a day and I Like the Country very well'. His postscript was 'You may cut this part'. When this wage is compared to the average earned by an agricultural labourer at the time, there is little wonder that James thought that if his wages were revealed they may have prejudiced his wife's chances of being paid relief.

Evidence of marital separation in Colyton can be found most readily in the total reconstitution from information given in the overseers' account book which was linked to the FRFs. In some cases it was explicitly stated, as in an entry of 1762, that one partner had left: 'pd William Harvey's wife when her husband left her'. In other cases, the marriage partner's house rent was paid separately or the wife was paid for her maintenance. In cases where the husband left the wife she was normally put under great immediate financial hardship and a large lump payment had to be made available to support her and the children. In permanent cases of separation, the wife often resumed use of her maiden name and a change of name in the overseers' account book could be identified. Such circumstances led to the pledge of goods to the parish by a woman in early eighteenth-century Axminster who had obviously been left with serious debts:

> I, Elizabeth Cross, of ye parish of Axminster . . . spinster for and in consideration of severall sumes of money already Receiv'd in ye absence of my Husband, John Cross, Junr and am still in want of severall sumes more to subsist my self and Children in his absence have Bargain'd sold & Deliver'd unto Wm Tucker etc [overseers] one brass pot and brass kettle one warming pan one Table baord and

fform one Standing Standking Bedsted, one feather Bed and what belong to ye same . . . for security of parish.[134]

Some tentative cases of marital separation have been excluded from this analysis. Where two unrelated people of different sex appear to have been paid together in the account book, and at least one was married, it does not seem unreasonable to assume they may have been separated and were having an extra-marital relationship. However, it is not possible to conclude that this was the case rather than an example of the overseer's shorthand. On the grounds given, eighty-eight cases of marital separation can be detailed in Colyton in the period 1741–69. Evidence of marital separation can be found for approximately 10 per cent of all marriages to have taken place in Colyton between 1725 and 1765. For seventy-six of the cases enough information can be pieced together to make some assumption about the reason for separation.

In thirty-three cases, the man seems to have instigated the separation. The primary reason seems to have been to work elsewhere and in half of these cases the man went into the militia. The underlying reason for the marriage dissolving was poverty. Matthew Gigg explained when his settlement was examined in 1755 that he was born in Axminster. When he was 10 he went with his father to Dalwood, where the family were tenants of Lord King. But 'his father failing & being originally bred a weaver, he went with him & wrought at that Business & has continued to do ever since'. He married in 1754 but lived with his wife only five or six weeks '& then left her for she being near her time'. He heard she 'went to the parish of Upottery where she was brought to bed of a son and sometime after she returned to their settlement parish of Ottery and later left the child to the parish'.[135] Settlement examinations record facts relating to residency, hiring, wages and renting. Those taking down the testimonials were not required to plumb the emotional reasons for decisions, but in this case it is apparent that Gigg's marriage was over before it had really started.

In six of the cases the wife probably made the first move to leave. In thirty-two cases it is not clear who left whom. In two cases the husband went into the military and then the wife also left Colyton abandoning her children. So, in the case of Elizabeth Abrahams, described as a 'soldier's wife' in 1767, the overseers 'paid for information against Elizabeth Abrahams for running away and leaving her children chargeable'.[136] Separation took place at any stage of the marriage and regardless of the age at which the couple had married. In five cases, separation took place immediately after marriage. The brides had been pregnant before marrying and had been persuaded to marry the husbands, who were not natives of Colyton, to remove them from the poor rate.[137] Sarah Perry had an illegitimate child in 1749. Ferdinand Stile was the father and the parish had to pay him 10s 'for and towards keeping Sarah Perry's child'. Clearly the overseers were not prepared to put up with this expense for long and decided that the best course of action was for them to be forced to marry. Consequently the next pertinent entry was 'pd for License to marry Ferdinand Stile to Sarah Perry'. Although the marriage was recorded in 1751 there is no evidence that they ever lived together and Ferdinand's payments 'to keep his wife's base child' were kept up. By the 1760s Sarah was living with another woman of similar age to herself and Ferdinand was not in sight. In a Tiverton settlement examination of June 1820, Mary Snipling, the wife of William Snipling, a weaver, said that she was about three months pregnant before they married 'and on her application to the sd William Snipling to marry her he [at] first refused it saying he had no money—and then she applied to the overseers there for the money for that purpose which they advanced—namely 3 shillings for publishing the banns and two pounds on the morning of the marriage—and the overseers ordered her out of town as soon as she was married'.[138]

In twenty of the Colyton cases destitute couples who were some years into their marriage separated to live in different dwellings in the parish. Husband and wife lived in shared houses in the town with others who were of the same age group and sex as themselves for a few years, while their children were boarded out or apprenticed. The couple were usually reunited, normally between two and four years after the separation, but in one case fourteen years hence. It seems likely that these separations were organised by the poor relief officers with the expectation, as became common in nineteenth-century workhouses, that husbands and wives would be separated. They certainly received their sanction since the overseers were prepared to pay two house rents. Perhaps these families simply could not be held together under the circumstances of declining domestic industry in the urban part of the parish, and dwindling pastoral agricultural employment in the rural areas.[139]

These cases can be distinguished from those which occurred as a form of 'popular divorce'. Generally the man abandoned his wife to live with another woman and had illegitimate children with her, although either or both parties could have had children. George and Rose Farrant married in 1742. It was George's second marriage and they had one child called Sarah. From April 1744, twenty months after the marriage, George and Rose were being given separate payments by the overseers. George then disappeared and was not heard of until 1753 when he came back to live in Colyton. His rent was then paid by the overseer to John Ford who was, paradoxically, either the father or brother of his 'wife'. John Ford gave George 'houseroom' while Rose lived separately, and in 1756 the overseer notes: 'pd Rose Ford in necessity when Mr Berry turned her and Family out of his house'. Rose was sometimes referred to as Farrant, but in the 1760s more generally as 'Ford', her maiden name. She took in washing, tended sick people and got constant relief from the parish. By 1764 she lived with a group of other would-be or actual single women. The overseers chose to call her 'base wife' in the early 1750s because of the string of four children she gave birth to by another partner in George's absence. These were all recorded by the vicar as son or daughter of George when clearly this was not possible.[140]

The form of separation where a common law marriage was formed after the first marriage broke down was a response both to the skewed sex ratio and the lack of any divorce procedure which was accessible to the poor. In the mid-eighteenth century there were at least five women to every four men living in Colyton. There was a proportion of women who were either single all their lives, or who married at very late ages. These were generally poor women. It seems likely that the existence of these women in Colyton always created the possibility for alternative relationships to be established. They created a town-based nexus of poverty and loosely structured living arrangements. They relied on the diminishing profits of declining domestic industry and parish organised jobs, or applied for poor relief. These women constituted what has been pejoratively termed the 'bastardy prone sub-society' in Colyton.[141]

There are some grounds for believing that popular divorce became more common among the poor towards the end of the eighteenth century.[142] At the same time, it was not legally possible for couples so separated to remarry, and the result was common law marriage.[143] Settlement examinations of Devon, among other sources, show that what constituted a marriage in law was often confused and a variety of relationships were popularly thought to be acceptable. In some correspondence from the overseers of Colyton to the Taunton poor law officers, the case of John Pavey was reported. John Pavey was committed to Bridewell for deserting his wife and child and leaving them chargeable to the parish. When he was cross-examined in 1808 he admitted that his marriage to Mary Pavey at Taunton must be null and void since he had another wife living in Colyton. John Pavey stated in his defence that Anne Broughton ('this wife nowe living here') was the sister of a former wife by whom he had a child which was now chargeable to the parish, that he was informed that his marriage with Anne Broughton was therefore illegal, and that he thought he had been put into 'spiritual court' (as he termed it), meaning that the marriage had been set aside.[144]

The figure of 10 per cent of couples subsequently separating from the marriages which took place in the parish in the period 1725–65 is not as high as D.A. Kent found for eighteenth-century Westminster but it is higher than Snell has found for other areas of the country.[145] When we add to this a high rate of pre-nuptial pregnancy from the second half of the seventeenth century, with a third of all children being born within eight months of marriage,[146] and also in comparison with other areas of the country a relatively high illegitimacy rate, especially after 1675, we are identifying important characteristics of a local urban demographic regime.

Supporting the Aged

In 1685 John Pinney wrote to Hester:

> My yongest & for that usually ye dearest to parents. I have nothing, I value nothing but for yor Good. & when yu desired to come hither, I thought it would have bin to yor loss. and denyed myselfe of ye comfort of yor prsence, wch you impute to my disaffection most unjustly: for I have no Externall comfort under heaven like to my children: & had it not bin for their Good, I had not mourned sollitary here, where any child I have shall be most welcome & none more, then you my yongest daughtr oh child! wrong not a grieved father who is willing to sacrifice his life for yors & is so much afflicted for ye affliction of his children; who I hoped would have bin [a] comfort to me in my old age. yu shall never have just cause for yor Complaint if what I have or can doe, can assure yu of my true affection to yu.[147]

As he grew older, John Pinney cast his youngest and dearest daughter in the role of family carer. It was a position Hester was unwilling to take on. Although she probably always perceived the family farm as her real home, she became a successful businesswoman who lived in London and only made occasional visits to her parents. Four years later Nathaniel was trying to persuade his father that on his return from Dublin he should live not at the farm but in a house in Crewkerne. He wanted John to ask his congregation in Crewkerne, where he preached, to pay him: 'Then next take a small house and that wch is warme, by what I heare none better then that of dashoods wthout a garden and stable for wch I like it the better The market is the best garden and yor horse pray keepe at an Inn at soe much aweeke, otherwise you must keepe aman and bee at ye trouble and charge of hay straw oates.'[148] He suggested using the horse only for pleasure for John to make trips to view the estate. Nathaniel may have had his own ends in view, perhaps seeking to take up residence at the farm himself, but we know from other correspondence that he was reluctant to give up the life of a city merchant for bucolic boredom. John did not follow Nathaniel's advice and lived with Nathaniel and his wife, Naomi, after their marriage until his death. Nevertheless, Nathaniel's suggestions seem remarkably modern—while a seventeenth-century town house bore little resemblance to modern-day sheltered housing the practical planning is the same: you ought to have some recompense for all that voluntary work, use your central heating, give up the garden and shop at the supermarket, do you really need to use the car at your age? And don't do your own car maintenance either, take it to the garage!

For the poor and propertyless there are many parallels between care at the beginning of life and at the end. By contrast with those of higher-status groups, the elderly were not considered to be the responsibility of their relations, but the concern of the community as a whole. Death was a public affair which took place outside of the home and involved the participation of community-appointed helpers. It is also possible to chart a change from a welfare system which organised unrelated people to care for the ailing and elderly, to one with an emphasis on a kin-based support system in Colyton. For the nineteenth century, the census returns indicate that families were extended to take in aged parents, and occasionally, married children.[149] Daughters, in particular, provided care for their elderly parents.[150] Only two elderly poor men who had children in the parish were living alone, and aged people who had no relatives in the town had lodgers living with them.[151]

David Thomson has described the growing legislation of the eighteenth century which defined kin obligations for welfare, and some other studies indicate that the change was not confined to England.[152] The aged seem to have gradually withdrawn from working life in the past, but at some point complete retirement from working had to be necessary. In the overseers' account book this normally came within the category of payments for 'sickness'. In April 1746, for example, payments are made to 'Old Richard Butt in sickness, his labour being done'. In Colyton, instructions were given in 1847 to the relieving officers that court action was to be taken against adult children who were not willing to support their parents.[153] This seems to have been normal practice in Devon at the time as several orders were found among the settlement examination sample used in this study. At the Newton Abbott petty sessions in November 1864, an order was made to William Rolleston, a grocer, of St Andrew parish in Plymouth, to support his mother who was chargeable to the parish of Chudleigh, 'a poor and impotent person not able to work and maintain herself'.[154] Her son was thought to be of sufficient means to relieve and maintain her, and he was ordered to pay 9d weekly.

In a settlement case at Chudleigh in May 1859, Mary Soper, a 69-year-old poor woman, said: 'About ten or eleven years ago my Husband was unable to maintain me and with his consent I went into service to maintain myself and have maintained myself without any assistance from my Husband . . . my Husband is now living in the Parish of Hennock and is unable to maintain Himself, his friends maintain him I believe'. Her 76-year-old husband said: 'I have no Property, am unable to maintain myself and have been living with different members of my Family for 8 or 9 years past (in the parish of Stoketeignhead and Hennock) who have helped to maintain me'.[155] The assumption that kin, and married children in particular, were to be resorted to by the aged or sick runs through documents from this period. Sarah Rendel, a widow, examined in Chudleigh in February 1838, said that she must have parish relief because 'I have maintained myself for some years by going out to Nurse, but I am now very bed [bad], and I cannot support myself, and my children are unable to support me'.[156]

A letter written to the Colyton overseer in 1798 indicates that the old system, by which invalids were boarded out by the parish to people who were supposed to care for them, was perhaps under strain.[157] It is not clear who wrote it but thankfully his instructions on destroying the letter were never carried out:

> I forgot to tell you yesterday that Nelly has almost lost the use of her right arm. I am forced to dress her, as she cannot even put on her cap without my help and is very weak otherways. I am shure, that I have had two Parish charges on me for years. I had Wm. Batt till he went to Mr Spurway. Nelly has had a greadle [great deal] of sickness and a bag [bad] leg for years, which has been very expensive to me. I bore it as long as I could till at last I went to Sir John & told him the miserable state she was in, and he was so good to go himself to Mr Lewes, who came and told me that in two days it would have been to late as it was going on very fast towards a mortification. She kept her bed for six week & I was at the expense to have a woman to tend her, Sir John made an order that she should half [have] half a Crown per week, but the Gentlemen soon altered it to eighteen pence.
>
> You will be so kind as to tell them this but pray burn this as soon as read as it is so badly wrote.
>
> Compliments to Mrs P.

'Nelly' seems likely to have been Eleanor Batt, who was 53, and in fact went on to live for another twenty one years. She was always single but had an illegitimate child in 1779 with Robert Beer, with whom she was then living.[158] William Batt was her brother. Such documents raise more questions than they answer.[159] As the first line indicates, much communication about poor relief matters was face-to-face and goes unrecorded. This writer is ashamed of his or her style, which seems to consist of copied words from a copybook. The other notable fact is the difference of opinion about the level of poor relief to be given to Eleanor between the seemingly arbitrary gesture by the lord of the manor and the overriding but less generous decision made by the vestry. The deference to 'Sir John', and his personal involvement in this case, are striking.

In the eighteenth century the sick and aged poor were not looked after at home. They were in fact likely to be moved around the village, being lodged and given temporary houseroom by different people until someone could be found to care for them on a semi-permanent basis. The experience of the poor was in contrast to the middle classes, who died at home. As Gittings comments, for them home was 'the traditional place for entering the world and leaving it'.[160] The poor usually died after being moved to the house of a carer. Charles Bull died in 1767 at the age of 21. He was the second son of a family of seven children. Despite the fact that at the time of his death both parents and all six siblings were alive, he did not die at home. He was lodged with Mary Newton when he became ill, and she was paid the enormous (in terms of female earnings for the time) sum of 9s for that particular week. After his death he was laid out by Bett Barrett. From 1768, paupers were taken to the workhouse to die. When a pauper died the coffin was usually supplied by the parish at a cost of 7s 6d. There would also be a shroud, a bell tolled at church and liquor (and sometimes even food) for the mourners.[161]

Waking, which seems to have died out for the middle classes after the Reformation, was common for the very ill among the poor and took place prior to, rather than after, death. It was a shared activity normally carried out by women. In 1684 Joane Viney, a married woman of Honiton, was at the house of Phillip Abbott 'to wake with his wife who then lay sick' and was suspected of stealing money from his pockets.[162] People who were waked were not necessarily on their deathbed.[163] Hugh Newton was 63 in October 1758 when he fell sick. A bed was rapidly set up for him in someone's house and the aforementioned Rose Farrant was given the job of tending him. Grace Calley waked with him but Hugh did not die until ten years later. Charity Penny was waked in June 1758. By July she had recovered and was being removed to Sturminster Newton. By 1763 she was back in Colyton and was being paid for doing waking herself!

In the late eighteenth century, the elderly could resort to the Colyton Friendly Society, instituted in 1786.[164] Admittance was based on a subscription of 3s 3d. Each meeting cost 2s 3d, and 3d had to be spent on liquor whenever they met. Such levels of payment would have made membership prohibitive for the poor. A member who was rendered incapable of working received 7s weekly for three months if a nurse was required. Without a nurse, he received 3s 6d weekly. After the three months, he would receive 4s 6d weekly if he was bedridden, but 2s 6d if he could walk, 'provided it shall not have proceeded from the Venereal Disease, from Riots, from Fighting, or from any violent exercise'. Upon death £3 would be paid to the man's widow or representative. There were also attempts to start a pension scheme: 'Every member to have subscribed 25 years arriving at the age of 65 shall receive weekly sums as members present at the annual meeting think proper and be allowed to follow his usual employment'. For swearing or being intoxicated at a meeting, the forfeit was 6d. By 1803 this friendly society had ninety members.[165] In the same year as the friendly society was instituted, a Burial Board was incorporated which had a similar membership drawn from respectable tradespeople, craftsmen and social classes above them. Membership was popular, and men were admitted at the ages of 19 or 20.[166]

For the Old Poor Law period, there are no complementary documents for feoffee and poor law relief which would make it possible to estimate what proportion of the population were in receipt of one type of relief or the other.[167] However, it is clear that the comprehensive provision for the poor in Colyton should be taken into account in providing a balanced picture of the local economy in Colyton. Among the poor, for whom there is most evidence of family and social life in Colyton, the involvement of the relief system was all important. Apart from providing the support for 'vital' events by paying for births, subsidising weddings and organising the financial aspects of funerals, the authorities were instrumental in these activities so as to invest them with a particular 'public' significance that stood outside any familial involvement.

The History of the Family in Colyton

This chapter has highlighted some of the aspects of family, household and life-cycle in Colyton for which there is recorded information. There are few documents that can give us more than a glimpse of ordinary family life and the parish papers available tend to emphasise disjunctures and points of discordance. In the face-to-face system in which overseers distributed relief in Colyton, relationships were on public view. There was no anonymity to hide common law arrangements and to protect the reputation of the parents of illegitimate children. Of course, the type of relief also depended on the government of the parish. We have seen that there were two tiers of poverty in late seventeenth-century Colyton, with a group of 'honorable poor' and those who were not relieved at all. In the eighteenth century the balance of power in the parish moved back to the vestry and the manorial lord and the resulting poor law system was possibly less partisan and more inclusive.

Historians and sociologists have produced a corpus of writings that view the concept and the reality of 'family' as enduring through time.[168] An older generation of 'pessimist' historians thought that the industrial revolution shattered the stable agrarian labourer's family. This view has been replaced by those who believe that industrialisation strengthened kin ties.[169] The family is presented as an institution that has weathered civil and social unrest, economic and religious onslaught and emerged unscathed. This 'family' in question is the nuclear family and the weight of literature allows little room for diversity from this model. Indeed, the prevailing assumption seems to be that although wealthier households might be 'extended' by the presence of servants, the structure of the family in fact varied little between socio-economic groups. This is the impression given by listings and census and is emphasised in reconstitution studies which take family events, normally a marriage, as their starting point, and from there, facts about the family are collected on to an FRF which represents the 'typical' nuclear model. The evidence in this chapter suggests, however, that among the poor, the 'nuclear family' (which is still seen as the 'traditional' support system today) was often not the abiding schema for life. Not only did it fail to function as a safety net in terms of welfare provision, but it does not seem apposite to view the family as a work unit, and since spinsterhood, prenuptial pregnancy and illegitimacy were most common among the poor, it is also questionable how important it was as a procreative unit. The economic well-being of the poor was heavily dependent upon parish poor relief provisions and stipulations; their opportunities for employment were subject to the the gender-specific nature of the labour market in Colyton, and their reproduction depended upon the structure of Colyton's population, particularly the availability of marital partners and the access to occasional work.

Family life was affected by the poor relief system in towns like Colyton. Under an inclusive and selective system, overseers not only provided vital supplementary resources for a whole section of the population, and to a certain extent regulated labour supplies by the implementation of the settlement laws, but they also supervised a welfare system which influenced the 'private' acts of birth, marriage and death. A reliance on male real wages and male employment in agriculture and industrial sectors of the British economy has dominated economic history. In fact, it was the female sectors of employment that had the greatest influence on Colyton's demography in the seventeenth and early eighteenth centuries. Poor relief systems also benefited women, and, until the second half of the eighteenth century certainly, worked to maintain their precarious independence. Female-dominated households have been seen by sociologists to be a feature of modern-day life in urban poor districts: part of an identifiable 'poverty culture'.[170] However, some of the characteristics of these households can be studied in the town area of Colyton, and it can be suggested that they occur wherever areas of women's work with relatively low wages predominate.[171] In the period from the mid-seventeenth century until the last quarter of the eighteenth century Colyton most obviously takes on the characteristics of an industrial parish and many of the aspects described in this chapter result from this. Oscar Lewis's classic portrayal of the 'poverty culture' is an urban subculture which could arise when a socio-economic system is in transition.[172] Two of the features of this culture are increases in extra-legal family formation, and matrifocal family structures, as women are able to gain some economic power. From the seventeenth century appreciable amounts of long-term poverty became apparent in Colyton, and a permanently poor section of the community developed.[173] This becomes more obvious in the surviving eighteenth-century records. Under circumstances where, for the last hundred years, poor women had married at a late age if at all, and where women's employment had been plentiful, the single woman was not an unusual figure in the eighteenth-century community. It is not surprising that when women's employment chances fell, they were supported by the welfare agencies.

Aside from the socio-legal difficulties always faced by women, it is only from perceptions based on the last two centuries of near universal marriage that women have come to be viewed as always requiring the support of a family system. At the same time if we are to redress the balance away from the current historiography that exalts marriage and the family as the most historically valid and universally relevant schema for production and reproduction, we must reconsider the view that consequently sees illegitimate births and marital separation as hints of discordance, as points of stress at the edge of an otherwise perfectly functioning system. Even though much has been written on the comprehensiveness of the poor relief system, naturally vulnerable groups such as spinsters have been seen to be cut out of an illusory familial support system. For the poor marriage was not meaningful in an economic sense. The poor did not bring resources into the marriage and seem to have had practically no resources to share within the union. There is no evidence that work was construed as a partnership and men and women worked in different employment spheres. There must have been some perception by the overseers of a need to accommodate sex-specific employment patterns in the seventeenth and eighteenth centuries, which, in an industrialising and changing England, demanded mobile workers.

The material basis for marriage seems much more apposite when reviewing the more scant evidence for the propertied sections of society, and reflects a growing social differentiation in the parish. The family was the central institution for resource concentration and many tensions centred on the fact that the extended family was also composed of business associates, or actors in the complex relationships surrounding inheritance.[174] Here too there were illicit relationships and single women who stayed outside fraught familial projects, as we can see in the life of Hester Pinney.

The 'family economy' model, which historians Snell and Hill suggest was important between 1690 and 1750, was precluded for the poor by the skewed sex ratio of Colyton, as well as socio-structural constraints on this type of household production.[175] Analysis of the overseers' account book for Colyton shows that functions which the modern family undertakes were often irrelevant to the eighteenth-century poor family.[176] To go through the life-cycle: mothers did not always nurse their own children, they were put out to other people while these women took care of other children; the years that children lived with their parents could be few before they were apprenticed; families did not nurse their own sick; siblings maintained no connection with each other and children did not look after their aged parents. Dying people were generally removed from their home rather than being allowed to die in it. Yet more surprising are the cases where a sick child was removed from the household, and died elsewhere, while the mother took in an unrelated lodger. With present-day perceptions it seems strange that commonplace familial relations should exact a price, and indeed that they should fall so far within the commercial realm at all. But family relationships were material relationships as well as loving exchanges in seventeenth- and eighteenth-century Colyton.

As we saw in Chapter 4, in the 1780s more work became available for men in the arable sector in Colyton. Wages were high for day work but unemployment predominated in winter and, as prices rose, allowances from the poor relief authorities were increasingly resorted to. Constant supplements were assured by the parish to those with a settlement, and whereas some men travelled to try to find temporary work away from Colyton after the harvest, those with large families often found it advantageous to stay put. Although the evidence is lacking for Colyton, it seems to be on the heavily supplemented male wage that family security was increasingly based. Poverty, derived from endemic male under-employment, was assuaged by direct cash payments and gradually the payments to females for caring jobs were eroded. As a result, for labourers as much as for professionals and the middle class, economic structures and social responses underlay the patriarchial family of the nineteenth century.

Overview of Part Three

Chapter 5 analysed the demographic characteristics of the parish by relating the population patterns to the 'total reconstitution'. The picture to emerge is a good fit with the economic situation described in Part 2: health and wealth were inextricably connected. The predominance of women, the high level of migration, the marriage patterns and the relatively high death rates all point to the intensification of production in the parish as the seventeenth century unfolded. Chapters 6 and 7 describe different aspects of the control of the poor and of family life in Colyton. The results serve to underline the fact that although Colyton had a wood-pasture economy it is a fallacy to see the social structure of the parish as being egalitarian. Although Chapter 2 suggested the tradition of independent thought in Colyton, many people's livelihoods and family life were dependent because they lived as lodgers, servants, apprentices, paupers or incapable aged. Finally this section has developed the economic arguments of Part 2 that suggested that in the eighteenth century Colyton became more socially stratified as the 'middling' group in the parish lost both political and economic power. The last task is to consider the picture that emerges when we have assembled and assimilated all of the findings about Colyton's history. We need then to ask what they mean when compared with similar socio-economic historical studies of parishes that have been carried out for England and for other countries.

Epilogue

Reinterpreting Colyton
Explaining Population Change in the Parish

> The problem of all social historians who seek to provide more than a sketch of a past society—that vast energies may be expended on the demonstration of a crucial point which may then be assimilated instantly, even dismissed contemptuously—is unlikely to diminish. The village study is, for those who undertake it, something of a Pilgrim's Progress, requiring faith, grit and a capacity to take hard knocks.
>
> (K. Wrightson, 'Villages, Villagers and Village Studies', 1975: 639)

As this book has shown, the sources available for the history of Colyton are less than perfect and in order to produce a full examination of a small community we must be as aware of both the need to interpret gaps and silences in the records as well as consideration of the reasons why contemporaries sometimes produced copious and pristine recordings of information and why these records survived. As a means to understanding, it is necessary for social and economic historians to examine the political and religious histories of the parishes they research. As W.G. Hoskins put it, the ultimate ideal of the local historian is to 'restore the fundamental unity of human history'.[1] This cannot be achieved by an economic or demographic history which is devoid of human actors, a social history which pays no attention to wider political context, or a political history which gives no credence to the agency of ordinary individuals. Scores of early modern Colytonians have been presented here. With no wish to return to the era of the history of the 'great man', we are left with the impression that the actions of ordinary people such as Roger Satchell or Ann Blackaller were of enduring importance in shaping the history of their community.

Not only must the historian of the local community research at the interface, he or she should also be prepared to interlink documents, by means such as a total reconstitution, to gain a greater depth of understanding about both individual and group action and to uncover more of the social and gender relations within regional and local settings. As such the whole investigation resembles an old jigsaw recovered from the drawers after several years. While there will always be missing pieces, hopefully the sum is greater than the parts in any case. But Hoskins's 'full mastery of the facts', mentioned at the outset of this study, remains an unobtainable goal.

Population Change and Society in Colyton

A large part of this book has tried to explain why Colyton had a low fertility/high mortality regime during the period c.1630–c.1720 as opposed to the high fertility/relatively low mortality which both precedes and follows it. Colyton, like other present-day English rural villages in Devon, was an industrial community in the seventeenth century. Wrigley and Schofield found that manufacturing parishes showed a notable drop in age at marriage whereas agricultural parishes showed the least change in this period. The economic and demographic histories of Colyton are inseparably linked through the nexus of the sex ratio. The synthesis produced from the Colyton data rests on the differing employment and welfare influences on men and women. It points to the sex ratio as the crucial mechanism of mediation between population change and local economic circumstances. The implication of this is that the key to population expansion is a reasonably stable population. The conditions for this did not exist in Colyton for much of the period covered here. The status attributes derived from the total reconstitution set up some sort of criteria about how long different sections of the population had to wait before marrying. The age of marriage was found to be partly a function of the local marriage opportunities which meant that women from poor families often married at late ages or not at all. This was a fertility depressing system and the pattern was amplified by remarriage trends. Several preconditions must exist for the sex ratio to have the effect of suppressing population growth. First, women's wages must be too low to support a family. What is already known about the socio-legal restraints on women suggests that this was the case, and the wage evidence which can be collected for Colyton confirms it. Secondly, emigration and immigration need to be unrestrained. This was the case in an 'open' parish like Colyton. Thirdly, men and women must operate in different spheres or gender-differentiation of the population would not occur. This was the case in Colyton where the concept of the family as an integrated work unit seems to have been irrelevant for the lower rungs of the hierarchy at any stage in the parish's history.

The different demographic effects of 'masculine' and 'feminine' sex ratios also needs further exploration. Models have not been made of the effects of unbalanced sex ratios on population change. Thompson suggested that low sex ratios would take effect earlier than high ratios, but he was considering broad 'social' effects rather than strictly demographic consequences.[2] The evidence from Colyton suggests that the ratio of 80 may be a cut-off point below which population growth is inhibited. Mildly imbalanced sex ratios, of between 80 and 95 for instance, might act as a population stimulus. The period of wheat and wool economy in Colyton led to a 'masculine sex ratio' before 1650, and brought about a rise in baptisms of greater magnitude than the late eighteenth-century rise. Since the sex ratio at that time was not skewed drastically towards males, questions are raised as to the point at which a mildly unbalanced ratio combined with economic buoyancy would encourage population growth.

It seems likely that the craft and labourer groups did not have such variable demographic behaviour over time as the poor in Colyton. The change in marriage ages (and probably in proportions marrying) of poor women were most decisive over the period of this study and this suggests that future research on local communities might profitably concentrate on a limited reconstitution of the poor to research their demographic behaviour, carrying the analysis into the nineteenth century with a comprehensive series of poor law records. One implication of the research into Colyton is that the importance of women's work in the past should be re-evaluated. While the male wage and male work has been stressed in economic history from the mid-eighteenth century, the involvement of women in relatively low paid domestic work, who formed female-predominant 'urban' communities, has been largely overlooked.

While the finding that the further down the social scale a person was the longer he or she might wait to marry immediately suggests a Malthusian explanation, resources as a whole were not in short supply in the parish after the plague. As Dyer points out in a survey of market towns in early modern England, previously forested areas with wood-pasture economies which combined cattle raising, dairying, rural crafts and industries were generally growing in population in the seventeenth century because they offered land newly cleared from woodland and extra employment in the industrial sphere.[3] In fact, there had been a Boserupian reaction to the population increase from the late sixteenth century with the pressure of population forcing economic progress.[4] With an influx of migrants, why was Colyton's level of population in stasis or decline? Counteracting the possibilities of expansion in the margins of the parish were outbreaks of virulent mortality. Plague is an urban disease and this is very significant. Some aspects of Colyton's late seventeenth-century demography are most accurately described as 'urban': the high mortality of the parish and the skewed sex ratio in particular. Chris Galley has recently outlined models of urban demography as multi-explanatory and stresses that the demographic behaviour of migrants and natives may look different.[5] The first historical views of Colyton placed it within a rural framework and the interpretation of family limitation rested on there being a limited number of economic 'slots' within the parish. Levine also described a 'peasant' situation with proto-industry grafted onto a rural framework. But it was what was happening in Colyton town which most affected the demographic picture. Lace-making was big business. Colyton saw a mini 'industrial revolution' in the seventeenth century and as the parish urbanised it became less healthy and less moral. Mortality rose, as did illegitimacy. Pauperism was widespread, and relief distribution was the result of a discretionary project of the middling Dissenting people and a way of imposing a sense of control.

For the middling orders Puritanism provided the ideological basis for restraint in family formation and size, with concern to keep the patrimony intact the most immediate and pressing influence. The strength of Dissent in the parish and the incorporatism of self-government by the feoffees was so all-pervading that it cast a strong influence over most of the local yeomanry. There was a great deal of local interest in luxury production and retail trades, but essentially the 'industrious revolution' was still within a traditional context. Wealth from trade was transitional; ultimately it could only be secured by landholding, and as we have seen in the case of the plots on Colyford Meadow, land was a scarce commodity. It was important to temper prosperity with prudence, for unexpected disease or death, a bad marriage, crop failure, a foreign war or a shipwreck or piracy might all reverse family fortunes. We know that trade cycles, fighting armies, plague, political upheavals and religious persecution plus a rush of support for an unsuccessful rebellion did so in the Colyton context. As such the restraint and restriction imbued in local people from their prolonged period of youth in schooling and apprenticeship created a sense of anxiety and caution that remained with them into later life. For those people fortunate enough not to be struck down by any of the disasters which might befall a local community, longevity also held a price for their descendants. The marriage of John and Jane Pinney lasted for forty-eight years, and John Pinney was 85 when he died in 1705. Although their son Nathaniel and his wife had lived with the widowed John for the last decade or so of his life, and managed the farm, Nathaniel had no real independence and suffered untold frustration until he was well into middle age. A religion of restraint suited this set of circumstances.⁶ Extreme Protestantism still pervaded the parish in a vestigal form, long after the divisions of the seventeenth century. There is evidence from the second half of the nineteenth century of the enthusiastic way in which Guy Fawkes was burned every year. In 1854 Colyton's residents were accused of lawbreaking on 5 November by rolling burning tar barrels through the streets and letting off fireworks. On Guy Fawkes Day 1883 George Bull, a mason's labourer, was so keen to join in that he stole a petroleum barrel from Colyton's chemist but claimed he found it on the highway.⁷ When the Oxford Movement started to impinge on Colyton with the Reverend Mamerto Gueritz in the 1860s, effigies of Mr Gueritz and the curate were burned in the streets after a mass at Colyton church.

This interpretation suggests a worrying sort of economic apartheid, whereby the demography of the lower orders is determined by population imbalance, and that of the middling orders and upwards is determined by inheritance and by an intellectual impetus which suggested that restraint meant success. Essentially, we find that class divisions determined life experiences in Colyton. As we have seen, however, by Monmouth's rebellion, strongly Protestant influences certainly affected the poor. This may in part reflect deference, as a strategy for the receipt of relief. Of course, we have too little evidence on differing cultural attitudes between incomers and natives, although we can imagine that some of the migrants may have gravitated towards Colyton because of religious proclivities as well as economic opportunities.⁸ We can suggest that many of the incomers represented an underclass, exacerbated by the fact that they were mainly women who may have been seen to have undercut some of the work of local men in crafts, in a similar process that happened on a larger scale in the mass production of the 1820s and 1830s in industries such as tailoring. In a situation of a plenitude of cheap labour, small-scale capitalism soon burgeoned. We can detect an underlying concern throughout the late seventeenth century about what constitutes a community. In the 1689 case of Mr Mayowe, the pretend vicar who stalked the parish of Membury immediately after Monmouth's rebellion, we are aware that when he evoked the gospel of John and the story of the woman of Samaria, his message was really that of the biblical story: the meaning of love and the definition of the community.⁹ Many of Mayowe's muddled actions, and those of his supposed parishioners, reflect the contrast between the ecclesiastical parish and the parish of Dissenters. How could a community of Dissenters operate when it spilled across parish boundaries? This flew in the face of increasing regulation, such as the settlement laws, which were enforced on the basis of the parish. Moreover, with the stress on order and discipline, how were self-reliance and independence to be fostered among citizens?

Indeed, the ethos of corporatism, even if it represented an umbrella for many fissures and factions, gave way to individualism in the early eighteenth century. Nonconformity lost its potency as a political force and became the religion of the respectable, urban middling orders. To an important degree the county administration and national laws began to impinge much more directly on Colyton. The effective end of feoffee control of poor relief came in the early 1740s. From the mid-eighteenth century, parishes fought bitterly and sometimes went as far as preparing lengthy legal cases over settlement issues. In 1765 one case referred to the settlement of a servant formerly resident in a house which belonged to the Marwood family located across the borders of three parishes.[10] As the part of the house which stood in Colyton consisted of a dairy and some offices, the dispute was between Southleigh and Farway. It soon centred on the position of the servant's bed and table. At length the case was decided on the basis of where the servant's head lay when he was in bed. His bed was actually located in both parishes but not his pillow. Finally, it was decided that as his head and the upper part of his body lay in Farway when he slept they should take charge of him.

During the period 1730–80 Colyton seemed to lie in the economic doldrums. Lace-making had waned and on a more general level the parish now seemed to become isolated from colonial trades. Families who had seen spectacular social and economic success moved away from the parish. Farms that had remained intact survived but it was not until the high price years after 1780 that they again thrived. Perhaps it was during these years that Colyton's poor roads and silted estuary had a real effect on the vitality of the local economy. The community had lost the cut and thrust of local trader competition, of a business ethic sparked by Protestant fervour. As a town, by the end of the eighteenth century Colyton developed more gentrified characteristics—new architecture, more resident physicians and even a man-midwife.[11] The rising influence of the lord of the manor in the second half of this century is a useful corrective to a 'Whig' view of history that is sometimes applied to parish studies. The Colyton experience does not show progress towards greater democracy and a more diverse economy as time rolled forward in the period covered by this book.

In the course of the eighteenth century Colyton women joined in the long national fall in average age at marriage. Colyton's 'mini industrial revolution' and the distinctive evolution of 'urban characteristics' in the local population had passed. In the eighteenth century deindustrialisation meant women married at earlier ages. The effect of the sex ratio in inhibiting marriage was less important and women no longer had such active business lives. My interpretation departs from David Levine's in terms of chronology and effects. The rise in marriages and baptisms in Colyton occurred when the constraint of an unbalanced population was lifted. Whereas marriages appear to increase in number before baptisms, this was largely an artificial result of the 'low' in recording which continued until the mid-eighteenth century. It was effectively precluded by Hardwicke's Act of 1753/4, as well as a loss of popularity for nonconformism. This accounts for the apparent boom in marriages in the second half of the eighteenth century. The significant rise in baptisms dating from the 1780s represents Colyton's population 'take-off'. If the crux of a local study is to relate the results to country-wide patterns, then the task of explaining 'population take-off', even if this was a limited phenomenon in deindustrialising Colyton, must be attempted.

The period from 1780 to 1820 appears to be vital in explaining population growth as marriage ages fell at the same time as the sex ratio became more balanced. Relatively high wages for males in arable agriculture followed a decline of work in domestic industry (in lace-making and wool-spinning) for females. Women were given various parish-organised caring jobs in the 1760s as they increasingly fell on the poor rates. The male opportunities led to a reversal in the sex ratio as more men stayed in Colyton in the 1780s. From the 1790s, more people married and at younger ages. Against a background of year-round family allowances and child apprenticing, labourers were able to raise large families. So why did this latter change occur in Colyton? First, there was a twenty-year period of arable agriculture at the end of the eighteenth century. As this created opportunities for men, the distorted sex ratio eased a fraction. In the second half of the eighteenth century women's employment was eroded by the decline of domestic industry. Women were maintained, on a sporadic basis, by parish relief and casual jobs. At the end of the century the introduction of family allowances put this relief on a family basis. Payments were made to the male head of household and made family formation among the lower classes a more realisable prospect. Combined with female unemployment, these allowances made birth spacing an irrelevancy for wives. Moreover, and perhaps of greatest importance, by the end of the eighteenth century religion no longer determined marital partners or influenced age at marriage.

In the late eighteenth century there is a change in the type of migration reflected in the Colyton settlement examinations. Young men seem to have found work on Colyton farms more easily, particularly work by the day or week. This probably reflects some job opportunities on arable farms in Colyton. There were a class of craftsmen and 'decayed tradesmen' whom the feoffees and poor officers tried to help. Some of their correspondence indicates what led people to migrate from Colyton. There is a letter from James Anning, a joiner, to the overseers of the poor. It does not bear a date, but he seems likely to have been the man who baptised children in 1791 and 1795 and then disappeared from the reconstitution. He had pawned his tools for £2 18s 6d and said:

> Not ben able to maintaine my familey in England i am Now got to Guernsey to Better Myself and my Famley which I have Greate Incouragement and if i have my troth i shall be able to maintain them in a chreaditable maner, after i have my tools and a fue cloths fit to go before a Gentleman to work, and after that if i have my troth i will never trouble you more and if Please God i have to Return i shall have no objection to pay you 40 or 50 shillings but i cannot do without my tools which i solde to support my family and on this condison to have them againe for the same money when i coulde Rise it.[12]

James Anning presents a clear contrast with the prospects open to his erstwhile carpentering predecessors, Isaac and Zachary Drower: the late eighteenth-century parish did not present the same sort of industrious possibilities. The feoffees also occasionally provided support for emigration. On Christmas Eve 1827 they granted £10 to Richard Pratt to convey himself and his family to America.[13] In 1838 the parish paid £20 for the fare of three orphaned children who were going to live with their uncle in Upper Canada.[14] In the French Wars, men were often in the navy for eight or nine years before they married. John Turner, a weaver, examined in Colyton in 1815, said that at the age of 20 he 'agreed with a man at Colyton to go in the militia'.[15] He served with the First Devon militia in the Napoleonic Wars. Many were 'impressed' into the service or chosen by ballot. Matthew Lilley said in his settlement examination in 1790 at Colyton that he was chosen by lot to serve in the east Devon militia for five years.[16]

The parish became more rural but nevertheless some rural workers were lured to London. Thomas Clarke was born in Axmouth and in the customary manner was apprenticed at the age of 10 to Robert Bartlett of Roosdown in Colyton.[17] He was then in various hirings but in 1822, aged 18, he went to London, and entered into the employment of his cousin as a shop boy. His cousin was a grocer in Holborn and Clarke was paid 2s 6d a week plus board and lodging. But his cousin soon moved to St Pancras and dismissed Clarke because he was dissatisfied with his conduct. We can only speculate on the circumstances here; perhaps Clarke was overwhelmed by the delights of the capital or perhaps his background in agriculture ill-fitted him for a metropolitan shop. His cousin had certainly encouraged the move as he had given him a guinea on coming to London for travelling expenses and furnished him with clothes which were deducted out of his wages. Once dismissed, Clarke lived and worked with a silk-trimming manufacturer in St Lukes, Middlesex, but finally, perhaps disillusioned with his prospects, returned to Shute as a day labourer and was forced to apply for poor relief. It was not solely men who made such moves. Frances Newcombe wrote back to her settlement parish of Sidmouth in 1834.[18] She had been a servant in Yorkshire, Essex and Bath but now lived in London where she had been a 'work Woman' for an upholsterer in Gerrard Street, Soho, before she was taken ill. She now sought to be taken on in a shop back in this seaside parish.

Such cases, pinpointing the experience of unremarkable mobile people in east Devon, draw attention to the question of the typicality of Colyton as an experiment in the reconstruction of demographic experience. Put crudely, in the seventeenth and eighteenth centuries the parish does not resemble an ideal reconstitution parish with so much trade, in and out mobility and cross-parish religious affiliation. But this is perhaps to miss the point: the typical English parish probably cannot conform to all the 'rules' of reconstitution because the lives of ordinary inhabitants were transient and their relationship to the Anglican church was more discerning than we have perhaps given them credit for.

Colyton in Wider Perspective

The research of the Cambridge Group has stressed the homogeneity of the English demographic regime. As Wrigley and others have recently commented, 'England appears to have been a singularly homogeneous society in those aspects of social and personal behaviour which influenced fertility characteristics in early modern times'.[19] This finding apparently contrasts with the distinctiveness of local communities as highlighted by local and social historians. In the case of Colyton, the broad patterns of demographic change were replicated in other parishes that have been studied but the population trends appear to have been more intense than the national picture, especially in the case of the later age of marriage at the end of the seventeenth century.

The closest comparative local economy to Colyton which has been subject to detailed analysis is in fact not in England, but Myron Gutmann's study of the Verviers region of Belgium.[20] Gutmann found that despite immigration and industry in the period c.1675–1720 marriage ages remained high, contrasting with both the findings of proto-industrial theorist Mendels, and Levine's results for the four communities he studied. Gutmann believed that the patterns in Verviers related to 'culture' not economic change. Marriage ages remained high because there were limits to the amount of industrial work, and agriculture maintained its underlying importance. Wherever agriculture remained a viable alternative to industry there were mixed social environments. The description he ascribes to this, which might equally apply to Colyton, was that this was 'a hybrid society'. He was able to differentiate marriage by occupation for six communities in Verviers. He found that males and females from the groups of 'farmers' and 'spinners' married at

Plate 8. The Old Church House (1612).
(D. Sharpe)

the highest ages whereas industrial households had the lowest age at marriage, comprising weavers and workers in trade and transport. The spinners he saw as a group of outsiders due to the number of them who lived in female-headed households. He also found that the income from industry allowed peasants to retain their land. As they existed in interlocked systems of credit which meant they borrowed from larger farmers, without the income from industry in the end they would have had to sell out. Verviers also had an integral poor relief system which, in effect, recognised the roles played by the agricultural and industrial sectors of the population by the agriculturalists supporting the industrialists during periods of economic downturn. A similar picture was found in the tiny town of Comines in French Flanders, where intensive agriculture on small parcels of land flourished alongside industry. There age at marriage remained high, especially among the agricultural sectors of the population.[21] Gay Gullickson's detailed study of proto-industrialisation in Auffay in France provided a detailed picture of the effects of gender-differentiated employment patterns which also compares with Colyton.[22] In Auffay population grew but marriage ages remained very high until the 1780s because cottage industry prior to that date was limited to women. Another comparison can be made with the Twente region of the Netherlands recently analysed by Hendrickx.[23] He also found that both agriculture and industry were important in the local economy and neither had an overriding effect on demography. The most obvious differences were found between Catholic and Protestant sectors of the population. Hendrickx has commented that proto-industry was essentially a type of self-organisation to alleviate poverty and discovers that infant and child mortality actually improved with industrialisation. Two basic points emerge from these academic studies. The first is that detailed investigation of parishes simply accentuates differences between them.[24] The second is that historical demographers perhaps need to pay much greater attention to religion in explaining population patterns.

All of these communities differ from the classic study of proto-industrialisation undertaken by Braun on the Zurich Highlands, where he found much independence of women but poor land that would not sustain farming.[25] Colyton's economy and demography also contrast with many of the classic studies undertaken of English parishes which are situated in the Midlands or eastern counties.[26] The overall process of seventeenth-century proletarianisation was similar in Colyton and the Essex village of Terling, but differences in female and male employment and inheritance practices made a significant contrast between the demographic experiences of these parishes.[27] Terling had lower than average marriage ages for women but no employment for them. In Terling land was normally equally shared between inheriting children whereas Colyton's three-life leases were a means to keep estates intact. Finally, an examination of 'culture' reinforces the differences. Seventeenth-century Terling was characterised by the division between 'godly' and 'good honest men', whereas Colyton had a more fractured system of local authority yet a more pervading purist Protestant culture. This probably meant that restraint and social discipline were a more acceptable part of the local ethos. The in-depth study of early modern Whickham in County Durham in fact revealed another contrasting type of parish to Colyton. In Whickham, industrialisation meant a predominance of men, but there was also high mortality and a very high level of immigration.

We might expect that Colyton would be most similar to other wood-pasture parishes on the western side of England. David Hey's detailed study of the North Shropshire parish of Myddle described a woodland parish with pastoral-based agriculture, early enclosure, and many free tenures and long leases which had developed from forest clearings.[28] But there was no industry, only a very small artisan community and no nonconformity before the nineteenth century. Skipp's study of the forest of Arden in Warwickshire also does not extend beyond the mid-seventeenth century.[29] Skipp finds the industrialisation of this area to have been a response to ecological crisis from population pressure when price rises lead to population growth. Colyton, however, was both more rich in resources and more poverty-stricken than either Arden or, indeed, Verviers. It is much more of a 'hybrid' society than either Myddle or Arden. The turning points in the demographic regime of c.1630 and c. 1720 define the point where nonconformity and industriousness exerted such a hold on the town area of the parish. For the rural parts of the parish, however, the disruptions and dislocations of the seventeenth century brought a tenacious desire for farmers to hold on to their land, extend it if possible, but to keep their farms intact whatever transpired. Ultimately, it was the success of this strategy among the most ambitious families that determined the later character of the parish. In the last resort, Colyton had some of the best land and a relatively well educated population but some of the poorest inhabitants. It is the interface between the rural and industrial sectors of the parish which determined the demographic history of Colyton. Written on a larger canvas, it may have been the interaction between rural and industrial sectors of the English economy as a whole that determined national population trends and cancelled out the contrasting experiences of different parishes.

If Colyton bears only slight resemblance to other historical communities, can the parish be situated in terms of contemporary comparisons? I cast my mind through places I have travelled and Filadelfia in the Middle Chaco of Paraguay came to mind. Filadelfia is a Mennonite community and I travelled there on a bus with strait-laced and straight-faced Mennonites at the front, and drunken Indians at the back. Whereas the Mennonites looked extremely healthy and hearty, the same could not be said for the Indians. I arrived to find clinically modern houses with orchards and paddocks interspersed with co-operative industries and some of the most up-to-date farm machinery I had seen in South America. There were only two places to stay: an expensive efficient Mennonite hotel with squeaky clean rooms or an insect-ridden shack at the back, where decrepit beds cost $3 each and were clearly aimed at Indian incomers. This economically successful community incorporated an Indian mission station with small brick houses but other Indians lived in appalling conditions under black plastic. Very little Spanish was spoken: the language of the Mennonites was German and the Indians spoke Guarani. Early modern Colytonians were, of course, unable to realise such an ultra-Protestant community and there was none of the racial imperialism found in Filadelfia. But the economic organisation and insularity, justified by biblical precepts, was undoubtedly similar.

Colyton has taken a central place in population history studies. This 'microscopic' study of the community stands at the end of a forty-year collective endeavour to pull together threads of knowledge about Colyton's history and to use them to examine the finer details of demographic and social change. Such a venture must overcome many obstacles, some of which, in the absence of documentary material and the implausibility of uncovering real evidence of fertility strategies, will remain unsurmountable. Yet a deep interest in one community is justified by the discovery of historical change that was certainly of more than local importance, and is perhaps of regional, national and even international significance.

Appendix

The Methodology of Total Reconstitution

The period for this study was taken as that of the original reconstitution, with the year from which all the registers date, 1538, as the starting point.[1] The analysis extended to the end of the 'parish register' reconstitution period in 1837, with the linkage of the 1832 tax assessment. However the pre-1800 analysis is more intensive. The reconstitution has been extended through the census years of the nineteenth century by Jean Robin.[2] The FRFs that extend into the period on which she has worked have purposely been excluded from this study. Thus the numbers in the cohort 1800–37 which were used here are considerably smaller than the full sample. Where the results in this last cohort were felt not to be representative, they have been excluded. The FRFs have been organised into seven cohorts: 1538–49, 1550–99, 1600–49, 1650–99, 1700–49, 1750–99 and 1800–37. These cohort divisions follow those most commonly used for statistical work on Colyton.[3]

The total reconstitution process involved four stages. The first was collation and assessment of sources for their quality and usefulness. Sources which did not mention any names could be excluded immediately. Priority was given to sources that mentioned occupations and wealth levels. Tax assessments, for example, were an ideal source. Secondly, the information from the documents was put onto index cards. These were sorted according to surname sets into rough cohort groupings. In the cases where several people had the same name, they were sorted into chronological order. Thirdly, the index cards were linked to their respective FRF and surnames were standardised to the form they took on the FRF to avoid further confusion. The cards of two people who had the same name and lived at the same time, such as fathers and sons, could now be sorted out. Family index cards were grouped together as they appeared on the FRF. At this point cards were sorted into final

APPENDIX: THE METHODOLOGY OF TOTAL RECONSTITUTION

cohort groups according to the FRF date, which is either the date of marriage, or in the case of 'dummy' FRFs the date of first child's baptism. Lastly the FRF/card conjunctions were sorted into status groupings. Preferably the group chosen was based on a wealth indication, but where this was not available, occupation attributes are used. After that the definition of group could depend on more tentative indications. Clearly the choice of the status-specific groupings embraced a welter of methodological problems and as there is no precedent for this type of analysis any division runs a risk of oversimplification. The preferred defining characteristics were: an indication of amount of land owned or leased, a list of possessions such as would be found in an inventory, a comment on wages received, a note of the amount of tax paid, or an entry that the person in question received poor relief or their children were made pauper apprentices. Failing these, an assumption of social grouping would be made from a source where occupation was mentioned. Occupational labels were assigned secondary status because of the problems attached to their use. For example, Ralph Seaward, described as a carpenter in his will in 1669, was nevertheless the owner of three houses and of substantial 'middling' wealth. His position might then more realistically have been defined as 'property developer' in current-day terms.[4] Only at the last resort would more subjective indicators, such as a description of a person as a 'poor man', be used. While for some people a status categorisation had to be based on a single incidence in the records, others had several entries. If there was a conflict in the information, for example between a man who is recorded as a 'craftsman' on marriage but as a 'labourer' later, the attribute nearest to his marriage defined his grouping since the behaviour of the young adult age group was seen as most crucial in this study. Normally the evidence was sufficient to put an individual clearly in a particular category. It was generally difficult to give women a status attribute since they were rarely given occupational labels and the social and legal system effectively precluded them from appearing in many of the documents which indicate landholding. It was regrettably necessary, then, to give women their father's status group until marriage and their husband's group at marriage and thereafter.

The following is a full list of the documents used in the total reconstitution to determine the status attributes of FRFs. Reference numbers and locations of these documents are given in the Bibliography. In Table A.1 the stars indicate the statuses derived from the respective documents. Table A.2 shows how status was derived in the first section of listings. Table A.3 identifies the documents which give an occupation rather than, or in addition to, a wealth level. Over the entire period of the reconstitution, linkage was given to a total of 2,185 FRFs. These were status linked as follows:

APPENDIX: THE METHODOLOGY OF TOTAL RECONSTITUTION

Gentry	610
Crafts	498
Labourer	496
Poor	581

Of these, linkage could be given to 1,242 FRFs with marriages. These were linked as follows:

Gentry	294
Crafts	296
Labourer	306
Poor	346

Any labelling system is open to subjective interpretation; 'gentry', 'crafts', 'labourer' and 'poor' are chosen to give easy reference to the socio-economic classification and describe the majority of individuals in that group. The four-part hierarchy seems to be an accurate representation of Colyton society through the time period in question.

Table A.1 Status Derivation of Total Reconstitution documents

Reconstitution documents	Gentry	Crafts	Labourer	Poor
Taxation documents				
1524 Lay subsidy	*	*	*	*
1543/5 Subsidy	*	*	*	–
1547 Survey of tenants	*	*	*	–
1582 Subsidy	*	*	*	–
1592 Subsidy	*	*	*	–
1620/1 Subsidy	*	*	*	–
1624 Devon subsidy roll	*	*	–	–
1636 Ship money	*	*	*	–
1674 Hearth tax	*	*	*	*
1684 Yearly rent of Colyton manor	*	*	–	–
1702/3 Rental of Colyford borough	*	*	–	–
1726 Colyton church rate	*	*	*	*
1780 Land tax	*	*	*	–
1798 Land tax	*	*	*	–
Late eighteenth-century poor rates	*	*	*	*
1819 Poor rate assessment	*	*	*	*
1832 Land tax	*	*	*	–
Court roll material and manor surveys				
1550 Colyton manor court roll	*	*	–	–
1553 Colyton manor court roll	*	*	–	–
1592–1685 Whitwell court/ estreat rolls	*	*	–	–
1544–1682 Whitwell manor	*	*	–	–

320

APPENDIX: THE METHODOLOGY OF TOTAL RECONSTITUTION

1606 Whitwell survey	*	*	—	—
1578–1639 Deeds	*	*	—	—
Drake deeds	*	*	—	—
Sampson accounts	*	*	*	—
Rolle papers	*	*	—	—
Petre cottage leases 1655–1690	—	—	*	*
1761–1815 Carew-Pole rentals	—	*	*	*
1787 Receipts for expenses on Colyton estates	—	*	*	—
1793–1806 Carew-Pole miscellaneous bills	*	*	*	—
1789–1794 Carew-Pole account books	*	*	*	—
1785 Carew-Pole miscellaneous receipts	*	*	*	—
1622–1679 Lease book of manor of Yardbury	—	*	*	—
1665–1825 Dean and Chapter of Exeter items	*	*	*	—
Probate and ecclesiastical material				
Probate inventories	*	*	—	—
Special inquisition	*	—	—	—
Special inquisition	*	—	—	—
PCC. wills	*	—	—	—
Marriage bonds	*	*	*	*
Chamber of Feoffees records				
1579–1720 Churchwarden's fabric accounts and bills	—	*	*	*
1659–1699 Bailiff's accounts	—	*	*	*
1682–1683 & 1698–1699 Receipts and payments to the poor	*	*	*	*
1704 Colyton bridge building account	—	*	*	—
1573 Rent demand	*	—	—	—
Early seventeenth-century parish deeds	*	*	—	—
1611 Survey of parish lands	*	*	—	—
1649 Indenture	*	*	—	—
1618 Indenture and draft lease	*	*	—	—
1556–1558 Rentals	*	*	—	—
1659–1700 Parish chamber leases	—	—	*	*
1684–1685 Bills and rentals	—	*	—	—
1708 Receipt for payment of house	*	—	—	—
c.1792 Copy of feoffee charter	*	*	*	—
1766–1853 Feoffees' minute book	*	*	*	*
Town administration records				
1740–1770 Overseers' account book	—	*	—	*
1664–1742 Settlement certificates	—	—	*	*
1700–1829 Settlement certificates	—	—	*	*

APPENDIX: THE METHODOLOGY OF TOTAL RECONSTITUTION

1765–1854 Settlement examinations	–	–	*	*
1700–1854 Removals to Colyton	–	–	*	*
1742–1810 Papers relating to settlement	–	–	*	*
1830 Appeals against poor rate assessment	–	–	*	*
1793–1799 Bastardy examinations	–	*	*	*
1772–1831 Bastardy examinations	–	*	*	*
1590–1744 Bastardy bonds	–	*	*	*
1777–1779 Bastardy bonds	–	*	*	*
1771–1834 Maintenance payments	–	*	*	*
1790 Other bastardy papers	–	*	*	*
1662–1737 Constable's presentments for hundred of Colyton	–	–	*	*
1664–1685 Constable's warrants	–	–	*	*
1683 Constable's account	–	–	*	*
1680 Petty constable's accounts	–	–	*	*
1598–1711 Apprenticeship register	*	*	–	*
1800–1830 Register of poor apprentices	*	*	*	*
1647–1741 Apprenticeship indentures	*	*	–	*
1758–1779 Apprenticeship bonds	*	*	–	*
1772–1796 Miscellaneous apprenticeship bonds	*	*	*	–
1764 Private apprenticeship records	*	*	*	–
1586–1741 Apprenticeship indentures	*	*	*	*
1767–1778 Colyton churchwarden's accounts	–	*	*	–
1786–1790 Hemp and flax bounty papers	–	*	*	–
1809–1838 Burial board account book	–	*	*	–

Table A.2 Status Derivation in the listings

		Gentry	Crafts	Labourer	Poor
1524	Lay subsidy	>20s	5s–20s	1s–4s	<1s
1543/5	Subsidy	>10s	£2–10	<£1	
1547	Survey of tenants	Amount of acreage			
1582	Subsidy	>2s8d	16d–2s8d	<16d	
1592	Subsidy	>2s8d	16d–2s8d	<16d	
1620/1	Subsidy	>7s	1s6d–7s	<1s6d	
1624	Devon subsidy roll	Gives some occupations			
1636	Ship money	>5s	2s–5s	<1s	

322

APPENDIX: THE METHODOLOGY OF TOTAL RECONSTITUTION

1674	Hearth tax	6–20s	3–5s	1–2s	Pauper
1684	Yearly rent of Colyton Manor	Indications of Acreage			
1702/3	Rental of Colyton borough	Indications of Acreage			
1726	Colyton church rate	>5s	1s–5s	1d–1s	<1d
1780	Land tax	>20s	5s–20s	<5s	
1798	Land tax	>20s	5s–20s	<5s	
Late 18th century	Poor rates	>10s	1s–10s	<1s	Pauper
1819	Poor rate assessment	>10s	1s–10s	<1s	Pauper
1832	Land tax	>£5	£1–£5	<£1	

Table A.3 Documents giving occupations

1624 Devon subsidy roll
1550 Colyton manor court roll
1553 Colyton manor court roll
1578–1639 Deeds
Drake deeds
Sampson accounts
Rolle papers
1787 Receipts for expenses on Colyton estates
Probate inventories
PCC. wills
Marriage bonds
1579–1720 Churchwarden's fabric accounts and bills
1659–1699 Bailiff's account
1766–1853 Feoffees' minute book
1740–1770 Overseers' account book
1767–1778 Colyton churchwarden's accounts
1590–1744 Bastardy bonds
1777–1779 Bastardy bonds

All the Colyton records were linked by hand with the aid of computer-produced indexes of the FRFs. The reconstitution was punched into a computer some years ago. Since the technology available then was less sophisticated than today, only certain aspects of the FRFs were entered. Alphabetical indexes of husbands, wives and children by surname were used. An inherent disadvantage of the reconstitution method is that it highlights family relationships. Individuals without a legitimate relationship to the married couple are excluded. However, illegitimate births were added into the data using an index compiled by Tony Wrigley. Since 1990 automated reconstitution has been a possibility.[5]

But when the Colyton total reconstitution was carried out the process remained clumsy and costly by machine and the diverse spelling of names was a particular problem.[6] The Russell SOUNDEX code was the most promising method of nominal linkage by machine. SOUNDEX was appreciably quicker than hand methods. Katz and Tiller found it took only a tenth of the time it had taken to link the 1861 Hamilton, Ontario census by hand.[7] However, the code is not satisfactory for the linkage of names further back in the past. When tested on Colyton by hand methods, Wrigley identified 986 spellings comprising 244 different christian names in the Colyton register over the period 1538–1640. SOUNDEX failed to assign 14 per cent of the spellings and erroneously conflated 35 per cent of names. This was obviously found to be 'an entirely unacceptable error rate'.[8]

Name problems do still exist when documents are linked by hand. In seventeenth-century parish documents like poor law accounts, spellings are even more diverse than in the parish registers. To help overcome this, a system of phonetic linkage was used in this part of the Colyton project. This aimed to take the linguistic development of the local dialect into account and certain idiosyncratic patterns could be identified. From this some 'name' rules could be drawn up and applied loosely.[9] Surname shortening is a frequently encountered name change in the Colyton data. Thus over time, the very common Colyton surname of 'Batstone' became Battey, then Batt. Presumably there was an element of sheer laziness in this but the variations on this name served to distinguish different family branches and may have been applied as colloquial nicknames. Other examples of the 'y' shortening are Clotworthie becoming Clittery, Goulsworthy becoming Gollsey, Husway or Hussey becoming simply Hooy, and Killander becoming Kelly. Some names are just shortened. For example, Hooper became Hoop and Quinton became Quint. Some permutations certainly reflect local dialect: Cauley and Cawley are the same as Calie and Calley, as are Lowde and Lewd (!). Other names could change completely. While Ticken, Tigon and Tirken are recognisable as species of the same name, the links between Turle, Tirrel, Tyall and Turvell are perhaps not so obvious. Similarly Salway or Zalway became Samwayes or Zamwayes and eventually just Samis.

Changes in the first letter of the surname provide much confusion in linking. Not surprisingly 'H' may or may not appear, thus Alstone, Halson and Halstone are all the same name. Similarly 'C' and 'K' were interchangeable. Kerby could be Corby or even Corky. Abbreviation sometimes started from the beginning of the name, hence Spurway became Purway in some cases. In the nineteenth century the common name in Colyton of Restorick went to Restadick and then just Stadick. Some letters were often reversed, so Crocker and Corker were the same names. Another problem is 'alias' names, as in the case of 'Tucker alias

Baker' or 'Kerby alias Pyper'; either surname might be used without the other. The reason for these names is not clear but may reflect an illegitimate line in some cases.[10] Some female Christian names were interchangeable, for example Joan, Joanne and Jane, and also Hannah, Joanna and Susannah. It is noticeable that the names subject to most permutations were those of the poor. This group were least likely to write their own names, thus establishing some sort of spelling precedent for themselves.

Notes

Bibliographical and Note Conventions

Manuscripts: in the Notes, all references begin with an abbreviated version of their archive; they are arranged by archive in the Bibliography.

Unpublished and Published Sources: author/date references are provided in the Notes, with full references in the Bibliography.

Books and articles appear together in the Bibliography. Places of publication are provided except where it is London.

Prologue

1. Wrigley, Davies, Oeppen and Schofield 1997.
2. Vann 1999: 101. Vann is drawing on the anthropological use of 'thick description' as employed by Geertz 1973: 6–9.
3. Crafts and Ireland 1976: 610.
4. Spufford 1974: 350, 352 warns against placing too much emphasis on economic factors in reconstructing the life of the ordinary villager.

Chapter 1. Interpreting Colyton

1. Pulman 1875: 507.
2. Hoskins and Finberg 1952: 304–322.
3. Hoskins 1954: 108; Kowaleski 1995: 357, 368.
4. Arkell 1982.
5. Laslett 1973: 100.
6. DRO 3483A/PR1.
7. Wrigley 1966a: 82–109. The early stages of the research are summarised by Clapp 1982: 4–8. For the wider implications of Colyton research see Ladurie 1979: 223–234. Also see Landers 1993: 97–127, who urges a broader context for demography embracing high politics, and stresses the importance of mortality.
8. Wrigley 1968: 546–580; Wrigley 1972: 199–221; Wrigley 1975: 299–316; Wrigley 1977a: 281–312; Wrigley 1977b: 9–21.
9. Wrigley and Schofield 1981.
10. Wrigley 1981: 137–185, quoted 145–146.
11. Weir: 1984: 340–354, quoted 349.
12. For significant exceptions see Reay 1996, and Hudson and King 2000: 706–741.
13. See criticisms by B. Hill 1989a; Mackinnon 1995.
14. Henry 1961: 81–91.
15. Macfarlane, Harrison and Jardine 1977.

16. Reference can be made to a wide selection of studies that incorporate nominal linkage. For example, for the early modern period Rutman and Rutman 1979: 153–182 used prosopographic methods to outline the lives of as many people as possible who resided in Middlesex County, Virginia, between 1650 and 1750. They describe the pitfalls they identified on p. 176. On a much smaller scale Chaytor 1980: 25–60 employed a linkage method to listings, deposition books, wills and debt lists for four families in Ryton in County Durham in the sixteenth century. This was strongly criticised by Houston and Smith 1982: 120–131. Prior 1982 produced a total reconstitution of one street, Fisher Row in Oxford. Johansen 1987: 297–305 and Johansen n.d. exploit the method of 'house repopulation' for the urban environment of Odense in Denmark. In some countries very detailed documents have proved to be a short cut towards producing collective biographies. Knodel and Shorter 1976: 115–154 and Knodel 1988, for example, used the German 'Ortssippenbuch' which provided a nominal linkage basis of ready-made genealogies.

17. Hareven 1974: 322–329; Hareven 1977: 339–349.

18. Åkerman 1977: 160–170; S. King 1996.

19. C. Wilson 1982: 124 comments on this problem.

20. Levine 1996: 105.

21. Norton 1980: 11–12. Rogers 1988 considers Swedish family reconstitution methodology and is optimistic about the effects of migration.

22. The names of these groups do not always capture the full range of occupations or wealth levels contained within them, and conversely, in some cases the labels exaggerate the prevalence of this actual group in Colyton. For example, 'gentry' embraces the elite of Colyton society and includes wealthy yeoman farmers as well as better-off clothiers. See the Appendix for how these groups were derived.

23. DRO Box 1, Marriage bonds.

24. B.M.S. Campbell 1981: 145–154 argues that lay subsidies provide a fuller enumeration of the adult population than has been hitherto realised.

25. Much appreciation is owed to T.L. Stoate, who has transcribed and privately printed several Devon listings: the 1524 subsidy roll, the 1543/4 subsidy roll, the muster roll of 1569 and the Hearth Tax of 1674. See Stoate and Howard 1977; Stoate 1979; Stoate 1982; Stoate 1986.

26. In particular, for the communities of the Forest of Arden and of Terling in Essex, see Skipp 1978; Wrightson and Levine 1979. Some attempts have been made to assess the reliability of Hearth Tax returns. Tom Arkell found by comparing the Hearth Tax with surviving overseers' accounts for twelve parishes in Warwickshire that very few poor households were missing. See Arkell 1986–7. For a different view see Husbands 1985.

27. The Pinney papers are in Bristol University Library Special Collections.

28. G. Roberts 1848. See also Wolffe 1997: 179–196.

29. Anderson Smith 1901. I am very grateful to Mrs Gillian A. Falla and the Devon and Cornwall Record Society for this reference. The Moger-Murray abstracts are in the West Country Studies Library in Exeter. Cash 1966 contains transcripts of some wills of the very wealthy. See also Fry 1908 and Fry 1914. Wyatt 1997 shows that a comparable set of probate material, stored out of the country, has survived and been collected for the parish of Uffculme.

30. David Souden's file DCS EXON was initially used as an index.

31. White 1951: 34.

32. White 1951: 2.

33. Wrightson 1975b: 632–639.

34. Hollingsworth 1968: 415–432 and Hollingsworth 1969: 184, 190–194, who argued on p. 191 that overall for Colyton 'a fairly low standard of completeness existed

throughout'. Razzell 1994 casts doubt the Colyton registers from several aspects, in both his new and reprinted research: see 97–98, 119–145, 189–190 and 213. Regarding the early nineteenth-century registers Wrigley had replied in Wrigley 1975. See also Clapp 1982: 7–8. On the wider ramifications of parish register reliability see Wrigley 1997.

35. Wrigley 1977b: 9–21.

36. This is mentioned in DRO 3483A/PO13, the overseers' account book for 1740–70. For other parishes see Schofield 1984: 49–53; K.D.M. Snell 1984: 29–43; Souden 1984b: 11–28.

37. Bourgeois-Pichat 1951: Vol. II, 223–248, Vol. III, 459–480; R.E. Jones 1976: 305–318; Levine 1976: 107–122; Pitkänen 1977: 138–159; Wrigley 1977a: 281–312; Schofield and Wrigley 1979: 61–95; Finlay 1980: 26–41; Wrigley and Schofield 1981: 89–102.

38. Krause 1965: 379–393; Midi Berry and Schofield 1971: 453–464; Razzell 1972: 121–146.

39. Schofield and Wrigley 1979: 61–95.

40. DRO 3483A/PO24 Register of Pauper Apprentices.

41. Wrigley 1977a: 281–312. Also COLYFILE (statistical work carried out at the Cambridge Group for the History of Population and Social Structure).

42. E.P. Thompson 1963: 246; K.D.M. Snell 1985; 72–73.

43. Wall 1976: 73–90.

44. Southerden Burn 1829: 34 gives more details of this tax.

45. In London, for example, many non-regular marriages were performed at the Fleet Prison. See Lee Brown 1981: 117–136. For Nottinghamshire see Outhwaite 1990. See also Wrigley 1969b: 15–17 and Wrigley 1973b: 15–21; Gillis 1985: 136n.

46. Wrigley 1977a: 281–312. See also Wrigley 1969b: 15–17 and Wrigley 1973b: 15–21. Bradley 1973: 63–94 found that the parish registers of Eyam in Derbyshire showed very high baptism/marriage ratios between 1641 and 1660 and few illegitimate baptisms. He suggested that these were signs of clandestine marriage.

47. Schofield 1985: 2–20.

48. Wrigley 1978: 429–436; Lee Brown 1981: 117–136.

49. Souden 1981: 28.

50. Gillis 1985: 92 discusses these conditions.

51. Personal communication with Mrs Angela Doughty and Mrs Margaret Rowe at Devon Record Office, and with Mrs Audrey Erskine formerly at the Exeter Cathedral Library. But some incumbents were keen to perform irregular marriages. Chanter 1919: 258–260 describes the parish of Brushfield as a Gretna Green in the 1660s. The author found a scrap of paper in the Exeter Cathedral muniments written by the incumbent when he was called to order and asked to recall the marriages he had solemnised.

52. Wrigley and Schofield 1981: 89n.

53. DRO Chanter 874.

54. Welch 1959: 111–112.

55. The marriage registers were searched in DRO for Axmouth, Branscombe, Farway, Honiton, Musbury, Offwell, Seaton and Beer, Shute and Widworthy. The proximity of these parishes to Colyton can be readily discovered by reference to Map 3.

56. Axminster marriages do not start until 1695. Kilmington has no marriages recorded between 1589 and 1727. Northleigh parish registers only commence in 1697 and Southleigh's only begin in 1754.

57. Finlay 1980: 26–41 comments on distance affecting baptism registration. Although endogenous infant mortality rates were low in Colyton, there seems to have been a desire to baptise in the church. It is unlikely that geographical factors would ever have prevented anyone from having a ceremony in Colyton if they so wished.

58. Caffyn 1988: 60 found that Baptists in Sussex in the seventeenth and eighteenth centuries sometimes formalised marriages in parish churches after the birth of a child to establish the validity of the union in the civil courts.
59. Wickes 1990: 14.
60. Eyre Evans 1908: 89–91; Brushfield 1908: 119–120.
61. I am indebted to Jonathan Barry for clarification on this point.
62. DRO Marriage bonds, Box 1–6, 42. Large numbers of these documents are extant for Devon. They have been sorted according to date. A few years, 1689 for example, have disintegrated.
63. Clapp 1982: 4–9 reached the conclusion that the presence of occasional nonconformity might make the Colyton reconstitution less useful. While his suspicions about Dissent have proved correct, it is to be hoped that my later conclusions will show that the demographic data are useful nonetheless. I have also had personal communication with Mrs Ena Cummings regarding reconstitution the parish of Morchard Bishop. More generally, Wrigley and Schofield 1981: 89–95, Landers 1987: 59–76 and Vann and Eversley 1992 comment on Quakerism affecting registration patterns. The evidence presented here suggests that other nonconformist groups also had this effect. Caffyn 1988 uses Baptist genealogies and finds that Baptists certainly married within their own community before 1753. He associates nonconformity with a non-resident marryer pattern which is also indicated by the registers of Devon churches, since these may have had incumbents who were willing to tailor their wedding services to the requirements of nonconformists in order to validate their marriages in civil law. Some 70 per cent of Baptists in Sussex did marry in an Anglican church.

Chapter 2. Dissenting People

1. This might explain the Compton Census's deficiency in recording nonconformists. All the population shortfall of an estimated 600 were likely to be nonconformists.
2. Many other studies have also found Dissenters to constitute the 'middle' of local society, for example Spufford's study of Willingham 1974: 303. Caffyn 1988: 99, 166 found that Baptists were fully integrated into their Sussex communities in terms of officeholding and social life. For Devon, P.W.Jackson 1986: 120 finds that few servants or labourers were nonconformists, and Stoyle 1994: 91 finds husbandmen and labourers were more likely to be royalist.
3. Peskett 1974: 68–70.
4. White 1951: 7. For the background to dissent in the south-west in the 1540s, see Rowse 1941: 262–292.
5. Gowers 1970: 35. Much detail in the paragraphs to follow is drawn from Ian Gowers's excellent dissertation.
6. Gowers 1970: 52.
7. Gowers 1970: 183–186; see also Stoyle 1994: 189 and DRO Moger Papers Diocesan Records CC 181 (34) 1625.
8. Gowers 1970: 184–185.
9. For more details see Underdown 1985b.
10. DRO 67A PW1 Farway Churchwarden's Memoranda Book.
11. Gowers 1970: 100. For the geography of dissenting congregations later established see Jonathan Barry's mapping in Kain and Ravenhill 1999: 225.
12. Stoyle 1994: 190 says that Puritan lectures were established in Axminster and Honiton in 1613. Both Traske and his wife, Dorothy, whom he married in 1617, were teachers. In 1618 the couple were imprisoned for their Sabbatarian views: see Crawford and Gowing 2000: 93–94.

13. Gowers 1970: 161–162.
14. See Wolffe 1997: 179–196 for a recent summary of Yonge's career.
15. Cliffe 1993: 136.
16. Bodleian Library, Oxford, Tanner MSS, 141, fos 120–122 (The Clerk of Parliament's Papers) and personal communication with Mark Stoyle: Letter to the Bishop of Exeter, regarding Gould, clerk and churchwarden of Colyton, written in the early 1680s referring to the 1630s.
17. W. Hunt 1983: 146.
18. Stoyle 1994: 189.
19. DRO Chanter 867 Reynolds v Newbury (1616) and Chanter 867 Reynolds v Stocker (1619) and for a later case WCS Anstis MSS 1743 on Sampson, the churchwarden and the vicar taking six men to court for non-payment of tithes.
20. As Leland commented on his 1534–43 tour of Colyton, 'The Bisshop of Excester's Chauncelar is vicar of this town and hath a fair House ther'; cited in Pearse-Chope 1918: 79.
21. Noble 1970: 191; Scott Smith 1984: 17–27; Scott Smith 1985: 541–565 has analysed Puritan naming practices in New England. See also Tyacke 1979: 77–92; Main 1996: 1–28.
22. DRO 1637 Diocesan Records CC 178/1. See also Gowers 1970: 188–191.
23. This refers to 'A Necessary Doctrine and Erudition of any Christian Man' published in 1543. It placed heavy stress on observance of the Sabbath. See Hutton 1994: 78.
24. Hitchcock 1997: 54.
25. See Thomas 1971: 193–197.
26. Spufford 1974: 344. See also Collinson 1982: 249 on 'voluntary religion' and the gentry gadding between congregations.
27. FF 22/7 (2).
28. I am grateful to Dr Todd Gray for putting me in mind of this connection.
29. Barge 1932: 65–67.
30. Brown 1963: 219–243.
31. The most detailed biography is Rose-Troup 1930. However, Bridenbaugh 1968 argues that Frances Rose-Troup confused the Dorchester John White with the colonising activities of London barrister John White and thus misappropriates some of his activities. For the background on Dorchester, see Underdown 1993.
32. Rose-Troup 1930: 454, 458.
33. The literature on this subject is vast. For reference to some of the key articles in this debate see Breen and Foster 1973: 189–222; V.D.J. Anderson 1985: 339–383; and the replies and discussion of Anderson and Allen 1986: 406–424.
34. Rose-Troup 1930: 199, 229.
35. Hotten 1874.
36. Hotten 1874.
37. Anderson Smith 1901: PCC 3 April 1646.
38. Cresswell n.d. 10.
39. Gowers 1970: 204–206.
40. Pulman 1875: 507.
41. Stoyle 1994: 166.
42. Stoyle 1994: 87.
43. Howard 1973: 155; Stoyle 1994: 189.
44. Andriette 1971: 107, 110, 156.
45. Cited in Stoyle 1994: 148.
46. Wanklyn 1927.
47. This story also appears in Wilkin 1935: 20–26. Matthews 1948: 110 says that,

according to Walker In 1714, he was several times imprisoned. He was forced to sell his estate worth £60 a year to support his wife and ten children. In 1660 he became a schoolmaster in Somerset.
    48. Gillespie 1943: 16.
    49. Jackson 1986: 208.
    50. Brockett 1958: 32–59.
    51. DRO 235M/E3 Courtenay-Pole accounts. Cash book 1658–1665 contains a detailed account of the burial of Courtenay-Poles at Colyton. See also Hoskins 1954: 374 and Wolffe 1997: 215–220.
    52. National Trust n.d.; Russell 1959: 53–54.
    53. Jackson 1986: 120.
    54. Jackson 1986: 208.
    55. DRO QSBb 1656. See C. Hill 1972.
    56. DRO 1663 Chanter 869 Hallet vs Manly.
    57. Wilkin 1934a: 370. See also Matthews 1934: 530.
    58. Matthews 1934: 390–1; UBSC Pinney Papers, Account Book 1 1650–1668.
    59. Nuttall 1939: x.
    60. Windeatt 1885: 298–312. See also Chapman 1998: 73–4.
    61. Jackson 1986: 277.
    62. Little 1956: 65–66.
    63. This paragraph draws on Little 1956: 69.
    64. Finberg 1952: 372–3.
    65. Watts 1978: 229–232. See also DRO QS Order Book 1671.
    66. DRO QS 74/34/2.
    67. DRO QS Order Book 1675 Easter and Epiphany.
    68. DRO QSBb 1670 Michaelmas.
    69. DRO QSBb 1682 Easter, Case of Samuel Edwards.
    70. DRO QSBb 1684 Midsummer.
    71. DRO QS 15/86/1–12.
    72. Macdonald Wigfield 1980: 6.
    73. Bate 1908: 20–25, 62–65. I am grateful to Dr Jeremy Boulton for suggesting this reference.
    74. Jackson 1992: 117–129. Whiteman 1986 shows that the Compton Census underestimates nonconformity.
    75. 1670 QS 74/14 Colyton Conventicle.
    76. DRO QSBb Order Books Easter 1682, Michaelmas 1683 and Midsummer 1684.
    77. Jackson 1986: 181–2. Diocesan Records Principal Registry Papers Basket A 2574 shows that Tanner had interceded with the Bishop's Register in favour of two Colyton men in 1671.
    78. DRO 1674 Diocesan Records Principal Registry Papers Basket 2663.
    79. DRO Diocesan Records Principal Registry Papers Basket A2638, Thomas Tanner to Francis Cook the Younger.
    80. DRO 1674 Diocesan Records Princial Registry Papers Basket 2666. But Bagwell and Sampson's account for the feoffees suggests that they did pay for communion sack and provide books such as a common prayer book and book of homilies, articles etc., but they noted that 'when we provided wine for ye Communion at Christ Mr Tanner would not accept of it but sent for sack himselfe which was a loss to us wee charge nothing for either' (FF 14/1 1674). It is not clear whether Tanner sought better-quality wine or whether this was part of the dispute.
    81. Bodleian Library, Oxford, Tanner MSS, 141, fos 120–122 (The Clerk of Parliament's Papers) and communication with Mark Stoyle.

82. DRO QS 15/86/1–12 Petty Constables Presentments for Colyton 1683.
83. DRO Drake MSS 1700M/T70, T71.
84. DRO Diocesan Records Principal Registry Papers Basket A2574.
85. DRO QS Midsummer 1684 Certification from Colyton that Daniel Toupe received holy sacrament of Lord's Supper of the Church of England, in the parish church, according to his promise made to the Archdeacon at his visitation. This record also states that Colonel Pole at Honiton requested the Clerk of the Peace's favour for him.
86. Earle 1977: 13–17. I am lucky to have had access to the personal correspondence from Peter Earle to Tony Wrigley about the Sedgemoor rebels.
87. Earle 1977: 143; Underdown 1996: 26 also sees the rebellion as a class war given the absence of gentry and the documentation of remarks such as 'we will do the work without them, and then we will have their estates'.
88. Little 1956: 27.
89. DRO QSBb 1685 Midsummer.
90. Nuttall 1939: 19, John Pinney to Sarah Pinney 14/6/1685.
91. DRO QS 1/11 1667.
92. Wanklyn 1927: 195.
93. Earle 1977: 19.
94. DRO QSBb Michaelmas 1681; QSBb Misummer 1982.
95. Clifton 1984: 272.
96. DRO QSBb Midsummer 1685.
97. DRO QSBb Michaelmas 1685.
98. Clifton 1984: 252.
99. DRO Axminster Churchwarden's Account R7/2/Z3–7.
100. Macdonald Wigfield 1980.
101. Little 1956: 216.
102. Little 1956: 232.
103. Satchell's later details from Macdonald Wigfield 1980: 149.
104. DRO Drake MSS 1700M/W20.
105. Macdonald Wigfield 1980: 97. The other cases of Colyton men and the paragraphs to follow on Whicker and Bagwell are all based on Macdonald's Wigfield research. For more details see Macdonald Wigfield 1982.
106. Earle 1977: 110.
107. He had heavy debts of £300 which his brother became liable for. The brother lost the case to his widow who was given his small estate to sell. Macdonald Wigfield 1980: 114.
108. Yallop 1989: 109–127.
109. Pulman 1854: 434.
110. Earle 1977: 143–144; Macdonald Wigfield 1980.
111. Earle 1977: 144; Macdonald Wigfield 1980.
112. Earle 1977: 139.
113. Earle 1977: 143.
114. Earle 1977: 146–147.
115. Macdonald Wigfield 1980: 111.
116. UBSC, Pinney Papers, September 1685, Accounts and subsequent references throughout Azariah's correspondence.
117. Macdonald Wigfield 1980: 155.
118. Warne 1969: 93.
119. UBSC, Pinney Papers, Numbered Folders XX. Extract from 'An Account of the Ministers, Lecturers, Masters and Fellows of Colleges . . . who were ejected or silenced at the Restoration also by or Before the Act of Uniformity' by Edward Parry, London, 1713.

120. National Library of Wales, George Eyre Evans Bequest, Ref 13,595.
121. Brockett 1963: 145.
122. Eyre Evans 1908: 90; Warne 1969: 96.
123. Warne 1969: 96.
124. Pulman 1875: 507; Murch 1935: 322.
125. Eyre Evans 1898. There is also information in Windeatt 1885: 298–312 and W.B. Matthews 1911.
126. Brockett 1963: 81–82, 88.
127. Brockett 1963: 193.
128. Worth 1877: 276.
129. Anderson Smith 1901.
130. Jackson 1986: 341; Brockett 1958: 31–59.
131. Schofield 1972a: 122–125.
132. National Library of Wales, George Evans Bequest, Ref 13,595.
133. Warne 1969: 96.
134. Polwhele 1793: Vol. 3, 53, 314.
135. DRO Chanter 242B (1821) mentions that the Dissenters in Colyton, termed 'Independents', have two meeting houses, one of ancient standing, the other seceded from the first. An Independent chapel was built in 1814 for a working-class congregation. Their register contains just a few entries, relating to a small section of the population, which has now been incorporated into the reconstitution.
136. DRO 1687 Chanter 8298, Pearse vs Mayowe.
137. Spaeth 1985: 135.
138. Earle 1977: 225.
139. The power of ministers over the lives of their congregations is shown in the excommunication of Susanna Parr and Mary Allein in Exeter in 1657; see Edwards 1997: 1–16 and Crawford 1993: 152–153.
140. Underdown 1985b and in reply to this Morrill 1987: 451–467. Underdown 1987: 468–479 is the rejoinder. See also Underdown 1996 and the reply by Davie 1991: 1–31.
141. Stoyle 1994: 154.

Chapter 3. Industrious Dealers

1. Thirsk 1961: 70–88.
2. Levine 1977: 103–115.
3. Levine 1977: 106 analyses landholding by reference to DRO 123M/E77. He considered local trends in the woollen industry by some speculative observations as well as reference to Hoskins 1929. See the points made in the review article Outhwaite 1979: 229–237 on the inadequacy of the evidence for his case.
4. Levine 1977: 108n.
5. Wrigley and Schofield 1981; Wrigley, Davies, Oeppen, and Schofield, 1997.
6. Wrigley 1977b: 9–21.
7. Hoskins 1954: 63–64.
8. Wrightson and Levine 1979: 35.
9. Levine 1977: 116–126.
10. Arkell 1987: 23–48.
11. Hoskins 1938: 117.
12. Everitt 1990: 164.
13. G. Roberts 1847: ix. For good background on commercial shipping in south-west England see Childs 1997: 272–292.
14. Wanklyn 1927: 83.

15. Hoskins 1954: 106.
16. Hoskins 1954: 116.
17. Westcote 1630: 241.
18. Wolffe 1997: 191.
19. Clark and Slack 1976: 24–25.
20. Chartres 1973a and Chartres 1973b.
21. Dyer 1979: 132–133.
22. DRO QSBb Epiphany 1640.
23. 123M/E78 Late seventeenth-century survey book for the Borough of Colliton. As the DRO catalogue states this is a mistake: 'Borough' should read 'Manor'.
24. DRO QSBb Midsummer 1652 Case of Thomas Burges of Gittisham.
25. Polwhele 1797: Vol. 3, 309.
26. Lysons and Lysons 1822: 129–130.
27. Morris 1971: 245.
28. DRO QSBb Midsummer 1662.
29. WCS, Rev. J. Milles manuscript (microfilm).
30. Pearse-Chope 1918: 232. Presumably he was referring to 'gambadoes'—a large boot or gaitor attached to the saddle to protect the rider's legs and feet.
31. Hoskins 1938: 10.
32. DRO QSBb Michaelmas 1649.
33. The houses in Colyton are slate. Hoskins 1954: 260 says that Beer quarries were at their most active in the fifteenth and sixteenth centuries, drawing some workers from Colyton. They produced a fine stone much used for decorative interiors and may have stimulated local skill in stone dressing.
34. Pinneys letter 18/7/1684 to Mary Colemar.
35. DRO QSBb Michaelmas 1619.
36. DRO QSBb Ephiphany 1653.
37. DRO 3327A Add/PZ3 Microfilm MFC45, John Burwell's Book 1666– 1748, Ottery St Mary.
38. For a wider view see Zahedieh 1994: 257. For more details on Burwell and his trading activities with his brother, Henry see Tattersfield 1991: 124–125.
39. Tattersfield 1991: 15.
40. Morris 1971: 257.
41. DRO Exeter Quarter Sessions, Michaelmas 1693.
42. DRO QSBb 1647.
43. DRO QSBb Easter 1677.
44. DRO QSBb Michaelmas 1648.
45. Hoskins 1935: 89.
46. Wanklyn 1927: 81.
47. Tattersfield 1991: 230.
48. CRO PA/32/26 Receipts for for work at Shute, and PA/31/20 Receipts for expenses on Colyton Estates. Also DRO 1142B/EA32–38 Sampson accounts.
49. DRO 348A/PO13.
50. DRO 3327A/PO77.
51. DRO 235M/E2 Cash Book 1667.
52. F.J. Snell 1892: 254–259.
53. DRO QSBb Michaelmas 1656.
54. UBSC Pinney Papers, Azariah Pinney to Mary Colemar 18/7/1684.
55. UBSC Pinney Papers, Mary Pinney to Hester Pinney 9/9/1693.
56. UBSC Pinney Papers, Nathaniel Pinney to Hester Pinney 24/8/1696.
57. UBSC Pinney Papers, Bills.
58. UBSC Pinney Papers, Nathaniel Pinney to Hester Pinney 1/8/1720.

59. PRO PROB 4/1896.
60. DRO QSBb Epiphany 1673.
61. DRO QSBb 1640. Humphry Browne of Colyton, baker, was thought to have asked the wife of another baker to see pewter dishes for him.
62. DRO QSBb Easter 1638.
63. DRO QSBb Midsummer 1639.
64. DRO QSBb 1624, 1630 Epiphany.
65. Fortescue-Foulkes 1971: 48–71.
66. DRO QSBb 1648 Midsummer.
67. DRO PR518 Diocesan Records Surgeon's Licences 1661.
68. DRO PR518 Diocesan Records Surgeon's Licences. Letter to Francis Cooke from John Abbott 1675.
69. DRO PR518 20 June 1697.
70. DRO QS 499M/Q/57 List of Freeholders and Jurymen, Colyton hundred 1698. DRO Turner Collection 53/6 Box 16, Marriage Settlement of Ellis Veryard, batchelor of Physick, 1737.
71. Lysons and Lysons 1822: ccci. The reliability of the Lyson brothers as a source is validated by Hoskins 1966: 57.
72. PRO E179 96/183. See also Stoate 1979.
73. Lysons and Lysons 1822: ccc.
74. Pearse-Chope 1918: 77.
75. FF 22/10 (1). Haydon and Harrop 1997: 15 cite the Widworthy manorial court rolls which mention a fulling mill in Widworthy in 1549 belonging to the lord of the manor.
76. Fox 1999: 329.
77. DRO Feoffment found with 123M/E77.
78. Hoskins 1935: 12–13.
79. DRO QSBb Easter 1606, Robert Westcotte of Sidbury, tucker.
80. Blake 1915: 346.
81. Wyatt 1997: 45, 1/1/1623/4.
82. DRO 123M/E78.
83. Fortescue-Foulkes 1972: 111.
84. Seward 1970: 29–50. Export trends and other background information are to be found in Lipson 1921; Bowden 1956: 44–56; Clarke 1960; C. Wilson 1960: 209–221.
85. Coleman 1969: 417–429.
86. Levine 1977: 106–107.
87. Hoskins 1929.
88. Levine 1977: 108.
89. Hoskins 1929.
90. J.H. Bettey 1976: 297.
91. Westcote 1630: 60–61.
92. Inventory of William Hill, 2 June 1627. Copy in Colyton Library.
93. PCC 18 August 1629.
94. Roberts 1847–8: 56.
95. Gray 1988: 187–188.
96. Hamilton Rogers 1894: 70.
97. Lysons and Lysons 1822: ccci.
98. DRO QSBb Epiphany 1657; QSBb Easter 1658; and QSBb Epiphany 1658.
99. DRO QSBb Michaelmas 1636.
100. DRO QSBb Epiphany 1655.

101. DRO QSBb Epiphany 1639.
102. Bradley 1977: 63–94.
103. Schofield 1977: 95–126.
104. Personal communication with the late Dr H.J. Yallop, who helped me to distinguish types of wool-worker using his expert knowledge of local textiles.
105. Wrigley 1977b: 9–21. Kinvig 1915–16: 298 aruges that there was no change in woollen products in Devon at all over time.
106. Coleman 1969: 421–423.
107. CRO PE/29/1B.
108. PCC 8 June 1670 cited in Anderson Smith 1901. However, since it said 'wherein he liveth' it is questionable whether this was working or not.
109. White 1951: 12.
110. PCC will, 13 September 1651, cited in Anderson Smith 1901.
111. Thanks to Helene Sjunnesson, National Museum of Science and Technology, Stockholm, for her helpful comments on early paper production.
112. Pulman 1875: 507. This may be inaccurate as Havinden 1999: 343, based on Shorter's notes and published work, finds no seventeenth-century paper mills outside of Exeter and Plymouth and dates the earliest one in Colyton at 1732.
113. WCS Milles MS c.1750.
114. Cited in Hoare 1973: 50.
115. Shorter 1971: 27.
116. Shorter 1957: 153.
117. Stephens 1958: 135.
118. De Lacy Mann 1971: 104.
119. Hoskins 1935: 69.
120. Morris 1971: 245–246.
121. DRO 123M/E78, A Survey Book for the Burrough of Colliton.
122. Wyatt 1997: xxvii–xxvii.
123. The examples are in DRO 3483A/PO19. The use of settlement examinations and removal certificates to evaluate local migration patterns demands utmost care. See K.D.M. Snell 1985.
124. *A Tour through Great Britain by a Gentleman* (Daniel Defoe), 1721–4, reproduced by Pearse-Chope 1918: 147.
125. Ibid.: 145.
126. DRO 3483A/PO20.
127. Hoskins 1935: 76.
128. Chapman 1978: 12–14.
129. Colyton Church Rate 1726. Transcription by Devon and Cornwall Record Society. Copy kept at Cambridge Group.
130. Chapman 1978: 12–14. Chapman provides Vicary's goods as evidence of cloth-making but this equipment might be for cider-making. It is noticeable that most of the sergemakers mentioned in the inventories are nonconformists according to Eyre Evans: 1898.
131. WCS Milles MS c.1750. The replies for Colyton were sent in by Rev. George Anstis, the vicar.
132. Lysons and Lysons, 1822: 21.
133. P. Hunt 1984: 42.
134. Coxhead 1951: 19.
135. Lysons and Lysons 1822: ccciv.
136. DRO 3483A/PO13.
137. DRO EDRO/PO9–16.
138. DRO 3483A/PO16.

139. DRO 3327A/PO81 Ottery St Mary Settlement Examinations for the 1760s show many unemployed serge weavers.
140. W. Marshall 1796: Vol. I, 50 and Vancouver 1813: 567.
141. Polwhele 1797: Vol. III, 318.
142. Hoskins 1935: 55.
143. W.G. Maton, *Observations on the Western Counties of England, 1794–6*, reproduced in Pearse-Chope 1918: 234.
144. Cited in Hoare 1973: 8.
145. 1819 Poor Rate Assessment. Copy held at Cambridge Group.
146. Morris 1971: 135.
147. PRO 3483A/PO20.
148. DRO 43/18/1–3.
149. DRO 1466M/M1 1781.
150. CRO PA/32/37 receipts from the Shute Barton estate show that Philip Matthess purchased flax in bulk to manufacture ropes and twine. Crick 1908b: 344–352 gives details of hemp industry along the coast. See also Shorter 1950: 41–44.
151. Clapp 1982: 4–8.
152. Levine 1977: 108n.
153. Yallop 1992: 22–24.
154. Rapp 1975: 499–525. Thanks to Tony Antonovics for drawing this article to my attention.
155. Levey 1983: 17.
156. Blake 1915: 341–342.
157. Yallop 1992: 19.
158. Thirsk 1978.
159. Kussmaul 1990.
160. Spenceley 1973: 81–93.
161. Stoyle 1994: 202.
162. Emmison 1931: 102–116 mentions a memorandum from the parish of Eaton Socon in Befordshire which records the payment of 2d per week to a woman who taught poor children to make bone lace in 1596.
163. Palliser 1875: 356; Yallop 1992: 9.
164. Cited in Yallop 1992: 35.
165. Luton Museum and Art Gallery 1958: 10. For later examples see Buck 1964: 39–50. Kennett 1974: 111–118 describes lace-making in Bedford St Paul's workhouse.
166. De Vries 1993: 85–132.
167. E.L. Jones 1968: 58–71; Spenceley 1973: 81–93.
168. Westcote 1630: 61.
169. DRO QSBb Midsummer 1611.
170. DRO QSBb Epiphany 1621.
171. DRO QSBb Michaelmas 1628.
172. Cockburn 1976: 149. Devon Assizes at Exeter Castle, 12 March 1638.
173. DRO QSBb Midsummer 1638.
174. WCS Anstis microfilm 1743.
175. For further background information, see Levey 1983: 21.
176. Yallop 1992: 79–80.
177. Campbell 1969: 151.
178. DRO 235M/E3 Courtenay-Pole accounts.
179. DRO 235M/E2 Cash book 1658–1665.
180. Palliser 1875: 297–298. But Yallop 1992: 62–65 shows the commissioning of lace items of Royalists for political purposes.
181. Rose-Troup 1930: 229.

182. DRO QSBb Midsummer 1639.
183. Contained within the UBSC Pinney Papers.
184. UBSC Pinney Papers, Naomi Gay to Martha Gay (Nathaniel's fiancée) 1690.
185. Nuttall 1939; UBSC Pinney Papers.
186. Nicholls 1854.
187. Nuttall 1939: John Pinney to Rachel Pinney 28/3/1679.
188. A more detailed description of Hester and the Pinney's business is to be found in Sharpe 1999: 209–232.
189. Nuttall 1939: 14, John Pinney to Hester Pinney 4/9/1682.
190. Nuttall 1939: 36–37.
191. Nuttall 1939: 17–18, Jane Pinney to Sarah Pinney 11/6/1685.
192. Yallop 1992: 165; Palliser 1875: 363.
193. UBSC Pinney Papers, Accounts, September 1685.
194. This can be ascertained by comparison with Zahedieh 1994: 239–261.
195. Nuttall 1939: 24, August 1685.
196. UBSC Pinney Papers 1686 account.
197. UBSC Pinney Papers 1686 account.
198. UBSC Pinney Domestic Papers Dec 1690 Account for 1689.
199. Nuttall 1939: 20, John Pinney to Sarah Pinney 14/6/1685.
200. Nuttall 1939: 31, John Pinney to Sarah Pinney 30/11/1685.
201. The two Bristol retailers were Ann Christopher and Elizabeth Cupid, both widows and resident in the centre or port area of the city. See Ralph and Williams (eds) 1968: 87.
202. Personal communication with H.J. Yallop.
203. Inder 1971: 2.
204. Gill 1872: 216–243.
205. DRO QSBb Epiphany 1686.
206. Craig Muldrew's research has revealed the extent of credit networks in local economies. See Muldrew 1998.
207. DRO QSBb Epiphany 1638 concerns the case of money stolen from a Colyton mercer by an apprentice.
208. Wyatt 1997: 137, Samuel James 29 April 1682.
209. Cash 1966: 164–167, 23 January 1694/5.
210. DRO QSBb Easter 1662.
211. See Lemire 1997.
212. DRO QSBb Michaelmas 1681.
213. DRO QSBb Epiphany 1666.
214. DRO QS Order Book Michaelmas 1667.
215. All Hallows Museum, Honiton ND40 3/9/1689.
216. All Hallows Museum, Honiton DG 28/8/1690.
217. All Hallows Museum, Honiton ND42 28/12/1691.
218. All Hallows Museum, Honiton ND46 24/7/1697.
219. DRO 3327A/PO77 Ottery St Mary Settlement Certificate 1701.
220. DRO 239Aadd3/PO50.
221. DRO 2096A/PV3.
222. DRO 3483A/PO20.
223. DRO 3327A/PO81 1815 Ottery St Mary Settlement Case, Mary Salter.
224. Vancouver 1808: 394.
225. 1843 PP Children's Employment Commission (Trades and Manufactures) Vol. IX: 28.
226. DRO Chanter 869 Hallet vs Manly, Honiton 1663.
227. Spenceley 1973: 81–93, especially 85.

228. Hoskins 1929: 11 (1679); Hamilton 1878: 163 (1684).
229. Horn 1974: 779–796.
230. Earle 1989a: 328–353.
231. Sharpe 1995: 66–68.
282. Yallop 1992: 54.
233. Palliser 1875: 86–88.
234. Spenceley 1973: 81–93, especially 88. V&A 43/AZH Case of the Lace-makers in Relation to the Importance of Foreign Lace.
235. Hoare 1973: 53. Of course, women's domestic work may not have been fully enumerated in the census.
236. Yallop 1992: 67.
237. Yallop 1992: 69–70.
238. Morris 1971: 271. The poor quality of the thread was restated by Don Manuel Alvarez Espriella, alias Robert Southey, in 1802, reproduced in Pearse-Chope 1918: 309.
239. Levey 1983: 58.
240. Yallop, 1992: 84.
241. Lee 1904: 142.
242. DRO 3327A Ottery St Mary Vagrancy Orders 1769.
243. Climenson 1899: 59.
244. *Exeter's Flying Post* 14/11/1766.
245. See Travis 1993: 7–21.
246. P. Hunt 1984: 46.
247. *Exeter's Flying Post* 26/12/1816.
248. *Exeter's Flying Post* 27/2/1817.
249. Lysons and Lysons 1822: 281.
250. *Exeter's Flying Post* 3/7/1828; 28/8/1828; 27/8/1828; 10/7/1834; 18/12/1834.
251. DRO 20964A/PO21 Census of Sidbury taken 1829 between the months of August and November. The next revival came in the 1840s when lace came back into fashion after Queen Victoria's wedding dress was made from Honiton lace. PP Report XII 1843 on the Employment of Women and Children in Agriculture, found that 'lacemaking occupies a great many of the daughters of agricultural labourers in Devonshire and earnings are considerable'. Inder 1971: 9 reports that W.I. Gill of Colyton invented a new chromatic coloured lace which was first shown at a Society of Arts exhibition in 1849, and Hoare 1973, that in the early 1850s there were six or seven lace schools in Colyton. The trade was so lucrative that in PP Select Committee on Children's Employment: Factories, XVIII 1863: 251–252 the Reverend Mamerto Gueritz, vicar of Colyton, claimed that it diminished the wages of agricultural labourers, 'the farmers and employers giving less in proportion as the wives and daughters could earn something on which the family may be supported'.
252. Mies 1982a; Mies 1982b: 1–28.
253. Gill 1872: 216–243.
254. Prior 1985: 93–117.
255. DRO QSBb Epiphany 1689.
256. E.P. Thompson 1991: 504.
257. Hoskins 1935: 41.
258. DRO QSBb Epiphany 1646.
259. DRO QSBb Midsummer 1647.
260. DRO QSBb Epiphany 1641.
261. DRO 1669 Exeter QS, Book 65, folio 315. Thanks to Stuart Walsh for originally drawing my attention to this reference.

262. Nuttall 1939: 83, John Pinney to Hester Pinney 3/10/1691.
263. DRO QSBb Epiphany 1679.
264. Tattersfield 1991: 231.
265. Tattersfield 1991: 233.
266. FF 14/5g (1).
267. DRO Chanter 8298 Pearse vs Mayow 1687.
268. DRO QSBb Michaelmas 1648.
269. DRO QSBb Michaelmas 1648. See Bennett 1996.
270. Wanklyn 1927: 24–25.
271. Wanklyn 1927: 38, Trenchard 1994: 157–158.
272. A. Clark 1919: 12n.
273. DRO QSBb Michaelmas 1666 Petition of the inhabitants of Beer.
274. DRO QS 1666 144/3; QS 15/1/7.
275. The argument is similar here to that advance by Goldberg 1992, who finds women servants who move to urban areas for work to be involved in a low pressure (late marriage) regime.
276. Nuttall 1939: 67, Nathaniel Pinney to John Pinney 10/9/1689.
277. Underdown 1985a: 136.
278. There is an extensive literature on this subject. For a summary see Banks 1988.
279. Underdown 1985a: 116–137 argues that involvement in the market economy in dairying areas gave women a greater sense of independence.
280. DRO QSBb Michaelmas 1675.
281. Hoskins 1954: 366; Stoyle 1994: 82.
282. Davis 1987: 82. See also pp. 86–93 on male and female Protestant activities together after the Reformation. As Davis comments on p. 88, the reformed position on marriage provides a final illustration of the maxim 'together but unequal'.
283. DRO 3327A/PO81.
284. DRO 3327A/PO81.
285. For a recent view on this see Innes 1995.
286. C. Hill 1974: 99.
287. DRQ QSBb Easter 1614.
288. UBSC Pinney Papers, Nathaniel Pinney to Hester Pinney 6/2/1696.

Chapter 4. Resourcefulness

1. Fox 1975: 183.
2. Thirsk 1987.
3. DRO 123M/E/79 Petre Papers n.d. but probably eighteenth century.
4. White 1951: 2–8.
5. A copy of this is in the Feoffees Town Hall, FF 22/10.
6. Hoskins and Finberg 1952: 364–365.
7. Hoskins 1954: 373.
8. Hoskins and Finberg 1952: 396–404; 1953.
9. Fox 1972: 102.
10. Blake 1915: 344.
11. Polwhele 1797: Vol. II, 309.
12. FF 21/1–2.
13. PRO STAC 8 90/12 May 1607. DRO 123M/E87 Survey of Whitford 1613 in the Petre Papers details the tenants rights to common, furze, pasturing, etc.
14. SRO C/344.
15. DRO 1837 Diocesan Principal Registry List of Poor Rates.
16. Hoskins 1954: 63–64. The few inventories which describe the insides of the

houses of these large farmers show evidence of Hoskin's 'great rebuilding'. See Hoskins 1953: 44–59; G.V. Harrison 1985: 377–389.
    17. Hoskins 1954: 99.
    18. Clay 1981: 83.
    19. Bettey 1982: 46–47.
    20. DRO 3327A Add/Pz 3 Microfilm MFC 45 Manor Court Documents of Ottery St Mary.
    21. DRO Dean and Chapter Archives 2047–2055.
    22. Bettey 1982: 33–54.
    23. Hoskins 1938.
    24. Bouquet 1985: 27.
    25. Bouquet 1985: 30.
    26. In comparison with Whittle 1998: 35–40, the percentages of women tenants cited by Fox 1995: 133 suggests greater female landholding in east Devon than in other parts of country in the late medieval period, especially of farm holdings used for dairy production. In 1394–5 13 per cent of occupiers of farm holdings at Sidbury were women, 22 per cent at Dawlish in c.1385 and 20 per cent at Lympstone in 1525.
    27. However Williams 1963: 94–97 in field work on a north Devon village in 1958 found a lack of relationship between marriage and the transmission of farms. The transition from one generation to another was a protracted affair lasting several years on the farms of Ashworthy.
    28. For example, UBSC Pinney Papers, Azariah Pinney to John Pinney 18/7/1684; Nathaniel Pinney to John Pinney 10/9/1689.
    29. UBSC Pinney Papers, Nathaniel Pinney to Hester Pinney n.d. late 1690s.
    30. Hoskins 1938: 9.
    31. Hoskins 1954: 373.
    32. Hoskins 1954: 426.
    33. Fox 1972: 86.
    34. Fox 1975: 181–202.
    35. Fox 1972: 81–135.
    36. Lysons and Lysons 1822: 129 and 590 addendum.
    37. Kowaleski 1995: 41n., 328, 357.
    38. Kowaleski 1995: 369.
    39. Fox 1991: 157. For more details on farming improvements see Youings 1969: 164–174.
    40. Fox 1975: 192.
    41. Pearse-Chope 1918: 79.
    42. Norden 1728.
    43. MacCaffrey 1958: 162.
    44. G. Roberts 1848: 88.
    45. BM Add. MS 22/73.
    46. FF 16/10 (2).
    47. DRO Chanter 867.
    48. PRO E178/691; Mitchell Whitley 1903: 133–136.
    49. Kussmaul 1981: 98n.; Kussmaul 1990: 88.
    50. Marshall in 1796 cited in Hoskins 1938: 10.
    51. Fox 1972: 126.
    52. Gray 1995: xlv.
    53. Cheke 1959 describes the development of commercial cheese-making.
    54. Stanes 1990: 46.
    55. Polwhele 1797: Vol. III, 309.
    56. Finberg 1951.

57. Haydon and Harrop 1997: 67. For more details of the geology see Lysons and Lysons 1822: ccxlviii.
58. Stanes 1964: 272–273, 279–280. DRO Petre 123M/E80 is an interesting map of Borcombe, Colyton, a farm of just over 169 acres, showing land for improvement by marl or lyme by Lord Petre.
59. *DCNQ* Vol. V Part V (1909): 177.
60. See, for example, DRO DQS 15/1/3–4 Constables' Presentments report making of marl pits near Honiton and carrying away marl in 1664; DRO DQS 15/1/13 John Sheppard of Yarcombe presented for digging two dangerous marlepitts in the King's Highway in 1668.
61. PRO PROB 4 12717.
62. PRO PROB 4 9605.
63. PRO PROB 4 17599.
64. BM Add. MS 22/73.
65. Bettey 1973: 9–18 and Bettey 1976.
66. Fox 1995: 125–154.
67. Kowaleski 1990: 61.
68. Fox 1972: 126.
69. WCS Dean Milles Survey microfilm.
70. Wrigley 1977b: 9–21.
71. PCC 18 January 1691 cited in Anderson Smith 1901.
72. Hamer 1968: 61–69.
73. DRO 1466 M/M1Manor Court Book of Colyton 1770–85; DRO 1077M/ 6/1 Marker of Gittisham, Court book of Manor and Borough of Honiton still shows searchers and sealers of leather in the 1820s.
74. Hoare 1973: 50.
75. DRO QSBb Easter 1627.
76. DRO QSBb Epiphany 1634.
77. DRO QSBb Michaelmas 1698 mentions the tithingman lives in Shute and is a soapboiler.
78. ECR Chanter 867 1619 Raynolds v Bagwill mentions 3d per hogshead of cider being paid to the vicar 'by custom' for the last forty years. For more details see also Robinson 1981: 15–18; Lethbridge 1900: 142–194; and Hawker 1883: 237–245.
79. G.V. Harrison 1985: 377–389.
80. Nuttall 1939: 105; UBSC, John Pinney to Hester Pinney, October 1699.
81. PCC Will, 24 November 1642, cited in Anderson Smith 1901.
82. DRO Chanter 8298 Pearse vs Mayowe 1687. These cider houses would have been common in the region. DRO 1855A/PV1 Vestry Minute Book 1823–32 for Sidmouth records that parish pay to one John Evans was to be stopped on account or irregular conduct, he being found inebriated in a common unlicensed cider house.
83. Stanes 1969: 59. This estimate is by Stanes 1990: 61. Pearse-Chope 1918: 147 quotes from the *A Tour Through Great Britain By a Gentleman* (known to be Defoe, published in 1721–4 using material collected over the past three decades) which reported that 20,000 hogsheads of cider were being sent per year to London from Ottery alone.
84. DRO 1142B/EA37 Sampson account book 1755–81. In 1766 Sir George Yonge was elected MP for Honiton on a 'no-cider tax' vote. In celebration he provided a sheep to be roasted and seven hogsheads of cider. An ox adorned with flowers and gilt apples was led through the town attended by drums, fifes and a green banner of 'Yonge and Liberty and no Cider Tax'.
85. FF 17/7 Feoffees' Minute Book 1766–1853. Photocopy kept at Cambridge Group.

86. Fraser 1/94: 67.
87. UBSC Pinney Papers, 1737 Letter Folder 1X Box 19.
88. Coxhead 1972: 97–103; Ramsden 1945: 145–148.
89. Pearse-Chope 1918: 80.
90. Parkinson 1985: 19–62.
91. Parkinson 1985: 25.
92. Coxhead 1972: 98–99.
93. PCC Will, 27 April 1580, cited in Anderson Smith 1901.
94. These collections were not dated but William Pole died in 1635. His book was printed in 1791: 139–140.
95. Coxhead 1972: 99.
96. Dickinson 1987: 45.
97. The paragraphs to follow largely draw on Parkinson's excellent article. Parkinson 1985: 19–62.
98. Fox 1972: 108.
99. ECR Chanter 866 Reynolds vs Walrond 1636.
100. DRO 123M/E79.
101. SRO DD/WO62/6/5 John Willoughby vs Courtenay Pole 1678.
102. DRO Barnstaple Record Office 1142B/EC39 (1780).
103. *DCNQ* Vol. V Part V (1909).
104. Fox 1972: 97–98.
105. For example, see DRO QSBb Epiphany 1661 for a case with coneys and netts at Sidbury.
106. *Victoria County History of Dorset* 1908: 354.
107. Wanklyn 1927: 22–24.
108. Wanklyn 1927: 89.
109. Kowaleski 2000: 429–454; Gray 1988. An excellent short summary is provided by Gray 1999: 377–383.
110. Gray 1994.
111. Oswald 1985: 19–36.
112. F.J. Snell 1892: 258.
113. Gray 1988: 95. Noted by both the early seventeenth-century writers Westcote 1630 and Risdon 1811.
114. DRO QSBb Epiphany 1699.
115. DRO QSBb Michaelmas 1632.
116. Gray 1988: 53.
117. Risdon 1811: 34.
118. Risdon 1811: 31.
119. P. Hunt 1984: 44–45.
120. P. Hunt 1984: 48.
121. DRO 73A/PO44–348. Coffinswell Settlement Examinations 1740–1840.
122. Parkinson 1985: 40–45.
123. DRO QSBb Easter 1631.
124. DRO QSBb Midsummer 1656.
125. DRO QSBb Epiphany 1659–60.
126. DRO QS 96/9–10.
127. Fowles 1969: 70–71.
128. Fox 1995: 135.
129. Hoskins 1938: 178.
130. ECL Dean and Chapter 6056/2. Survey of the Manor of Colyton by James Bond 1696.
131. Chapple 1785: 17.

132. Schofield 1977: 95–126.
133. Blake 1915: 346.
134. DRO QSBb Michaelmas 1658.
135. DRO QSBb Midsummer 1684.
136. DRO QSBb Epiphany 1698.
137. DRO 1215A/PO1 Stockland Overseers' Account Book 1755. DRO 1077M/6/1 Marker of Gittisham 'The Act for enclosing lands in the manor and parish of Stockland' took place in 1807.
138. DRO 50M/I1–4 Papers of Marwood Tucker of Kilmington.
139. DRO 5301A/PV1 Vestry Minute Book for Kilmington 1732–1838.
140. P. Hunt 1984: 38–51.
141. Polwhele 1793: Vol. I, 309.
142. Cash 1966: 136–7. Inventory of Mary Bradforde of Colyton 3 June 1674.
143. BM Add. MS 22/73.
144. Skipp 1978.
145. Westcote 1630: 62.
146. ECL Dean and Chapter 6056/2.
147. BM Add. MS 22/73; A 1630 QSBb case from Membury involved a woman conveying empty and full bee butts.
148. *DCNQ* Vol. V, Part V (1909).
149. DRO QSBb 1629 Epiphany Case about John Mitchell of Northleigh.
150. DRO 3327A add2/PA1–2 Ottery St Mary Corporation Books give information for 1672 and 1691.
151. WCS Anstis MSS microfilm.
152. Gray 1995: xxiii, xlv. DRO 235M E5 Account Book of Sir William Pole 1718–23 also shows payments to local fisherwomen.
153. DRO QSBb Michaelmas 1624.
154. DRO 4262A/PO147. Eighteenth-century settlement certificates for Ottery St Mary (DRO 3327A/PO77) often mention 'potato ground'.
155. DRO EDRO/PO4.
156. Bettey 1976: 27.
157. Marshall 1796: Vol. V, 250–1.
158. Marshall 1796: Vol. V, 251.
159. This system seems peculiar to Dorset and east Devon and was described in Claridge's Dorsetshire' in Marshall 1796: Vol. V, 250–1. See also Claridge 1793.
160. As suggested in 'Stevenson's Dorsetshire' in Marshall 1796: Vol. V, 278–9, 'Some of the farmers let as many as a hundred dairy cows to three or four dairy-men; and in the last century it is probable that the labour of such a dairy was performed by half a dozen farmer's wives, who seemed it no drudgery, while they were permitted to consume a part of the produce'. See also Stevenson 1813.
161. DRO 365A/PO3–62.
162. DRO 365A/PO3–62 Case of William Baker 1846.
163. DRO 3483A/PO21 Examination for removal to Colyton.
164. EDRO/PO2 Membury settlement examination.
165. Polwhele 1797: Vol. 3, 309.
166. Vancouver 1813: 50.
167. DRO Chanter 866 Restorick vs Phillips.
168. Stanes 1964: 290, 297.
169. DRO Chanter 880, Gittisham. Two cases from other areas of the West Country reflect a preference for girls. DRO QSBb Easter 1674 Case of Thomas Austey of Clovelly regarding poor apprentices. He 'hath not any imployment for the said boy but would willingly take a maid'. He offered to pay 40s towards binding the boy elsewhere.

Similarly in the DRO QS Order Book Easter 1678 John Satterly had been bound apprentice in Moretonhampstead but his master Mr Tothill wanted to take a girl apprentice instead, which may reflect the fact that girls' role was seen as important in dairying (or that she was to be an indoor servant).

170. DRO QSBb Epiphany 1640.
171. DRO QSBb Midsummer 1645.
172. DRO QSBb Midsummer 1648.
173. Pounds 1973: 55–75.
174. Howkins 1994: 55. Personal communication from Alun Howkins 15/1/99.
175. Dunning and Bicknell DRO337 add 2/1/d George Harris farm account 1782.
176. DRO 3327A/PO91 Settlement case about Hosannah Clarke 1840.
177. For further details see Sharpe 1988: 152.
178. DRO EDRO/PO2.
179. PP Accounts and Papers (12), Volume 1, 1833: 124–125.
180. DRO 3483A/PO20.
181. CRO PA/32/27–29.
182. The reconstitution of Shute was carried out by Roger Sellman and presented to the Cambridge Group.
183. For further discussion of illegitimacy see Chapter 7.
184. FP Report on the employment of women and children in agriculture XII: 13.
185. K.D.M. Snell 1985: 414. Snell also stressed the importance of hiring fairs which provide a benchmark of comparison for wage rates. But fairs do not seem to have been the main method of recruitment in Devon. Marshall 1796: Vol. II, 108 said that there was no fixed time or place for hiring servants: 'When a servant is out of place, he makes enquiries among his acquaintances, and goes round to the farm houses to offer himself'. This direct, word-of-mouth approach seems to have been the main way of finding jobs in Colyton.
186. Vancouver 1808: 574.
187. Hoskins 1938: 95–98.
188. ECL Dean and Chapter Item 846.
189. Vancouver 1808: 53, 167–170.
190. This is shown by the receipts in DRO 1142B/EA Sampson Account Book for 1755–81.
191. Polwhele 1797: Vol. II, 278, 309.
192. Body 1965: 222–226.
193. P. Hunt 1984: 38–51.
194. Hoare 1973.
195. Lysons and Lysons 1822: 130.
196. Quoted in Hoare 1973: 20.
197. Minchinton 1969: 176.

Chapter 5. Demographic Experiences

1. The comprehensive results of reconstitutions carried out in many different areas of England are to be found in Wrigley, Davies, Oeppen and Schofield 1997. See Galley 1998 for a detailed examination of York.
2. K.D.M. Snell 1985: 62–63.
3. See for example, Gugler 1981: 49–64; Harriss and Watson 1987: 85–115; Pearson 1987: 116–130; Townshend and Momsen 1987: 27–82; Muntemba 1988: 407–428.
4. There are some exceptions, for example R. Thompson 1974a: 153–165. M. Anderson 1976: 55–78 described rural sex ratios and their effects on female marriage

chances and marriage ages. Souden 1984a: 133–168 and Souden 1987: 292–332 estimated sex ratios in burial registers and listings. Unbalanced populations are viewed as being of great significance in the demographic history of early America: see Walsh 1979: 126–152; Wells 1975; Moller 1945: 113–153. R. Thompson 1974a: 153–165 and Thompson 1974b extends this association but I am not happy with his association between a decline in the position of women in formal employment and low sex ratios, or his belief that female surplus necessarily gives rise to male chauvinism, patriarchy and declining social position of women.

5. Weir 1984: 340–354.

6. For the theoretical basis of this for the nineteenth century, see M. Anderson 1984: 377–393.

7. Souden 1981: 158. See also De Vries 1984: 178, 186 and van der Woude 1982: 55–75 on urban unbalanced sex ratios in the European context. Interestingly, Colyton had a similar sex ratio to burial to nearby Lyme Regis in 1697 at 70.1. Finlay 1981b: 141–142 believed that there was a surplus of males in the whole population in the early seventeenth century from measuring sex ratios at burial. He followed R. Thompson 1974a: 153–165 in believing that this changed to a female surplus in the second half of the century. This was indicated by Gregory King's findings from the Marriage Duty Act returns of 1694 that the ratio in London was 77, in cities and market towns 89, and in villages and hamlets 101. The ratio for the whole county for the population aged over 16 was 94.8. Souden 1987: 292–332 shows that predominantly arable villages in the south-east of England tended to be male-dominated. Dobson 1997: 129 finds the textile towns of North Essex have persistent outmigration of males in the seventeenth century. Kussmaul 1990 elucidates the wider patterns here.

8. Souden 1981: 142–144. Other work on Devon parishes confirms the pattern. Annett 1976: 69–125 found that there was emigration of young men from North Molton parish due to a lack of steady employment in the wool trade. He associated this with a drop in the birth rate after 1676. Finch 1979: 12–22 found a correlation between population fall and lack of work opportunities for able-bodied men in Hartland.

9. FF 15/1 Settlement certificates. DRO QS 7/1–42 Constables presentments for the hundred of Colyton.

10. Hindle 1998b: 71–91.

11. FF 15/1 and for the following cases.

12. This effect will be considered in greater detail below. The obverse situation has been found for London during this period: see Brodsky Elliott 1978: 222; Brodsky Elliott 1986: 122–154. The sex ratio in early seventeenth-century London was skewed towards males and the result seems to have been late male marriage and early female marriage for London-born women. These links have not been proven, however. Walsh 1979: 126–152 describes the extremely skewed sex ratio in early America as leading to native women marrying very early, between the ages of 16 and nineteen, and three widows marrying again for every widower who was able to marry again. For a more recent contrast with Colyton, Brody 1973: 95 describes the social problems of the skewed sex ratio in rural Ireland in the twentieth century. In the Irish census of 1956 the number of men per thousand women varied from 820 to 927. Irish females have always been more mobile than men in the twentieth century. High rates of male celibacy combined with low female marriage ages in local populations.

13. Erikkson and Rogers 1978 found an older woman/younger man marriage pattern among the propertyless farm labourers of east-central Sweden in the nineteenth century. This pattern has often been related to conscious fertility restraint, as the researches of the nineteenth-century rural sociologist Sundt showed. See Drake 1969.

14. There are comparisons here with the Weald of Kent in the early modern period: see Zell 1994.

15. Disruption in economic conditions in the wool areas has been seen as a major cause of emigration, but Salerno 1979: 31–52 found, by looking at emigrants leaving Wiltshire through a combination of passenger lists and parish records, that only 10 per cent of emigrants in the 1630s and 14 per cent in the 1650s were from textile-related trades. He suggested that there was usually a diverse occupational structure within textile areas which is certainly borne out by the Colyton picture.

16. DRO cited in Gray 1988: 179.

17. DRO 67A/PW1.

18. Hollingsworth 1969: 191 suggested such a scenario at an early stage of the Colyton analysis and with similar acumen pointed out that the nonconformity situation in the parish was an important consideration in understanding the demographic picture.

19. Allen 1981 showed in his study of migration to early America from Hingham in Norfolk, that periodic recurrence of plague frequently preceded a wave of emigration.

20. Gemery 1980: 179–231; Wrigley and Schofield 1981: especially 219–228.

21. Souden 1981: 23, 208.

22. Finlay 1976: 168–172 finds the sex ratio of the living population to be more skewed than the population at burial. His remark on pp. 168–169 that 'The historiography of the problem of the sex ratio in seventeenth-century England is not well known' still rings true. See also Finlay 1981b: 141–142.

23. Wrigley 1977c: 22–29.

24. FF 15/1 (1).

25. FF 15/1 (1).

26. FF 14/1b–k (1).

27. Campbell 1959: 63–89.

28. Galenson 1978: 499–540 and rebuttal by Campbell 1979: 264–284. Galenson 1981 estimated that there was a three to one ratio of men to women. Cressy 1987: 129 argues that it would cost between £30 and £50 for a family to emigrate, which was within the reach of modest artisans and husbandmen.

29. DSRO B7/M9/1–28. I am indebted to David Souden for pointing out the existence of these documents.

30. Widdowson 1969: 183–196 makes an interesting study of the transference of folklore from Devon to Newfoundland.

31. ECR Chanter 869 1663. See Stretton 1998: 149 on the origins of 'Ffloyde'.

32. Derouet 1980: 3–41 analysed demographic behaviour in France by comparing better-off with poorer peasants. Jutikkala 1987 used parish registers to differentiate the population of Turku in Finland by socio-economic class for the years 1826–44. He found no differences in fertility factors and some slight differences in mortality factors. Knodel 1988 used the Ortsippenbuch genealogies to produce reconstitutions of fourteen different villages in diverse districts of Germany. He was then able to analyse demographic change by occupational groups. The results presented here are merely suggestive in comparison with the scope of the work done by Knodel. The most significant attempt to analyse demographic data in this way in the British context is Reay 1996 and Hudson and King 2000: 706–741, who compared age of marriage by status in two textile townships. Differences were slight but they found later marriage for the wealthiest people involved in textiles and earlier marriage for the proletarianised textile workers.

33. Weir 1984: 340–354, Schofield 1985: 2–20.

34. Goldstone 1986: 5–33. He is supported by proto-industrial theorists. See for example Medick 1976: 291–315; Levine 1977.

35. K.D.M. Snell 1985: 349; Schofield 1985: 2–20.

36. The number of cases for women and men differ slightly from those produced by the Cambridge Group and used by Wrigley and Schofield. A few cases were removed

because a woman's baptism appears to have been incorrectly linked to a marriage. Some cases were added; six were put into the women's cohort for 1650–99, for example. This is because marriages which were discovered in another parish or mentioned in another document could be linked. The 1800–37 cohort is well short of cases since only a section of this cohort's FRFs were used in this study and no attempt was made to take the data through to 1849. There is a general the problem of small samples in this data. Where there were five or less cases the result has been omitted as it was not felt to be representative. This is a particular difficulty with the craft and labourer groups for women and men in the 1650–1749 period, and the pattern produced tends to reflect arbitrary figures which swing to an undue extent. This is unavoidable considering the nature of the enquiry into a single community.

37. Similar patterns have been found in Scandinavia. See Drake 1969.

38. Wrigley 1987: 248.

39. Although 'gentry' here embraces a wide group of the elite of the parish, comparison can be made with Hollingworth 1964: especially 8–27. He found age at marriage of peers rising over time from the mid-sixteenth century to the mid-twentieth century, and a considerable proportion of peers remaining celibate. He thought that the nobility married later than the rest of the population and argued for 'the general possibility that in every era age at marriage rises with social class'. This argument loosely holds for men in Colyton. Stone and Stone 1984: especially 86–104, found a rise in age of marriage and in the likelihood of never marrying as well as a fall in remarriage for heirs occurring in the second half of the seventeenth century.

40. It is instructive to compare the situation in Colyton with that of New England. Greven 1970: 246 finds that in Andover fathers were increasingly more likely to settle land on one son but fathers helped their brothers to buy land outside of Andover. On p. 270n he makes suggestive comments linking family life with politics and religion especially for displaced younger sons.

41. See Turner 1963 for a reconstruction of a marriage of a Colyton couple who were both illegitimate: Edward Deane, labourer, born 1570, and Katherine Manly.

42. Knodel 1988: 130n. found similarity in age of marriage across occupational categories in the German reconstitutions—especially for men—but in so far as there is a consistent pattern, labourers and their wives married later than other villagers. They may have sometimes opted for older wives who had had longer to accumulate their savings. He does not, however, attempt to measure 'poor' as distinct from 'proletarian' groups. He found that wives ages were more closely lined to occupation than husbands. This supports Hajnal 1982: 449–494, who also found a later age at marriage for labourers' wives than farmers' wives which, he believed was due to the labouring females spending a longer period in service before marriage.

43. Knodel 1988: 153–184 finds, based on the Ortsippenbuch from fourteen villages, that widowers had more chance of remarriage than widows, but there was little difference in the trends found for artisans, peasants or proletarians.

44. Wrigley and Schofield 1981: 211–227. Their intervals to marriage were confirmed by Holderness 1984: 423–442 and Griffith 1980: 479–496. Similar intervals were found in Salisbury. See Wright 1982: 231. By contrast, Brodsky Elliot 1978: 124 found that in London, where marriages of younger men and older women were common, remarriage was rapid for widows of craftsmen and tradesmen. A new interpretation of remarriage in Banbury is provided by Lauricella 1998.

45. Wrigley, Davies, Oeppen and Schofield 1997: 171–173.

46. Todd 1983: 140–146 and Todd 1985: 54–92 found for Abingdon in Berkshire that remarriage rates fell by half during the period 1540–1720. Whereas half of the widows remarried in the sixteenth century, only a quarter of them did so in the

period 1660–1720. She argued that this was due in part to increasing longevity of first marriages and in part to a shift in public opinion so that will-makers penalised remarryers, but the main reason was a transformation in institutionalised poor relief with widows and children being the main beneficiaries. See also Boulton 1990: 323–355 and the rejoinder by Todd 1994: 421–450. Griffith 1980: 479–496 also found that poor relief reduced the pressure to remarry in Aldenham.

47. Robin 1987: 307–342 finds that, by contrast, in nineteenth century Colyton widowhood alone did not qualify for assistance, but if a woman had dependent children and did not earn enough by lace-making to support them, relief would be provided for her.

48. Wrigley 1966a: 82–109. For a recent view see Vann 1999: 1–14, who raises the vexing question of why the ability to limit would have been lost.

49. For example, Hollingsworth 1969: 193–194 wrote that 'The class that married in Colyton parish church was highly selective at the period when family limitation and late marriage appear in the reconstituted family records, and one must wonder as to their social status and whether they even adhered strictly to the Anglian forms for the whole of their married lives'. For a detailed examination of the accuracy of the parish register, see Chapter 1.

50. Henry 1956: 75–81.

51. Morrow 1978: 419–436 and reply by Wrigley 1978: 429–436. In the response to Morrow in Wrigley and Schofield 1981: 433, Wrigley says 'I have sometimes thought that it would have captured the spirit of the discussion of the question in my original article if I had added a question mark at the end of the title'.

52. Wrigley, Davies, Oeppen and Schofield 1997: 449 revise their earlier assumptions that marital fertility was constant in early modern England. They argue that it rose in the eighteenth century thus magnifying changes in marriage age and fertility outside marriage, all of which were causing overall fertility to rise to a high peak in the nineteenth century. See p. 461 for affirmation of the family limitation argument for Colyton. The marital fertility stance represents a revision of the position of Wrigley 1981: 137–185, where the comment was made on p. 141: 'present evidence is strongly against the possibility that changes in marital fertility can take us far towards an explanation of the huge rise in fertility over all'. Knodel 1988: 247n. was in agreement for the period before 1800. The earlier work on the role of marital fertility in population change in England drew reinforcement from the research of Wilson. He claimed that birth intervals were similar in all places through time and could not be considered an important factor in population change, but his work concerned comparison between reconstituted communities and he did not attempt to measure marital fertility differences between communities. See C. Wilson 1982. See also Wrigley and Schofield 1983: 151–184, especially 168–175.

53. For example Scott Smith 1979 finds some family limitation in Hingham 1691–1715.

54. Wilson 1982: 151, 164–165. Fildes 1986: 352 found that the average age of weaning fell from 18 months in the early sixteenth century to 7.25 months by the late eighteenth century in England, but there was no change in Colyton.

55. Wenlock and Wenlock 1981: 261–8 in a study of a clinic in Europe commented that the very long breast-feeding period of 25–30 months extended birth intervals to create a 34–39 month cycle of births. Cumulative effects were also noticeable in undernourished women as the child demanded the breast more often to obtain its energy intake. This raises the prolactin levels and extends amenhorrea. Although Bongaarts 1980: 564–570 argues 'moderate chronic' malnutrition has only a minor effect on fertility, he also finds that every two months of breast-feeding produces an extra month of amenorrhoea. Knodel 1988 found very substantial variations in

marital fertility due to infant feeding practices, with high fertility in Bavaria where breast-feeding was not practised.

56. Dupaquier and Lachiver 1969: 1391–1406. As Wilson has noted, this technique can be problematic. See the discussion of levels of 'M' and 'm' in Wrigley, Davies, Oeppen and Schofield 1997: 457–461.

57. Flandrin 1976. But see Chapter 7 for the evidence of wet nursing in Colyton.

58. Since there was little change in these class-specific patterns of marital fertility between the first and second halves of the seventeenth century, the explanation given by Morrow 1978: 419–436 can be discounted. He argued that plague was responsible for family limitation in Colyton as it severely reduced the fecundity of survivors, giving rise to haemorrhaging, abortion and premature births. See also the rejoinder by Wrigley 1978: 429–436.

59. A. Maclaren 1984 argues that abortion was used as a birth control method despite being extra-legal. See also A. Maclaren 1981: 224–237 and A. Maclaren 1990. Knight 1977: 57–68 makes an argument along similar lines. Wrightson 1975a: 10–21, however, found in a study of Essex assize records that infanticide was a minority practice used only for the disposal of unwanted illegitimate babies in the early seventeenth century. However, see Gowing 1997: 87–115. Considering other time periods and geographical areas, Biller 1982: 3–26 argued for the adoption of a 'contraceptive mentality' in early medieval times and thought that the use of coitus interruptus was encouraged by parish priests. Harris and Ross 1987, who make cross cultural comparisons, see fertility as controllable in pre-industrial populations and believe 'natural' fertility is a misrepresentation.

60. DRO QSBb Michaelmas 1651.

61. DRO QSBb Midsummer 1682.

62. Riddle 1997.

63. Van der Walle 1997: 184 disagrees with Riddle. He argues that 'that plant substances were taken primarily to stimulate the natural processes of menstruation, and that their use as abortifacients was a rare deviation from the norm'. Rublack 1996: 57–80 finds coitus interruptus and self-abortion, using penny royal, to be very common.

64. DRO 1700M/W20 Will of Roger Satchell 7/10/1684.

65. G. Roberts 1848: 3.

66. Santow 1993: 772.

67. Cited in Santow 1995: 33. However, Wrigley, Davies, Oeppen and Schofield 1997: 493 argue the quantitative section of Santow's article rests upon a misapprehension from data processing.

68. The relationship between breast-feeding and low infant mortality is well established. See Knodel and van der Walle 1967: 109–132; R.E. Jones 1976: 305–318; R.E. Jones 1980: 239–250; Schofield and Wrigley 1979: 61–95; Lithell 1981: 182–194. Fildes 1980: 313–324 found that improvements in neo-natal feeding practices led to a fall in infant mortality in the second half of the seventeenth century in England.

69. Wrigley, Davies, Oeppen and Schofield 1997: 217, 273.

70. Wrigley 1968: 546–580.

71. Wrigley, Davies, Oeppen and Schofield 1997: 69, 72.

72. For a comparative attempt to analyse child mortality by status see Finlay 1981a: 67–80.

73. Knodel 1988: 74n.

74. Wall 1981a: 119–140 found no differential neglect of infants according to gender.

75. Perrenoud 1981: 89–104.

76. Polwhele 1793 Vol. III, 309–310.

77. WCS Dean Milles Survey
78. Dobson 1997: 130, 223, 225.
79. Pearse-Chope 1918: 145 (*A Tour through Great Britain by a Gentleman* (Daniel Defoe) published 1721–4). See also Pearse-Chope 1918: 309 (Don Manuel Alvarez Espriella alias Robert Southey 1802).
80. Polwhele 1793: Vol. I, 16.
81. FF 14/1b–k (1).
82. DRO 1466M/M1 1775.
83. Wrigley, Davies, Oeppen and Schofield 1997: 351.
84. Wrigley 1968: 271. See the figures in Levine and Wrightson 1991: 201. For an attempt to analyse death rates by age, class and gender see Perrenoud 1981: 89–104.
85. P.A. Slack 1972: 45–47.
86. Slack 1972: 49.
87. Slack 1972: 4–57.
88. Oswald 1977: 73–116.
89. Slack 1972: 57.
90. Slack 1972: 68.
91. Chambers 1969: 18–28.
92. Crafts and Ireland 1976: 598–623, especially 618.
93. Wrigley, Davies, Oeppen and Schofield 1997: 272–273.
94. Wrigley 1987: 264, 266.
95. Bailey 1996: 1–19. The research of Hatcher supports this: see Hatcher 1977 and Hatcher 1994: 3–25.
96. Lestaeghe 1980: 542.
97. Wrigley, Davies, Oeppen and Schofield 1997: 551.
98. G. Roberts 1848: 31–32, 59–64, 63–64, 96.
99. W. Hunt 1983: 83–84.
100. Vann and Eversley 1992: 128, 244.
101. Sharpe 1999: 209–232.

Chapter 6. Inside the Parish

1. See FF 14/1b–k (1).
2. DRO QSBb Epiphany 1634.
3. Morrill and Walter 1985: 137–165. For these processes in another detailed study of a parish see Nair 1988.
4. Wrightston and Levine 1979.
5. W. Hunt 1983.
6. Ingram 1985: 159.
7. Ingram 1984: 189.
8. Spufford 1995.
9. See also Spufford 1985: 41–57. See these debates summarised in the new postscript 'Terling Revisited' in Wrightson and Levine 1995: 197–221.
10. For example, see DRO 96M Rolle papers Box 33/1 Manor Court of Beer Presentments.
11. However, see Griffiths 1980: 260–283 and C. Harrison 1997: 43–59. The latter provides a straightforward revision of any idea that courts were a 'moribund jurisdiction' after the medieval period. I am grateful to Steve Hindle for providing these references.
12. DRO 3327A Add/Pz 3 Microfilm MFC 45 Lord of the Manor of Ottery St Mary.
13. DRO 3327 add.b/567 Ottery St Mary Manor Book 1795–1837.

14. DRO 1466M/M1 Manor Court Book for Colyton 1770–85.
15. UBSC Pinney Papers Folder 1X Box 20; Nathaniel Pinney to Hester Pinney 7/2/1701.
16. Wolffe 1997: 44.
17. DRO QSBb 1631. See S.K. Roberts 1985 for more details on the administrative structure.
18. DRO QSBb 1607; DRO 235M/E3 the Courtenay-Pole papers for 1670 mention 'sessions' at Colyton and Ottery.
19. SRO Trevelyn MSS 55/7/28.
20. SRO Trevelyn MSS 55/7/50.
21. DRO QSBb Michaelmas 1648.
22. W. Hunt 1983: 232. See also Jordan 1959.
23. WCS Anstiss MSS 1743.
24. Lysons and Lysons 1822: 590 Addendum.
25. National Trust 1996: 7.
26. DRO 1236A add2/PV1 Shute Vestry Book 1789–1803.
27. S. King 1997: 318–338.
28. DRO QSBb Easter 1661. For more detail see Henning 1983: 201–220.
29. Wilkin 1924b: 272.
30. Hoskins 1954: 187.
31. S.K. Roberts 1985: 158. The surviving wills of Devon justices that have survived show a similar drop in private bequests.
32. Brushfield 1899: 199–284.
33. Whitham 1984: 107–108. Another example is Great Torrington. PP Report of the Commissioners concerning Charities . . . The Public Charities of Great Torrington, Devon 1846: 3–4.
34. DRO QSBb Michaelmas 1607.
35. Wales 1984: 351–404; Wales n.d. Also see Slack 1988: especially 138–161. FF 16/8 (2).
36. ECR Starr vs Manson 1619.
37. DRO QSBb Midsummer 1631.
38. DRO QSBb Epiphany 1630.
39. DRO QSBb Michaelmas 1640.
40. DRO FF 16/15a–b (2).
41. 1646 (filed in DRO QSBb Epiphany 1648).
42. DRO QS 96/5 Petition of maimed soldier John Ffitz 1674.
43. Clark and Slack 1976: 150.
44. DRO QSBb Epiphany 1662. However we cannot be sure that such statements always come from the Puritan-minded. Loyal Anglicans could also use the moral language of the reformation of manners.
45. DRO QS1/11.
46. DRO DSQ 15/20/1–19.
47. DRO QSBb Easter 1663.
48. DRO QS Order Book of Midsummer 1668.
49. DRO QS 62/15/1/8; QS 62/15/2/1–2, 4–5; QS 62/15/13/1.
50. DRO QS Order Book 1666.
51. DRO QS Order Book Epiphany 1665.
52. DRO QS Order Book Epiphany 1671.
53. DRO QSBb Order Book 1/11 Easter 1671; Epiphany 1673; Easter 1674.
54. DRO QS Order Book Easter 1675.
55. DRO QSBb Michaelmas 1681.

56. 'Twenty Lessons to be Learned from London's Late Burning Written by Mr JP' (1666): 27.
57. DRO QSBb Midsummer 1684.
58. Hindle 1996: 125–149; Hindle 1998a: 67–96; and especially Hindle 2000.
59. DRO QS Order Books Michaelmas 1689.
60. DRO QS Order Books Michaelmas 1690 Petition of Edward Warden.
61. DRO QSBb 1693.
62. Macfarlane 1970.
63. FF 14/1bb–k (1) Feoffee Bailiff's Accounts 1659–1699.
64. Robin 1987: 7.
65. Levine and Wrightson 1991: 378.
66. FF 14/9a (1).
67. Overseers' records used were all in the DRO. Reference numbers as follows: 2954A/PO1, 2141A/PO3, 1237A/PO20, 2452M/A/PO1, 1633A/PO1, EDRO/PO1, 1235A/PO3, 1061/PW1, 2404A/PO1, 2165A/PO1, 1213A/PO1, 3167A/PO1, EDRO/PO2, 2922A/PO2, EDRO/PO2, 2994A/PO1–3, 3239A/PO1, 1927A/PO1, 271A/PO1, 285A/PO1, 1981A/PO1, 3420A/PO1, 2288A/PO1, 1464A/PO1, 1710A/PO1, 1095/PW1. The Colyton account is FF 14/9a–b (1). Compton census details appeared in Stanes 1974 and 1975: 18–27 and 4–17. While other population estimates are not readily available, there are inherent problems with using Compton census figures since, for example, the number given for Colyton does not seem to have been accurate. In this case the figures at least represent 'like' estimates in that the number of 'conformists', 'papists' and 'non-conformists' have been added together to produce the population excluding children.
68. The very early poor account of one of these sample parishes was analysed in Tovt 1928. In 1641, of twenty-eight people who received regular relief eight were widows. Seven men received regular payments but they were on average much lower than payments to women. Whereas most payments went to the elderly at the beginning of the seventeenth century, later on more children seemed to be listed.
69. Wales 1984: 351–404 shows for sample years taken from different Norfolk parishes that women frequently formed up to at least 60 per cent of parish paupers in the seventeenth century. Newman Brown 1984: 405–420 presents a complementary picture for Aldenham in Hertfordshire from 1630 to 1690 when the largest category of regular recipients were widows or widowers who accounted for more than 20 per cent of household heads. They made up about 60 per cent of regular adult collectioners and received a larger proportion than that of the relief disbursed. As was apparent in Colyton, little relief was distributed to young adults. J.E. Smith 1984: 429–450 covered a wider time period when analysing Lichfield in 1695, Cardington in 1782, Corfe Castle in 1790 and Ardleigh in 1796, and found a disproportionate number of widow-headed households were in receipt of poor relief.
70. Wales 1984: 351–404. This may not have included rent. A. Clark 1919: 73, 79 thought 2s a realistic figure.
71. DRO R7/2/Z3–7 Axminster Churchwarden's Account.
72. J.S. Taylor 1966: 122.
73. Hoskins 1954: 244.
74. See Anderson Smith 1901. PCC Wills, 14 October 1587, 7 November 1614, 8 June 1670; see also FF 15/12 (1), 28 July 1688. Isaac Grigg's will is mentioned in the Extract from the Parliamentary Report 1820: Hundred of Colyton, Devon—Parish Lands.
75. Todd 1983 finds a similar picture to that in Colyton. The poor relief structures were organised for women to be independent householders; wills made provision for it, almshouses were purposely built with small units for separate residency, or alternatively,

women were independent lodgers within people's houses. Wright 1982, however, found that in this earlier period single residency of women was usually a temporary arrangement.

76. FF 14/1b–k (1), 17/10 (4).
77. The details are contained in PRO E/179/245/14(4), PCC 1 June 1678; 1726 Colyton Church Rate. Devon and Cornwall Record Society Transcription. Wall 1981b: 303–320 in his analysis of listings finds that single and widowed men of all ages were less likely to be heading their own household than women in these groups. By contrast, however, Cooper 1986 found that in the poll tax taken in King's Lynn men were most likely to be solitaries and that living alone was a 'widespread and accepted condition'. It remains to be seen whether one reason for this pattern could have been a sex ratio skewed towards men in the eastern counties.
78. DRO 123M/L747.
79. SRO DD/WO Box 45 C/344.
80. J.T. Smith 1985: 33–34 describes these structures.
81. DRO Chanter 11042/3 1592.
82. Quoted in Eden 1797: 41.
83. L.C.C. n.d.: 92. Wall 1972: 159–203 suggests that King tabulated several families sharing a common roof.
84. CRO PE/29/1B.
85. DRO QSBb Michaelmas 1607.
86. Best 1857: 125.
87. Keene 1987 described subdivision of buildings like stables and outhouses in poor districts of London where single and widowed women were inmates.
88. DRO 3483A/PO13.
89. DRO EDRO/PO9–16.
90. DRO 3483A/PO20.
91. DRO 1142/BEA 32–38.
92. Lysons and Lysons 1822: 590 Addendum.
93. Pulman 1854: 446; see also DRO Chanter 232 for 1779.
94. DRO QSBb Midsummer 1629.
95. Gowers 1970: 254–255.
96. DRO QSBb Midsummer 1629.
97. Cash 1966: 136.
98. DRO Chanter 8298 Membury in 1687.
99. White 1951: 11.
100. DRO Diocesan Records PR510.
101. DRO Diocesan Records PR510 Letter from Thomas Tanner on behalf of Mr Butter, 1672.
102. DRO Diocesan Records PR510 Letter from Thomas Tanner to Francis Cook the younger, 1673.
103. Brockett 1958: 32–59.
104. Eyre Evans 1898.
105. DRO 3483A/PE1.
106. DRO 3483A/PO13.
107. DRO 3483A/PO23.
108. DRO 3483/PO15.
109. PP Abstract of Answers and Returns, 'An Act for Procuring Returns Relative to the Expense and Maintenance of the Poor in England' (1803) VIII Devon: 98–116.
110. Phelps-Brown and Hopkins 1956: 179–196.
111. DRO 3483A/PO12.

112. Accounts do exist of collections for the poor rate. They are catalogued DRO 3483A/PO1–4.
113. J.S. Taylor 1966. See also Hoare 1973: 9, 20, 22. Body 1965: 202 finds that family allowances started to be paid in west Dorset and east Devon from 1792.
114. All the information in the paragraphs to follow was drawn from the Overseers' Account Book, DRO 3483A/PO13.
115. DRO 2096A/PF1 Sidbury Poor Relief Book 1783–1803.
116. Robin 1990: 211. This restriction seems to have been an aspect of new poor law policy. See K.D.M. Snell 1985: 114–124. The promotion of 'self-sufficiency' for the labourer was not an aspect of new poor law philosophy and it is interesting that the feoffees should step in to provide the means for this.
117. FF 17/7 Feoffees' Minute Book 1766–1853. Razzell 1965: 312–332 and Razzell 1977 claim the controlling of smallpox was a major factor in the eighteenth-century mortality decline.
118. DRO 1142/BEA Sampson Account Books 32–38 1755–81. Soap production in the United Kingdom increased twice as fast as the rise in population between 1760 and 1790. See Mathias 1969: 218.
119. S.K. Roberts 1985: 191–193.
120. DRO 3483A/PO15 Answers to queries about poor law administration in Colyton 1775/6.
121. DRO 3483A/PO17 Workhouse Committee Notes.
122. DRO 1142/BEA Sampson Account Book 32–38, 1755–81 20 April 1772.
123. DRO 3483A/PO16 Workhouse Inventory.
124. PP 'Abstract of Answers and Returns 1803'.
125. CRO PO/34/41 Rules of Colyton Workhouse.
126. FF 17/7 Feoffees' Minute Book 1766–1853 and contains all the references to follow.
127. Robin 1990: 193–218 and especially Robin 2000.
128. Robin 1990: 193–218.
129. DRO 3327A/PO81 Examination of Martha Roe, Ottery St Mary 1749.
130. DRO 3327A/PO81 Settlement Examination, Ottery St Mary 1767.
131. DRO 3483A/PO13.
132. K.D.M. Snell 1985: 45 found unemployment in May to be a typically pastoral pattern.
133. FF 17/7 Feoffees' Minute Book 1766–1853; Robin 1990: 193–218. Hoare 1973: 71. Similar Christmas disbursements were probably made in other parishes and account for January 'lows'. See K.D.M. Snell 1985: 92 for graphs of poor relief in Ardleigh and St Osyth, for example.
134. DRO 3483A/PO13 Overseers' Account Book. All the details about the poor in eighteenth-century Colyton came from this source.
135. Brushfield 1897: 291–349 explains that the removal of vermin was statutory from Tudor times but local authorities organised how it was to be executed and consequently rates of payment varied between parishes. This reference was suggested to me by Amy Erickson.
136. FF 17/7 Minutes and account book 1766–1853.
137. See K.D.M. Snell 1985: 414.
138. DRO 3483A/PO13.
139. Wear 1987 analysed the care network in this city parish.
140. Schofield 1985: 19; K.D.M. Snell 1985: 348; Gillis 1985: 113.
141. DRO 3483A/PO21.
142. DRO 3483A/PO20. Huzel 1980: 367–381 argued that family allowances made no difference to crude marriage rates but his analysis seems to have been flawed

because the parishes he used were not differentiated in a socio-economic manner. Hawker 1882: 329–336 reported a conversation with an old South Devon labourer who told him that he had had a large family and had received parish pay for every one of his children after the first so that, as he put it, 'they didn't hurt me much'. There is a large literature on 'Speenhamland' type policies and their local applications. See, for example, T.D. Marshall 1968: Oxley 1974.

143. DRO 3483A/PO45.
144. See Hitchcock, King and Sharpe 1997 for many more examples.

Chapter 7. Viable Households

1. M. Hunt 1996.
2. UBSC Pinney Papers, John Pinney to Hester Pinney 16/8/1688; Azariah Pinney to John Pinney Junior 28/8/1711.
3. Ingram 1984: 177–193.
4. A. Wilson 1985: 129–144.
5. Fildes 1986.
6. Wrigley 1977a: 281–312.
7. DRO 3483A/PO13.
8. FF 15/3 (1) and DRO 3483A/PO32.
9. Erickson 1993: 50.
10. Fitzroy Jones 1952: 72–105 found for the poor accounts of Trull in Somerset that childbirth assistance was only established after 1758.
11. D. Maclaren 1979: 427–441. For another local study see G. Clark 1985: 25–33.
12. Fildes 1986: 153.
13. DRO Chanter 872.
14. DRO Chanter 878.
15. Colyton parish magazine, September 1907.
16. These details are derived from the linkage of the overseers account book DRO 3483A/PO13 to the reconstitution.
17. DRO 3483/PO21.
18. DRO EDRO/PO9–16 1 May 1820.
19. DRO R4/1/PO16 26 May 1813.
20. DRO 3483A/PO21 22 May 1847.
21. UBSC Pinney Papers, Account 28/11/1689 sent by Nathaniel Pinney to John.
22. FF 15/1.
23. UBSC Pinney Papers, Azariah Pinney to Hester Pinney 31/8/1704.
24. Dunlop and Denham 1912 provide the statutory background to apprenticeship.
25. Personal communication with the feoffees indicates that helping Colyton teenagers to acquire job training remains an aspect of their charity today.
26. Coate 1958: 23, 26.
27. FF 14/3 (1).
28. Gray 1992: 76.
29. By contrast, Schofield 1970: 261–274 found in the 1782 listing for the parish of Cardington in Bedfordshire that most children up to the age of 14 lived at home because of the domestic lace-making and textile-spinning. In the 15–19 age group only 22 per cent of boys lived at home, but 71 per cent of girls did so.
30. FF 14/3 (1).
31. Clapp 1982: 4–9 believed the amount of fighting had a significant effect on

mortality. Oswald 1977: 75-116 described epidemics in Devon and chronicled the outbreak of typhus.

32. Schofield 1977: 97–126. Hoskins 1966: 150 argues that 1592/3 were also plague years in Colyton but this cannot be confirmed as the mortality in those years contained a high proportion of infant deaths. The plagues of 1570 and 1590 described in Pickard 1947 had no effect in Colyton. For further information see Slack 1985: 83–99, 183.

33. Few attempts have been made to look closely at pauper apprentices. Recent exceptions are Lane 1996; K.D.M. Snell 1985: 228–319; and Wales 1986. Wales has evidence from Cawston in Norfolk that children could not fully recompense their expense by their labour as their cost outweighed their work value.

34. K.D.M. Snell 1985: 20–21, 48. Snell's graphs, which show the seasonal distribution of unemployment for both eastern and western counties, indicate that unemployment was lowest in late summer.

35. Marshall 1796: Vol. II, 227.

36. See Pinchbeck and Hewitt 1969: 223n.

37. FF 15/3 (1); DRO 3483A/PO32.

38. DRO 3483A/PO13.

39. This confirms the findings of Wales that poor law officers turned their attention from younger to older children during the seventeenth century. See Wales 1986. It may have been an earlier custom to put children out when they were young: in 'A relation or rather a true account of the island of England . . . about the year 1500' (Camden Society 1847: 24–25) the anonymous Italian comments on the phenomenon of the English sending their children away from their families between the ages of 7 and 9 years.

40. K.D.M. Snell 1985: 324–325.

41. Yarborough 1979: 67–82 estimated that adolescents entered apprenticeship in sixteenth-century Bristol between the ages of 14 and 16. Newman Brown 1984: 405–420 found that in Aldenham in the second half of the seventeenth century, 13 years and 11 months was the average age for boys and 13 years 7 months for girls. Erickson 1993: 51 found apprenticeship as young as 10 or 11 unusual.

42. Wall 1978: 181–202.

43. Brodsky Elliott 1978 found that the motivation for emigration for many London apprentices was the death of their father.

44. Vancouver 1808: 92–98 stressed that a lack of cottages delayed marriage in the west of England. Certainly instances are shown in the settlement examinations of young married couples moving in with their parents and it is possible that pressure of space and funds meant that a younger member of the family might be apprenticed.

45. DRO R4/1/PO16.

46. PP Abstract of Answers and Returns 1801, Accounts and Papers Volume XI 1812, Volume XV 1822.

47. Rutman and Rutman 1979: 153–182 for comparison with step-relations established under conditions of high mortality in early America. Ennew 1987 found that for street children in Peru, fictive family relationships develop as rich families take in poorer kin. The incidence of 'godparenthood' increases in periods of rapid social change.

48. DRO 3483/A/PO13.

49. Gillis 1974: 2–22; Thomas 1976: 214–218; Kussmaul 1981: 100n: K.D.M. Snell 1985: 322–332; Ben-Amos 1988: 41–64.

50. Wall 1978: 181–202.

51. Wall 1987: 77–101; Johansen n.d. confirms these urban/rural differences.

52. Wall 1987: 77–101. Wall finds it a universal rule for children to have left

home in their teens in 'pre-industrial' England. Industrialisation seems to have produced the situation where children spent prolonged periods of time in the parental home. See M. Anderson 1971; Katz and Davey 1975: 81–119.

53. Marshall 1796: Vol. I, 111.
54. K.D.M. Snell 1985: 261n.
55. DRO 3483A/PO20.
56. DRO 3483A/P21.
57. PP Report on the Employment of Women and Children in Agriculture 1843 XV: 47.
58. DRO 3033A/PO7–36.
59. DRO 3483A/PO20 and the following settlement examinations are contained in this collection.
60. DRO 3483A/PO21.
61. DRO 3483A/PO20.
62. PP 1834 Poor Law Report Answers to Rural Queries XXX Appendix BI Devon: 125a, 136a.
63. DRO QSBb Midsummer 1600.
64. DRO QSBb Midsummer 1599.
65. DRO QSBb Midsummer 1624.
66. DRO QSBb Midsummer 1630.
67. DRO QSBb Michaelmas 1641.
68. DRO EDRO/PO2.
69. DRO 3327A/PO81 Ottery St Mary Settlement Examination 1751.
70. EDRO Membury PO2.
71. Robin 2000: 50–54.
72. Wrightson 1982: 67–88.
73. Foyster 1999 for much greater discussion of these matters.
74. Nuttall 1939: 12, John Pinney to Rachel Pinney 11/7/1682.
75. UBSC Pinney Papers, Azariah Pinney to Mary Colemar 18/7/1684.
76. For the full details see Sharpe 1999: 209–232.
77. Nuttall 1939: 68, Nathaniel Pinney to John Pinney 10/9/1689.
78. Nuttall 1939: 89, Nathaniel Pinney to John Pinney 11/3/1690/1.
79. UBSC Pinney Papers, Azariah Pinney to his son, John, 11/1/1706/7.
80. UBSC Pinney Papers, Azariah Pinney to John Pinney 28/8/1711. The fact that Azariah had this story from Hester is evident from a letter of the same date from PP Azariah Pinney to Hester Pinney.
81. UBSC Pinney Papers, John Pinney Junior to Azariah Pinney 3/4/1713; Azariah Pinney to Hester Pinney 10/9/1713.
82. For a discussion of this see Erickson 1993: 79–101.
83. DRO ECR Chanter 866 Restorick vs Philips.
84. DRO Chanter 875 1675 Farrant vs Cox, Shute.
85. DRO Chanter 878 1679 Searle vs Moore, Northleigh.
86. Coate 1958: 28.
87. Hindle 1998b: 71–89.
88. UBSC Pinney Papers, Nathaniel Pinney's account book.
89. DRO QSBb Epiphany 1655.
90. DRO QSBb Michaelmas 1651.
91. DRO QSBb Midsummer 1653.
92. DRO QSBb Midsummer 1665 Information of Nicholas Gosling and Richard Bucknole of Membury.
93. DRO QSBb Epiphany 1666.
94. DRO QSBb Midsummer 1678.

95. Bettey 1976: 236–237.
96. Laslett 1977: 27, 30.
97. Slater 1984: 78.
98. Hufton 1984: 356.
99. Amussen 1988: 117.
100. On problems with FRFs and illegitimacy, see Wrigley, Davies, Oeppen and Schofield 1997: 54.
101. DRO 3483A/PO45.
102. Weir 1984: 349 thought that celibacy would be class-specific: 'Under the right conditions of income distribution, a fall in the wage could have its greatest impact on the prospects of every marrying for a part of the population and little impact on the rest'.
103. Studies of other welfare-dependent societies confirm that they tend to develop matrifocal and highly adaptive family structures. One example is Stack 1974, who describes a black ghetto in the mid-west USA. I am grateful to John Gillis for originally suggesting this reference.
104. Oosterveen, Smith and Stewart 1980: 89–90 show that over the period 1600–1789 17.3 per cent of married women were baptised in Colyton parish but that 42.3 per cent of unmarried mothers were. If we look over the entire reconstitution, the time period with the lowest population of unmarried mothers born in Colyton occurs in the second half of the seventeenth century (33.3 per cent), which is a further indication of the extent of migrancy and connection with the lace industry.
105. Oosterveen, Smith and Stewart 1980: 86–140.
106. Wrigley, Davies, Oeppen and Schofield 1997: 534.
107. Laslett and Oosterveen 1973: 255–285. For a more recent estimate of national illegitimacy see Adair 1996: 50.
108. S.K. Roberts 1985: 198–199; Levine and Wrightson 1980: 181. For comparison with a neighbouring parish with a 'low' of illegitimacy in the mid-seveteenth century, see Cumming 1981: 25–29.
109. Oosterveen, Smith and Stewart 1980: 113 also associate bastardy in the periods after 1750 in Colyton with labourers and those in receipt of poor relief.
110. Oosterveen, Smith and Stewart 1980: 86–140 find that 17.3 per cent of married women were born in Colyton, but 42.3 per cent of unmarried mothers were born there in the shorter period of 1600–1789. This is a clear contrast with Terling where those who produced illegitimate children tended to be the 'obscure'—perhaps transient servants rather than locals, see Wrightson and Levine 1979: 128.
111. Laslett and Oosterveen 1983: 255–285.
112. PRO E/315/86.
113. Levine 1977: 125–147; Levine and Wrightson 1980: 158–175.
114. DRO QSBb Midsummer 1649.
115. See Ingram 1981: 35–37; Ingram 1987.
116. DRO Chanter 870.
117. DRO Chanter 868.
118. DRO QSBb Midsummer 1675.
119. DRO 3327A/PO94 Affidavit at Ottery St Mary.
120. Wrigley 1981: 137–185; Hair 1966: 233–243; Hair 1970: 59–70 found national averages of 20 per cent of all brides prenuptially pregnant before 1700 and 40 per cent thereafter. Robin 1986: 113–124. In the nineteenth century prenuptial conception was particularly common, firstly among farmers and then agricultural labourers.
121. R. Thompson 1974a: 153–165 also makes the association between extramarital sex and bastardy with unbalanced sex ratios.

122. DRO 1201A/PO654–750.

123. Robin 1987: 338.

124. In another area of domestic industry, the chapelry of Culceth in Lancashire, Gandy found that a third of women had their first child out of wedlock. This was usually a phase in their fertility history and they went on to marry later. See Gandy 1978.

125. Robin 1987: 307–342.

126. Clapp 1976: 65–72 found in Wembworthy in Devon in a listing made in 1778 that there were no single householders. They were either married or widowed and only three households were extended by an elderly parent. Tranter 1967: 261–282 also found few singles in the listing made of Cardington in 1782. Significantly, the sex ratio seems to have been quite balanced there. M. Anderson 1984: 377–393 wrote that spinsters heading their own households were unusual in the mid-Victorian period.

127. Compare Robin 1987: 307–342 with DRO 3483A/PO21.

128. DRO EDRO/PO9–16.

129. DRO 3483A/PO13.

130. Levine 1977: 139.

131. Clark and Souden 1987.

132. DRO QSBb Epiphany 1675.

133. DRO R4/1/PO16.

134. DRO R7/2/24. For comparative cases giving pauper inventories see P. King 1997: 155–191.

135. DRO 3327A/PO81 Ottery St Mary settlement examinations 1755.

136. DRO 3483A/PO13.

137. S.W. Taylor 1985 finds that £4 or £5 was often spent on each enforced marriage.

138. DRO EDRO R4/1/2/PO16 Volume of settlement examinations for Tiverton St Peter 1804–25.

139. K.D.M. Snell 1985: 360n. used 289 cases of family desertion from settlement examinations and found that these families had more children than those which stayed together. The father was most likely to leave in his thirties when the poverty of having many young children was worst.

140. While the children could not legally be defined as illegitimate, the invention of paternity links by the vicar of course confounds accurate reconstitution and birth interval analysis in these cases.

141. The theory of the 'bastardy prone subsociety' was developed by Peter Laslett in the early 1970s (Laslett and Oosterveen 1973: 255–285) and has largely been left to stand since, although subsequent work by various authors seems to have used the concept as a catch-all for various types of sexual nonconformity. Robin 1987: 307–342 provided detail about the subsociety in nineteenth-century Colyton, showing that bastard-bearers were generally related and lived close to each other in the southern half of the town. For a more recent view, albeit one which subscribes to the old interpretation of economy and society in early modern Colyton, see Adair 1996, who places Colyton in the 'Highland' category reflecting relatively high illegitimacy compared to 'Lowland' parishes.

142. Menefee 1981 described the pageant of wife sales at markets and notes that this form of popular divorce became more common towards 1800. Thornton 1916: 54–55 found that wife sales were still common in Devon at the end of the thirteenth century. Gillis 1985: 209 argued that a set of secular divorce rights based on the return of the ring became established in the second half of the eighteenth century.

143. Gillis 1985: 110, 205–207 argues that common law marriages peaked in number around 1800. Newman 1979 found that 15 per cent of couples who were living

together in Ash between 1750 and 1834 had not been married. Even in societies where divorce is accessible, a certain number of married people will have 'illegitimate' children. Foster Hartley 1969: 793–798 found that in the Registrar General's report of the 1960s 26 per cent of illegitimate births in England and Wales were to 'married' women. Cohabitation in the past has been studied by Sogner 1978: 61–82; Berlanstein 1980: 360–374; Matovic 1986: 385–413; and Adair 1996: 178–179, who finds that it was rare.

144. DRO 3483A/PO46. A comparative case appeared in the diary of William Holland, a Somerset vicar, who reported in December 1809: 'I met the Botany Bay man who lived at the workhouse. He has had another child by his sister-in-law and in shoart they have lived together and the husband is in Botany Bay. He asked me about marrying her, but I said she ran a risk if the husband should come home, besides she was by law his sister. But he said "such do marry and it could not in the sight of God be worse than it is now" '. Quoted in Ayers 1984: 190.

145. Kent 1990: 27–42; K.D.M. Snell 1985: 359–364.

146. By comparison, Wrigley, Davies, Oeppen and Schofield 1997: 421 find reconstitutions for the country as a whole that 16.4 per cent of all births were prenuptially conceived in the period 1675–99, whereas 37.9 per cent were during 1800–25. However, Colyton conforms to this later pattern in the late seventeenth century.

147. Nuttall 1939: 32–33, John Pinney to Hester Pinney 1/12/1685.

148. Nuttall 1939: 70, Nathaniel Pinney to John Pinney 10/9/1689.

149. Wall 1986: 261–294; Ruggles 1987.

150. Robin 1984: 505–516.

151. Robin 1990: 207–208.

152. Thomson 1986a; 1986b: 355–378. Johansen 1976: 129–142 finds a contrast between rural and urban districts. In a reconstitution of twenty-six Danish parish registers, he found that about half of the over-sixties who had married children lived with them. By contrast Johansen 1987: 297–305 found in his 'repopulation' of the town of Odense that the elderly lived alone. Even those with married children living in the town had little connection with them and there were disputes when the adult children were called upon to pay maintenance or funeral expenses. Personal communication with Hans Christian Johansen revealed some parallels between Colyton and Odense with its declining economy based on glove manufacture.

153. Robin 1990: 208.

154. DRO EDRO/PO9–16. A similar order was made on John and William Southwood of Chudleigh in January 1840 to maintain their impotent mother at 1s 6d weekly.

155. DRO EDRO/PO9–16.

156. DRO EDRO/PO9–16.

157. DRO 3483A/PO45.

158. DRO 3483A/PO31. The maintenance payment of Robert Beer mentions Eleanor Batt 'who now lives with me'.

159. See essays by Sokoll, Sharpe and Taylor in Hitchcock, King and Sharpe 1997.

160. Gittings 1984: 103.

161. See DRO 3483A/PO13.

162. DRO QSBb Midsummer 1684.

163. The following cases are recorded in DRO 3483A/PO13.

164. CRO PO/34/40 Rules of Colyton Friendly Society. On the wider context of early friendly societies and their development within Devon and links with migrancy see Gorsky 1998: 489–511.

165. PP 'Abstract of Returns...1803': 115.

166. DRO 3483A/PG1 Burial Board Account Book 1809–38.

167. Robin 1990: 197 estimates that at a minimum, 56 per cent of male household heads in Colyton in 1861 received one of the two types of relief.

168. The literature on this subject is vast. See for example Laslett 1972; Wrightson 1982; Mount 1982; Wall, Robin and Laslett 1983. Recent interpreters have been more circumspect, however, for the early modern family (Tadmor 1996: 111–140) and for the family since 1830 (Davidoff, Doolittle, Fink and Holden 1999).

169. For examples of a variety of views see E.P. Thompson 1963; Young and Wilmott 1957; Young and Wilmott 1972; M. Anderson 1971; Laslett 1972.

170. Lewis 1968: especially 48–52.

171. Collins 1982: 127–146 describes a comparative case of female-headed households and 'spinster grouping' in early industrial Ulster.

172. Lewis 1968: especially 48–52.

173. Numbers of poor were high enough in England for Gregory King to think that almost half of the population in 1696 were decreasing the national wealth. Kumar 1988: 138–166 has collected various estimates of the numbers of poor.

174. Discussed in M. Hunt 1996.

175. K.D.M. Snell 1985: 62; B. Hill 1989b: 24–46.

176. DRO 3483/PO13.

Epilogue: Reinterpreting Colyton

1. Phythian-Adams 1993: 2; see also Pythian-Adams 1987.

2. R. Thompson 1974a: 153–164 thought that low ratios would be felt at 80 or 90, but high ratios only at 150.

3. Dyer 1979: 123–134.

4. Boserup 1970.

5. Galley 1995: 448–469.

6. Greven 1966: 234–256. See also Greven 1970. In Andover, as in Scott Smith's Hingham, very long life expectancy delayed male marriage due to inheritance. As a result the family structure of the second generation maturing in the 1670s and 1680s was a combination of the classical extended family and the nuclear family. Greven notes: 'the newly created conjugal unit of husband and wife live in separate households in close proximity to their parents and siblings and continue to be economically dependent in some respects upon their parents' (1970: 255). As a result of the continuing dependence of the second generation on the first, typical families in Andover were particularly patriarchial.

7. Robin 2000: 146. Hutton 1996: 406–407 reports that tar barrel running for Guy Fawkes continues in Ottery St Mary.

8. For a stimulating discussion see Rollison 1992 on cultural identities in the early modern period.

9. DRO 1687 Chanter 8298 Pearse vs Mayowe.

10. Polwhele 1797: Vol. III, 307.

11. An architectural survey of Colyton carried out in 1986 by Bob Machin and John Smith of Bristol University Extra Mural Studies Department showed that a number of new large houses were built at the end of the eighteenth century. See the communication of April 1986 to Richard Wall at the Cambridge Group on this matter.

12. DRO 3483A/PO45 Miscellaneous correspondence to the overseers.

13. FF 17/7.

14. DRO 3483A/PO37.

15. DRO 3483A/PO20.

16. DRO 3483A/PO20. Also see DRO 3483A/PO35 showing relief for militia men in the Napoleonic War period.

17. DRO 4262A/PO148 Shute Settlement Examination 1027.
18. DRO 1855A/PO42.
19. Wrigley, Davies, Oeppen and Schofield 1997: 507.
20. Gutmann 1988: 143–145, 160, 170–171.
21. Research of D. Terrier and P. Toutain cited in Gutmann 1988: 189.
22. Gullickson 1986.
23. Hendrickx 1997.
24. For further results, see Hudson and King 2000.
25. For a survey of relevant literature on this topic see Ogilvie and Cerman 1996.
26. Amussen 1988; Hoskins 1957; Howell 1983; Spufford 1974.
27. Wrightson and Levine 1979; Wrigley, Davies, Oeppen and Schofield 1997 suggest that the age of marriage declined most significantly in industrial parishes but minimally in agricultural parishes in the eighteenth century. Agricultural parishes simply look more static in demographic terms.
28. Hey 1974.
29. Skipp 1978.

Appendix

1. Marriages begin on 21 January 1539, baptisms on 20 October 1538 and burials on 28 October 1538. Noble 1970: 189–191 makes an assessment of the content of the registers.
2. Jean Robin has done extensive work on mid-nineteenth century Colyton. See particularly Robin 2000; but also Robin 1984: 505–516; Robin 1986: 113–124; Robin 1987: 307–342; Robin 1990: 193–218 and Robin 1995.
3. In some cases the total FRFs in certain categories are at variance with those found in the Cambridge Group files. This is because part of the project was conceived to be a check on the original reconstitution. The occasional mis-linkage which appeared on the original reconstitution could be eradicated on a copy of the machine entered parts of the FRFs. These were shown up when conflicting facts appeared in another document. The slightly modified edition of the reconstitution formed the basis of the tables presented here.
4. His will is in the George Eyre Evans Papers, National Library of Wales, Aberystwyth.
5. Schofield 1992.
6. The problems which still beset this endeavour in the mid-1980s are discussed in Newcombe and Kennedy 1962: 563–566; Winchester 1970: 107–124; Katz and Tiller 1972; Kelley, Skolnick and Yasuda 1972; Schofield 1972a: 122–125; Winchester 1973: 128–150; Jardine and Macfarlane 1978: 71–78; Seaman and Condran 1979.
7. Katz and Tiller 1972.
8. Schofield 1972b: 359–364, quoted on 363.
9. Rodgers 1979 gives an insight into historical dialect nuances particular to Devon.
10. Hosking 1998.

Bibliography

Bibliographical and Note Conventions

Manuscripts: in the Notes, all references begin with an abbreviated version of their archive; they are arranged by archive in the Bibliography.

Unpublished and Published Sources: author/date references are provided in the Notes, with full references in the Bibliography.

Books and articles appear together in the Bibliography. Places of publication are provided except where it is London.

Manuscripts

Public Record Office (PRO)

Listings
E179 96/183 1524 Lay Subsidy
E179 97/221 1541 Lay Subsidy
E179 98/253 1543/5 Subsidy
E179 99/316 1550 Subsidy
E179 100/387 1582 Subsidy
E179 101/408 1592 Subsidy
E179 102/460 1620/1 Subsidy
E179 102/463 1624 Devon Subsidy Roll
E179 245/14(4) 1636 Ship Money
E179 254/14(4) 1660 Poll Tax
HO 107/1862 1851 Census Enumeration

Court Rolls
E315/85 1550 Colyton Manor
E315/86 1553 Colyton Manor

Probate Inventories
PROB 4/20508 1692 Benedicta Burnard
PROB 4/9605 1685 John Burnard
PROB 4/20115 1675 Arthur Bury
PROB 4/4817 1669 Edward Drake
PROB 4/12717 1684 John Darby
PROB 4/12812 1667 Robert Guppy
PROB 4/17599 1671 John Marwood

PROB 4/4906 1691 Aaron Reed
PROB 4/10067 1677 Bartholomew Searle
PROB 4/12783 1684 Margaret Stainborough
PROB 4/6349 1672 Walter Vye
PROB 4/4896 1678 Edward Wilkins
PROB 4/9361 1663 Sir John Yonge
PROB 31/749/174 1786 Thomas Drake
E178/691 Special Inquisition
E178/5237 Special Inquisition

Court of Star Chamber
STAC 8 2/44
STAC 8 90/12
STAC 8 186/17
STAC 8 230/13
STAC 8 211/11
STAC 8 260/28
STAC 8 271/18
STAC 8 176/8
STAC 8 295/17
STAC 8 275/3
STAC 8 298/8

Court of Requests
REQ 2 199/49
REQ 2 253/44
REQ 2 271/14
REQ 2 280/29

Other
IR 29/9 Colyton Tithe Land Apportionment 1844

British Museum (BM)

Court Rolls
Add. MS 22/73 Whitwell and Farway manors 1544–1682
Add. MS 21/605 Whitwell Survey 1606
13883-5 Deeds and Manuscripts 1578–1639
Charters Add. 13834 Deeds
Charters Add. 13847 Deeds
Charters Add. 13849 Deeds
Charters Add. 13985 Deeds
Charters Add. 13914 Deeds

Victoria and Albert Museum (V&A)

Parliamentary Petition 1698: Case of the Lacemakers in Relation to the Importance of Foreign Lace

Bodleian Library, Oxford

Tanner MSS, 141, fos 120–122 (The Clerk of Parliament's Papers)

National Library of Wales
George Eyre Evans Bequest, Ref 13,595 Ralph Seaward's will 1669

University of Bristol Library Special Collections (UBSC)
Pinney Papers
'Twenty Lessons to be Learned from London's Late Burning Written by Me JP' (manuscript, 1666)
Account Book 1 1650–1668
Folder LX Box 19 Agreement of William Phelps of Thornscombe and Ralph Bartlett of Marshwood 1673
Letter from Azariah Pinney to Mary Colemar 18/7/1684
Letter from Mary Pinney to Hester Pinney 9/9/1693
Letter from Nathaniel Pinney to Hester Pinney 24/8/1696
Letter Folder 1X Box 19 1737
Numbered Folders XX. Extract from 'An Account of the Ministers, Lecturers, Masters and Fellows of Colleges . . . who were ejected or silenced at the Restoration also by or Before the Act of Uniformity' by Edward Parry, London, 1713
Letter from Nathaniel Pinney to Hester Pinney 1/8/1720

Devon Record Office (DRO)
Parish Registers
2749A/MF1–3 Axmouth
3483A/PR1 Colyton
239A/MF 2–3 Branscombe
1639A/MF 6–9, PR 5 Honiton
2718A/MF 1–3 Musbury
364A/MF 1–3 Offwell
3292A/F 3–5 Seaton and Beer
1236A/MF 1–5 Shute
365/A/MF 1–3 Widworthy
EDRO/PR1 Exeter; St Sidwells
EDRO/67/A MF 6–8 Farway

Listings
123M/E178 1547 Survey of Tenants of Colyton
123M/E77 Late 16th Century Survey of Tenants of Colyton
123M/E40–48 1684 Yearly Rent of Colyton Manor
Devon and Cornwall Record Society Transcription 1726 Colyton Church Rate
County Records: Colyton 1780 Land Tax
County Records: Colyton 1798 Land Tax
County Records: Colyton 1832 Land Tax
3483A/PO25 1819 Colyton Poor Rate Assessment

Court Rolls
123M/E87 Survey of Whitford 1613, Petre Papers
3327A Add/Pz 3 (microfilm) MFC 45 Manor Court Documents of Ottery St Mary.
3327add.b/567 Ottery St Mary Manor Book 1795–1837
1466 M/M1 Manor Court Book of Colyton 1770–85

Ecclesiastical Court
CC 181 (34)
CC 178/1
CC 180
Chanter 866–880
Chanter 8297–9
Chanter 232, Diocesan Survey 1779
Chanter 242B, Diocesan Survey 1821
Chanter 11042/1, 3, 63

Public Courts
QS Quarter Sessions Order Books 1686–1801
QSBb Quarter Sessions Bundles 1592–1699
QS 74/14; 74/34/1–3. Conventicle Acts Documents
QS 499M/Q/57 List of Freeholders and Jurymen, Colyton Hundred 1698

Family Estate Papers
50M/I1–4 Papers of Marwood Tucker of Kilmington
53/6 Box 16 Turner Collection, Marriage Settlement of Ellis Veryard, 1737
96M 15/10 Rolle Papers
96M 35/5 Rolle Map
123M/E78 Colyton Manorial Survey
123M/E79 Enclosure Concerning Rights of Tenants
123M/E80 Borcombe Map
123M/E87 Survey of Manor of Whitford 1613
123M/E595 Rental of Colyford 1702–1703
123M/L738–749 Petre Cottage Leases 1655–1690
123M/E1044 Felony Case 1655
235/E2 Cash Book 1667
235M/E3 Courtenay Pole Cash Book 1658–1665
235M E5 Account Book of Sir William Pole 1718–23
281/M/T249 Family Will 1607
1142B/EA32–38 Sampson Accounts
1142B/EC39 Henry Clarke's Examination, 1780.
1700M/T189 Drake Deeds
1077M/6/1 Marker of Gittisham, Court book of Manor and Borough of Honiton 1748–1893
1466M/M1 Manor Court Book of Colyton 1770–85
1700M/W20 Drake of Colyton, Copy of Will of Roger Satchell, Merchant, 1684
DD37597 (1598) Petition

Overseers Records
ACCOUNTS
3483A/PO13 Colyton 1740–1770
2954A/PO1 Abbotskerswell 1640–1693
2141A/PO3 Ashburton 1678–1697
1237A/PO20 Bere Ferrers 1633–1666
2452M/A/PO1 Bovey Tracey 1628–1667
1633A/PO1 Cheriton Fitzpaine 1676–1699
EDRO/PO1 Chudleigh 1598–1694
1235A/PO3 Churston Ferrers 1662–1671
1061A/PW1 Clayhidon 1688–1720

48/13/9/3 Cockington 1670–1750
2404A/PO1 Cullompton 1656–1758
2165A/PO1 Drewsteignton 1678–1710
1213A/PO1 Dunchideock 1680–1814
3167A/PO1 Farringdon 1685–1735
EDRO/PO2 Halberton 1685–1728
2922A/PO2 Hennock 1646–1692
EDRO/PO2 Instow 1671–1700
2994A/PO1–3 Kingswear 1654–1694
3239A/PO1 Marldon 1608–1699
1927A/PO1 Newton Ferrers 1598–1691
271A/PO1 Nymet Rowland 1667–1704
2096A/PV3 Sidbury 1722–1825
285A/PO Spreyton 1662–1725
1215A/PO1 Stockland 1755
1981A/PO1 Stoke Gabriel 1638–1672
3420A/PO1 Stoke in Teignhead 1619–1668
2288A/PO1 Tawstock 1675–1706
2914A/PO1 North Tawton 1655–1665
1464A/PO1 Upton Heillons 1653–1777
1710A/PO1 Warkleigh 1654–1713
1095A/PW1 Zeal Monachorum 1626–1685

SETTLEMENT RECORDS
3483A/PO19 Colyton Certificates 1700–1829
3483A/PO20 Colyton Examinations 1765–1854
3483A/PO21 Removals to Colyton 1761–1854
3483A/PO22 Removals from Colyton 1700–1854
3483A/PO23 Colyton Papers Relating to Settlement 1742–1810
4262A/PO147 Settlement Examination of John Spurway of Shute 1827
3327A/PO77; PO81, PO91 Ottery St Mary Settlement Records
EDRO /PO4 Dunsford Settlement Examination 1838
365A/PO3–62 Settlement Papers for Widworthy

EXAMINATIONS IN OTHER PARISHES
EDRO/PO9–16 Chudleigh 1663–1859
73A/PO44–348 Coffinswell 1740–1840
EDRO/PO11 Dartington 1716–1836
EDRO/PO4 Dunsford 1663–1840
1201A/PO654–750 Hartland 1657–1817
EDRO/PO2 Membury 1669–1852
3033A/PO7–36 Sherford 1720–1840
1597A/24/36 Totnes 1602–1844
R4/1/PO16 Tiverton St Peter 1685–1804

BASTARDY RECORDS
3483A/PO29 Colyton Examinations 1772–1831
3483A/PO30–31 Colyton Maintenance Payments 1771–1834
3483A/PO32 Colyton Bastardy Bonds 1777–1779
3483A/PO33–34 Colyton Bastardy Papers 1790

BIBLIOGRAPHY

Constable Presentments
QS 7/1–42 Presentments for Hundred of Colyton 1662–1737
PC1–3 Constable's Warrants 1664–1685
Q/S15/86/1–12 Constables Presentments for Colyton
DQS 15/1/3–4 Constables Presentments for Axminster; DQS 1668 15/1/13

Apprenticeship Documents
3483A/PO24 Colyton Apprenticeship Register 1598–1711
3483A/PO26 Colyton Indentures 1647–1741
3483A/PO27 Colyton Bonds 1758–1779
3483A/PO28 Colyton Miscellaneous Apprenticeship Records 1772–1796
3483A/PZ1–2 Colyton Private Indentures 1764
239A add3/PO50 Whimple Apprentice Indenture 1756

Other Poor Relief Records
3483A/PW2 Colyton Churchwarden's Accounts 1767–1778
R7/2/Z3–7 Axminster Churchwarden's Account
67A PW1 Faraway Churchwarden's Memorandum Book
3483A/PO1–4 Colyton Poor Rate Books 1818–1831
3483A/PO11–12 Colyton Appeals Against Poor Rate Assessment 1818
3483A/PO15 Colyton Queries about Poor Law Administration 1776
3483A/PO16 Colyton Workhouse Inventory 1779
3483A/PO17–18 Colyton Workhouse Committee Notes c.1790
3483A/PO35 Colyton Relief for Militia Men 1799–1814
3483A/PO36–37 Colyton Letters to the Overseers 1832–38
3483A/PO45–46 Colyton Miscellaneous Correspondence 1798–1835
5301A/PV1 Vestry Minute Book for Kilmington 1732–1838
1855A/PV1 Vestry Minute Book for Sidmouth 1823–32
1236A add2/PVI Shute Vestry Book 1789–1803
3327A/add2/PA1–2 Ottery St Mary Corporation Books
3327A Ottery St Mary Vagrancy Orders, Case of Mary Williams 1769
Diocesan Principal Registry List of Poor Rates 1837

Miscellaneous Documents
3483A/PG1 Colyton Burial Board Account Book 1809–1838
3483A/PE1 Colyton Sunday School Minute Book 1814
43/18/1–3 Hemp and Flax Bounty Papers 1786–1790
Boxes 1–6, 42 Marriage bonds
337 add 2/1d, Dunning and Bicknell, George Harris Farm Account 1782
3327A Add/PZ3 Ottery St Mary (microfilm MFC45) John Burwell's Book 1666–1748
20964A/PO21 Census of Sidbury taken 1829 between the months of August and November
337add/474 List of Feoffees Property in Honiton and District in 1760
PR510–510a Schoolmaster's Licences
PR518 Diocesan Records Surgeon's Licences 1661
Diocesan Records Principal Registry Papers Basket A 2574, A2638, 2663, 2666

Cornwall Record Office (CRO)

Carew-Pole Papers from Antony House
PM/27 Carew Pole Rentals 1761–1815
CA/H/115–116 Workfolk's Wages 1673–1691

CA/H/117 Hiring Agreements 1692–1714
PA/31/20 Receipts for expenses on Colyton Estates 1787
PA/32/25 Late Eighteenth-Century Poor Rates and Taxes
PA/32/26 Receipts at Shute Barton 1791–1794
PA/32/27–29 Day Wages at Shute 1794–1796
PA/32/30 Peter Palmer's Account Book 1786–1798
PA/32/31 Shute Household Expense Book 1806–1808
PA/32/34 Miscellaneous Bills 1793–1806
PA/32/35–36 Account Books 1789–1794
PA/32/37 Miscellaneous Receipts 1785
PA/32/40 Legal Papers 1655
PE/29/1B Lease Book of Manor of Yardbury 1622–1679
PO/34/40 Rules of Colyton Friendly Society 1786
PO/34/41 Rules of Colyton Workhouse c.1790
PO/34/42 Colyton Bastardy Examinations 1793–1799
PO/34/43 Scheme for Apprentices at Shute

Dorset Record Office (DSRO)

B7/M9/1–28 List of Indentured Servants leaving Lyme Regis 1683–1689

Somerset Record Office (SRO)

C/344 1592–1685 Whitwell Court and Estreat Rolls
DD/WO62/6/5 Willougby vs Courtenay Pole 1678
DD/WO36, 45, 53–56, 62 Trevelyan manuscripts relating to Colyton

Dean and Chapter Archives: Exeter Cathedral (ECL)

Items 837–846 Dean and Chapter of Exeter 1665–1825
6056/2 Survey of the manor of Colyton by James Bond 1696
2047–2055 Manorial records of Sidbury

Westcountry Studies Library, Exeter (WCS)

Rev. J. Milles manuscript c.1750 (microfilm)
Anstis MSS Court of Exchequer case (microfilm)
Exeter's Flying Post newpaper 14/11/1766; 26/12/1816; 27/2/1817; 3/7/1828; 28/8/1828; 27/8/1828; 10/7/1834; 18/12/1834

Colyton Chamber of Feoffees, Colyton Town Hall (FF)

14/1b–k (1) Bailiff's Accounts 1659–99
14/2 (1) Colyton Bridge Building Account 1704
14/3 (1) Apprenticeship Clothing Accounts 1647
14/5g (1) Building Bonds
14/7–14/8a–v (1) Churchwarden's Fabric Accounts 1579–1720
14/9a–b (1) Receipts and Payments to Poor 1682/83, 1698/99
14/10 (1) Constable's Account 1683
15/1 (1) Settlement Certificates 1664–1742
15/3 (1) Bastardy Bonds 1590–1744
15/4 (1) Register of Poor Apprentices 1800–1830
15/5 (1) Apprenticeship Indentures 1586–1741

15/6 9 (1) Petty Constable's Accounts 1680
15/12 (1) Will of Thomas Holmes 1670
16/3 (2) Rent Demand 1573
16/5 (2) Maintenance Payment
16/8 (2) Inquisition into Feoffees
16/9 (2) Deeds Belonging to Parish of Colyton
16/10 (2) Feoffees Letting Terms of Properties
16/11a–b (2) Bond of Obligation
16/12a (2) Surveys of Parish Lands 1665
16/14 (2) Rents of Parish Lands
16/15 (2) Parish Money for Setting to Work 1641
16/16 (2) Uses of Parish Lands, Funds etc.
16/17 (2) Indenture of Robert Dolbiar 1649
16/18 (2) Indenture and Draft of Lease 1600
16/19 (2) Estimate of Repairs to Umborne Bridge 1768
16/34 (2) Rentals
17/3 (4) Accounts of Feoffee Funds 1825–1885
17/7 Feoffees Minute Book 1766–1853
17/9 (4) Rentals 1556–1558
17/10 (1) List of Parish Chamber Leases 1659–1700
18/1 (4) Bills and Rentals 1684–1685
21/1a–c/2 (2) Dispute over Lands Purchased 1817
22/4 (2) Receipt of Payment for House 1708
22/5 (2) Papers about Lease 1708
22/7 (2) Benefit of a Planting in New England 1623
22/8 (2) Deeds of Lands in Honiton
22/10 (1) Copy of Feoffees' Charter c.1792

Colyton Library

Copy of the Inventory of William Hill, 1627

All Hallows Museum, Honiton

Apprentice Indentures
ND40 3/9/1689
DG 28/8/1690
ND42 28/12/1691
ND46 24/7/1697

Parliamentary Papers (PP)

Abstract of the Answers and Returns 8, 1803, 98–116.
Accounts and Papers 11, 1812.
Accounts and Papers 15, 1822.
Accounts and Papers 12:1, 1833, 124–5.
Select Committee on Poor Rate Returns 5, 1822.
Select Committee on Poor Rate Returns 4, 1825.
Extract from Parliamentary Report 1820: Hundred of Colyton, Devon—Parish Lands. Colyton, 1857.
Report of the Commissioners Concerning Charities . . . Containing that Part which Relates to the County of Devon 1, 1826.
Poor Law Report Answers to Rural Queries 30: Appendix BI Devon 1834.

Report of the Commissioners concerning Charities . . . the Public Charities of Great Torrington, Devon, 1846.
Reports of the Special Assistant Poor Law Commissioners on the Employment of Women and Children in Agriculture, 12 & 15, 1843.
Select Committee on Children's Employment: Factories, 18, 1863.

Theses and Papers

Bettey, J.H., 'Agriculture and rural society in Dorset 1570–1670' (Ph.D. thesis, University of Bristol, 1976).
Body, G.A., 'The administration of the poor laws in Dorset 1760–1834: with special reference to agrarian distress' (dissertation kept at Dorset Record Office, 1965).
Brodsky Elliott, V., 'Marriage and mobility in pre-industrial England' (Ph.D. thesis, University of Cambridge, 1978).
Chartres, J.,'The place of inns in the commercial life of London and western England 1660–1760' (D.Phil. thesis, University of Oxford, 1973a).
COLYFILE Collation of Colyton statistical data held at Cambridge Group.
Cooper, S., 'Family, household and kinship in seventeenth century Kings Lynn' (seminar paper given at Cambridge Group, June 1986).
DCS.EXON Index of Ecclesiastical Court Depositions for Diocese of Exeter (computer file in the possession of David Souden).
Ennew, J., 'Fictive kin and entry to the employment market' (seminar paper delivered at Cambridge Group, February 1987).
Finlay, R.A.P., 'The population of London 1580–1650' (Ph.D. thesis, University of Cambridge, 1976).
Gandy, G.N., 'Illegitimacy in a handloom weaving community: fertility patterns in Culceth, Lancashire 1781–1860' (D.Litt. thesis, University of Oxford, 1978).
Gillespie, Rev. J.T., 'Presbyterianism in Devon and Cornwall in the seventeenth century' (M.A. thesis, University of Durham, 1943).
Gowers, I.W., 'Puritanism in the county of Devon between 1570 and 1641' (M.A. thesis, University of Exeter, 1970).
Gray, T., 'Devon's coastal and overseas fisheries and New England migration 1597–1642' (Ph.D. thesis, University of Exeter, 1988).
Gray, T., 'The fishwife in the south-west 1540–1650' (paper at Gender and Material Culture conference, University of Exeter, July 1994).
Hoare, N.F., 'The community of Colyton and its poor 1800–1850' (M.A. dissertation, University of Leicester, 1973).
Hosking, J., 'Fictive families: illegitimacy and inheritance in West Cornwall' (paper delivered at The Social History Society Conference, University of Nottingham, 1998).
Hoskins, W.G., 'The rise and decline of the serge industry in the south-west of England, with special reference to the eighteenth century' (M.Sc. dissertation, University College, Exeter, 1929).
Hoskins, W.G., 'The ownership and occupation of land in Devonshire 1650–1800' (Ph.D. thesis, University of London, 1938).
Husbands, C.R., 'The hearth tax and structures of the English economy' (Ph.D. thesis, University of Cambridge, 1985).
Jackson, P.W., 'Nonconformists and society in Devon 1660–1689' (Ph.D. thesis, University of Exeter, 1986).
Johansen, H.C., 'Urban and rural households in Denmark in the late eighteenth century' (paper kept in library of Cambridge Group, n.d.)

Keene, D., 'The poor and their neighbours in sixteenth-and seventeenth-century London' (seminar paper at Cambridge Group, January 1987).
Lauricella, S.,'Economic and social influences on marriage in Banbury 1730–1841' (Ph.D. thesis, University of Cambridge, 1998).
L.C.C., 'Burn's Journal: The Earliest Classics: Pioneers of Demography . . . works of J. Gaunt and G. King' (unpublished manuscript n.d.).
Matthews, W.B., 'A shorter history of George's Meeting, Colyton' (unpublished manuscript kept at DRO 3242D/23, 1911).
Newman, A.E., 'The old poor law in East Kent 1606–1834: a social and demographic analysis' (Ph.D. thesis, University of Kent, 1979).
Seaman, J. and Condran, G.A., 'Nominal record linkage by machine and hand: an investigation of linkage techniques using the manuscript census and the death register, Philadelphia, 1880' (copy in Cambridge Group Library of paper presented at American Statistical Association meeting, Washington, 1979).
Sharpe, P., 'Gender-specific demographic adjustment to changing economic circumstances: Colyton 1538–1837' (Ph.D. thesis, University of Cambridge, 1988).
Slack, P.A.,'Some aspects of epidemics in England 1485–1640' (D.Phil. thesis, Oxford University, 1972).
Souden, D.C., 'Pre-industrial English local migration fields' (Ph.D. thesis, University of Cambridge, 1981).
Spaeth, D.A., 'Parsons and parishoners: lay–clerical conflict and popular piety in Wiltshire villages 1660–1740' (D.Phil. thesis, Brown University, 1985).
Taylor, J.S., 'Poverty in rural Devon 1780–1840' (Ph.D. thesis, Stanford University, 1966).
Taylor, S.W., 'Family formation and the old poor law in eighteenth-century Berkshire: some findings of a modified family reconstitution project' (paper kept at Cambridge Group Library, 1985).
Thomson, D., 'The Poor Law Act of 1601—foundation of the welfare state?' (seminar paper at Oxford University, 1986a).
Todd, B.J., 'Widowhood in a market town: Abingdon 1540–1720' (D.Phil. thesis, University of Oxford, 1983).
Tovt, C., 'Bovey Tracey: church rates and poor rates 1596–1729' (paper for circulation deposited in Westcountry Studies Library, Exeter, 1928).
Wales, T., 'The rise of parish relief 1560–1700' (draft chapter of thesis kept at Cambridge Group, n.d.).
Wales, T., 'Child labour, begging and apprenticeship in early modern England' (paper at the workshop on The History of Apprenticeship and Child Labour, University of Essex, 1986).
Wear, A., 'The sick poor in St Bartholomew's Exchange in London c.1590–1676', (seminar paper at Cambridge Group, 1987).
Wilson, C., 'Marital fertility in pre-industrial England 1550–1849' (Ph.D. dissertation, University of Cambridge, 1982).
Wright, S.J., 'Family life and society in sixteenth-and early seventeenth-century Salisbury' (Ph.D. thesis, University of Leicester, 1982).

Published Primary and Secondary Sources

Adair, R., *Courtship, Illegitimacy and Marriage in Early Modern England* (Manchester, 1996).
Åkerman, S., 'An Evaluation of the Family Reconstitution Technique' *Scandinavian Economic History Review*, 25 (1977), 160–170.
Allen, D.G., *In English Ways: The Movement of Societies and the Transferral of English Local*

Law and Custom to the Massachusetts Bay in the Seventeenth Century (Williamsburg, 1981).
Amussen, S.D., *An Ordered Society: Gender and Class in Early Modern England* (Oxford and New York, 1988).
Anderson, M., *Family Structure in Nineteenth-Century Lancashire* (Cambridge, 1971).
Anderson, M., 'Marriage Patterns in Victorian Britain—an Analysis Based on Registration Data for England and Wales (1861)' *Journal of Family History*, 1 (1976), 55–78.
Anderson, M., 'The Social Position of Spinsters in Mid-Victorian Britain' *Journal of Family History*, 9 (1984), 377–393.
Anderson, R.C, and Allen, D.G., 'Communications: On English Migration to Early New England' *New England Quarterly*, 59 (1986), 406–424.
Anderson, V.D.J., 'Migrants and Motives: Religion and the Settlement of New England 1630–1640' *New England Quarterly*, 58 (1985), 339–383.
Anderson Smith, S., *Extracts from Wills Proved in P.C.C. Relating to the Parishes of Shute and Colyton, Co. Devon* (1901).
Andriette, E.A., *Devon and Exeter in the Civil War* (Newton Abbot, 1971).
Annett, N., 'North Molton: The Pre-Census Population' *TDA*, 108 (1976), 69–125.
Arkell, T., 'Multiplying Factors for Estimating Population Totals from the Hearth Tax' *LPS*, 28 (1982), 51–57.
Arkell, T., 'Assessing the Reliability of the Warwickshire Hearth Tax returns of 1662–74' *Warwickshire History*, 6 (1986–7), 183–197.
Arkell, T., 'The Incidence of Poverty in England in the Later Seventeenth Century' *Social History*, 12 (1987), 23–48.
Austen, J., *Persuasion* (1818).
Ayers, J. (ed.), *Paupers and Pigkillers: The Diary of William Holland, a Somerset Parson 1799–1818* (Gloucester, 1984).
Bailey, M., 'Demographic Decline in Late Medieval England: Some Thoughts on Recent Research' *EHR*, 59 (1996), 1–19.
Baldock, S.F., 'Farmhouse Cider-Making Equipment in the County of Devonshire' *DH*, 19 (1979), 2–8.
Banks, S., 'Nineteenth-Century Scandal or Twentieth-Century Model? A New Look at "Open" and "Close" Parishes' *EHR*, 41 (1988), 51–73.
Barge, A.M., 'Emigration from Devon and Cornwall 1623–1638' *DCNQ*, 17 (1932), 65–67.
Barry, J., 'Religion and the Spread of Nonconformity before 1800' in R. Kain and W. Ravenhill (eds), *Historical Atlas of South-West England* (Exeter, 1999), 220–227.
Bate, F., *The Declaration of Indulgence 1672: A Study in the Rise of Organised Dissent* (1908).
Ben-Amos, I.L., 'Service and the Coming of Age of Young Men in Seventeenth-Century England' *Continuity and Change*, 3:1 (1988), 41–64.
Bennett, J.M., *Ale, Beer and Brewsters in England: Women's Work in a Changing World, 1300–1600* (New York, 1996).
Berlanstein, L.R., 'Illegitimacy, Concubinage, and Proletarianization in a French Town 1760–1914' *Journal of Family History*, 5 (1980), 360–374.
Best, H., *Rural Economy in Yorkshire in 1641* (Durham, 1857 edn).
Bettey, J.H., 'Sheep, Enclosures and Watermeadows in Dorset Agriculture in the Sixteenth and Seventeenth Centuries' in M. Havinden (ed.), *Husbandry and Marketing in the South-West 1500–1800* (Exeter Papers in Economic History, University of Exeter, 1973), 9–18.
Bettey, J.H., 'Land Tenure and Manorial Custom in Dorset 1570–1670' *Southern History*, 4 (1982), 33–54.

Biller, P.P.A., 'Birth Control in the Medieval West in the Thirteenth and Early Fourteenth Centuries' *Past and Present*, 94 (1982), 3–26.
Blake, W.J., 'Hooker's Synopsis Chorographical of Devonshire' (1600) *TDA*, 47 (1915), 334–348.
Bonfield, L., Smith, R. and Wrightson K. (eds), *The World We Have Gained* (Oxford, 1986).
Bongaarts, J., 'Does Malnutrition Affect Fecundity?' *Science*, 288 (1980), 564–570.
Boserup, E., *Women's Role in Economic Development* (1970).
Boulton, J., 'London Widowhood Revisited: The Decline of Female Remarriage in the Seventeenth and Eighteenth Centuries' *Continuity and Change*, 5 (1990), 323–355.
Bouquet, M.R., *Family, Servants and Visitors: The Farm Household in Nineteenth and Twentieth-Century Devon* (Norwich, 1985).
Bourgeois-Pichat, J., 'La Mesure de la Mortalité Infantile' *Population*, 6:2 (1951), 233–248, and 6:3 (1951), 459–480.
Bowden, P.J., 'Wool Supply and the Woollen Industry' *EHR*, 2nd ser., 9 (1956), 44–58.
Bradley, L., 'Common Law Marriage: A Possible Cause of Underregistration' *LPS*, 11 (1973), 43.
Bradley, L., 'The Most Famous of all English Plagues: A Detailed Analysis of the Plague at Eyam 1665–6', in Local Population Studies: a Supplement (ed.), *The Plague Reconsidered: A New Look at its Origins and Effects in Sixteenth and Seventeenth-Century England* (1977), 63–94.
Breen, T.H. and Foster, S., 'Moving to the New World: The Character of Early Massachussetts Immigration' *William and Mary Quarterly*, 30 (1973), 189–222.
Bridenbaugh, C., *Vexed and Troubled Englishmen 1590–1642* (Oxford, 1968).
Brockett, A.A., 'Nonconformity in Devon in the Eighteenth Century' *TDA*, 90 (1958), 31–59.
Brockett, A.A., *Nonconformity in Exeter 1650–1875* (Manchester, 1963).
Brodsky Elliot, V., 'Widows in Late Elizabethan London: Remarriage, Economic Opportunity and Family Orientations' in L. Bonfield, R. Smith, and K. Wrightson (eds), *The World We Have Gained* (Oxford, 1986), 122–154.
Brody, H., *Inishkillane: Change and Decline in the West of Ireland* (1973).
Brown, R.D., 'Devonians and New England Settlement before 1650' *TDA*, 45 (1963), 219–243.
Brushfield, T.N., 'On the Destruction of "Vermin" in Rural Parishes' *TDA*, 29 (1897), 291–349.
Brushfield, T.N., 'Aids to the Poor in a Rural Parish' *TDA*, 31 (1899), 199–284.
Brushfield, T.N., 'Colyton Marriages in Exeter Cathedral' *DCNQ*, 5 (1908), 119–20.
Buck, A., 'The Teaching of Lace-making in the East Midlands' *Folk Life*, 4 (1964), 39–50.
Burn, R., *The Ecclesiastical Law* (1824).
Caffyn, J., *Sussex Believers: Baptist Marriage in the Seventeenth and Eighteenth Centuries* (Worthing, 1988).
Camden Society, 'A Relation or Rather a True Account of the Island of England . . . about the year 1500, by an Italian' *Camden Society Series*, 37 (1847), 24–25.
Campbell, B.M.S., 'The Population of Early Tudor England: A Re-evaluation of the 1522 Muster Returns and the 1524 and 1525 Lay Subsidies' *Journal of Historical Geography*, 7:2 (1981), 145–154.
Campbell, M., 'Social Origins of Some Early Americans' in J.M. Smith, (ed.), *Seventeenth-Century America*, (Williamsburg, Va. 1959), 63–89.
Campbell, M., 'Middling People or Common Sort? The Social Origins of some Early Americans Re-examined' *William and Mary Quarterly*, 36:2 (1999), 264–286.

Campbell, R., *The London Trademan* (London, 1747; Newton Abbot 1969).
Cash, M. (ed.), *Devon Inventories of the Sixteenth and Seventeenth Centuries* (Devon and Cornwall Record Society Series, vol. 11, Exeter, 1966).
Chambers, J.D., 'Some Aspects of E.A. Wrigley's *Population and History*' *LPS*, 3 (1969), 18–28.
Chanter, J.F., 'Irregular Marriages at Brushford (1662–1669)' *DCNQ*, 7 (1919), 258–260.
Chapman, G., *A History of Axminster to 1910* (Honiton 1998).
Chapman, S.D. (ed.), *The Devon Cloth Industry in the Eighteenth Century: Sun Fire Office Inventories of Merchants and Manufacturer's Property 1726–1770* (Devon and Cornwall Record Society Series, vol. 23, Exeter, 1978).
Chapple, W., *A Review of Part of Risdon's Survey of Devon* (Barnstaple 1785; 1970 edn).
Charles, L. and Duffin, L. (eds), *Women and Work in Pre-industrial England* (Dover, 1985).
Chartres, J., 'Markets and Marketing in Metropolitan Western England in the Late Seventeenth and Eighteenth Centuries' in M. Havinden, (ed.), *Husbandry and Marketing in the South-West 1500–1800* (Exeter Papers in Economic History, University of Exeter, 1973b), 63–74.
Chaytor, M., 'Household and Kinship: Ryton in the Late Sixteenth and Early Seventeenth Centuries' *History Workshop Journal*, 10 (1980), 25–60.
Cheke, V., *The Story of Cheesemaking in Britain* (1959).
Childs, W.R. 'The Commercial Shipping of South-Western England in the Later Fifteenth-Century' *The Mariner's Mirror*, 83 (1997), 272–292.
Clapp, B., 'Wembworthy: A Devon Parish in the Eighteenth Century' in W. Minchinton, (ed.), *Population and Marketing: Two Studies in the History of the South-West* (Exeter, 1976), 65–72.
Clapp, B., 'The Place of Colyton in English Population History' *DH*, 24 (1982), 4–8.
Claridge, J., *General View of the Agriculture of the County of Dorset* (1793).
Clark, A., *Working Life of Women in the Seventeenth Century* (1919; 1968 edn; repr. 1992).
Clark, G., 'Nurse Children in Bedfordshire' *Berkshire Old and New*, 2 (1985), 25–33.
Clark, P. and Slack, P., *English Towns in Transition* (Oxford 1976).
Clark, P. and Souden, D.C. (eds), *Migration and Society in Early Modern England* (1987).
Clarke, E.A.G., *The Ports of the Exe Estuary 1660–1860* (Exeter, 1960).
Clay, C., 'Lifeleasehold in the Western Counties of England 1650–1750' *Agricultural History Review*, 29 (1981), 83–96.
Cliffe, J.T., *The Puritan Gentry Beseiged 1650–1700* (1993).
Clifton, R., *The Last Popular Rebellion* (1984).
Climenson, E.J., (ed.), *Passages from the Diaries of Mrs Lybbe Powys of Hardwick House, Oxon 1756–1808* (1899).
Coate, M., 'The Corporation of the Church of St Mary of Ottery' *TDA*, 40 (1958), 18–30.
Cockburn, J.S. (ed.), *Western Circuit Assize Orders 1629–1648: A Calendar* (Royal Historical Society Camden 4th Series, 17, 1976).
Coleman, D.C., 'An Innovation and its Diffusion: The New Draperies', *EHR*, 22 (1969), 417–429.
Collins, B., 'Proto-industrialization and Pre-Famine Emigration' *Social History*, 7 (1982), 127–146.
Collinson, P., *The Religion of the Protestants: The Church in English Society 1559–1625* (Oxford, 1982).
Colyton Parish Magazine (September 1907).
Coxhead, J.R.W., *The Romance of the Wool, Lace and Pottery Trades in Honiton* (Exmouth, 1951).

Coxhead, J.R.W., 'Axmouth Haven — East Devon's Lost Harbour' *DCNQ*, 32:1 (1972), 97–103.
Crafts, N.F.R. and Ireland, N.J., 'Family Limitation and the English Demographic Revolution: A Simulation Approach' *Journal of Economic History*, 36 (1976), 598–623.
Crawford, P., *Women and Religion in England 1500–1720* (1993).
Crawford, P. and Gowing, L., *Women's Worlds in Seventeenth-Century England* (2000).
Cresswell, B.F., *Colyton: The Church and People in Past Times* (Honiton, n.d.).
Cressy, D., *Coming Over: Migration and Communication between England and New England in the Seventeenth Century* (Cambridge, 1987).
Crick, M.M., 'Fisheries' in *VCH: Dorset* (ed. William Page, 1908a) Vol. II, 354.
Crick, M.M., 'The Hemp Industry' in *VCH: Dorset* (ed. William Page, 1908b) Vol. II, 344–52.
Cumming, E., 'Illegitimacy and Bridal Pregnancy in Ottery St Mary 1602–1837' *DH* 23 (1981), 25–29.
Davidoff, L, Doolittle M, Fink, J. and Holden, K., *The Family Story: Blood, Contract and Intimacy 1830–1960* (Harlow, 1999).
Davie, N., 'Chalk and Cheese? "Fielden" and "Forest" Communities in Early Modern England' *Journal of Historical Sociology*, 4:1 (1991), 1–31.
Davis, N.Z, 'City Women and Religious Change' in *Society and Culture in Early Modern France* (1987) 65–96.
DCNQ, Vol. V Part V (1909).
Defoe, D., *Tour Through the Whole Island of Great Britain 1724–6* (1971 edn).
de Lacy Mann, *The Cloth Industry in the West of England from 1640 to 1880* (Cambridge, 1971).
Derouet, B., 'Une Démographie Différentielle: clés pour un Système Autorégulateur des Populations Rurales d'Ancien Régime' *Annales ESC*, 35:1 (1980), 3–41.
De Vries, J., 'Between Purchasing Power and the World of Goods: Understanding the Household Economy in Early Modern Europe' in J. Brewer and R. Porter (eds), *Consumption and the World of Goods* (1993), 85–132.
Dickinson, M.G. (ed.), *A Living from the Sea: Devon's Fishing Industry and its Fishermen* (Exeter, 1987).
Dobson M.J., *Contours of Death and Disease in Early Modern England* (Cambridge, 1997).
Drake, M., *Population and Society in Norway 1735–1865* (Cambridge, 1969).
Dunlop, T. and Denham, R.D., *English Apprenticeship and Child Labour* (1912).
Dupaquier, J. and Lachiver, I., 'Sur les debuts de la Contraception en France au les deux Malthusianismes' *Annales ESC*, 24 (1969), 1391–1406.
Dupaquier, J., Helin, E., Laslett, P., Livi–Bacci, M. and Sogner, S., *Marriage and Remarriage in Populations of the Past* (1981).
Dyer, A.D., 'The Market Towns of Southern England 1500–1700' *Southern History*, 1 (1979), 123–34.
Earle, P., *Monmouth's Rebels: The Road to Sedgemoor 1685* (1977).
Earle, P., 'The Female Labour Market in London in the Late Seventeenth and Early Eighteenth Centuries' *Economic History Review*, 42 (1989a), 328–353.
Earle, P., *The Making of the English Middle Class* (1989b).
Eden, F.M., *The State of the Poor* (1797; abridged 1928 edn).
Edwards, K.L., 'Susanna's Apologie *and the Politics of Privity*' *Literature and History*, 6:1 (1997), 1–16.
Emmison, F.G., 'Poor Relief Accounts of Two Rural Parishes in Bedfordshire 1563–1598' *EHR*, 3 (1931), 102–116.
Erickson, A.L., *Women and Property in Early Modern England* (1993).
Everitt, A., 'Farm Labourers 1500–1640' in C. Clay, (ed.), *Rural Society: Landowners,*

Peasants and Labourers 1500–1750: Chapters from the Agrarian History of England and Wales, Vol. II (Cambridge 1990), 161–245.
Eyre Evans, G., *Colytonia: A Chapter in the History of Devon* (Liverpool, 1898).
Eyre Evans, G., 'Colyton Marriages in Exeter Cathedral' *DCNQ*, 5 (1908), 89–91.
Fildes, V. (ed.), *Women as Mothers in Pre-industrial England* (1980).
Fildes, V., *Breasts, Bottles and Babies* (Edinburgh, 1986).
Finberg, H.P.R., *Tavistock Abbey* (Cambridge 1951).
Finberg, H.P.R., 'A Chapter of Religious History' in W.G. Hoskins and H.P.R. Finberg (eds), *Devonshire Studies* (1952), 372–373.
Finch, G., 'The Population of Hartland in the Sixteenth and Seventeenth Centuries' *DH*, 19 (1979), 12–22.
Finlay, R.A.P., 'Distance to Church and Registration Experience' *LPS*, 24 (1980), 26–41.
Finlay, R.A.P., 'Differential Child Mortality in Pre-industrial England: The Example of Cartmel, Cumbria 1600–1750' *Annales de Démographie Historique* (1981a) 67–80.
Finlay, R.A.P., *Population and Metropolis: The Demography of London 1580–1650* (Cambridge, 1981b).
Fitzroy Jones, I., 'Aspects of Poor Law Administration, Seventeenth to Nineteenth Centuries, from Trull Overseers Accounts' *Proceedings of the Somersetshire Archaeological Society*, 95 (1952), 72–105.
Flandrin, J.L., *Families in Former Times: Kinship, Household and Sexuality* (Cambridge, 1976).
Fletcher, A. and Stevenson J. (eds), *Order and Disorder in Early Modern England* (Cambridge, 1985).
Fortescue-Foulkes, R., 'The Marwoods of Honiton and Colyton: Physicians to Royalty' *DCNQ*, 27 (1971), 48–71.
Fortescue-Foulkes, R., 'The Marwoods of Honiton and Colyton Part III' *DCNQ*, 32 (1972), 110–113.
Foster Hartley, S., 'Illegitimacy among "Married" Women in England and Wales' *Journal of Marriage and the Family*, 31 (1969), 793–798.
Fowles, J., *The French Lieutenant's Woman* (1969).
Fox, H.S.A., 'Field Systems of East and South Devon: Part 1: East Devon' *TDA*, 104 (1972), 81–135.
Fox, H.S.A., 'The Chronology of Enclosure and Economic Development in Medieval Devon' *EHR*, 28 (1975), 181–202.
Fox, H.S.A., 'The Occupation of the Land: Devon and Cornwall' in *The Agrarian History of England and Wales* (Vol. III 1348–1500 ed. Edward Miller) (Cambridge, 1991), 152–174.
Fox, H.S.A., 'Servants, Cottagers and Tied Cottages During the Later Middle Ages: Towards a Regional Dimension' *Rural History*, 6:2 (1995), 125–154.
Fox, H.S.A. 'Medieval Rural Industry' in R. Kain and W. Ravenhill (eds), *Historical Atlas of South-West England* (Exeter, 1999), 322–329.
Foyster, E.A., *Manhood in Early Modern England* (Harlow, 1999).
Fraser, R., *General View of the County of Devon with Observations on the Means of its Improvement drawn up for the Board of Agriculture* (1794).
Fry, E.A., *Calendars of Wills Relating to Devon and Cornwall* Vol. I (1908), Vol. II (1914).
Galenson, D., *White Servitude in Colonial America* (Cambridge, 1981).
Galenson, D., 'Middling People or Common Sort? The Social Origins of some Early Americans Re-examined' *William and Mary Quarterly*, 35:3 (1978) 499–540.
Galley, C., 'A Model of Early Modern Urban Demography' *EHR* 48 (1995), 448–469.
Galley, C., *The Demography of Early Modern Towns: York in the Sixteenth and Seventeenth Centuries* (Liverpool, 1998).

Geertz, C., *The Interpretation of Cultures* (1973).
Gemery, H.A., 'Emigration from the British Isles to the New World 1630–1700: Inferences from Colonial Population' *Research in Economic History*, 5 (1980), 179–231.
Gill, H.S., 'Devonshire Tokens Issued in the Seventeenth Century' *TDA*, 5 (1872), 216–243.
Gillis, J.R., *Youth and History: Tradition and Change in European Age Relations 1770–Present* (1974).
Gillis, J.R., *For Better, For Worse: British Marriages 1600 to the Present* (1985).
Gittings, C., *Death, Burial and the Individual in Early Modern England* (Beckenham, 1984).
Glass, D.V. and Eversley, D.E.C. (eds), *Population in History: Essays in Historical Demography* (1965).
Goldberg, P.J.P., *Women, Work and Lifecycle in a Medieval Economy: Women and Work in York and Yorkshire c.1300–1520* (Oxford, 1992).
Goldstone, J.A., 'The Demographic Revolution in England: A Re-examination' *Population Studies*, 40:1 (1986), 5–33.
Gorsky, M., 'The Growth and Distribution of English Friendly Societies in the Early Nineteenth Century' *EHR*, 51 (1998), 489–511.
Gowing, L., 'Secret Births and Infanticide in Seventeenth-Century England' *Past and Present*, 156 (1997), 87–115.
Gray, T. (ed.)., *Harvest Failure in Cornwall and Devon: The Book of Orders and the Corn Surveys of 1623 and 1630–1* (Institute of Cornish Studies, 1992).
Gray, T. (ed.)., *Devon Household Accounts 1627–59* Part 1 (Devon and Cornwall Record Society Series, 38, 1995).
Gray, T., 'Fisheries, Exploration, Shipping and Mariners in the Sixteenth and Seventeenth Centuries' in R. Kain and W. Ravenhill (eds), *Historical Atlas of South-West England* (Exeter, 1999), 377–383.
Greven, P.J., 'Family Structure in Seventeenth-Century Andover, Massachusetts' *William and Mary Quarterly*, 3rd series, 23 (1966), 234–256.
Greven, P.J., *Four Generations; Population, Land and Family in Colonial Andover, Massachussetts* (Ithaca 1970).
Griffith, J.D., 'Economy, Family and Remarriage', *Journal of Family Issues*, 1:4 (1980), 479–496.
Griffiths, M., 'Kirtlington Manor Court 1500–1650' *Oxoniensia*, 14 (1980), 260–283.
Gugler, J., 'The Rural–Urban Interface and Migration' in A. Gilbert, and J. Gugler, *Cities, Poverty and Development: Urbanization in the Third World* (1981), 49–64.
Gullickson, G., *Spinners and Weavers of Auffay* (Cambridge, 1986).
Gutmann, M.P., *Toward the Modern Economy: Early Industry in Europe 1500–1800* (Philadelphia, 1988).
Hair, P.E.H., 'Bridal Pregnancy in Rural England in Earlier Centuries' *Population Studies*, 20 (1966), 233–243.
Hair, P.E.H. 'Bridal Pregnancy in Earlier Rural England: Further Examined' *Population Studies*, 24 (1970), 59–70.
Hajnal, J., 'Two Kinds of Pre-industrial Household Formation Systems' *Population and Development Review*, 8 (1982), 449–494.
Hamer, J.H., 'Trading at Saint White Down Fair 1637–1649' *Somerset Archaeology and Natural History*, 112 (1968), 61–69.
Hamilton, A.H.A., *Quarter Sessions from Queen Elizabeth to Queen Anne: Illustrations of Local Government and History drawn from Original Records Chiefly of the County of Devon* (1878).
Hamilton Rogers, W.H., *West Country Stories and Sketches: Biographical and Historical* (Exeter, 1894).

Hareven, T.K., 'The Family as Process: The Historical Study of the Family Cycle' *Journal of Social History*, 7:3 (1974), 322–329.
Hareven, T.K., 'The Family Lifecycle in Historical Perspective' in J. Ousiener, (ed.), *The Family Life Cycle in European Societies* (The Hague, 1977), 339–349.
Harris M. and Ross, E.B., *Death, Sex and Fertility: Population Regulation in Pre-industrial and Developing Societies* (New York, 1987).
Harriss, B. and Watson, E., 'The Sex Ratio in South Asia' in J.H. Momsen, and J. Townshend (eds), *Geography of Gender in the Third World*, (1987), 85–115.
Harrison, C., 'Manor Courts and the Governance of Tudor England' in C. Brooks, and M. Lobban (eds), *Communities and Courts in Britain 1150–1900* (1997).
Harrison, G.V., 'The South-West' in J. Thirsk, (ed.), *The Agrarian History of England and Wales*, Vol. V (Cambridge, 1985), 377–389.
Hatcher, J., *Plague, Population and the English Economy, 1348–1530* (1977).
Hatcher, J., 'England in the Aftermath of the Black Death' *Past and Present*, 144 (1994), 3–25.
Havinden, M. 'The Woollen, Lime, Tanning and Leather-working, and Paper-making Industries, c.1500–c.1800' in R. Kain, and W. Ravenhill (eds), *Historical Atlas of South-West England* (Exeter 1999), 338–344.
Hawker, T., 'The Devonshire Farm Labourer Now and Eighty Years Ago' *TDA*, 14 (1882), 329–336.
Hawker, T., 'Devonshire Cyder' *TDA*, 15 (1883), 237–245.
Haydon, E. and Harrop J.,(eds), *The Widworthy Manorial Court Rolls 1453–1617* (Honiton, 1997).
Hendrickx, F.M.M., *In Order not to Fall into Poverty: Production and Reproduction in the Transition from Protoindustry to Factory Industry in Borne and Wierden (The Netherlands) 1800–1900* (Nijmegen, 1997).
Henning, B.D., *The History of Parliament: The House of Commons 1660–1690* Vol. I (1983).
Henry, L., *Anciennes Familles Genevoises: étude Demographique: XVIe–XXe Siècle* (Paris, 1956).
Henry, L., 'Some Data on Natural Fertility' *Eugenics Quarterly*, 8:2 (1961), 81–91.
Hey, D.G., *An English Rural Community: Myddle under the Tudors and Stuarts* (Leicester 1974).
Hill, B., 'The Age of Marriage and the Demographers' *History Workshop Journal*, 29 (1989a), 129–147.
Hill, B., *Women, Work and Sexual Politics in Eighteenth-Century England* (Oxford, 1989b).
Hill, C., *The World Turned Upside Down* (1972).
Hill, C., 'Protestantism and the Rise of Capitalism' in C. Hill, *Change and Continuity in Seventeenth-Century England* (1974), 81–102.
Hindle, S., 'Exclusion Crises: Poverty, Migration and Parochial Responsibility in English Rural Communities c.1560–1660' *Rural History*, 7 (1996), 125–149.
Hindle, S., 'Power, Poor Relief and Social Relations in Holland Fen c.1600–1800' *Historical Journal*, 41:1 (1998a), 67–96.
Hindle, S., 'The Problem of Pauper Marriage in Seventeenth-Century England' *Transactions of the Royal Historical Society*, 7 (1998b), 71–89.
Hindle, S., *The State and Social Change in Early Modern England, c.1550–1640* (2000).
Hitchcock, T., English Sexualities 1700–1800 (1997).
Hitchcock, T., King, P. and Sharpe P. (eds), *Chronicling Poverty: The Voices and Strategies of the English Poor 1640–1840 (1997).*
Holderness, B.A., 'Widows in Pre-industrial Society: An Essay upon their Economic Functions' in R.M. Smith (ed.), *Land, Kinship and Lifecycle* (Cambridge, 1984), 423–442.

Hollingsworth, T.H., *The Demography of the British Peerage* (Population Studies Supplement), 18:2 (1964).
Hollingsworth, T.H., 'The Importance of the Quality of the Data in Historical Demography' *Daedalus* (1968), 415–432.
Hollingsworth, T.H., *Historical Demography* (New York, 1969).
Horn, P., 'Child Workers in the Pillow Lace and Straw Plait Trades of Victorian Buckinghamshire and Bedfordshire' *Historical Journal*, 17:4 (1974), 779–796.
Hoskins, W.G., *Industry, Trade and People in Exeter 1688–1800* (Manchester, 1935).
Hoskins, W.G., 'The Reclamation of the Waste in Devon 1550–1800' *EHR*, 13 (1943), 80–92.
Hoskins, W.G. and Finberg, H.P.R. (eds), *Devonshire Studies* (1952).
Hoskins, W.G., 'The Rebuilding of Rural England 1570–1640' *Past and Present*, 4 (1953), 44–59.
Hoskins, W.G., *Devon* (1954).
Hoskins, W.G., *The Midland Peasant: the Economic and Social History of a Leicestershire Village* (1957).
Hoskins, W.G., *Old Devon* (Newton Abbot 1966).
Hotten, J.C., *Hotten's List of Emigrants* (Washington, 1874).
Houston, R. and Smith, R.M., 'A New Approach to Family History?' *History Workshop Journal*, 14 (1982), 120–131.
Howard, A.J. (ed.) *The Devon Protestation Returns* (Exeter, 1973).
Howell, C., *Land, Family and Inheritance in Transition, Kibworth Harcourt 1280–1700* (Cambridge, 1983).
Howkins, A., 'Peasants, Servants and Labourers: The Marginal Workforce in British Agriculture c.1870–1914' *Agricultural History Review*, 42 (1994), 49–62.
Hudson P. and King S., 'Two Textile Townships: A Comparative Demographic Analysis' *EHR*, 53 (2000), 706–741.
Hufton, O., 'Women without Men: Widows and Spinsters in Britain and France in the Eighteenth Century' *Journal of Family History*, 9:4 (1984), 355–376.
Hunt, M., *The Middling Sort: Commerce, Gender and the Family in England 1680–1780* (Berkeley, 1996).
Hunt, P. (ed.), 'Rev. John Swete's Picturesque Sketches of Devon (1792–1801)' in *Devon's Age of Elegance, Described by the Diaries of the Reverend John Swete, Lady Paterson and Miss Mary Cornish* (Exeter, 1984).
Hunt, W., *The Puritan Moment: the Coming of Revolution in an English County* (Cambridge, Mass., 1983).
Hutton, R., *The Rise and Fall of Merry England* (Oxford, 1994).
Hutton, R., *The Stations of the Sun* (Oxford, 1996).
Huzel, J.P., 'The Demographic Impact of the Old Poor Law: More Reflections on Malthus' *EHR*, 32 (1980), 367–381.
Inder, P.M., *Honiton Lace* (Exeter Museum Publication No. 55, 1971).
Ingram, M., 'Spousals Litigation in the English Ecclesiastical Courts c.1350–c.1640' in R.B. Outhwaite (ed.), *Marriage and Society* (1981), 35–57.
Ingram, M., 'Religion, Communities and Moral Discipline in Late Sixteenth and Early Seventeenth-Century England: Case Studies' in K. von Greyerz (ed.), *Religion and Society in Early Modern Europe 1500–1800* (1984), 177–193.
Ingram, M., 'The Reform of Popular Culture? Sex and Marriage in Early Modern England' in B. Reay (ed.), *Popular Culture in Seventeenth-Century England* (London, 1985).
Ingram, M., *Church Courts, Sex and Marriage in England, 1570–1640* (Cambridge, 1987).
Innes, S., *Creating the Commonweath: The Economic Culture of Puritan New England* (New York, 1995).

Jackson, P., 'Nonconformity and the Compton Census in Late Seventeenth-Century Devon' in K. Schürer K., and T. Arkell (eds), *Surveying the People* (1992), 117–129.

Jardine, C.J. and Macfarlane, A.D.J., 'Computer Input of Historical Records for Multi-source Record Linkage', in M.W. Flinn (ed.), *Proceedings of the Seventh International Economic History Congress* (1978), 71–78.

Johansen, H.C., 'The Position of the Old in the Rural Household in a Traditional Society' *Scandinavian Economic History Review*, 24 (1976), 129–142.

Johansen, H.C., 'Growing Old in an Urban Environment' *Continuity and Change*, 2:2 (1987), 297–305.

Jones, E.L., 'Agricultural Origins of Industry' *Past and Present*, 10 (1968), 58–71.

Jones, R.E., 'Infant Mortality in Rural North Shropshire 1561–1810' *Population Studies*, 30 (1976), 305–318.

Jones, R.E., 'Further Evidence on the Decline of Infant Mortality in Preindustrial England' *Population Studies*, 34 (1980), 239–250.

Jordan, W.K., *Philanthropy in England 1480–1660* (1959).

Jutikkala, E., *Social Differences in Pre-industrial Demography: A Case Study on a Middle-Sized Town* (Helsinki, 1987).

Kain, R. and Ravenhill, W. (eds), *Historical Atlas of South-West England* (Exeter, 1999).

Katz, M.B. and Davey, I.E., 'Youth and Early Industrialization in a Canadian City' in J. Demos and S.S. Boocock (eds), *Turning Points: Historical and Sociological Essays on the Family* (Chicago, 1975), 81–119.

Katz, M.B. and Tiller, J., 'Record Linkage for Everyman: A Semi-Automated Process' *Historical Methods Newsletter*, 4:5 (1972), 144–150.

Kelley, R., Skolnick, M.H. and Yasuda, N., 'A Combinational Problem in Linking Historical Records' *Historical Methods Newletter*, 6:1 (1972), 10–16.

Kennett, D.H., 'Lace-making by Bedfordshire Paupers in the Late Eighteenth Century' *Textile History*, 5 (1974), 111–118.

Kent, D.A., ' "Gone for a Soldier": Family Breakdown and the Demography of Desertion in a London Parish, 1750–91' *LPS*, 45 (1990), 27–42.

King, P., 'Pauper Inventories and the Material Lives of the Poor in the Eighteenth and Early Nineteenth Centuries' in T. Hitchcock, P. King, and P. Sharpe (eds), *Chronicling Poverty: The Voices and Strategies of the English Poor, 1640–1840* (1997), 155–191.

King, S., 'Historical Demography, Lifecycle Reconstruction and Family Reconstitution: New Perspectives' *History and Computing*, 8:2 (1996), 62–77.

King, S., 'Reconstructing Lives: The Poor, the Poor Law and Welfare in Calverley 1650–1820' *Social History*, 22:3 (1997), 318–338.

Kinvig, R.H., 'The Historical Geography of the West Country Woollen Industry' *The Geographical Teacher*, 8 (1915–16), 298.

Knight, P., 'Women and Abortion in Victorian and Edwardian England' *History Workshop Journal*, 4 (1977), 57–68.

Knodel, J.E., *Demographic Behaviour in the Past: A Study of Fourteen German Village Populations in the Eighteenth and Nineteenth Centuries* (Cambridge, 1988).

Knodel, J.E. and Shorter, E., 'The Reliability of Family Reconstitution Data in German Villages' *Annales de Démographie Historique* (1976), 115–154.

Knodel, J.E. and van der Walle, E., 'Breast-feeding, Fertility and Infant Mortality: An Analysis of some Early German Data' *Population Studies*, 21 (1967), 109–132.

Kowaleski, M., 'Town and Country in Late Medieval England: The Hide and Leather Trade' in P.J. Corfield and D. Keene (eds), *Work in Towns 850–1850* (Leicester, 1990), 57–73.

Kowaleski, M., *Local Markets and Regional Trade in Medieval Exeter* (Cambridge, 1995).

Kowaleski, M., 'The Expansion of the South-Western Fisheries in Late Medieval England' *EHR*, 53 (2000), 429–454.
Krause, J.T., 'The Changing Adequacy of English Registration 1690–1837' in D.V. Glass, and D.E.C. Eversley (eds), *Population in History: Essays in Historical Demography* (1965), 379–393.
Kumar, K., 'From Work to Employment and Unemployment: The English Experience' in R.E. Pahl (ed.), *On Work: Historical, Comparative and Theoretical Approaches* (Oxford 1988), 138–166.
Kussmaul, A., *Servants in Husbandry in Early Modern England* (Cambridge, 1981).
Kussmaul, A., *A General View of the Rural Economy of England 1538–1840* (Cambridge, 1990).
Ladurie, E. Le Roy, 'From Waterloo to Colyton' first published in the *Times Literary Supplement* (8 September 1966), 791 and reprinted in E.L. Ladurie, *The Territory of the Historian* (Brighton 1979), 223–234.
Landers, J., 'Mortality and Metropolis: The Case of London 1675–1825' *Population Studies*, 41 (1987), 59–76.
Landers, J., 'From Colyton to Waterloo: Mortality, Politics and Economics in Historical Demography' in A. Wilson (ed.), *Rethinking Social History* (Manchester 1993), 97–127.
Lane, J., *Apprenticeship in England 1600–1914* (1996).
Laslett, P. (ed.), *Household and Family in Past Time* (Cambridge 1972).
Laslett, P. (ed.), *The Earliest Classics: Works by J. Graunt and G. King* (Farnborough, 1973).
Laslett, P., 'Parental Deprivation in the Past: A Note on the History of Orphans in England' *LPS*, 13 (1974), 11–18.
Laslett, P., *Family Life and Illicit Love in Earlier Generations* (Cambridge, 1977).
Laslett, P., 'Comparing Illegitimacy over Time and between Cultures', in P. Laslett, K. Oosterveen and R.M. Smith (eds), *Bastardy and its Comparative History* (1980), 1–70.
Laslett, P., *The World we have Lost—Further Explored* (1983).
Laslett, P., Oosterveen K. and Smith, R.M. (eds), *Bastardy and its Comparative History* (1980).
Laslett, P. and Oosterveen, K., 'Long Term Trends in Bastardy in England', *Population Studies*, 27 (1973), 255–285.
Lee, C., 'Hand-made Lace and Nett: Ebb and Flow' *TDA*, 36 (1904), 135–143.
Lee Brown, R., 'The Rise and Fall of the Fleet Marriages' in R.B. Outhwaite (ed.), *Marriage and Society* (1981), 117–136.
Lemire, B., *Dress, Culture and Commerce: The English Clothing Trade before the Factory 1660–1800* (1997).
Lestaeghe, R., 'On the Social Control of Human Reproduction' *Population and Development Review*, 6 (1980), 527–548.
Lethbridge, R., 'Apple Culture and Cider-making in Devonshire' *TDA*, 32 (1900), 142–194.
Levey, S.M., *Lace: A History* (1983).
Levine, D., 'Deindustrialization and Changing Marital Habits in Colyton' *LPS*, 13 (1974), 52.
Levine, D., 'The Reliability of Parochial Registration and the Representativeness of Family Reconstitution' *Population Studies*, 30 (1976), 107–122.
Levine, D., *Family Formation in an Age of Nascent Capitalism* (New York, 1977).
Levine, D., 'Assymetrical Non-linear Population Dynamics' in R. Leboutte (ed.), *Proto-industrialization* (Centre for International Economic History, University of Geneva 1996), 93–105.
Levine, D. and Wrightson, K., 'The Social Context of Illegitimacy in Early Modern

England' in P. Laslett, K. Oosterveen and R.M. Smith (eds), *Bastardy and its Comparative History* (1980), 158–175.

Levine, D. and Wrightson, K., *The Making of an Industrial Society: Whickham 1560–1765* (Oxford, 1991).

Lewis, O., *La Vida* (1968).

Lipson, E., *The History of the Woollen and Worsted Industries* (1921).

Lithell, U.B., 'Breast-feeding Habits and their Relation to Infant Mortality and Marital Fertility' *Journal of Family History*, 6 (1981), 182–194.

Little, B., *The Monmouth Episode* (1956).

Local Population Studies (ed.), *The Plague Reconsidered: A New Look at its Origins and Effects in Sixteenth and Seventeenth-Century England* (Matlock, 1977).

Luton Museum and Art Gallery, *Pillow Lace in the East Midlands* (1958).

Lysons, D. and Lysons, S., *Magna Britannia being a Concise Topographical Account of the Several Counties of Great Britain* 6 vols (1822).

MacCaffrey, W.T., *Exeter 1540–1640* (Cambridge, Mass., 1958).

Macdonald Wigfield, W. *The Monmouth Rebellion* (Bradford on Avon, 1980).

Macdonald Wigfield, W., 'The Devon Contingent in Monmouth's Army' *DH*, 24 (1982), 15–17.

Macfarlane, A., *Witchcraft in Tudor and Stuart England: A Regional and Comparative Study (1970)*.

Macfarlane, A., Harrison, S. and Jardine, C., *Reconstructing Historical Communities* (Cambridge, 1977).

Mackinnon, A., 'Were Women Present at the Demographic Transition? Questions from a Feminist Historian to Historical Demographers' *Gender and History*, 7 (1995), 222–240.

Maclaren, A., 'Barrenness against Nature: Recourse to Abortion in Preindustrial England' *Journal of Sex Research*, 17:3 (1981), 224–237.

Maclaren, A,. *Reproductive Rituals* (New York, 1984).

Maclaren, A., *The History of Contraception from Antiquity to the Present Day* (Oxford, 1990).

Maclaren, D., 'Nature's Contraceptive . . . Wet Nursing and Prolonged Lactation: The Case of Chesham, Buckinghamshire 1578–1601', *Medical History*, 23 (1979), 427–441.

Main, G.L., 'Naming Children in Early New England' *Journal of Interdisciplinary History*, 27 (1996), 1–28.

Marshall, T.D., *The Old Poor Law 1795–1834* (1968).

Marshall, W., *Rural Economy of the West of England*, Vols I–V (1796; repr. Newton Abbot 1970).

Mathias, P., *The First Industrial Nation: An Economic History of Britain* (1969).

Matovic, M.R., 'The Stockholm Marriage: Extra-legal Family Formation in Stockholm 1860–1890' *Continuity and Change*, 1:3 (1986), 385–413.

Matthews, A.G., *Calamy Revised* (Oxford, 1934).

Matthews, A.G., *Walker Revised: Being a Revision of John Walker's Sufferings of the Clergy During the Grand Rebellion 1642–60* (Oxford, 1948).

McBride T.M., *The Domestic Revolution* (1976).

Medick, H., 'The Protoindustrial Family Economy: The Structural Function of Household and Family during the Transition from Peasant Society to Industrial Capitalism' *Social History*, 2 (1976), 291–315.

Menefee, S.P., *Wives for Sale: An Ethnographic Study of British Popular Divorce* (Oxford, 1981).

Midi Berry, B. and Schofield R.S., 'Age at Baptism in Pre-industrial England' *Population Studies*, 25 (1971), 453–464.

Mies, M., *The Lace Makers of Narsapur: Indian Housewives Produce for the World Market* (1982a).
Mies, M., 'The Dynamics of the Sexual Division of Labour and the Integration of Rural Women into the World Market' in L. Benería (ed.), *Women and Development: The Sexual Division of Labour in Rural Societies* (New York, 1982b), 1–28.
Minchinton, W., 'The Economic History and Industrial Archaeology of Devon since 1700' in F. Barlow (ed.), *Exeter and its Region* (Exeter 1969), 175–193.
Minchinton, W., *Population and Marketing: Two Studies in the History of the South-West*, (Exeter Papers in Economic History, 11, Exeter, 1976).
Mitchell, B.R. and Deane P., *Abstract of British Historical Statistics* (Cambridge, 1962).
Mitchell Whitley, H., 'An Inventory of the Goods of John Strowbridge of Hobrayne, 1576' *DCNQ*, 2 (1903), 133–136.
Moller, H., 'Sex Composition and Correlated Culture Patterns in Colonial America' *William and Mary Quarterly*, 2 (1945), 113–153.
Morrill, J., 'The Ecology of Allegiance in the English Revolution' *Journal of British Studies*, 26 (1987), 451–467.
Morrill, J.S. and Walter, J.D., 'Order and Disorder in the English Revolution' in A.J. Fletcher and J. Stevenson (eds), *Order and Disorder in Early Modern England* (1985), 137–165.
Morris, C (ed.) *The Journeys of Celia Fiennes* [1698] (1971).
Morrow, R.B., 'Family Limitation in Pre-industrial England: A Reappraisal' *EHR*, 31 (1978), 419–436.
Mount, F., *The Subversive Family* (1982).
Muldrew, C., *The Economy of Obligation* (1998).
Muntemba, S., 'Women as Food Producers and Suppliers in the Twentieth Century: The Case of Zambia' in R.E. Pahl (ed.), *On Work: Historical, Comparative and Theoretical Approaches* (Oxford, 1988), 407–427.
Murch, J., *A History of the Presbyterian Churches in the West of England* (1935).
Nair, G., *Highley: The Development of a Community 1550–1880* (Oxford, 1988).
National Trust leaflet, *Loughwood Meeting House* (n.d).
National Trust leaflet, *Shute Barton* (1996).
Newcombe, H.B. and Kennedy, J.M., 'Record Linkage' *Communications of the Association for Computing Machinery*, 5 (1962), 563–566.
Newman Brown, W., 'The Receipt of Poor Relief and Family Situation, Aldenham, Hertfordshire, 1630–90' in R.M. Smith (ed.), *Land, Kinship and Life Cycle* (1984), 405–420.
Nicholls G., *A History of the English Poor Law* Vol. I (1854; repr. 1967).
Noble, A.H., 'The Register of the Parish of Colyton, Devon' *TDA*, 102 (1970), 189–191.
Norden, J., *Speculi Brittaniae Pars* (1728, repr. 1966).
Norton, S.L., 'The Vital Question: Are Reconstituted Families Representative of the General Population?' in B. Dyke. and W.T. Morrill (eds), *Genealogical Demography* (1980), 11–12.
Nuttall G.F. (ed.), *Letters of John Pinney 1679–1699* (Oxford, 1939).
Ogilvie, S.C. and Cerman, M., *European Proto-industrialization* (Cambridge, 1996).
Oosterveen, K., Smith, R.M. and Stewart, S., 'Family Reconstitution and the Study of Bastardy: Evidence from Certain English Parishes' in P. Laslett, K. Oosterveen, K. and R.M. Smith (eds), *Bastardy and its Comparative History* (1980), 86–93.
Oswald, N.C., 'Epidemics in Devon 1538–1837' *TDA*, 109 (1977), 73–116.
Oswald, N.C., 'Devon and the Cod Fishery of Newfoundland' *TDA*, 115 (1985), 19–36.
Outhwaite, R.B., 'Population Change, Family Structure and the Good of Counting' *Historical Journal*, 22:1 (1979), 229–237.

Outhwaite, R.B., 'Sweetapple of Fledborough and Clandestine Marriage in Eighteenth-Century Nottinghamshire' *Transactions of the Thoroton Society of Nottinghamshire*, 87 (1990), 35–46.
Oxley, G.W., *Poor Relief in England and Wales* (Newton Abbot, 1974).
Palliser, B., *The History of Lace* (1875).
Parkinson, M., 'The Axe Estuary and its Marshes' *TDA*, 117 (1985), 19–62.
Pearse-Chope, R. (ed.), *Early Tours in Devon and Cornwall* (1918)
Pearson, M., 'Old Wives or Young Midwives: Women as Caretakers of Health: The Case of Nepal' in J.H. Momsen and J. Townshend (eds), *Geography of Gender in the Third World* (1987), 116–130.
Perrenoud, A., 'Surmoralité Féminine et Condition de la Femme (XVIIe–XIX Siecles) Une Véification Empirique' *Annales de Démographie Historique* (1981), 89–104.
Peskett, H., 'Heresy in Axminster in 1535' *DCNQ*, 33 (1974), 68–70.
Phelps-Brown, E.H. and Hopkins S.V., 'Seven Centuries of the Prices of Consumables Compared with Builder's Wage Rates' *Economica*, 23 (1956), 296–314.
Phythian-Adams, C., 'Rethinking Local History' *English Local History Occasional Paper*, 4th series, 1 (Leicester, 1987).
Phythian-Adams, C., *Societies, Cultures and Kinship 1580–1850: Cultural Provinces and English Local History* (Leicester, 1993).
Pickard, R., *The Population and Epidemics of Exeter in Pre-Census Times* (Exeter, 1947).
Pinchbeck, I. and Hewitt, M., *Children in English Society*, Vol. I (1969).
Pitkänen, K. 'The Reliability of the Registration of Births and Deaths in Finland in the Eighteenth and Nineteenth Centuries: Some Examples', *Scandinavian Economic History Review*, 25:1 (1977), 138–159.
Pole, W., *Collections Towards a Description of the County of Devon* [pre-1635] (1791).
Polwhele, R., *The History of Devonshire* Vols I–III (1793–7; repr. Dorking 1977).
Pounds, N.J.G., 'Barton Farming in Eighteenth-Century Cornwall' *Journal of the Royal Institution of Cornwall*, 7 (1973), 55–75.
Prior, M., *Fisher Row* (Oxford, 1982).
Prior, M., 'Women and the Urban Economy: Oxford 1500–1800' in M. Prior (ed.), *Women in English Society 1500–1800* (1985), 93–117.
Pulman, G.P.R., *The Book of the Axe* (1854; reprinted 1875).
Ralph, E., and Williams M.E. (eds), *The Inhabitants of Bristol in 1696* (Bristol Record Society, Vol. 25, 1968).
Ramsden, Lt Colonel J.V., 'Axmouth Haven', *TDA*, 77 (1945), 145–148.
Rapp, R.T., 'The Unmaking of the Mediterranean Trade Hegemony: International Trade Rivalry and the Commercial Revolution' *Journal of Economic History*, 35 (1975), 499–525.
Razzell, P.E., 'Population Change in Eighteenth-Century England—a Re-interpretation', *EHR*, 18 (1965), 312–332.
Razzell, P.E., 'The Evaluation of Baptism as a Form of Birth Registration through Cross-matching Census and Parish Register Data: a Study in Methodology' *Population Studies*, 26 (1972), 121–146.
Razzell, P.E., *The Conquest of Smallpox* (Firle, Sussex, 1977).
Razzell, P.E., *Essays in English Population History* (1994).
Reay, B., *Microhistories: Demography, Society and Culture in Rural England 1800–1930* (Cambridge, 1996).
Riddle, J.M., *Eve's Herbs: A History of Contraception and Abortion in the West* (Cambridge, Mass., 1997).
Risdon, T., *The Chorographical Description of the County of Devon*, (written pre-1640, first published 1714; 1811 edn).

Roberts, G. (ed.), *The Diary of Walter Yonge esq. Written at Colyton and Axminster, Co. Devon from 1604 to 1628* (Camden Society Series, 1848).
Roberts, M., 'Sickles and Scythes: Women's Work and Men's Work at Harvest Time' *History Workshop Journal*, 7 (1979), 3–28.
Roberts, S.K., *Recovery and Restoration in an English County 1646–1670* (Exeter, 1985).
Robin, J., 'Family Care of the Elderly in a Nineteenth-century Devonshire Parish' *Ageing and Society*, 4:4 (1984), 505–516.
Robin, J., 'Prenuptial Pregnancy in a Rural Area of Devonshire in the Mid-Nineteenth century: Colyton 1851–1881' *Continuity and Change*, 1:1 (1986), 113–124.
Robin, J., 'Illegitimacy in Colyton 1851–1881' *Continuity and Change*, 2:2 (1987), 307–342.
Robin, J., 'The Relief of Poverty in Mid-Nineteenth Century Colyton' *Rural History*, 1 (1990), 193–218.
Robin, J., 'From Childhood to Middle Age: Cohort Analysis in Colyton 1851–1891' (Cambridge Group for the History of Population and Social Structure Working Paper, 1, 1995).
Robin, J., *The Way We Lived Then* (Aldershot, 2000).
Robinson, R., 'Early Eighteenth-century Cider Production at Bearscombe Farm, South Devon' *DH*, 23 (1981), 15–18.
Rodgers, N., *Wessex Dialect* (Bradford-on-Avon, 1979).
Rogers, J., 'Family Reconstitution: New Information or Misinformation?' *Meddelande Från Familjehistoriska Projecktet*, 7 (Historical Institute, Uppsala University, 1988).
Rollison, D., *The Local Origins of Modern Society: Gloucestershire 1500–1800* (1992).
Rose-Troup, F., *John White* (1930).
Rowse, A.L., *Tudor Cornwall* (1941).
Rublack, U., 'The Public Body: Policing Abortion in Early Modern Germany' in L. Abrams and E. Harvey (eds), *Gender Relations in German History* (1996), 57–80.
Ruggles, S., *Prolonged Connections: The Rise of the Extended Family in Nineteenth-century England and America* (Madison, Wis., 1987).
Russell, J.P., 'The Loughwood Meeting House and the Founding of the Baptist Church at Kilmington and Loughwood' *DCNQ*, 33 (1959), 53–54.
Rutman, B. and Rutman, A.H., 'Now-wives and Sons in Law: Parental Death in a Seventeenth-century Virginia County', in T.W. Tate, and D.L. Ammerman (eds), *The Chesapeake in the Seventeenth Century* (New York, 1979), 153–182.
Saito, O., 'Who Worked When: Lifetime Profiles of Labour Force Participation in Cardington and Corfe Castle in the Late-Eighteenth Century and Mid-Nineteenth Centuries', *LPS*, 22 (1979), 14–30.
Salerno, A., 'The Social Background of Seventeenth Century Emigration to America' *Journal of British Studies*, 19:1 (1979), 31–52.
Santow, G., '*Coitus Interruptus* in the Twentieth Century' *Population and Development Review*, 19 (1993), 767–792.
Santow, G.,'*Coitus interruptus* and the Control of Natural Fertility' *Population Studies*, 49 (1995), 19–43.
Schofield, R.S., 'Age-Specific Mobility in an Eighteenth-Century Rural English Parish', *Annales de Démographie Historique* (1970), 261–274.
Schofield, R.S, 'Representativeness and Family Reconstitution', *Annales de Démographie Historique* (1972a), 122–125.
Schofield, R.S., 'The Standardisation of Names and the Automatic Linking of Historical Records' *Annales de Démographie Historique* (1972b), 359–364.
Schofield, R.S., 'An Anatomy of an Epidemic—Colyton, November 1645 to November 1646', in Local Population Studies Supplement (ed.), *The Plague Revisited* (Matlock, 1977), 95–126.

Schofield, R.S., 'Traffic in Corpses: some Evidence from Barming, Kent 1788–1812', *LPS*, 33 (1984), 49–53.

Schofield, R.S., 'English Marriage Patterns Revisited' *Journal of Family History*, 10 (1985), 2–20.

Schofield, R.S., 'Automated Family Reconstitution: The Cambridge Experience' *Historical Methods*, 25 (1992), 75–79.

Schofield, R.S. and Wrigley, E.A., 'Infant and Child Mortality in England in the Late Tudor and Early Stuart period', in C. Webster (ed.), *Health, Medicine and Mortality in the Sixteenth Century* (Cambridge, 1979), 61–95.

Schofield, R.S. and Wrigley, E.A.W., 'Remarriage Intervals and the Effect of Marriage Order on Fertility' in J. Dupaquier, E. Helin, P. Laslett, M. Livi-Bacci and S. Sogner (eds), *Marriage and Remarriage in Populations of the Past* (1981), 211–227.

Scott Smith, D., 'The Demographic History of Colonial New England' in M. Vinovskis (ed.), *Studies in American Historical Demography* (New York, 1979) (reprinted from *Journal of Economic History*, 1 (1972), 165–183).

Scott Smith, D., 'Child-Naming Practices as Cultural and Familial Indicators' *LPS*, 32 (1984), 17–27.

Scott Smith, D., 'Child-Naming Practices, Kinship Ties and Change in Family Attitudes in Hingham, Massachusetts 1641 to 1880' *Journal of Social History*, 18 (1985), 541–566.

Seward, D., 'The Devonshire Cloth Industry in the Early Seventeenth Century' in K. Burt (ed.), *Industry and Society in the South West* (Exeter Papers in Economic History, Exeter, 1970), 29–50.

Sharpe, P.,'Time and Wages of West Country Workfolks in the Seventeenth and Eighteenth Centuries' *LPS*, 55 (1995), 66–68.

Sharpe, P.,'Dealing with Love: The Ambiguous Independence of the Single Woman in Early Modern England' *Gender and History*, 11:2 (1999), 209–232.

Shorter, A.H., 'Flax-growing in Devon in the Eighteenth and Early Nineteenth Centuries' *DCNQ*, 24 (1950), 41–44.

Shorter, A.H., *Paper Mills and Paper Makers in England 1495–1800* (Hilversum, 1957).

Shorter, A.H., *Papermaking in the British Isles: An Historical and Geographical Study* (Newton Abbot, 1971).

Skinner, A.J.P. (ed.), *The Register of Baptisms, Marriages and Burials of Colyton, Devon 1538–1837* (Exeter, Devon and Cornwall Record Society Series, 1928).

Skipp, V.H.T., *Crisis and Development: An Ecological Case Study of the Forest of Arden 1570–1674* (Cambridge, 1978).

Slack, P., *The Impact of Plague in Tudor and Stuart England* (Oxford, 1985).

Slack, P., *Poverty and Policy in Tudor and Stuart England* (1988).

Slater, M., *Family Life in the Seventeenth Century: The Verneys of Claydon House* (1984).

Smith, J.E., 'Widowhood and Ageing in Traditional English Society' *Ageing and Society*, 4 (1984), 429–450.

Smith, J.T., 'Short-lived and Mobile: Houses in Late Seventeenth-Century England' *Vernacular Architecture*, 16 (1985), 33–34.

Smith, R.M., 'Families and their Property in Rural England 1250–1800' in R.M. Smith (ed.), *Land, Kinship and Lifecycle* (Cambridge, 1984a), 31–38.

Smith, R.M., 'The Structured Dependence of the Elderly as a Recent Development: Some Sceptical Historical Thoughts' *Ageing and Society*, 4 (1984b), 409–420.

Smith, T.C., *Nakahara: Family Farming and Population in a Japanese Village 1717–1830* (Stanford, Ca., 1977).

Snell, F.J., 'A Devonshire Yeoman's Diary' *The Antiquary*, 26 (1892), 254–259.

Snell, K.D.M., 'Parish Registration and the Study of Labour Mobility' *LPS*, 33 (1984), 29–43.

Snell, K.D.M., *Annals of the Labouring Poor* (Cambridge, 1985).
Sogner, S., 'Illegitimacy in Old Rural Society: Some Reflections on the Problems arising from two Norwegian Family Reconstitution Studies' in S. Åkerman, H.C. Johansen and D. Gaunt (eds), *Social and Economic Studies in Historical Demography in the Baltic Area* (Odense, 1978), 61–82.
Souden, D.C., 'Migrants and the Population Structure' in P. Clark (ed.), *The Transformation of English Provincial Towns* (1984a), 133–168.
Souden, D.C., 'Movers and Stayers in Family Reconstitution Populations' *LPS*, 33 (1984b), 11–28.
Souden, D.C., 'East, West—Home's Best? Regional Patterns in Migration in Early Modern England' in P. Clark and D.C. Souden (eds), *Migration and Society in Early Modern England* (1987), 292–332.
Southerden Burn, J., *The History of Parish Registers in England* (1829; Wakefield 1976 edn).
Spenceley, G.F.R., 'The Origins of the English Pillow Lace Industry' *Agricultural History Review*, 21:2 (1973), 81–93.
Spufford, M., *Contrasting Communities: English Villagers in the Sixteenth and Seventeenth Centuries* (Cambridge, 1974).
Spufford, M., 'Puritanism and Social Control?' in A. Fletcher and J. Stevenson (eds), *Order and Disorder in Early Modern England* (Cambridge, 1985), 41–57.
Spufford, M., (ed.) *The World of Rural Dissenters 1520–1725* (Cambridge, 1995).
Spurr, J., 'From Puritanism to Dissent 1660–1700' in C. Durston and J. Eales (eds), *The Culture of English Puritanism 1560–1700* (1996), 234–265.
Stack, C.B., *All Our Kin: Strategies for Survival in a Black Community* (New York, 1974).
Stanes, R., 'A Georgicall Account of Devonshire and Cornwall, Samuel Colepresse (1667)', *TDA*, 96 (1964), 269–302.
Stanes, R., 'Devon Agriculture in the mid-Eighteenth Century: the Evidence of the Milles Enquiries' in M.A. Havinden and C.M. King (eds) *The South-West and the Land* (Exeter Papers in Economic History, University of Exeter, 1969), 43–65.
Stanes R. (ed.), 'The Compton Census for the Diocese of Exeter 1676: Part 1 and 2.' *DH*, 9 and 10 (1974 & 1975), 18–27, 4–17.
Stanes, R., *The Old Farm: A History of Farming in the West Country* (Exeter, 1990).
Stephens, W.B., *Seventeenth-Century Exeter: A Study of Industrial and Commercial Development 1625–1688* (Exeter, 1958).
Stevenson.W., *General View of the Agriculture of the County of Dorset* (1813).
Stoate, T.L. and Howard, A.L. (eds), *Devon Muster Roll, 1569* (Exeter, 1977).
Stoate, T.L. (ed.), *1524 Lay Subsidy* (Exeter, 1979).
Stoate, T.L. (ed.), *Devon Hearth Tax 1674* (Exeter, 1982).
Stoate, T.L. (ed.), *Devon Subsidy Rolls 1543–5* (Exeter, 1986).
Stone, L. and Stone, J.C.F., *An Open Elite? England 1540–1880* (Oxford, 1984).
Stoyle, M., *Loyalty and Locality: Popular Allegiance in Devon during the English Civil War* (Exeter, 1994).
Stretton T., *Women Waging Law in Elizabethan England* (Cambridge, 1998).
Tadmor, N., 'The Concept of the Household-Family in Eighteenth-Century England' *Past and Present*, 151 (1996), 111–140.
Tattersfield, N., *The Forgotten Trade* (1991)
Tawney, R.H., *Religion and the Rise of Capitalism* (1987).
Taylor, J.S., 'The Impact of Pauper Settlement 1691–1834', *Past and Present*, 73 (1976), 42–74.
Thirsk, J., 'Industries in the Countryside' in F.J. Fisher (ed.), *Essays in the Economic and Social History of Tudor and Stuart England* (Cambridge, 1961), 70–88.
Thirsk, J., *Economic Policy and Projects* (Oxford, 1978).

Thirsk, J., *England's Agricultural Regions and Agrarian History 1500–1750* (1987).
Thomas, K., 'Age and Authority in Early Modern England' *Proceedings of the British Academy*, 62 (1976), 214–218.
Thomson, D., 'Welfare and the Historians' in L. Bonfield, R.M. Smith and K. Wrightson (eds), *The World We Have Gained* (Oxford, 1986b), 355–378.
Thompson, E.P., *The Making of the English Working Class* (1963)
Thompson, E.P., *Customs in Common* (1991).
Thompson, R., 'Seventeenth-Century English and Colonial Sex Ratios: a Postscript' *Population Studies*, 28 (1974a), 153–165.
Thompson, R., *Women in Stuart England and America: A Comparative Study*, (1974b).
Thornton, W.H., 'The Devonshire Matrimonial Market' *DCNQ*, 4 (1916), 54–55.
Todd, B.J., 'The Remarrying Widow: A Stereotype Reconsidered' in M. Prior (ed.), *Women in English Society 1500–1800* (1985), 54–92.
Todd, B.J., 'Demographic Determinism and Female Agency: The Remarrying Widow Reconsidered . . . Again' *Continuity and Change*, 9 (1994), 421–450.
Townshend J. and Momsen, J.H., 'Towards a Geography of Gender in Developing Market Economies' in J.H. Momsen and J. Townsend (eds), *Geography of Gender in the Third World* (1987), 27–82.
Tranter, N.L., 'Population and Social Structure in a Bedfordshire Parish: the Cardington Listing of Inhabitants 1782' *Population Studies*, 3 (1967), 261–282.
Travis, J.F., *The Rise of the Devon Seaside Resorts 1750–1900* (Exeter, 1993).
Trenchard, D., *Women of Dorset: Famous and Forgotten Women from the Dark Ages to the Present Day* (Tiverton, 1994).
Turner, D., 'An East Devon Family 1570–1646' *DCNQ*, 29 (1963), 47–49.
Tyacke, N., 'Popular Puritan Mentality in Late Elizabethan England' in A.G.R. Smith and N. Tyacke (eds), *The English Commonwealth 1547–1640* (Leicester, 1979), 77–92.
Underdown, D., 'The Taming of the Scold: the Enforcement of Patriarchal Authority in Early Modern England', in A. Fletcher and J. Stevenson (eds), *Order and Disorder in Early Modern England*, (Cambridge 1985a), 116–137.
Underdown, D., *Revel, Riot and Rebellion: Popular Politics and Culture in England 1603–1660* (Oxford, 1985b).
Underdown, D., 'A Reply to John Morrill' *Journal of British Studies*, 26 (1987), 468–479.
Underdown, D., *Fire from Heaven: Life in an English Town in the Seventeenth Century* (1993).
Underdown, D., *A Freeborn People* (Oxford, 1996).
Vancouver, C., *General View of the Agriculture of the County of Devon* (1808; 1813 edn).
van de Walle, E., 'Flowers and Fruits: Two Thousand Years of Menstrual Regulation' *Journal of Interdisciplinary History*, 28:2 (1997), 183–203.
van der Woude, A.M., 'Population Developments in the Northern Netherlands (1500 to 1800) and the Validity of the Urban Graveyard Effect' *Annales de Démographie Historique* (1982), 55–75.
Vann, R.T., 'Unnatural Fertility, or Whatever Happened in Colyton? Some Reflections on English Population History from Family Reconstitution 1580–1837' *Continuity and Change*, 14 (1999), 91–104.
Vann, R.T. and Eversley, D., *Friends in Life and Death: The British and Irish Quakers in the Demographic Transition* (Cambridge, 1992).
Victoria County History of Dorset Vol.II ed. William Page (1908).
Wales, T., 'Poverty, Poor Relief and the Lifecycle: Some Evidence from Seventeenth-Century Norfolk' in R.M. Smith (ed.), *Land, Kinship and Life Cycle* (Cambridge, 1984), 351–404.

Wall, R., 'Mean Household Size from Printed Sources' in P. Laslett (ed.), *Household and Family in Past Time* (Cambridge, 1972), 159–203.
Wall, R., 'Reconstitution and Census: Colytonians in Parish Register and Enumerator's Book' in W. Minchinton (ed.), *Population and Marketing: Two Studies in the History of the South-West* (Exeter Papers in Economic History, 11, Exeter, 1976), 73–90.
Wall, R., 'The Age at Leaving Home' *Journal of Family History*, 3:2 (1978), 181–202.
Wall, R., 'Inferring Differential Neglect of Females from Mortality Data' *Annales de Démographie Historique* (1981a), 119–140.
Wall, R., 'Women Alone in English Society' *Annales de Démographie Historique* (1981b), 303–20.
Wall, R., 'Work, Welfare and the Family: Farmers and Labourers of Colyton in a Comparative Perspective', in L. Bonfield, R.M. Smith and K. Wrightson (eds), *The World we have Gained* (Oxford, 1986), 261–294.
Wall, R., 'Leaving Home and the Process of Household Formation in Preindustrial England' *Continuity and Change*, 2:1 (1987), 77–101.
Wall, R., Robin, J. and Laslett, P. (eds), *Family Forms in Historic Europe* (Cambridge, 1983).
Walsh, L.S., ' "Till Death Us Do Part": Marriage and Family in Seventeenth-Century Maryland' in T.W. Tate and D.L. Ammerman (eds), *The Chesapeake in the Seventeenth Century* (New York, 1979), 126–152.
Wanklyn, C., *Lyme Regis: A Retrospect* (1927).
Warne, A., *Church and Society in Eighteenth-Century Devon* (Newton Abbot, 1969).
Watts, M.R., *The Dissenters*, Vol. I (Oxford, 1978).
Weir, D.R., 'Rather Never Than Late: Celibacy and Age at Marriage in English Cohort Fertility' *Journal of Family History*, 9:4 (1984), 340–354.
Welch, C.E., 'The Division of Colyton and Shute in 1658' *DCNQ*, 28 (1959), 111–112.
Wells, R.V., *The Population of the British Colonies in America before 1776: A Survey of Census Data* (Princeton, 1975).
Wenlock, R.J. and Wenlock, R.W., 'Maternal Nutrition, Prolonged Lactation and Birth Spacing in Ethiopia' *Journal of Biological Science*, 13:3 (1981), 261–268.
Westcote, T., *A View of Devonshire in 1630* (1630).
Whetham, C.D. and M., *A Manor Book of Ottery St Mary* (1913).
White, R.G.C., *The History of the Feoffees of Colyton 1546–1946* (Bridport, 1951).
Whiteman, A. (ed.), *The Compton Census of 1676: A Critical Edition* (Oxford, 1986).
Whitham, J., *Ottery St. Mary* (Chichester, 1984).
Whittle, J., 'Inheritance, Marriage, Widowhood and Remarriage: a Comparative Perspective on Women and Landholding in North-East Norfolk 1440–1580' *Continuity and Change*, 13:1 (1998), 35–40.
Wickes, M. (ed.), *Devon in the Religious Census of 1851* (Exeter, 1990).
Widdowson, J.D.A., 'A Survey of Current Folklore Research in Newfoundland' *TDA*, 101 (1969), 183–196.
Wilkin, W.H., 'The Rev. John Wilkins of Colyton' *DCNQ*, 18 (1934a), 370–371.
Wilkin, W.H., 'Notes on the Members for Honiton 1640–1868' *TDA*, 66 (1934b), 253–278.
Wilkin, Major W.H., 'Colyton Parish: Vicars since 1525' in *Pulman's Weekly News*, 5/3/1935, 20–26.
Williams, W.M., *A West Country Village: Ashworthy, Family, Kinship and Land* (1963).
Wilson, A., 'Participant or Patient? Seventeenth-century Childbirth from the Mother's Point of View' in R. Porter (ed.), *Patients and Practitioners: Lay Perceptions of Medicine in Pre-industrial Society* (Cambridge, 1985), 129–144.

Wilson, C., 'Cloth Production and International Competition in the Seventeenth Century' *EHR*, 13 (1960), 209–221.

Winchester, I., 'The Linkage of Historical Records by Man and Computer: Techniques and Problems' *Journal of Interdisciplinary History* 1:1 (1970), 107–124.

Winchester, I., 'A Brief Survey of the Algorithmic, Mathematical and Philosophical Literature Relevant to Historical Linkage' in E.A. Wrigley (ed.), *Identifying People in the Past* (1973), 128–150.

Windeatt, E., 'Early Nonconformity in the Neighbourhood of Seaton' *TDA*, 17 (1885), 298–312.

Wolffe, M., *Gentry Leaders in Peace and War* (Exeter, 1997).

Worth, R.N., 'Puritanism in Devon and the Exeter Assembly' *TDA*, 9 (1877), 250–291.

Wrightson, K., 'Infanticide in Earlier Seventeenth-Century England' *LPS*, 15 (1975a), 10–21.

Wrightson, K., 'Villages, Villagers and Village Studies' *Historical Journal*, 13 (1975b), 632–639.

Wrightson, K., 'The Nadir of English Illegitimacy in the Seventeenth Century' in P. Laslett, K. Oosterveen and R.M. Smith (eds), *Bastardy and its Comparative History* (1980), 176–191.

Wrightson, K., *English Society 1580–1680* (1982).

Wrightson, K. and Levine, D., *Poverty and Piety in an English Village: Terling 1525–1700* (New York, 1979; second edn Oxford, 1995).

Wrigley, E.A., 'Family Limitation in Pre-industrial England' *EHR*, 19 (1966a), 82–109. Reprinted in E.A. Wrigley, *People, Cities and Wealth* (Oxford, 1987), 242–270.

Wrigley, E.A., *An Introduction to English Historical Demography* (1966b).

Wrigley, E.A., 'Mortality in Pre-industrial England: An Example of Colyton, Devon over Three Centuries' *Daedalus*, 97 (1968), 546–580.

Wrigley, E.A., *Population and History* (1969a).

Wrigley, E.A., 'Baptism/Marriage Ratios in Late Seventeenth-century England' *LPS*, 3 (1969b), 15–17.

Wrigley, E.A., 'Some Problems of Family Reconstitution using English Parish Register Material: the Example of Colyton' in *Demography and Economy* (Paris, 1972), 199–221.

Wrigley, E.A. (ed.), *Identifying People in the Past* (1973a).

Wrigley, E.A., 'Clandestine Marriage in Tetbury in the Late Seventeenth Century' *LPS*, 12 (1973b), 15–21.

Wrigley, E.A., 'Baptism Coverage in Early Nineteenth-Century England: the Colyton Area' *Population Studies*, 29 (1975), 299–316.

Wrigley, E.A., 'Births and Baptisms: The Use of Anglican Baptism Registers as a Source of Information about the Number of Births in England before the Beginning of Civil Registration' *Population Studies*, 31:2 (1977a), 281–312.

Wrigley, E.A., 'The Changing Occupational Structure of Colyton over Two Centuries' *LPS*, 18 (1977b), 9–21.

Wrigley, E.A., 'A Note on the Life-Time Mobility of Married Women in a Parish Population in the Later Eighteenth Century' *LPS*, 18 (1977c), 22–29.

Wrigley, E.A., 'Marital Fertility in Seventeenth-Century Colyton: A Note', *EHR*, 31 (1978), 429–436.

Wrigley, E.A., 'Marriage, Fertility and Population Growth in Eighteenth-Century England' in R.B. Outhwaite (ed.), *Marriage and Society* (1981), 137–185.

Wrigley, E.A., *People, Cities and Wealth* (Oxford, 1987).

Wrigley, E.A., 'How Reliable is our Knowledge of the Demographic Characteristics of the English Population in the Early Modern Period?' *Historical Journal*, 40.3 (1997), 571–595.

Wrigley, E.A. and Schofield, R.S., *The Population History of England 1541 to 1871* (Cambridge, 1981).

Wrigley, E.A. and Schofield, R.S., 'English Population History from Family Reconstitution: Summary Results 1600–1799' *Population Studies*, 37 (1983), 157–184.

Wrigley, E.A., Davies, R.S., Oeppen, J.E., and Schofield, R.S., *English Population History from Family Reconstitution 1580–1837* (Cambridge, 1997).

Wyatt, P (ed.), *The Uffculme Wills and Inventories 16th–18th centuries* (Exeter, Devon and Cornwall Record Society, 40, 1997).

Yallop, H.J., 'Honiton and William, Prince of Orange' *TDA*, 121 (1989), 109–127.

Yallop, H.J., *The History of the Honiton Lace Industry* (Exeter, 1992).

Yarborough, A., 'Apprentices as Adolescents in Sixteenth-Century Bristol' *Journal of Social History*, 13:1 (1979), 67–82.

Youings, J., 'An Economic History of Devon 1300–1700' in F. Barlow (ed.), *Exeter and its Region* (Exeter, 1969), 164–174.

Young, M. and Wilmott, P., *Family and Kinship in East London* (1957).

Young, M. and Wilmott, P., *The Symmetrical Family: A Study of Work and Leisure in the London Region* (1972).

Zahedieh, N., 'London and the Colonial Consumer in the Late Seventeenth Century' *EHR*, 47 (1994), 239–261.

Zell, M., *Industry in the Countryside: Wealden Society in the Sixteenth Century* (Cambridge, 1994).

Glossary

barton a farm in the demense of the manor.
bid-ale an ale for the benefit of a person in the community to which a general bidding was given.
bobbin lace lace made on a pillow with bobbins.
borough a town with a municipal corporation and special privileges conferred by royal charter. Also a town which sends representatives to parliament.
calamanco a glossy woollen cloth, twilled and chequered on the warp so that the checks are seen on one side only.
chain as a term used in weaving, the warp.
Compton Census a religious census of 1676, commissioned by the Earl of Danby but executed by Bishop Compton of London.
conventicle a clandestine or illegal meeting, or a reference to a non-conformist or Dissenting meeting house.
copyholder holder of the tenure of lands being parcel of a manor 'at the will of the lord according to the custom of the manor' by copy of the manorial court-roll.
damask a rich fabric with elaborate patterns.
Dissenter one who disagrees in matters of religious belief and worship and separates himself from the communion of the Church of England.
dummy marriage an assumed marriage date based on the birth of the couple's first child.
endogenous infant mortality death of an infant assumed to be arising from causes connected with its birth.
estover 'necessaries allowed by law', usually wood for repairs allowed to the tenant from the landlord's estate.
family reconstitution a technique by which records concerning the vital events of all members of a family are linked to each other. Recorded on a **family reconstitution form (FRF)**.
feoffee one of a board of trustees holding land for public and charitable purposes.
fulling mill a mill in which cloth is treaded and beaten to cleanse and thicken it by being pressed by rollers and cleansed with soap or fuller's earth.
galume (galloon) lace a narrow, close-woven ribbon or braid used for trimming articles of apparel.
grist mill a mill for grinding corn.
hayes/hayne an enclosure.
Hearth Tax tax collected from 1662 to 1689 with local assessment based on the number of hearths in a house, thus providing information on households.
heriot a render due on the death of a tenant, usually paid by a widow for her holding.
kersey a narrow, coarse woollen cloth woven from long wool.
Land Tax parochial tax assessments for the late eighteenth and early nineteenth centuries, providing information about land distribution.

GLOSSARY

Lay subsidy tax assessments carried out at various dates.
linney (or lynney) a lean-to, two-storied barn with the ground floor open and used for animals and the upper storey for storing hay etc.
linsey-woolsey a textile of mixed wool and flax.
nail a length of cloth measuring a sixteenth of a yard.
needlepoint point lace made with a needle.
nonconformist [in the seventeenth century sense] one who while adhering to the doctrine of the Church of England, refused to conform to its discipline and practice. In this book I have used the term as synonymous with dissenter (q.v.) in the eighteenth century.
parish register aggregate analysis by simple totals of events rather than a technique like family reconstitution which subdivides the population.
peculiar a parish removed from the usual ecclesiastical system and placed under the direct jurisdiction of the Bishop or the Dean and Chapter.
point-maker a lace-maker, in the sense that points was used to describe all lace, or maker of cords for lacing up clothes.
Poll Tax tax on number of heads.
portion the property a bride takes into marriage, also known as a dowry.
portreeve chief officer of a borough (except the mayor in some cases).
potwallers in some English boroughs before 1832 (in this case, Honiton) a man qualified for a Parliamentary vote as a householder. The test of this was that he possessed a separate fireplace on which food was cooked for himself and his family.
poundhouse pounding apparatus possibly for cider.
pressing iron and shears presumably the area in which the final presentation of cloth was carried out.
Protestation Oath—in February 1641/2 all men aged 18 and over were asked to swear to maintain and defend 'the true, reformed Protestant religion', 'the Power and Privilege of Parliament' and 'the lawful Rights and Liberties of the Subjects'.
Puritan a member of that party of English Protestants who regarded the reformation of the church under Elizabeth as incomplete and called for its further 'purification' from unscriptural and corrupt forms and ceremonies retained from the unreformed church. Subsequently often applied to those who separated from the Established Church on points of ritual, polity or doctrine.
rackrent a level of rent, equal (or almost equal) to the annual value of the land.
serge a woollen fabric often with the warp of worsted and the woof of wool and used to make clothing.
settlement legal residence in a particular parish conferring the right to poor relief from the poor rates. From 1662 parishes issued certificates designating settlement rights to people according to settlement law.
Ship Money an ancient tax levied in time of war on the ports and maritime towns, cities and counties of England to provide ships for the king's service. It was revived by Charles I, with an extended application to inland counties, but abolished by statute in 1640.
spousal usually colloquially refers to a betrothal and what we would in modern terms describe as an engagement.
skaining turn an implement to measure or store a quantity of thread or yarn wound to a certain length on a reel.
skillet a metal cooking utensil with a long handle.
squire a country gentleman or landed proprietor.
status used in this book as a socio-economic classification, partly influenced by income but also denotes both a position in the social system and the honour or prestige denoted by this position.

stock a designated sum of money or goods to be used for the employment of the poor.

tithe a grant of a tenth of one's earnings to the church.

tithing(man) a rural division, originally a company of ten householders. The tithingman was, anciently, the headhouseholder of this group. In early modern Colyton, the term denotes the equivalent of the parish peace-officer or petty constable.

total reconstitution an enhanced method of family reconstitution involving linking information from documents other than the parish registers.

tucker/tucking mill another name for a fuller, or cloth finisher, and the mill where it is carried out.

turbary a piece of land where peat or turf may be dug for fuel usually by common right.

wood-pasture areas of cleared woodland, usually under permanent pasture. Such areas are characterised by heavy land, many commons, dispersed settlement, weak social control, large parishes, inmigration, much industry, radical politics and Dissenting religion.

worsted a woollen fabric or stuff made from well-twisted yarn spun of long-staple wool combed to lay the fibres parallel.

yeoman a man owning or cultivating a small estate, a freeholder under the rank of gentleman.

Index

Where a page reference appears in bold, this indicates illustrative material relevant to the index entry.

Abbot, John, 216
Abbott, Mary and Elizabeth, 103
Abrahams, Elizabeth, 255, 292
Abrahams, Samuel, 258
Act of Uniformity 1662, 45
Alford, Gregory (Mayor of Lyme), 41, 46–7, 53, 55, 113
American Wars, impact on industries, 89, 107
Anning, James, 311–12
Anning, Mary (known as Facey), 282
apprenticing of middle classes, 258, 265–6
apprenticing of poor, 257–67, **259**, 270
   age at, 257, 258, 263–4, **263**, 267, 270, 357
   family circumstances, 264–7, **264, 265,** 357
   in farm labour, 152, 262–3, 344–5
   favoured by feoffees, 251, 257
   hardship as cause, 259–60
   impact of plague, 260–1
   indentures, 266, 267
   independence and marriage of, 267, 269
   as paid employment, 268, 269–70
   payments for, 263
   registers of, 17, 19, 75, 251, 257, 261
   to relatives, 266, 270
   seasonal patterns, 261–2, **262**
   as settlement criterion, 266
   sex ratios and differences, 259, **260**, 266, 356
   as statutory function, 257, 258, 259
   in trades, 103–4, 171, 270
Arden (Warwickshire), 316
Ascott, Nathaniell, 286
Auffay (France), 315
Auton, Susannah, 230–1
Awliscombe parish, 219–20, 270
Axe estate, provision of marriage portions, 278–9
Axe Estuary, 5, 134, **137**

efforts to reopen, 134–5, 138
impact of loss of harbour, 135
inland fishery, 138
marshes *see* salt marshes and meadows
quay constructed, **136**, 138
silting, 71, 134
Axminster, 30, 71, 73, 329
   Anglican clergy, 31
   carpet factory, 89
   in Civil War, 40
   Independent congregations, 46
   overcrowded, 201
   Royalist garrison, 82, 83
Axmouth, 32–3, 71, 134
   early trade centre, 77, 134
   loss of fishing community, 135
   Parliamentary garrison, 41
   Puritans, 32, 34, 40
   tannery, 130

Bagwell, Francis (churchwarden), 49
Bagwell, John, 48
Bagwell, Peter, 56–7, 124
Bagwill, Joel (of Offwell), 151
Bailes, John (informer), 58
Baker, William (of Widworthy), 151
Bale, Walter and Elinora, 286
Balster, Abraham, 62
baptism register, 18, 19, 27, 189, 193, 328
   as registration for poor relief, 20
Baptists, 29, 43, 47, 60
   see also Dissenters
Barnard, Jane and John, 280
Baron, Dorothy, 101–2
Barrett, John, Elizabeth and Mary, 170
Bartlett, Anna, John and Samuel (of Whimple), 104
bastardy records *see* recording of *under* children, illegitimate
Batstone, Thomas, 269–70
Batt, Eleanor, 297–8

397

Batt, James (of Uffculme), 88
Batt, Joane, 229
Batt, William, 297
Batten, James, 195
Bawden, Jayes, 285
Beavis, Jane, 165
Beer, 144, 201, 334
Beer, George (of Honiton), 108
Bennett, Elisha, 91
Berry, Jane and William, 289
Berry, William, 89
Bird, George, 224–5
Bird, Stephen (overseer), 220
Bird, William (lace dealer), 101
birth *see* childbirth
birth control, 189–97
  through abortion, 193, 195, 196–7, 350
  through breast feeding, 192, 193, 255, 349–50
  through coitus interruptus, 37, 193, 197
  see also fertility
birthplace records for poor relief, 20
birthrates *see* fertility
Bishop, Hannah, 103
Bishop, William, 243
Blackaller, Ann, 112, 113, 305
Blackaller, Thomas (physician), 77
Blackaller, William, 112, 113
Blackmore, Thomas (alias Hill), 77, 153
Boden, John (glover), 131
Bole, Isaac, 243
Bole, Joan, 246
Bole, William, 268
Bond, Edward (constable), 48
Bord, Henry (of Widworthy), 114, 213
Bowder, William (of Honiton), 108
Brackley, Deborah (of Lamerton), 193
Bradforde, Mary (manorial tenant), 149
Bright, Thomas, 270
Browne, Robert (Colyton manor), 212
Buckland, John (feoffee), 79
Buddlehayes farm, 17, 127
Bull, Elizabeth, baptism of, 19
Bully, Mary, spoused to John Hart, 286–7
Burd, Maria, 254
Burd, William, 119
burials register, 19, 23, 27, 162, 260
Burnard, John, 220
Burrough, Mary (midwife), 195
Burwell, John, 73, 76, 92
Butler, James (schoolmaster), 232–3
Byrde, John (feoffee), 79

Cambridge Group for the History of Population and Social Structure, 2–3, 8, 11, 21, 313
Card, Mary, 47
Carew, Peter, 254
Carew-Pole family *see* Pole family

Carmel, Grace, 273
Carpenter, John, 104
Carter, John (customs officer), 112
Castle, Nicholas (of Axminster), 73
cattle droving *see* droving *under* pastoralism
Cawley, Edward, 131
census data for Colyton, 14, 20, 318
  Compton Census, 8, 48, 106, 329, 353
Chamber of Feoffees *see* Feoffees, Chamber of
Chard, William (of Honiton), 103
child mortality *see* mortality, child; mortality, infant
child raising, 253, 254, 257
  training *see* apprenticing; schools
  weaning, age at, 255
  wet nursing, 192, 193, 252, 254–6
child status, 257
  achievement of independence, 267–8, 274, 290, 308, 357–8, 362
childbirth, 252–4
children, illegitimate, 283–4, **284**
  apprenticing of, 263, 266
  as challenge to social order, 281
  with father's name, 282
  maintenance of, 252–3, 289, 293
  recording of, 17, 19, 251, 323
  see also illegitimate mothers
Chubb, Matthew, 280
Chudleigh parish closed to migration, 116
churchwardens, 35, 49, 50, 222
cider houses, 132, 342
cider production 130, 131–2, **133**, 342
Civil Wars, 30, 40–1, 209
  local disruption, 82–3, 147, 219, 260
  men killed, 115, 147, 163
  women's involvement with, 114
Clapp, Thomas (constable), 48
Clarke, Henry (cottager), 140, 142
Clarke, John, 271
Clarke, Thomas, 312
Cleeve, John, 77
Clegg, William, 54–5
Cleveland, Daniel (of Honiton), 59, 75
Clode, James, 280
cohorts *see under* family reconstitution for Colyton
Colcombe, in Civil War, 209, 216
Collier, Mary, 245–6
Collings, John (constable), 220
Collins, Robert, 47, 220
Collyns, Thomas, 22, 41, 45, 330–1
colonies, 38–9
  emigration to, 30, 39–40, 169, 170–1, 312, 347
  penal, 56–7
  trade with, 3, 71, 74–5, 100
Coly River, 5, 79, 87–8, 131

INDEX

Colyford, 5, 71, 72, 132, 157, 212–13
Colyford Common, 142
Colyford Meadow, 138, 140–2, **141**, 158
Colyton (town), 5, **6**, 134, **156**
  as centre for Dissenters, 34, 41, 49
  gentrification, 310
  impact of plague, 84–5, 147, 219, 260, 307–8
  industries, 106, 118, 131, 306, 308
  as market town, 71, 72, 73, 119, 127
  Monmouth Rebellion and Civil Wars, 41, 51–2, 54–5
  poverty, times of, 147, 157
  riot against customs officials, 112–13, 117
  saltworks, 144
  transport limitations, 73, 77
  water supply, 201
Colyton, Lazarus, 20, 255
Colyton church, 17
  attendance laws, 46, 50
  avoided for marriage ceremonies, 20–1, 22, 23, 349
  baptism records without marriage records, 12
  Courtney–Pole tombs, **42**, 43, 331
  rates and taxes for repairs, 15, 30, 89, 229
Colyton Friendly Society, 298–9, 361
Colyton hundred, 212, 220
Colyton manor, 121, 149–50, 211–12
Colyton Parish, **xvi**, 8, 16, 23–4, 120–1, 157, 160
  chapelries, 8, 23
  comparable studies, 313–16
  documentation of, 14–27, 30, 214, 251–2, 305–6, 319
  economic peak, medieval, 71, 77, 118
  employment opportunities, 169
  factional divisions, 49, 211, 220, 233
  marshes as source of malaria, 200–1, 202
  official positions hard to fill with Anglicans, 49, 220
  open to migration, 116, 169, 232
  peculiar of the Dean and Chapter of Exeter, 16, 22, 36
  rebels *see under* Monmouth Rebellion
  support of poor, 82, 84, 219, 220
  tithes, 127, 150, 213
  typicality of, 10, 11, 63, 121, 157
  urban characteristics, 307–8, 310
  vicars, appointments and ejections, 22, 36, 41
Colyton Parish Registers, 8, 14, 18–20
  aggregated data, 9, **9**
  baptisms *see* baptism register
  burials *see* burials register
  commencement of, 318, 363
  completeness of, 18–19, 20–2, 26–7, 327–8

copied to parchment and bound, 8, 14, 18
  marriages *see* marriage register
  nominal linkage to other sources, 11, 14, 18
  residents without records, 26–7, **26**
  see also unrecorded *under* marriages
commons, 121, 147–9
  access to, 123, 124, 142, 148, 149
  controlled by landowners, 123, 124, 127, 147, 210
  dwellings for the poor on, 229–30
  enclosures of, 148–9
  wastes, resources of, 142
Commonwealth period, 41, 43
Compton census *see under* census data for Colyton
control
  as attribute of Puritanism, 279, 284
  through poor relief, 221, 237–8
  as reaction to insecurity, 210–11, 219, 238, 308
Conventicle Acts, 46–9, 51
Copp, Gilbert, 52
Cornish, Joseph (schoolmaster), 233
cottagers, 146–7, 149, 150, 158
  access to commons *see under* commons
  cloth work, 146
  dairying, 150–2
  diversity of production, 149–50
  impact of Civil War, 147
  as labour force, 152–4, 162
  pasturage, 146
  see also labourers, farm
Coul, Catherine, 289
Courtenay, Henry (Marquis of Exeter), 16
  execution in 1538, 16, 122
Courtenay-Pole family *see* Pole family
Cox, Elizabeth, Jane and Mary, 51
Cox, John (farmer), 218
Cox, John (of Shute), 278
Cox, Philip, 56
crafts status group, 12–13, 320–3
  birth intervals, 193
  impact of plague, 85
  numbers without parish records, 26–7, **26**
  representation in marriage records, 23, 27
craftsmen, 158
  as Dissenters and Puritans, 78, 94
  for local trade, 75, 258
  from poor relief training and work, 75
  specialist, 76
Croker, William (of Beer), 115
Cross, Deborah, 265–6
Crow, Ann, marriage to Robert Sandy, 24–5
Culme, Thomas (of Colyton), 218
Curteise, Christian, 272
customs officers and riot over confiscated cloth, 112, 113

399

dairying, 129–30, 150–2, 160
  leasing of cows and dairies, 150–2
  products sold by women, 115–16
  see also pastoralism
Daniel, Joane (of Axminster), 113–14
Darby, John, 129–30
Darke, Robert (of Honiton), 103
Davis, Mary, 238
Deane, John, Sarah and children, 255–6
death customs, 298
Defoe, Daniel, 88
deindustrialisation, 91, 157, 158, 160, 173, 214
demographic trends, 8–9, **9**, 10, 190, 204–5, 207, 306–8, 310–11
  pressure on land from population growth, 169
Dene, Arthur (curate), 25
Denning, Widow and Thomazine, 230–1
Devon, 5, 7
  industries, 67, 88
  plague epidemics, 202–3
  records for parishes other than Colyton, 15
  Records Office, bombed in 1942, 16
  sex ratios, 346
Diamont, Mary, 280–1
Dissent, 29
  anti-authoritarian, 30, 40–1, 251, 309
  philosophy of discipline, 206, 207, 261, 279, 308–9
  as reason for non-Anglican marriages, 27, 28
  work ethic, 94, 108, 118–19, 219–20, 261
Dissenters, 25, 29–30, 32, 43, 309–10
  acts of, 31–4, 35–6, 63
  decline of, 60–1, 159, 209, 214
  emigration to New World, 30, 39–40
  illegal marriages, 31, 62
  middle class, 29–30, 39, 50, 329
  migration of, 210
  nonconformist academies, 46, 60, 233–4
  persecution of, 30, 46, 47, 209, 222
  as political force, 29, 40, 52, 64, 310
  records and registers of, 20, 27, 30, 48–9
  as traders, 69
  unity lacking, 43, 210–11, 275
  women, 50–1, 111, 172
  see also Baptists; Independents; Presbyterians; Puritanism; Quakers
domestic industry *see* industry *under* households
Dorchester, 40, 81
Dorchester Company, 38, 39
Drake, Alice (widow), 49
Drake, Edward (at Lyme, 1642), 41
Drake, Edward (land in 1680), 142
Drake, Reverend Francis (of Seaton), 200

Drake family leases, 122
droving *see under* pastoralism
Drower, Isaac, 13–14, 28, 70, 312
Drower, Jane, marriage to Samuel Sweetland, 24
Drower, Zachariah, 14, 28, 57–8, 86, 312
Dunscombe, Nicholas, 131
Dwight, Bernard, 48
Dyer, Robert, 86

East, Dorothy (of Luppitt), 74, 223
ecclesiastical courts, records of, 16, 61
  matrimonial cases, 286
Edwards, Joan, 245, 255
Edwards, William, 238
elderly, care of, 296–8, 361
  poor relief payments, 225, 227
enclosures, medieval, 8, 123–4, 126–7
Erle, Sir Walter, 32, 39
Erle family and Axe harbour, 135
Estreat Rolls 1625–35, 123
Exeter, 72, 165
  nonconformist academy, 60, 233
  wool markets, 78, 87, 88, 89
Exeter Assembly, 41–3
Exeter Cathedral, 16, 22, 25, 36

family as an institution, 299–302
  impact of family allowances, 234, 246–8, 290, 300, 302, 311, 355–6
  variation with class, 301–2
  of work, 306–7
family names linkage, 11, 318, 327
  standardisation of names, 318, 324
family reconstitution, 8, 11, 27, 318
  nominal linkage *see* family names linkage
  sources other than parish registers, 10, 11
family reconstitution for Colyton, 318–20, 323
  cohorts, 318, 363
  cohorts, summary data for, 12–13, **13**
  individuals with inferred details, 12, 26–7, **26**, 178, 179–80, 183
  status groups *see* crafts status group; gentry status group; labourer status group; poor status group; status groups
  typicality of population with complete records, 12
Farmer, James, 238
farmers, 121, 150–2
farmhouses, 123
farming, 8, 126–7, 129–30, 157–8
  cider apples *see* cider production
  cropping, 127
  dairying *see* dairying
  employment *see* labourers, farm
  grain production, 127, 155–6, 157

hops, 156
inheritance of, 124–6, 341
land improvement and hedging, 123, 129, 130
lease of pasture, 130, 131
textile manufacture, 130
tools, unsophisticated, 125, 158
  see also pastoralism
Farrant, George and Rose, 293–4
Farrant, Mary, 278
Farway, 8, 24, 147
Feoffees, Chamber of, 12, 16, 79, 122, 213
administration of private charities, 228
apprenticeships see apprenticing of poor
charter, 15, 16, 17, 237
declines, 213–14, 237
election of Feoffees, 16–17, 213
emigration funded, 312
estates purchased and leased, 16–17, 36, 122
funds, use of, 17, 73, 213
Muster Master and armoury, 52
poverty relief see poor relief, feoffee administration
resistance of Dissenters sanctioned, 35, 213
unifying force, 45, 65, 122, 209, 308
water supplies, 201
fertility, 10, 169, 174
birth intervals, 173, 192–3, **194**, **195**
contraceptive methods see birth control
impact of infectious diseases, 203
impact of insecurity, 205–6
limitation of family size, 189, **190**, 349
Ffitz, John (Royalist soldier), 219
Fiennes, Celia, 72, 74, 87, 106
firewood see under woodlands
fishing, maritime, 143–4
flax production, 91, 95, 337
  see also textile industries
Flood, Ann, Ann (daughter) and Hester, 51
Flood, Florans, Dorothy and Ann, 170
Ford, Jane, 231
Ford, Susannah (of Axmouth), 165
Forde, Martha, Christian and John (of Honiton), 103
Ford Abbey, 46–7, 52
Freeman, Deborah (of Bicton), 104
French, William (of Colyford), 171
French wars, impact of, 89, 156, 166
Froom, Elizabeth, 153
Fry, William (of Honiton), 216
Fry, William (of Yorty), 39
Fursey, Elenor and Rafe (of Farway), 145

Gammage, Elenor, 281
Gander, Anstis, 280
Gates, Thomas (in Virginia), 40
gentry and yeomen, 121, 122, 132–4, 158, 160
apprentices, 152, 262–3, 344–5
cider production, 130, 132
consumer spending, 75–6
impact of plague, 85
influence of, 38, 51, 126
interest in trade, 75, 92, 93–4
labour employed see labourers, farm
Puritans supported, 33–5, 38, 50, 63, 308, 332
rise of, 124, 130
sheep farming and wool trade, 75, 122–3
gentry status group, 12–13, 15, 16, 320–3, 327
age at marriage later for men, 178, **184**, 348
age of marriage for women, 178, **184**, **185**
fertility, 192, 193
infant mortality, 199
parish records of, 18, 24, 26–7, **26**
George's Meeting House, 59, 60, 61
Gigg, Matthew, 292
Gilbert, Sir Humphrey, 135
Gill (churchwarden), 37–8
Gill, Esther, 90
Gillard, Mary Ann, 269
Goff, Samuel, 244
Gold, Anne, 153, 272–3
Good, John (feoffee), 213
Goodman, Sarah, 245
Gosling, Margaret, 255
Gould, John (churchwarden), 35, 50, 58, 221
Goyings, Samuel, 96
Gundry, Hugh, 279, 286
Gundry, Hugh (preacher), 34–5
Gundry, William, 278
Gundry family lease, 126

Hake, William, 25
Hall, Gideon, 132
Hallett, Rebecca, 231
Ham, Henry (of Luppitt), 48
Ham, Jane, 74, 223
Ham, William (of Tiverton), 82
Hardwicke Act 1753, 21, 64, 311
Hardy, George, 32–3
Harper, Edward, 25
Harper, George, 269
Harries, Richard, 151–2
Harris, Susan, 273
Hart, John, 286–7
Hart, Sarah (of Otterton), 105
Harvey, Hannah and William, 282
Harvy, Richard (vicar of Axmouth), 32
Hawker, Alice, marriage to Edward Harper, 25
Hawker, Pol, 90

Hawkins, Robert, 47–8
Hayman, Syth, 272
Hayne, Morgan, 271–2
Hearth Tax (1674) records, 8, 15, 69, 327
  division between landed and landless, 124, 157
  extent of poverty, 70, 221, 224, 225
Henry, Marquis of Exeter *see* Courtenay, Henry (Marquis of Exeter)
Henry, Louis, 11
Hewes, John, 82–3, 84
Hill, William (vicar at Colyton), 81–2
Hitchcock, Majdalene, 282
Hoare, Eliza, 256
Hoare, Jane, 52
Hoare, John, 257
Hoare, Moll, marriage to Hugh Gundry, 279, 286
Hoare, William, 208–9, 256
Hollet, Ruth (of Honiton), 103
Holmes, John and Thomas, 86
Holwill, John (constable), 48
Honiton, 34, 72–3, 216–17, 329
  coronation celebrations, 110
  lace industry, 94, 95–6, 106, 108, 217, 339
  Presbyterians, 48–9, 59
  prison, 236
  serge manufacture, 88, 89
  water supply, 201
Honnywell, William (yeoman), 75–6, 144
Hooke, William, 148
Hooke, William (vicar of Axmouth and Taunton, Massachusetts), 38, 40
Hooker, John, 67, 79, 92, 127
Hooper, Henry, 48
Hooper, Jane, 278
Hore, Mary (of Axmouth), 165
Hoskins, W.G., 3, 5, 305
Hoskyns, George, 122–3
households
  for apprentice children, 265, 269–70
  dependent on welfare and charity, 270
  domestic industry in, 95, 108, 231, 270, 290
  women as head of, 300, 362
houses, for poor, 229–32
  on commons and wastes, 229–30
  crowded, 169, 201, 230, 265, 357
  parish chamber, 229, 235
  shared, 230–1, 293

illegitimate children *see* children, illegitimate
illegitimate mothers, 285–6, **286**, 294–5, 359, 360–1
  impact of economic difficulties, 288–9
  punishment of, 284
  related, 283, 360

  servants as, 287
  subsequent marriages, 289, 360
  from unbalanced sex ratio, 289, 359
  see also children, illegitimate; prenuptial pregnancy; women, single
Independents, 25, 29, 333
  see also Dissenters
infant mortality *see* mortality, infant
infectious diseases, 198, 200–1, 202, 203, 260
  inoculations for smallpox, 215, 235–6
  linked to market towns, 198, 203–4
  see also malaria; plague
insecurity, reactions to, 210–11, 219, 238, 308, 316

James, Samuel, 102
Jeffries, Judge, 55–6
Jewell, George, 193
Jewell, Melanthon, 31–2
Johns, Eleanor, 256

Kemer, Elizabeth, 217–18
Kerbie, John (constable), 218
Kerridge, John, 59–60
Kilmington, 42, 123, 148
King, Gregory, 8
Knight, Robert (b. 1757), 255
Knight, Robert, 218–19
Knolls, William (vicar of Axminster), 31
Knowles, John (weaver), 230

labourers, farm, 152–4, 158, 345
  apprenticed, 262–3
  in arable agriculture, 166, 290, 311
  day labourers, 152–3, 154, 173, 311
  migratory, 165, 290–1
  numbers, 153–4
  wages, 154–5, 291, 302, 311
  women, 125, 153, 154, 158
labourers, industrial, 270
labourers status group, 12–13, 320–3
  age at marriage, 173, 185, 348
  birth intervals, 193
  child mortality, 199
  impact of plague, 85
  numbers without parish records, **26**, 27
  representation in marriage records, 24, 27
lace, as an investment, 98
lace industry, 92–4, 162, 308
  associated businesses, 102
  bone lace production, 94, 95, 97
  decline of, 106–8
  and Pole tombs, **42**, 43
  protected, 92, 97, 106, 112, 171
  see also textile industries
lace trade
  with colonies, 92, 97, 100

402

in local area, 94, 97–8, 101, 102, 338
  with London, 93, 95, 97, 105, 106
  in secondhand lace, 98, 100, 102
  for tourist trade, 97, 107
lace-making, 97, 106, 108, 170
  apprenticeships and schools, 103–4, 270
  bobbin method, 96–7, 105
  conditions and impact on health, 100, 104–5
  in India, 108
  marriage age associations, 68, 108, 274
  mechanisation, 107, 108
  by men, 96, 103
  and migration, 96, 104, 170, 210
  payment for, 105–6, 116, 339
  relationships with shopkeepers, 101–2
  relationships with traders, 99
land, 126
  as basis for socioeconomic status, 121, 157, 158, 274–5, 308
  freehold *see* gentry and yeomen
  impact of French Wars, 155–6
  improvement of, 129
  lease of *see* cottagers; tenant farmers
  ownership of, 121
  shortage perceived, 122, 123, 126, 158, 308
  wool farmers increase holdings of, 123, 127
Land Tax records, 15
  indicator of small and large holdings, 157, 158
landless, 126, 158
  involved in cloth making, 79
Landley, Elinor, 280
Laud, Archbishop W., 35
  opposition to, 31, 40
lay subsidies, 15, 327
leases *see* manorial system; tenant farmers
Legg, Elizabeth, 255
Leighton, Elizabeth, 90
Levermore, Richard, 216
Levine, David, 67–8, 73, 81, 92, 118, 308, 310
Lewes, John (shoemaker), 229
Lewson, Robert (of Colyton), 77
Leyman, Walter, 33
London, 203, 346
  trade with, 76, 99, 105, 118, 129
Long, Elizabeth, 245
Long, Grace, 231
Loughwood Meeting House, Kilmington, 42, 44
Lovehayne Common, 123, 149
Lovehayne farm, 17, 127, 132
Loveridge, John and Charlotte, 268
Loveridge, Robert and Mary, 247–8
Lovett, Elizabeth and William (of Widworthy), 114, 212

Lugg, John, 282
Lymbrey, Grace, 50, 60
Lymbrey, William, 50, 60
Lyme Regis, 33–4, 142–3
  arrival of Monmouth, 53
  nonconformist schools, 46
  marriage registrations, 63
  Parliamentary garrison, 41, 82, 83, 209
  as port, 142–3
  separatist and Independent congregations, 41, 46
  siege, 41, 114
  trade with colonies, 71, 75
  wool cloth production, 81

malaria, 200–1, 202
Mallock, Richard, 39
Mallocke, Reverend (at Farway), 24
manorial system, 121, 124
  continuing influence, 209, 211, 310
  courts, 211, 351
  leasehold systems, 124–5
  rights of tenants, 121–2
  see also tenant farmers
Manson, Dr, 40
marital separation, 290–5
  children as paupers, 292
  desertion and divorce, 293, 294, 360
Markes, Charles, 287
market towns, 71–2
  and infectious diseases, 198, 203–4
Markhill, Alys, 149
marl pits, 129, 342
marriage, age at, 9, 26, 174–86, **175**, **186**, 280, 306, 311
  for apprentices, 267
  impact of unbalanced sex ratios, 167–8, 175, 184–5, 186
  impact of wage levels, 10–11, 68, 108, 172–3
  as indicator of population trend, 10, 306
  validity of data, 28, 178, 347–8
  variations within gender, 11, 173, 175, 186
  see also under status groups
marriage, legality of, 21, 22, 64, 329
marriage, place of, 21, 25, 166–7, 328
marriage, season of, 128–9, **128**
Marriage Duty Act 1695, 8, 346
marriage register, 18
  decline in number recorded, 1650–1750, 9, 18, 20–1, 23
  individuals with record of marriage only, 21–2, **22**, 170
marriages, 274–5, 278–9, 301
  bonds, 26, 329
  of Colyton born, 165–7, **166**
  common law, 293–4, 301, 360
  enforced, 292–3, 360

impact of access to land, 168, 274, 346
performed by Justices of the Peace, 22–3
proportion recorded in parish documents, 21, 328
spousal and wedding customs, 286
unrecorded, 23–7, **23**, 29, 30, 62–3, 68, 174, 179–80, 183
Marwood, John (Monmouth rebel), 58
Marwood, John (yeoman), 130
Marwood, Thomas (feoffee), 213
Marwood, Thomas (physician), 77
Marwood family occupations, 80
Mathew, Christopher, 145
Maunder, John (feoffee), 79
Maynard, James, 89
Maynard, Mary, 107
Mayne, William, 255
Mayowe, curate, 61–2, 113–14, 309
Membury, 59, 61–2
men
  emigration to colonies, 170–1
  marriage to older women, 167, 175
  marriageable, 274–5
  remarriage, 167–8, 188, 244, 348
Michell, William, 255
migration and mobility, 116, 309, 312–13
  as cause of crowding, 169, 201
  for economic opportunities, 10, 164, 165, 169, 170, 346
  following preachers, 210
  impact on local records, 12, 25, 27, 70
  impact on sex ratios, 10, 164–5, 170
  as life cycle stage, 164
  of men, 165, 171
  patterns according to sex, 165, 172
  of textile workers, 88, 96, 104, 170, 210
Milles, Dean J., survey, 72–3, 86, 89, 131, 144, 200
Mills, Ann, marriage to William Hake, 25
Minifie, Emlin, 84, 280
missing marryers *see* unrecorded *under* marriages
Mitchell, Elizabeth, 152
Mitchell, Hannah, 287
Mitchell, Humphrey, 58
Mitchell, Phil (feoffee), 213
mobility *see* migration and mobility
Monmouth, Duke of, 51, 52–3
Monmouth Rebellion, 29, 30, 51, 53, 209, 309
  loss of marriageable men, 169
  for Protestant cause, 48, 54, 55
  rebels, 54–8, 62–3
Morgaine, Joane, 286
Morgan, John (paper maker), 87
mortality, adult, 9, 202, 265–6, 356–7
mortality, child, 9173–4, 198–200, 252
mortality, infant, 162–3, 173–4, 198–200, **198**, 252

and breastfeeding, 200, 350
recording of, 19, 200–1
musters, 52, 208, 209, 212, 327
Myddle (Shropshire), 316

New England Puritan colony, 39–40
Newbery, Robert, 280
Newbury, Mary, 253
Newbury, Samuel, 268
Newbury, Sarah, 88, 231
Newcombe, Frances, 312–13
Newfoundland, 39, 93, 143, 144, 171
Newton, John, 40
nonconformists *see* Dissenters
non–marryers, 173, 281–2
  status groups of, 282–3, **283**
  see also illegitimate mothers; women, single
Northleigh, 8, 146

Ottery St Mary, 34
  in Civil War, 40
  feoffees, 217, 257–8
  industries and trade, 75, 89–90, 220, 342
  lands controlled by manor, 124–5, 211
  persecution of Dissenters, 47–8
  prison, 236
  tithes collected, 150
  vegetable growing, 150
  water supply, 201
Overmarss, Anthony, 78

paper making, 86–7
  see also textile industries
parishes, open and closed to migration, 116–17
Parsons, Henry, 31
Parsons, Thomas (constable), 48
Parsons, Thomas, 86
Parsons, Thomas (of Membury), 47
pastoralism, 122–3, 130
  droving, 130–1
  employment in, 92–3, 162
  growth of, 127, 130
  textile trade as cottage industry, 116, 130, 339
  see also dairying
Paul, Alice, marriage to William Zalway, 282
Pavey, John and Mary, 294
Pease, Mary (incomer), 195–6
Pennington, Thomas, 280
Perram, George and John, 52
Perry, Richard (of Farway), 77
Perry, Sarah, 292–3
Person, Amy, 37
Petre family papers, 15, 340
Phelps, William, 132–4

Pinckley, Thomas, 96
Pinney, Azariah, 29, 73, 76
  marriage, 250, 275
  Monmouth rebel, 29, 100
  in Nevis, 59, 100, 257, 258
Pinney, Dorothy, 37
Pinney, Hester, 99, 100, 112, 115, 206, 275
  mistress of George Booth, 275, 279–80
Pinney, Jane, 99
Pinney, John, 52, 99, 101, 208, 221
  ejected, 45–6, 98
  family farm lease, 125–6
  lace dealer, 98, 100
  marriages of children, 275–6
  old age, 295, 308
Pinney, John (son of Azariah), 250, 277–8
Pinney, Mary, 76
Pinney, Nathaniel, 29, 73, 77, 100, 115, 119, 126, 250, 308
  marriage, 275–7
Pinney, Rachel, 98–9, 275
Pinney, Sarah, 98–9, 275
Pinney family, 15, 76, 118
  lace traders, 98–101, 106
  money lending, 100–1
  trade with West Indies, 100
Pitfield, Hannah, 267
Pitman, Dr Henry, 56–7
Pitts, Joseph, 58
plague, 84–5, 147, 219, 260–1, 357
  and emigration, 169
  impact on fertility, 189, 198, 350
  recurrence of, 202–3
Pole, Elizabeth (émigré), 39, 40
Pole, Lady Elizabeth, tomb of, **42**, 43, 97
Pole, Sir John, tomb of, **42**, 43, 97
Pole, Sir John William de la, 157, 158–9, 214–15
Pole, William (émigré), 39, 40
Pole, Sir William (d. 1635), 39, 135, 138, 343
Pole, Sir William (1678–1758), 214
Pole family, 15, 154, 211, 214
  lace purchases, 97
  leases, 122
Poll Tax (1660), records, 15
poor, 70, 217, 225
  access to commons, 148, 149
  control of, 220–1, 279, 292–3, 308
  divorce, 294, 360
  impressed as soldiers, 145
  loyalties divided, 216–17, 221
  in old age, 225, 227, 296–8
  in open and closed parishes, 116–17
  parish support for children of, 19, 61
  support for Puritanism, 37, 38, 309
poor relief, 215, 217, 220, 226–7, 299
  birth parish responsibility, 20, 226
  documents, 14, 17, 19, 20
  housing *see* houses, for poor; workhouses
  impact on family structures, 222, 300, 355–6
  as means of control, 220–1, 308
  national parish system, 217, 222
  rent payments, 221, 223–4
  for sickness and death, 298, 299, 302
  value of, 226–7, **226**
  women as recipients, 164, 173, 188, 225, **225**, 227–8, 300, 349, 353–4
poor relief, feoffee administration of, 213, 217–18, 223–4, 237–9
  allowance scheme, 238–9
  Christmas dole, 243, 355
  enforced marriages, 292–3
  job creation, 90, 94, 235, 236
  outrelief preferred to workhouse, 236
  parish chamber maintained, 229
  payments to women and children, 224
  relief in kind, 221, 238
  selective, 218, 224, 225
poor relief, parish administration of, 234, 241, 310
  amounts paid, 234, **239**, **242**
  family allowances, 234, 246–8, 290, 300, 311, 355–6
  job creation, 235
  payment for welfare work, 236, 244–6, **245**, 311
  relief in kind, 235, 243
  relief to non-resident parishioners, 248
  seasonal patterns, 240–1, **240**, **241**, **242**, 243
  smallpox inoculations, 215, 235–6
  supplements to earned income, 248
poor relief overseers
  partiality of, 220–1
  records, 17, 19–20, 214, 222, 225, 234, 240
  significance of position, 221–2
poor status group, 12–13, 15, 320–3
  age at marriage, 281
  baptism of children, 19–20
  as driver of demographic trends, 307
  impact of plague, 85
  non-marrying women, 282–3
  number without parish registration, 26
  representation in marriage registers, 23, **23**, **24**
population data *see* demographic trends
Pound, Bartholomew, 290
Power, Nathaniel, 269–70
Pratt, Richard, 312
prenuptial pregnancy, 286, 287–8, **288**, 359, 361
  and marital separation, 292–3
  see also children, illegitimate; illegitimate mothers

INDEX

Prerogative Court of Canterbury, record of wills, 16
Presbyterians, 29–45, 47, 48, 59, 60
  money lending, 76, 101
  see also Dissenters
Prideaux, Edmund, 32, 35, 46–7, 52–3
Pring, Edward, 280, 359
probate documents lost, 16
prostitution, rural, 193, 280, 290
Protestant work ethic *see* work ethic *under* Dissent
Protestantism *see* Dissent; Puritanism
Protestation Oath 1641, 8, 41
Pulman, John (tailor), 216
Purchase, Dorothy, 287
Puritan Clergy, 22, 25, 32
  eviction of, 31, 45–6
Puritanism, 209
  associated with fertility decline, 197
  associated with lack of access to land, 34, 121, 124
  Christian names, 36, 330
  concern for social welfare, 217, 221, 308
  in market towns and lace industry, 63, 94
  marriage and family, 116, 251
  popular support for, 33–5, 37, 38, 40, 63
  see also Dissent; Dissenters; Quakers

Quakers, 29, 43, 206
  see also Dissenters; Puritanism

Raddon, William, 47
Radford, Reuben, 154
Reed, Aaron, John and Rebekah, 131
Reede, Francis, 31
Restoration 1660, 25, 43, 48
Restorick, Benedicta, 252
Restorick, John, 278
Restorick, Joseph, 91, 252
Restorick, Mary, 246
Richards, Martha (of Honiton), 103
rivers, 73, 87, 112, 160, 201
roads, 17, 73, 310
Rode, Roger and Julian, 216
Rodgers, Christopher, 223
Roe, Martha and William, 239
Rogers, Nicholas (of Membury), 232
Rolle family papers, 15
Rolls, Mary (of Exeter), 103–4
Roost, William and Thomasine, 152
Routley, Mary, 256
Royers, John (of Shute) 72
Rudge, James, 94
Rulty, John (of Colyton), 145
Rutley, Edward, 271

St Sidwells (Exeter), Colyton marriages at, 25

salt marshes and meadows, 131, 134, **136**, 138–40
  as source of diseases, 200–1, 202
Salter, Mary and George, 104–5
Salter, William, 19, 47
Salway, John (curate at Shute), 36–8, 197
Samon, Philip, 30
Sampson, Thomas (churchwarden), 49
Sampson family, 15, 122, 132, 231
Sanday, Robert (slave in Barbados), 56
Sandy Ann, baptism at Colyton, 25
Sandy, Robert, marriage at Seaton and Beer, 24–5
Satchell, John (of Honiton), 95–6
Satchell, Roger, 48, 124, 195–7, 305
  Monmouth rebel, 53, 55, 56, 196
  overseer of the poor, 221, 222
Scarr, John, 167
schoolmasters, 232
schools, 17, 232–4
  nonconformist academies, 46, 60, 233
Scriven, William, 270
Searell, Robert and Hugh (of Honiton), 95
Searle, Edward and Ellen, 278
Seaton, 131, 135, 144, 200
  poor relief, 218
  sea watches, 212
Seaton and Beer parish, 24–5, 40, 328
Seaton Marsh, reclamation of, 138–40, **139**, 144, 200
Seaward, Mary (of Axminster), 110
Seaward, Ralph, 319
Seaward, Thomas (of Axmouth), 150
Seaward, Thomas (of Colyton), 147
Sedgemoor battlefield 1685, 14, 54
Settlement Laws, requirements and enforcement of, 20, 61, 165, 239–40, 266
  records, 17, 165, 170, 171
Seward, Johane, marriage to John Scarr, 167
sex ratios, 10, 162
  of apprentices, 259, **260**
  at burial, 162–4, **163, 164**, 167, **168**
  impact on marriages, 165–6, 184–5, 281, 289
  impact of migration, 10, 306
  impact on population growth, 306, 307
  unbalanced, 162, 170, 172, 207, 346
Sexton, Elizabeth, 272
Shakell, Roger (of Colyton), 230
sheep farming *see* pastoralism
sheep stealing, 147
Ship Tax levies, 15, 40, 229
Short, Reverend Ames (separatist), 41, 46
Shute Barton, 154, 214, **215**
Shute chapelry, 8, 23, 24, 25, 36–7, 328
Shute House, 214
Sidbury, 108, 146–7

INDEX

lace school, 104
  tenant farmers, 125, 341
  workhouse, 236
Sidmouth, 95, 107, 144
Skiffes, John, 59
Skinner, Daniel, 273
Slade, Roger, 31
slave trade (West Africa), 74
slavery as punishment for rebels, 56–7, 58–9
Smith, Joane, 280
Smith, Captain John, 39
Smith, Nathaniel, 59
Snell, Ann, 88, 231
Snipling, Mary and William, 293
soap making, 131, 236, 342
social mobility and insecurity, 209–10
social stratification, 69–70, 157, 160, 209, 210, 251, 303, 309
  impact of access to land, 121, 157, 158, 274–5, 308
socioeconomic status *see* status groups
soldiers
  behaviour during Civil War, 82–3, 219, 280
  behaviour in pursuit of Monmouth rebels, 58, 101
  billeted at Colyton, 285
  link with infectious diseases, 202, 203
  men disabled as, 103, 115, 219
  recruited and impressed, 145, 166, 169, 171, 312
  separation from wives, 292
Soper, Mary, 117
Southcombe, Jane and Nathaniel, 254
Southcott, Thomas, 39
Southleigh, 8, 25
Speed, Joseph (shoemaker), 55
Sprague, John (mason), 55
Spurway, John (of Shute), 150
Spurway, John, 89
Stamp Act 1783–94, 20
Starrs, Elizabeth, 142
status groups, 12–13, 69, 172, 319–20, **320–3**, 327
  and age at first marriage, 172–86, **175**, **180**, **184**, 348
  and age at first marriage for men, 177, 178, **179**, 182–3, **182**, **183**
  and age at first marriage for women, 175, **176**, 178, **178**, **181**, 183
  analysis by, 10, 12–13, **13**
  and child and infant mortality, 173–4, 198–200, **198**, **199**, **200**
  and fertility, 174, 191–5, **191**, **192**, **194**, **195**
  impact of Chamber of Feoffees, 122
  impact of access to land, 121, 157, 158
  and remarriage, 174, 186–9, **187**

unknown group, 174, 185–6, **186**
  see also crafts status group; gentry status group; labourer status group; poor status group
Stedham, Honor, 285
Stevens, Bartholomew, 31
Stocker, William, 48, 83
Stockland, dispute over common, 148
Strowbridge, John, 122, 127–8
Strowbridge family leases, 122
Sweete, Nathaniel, 77, 272
Sweetland, John, 112
Sweetland, Robert, baptism, 24
Sweetland, Samuel, marriage, 24
Swete, Reverend John, 89, 144, 157
Sydenham, Charles (customs officer), 112

Tanner, Thomas (vicar of Colyton), 47, 232–3, 331
  problems with churchwardens, 49–50, 331
tanneries, 130–1
Taunton, 63, 233
Taunton, Massachusetts, 40
taverns, as places of business, 113–14, 115
  frequented by women, 99, 111, 113, 115
tax assessment documents, 318
Taylor, Mary, 284
Teape, Ralph, 147
tenant farmers
  leasehold systems, 124–5, 156–7
  leases, inheritance of, 125–6, 265–6, 274
  rights of, 121–2, 123, 148, 340
  women as, 125, 341
  see also manorial system
Terling (Essex), 315–16
textile industries, 78, 87, 91, 169
  attracted migrant workers, 70, 96, 104
  see also flax production; lace industry; paper making; wool industry
Thompson, Nicholas (doctor), 54
Thrale, Zachariah, 280–1
tobacco, 74–5, 77, 95
Toleration Act 1688, 43, 59
Toods, Bridgett, 223
Toupe, Daniel, 50, 51, 75, 332
Toupe, Mary, 50
Towgood, Matthew, 60, 233
Towgood, Reverend Stephen, 51, 52, 53–4, 58
trade, 69, 308
  in agricultural produce, 72–3
  in manufactured goods, 74
  with colonies, 3, 71, 74–5, 100
  links with infectious diseases, 203–4
  merchants marks, 108
  in tobacco, 74
  women in, 108–10
trade tokens, 101, 108–10

INDEX

Traske, John (heresy charge), 34, 329
Trawle, Mary, marriage to Isaac Drower, 14
Trevelyan, Sir John, 144
Troude, John (of Upottery), 47
Tucker, Deborah (of Exeter), 102
Tucker, James and Hannah, 151
Tucker, Joseph (alias Baker), 229
Turner, John, 284
Turner, John (apprentice of Colyton), 91
Twente region, Netherlands, 315
typhus *see* infectious diseases

unemployment, seasonal, 240–3, 248, 262, 302
unmarried mothers *see* illegitimate mothers

vermin collection payments, 243–4, 355
Verviers (Belgium), 313–15
Vicary, Elizabeth, 89, 336
Vye, Jane, 108, **109**
Vye, Walter, 261

wage dependency and poverty, 225, 228
wage rates, 10, 154–5, 291, 302, 311
  for women, 68, 105–6, 307
Wallop, Henry (MP), 99
Ware, Mary, 269
Warmington, Collan, 268
Warren, Nicholas, 58
Warren, Richard (of Axmouth), 150
wastes *see under* common land
Watchcombe, 8, 243, 244
Weekes, Alice (of Colyton), 80
Weekes, Anne, 272
West Africa trade, 71, 74
West Indies, 56–7, 100
Westcote, T., 80, 81, 83, 93, 95, 127
Westcotte, Robert, 79
Weston, William, 269
Wey, Henry (from Cullompton), 88
Whicker, John, escape from West Indies, 56–7
White, John, 38, 39–40, 97, 330
Whitwell Common, 140
Whitwell Farm, 153
Whitwell manor, 15
widows, 115, 228
  loss of estate with illegitimate births, 281
  remarriage of, 25, 26, 168, 186, 188, 348–9
  in shared houses, 230–1
  see also illegitimate mothers; women
Widworthy, 8, 25, 90, 129
Wilkins, Edward, 45, 77, 229
Wilkins, John (Puritan vicar), 22, 41, 45
Williams, Mary, 106–7
Willoughby family records, 129
  reclamation of Seaton Marsh, 138–40, **139**

wills, records of, 16
Winston, Agnes (of Honiton), 105
Winthrop papers, 97
Wishlade, Agnes, 230–1
witchcraft trial, 223
Wollacott, Jeffrey (of Exeter), 103–4
women,
  in Civil War, 114
  as farm labourers, 125, 153, 154, 158
  independence of, 115–17, 118, 301
  as migrants, 165, 170, 171–2
  records and status of, 14–15, 319
  in riots, 112–13, 117
  in taverns, 99, 111, 113, 115
  as traders, 108, 110, 111–12
  travel, 101, 111–12
  wages for, 68, 154–5, 307
  work for, 89, 92–3, 208–9, 246, 307
  see also illegitimate mothers; widows
women, single, 10, 115, 281–2, 301
  emigration to New World, 40
  in lace trade, 98–9
  late marriage with high employment, 115, 118
  living arrangements, 229, 230, 353–4
  marriage outside of Colyton, 168
  poverty likely, 283, 290
  see also illegitimate mothers; widows
Woodgate, Henry (from Exeter), 88
woodlands, access to, 123, 148
  firewood, 148, 235
wool industry, 78–9, 85, 91, 88, 118
  collapse of, 67–8, 91, 162
  cyclic nature, 82, 86, 87, 90
  development of, 79–80, 81, 83, 85–6, 89
  impact of Civil War, 82–4
  impact of plague, 84, 85, 260
  serge production, 80–1, 87, 89
  spinning, organisation of, 83–4
  workers, 79, 80
  see also textile industries
wool production, 122–3
Woolmington, John, 58
work agreement and payment records, 17
workhouses, 17, 90, 236–7
Worth, Richard, 30
Worthell, John, 223
Wrigley, Tony, 8–9, 10, 11
Wyatt, David, 281

yeomen *see* gentry and yeomen
Yonge, Sir George (MP), 342
Yonge, Jane, marriage to Richard Mallock, 39
Yonge, John, 39, 71
Yonge, Walter, 31, 39, 40, 53, 71
  diary, 15–16, 35, 82, 127, 197, 205–6
Yonge family, 34, 118, 122, 123